RACE, LANGUAGE AND CULTURE

FRANZ BOAS

Race,
Language
and Culture

THE FREE PRESS, *New York*
COLLIER-MACMILLAN LIMITED, *London*

035375

Collier-Macmillan Canada, Ltd., Toronto, Ontario

FIRST FREE PRESS PAPERBACK EDITION 1966

Second printing January 1968

PREFACE

ANTHROPOLOGY, the science of man, is often held to be a subject that may satisfy our curiosity regarding the early history of mankind, but of no immediate bearing upon problems that confront us. This view has always seemed to me erroneous. Growing up in our own civilization we know little how we ourselves are conditioned by it, how our bodies, our language, our modes of thinking and acting are determined by limits imposed upon us by our environment. Knowledge of the life processes and behavior of man under conditions of life fundamentally different from our own can help us to obtain a freer view of our own lives and of our life problems. The dynamics of life have always been of greater interest to me than the description of conditions, although I recognize that the latter must form the indispensable material on which to base our conclusions.

My endeavors have largely been directed by this point of view. In the following pages I have collected such of my writings as, I hope, will prove the validity of my point of view.

The material presented here is not intended to show a chronological development. The plan is rather to throw light on the problems treated. General discussions are followed by reports on special investigations on the results of which general viewpoints are based.

On the whole I have left the statements as they first appeared. Only in the discussion of the problems of stability of races and of growth which extend over many years, has scattered material been combined. In these the mathematical problems have been omitted and diagrams have been substituted for numerical tables. Here and there reviews and controversies have been included where they seemed relevant and of importance for the clearer statement of theories.

The terms "race" and "racial" are throughout used in the sense that they mean the assembly of genetic lines represented in a population.

It is natural that the earlier papers do not include data available at the present time. I have not made any changes by introducing new material because it seemed to me that the fundamental theoretical treatment of problems is still valid. In a few cases footnotes in regard to new investigations or criticisms of the subject matter have been added.

I have included two very early general papers at the end of the book because they indicate the general attitude underlying my later work.

I wish to express my sincere thanks to Dr. Alexander Lesser whose help and advice in the selection of material has been of greatest value.

FRANZ BOAS

Columbia University
November 29, 1939

TABLE OF CONTENTS

RACE

ILLUSTRATIONS

CHANGES IN BODILY FORM OF DESCENDANTS OF IMMIGRANTS

THE TEMPO OF GROWTH OF FRATERNITIES

GROWTH

RACE

RACE AND PROGRESS [1]

PERMIT me to call your attention to the scientific aspects of a problem that has been for a long time agitating our country and which, on account of its social and economic implications, has given rise to strong emotional reactions and has led to varied types of legislation. I refer to the problems due to the intermingling of racial types.

If we wish to reach a reasonable attitude, it is necessary to separate clearly the biological and psychological aspects from the social and economic implications of this problem. Furthermore, the social motivation of what is happening must be looked at not from the narrow point of view of our present conditions but from a wider angle.

The facts with which we are dealing are diverse. The plantation system of the South brought to our shores a large Negro population. Considerable mixture between White masters and slave women occurred during the period of slavery, so that the number of pure Negroes was dwindling continually and the colored population gradually became lighter. A certain amount of intermingling between White and Indian took place, but in the United States and Canada this has never occurred to such a degree that it became an important social phenomenon. In Mexico and many parts of Central and South America it is the most typical case of race contact and race mixture. With the development of immigration the people of eastern and southern Europe were attracted to our country and form now an important part of our population. They differ in type somewhat among themselves, although the racial contrasts are much less than those between Indians or Negroes and Whites. Through Mexican and West Indian immigration another group has come into our country, partly of South European, partly of mixed Negro and mixed Indian descent. To all these must be added the East Asiatic groups, Chinese, Japanese and Filipinos, who play a particularly important rôle on the Pacific Coast.

[1] Address of the president of the American Association for the Advancement of Science, Pasadena, June 15. *Science*, N.S., vol. 74 (1931), pp. 1-8.

The first point in regard to which we need clarification refers to the significance of the term race. In common parlance when we speak of a race we mean a group of people that have certain bodily and perhaps also mental characteristics in common. The Whites, with their light skin, straight or wavy hair and high nose, are a race set off clearly from the Negroes with their dark skin, frizzly hair and flat nose. In regard to these traits the two races are fundamentally distinct. Not quite so definite is the distinction between East Asiatics and European types, because transitional forms do occur among normal White individuals, such as flat faces, straight black hair and eye forms resembling the East Asiatic types; and conversely European-like traits are found among East Asiatics. For Negro and White we may speak of hereditary racial traits so far as these radically distinct features are concerned. For Whites and East Asiatics the difference is not quite so absolute, because a few individuals may be found in each race for whom the racial traits do not hold good, so that in a strict sense we cannot speak of absolutely valid hereditary racial traits.

This condition prevails to a much more marked extent among the different, so-called races of Europe. We are accustomed to speak of a Scandinavian as tall, blond and blue-eyed, of a South Italian as short, swarthy and dark-eyed; of a Bohemian as middle-sized, with brown or gray eyes and wide face and straight hair. We are apt to construct ideal local types which are based on our everyday experience, abstracted from a combination of forms that are most frequently seen in a given locality, and we forget that there are numerous individuals for whom this description does not hold true. It would be a rash undertaking to determine the locality in which a person is born solely from his bodily characteristics. In many cases we may be helped in such a determination by manners of wearing the hair, peculiar mannerisms of motion, and by dress, but these are not to be mistaken for essential hereditary traits. In populations of various parts of Europe many individuals may be found that may as well belong to one part of the continent as to another. There is no truth in the contention so often made that two Englishmen are more alike in bodily form than, let us say, an Englishman and a German. A greater number of forms may be duplicated in the narrower area, but similar forms may be found in all parts of the continent. There is an overlapping of bodily form between the local groups. It is not justifiable to assume that the individuals that do not fit into the ideal local type which we construct from general impressions are foreign elements in the population, that their presence is always due to intermixture with alien types. It is a fundamental characteristic of all local populations that the individuals differ among themselves, and a closer study shows that this is true of animals as well as of men. It is, therefore, not quite proper to speak in these cases of traits that are hereditary in the racial type as a whole, because too many of them occur also in other racial types. Hereditary racial traits should be shared by the whole population so that it is set off against others.

The matter is quite different when individuals are studied as members of their own family lines. Racial heredity implies that there must be a unity of descent, that there must have existed at one time a small number of ancestors of definite bodily form, from whom the present population has descended. It is quite impossible to reconstruct this ancestry through the study of a modern population, but the study of families extending over several generations is often possible. Whenever this study has been undertaken we find that the family lines represented in a single population differ very much among themselves. In isolated communities where the same families have intermarried for generations the differences are less than in larger communities. We may say that every racial group consists of a great many family lines which are distinct in bodily form. Some of these family lines are duplicated in neighboring territories and the more duplication exists the less is it possible to speak of fundamental racial characteristics. These conditions are so manifest in Europe that all we can do is to study the frequency of occurrence of various family lines all over the continent. The differences between the family lines belonging to each larger area are much greater than the differences between the populations as a whole.

Although it is not necessary to consider the great differences in type that occur in a population as due to mixture of different types, it is easy to see that intermingling has played an important part in the history of modern populations. Let us recall to our minds the migrations that occurred in early times in Europe, when the Kelts of Western Europe swept over Italy and eastward to Asia Minor; when the Teutonic tribes migrated from the Black Sea westward into Italy, Spain and even into North Africa; when the Slav expanded northeastward over Russia, and southward into the Balkan Peninsula; when the Moors held a large part of Spain, when Roman and Greek slaves disappeared in the general population, and when Roman colonization affected a large part of the Mediterranean area. It is interesting to note that

Spain's greatness followed the period of greatest race mixture, that its decline set in when the population became stable and immigration stopped. This might give us pause when we speak about the dangers of the intermingling of European types. What is happening in America now is the repetition on a larger scale and in a shorter time of what happened in Europe during the centuries when the people of northern Europe were not yet firmly attached to the soil.

The actual occurrence of intermingling leads us to consider what the biological effect of intermixture of different types may be. Much light has been shed on this question through the intensive study of the phenomena of heredity. It is true we are hampered in the study of heredity in man by the impossibility of experimentation, but much can be learned from observation and through the application of studies of heredity in animals and plants. One fact stands out clearly. When two individuals are mated and there is a very large number of offspring and when furthermore there is no disturbing environmental factor, then the distribution of different forms in the offspring is determined by the genetic characteristics of the parents. What may happen after thousands of generations have passed does not concern us here.

Our previous remarks regarding the characteristics of local types show that matings between individuals essentially different in genetic type must occur in even the most homogeneous population. If it could be shown, as is sometimes claimed, that the progeny of individuals of decidely distinct proportions of the body would be what has been called disharmonic in character, this would occur with considerable frequency in every population, for we do find individuals, let us say, with large jaws and large teeth and those with small jaws and small teeth. If it is assumed that in the later offspring these conditions might result in a combination of small jaws and large teeth a disharmony would develop. We do not know that this actually occurs. It merely illustrates the line of reasoning. In matings between various European groups these conditions would not be materially changed, although greater differences between parents would be more frequent than in a homogeneous population.

The essential question to be answered is whether we have any evidence that would indicate that matings between individuals of different descent and different type would result in a progeny less vigorous than that of their ancestors. We have not had any opportunity to observe any degeneracy in man as clearly due to this cause. The high nobility of all parts of Europe can be shown to be of very mixed origin. French, German and Italian urban populations are derived from all the distinct European types. It would be difficult to show that any degeneracy that may exist among them is due to an evil effect of intermating. Biological degeneracy is found rather in small districts of intense inbreeding. Here again it is not so much a question of type, but of the presence of pathological conditions in the family strains, for we know of many perfectly healthy and vigorous intensely inbred communities. We find these among the Eskimos and also among many primitive tribes among whom cousin marriages are prescribed by custom.

These remarks do not touch upon the problem of the effect of intermarriages upon bodily form, health and vigor of crosses between races that are biologically more distinct than the types of Europe. It is not quite easy to give absolutely conclusive evidence in regard to this question. Judging merely on the basis of anatomical features and health conditions of mixed populations there does not seem to be any reason to assume unfavorable results, either in the first or in later generations of offspring. The mixed descendants of Europeans and American Indians are taller and more fertile than the pureblood Indians. They are even taller than either parental race. The mixed blood Dutch and Hottentot of South Africa and the Malay mixed bloods of the Island of Kisar are in type intermediate between the two races, and do not exhibit any traits of degeneracy. The populations of the Sudan, mixtures of Mediterranean and Negro types, have always been characterized by great vigor. There is also little doubt that in eastern Russia a considerable infusion of Asiatic blood has occurred. The biological observations on our North American mulattoes do not convince us that there is any deleterious effect of race mixture so far as it is evident in anatomical form and function.

It is also necessary to remember that in varying environment human forms are not absolutely stable, and many of the anatomical traits of the body are subject to a limited amount of change according to climate and conditions of life. We have definite evidence showing changes of bodily size. The stature in European populations has increased materially since the middle of the nineteenth century. War and starvation have left their effects upon the children growing up in the second decade of our century. Proportions of the body change with occupation. The forms of the hand of the laborer and that of the musician reflect their occupations. The changes in head form that have been observed are analogous to those observed in animals under varying conditions of life, among lions born in captivity or among rats fed with different types of diet. The extent to which geographical and social environment may change bodily form is not known, but the influences of outer conditions have to be taken into consideration when comparing different human types.

Selective processes are also at work in changing the character of a population. Differential birth-rate, mortality and migration may bring about changes in the hereditary composition of a group. The range of such changes is limited by the range of variation within the original population. The importance of selection upon the character of a population is easily overestimated. It is true enough that certain defects are transmitted by heredity, but it cannot be proved that a whole population degenerates physically by the numerical increase of degenerates. These always include the physically unfit, and others, the victims of circumstances. The economic depression of our days shows clearly how easily perfectly competent individuals may be brought into conditions of abject poverty and under stresses that only the most vigorous minds can withstand successfully. Equally unjustified is the opinion that war, the struggle between national groups, is a selective process which is necessary to keep mankind on the onward march. Sir Arthur Keith, only a week ago, in his rectoral address at the University of Aberdeen is reported to have said that "Nature keeps her human orchard healthy by pruning and war is her pruning hook." I do not see how such a statement can be justified in any way. War eliminates the physically strong, war increases all the devastating scourges of mankind such as tuberculosis and genital diseases, war weakens the growing generation. History shows that energetic action of masses may be released not only by war but also by other forces. We may not share the fervor or believe in the stimulating ideals; the important point is to observe that they may arouse the same kind of energy that is released in war. Such a stimulus was the abandonment to religion in the middle ages, such is the abandonment of modern Russian youths to their ideal.

So far we have discussed the effects of heredity, environment and selection upon bodily form. We are not so much concerned with the form of the body as with its functions, for in the life of a nation the activities of the individual count rather than his appearance. There is no doubt in my mind that there is a very definite association between the biological make-up of the individual and the physiological and psychological functioning of his body. The claim that only social and other environmental conditions determine the reactions of the individual disregards the most elementary observations, like differences in heart beat, basal metabolism or gland development; and mental differences in their relation to extreme anatomical disturbances of the nervous system. There are organic reasons why individuals differ in their mental behavior.

But to acknowledge this fact does not mean that all differences of behavior can be adequately explained on a purely anatomical basis. When the human body has reached maturity, its form remains fairly stable until the changes due to increasing age set in. Under normal conditions the form and the chemical constitution of the adult body remain almost stable for a number of years. Not so with bodily functions. The conditions of life vary considerably. Our heart beat is different in sleep and in waking. It depends upon the work we are doing, the altitude in which we live, and upon many other factors. It may, therefore, well be that the same individual under different conditions will show quite different reactions. It is the same with other bodily functions. The action of our digestive tract depends upon the quality and quantity of the food we consume. In short, the physiological reactions of the body are markedly adjusted to conditions of life. Owing to this many individuals of different organic structure when exposed to the same environmental conditions will assume a certain degree of similarity of reaction.

On the whole it is much easier to find decided differences between races in bodily form than in function. It cannot be claimed that the body in all races functions in an identical way, but that kind of overlapping which we observed in form is even more pronounced in function. It is quite impossible to say that, because some physical function, let us say the heart beat, has a certain measure, the individual must be White or Negro—for the same rates are found in both races. A certain basal metabolism does not show that a person is a Japanese or a White, although the averages of all the individuals in the races compared may exhibit differences. Furthermore, the particular function is so markedly modified by the demands made upon the organism that these will make the reactions of the racial groups living under the same conditions markedly alike. Every organ is capable of adjustment to a fairly wide range of conditions, and thus the conditions will determine to a great extent the kind of reaction.

What is true of physiological function is equally true of mental function. There exists an enormous amount of literature dealing with mental characteristics of races. The blond North-Europeans, South Italians, Jews, Negroes, Indians, Chinese have been described as though their mental characteristics were biologically determined. It is true, each population has a certain character that is expressed in its behavior, so that there is a geographical distribution of types of behavior. At the same time we have a geographical distribution of anatomical types, and as a result we find that a selected population can be described as having a certain anatomical type and a certain kind of behavior. This, however, does not justify us in claiming that the anatomical type determines behavior. A great error is committed when we allow ourselves to draw this inference. First of all it would be necessary to prove that the correlation between bodily form and behavior is absolute, that it is valid not only for the selected spot, but for the whole population of the given type, and, conversely, that the same behavior does not occur when the types of bodily build differ. Secondly, it would have to be shown that there is an inner relation between the two phenomena.

I might illustrate this by an example taken from an entirely different field. A particular country has a specific climate and particular geological formation. In the same country is found a certain flora. Nevertheless, the character of soil and climate does not explain the composition of the flora, except in so far as it depends upon these two factors. Its composition depends upon the whole historical evolution of plant forms all over the world. The single fact of an agreement of distribution does not prove a genetic relation between the two sets of observations. Negroes in Africa have long limbs and a certain kind of mental behavior. It does not follow that the long limbs are in any way the cause of their mental behavior. The very point to be proved is assumed as proved in this kind of argumentation.

A scientific solution of this problem requires a different line of approach. Mental activities are functions of the organism. We have seen that physiological functions of the same organism may vary greatly under varying conditions. Is the case of mental reactions different? While the study of cretins and of men of genius shows that biological differences exist which limit the type of individual behavior, this has little bearing upon the masses constituting a population in which great varieties of bodily structure prevail. We have seen that the same physiological functions occur in different races with varying frequency, but that no essential qualitative differences can be established. The question must be asked whether the same conditions prevail in mental life.

If it were possible to subject two populations of different type to the same outer conditions the answer would not be difficult. The obstacle in our way lies in the impossibility of establishing sameness of conditions. Investigators differ fundamentally in their opinion in regard to the question of what constitutes sameness of conditions, and our attention must be directed, therefore, to this question.

If we could show how people of exactly the same biological composition react in different types of environment, much might be gained. It seems to me that the data of history create a strong presumption in favor of material changes of mental behavior among peoples of the same genetic composition. The free and easy English of Elizabethan times contrast forcibly with the prudish Mid-Victorian; the Norse Viking and the modern Norwegian do not impress us as the same; the stern Roman republican and his dissolute descendant of imperial times present striking contrasts.

But we need more tangible evidence. At least in so far as intelligent reaction to simple problems of everyday life is concerned, we may bring forward a considerable amount of experimental evidence that deals with this problem. We do not need to assume that our modern intelligence tests give us a clue to absolutely biologically determined intelligence—whatever that may mean—they certainly do tell us how individuals react to simple, more or less unfamiliar, situations. At a first glance it would seem that very important racial differences are found. I refer to the many comparative tests of the intelligence of individuals of various European types and of Europeans and Negroes. North Europeans tested in our country were found as a whole decidedly superior to South Europeans, Europeans as a whole to Negroes. The question arises, what does this mean? If there is a real difference determined by race, we should find the same kind of difference between these racial types wherever they live. Professor Garth has recently collected the available evidence and reaches the conclusion that it is not possible to prove a difference due to genetic factors, that rather all the available observations may be easily explained as due to differences in social environment. It seems to me the most convincing proof of the correctness of this view has been given by Dr. Klineberg, who examined the various outstanding European types in urban and rural communities in Europe. He found that there is everywhere a marked contrast between rural and urban populations, the city giving considerably better results than the country and that furthermore the various groups do not follow by any means the same order in city and country ; that the order rather depends upon social conditions, such as the excellence of the school systems and conflicts between home and school. Still more convincing are his observations on Negroes. He examined a considerable number of Negroes in southern cities who had moved to the city from rural districts. He found that the longer they lived in the city the better the results of the tests came to be, so that Negroes who had lived in the city for six years were far superior to those who had just moved to the city. He found the same result when studying Negroes who had moved from the south to New York, an improvement with the time of residence in New York. This result agrees with Brigham's findings for Italians who had lived for varying periods in the United States. It has often been claimed, as was done in the beginning by Brigham, that such changes are due to a process of selection, that more poorly endowed individuals have migrated to the country in late years and represent the group that has just come to the city. It would be difficult to maintain this in view of the regularity with which this phenomenon reappears in every test. Still, Dr. Klineberg has also given definite evidence that selection does not account for these differences. He compared the records of the migrating groups with those who remained behind. The records collected in Nashville and Birmingham showed that there is no appreciable difference between the two groups. The migrants were even a little below those who stayed at home. He also found that the migrants who came to New York were slightly inferior to those who remained in the South.

I have given these data in some detail, because they show definitely that cultural environment is a most important factor in determining the results of the so-called intelligence tests. In fact, a careful examination of the tests shows clearly that in none of them has our cultural experience been eliminated. City life and country life, the South and the North present different types of cultural background to which we learn to adapt ourselves, and our reactions are determined by these adaptations, which are often so obscure that they can be detected only by a most intimate knowledge of the conditions of life. We have indications of such adaptations in other cases. It would seem that among the Plains Indians the experience of girls with bead work gives to them a superiority in handling tests based on form. It is highly desirable that the tests should be examined with greatest care in regard to the indirect influence of experience upon the results. I suspect strongly that such influences can always be discovered and that it will be found impossible to construct any test in which this element is so completely eliminated that we could consider the results as an expression of purely biologically determined factors.

It is much more difficult to obtain convincing results in regard to emotional reactions in different races. No satisfactory experimental method has been devised that would answer the crucial question, in how far cultural background and in how far the biological basis of personality is responsible for observed differences. There is no doubt that individuals do differ in this respect on account of their biological constitution. It is very questionable whether the same may be said of races, for in all races we find a wide range of different types of personality. All that we can say with certainty is that the cultural factor is of greatest importance and might well account for all the observed differences, although this does not preclude the possibility of biologically determined differences. The variety of response of groups of the same race but culturally different is so great that it seems likely that any existing biological differences are of minor importance. I can give only a few instances. The North American Indians are reputed as stoic, as ready to endure pain and torture without a murmur. This is true in all those cases in which culture demands repression of emotion. The same Indians, when ill, give in to hopeless depression. Among closely related Indian tribes certain ones are given to ecstatic orgies, while others enjoy a life running in smooth conventional channels. The buffalo hunter was an entirely different personality from the poor Indian who has to rely on government help, or who lives on the proceeds of land rented by his White neighbors. Social workers are familiar with the subtle influence of personal relations that will differentiate the character of members of the same family. Ethnological evidence is all in favor of the assumption that hereditary racial traits are unimportant as compared to cultural conditions. As a matter of fact, ethnological studies do not concern themselves with race as a factor in cultural form. From Waitz on, through Spencer, Tylor, Bastian, to our times, ethnologists have not given serious attention to race, because they find cultural forms distributed regardless of race.

I believe the present state of our knowledge justifies us in saying that, while individuals differ, biological differences between races are small. There is no reason to believe that one race is by nature so much more intelligent, endowed with great will power, or emotionally more stable than another, that the difference would materially influence its culture. Nor is there any good reason to believe that the differences between races are so great that the descendants of mixed marriages would be inferior to their parents. Biologically there is no good reason to object to fairly close inbreeding in healthy groups, nor to intermingling of the principal races.

I have considered so far only the biological side of the problem. In actual life we have to reckon with social settings which have a very real existence, no matter how erroneous the opinions on which they are founded. Among us race antagonism is a fact, and we should try to understand its psychological significance. For this purpose we have to consider the behavior not only of man, but also of animals. Many animals live in societies. It may be a shoal of fish which any individuals of the same species may join, or a swarm of mosquitoes. No social tie is apparent in these groups, but there are others which we may call closed societies that do not permit any outsider to join their group. Packs of dogs and well-organized herds of higher mammals, ants and bees are examples of this kind. In all these groups there is a considerable degree of social solidarity which is expressed particularly by antagonism against any outside group. The troops of monkeys that live in a given territory will not allow another troop to come and join them. The members of a closed animal society are mutually tolerant or even helpful. They repel all outside intruders.

Conditions in primitive society are quite similar. Strict social obligations exist between the members of a tribe, but all outsiders are enemies. Primitive ethics demand self-sacrifice in the group to which the individual belongs, deadly enmity against every outsider. A closed society does not exist without antagonisms against others. Although the degree of antagonism against outsiders has decreased, closed societies continue to exist in our own civilization. The nobility formed a closed society until very recent times. Patricians and plebeians in Rome, Greeks and barbarians, the gangs of our streets, Mohammedan and infidel, and our modern nations are in this sense closed societies that cannot exist without antagonisms. The principles that hold societies together vary enormously, but common to all of them are social obligations within the group, antagonisms against other parallel groups.

Race consciousness and race antipathy differ in one respect from the social groups here enumerated. While in all other human societies there is no external characteristic that helps to assign an individual to his group, here his very appearance singles him out. If the belief should prevail, as it once did, that all red-haired individuals have an undesirable character, they would at once be segregated and no red-haired individual could escape from his class no matter what his personal characteristics might be. The Negro, the East Asiatic or Malay who may at once be recognized by his bodily build is automatically placed in his class and not one of them can escape being excluded from a foreign closed group. The same happens when a group is characterized by dress imposed by circumstances, by choice, or because a dominant group prescribe for them a distinguishing symbol—like the garb of the medieval Jews or the stripes of the convict—so that each individual no matter what his own character may be, is at once assigned to his group and treated accordingly. If racial antipathy were based on innate human traits this would be expressed in interracial sexual aversion. The free intermingling of slave owners with their female slaves and the resulting striking decrease in the number of full-blood Negroes, the progressive development of a half-blood Indian population and the readiness of intermarriage with Indians when economic advantages may be gained by such means, show clearly that there is no biological foundation for race feeling. There is no doubt that the strangeness of an alien racial type does play an important rôle, for the ideal of beauty of the White who grows up in a purely White society is different from that of a Negro. This again is analogous to the feeling of aloofness among groups that are characterized by different dress, different mannerisms of expression of emotion, or by the ideal of bodily strength as against that of refinement of form. The student of race relations must answer the question whether in societies in which different racial types form a socially homogeneous group, a marked race consciousness develops. This question cannot be answered categorically, although interracial conditions in Brazil and the disregard of racial affiliation in the relation between Mohammedans and infidels show that race consciousness may be quite insignificant.

When social divisions follow racial lines, as they do among ourselves, the degree of difference between racial forms is an important element in establishing racial groupings and in creating racial conflicts.

The actual relation is not different from that developing in other cases in which social cleavage develops. In times of intense religious feeling denominational conflicts, in times of war national conflicts take the same course. The individual is merged in his group and not rated according to his personal value.

However, nature is such that constantly new groups are formed in which each individual subordinates himself to the group. He expresses his feeling of solidarity by an idealization of his group and by an emotional desire for its perpetuation. When the groups are denominational, there is strong antagonism against marriages outside of the group. The group must be kept pure, although denomination and descent are in no way related. If the social groups are racial groups we encounter in the same way the desire for racial endogamy in order to maintain racial purity.

On this subject I take issue with Sir Arthur Keith, who in the address already referred to is reported to have said that "race antipathy and race prejudice nature has implanted in you for her own end—the improvement of mankind through racial differentiation." I challenge him to prove that race antipathy is "implanted by nature" and not the effect of social causes which are active in every closed social group, no matter whether it is racially heterogeneous or homogeneous. The complete lack of sexual antipathy, the weakening of race consciousness in communities in which children grow up as an almost homogeneous group; the occurrence of equally strong antipathies between denominational groups, or between social strata—as witnessed by the Roman patricians and plebeians, the Spartan Lacedaemonians and Helots, the Egyptian castes and some of the Indian castes—all these show that antipathies are social phenomena. If you will, you may call them "implanted by nature," but only in so far as man is a being living in closed social groups, leaving it entirely indetermined what these social groups may be.

No matter how weak the case for racial purity may be, we understand its social appeal in our society. While the biological reasons that are adduced may not be relevant, a stratification of society in social groups that are racial in character will always lead to racial discrimination. As in all other sharp social groupings the individual is not judged as an individual but as a member of his class. We may be reasonably certain that whenever members of different races form a single social group with strong bonds, racial prejudice and racial antagonisms will come to lose their importance. They may even disappear entirely. As long as we insist on a stratification in racial layers, we shall pay the penalty in the form of interracial struggle. Will it be better for us to continue as we have been doing, or shall we try to recognize the conditions that lead to the fundamental antagonisms that trouble us?

MODERN POPULATIONS OF AMERICA[1]

I HAVE been asked to speak on the modern populations of America, and I confess that I feel some hesitation in taking up this important subject. The scientific problems involved are of great and fundamental importance; but unfortunately materials for their discussion have hardly been collected at all, and I do not see any immediate prospect of their being gathered on a scale at all adequate.

We may distinguish three distinct types of populations in modern America. The first type includes those that are entirely or almost entirely descendants of European immigrants, such as the population of the northern United States, of Canada, and of the Argentine; a second type is represented by populations containing a large amount of Indian blood, like those of Mexico, Peru, and Bolivia; and a third type includes populations consisting essentially of mixtures of Negroes and other races. In this last group we may again distinguish between populations in which the mixture is essentially Negro and White and those in which we find a strong mixture of Negro and Indian, or Negro, Indian, and White. Examples of these are the populations of the Southern States, of the West Indies, of some districts of Central and South America, like parts of Brazil, and of certain localities on the west coast of South America.

It will easily be recognized that the mixed populations who are descendants of American Indians and Europeans are found essentially in those large areas in which the aboriginal population at the time of the Conquest was dense. This was the case particularly in Mexico and in the Andean highlands. The extermination of the native population has occurred only in those areas in which at the time of the Conquest the Indian population was very sparse or where a dense population lived in a limited territory, as in the West Indies. The Negro populations occur in all those areas in which there was a long-continued importation of African slaves.

[1]From *Proceedings of the 19th International Congress of Americanists, Washington, December, 1915* (Washington, D. C., 1917), pp. 569–575.

The development of these populations depended to a great extent upon the very fundamental difference in the relations between the Anglo-Saxon European immigrants and the Latin American immigrants. While among the former intermarriages or unions between women of European descent and members of the foreign races were rare, intermixture was not so limited in Latin American countries; and unions between European men and women of foreign races, or of European women and men of foreign races, have always been of more nearly equal frequency. The importance of this difference is great, because in the former case the number of individuals with European blood is constantly increasing, because the children of the women of the White population remain White, while the children of the women of the Negro or Indian population have on the average a considerable amount of infusion of White blood. This must necessarily result in a constant decrease of the relative amount of non-European blood in the total population. This phenomenon may be disturbed to a certain extent by differences in fertility or mortality of the mixed populations, but it is not likely that the total result will be influenced by such differences. In those cases, on the other hand, in which White women marry members of foreign races, or at least half-blood descendants of foreign races, a thorough penetration of the two races must occur; and if marriages in both directions are equally frequent, the result must be a complete permeation of the two types. There is very little doubt that the rapid disappearance of the American Indian in many parts of the United States is due to this peculiar kind of mixture. The women of mixed descent are drawn away from the tribes with a fair degree of rapidity, and merge in the general population; while the men of mixed descent remain in the tribe, and contribute to a continued infusion of White blood among the natives.

The claim has been made, and has constantly been repeated, that mixed races—like the American Mulattoes or the American Mestizos— are inferior in physical and mental qualities, that they inherit all the unfavorable traits of the parental races. So far as I can see, this bold proposition is not based on adequate evidence. As a matter of fact, it would be exceedingly difficult to say at the present time what race is pure and what race is mixed. It is certainly true that in the borderland of the areas inhabited by any of the fundamental races of mankind mixed types do occur, and there is nothing to prove that these types are inferior either physically or mentally. We might adduce, as an example,

Japan, a country in which the Malay and the Mongol type come into contact; or the Arab types of North Africa, that are partly of Negro, partly of Mediterranean descent; or the nations of eastern Europe, that contain a considerable admixture of Mongoloid blood. In none of these cases will a careful and conscientious investigator be willing to admit any deteriorating effect of the undoubted mixture of different races. It is exceedingly difficult in all questions of this kind to differentiate with any degree of certainty between social and hereditary causes. On the whole, the half-bloods live under conditions less favorable than the pure parental races; and for this reason the social causes will bring about phenomena of apparent weakness that are erroneously interpreted as due to effects of intermixture. This is particularly true in the case of the Mulatto population of the United States. The Mulatto is found as an important element in many of our American cities where the majority of this group form a poor population, which, on the one hand, is not in a condition of social and economic equality with the Whites, while, on the other hand, the desire for improved social opportunity creates a considerable amount of dissatisfaction. It is not surprising that under these conditions the main characteristics of the group should not be particularly attractive. At the same time the poverty that prevails among many of them, and the lack of sanitary conditions under which they live, give the impression of hereditary weakness.

The few cases in which it has been possible to gather strictly scientific data on the physical characteristics of the half-bloods have rather shown that there may be a certain amount of physical improvement in the mixed race. Thus the investigation of half-blood Indians in the United States which I undertook in 1892 showed conclusively that the physical development of the mixed race, as expressed by their stature, is superior to that of both the White and Indian parents. I also found that the fertility of half-blood women was greater than that of the full-blood Indian women who live practically under the same social conditions. The latter conclusion has been corroborated by a much wider investigation, included in the last Census of the United States. Professor Dixon, under whose auspices the data were collated, not only found that the half-blood women were more fertile than the full-blood women, but he also discovered that the number of surviving children of half-blood women was greater than the number of surviving children of full-blood women. This seems to indicate a greater vigor even more clearly than the data found by a study of the stature of the half-blood race. During the present year I have been able to make an investigation of the population of Puerto Rico; and here a similar phenomenon appears in a comparison between the Mulatto population and the White population. In a study of children it was found that the Mulattoes excel in physical development the children of pure Spanish descent, and that their development is more rapid. Evidently the rapidity of development of the Mulatto, and his better physique, are phenomena that are closely correlated.

A number of tests have been made of the mental conditions of Mulatto children. These, however, I do not consider as convincing, because the differences found are slight, and because, furthermore, the retardation of development due to less favorable social conditions has not sufficiently been taken into account. There is also much doubt in regard to the significance of certain differences in the resistance to pathogenic causes that has been observed in different races. Judging from a general biological point of view, it would seem that an unfavorable effect of mixture of races is very unlikely. The anatomical differences between the races of man that we have to consider here are at best very slight, certainly less than those found in different races of domesticated animals. In the case of domesticated animals, no decrease of vigor has been observed when races are crossed as closely allied as races of man. Since man must be considered anatomically as a highly domesticated species, we may expect the same conditions to prevail, and by analogy there is no reason to suppose any unfavorable effects.

Attention should be called here to a peculiar condition of society in all those regions where the old aboriginal population contributes a large amount to the modern population. In all these cases we observe a continuity of tradition that leads back to pre-Columbian times. It may be that the ancient religious ideas and that much of the oral tradition of the people have been lost and that their place has been taken by ideas imported from Europe. Nevertheless a vast amount of the old customs survives. This may be readily seen by a study of the habitations and of the household utensils in Mexico and in Peru. It is quite obvious that in these cases the ancient tradition survives; and this fact is merely an indication of the tremendous force of conservatism that binds the people of modern times to their past. It is no wonder that in these cases the obstacles to the diffusion of modern ideas are much greater than in those populations that derive their origin entirely from European sources. This is so much more the case, since the European immigrant breaks completely with his past, and develops in a new environment and according to new standards of thought.

The investigation of the ideas and beliefs of the American Negroes throws an interesting side-light on these conditions. Unfortunately this subject has received very slight attention, and it is hardly possible to state definitely what the conditions are in various parts of the continent. It is quite clear, however, that the Negroes, owing to their segregation, have retained much of what they brought from Africa. In this case there is no continuity in the material life, because the houses, household utensils, and other objects are all derived from European sources, while many of the old tales and old religious ideas seem to survive, much modified, however, by American conditions. Owing to the fact that the coast tribes of Africa have been long under the influence of Portuguese civilization, a certain assimilation of Negro ideas had developed; and in all probability this accounts for the similarity of ideas found among American Negroes and Indians of Latin America, so far as these have adopted ideas imported by Spaniards and Portuguese of the sixteenth and seventeenth centuries.

Another question relating to the physical type of the mixed populations relates to the question of how far a new type results from their intermingling. Of recent years there has been much discussion in regard to this problem. Galton and his adherents maintain that in a mixture of types a new intermediate type will develop analogous to the appearance of the mule as a result of mixture between horse and donkey. Other investigators, following the important observations of Mendel and his successors, claim that no permanent new type develops, but that the so-called "unit" characters of the parents will be segregated in the mixed population. Assuming, for instance, the blue eye of the North European to be a "unit" character, it is assumed that in the mixed type there will always remain a certain group with blue eyes. More specifically it is claimed that among the descendants of couples in which one parent has blue eyes, the other pure brown eyes, one-fourth of the total number from the second generation on will have blue eyes, while the rest will have brown eyes. In order to avoid technicalities, we might perhaps say that in these cases there must be a certain degree of alternating inheritance, in so far as in a mixed population some individuals will resemble in their traits the one parental race, while others will resemble the other. Some investigators claim that the existence of this type of inheritance—so-called "Mendelian" inheritance—has been definitely proved to exist in man.

It is hardly possible at the present time to answer this important problem with any degree of definiteness, although in regard to a number of traits sufficient evidence is available. I pointed out before that in the case of stature the half-blood shows a tendency to exceed both parental types; in other words, that a new distinctive form develops. On the other hand, the investigation of eye-color has shown that while intermediate eye-colors do occur, there is a decided tendency for a number of individuals to reproduce either the blue eyes of northern Europe or the very dark eyes of other races. In regard to skin-color the evidence is not clear. A certain permanence of type has also been found in the head form. Some types of man may be characterized by the ratio of the longitudinal to the transversal diameter of the head. Sometimes both are not very different, while in other cases the head is very narrow and at the same time very long. It has been found that when two types intermingle in which the parental races show material differences in head form, then a great variety of head forms will occur among the descendants, indicating a tendency to revert to the parental types. Whether or not the classical ratios of Mendelian inheritance prevail is a question that it is quite impossible to answer. On the whole, it seems much more likely that we have varying types of alternating inheritance rather than true Mendelian forms.

If further investigation should show that the tendency to such alternating inheritance is found in mixed types throughout, and that the different features belonging to the distinctive parental types have only slight degrees of correlation, it would follow that in a mixed type we may expect the occurrence of a great variety of combinations of parental types; and we may expect, perhaps, a certain loosening of those correlations that are characteristic for the parental races. This question, however, has never been investigated, and cannot be answered with any degree of certainty.

These questions have also a bearing upon the characteristics of the populations of pure European descent that are developing in our country. In earlier times the provenience of the settlers in each particular area was fairly uniform. In the United States we find settlers from England; in the Argentine, those from Spain; but the rapid increase of population in Europe, and the attractiveness of economical conditions in America, have brought it about that the sources of European immigration have become much wider. In the Argentine Republic we find an immigration coming principally from the shores of the Mediterranean. The modern population of the United States is drawn from all parts of Europe, the most recent influx being principally from southeastern, southern, and eastern Europe. The racial composition of the population of Europe is not by any means uniform; but we find distinctive local types inhabiting the various parts of the continent. The differences between a dark-eyed, black-haired, swarthy South Italian, and a blond, tall, blue-eyed Scandinavian and a short-headed, gray-eyed, tall Servian, are certainly most striking. This fact has led to the assertion that nothing like the modern intermixture of European types has ever occurred in the past in any part of Europe.

Attention should be called here to a peculiar difference between the composition of our American population and that of European populations. After individual land-tenure had developed, and agriculture had become the basis of life of all European peoples, a remarkable permanence of habitat developed in all parts of Europe. In place of the waves of migration that marked the end of antiquity, a local development of small village communities set in, which, after they were once established, came to be exceedingly permanent. The members of these communities were only slightly increased from the outside, and thus a period of inbreeding set in that is equaled only by the amount of inbreeding characteristic of small isolated primitive tribes. It is difficult to obtain exact information in regard to this process; but the investigation of genealogies of a few European communities shows that it has been very marked. It is therefore clear that when we compare, let me say, the population of a small Spanish village and that of a South Italian village, we may find in both communities what appears to the observer as the same type; but we find at the same time that the actual lines of descent of these two groups have been quite distinct for many generations. A peculiar result is found wherever this type of inbreeding occurs. Since all the families are interrelated, it is clear that all the families are very much alike, and that practically any family may be selected and considered as the type of the population that is being investigated. Wherever these conditions do not prevail, and where the ancestry of the various parts of the population is quite distinct, a single family can never be considered as representative of the whole population, and we may expect considerable differences to occur between the family lines. This coming together of distinct lines is characteristic of all the industrial districts of Europe and also of the populations of European descent in America. Thus in the Argentine Republic the people of Spanish and of Italian communities will be brought together. In the United States we find side by side families of English, Irish, French, Spanish, German, Russian, and Italian descent, each of which represents the type of the locality from which it comes. In other words, the family lines composing American populations are much more diverse than those found in the rural communities of Europe.

From a biological point of view there is little doubt that this condition must have an effect upon the physical characteristics of the whole population. Observations are not available, except those bearing upon the relation of sexes in the Argentine Republic. According to the last Argentine census, it has been found that the relation of sexes of children found in families of pure Italian or pure Argentine descent shows considerable differences when compared with that found in families of mixed Italo-Spanish descent, and it may very well be that this has to do with the disturbances of the lines of descent which we have just discussed.

No investigations are available on the physical characteristics of individuals of mixed European descent. All we know is that the alternating inheritance referred to before may be observed also in the descendants of a single people. Thus, for instance, it has been shown that when a long-headed Russian Jew marries a short-headed Russian Jewess, the children resemble in part the father, in part the mother, so that here also a certain reversion of type may be noticed. It has also been found that the laws of inheritance of eye-color are similar to those referred to before. There is therefore every reason to assume that the same laws of inheritance prevail in a mixture of European peoples that have been observed in a mixture of different races.

A word should be said in regard to the claim that the mixture of European types that is characteristic of the population of modern America is of a unique character. The events that occurred in prehistoric Europe do not favor this assumption, because the European continent at that time was the scene of constant migration and of constant intermingling of different peoples. The contrast between medieval conditions and ancient conditions appears, for instance, very clearly in Spain. The oldest inhabitants of the Iberian Peninsula of which we know were overlaid successively by Phenicians, Romans, Kelts, Teutonic tribes, and Moorish people from northern Africa, which resulted in an enormous infusion of blood from all parts of Europe. With the Spanish victories over the Moors and the driving away of the Jews, a period of inbreeding set in which has lasted up to the present time. Similar conditions obtain in eastern Europe, where waves of migrations of Slavic, Teutonic, Finnish and Mongol peoples may be traced, each of which represented a certain definite local type. In short, the whole early history of Europe is one continued series of shifts of populations, that must have resulted in an enormous mixture of all the different types of the continent.

The important question arises whether the types that come to America remain stable and retain their former characteristics. A number of years ago I investigated this question, and reached the conclusion that a number of definite, although slight, changes are taking place; more particularly, that under American geographical and social conditions the width of the face decreases, and the head form undergoes certain slight changes. My observations are corroborated by the evidence that may be obtained from studies of European city populations. The differences in social environment there are probably the same as those that I have observed in the city of New York; and the observations also indicate a certain difference between the city population and the country population which cannot be explained by mixture or by selection.

Quite recently I investigated this question in Puerto Rico, and found that the type of the modern population does not conform to any of the ancestral types. The population is derived very largely from Spanish sources, so much so that among the individuals whom I measured a large percentage were sons of Spanish-born fathers. Besides this, we find a considerable infusion of Negro blood, and I presume also a certain survival of Indian blood. The ancestral types, except the Indians, are decidedly long-headed. The Indian blood cannot be very considerable; nevertheless we find that the Puerto Ricans of today are as short-headed as the average of the French of the Auvergne. We may therefore conclude that the movement of populations from Europe to our continent is accompanied by certain changes of type, the extent of which cannot be definitely determined at the present time.

I cannot conclude my remarks without at least a brief reference to the modern endeavors to improve the physical type of the people. It has been claimed that the congestion in modern cities and other causes are bringing about a gradual degeneration of our race, which advocates of eugenics desire to counteract by adequate legislative measures. It is certainly right to try to check the spread of hereditary defects by such measures, but the movement as it is now conceived is not free of serious dangers. First of all, it would seem that the fundamental thesis of the degeneracy of our population has never been proved. Our statistics permit us to count the number of defective individuals, which of course appears to increase with the rigidity of examination. On the other hand, our statistics do not allow us to count the individuals of unusual physical or mental development. It is obvious that, even if the method of counting should remain the same, there would be an apparent increase in the number of defectives if the variability of the total population should increase; in other words, if not all should conform to a standard, but a considerable number should be inordinately gifted, another number inordinately deficient. This would not necessarily mean a degeneration of the population, but would merely be an expression of increased variability. More serious is the question whether the principles of eugenics conform to the natural development of the human species. The fundamental motive that prompts us to advocate eugenic measures is perhaps not so much the idea of increasing human efficiency as rather to eliminate human suffering. The humanitarian idea of the elimination of suffering, which conforms so well with our sentiments, seems, however, opposed to the conditions under which species thrive. What is an inconvenience today will be suffering tomorrow; and the effect of an exaggerated humanitarianism may be to make mankind so sensitive to suffering that the very roots of its existence will be endangered. This consideration ought to receive the most careful attention of those who try to predetermine the development of our populations by legislative devices.

REPORT ON AN ANTHROPOMETRIC INVESTIGATION OF THE POPULATION OF THE UNITED STATES[1]

CHARACTERISTICS OF THE POPULATION OF THE UNITED STATES

THE White population of the United States differs from that of Europe not so much in character as in the mode of assemblage of its component elements. The important theoretical and practical problems that arise in a study of the biological characteristics of our population relate largely to the effects of the recent rapid migrations of the diverse types of Europeans. The problem is further complicated by the presence of a large Negro population, of small remnants of Indian aborigines, and by a slight influx of Asiatics.

It would be an error to assume that the intermingling of different European types is a unique historical phenomenon which has never occurred before. On the contrary, all European nationalities are highly complex in origin. Even those most secluded and receiving the least amount of foreign blood at the present time have in past times been under entirely different conditions. An excellent example of this kind is presented by Spain. The Iberians are the earliest substratum of population with which we are acquainted. The coast population was undoubtedly affected by a certain amount of intermixture with Phenician and Greek colonists. There followed a number of migrations of Keltic tribes from northwestern Europe and a thorough colonization of the peninsula by Rome. The Teutonic tribes which invaded Spain came in part from the regions of the Black Sea. Later

[1] The following paper deals with purely anthropometric problems. It was intended to show the kinds of information needed for understanding the meaning of bodily build of individuals in relation to their descent and social environment. For this reason the important questions relating to relative fertility as bringing about changes in the constitution of the population and the problems involved in the hereditary characteristics of pathological characteristics, physiological and psychological traits determined by the genetic character of the individual were not touched upon. The whole problem should be solved by a consideration not only of the anthropometric traits, but also by a detailed study of heredity, of functions of the body and of the differential constitution of the population. Since the paper was written much valuable work has been done in this direction, particularly by the Population Association of America. *Journal of the American Statistical Association,* vol. 18 (June, 1922), pp. 181–209.

on we can trace waves of migration from northern Africa, which attained their greatest importance during the time of the Moorish empires. With the development of medieval conditions and the expulsion of the Moors and the Jews, the population of Spain became stable and there was no further disturbance due to important migrations. It is therefore evident that the present population of Spain contains elements derived from practically all parts of Europe and from northern Africa.

Similar conditions may be observed in Great Britain, where there is also clear evidence of a large number of waves of migration. In prehistoric times we find a long-headed type, quite different in appearance and in customs from a later round-headed type. With the beginning of historic times we observe first Roman colonization, then waves of migration entering Great Britain from all parts of the North Sea, from Scandinavia and northern Germany, and, finally, the influx of the Normans. With this event extended migration ceased and the population of the island was gradually welded into the modern English.

Migrations of this kind may be recognized even in very early times. After sweeping over the older population of Greece, north European types established themselves in the Balkan Peninsula and on the Aegean Islands during the so-called Doric migration, which occurred a thousand years before our era. Later on the movements of the Finnish ancestors of the Bulgarians and the migrations of the south Slavic peoples added to the intermixture of types in the eastern European peninsula.

It might seem that a few countries in Europe were not so much exposed to intermixture as those previously mentioned, and it is particularly assumed that Sweden and Norway represent a very homogeneous population. Still, we may recognize here also a considerable differentiation of local types. An investigation of the districts nearest to Finland shows very clearly an approach to the Finnish type which may be due to intermixture. In southern Norway is encountered a strongly aberrant type whose origin cannot be historically determined. In the northern area the Lapps present a foreign element. In later times immigrations were not by any means rare. Thus the development of the mining industry brought in a great many Walloons; and the nobility, at least, is a composite of descendants of natives from many parts of Europe. Historical evidence shows that the central parts of Europe over which migrations have swept periodically were, even more than the outlying districts, exposed to intermixture of different types.

Intermixture in Europe was largely confined to antiquity, although in some parts it continued into the Middle Ages, whereas the intermingling of different local types in the United States is recent. Owing to the social conditions in ancient Europe amalgamation of distinct elements may have been rather slow. Notwithstanding the relatively small numbers of migrating individuals, it may have taken several generations for the intrusive and native populations to become merged. In the United States, owing to the absence of hereditary social classes, the amalgamation is on the whole more rapid and involves larger numbers of individuals than the intermixture which took place in earlier periods in the Old World.

The impression that the population of European countries is comparatively speaking "pure" in descent is founded on its stability. In northern and central Europe this condition developed after individual hereditary landholding was substituted for the earlier forms of agricultural life, and with the attachment of the serf to the soil which he inhabited. These conditions prevailed in the Mediterranean area even in antiquity, but in the northern parts of Europe they did not develop until the Middle Ages, when the more or less tribal organization of the people gave way to feudal states. During the period when the Keltic and Teutonic tribes moved readily from place to place a vast amount of mixture occurred in all parts of Europe. Later on, when families became settled, those parts of the populations which were proprietors of the soil, or otherwise attached to the soil, became stationary, and consequently intermixture between distant parts of the continent became much less frequent than in previous times. On the other hand, the mutual permeation of neighboring communities probably became much more thorough.

These conditions of stability continued until by the development of cities diverse elements were brought together in the same community. This process became important with the growth of modern industrialism and with the concomitant growth of urban populations that were drawn together from large areas. Investigations made in different parts of Europe, particularly in Italy [1] and in Baden,[2] show differences in type between city populations and those of the open country. These

---

[1] Ridolfo Livi, *Antropometria Militare* (Rome, 1896), p. 87 *et seq.*

[2] Otto Ammon, *Zur Anthropologie der Badener* (Jena, 1899), p. 641.

may in part be explained by the strong intermixture of types drawn from a wide area which assemble and intermarry in the city. Observations of the population of Paris [1] indicate the same kind of intermixture of north European and central European types.

The settlement of the unoccupied districts of the United States has brought about an intermixture of types similar to that occurring in modern city populations, because settlers from different parts of Europe may dwell in close proximity in newly opened countries. Although in many cases we find a strong cohesion of farmers who come from the same European country, there is also a great deal of scattering.

It should, therefore, be understood that the problems presented by the population of the United States do not differ materially from the analogous European problems. The differences are due to the larger numbers of individuals involved in the whole process, in its rapidity, in its extension over rural communities, and in the forms of cohesion between members of the same group which are dependent upon the mode of settlement of the country. The process resembles earlier European mixtures in so far as many diverse European types are involved. In modern Europe only European types enter into the mixture, but a number of races morphologically removed from the White race enter into certain phases of the problem in America. Even this aspect of the problem was probably present in antiquity when slaves of foreign races formed a considerable part of the population.

The long continued stability of European populations which set in with the beginning of the Middle Ages and continued, at least in rural districts, until very recent times, has brought about a large amount of inbreeding in every limited district. In default of detailed statistical information in relation to the development of populations it is impossible to give exact data, but a cursory investigation shows that inbreeding of this type must have occurred for a very long time. The theoretical number of ancestors of every living individual proceeds by multiplication by two from generation to generation back, so that ten generations (or approximately 300 or 350 years) ago every single individual would have had 1,024 ancestors. Therefore, about 600 or 700 years ago there would be more than 1,000,000 ancestors for each individual. Considering the stability of population, and the fact that brothers and sisters have the same ancestors, such an increase in the number is, of

[1] Franz Boas, "The Cephalic Index," *American Anthropologist,* N. S., vol. 1 (1899), p. 453.

course, entirely impossible, and it necessarily follows that a very large number of individuals in the ancestral series must be identical, which means that there must have been a large amount of inbreeding.

The "loss of ancestors" becomes the greater the further back we go in the ancestry and the more stable the population. It is obvious that particularly in the landholding group of families which remains from generation to generation in the same place, there must have been much inbreeding. Statistical information is available only for a few village communities and for the high nobility of Europe. The genealogies of all these families demonstrate that the decrease in the number of ancestors is very considerable. The calculations for the high nobility of Europe [1] show that in the sixth ancestral generation there are only 41 ancestors instead of 64; in the twelfth generation, only 533 instead of 4,094. These numbers seem to be quite similar to those found in the stable village communities of Europe. Owing to this intermixture and to the similarity of descent of the families constituting the population, each family represents fairly adequately the whole population, or as we might express it, the whole population is homogeneous, in so far as all the families have the same kind of descent. On the other hand, in a population that results from recent migration and in which individuals from the most diverse parts of the world come together, a single family will not be representative of the whole population, because entirely different ancestral lines will be present in the various families. Therefore the population will be heterogeneous in so far as the different families belong to different lines of descent. To illustrate this point we might assume a community consisting of Whites and Negroes in which the Whites always intermarry among themselves, and the Negroes among themselves. Obviously in such a population, a single family would not be representative of the whole community, but only of its own fraction. On the other hand, if we had a community in which Whites and Negroes had intermarried for a long time, as is the case among the so-called Bastards of South Africa—a people very largely descended from Dutch and Hottentots and in which this intermingling has continued for a long time—we have a homogeneous population in so far as every family represents practically the same line of descent. [2]

[1] Ottokar Lorenz, *Lehrbuch der gesammten wissenschaftlichen Genealogie* (Berlin (1898), p. 289 *et seq.,* pp. 308, 310, 311.

[2] Eugen Fischer, *Die Rehobother Bastards* (Jena, 1913) ; Franz Boas, "On the Variety of Lines of Descent Represented in a Population," *American Anthropologist* N. S., vol. 18 (1916), p. 1 *et seq.*

It will therefore be seen that homogeneity is not by any means identical with purity of race. In the case of a homogeneous population of mixed descent we may expect, on the whole, a high degree of variability in the family, while all the families will be more or less alike. On the other hand, in a heterogeneous population in which each part is, comparatively speaking, "pure," we may expect a low variability of each family with a high variability of the families constituting the whole population. On account of its migratory habits the American city population must be heterogeneous. Heterogeneous are also the immigrants and their immediate descendants, whereas in the stationary populations of New England villages and of the Kentucky mountains we have presumably homogeneous groups.

HEREDITY

For determining the characteristics of a population knowledge of the laws of heredity is indispensable. Ordinarily the term heredity in relation to racial [1] characteristics is used in a somewhat loose manner, and we should distinguish clearly between the hereditary stability of a population and the hereditary characteristics which determine the bodily form and functions of an individual. The concept of hereditary stability in a population can mean only that the distribution of forms which occur in one generation will be repeated in exactly the same way in the following generation. This is clearest in the case of a homogeneous population as defined before. In every population varying bodily forms of individuals will occur with characteristic frequencies. In an undisturbed homogeneous population we must necessarily assume that each generation will show the same characteristic distribution of individual forms. If it did not do so there would be a disturbance of the hereditary stability.

Conditions are quite different in a heterogeneous population like that of the United States. Owing to intermarriages between the various constituent types there must be a tendency toward greater homogeneity, setting aside, of course, the influx of new immigrants. Experience shows that no matter how rigid may be the social objection to intermarriages between different groups, or how strong the pressure to bring about marriages between members of the same group, they will not prevent the gradual assimilation of the population. An instance of this kind is

---

[1] The terms "race" and "racial" are here used in the sense that they mean the assembly of genetic lines represented in a population.

presented by the castes of India in Bengal. Notwithstanding the rigid endogamy of castes it has been observed that the highest castes are similar in type to the peoples of Western Asia, while the lower down in the scale of castes we go the more this type becomes mixed with the older substratum of the native population.[1] This can be explained only by intermarriage between the different castes which must have occurred notwithstanding the rigid laws forbidding it. The less the tendency toward segregation of different groups, the more rapid will be the approach toward homogeneity. Therefore notwithstanding the laws of hereditary stability in individual strains, there cannot be a hereditary stability of a heterogeneous population until homogeneity has been attained. It may even be considered doubtful whether a disturbance of the distribution of bodily forms may not occur as an effect of the intermingling of two populations similar or even identical in type, but of different ancestry, in which, therefore, a heterogeneity of ancestry exists.[2]

Thus it will be seen that the physiological laws of heredity are quite different from the statistical expression of the effects of heredity upon a large population. The latter depends upon both the biological laws of heredity and the peculiar social structure of the population which is being considered. These two aspects of heredity must be kept clearly apart.

Unfortunately, the laws of heredity in man are not clearly known, and it is not yet possible without overstepping the bounds of sound, critical, scientific method to apply them to the study of the characteristics of a population. A considerable amount of preliminary fundamental work must be done before we can proceed to the explanation of special complex phenomena. One fundamental point of view may be considered as established, namely, that when a definite couple of parents is given, the probability of occurrence of a given form among the descendants of this couple is fixed. In man it is not easy to demonstrate this fact because the number of children for each couple is small. If we assume, however, an organism in which each parental couple has an infinitely large number of offspring, the laws of heredity may be so expressed that each form that occurs among the offspring

[1] H. H. Risley and E. A. Gait, *"Census of India, 1901* (Calcutta, 1903, vol. 1, pp. 489 *et seq.*

[2] M. D. and Raymond Pearl, "On the Relation of Race Crossing to the Sex Ratio," *Biological Bulletin,* vol. 15 (1908), pp. 194 *et seq.*

has a definite probability. In man these laws can be investigated only by combining many families in which both parents, or at least one of the parents, has the same characteristic form, although in this case the phenomenon is obscured by the fact that the same form in the parent does not necessarily mean the same ancestry.[1] Observation of various features of the body of man shows that the simple forms of Mendelian heredity are not often applicable. It is true that in a number of cases of pathological modifications, the validity of the simple Mendelian formulas has been established. Even in these cases the number of observations is not sufficient to determine whether we are dealing with exact Mendelian ratios or with approximations. Practically all other cases are still open to doubt. Even in the case of eye color, which has been claimed to be subject to a simple Mendelian ratio with dominance of brown over blue, the available figures are not quite convincing.[2] For the more complex variable measurements of the body simple Mendelian ratios are certainly not applicable. Up to the present time the complex laws governing the frequencies of occurrence of bodily forms among descendants of an ancestral line are not known.

The investigation of any population must, therefore, take into consideration the detailed study of the laws of heredity.

THE INFLUENCE OF ENVIRONMENT

In settling in the United States the immigrants have been brought into a new environment, geographically as well as socially, and the question arises whether the new environment exerts an influence upon bodily form and functions. It has been customary to consider certain features of bodily development as absolutely stable, and anthropologists have characterized modern human types as "permanent forms" which have lasted without variation from the beginning of our modern geological period up to the present time. It is fairly easy to show that in this view exaggerated importance is ascribed to the phenomena of observed hereditary stability.

We know that the bulk of the body of an adult depends to a certain extent upon the more or less favorable conditions under which the child

[1] Franz Boas, "On the Variety of Lines of Descent Represented in a Population," *loc. cit.*

[2] Helene M. Boas, "Inheritance of Eye Color in Man," *American Journal of Physical Anthropology*, vol. 2 (1919), pp. 15 *et seq.*

grows up. It has been shown that malnutrition or pathological conditions of various kinds may retard growth, and that the retardation may be so considerable that it cannot be made up by long continued growth. As a matter of fact, the bulk of the body at the time of birth is so small as compared to the bulk of the body of the adult that it is easy to understand that environmental conditions must exert a considerable influence upon its development. Proof of this is the gradual increase of stature during the past fifty years, until 1914, which has been demonstrated by investigations in a number of countries in Europe, and the difference in stature which is found in the same nationality for people living under different economic conditions.[1]

Since many proportions of the body are related to stature and bulk, these will also undergo modifications due to environmental conditions. The influence of environment is not so obvious in those cases in which the bodily form is practically determined at the time of birth, or in those in which the total growth from the time of birth until the adult stage is very slight. It might be assumed that in all cases of this type heredity alone determines the characteristic form of the body.

From a wider point of view the assumption that environment has no influence upon the form of the body does not seem justified. It must be understood that the question of stability or instability of the body in relation to environmental influences has no relation to the question of the inheritance of acquired characteristics. Even if we should adhere most rigidly to the dogma of the impossibility of the transmission of acquired characteristics, we must admit that a modification of the bodily form of the individual is easily conceivable without the necessity of assuming any modification of the germ plasm owing to individually acquired variation. We should rather have to say that adaptability of a definite type is one of the hereditary characteristics of the germ plasm. The problem involved is readily understood in the case of plants which appear in strongly modified form according to the environment in which they grow. In many cases the amount of hairiness, the form of the leaves, etc., are subject to the degree of moisture of the soil, and an accurate description of the species would therefore involve a statement that the plant has a certain degree of hairiness, dependent as a definite

---

[1] Rudolf Martin, *Lehrbuch der Anthropologie* (Jena, 1914), p. 225. Second edition (Jena, 1928), vol. 1, p. 297.

function upon the moisture of the soil, or that the leaves have a certain form dependent upon outer circumstances. In other words, the plant has a definite form only under a definite environment, and with changing environment, the form changes.

We may include under the group of environmental effects also all those variants of form and function that are dependent upon social habits which influence the organism. An influence upon bodily form is exerted by the habitual uses to which groups of muscles are put. Thus the rest position of the lower jaw is different in different areas. The English seem to hold the lower jaw a little farther forward than the Americans. The people of the western states relax the soft palate more than those of the North Atlantic area. The facial expression is determined by the development of the groups of facial muscles; the variations of certain aspects of the form of the hand and the foot are of this kind. The functioning of organs is even more markedly dependent upon habits, particularly upon habits firmly established during childhood. This is illustrated by the characteristic gait of individuals and of whole groups of people; by the involuntary movements in response to certain stimuli; by many of the expressive movements of the body; by habits of articulation; and by the dexterity and accuracy of movements obtained by early training.

Since we recognize the influence of environment upon the form of body including such features as bulk of body, or muscular forms and the functioning of organs, it seems justifiable to define racial characteristics as we do those of a variable plant, namely, by stating that under definite environmental conditions the bodily form of a race and its functioning are such as we observe, without prejudging the question in how far modifications in form and function may result from changing environment. The actual problem, then, would be to determine whether and how far the traits of the body may be so influenced. We should also bear in mind that it is perfectly conceivable that there may be congenital modifications in forms which are nevertheless not hereditary.[1] Constitutional changes in the body of the mother may bring about modifications in prenatal growth which to the superficial observer might give the impression of hereditary changes. These considerations demonstrate that it is necessary to consider this problem in any thorough investigation of the characteristics of the American population.

[1] Cf. *infra* p. 47.

The question must be asked in how far selective agencies may determine the movements of the population, including immigration and emigration, the settlement of the western parts of the United States by the inhabitants of the eastern states, and the migration from country to city. Besides migration, the selective influences of mating, of mortality, and of fertility have to be taken into account. Of late years much stress has been laid upon the effect of selection upon the constitution of a population.

The effect of selection as determined by bodily form can be investigated to advantage only in a homogeneous population. When every family may be considered as representative of the whole population, and when all strata of society present the same physical characteristics, selective forces that are based on social stratification will not influence the selective results, because all social strata will be alike. If it should be found that groups representing different bodily forms have different tendencies to migrate, or different rates of mortality or fertility, we might have an expression of the direct dependence of selection upon bodily form.

As a matter of fact, however, homogeneous populations do not exist anywhere in the world. A greater or less amount of heterogeneity has always been observed, and heterogeneity in our modern civilization, at least, is always connected with social stratification. In a heterogeneous population like that of the United States the difficulties in the way of determining a direct relation between selective influences and bodily form are almost insurmountable. If, for instance, descendants of a certain nationality are attracted to a particular area, as the Scandinavians to the northwest, the Hungarians to the mines of Pennsylvania, the Mexicans to the southern borderland of the United States, or the French Canadians to the New England states and northern New York, we must remember that each one of these social groups represents a certain physical type and that there will be, therefore, an apparent relation between selection and physical type which in reality is based on social factors.

Similar observations may be made with regard to selective mating. Since mating depends upon social contact, marriages will occur among the groups that associate together. Wherever nationalities cluster together, where denominational or racial considerations act as endogamic restrictions, there will be selective mating of similar types due to social heterogeneity. Besides this there may be a certain amount of selection that unites tall with tall or expresses the sexual attractiveness of other bodily features.

Social heterogeneity exerts an influence also upon the mortality and the fertility of different groups. The more recent immigrants are on the whole less well-to-do than the earlier immigrants and their descendants. We know that there is a relation between fertility and economic well-being and we find, therefore, that the number of children of the more recent immigrants is greater than that of the descendants of earlier immigrants, so that, setting aside the question of mortality, there would be a shifting in the distribution of the population in favor of later immigrants. Since the earlier immigrants represent the northwestern European type and the later immigrants the south and east European types, there will appear in this case also a selection according to bodily form, which is due not to the direct relation between physical characteristics and fertility, but rather to the fact that the one economic group is composed of one type, and the other economic group of another type. In many cases the relation between descent and social stratification is so complex that it easily escapes our notice, and for this reason we may observe phenomena of selection apparently related to bodily form but actually due to obscure social causes that are discovered with great difficulty only.

On the other hand it cannot be denied that in some cases at least there must be a direct relation between bodily form and physiological function on the one side and selective processes on the other. It is, for instance, quite obvious that in the settlement of the new western countries a certain bodily and mental vigor was necessary to enable a person to undertake the venture. It has often been pointed out, although it has never been proven empirically, that in this way there must have been a selection from the inhabitants of the New England villages who migrated westward and that the emigrants represented a physically superior type. Even though this conclusion is not based on observation it seems highly probable. To the same group of phenomena would belong the supposed greater susceptibility to certain forms of disease of slightly pigmented individuals, as compared with the greater power of resistance of brunet individuals. I am not by any means convinced that incontrovertible proof of this assumption has been given; but if it were true that the constitution of the blond is weakened by exposure to intense sunlight, there might be a selective influence of this kind when a people move from the cloudy temperate zones to the brilliant sunlight of more southern and more arid climes.

In considering the selective influences of environment it should be borne in mind that the human body is so constituted that all its organs can operate adequately under widely varying circumstances. Our lungs are able to supply the needs of our body under the air pressure that prevails at the level of the sea, and they operate adequately at an elevation of 20,000 feet where the air is highly rarefied. The heart can adjust itself to the variation in demands made upon it, either in sedentary life at the level of the sea, or in active life in high altitudes. Our digestive organs may adapt themselves to a purely vegetable diet or again to a purely meat diet. Our central nervous system is also capable of adjusting itself to the most varied conditions of life. As long, therefore, as the conditions of environment do not exceed very elastic limits, it is not probable that selective influences would become operative to any very great extent, at least not in so far as they are determined solely by the form and functioning of the organs of the body.

RACIAL AND INDIVIDUAL DIFFERENCES

An investigation of the bodily forms of the individuals constituting a race, homogeneous or heterogeneous, shows that they differ considerably among themselves in every single feature, such as pigmentation, form of hair, size and proportions of the body, physiological reactions. These differences are measurable and express the degree of variability of the race. A complete presentation of the characteristics of a race would contain a statement of the relative frequency of each particular bodily form which occurs among the individuals constituting the race. When comparing, from the point of view of anatomical or physiological characteristics, the racial types of Europe which constitute the bulk of the American population, it appears that the range of variation for the different types is of such a character that a great many individuals belonging to one type correspond to other individuals belonging to another type. In other words, there are certain forms common to all populations of Europe. To give an example: We find strongly contrasting head forms in northern Italy and in Sardinia. Nevertheless an investigation of the distribution of head forms in each one of these districts shows that 27 per cent of the population may belong either to Sardinia or to northern Italy. In other words, there is a very considerable amount of overlapping of bodily form between neighboring types, and it is only when we consider races that are fundamentally different that we find certain characteristics that do not overlap. Comparing, for instance, the blond north European White and the dark Sudanese Negro, there is no overlapping with regard to pigmentation, form of hair, form of nose, form of lips, etc. If, on the other hand, we proceed by steps from northern Europe to the Sudan, a great many intermediate and overlapping steps between these extreme forms will be found, so that only the extremes would really be entirely separate. While it may be that two races are quite distinct with regard to certain features, there are always other features with regard to which the differences are so slight that the assignment of any one individual to either one race or the other would be beset with doubt.

It has been customary to express the differences between racial types by the difference between the averages of each type or between the modes (the most frequent values) that are characteristic for each type. It is easily shown that such a description in misleading. If we wish to express the difference between two individuals, each of whom has constant characteristics, we may proceed in this manner. If one individual measures 170 cm. and another 165 cm., the difference between them is 5 cm. If, however, a certain population has an average stature of 170 cm., and another population an average stature of 165 cm., we cannot say that the difference between the two is 5 cm., because if there is a wide range of variability there will be a large number of individuals among the taller population who have exactly the same statures as individuals of the shorter population. To give arbitrarily selected figures, the one may range perhaps from 150 to 190 cm., the other from 145 to 185 cm. In this case an individual that measures anywhere between 150 and 185 cm. might belong to either class. It must, therefore, be clear that if we speak of differences between two races we do not necessarily mean differences between individuals, and these two concepts must be kept clearly apart. The bulk of our modern literature concerning racial differences is open to misinterpretation owing to a lack of a clear understanding of the significance of the term "difference" as applied on the one hand to individuals and on the other hand to races. The generalization, which is often made (to use our previous instance), that the one population is 5 cm. shorter than the other is often interpreted as meaning that this implies a characteristic of all the individuals of a race, while actually a single selected individual of the shorter race may be much taller than a single selected individual of the taller race. This is equally true of all those anatomical, physiological, and psychological characteristics which exhibit overlapping of individuals. It is also true of those that show no overlapping, because the difference between two selected representative individuals may vary within wide limits. If it is stated that the Whites have larger brains than the Negroes, this does not mean that every White person has a larger brain than any Negro, but merely that the average of the Negro brains is lower than the average of the brains of the Whites. With regard to many characteristics of this kind, we find that the difference between the averages of different races is insignificant as compared to the range of variability that occurs within each race.

An additional point should be considered in connection with this phenomenon. Most of the anatomical characteristics of the body are stable throughout adult life, until senile degeneration begins. On the other hand, physiological and psychological functions are not the same in the same individual at all times. They vary strongly with environmental conditions and particularly with different demands made upon the organism. The variability of physiological and psychological responses is therefore much greater than the variability of anatomical form, because the two former combine the variability due to the difference in the functioning in various individuals with the variations of response under varying conditions. When comparing racial types we must therefore avoid expressing a difference of types simply as a difference of averages.

Another point must be considered which may be illustrated by an example. Let us assume that in one area the color of the hair varies from black to dark brown with an average value on a certain definite shade, and that in another population the color of the hair varies from dark blond to very light blond with an average on a certain shade of blond. In this case the two distributions will not overlap at all. On the other hand, let us assume that we have two populations with the same average shades of brown and of blond as before, but in the one a variation which begins with black and extends into blond shades, and in the other a pigmentation which begins with a very dark brown and extends into very light blond, so that the two overlap. Obviously the two differences will not impress us as the same, notwithstanding the fact that the two averages remain the same. It is therefore indispensable that in an investigation of this kind the significance of the difference between two populations should be clearly expressed, and that the impression should be avoided that the difference between racial types is identical with the difference between individuals.

Still another point deserves attention. Many writers assume that an individual of a certain type represents the same biological type regardless of the racial group to which he belongs. To give an example: a round-headed person of the Tyrols is equated with a round-headed person of southern Italy, at least in so far as the form of the head is concerned. Even if we assume that the round-headedness of the two individuals is of the same kind, this inference is not tenable. It is true that by chance the two individuals may belong to the same lines of descent, but a study of a series of homologous individuals shows that genetically, and therefore physiologically, they are not the same notwithstanding the sameness of the particular trait that is made the subject of study. When we select, for instance, individuals with the same head index of 82 in a population that has the average head index of 85, the children of the selected group will be found to have an average head index of 84; when we select individuals with the same head index of 82 in a population that has the average head index of about 79, the children of the selected group will be found to have an average head index of about 80, for the reason that there will be in each case reversions to the average type of the population to which the selected group belongs. In other words, the individuals which are selected from any population must always be considered as part of this population and cannot be studied as though they were an independent group.

EUGENICS

One of the reasons for the special stress that is laid upon race investigations is the fear of race degeneration. It is assumed that the intermixture between different racial types and the rapid increase of the poorest part of the population have a deteriorating effect upon the nation. In the introductory remarks I have tried to show that there is little reason to believe that racial intermixture of the kind occurring in the United States at the present time should have a deteriorating effect. I do not believe that it has been adequately proved that there is a clearly marked tendency toward general degeneration among all civilized nations. In modern society the conditions of life have become more varied than those of former periods. While some groups live under most favorable conditions that require active use of body and mind, others live in abject poverty and their activities have more than ever before been degraded to those of machines. At the same time the variety of human activities is much greater than it used to be. It is therefore quite intelligible that the functional activities of each nation must show an increased degree of differentiation, a higher degree of variability. Even if the general average of the mental and physical types should remain the same, there must be a larger number now than formerly who fall below a certain given low standard, and also a larger number who exceed a given high standard. The number of defectives can be counted by statistics of poor relief, delinquency, and insanity, but there is no way of determining the increase of those individuals who are raised above the norm of a higher standard, and they escape our notice. It may therefore very well be that the number of defectives increases without influencing the value of a population as a whole, because it is merely an expression of an increased degree of variability.

Furthermore, arbitrarily selected absolute standards of value do not retain their significance. Even if no change in the absolute standard should be made, the degree of physical and mental energy required under modern conditions to keep oneself above a certain minimum of achievement is greater than it used to be. This is due to the greater complexity of our life and to the increasing number of competing individuals. Greater capacity is required to attain a high degree of prominence than was needed in other periods of our history. The claim that we have to contend against national degeneracy must, therefore, be better substantiated than it is now.

The problem is further complicated by the advance in public hygiene which has resulted in lowering infant mortality and has thus brought about a change in the composition of the population, in so far as many who would have succumbed to deleterious conditions in early years enter into the adult population and must have an influence upon the general distribution of vitality.

Notwithstanding the doubtful basis of many of the assertions relating to degeneracy, the problem of eugenics is clearly before the public, and the investigation of racial and social types cannot be separated from the practical aims involved in the eugenic movement.

The fundamental thought underlying eugenic theory is that no environmental influences can modify those characteristics which are determined by hereditary nature. *Nurture*, it is said, cannot overcome *nature*.

We should recall here what has been said before regarding the difference between the characteristics of hereditary strains and those of races, and that while it is true that strains differ greatly in physical and mental vigor and in specific characteristics, it is not equally true of races as a whole, because strains which are very much alike in all these characteristics are found in every single race. Even if it is not possible to prove with absolute certainty the complete identity in mental traits of selected strains belonging to races as diverse as Europeans and Negroes, there is not the slightest doubt that such identity prevails among the various European types. Eugenics, therefore, cannot have any possible meaning with regard to whole races. It can have a meaning only with regard to strains. If the task of the eugenist were the selection of that third of humanity representing the best strains, he would find his material among all European and Asiatic types, and very probably among all races of man; and all would contribute to the less valuable two-thirds.

As an objection to this point of view it is sometimes claimed that closely allied animal types are so different in their physical make-up and mental characteristics that members of one race can be clearly differentiated from those of another race. It is, for instance, said that the race horse and the heavy dray horse are so different in character that no matter what may be done to the dray horse its descendants can never be transformed into race horses. This is undoubtedly true, but the parallelism between the races of dray horses and race horses on the one hand and human races on the other is incorrect. The races of horses are developed by careful selection, by means of which physical and mental characteristics are fixed in each separate strain, while in human races no such selection occurs. We have rather a racial panmixture, which brings it about that the racial characteristics are distributed irregularly among all the different families. As a matter of fact, dray horses and race horses correspond to family strains, not to human races, and the comparison is valid only in so far as race horses and dray horses are compared to the characteristics of certain family lines, not to human races as a whole. In Johannsen's terminology the human races are to a much greater extent phenotypes than races of domesticated animals.

For this reason the task of eugenics cannot be to devise means to suppress some races and to favor the development of others. It must rather be directed to the discovery of methods which favor the development of the desirable strains in every race.

This problem can be attacked only after the solution of two questions. First of all, we have to decide what are the desirable characteristics; and secondly, we must determine what characteristics are hereditary. With regard to the former question, we shall all agree that physical health is one of the fundamental qualities to be desired; but there will always be fundamental disagreement as to what mental qualities are considered desirable—whether an intense intellectualism and a repression of emotionalism or a healthy development of emotional life is preferable. Obviously, it is quite impossible to lay down a standard that will fit every person, every place, and every time, and for this reason the application of eugenic measures should be restricted to the development of physical and mental health. Even if it were possible to control human mating in such a way that strains with certain mental characteristics could be developed, it would seem entirely unjustifiable for our generation to impose upon future times ideals that some of us may consider desirable. It might furthermore be questioned whether the interests of humanity will be better served by eliminating all abnormal strains which, as history shows, have produced a number of great men who have contributed to the best that mankind has done, or by carrying the burden of the unfit for the sake of the few valuable individuals that may spring from them. These, of course, are not scientific questions, but social and ethical problems.

For the practical development of eugenics it is indispensable to determine what is hereditary and what is not. The ordinary method of determining heredity is to investigate the recurrence of the same phenomenon among a number of successive generations. If, for instance, it can be shown that color-blindness occurs in successive generations, or that certain malformations like polydactylism are found repeatedly in the same family, or that multiple births are characteristic of certain strains, we conclude that these are due to hereditary causes; and if parents and children have the same head form or the same or similar statures, we decide that these similarities also are due to heredity. It must be recognized that in many of these cases alternative explanations are conceivable. If, for instance, a family lives under certain economic conditions which are repeated among parents and children, and if these economic conditions have a direct influence upon the size of the body, the similarity of stature of parents and children would be due to environment and not to heredity. If a disease is endemic in a certain locality and occurs among parents and children, this is not due to heredity but to the locality which they inhabit. In other words, wherever the environmental conditions have a marked influence upon bodily characteristics, and wherever these environmental conditions continue for a number of generations, they have an effect that is apparently identical with that of heredity. In many cases the causes are so obvious that it is easy to exclude persistence of characteristics due to environment. Under other conditions the determination of the causes is not so easy.

It is still more difficult to differentiate between heredity and congenital features. For example, if a child before birth should be infected by its mother, there might be the impression of a hereditary disease, which, however, is actually only congenital in the sense that it is not inherent in the structure of the germ plasm. Although the distinction between environmental causes as previously defined and hereditary causes is generally fairly easy, the distinction between congenital causes and true hereditary causes is exceedingly difficult, in many cases impossible. The long continued discussions relating to hereditary transmission of disease are a case in point. Most of these questions cannot be solved by statistical inquiries, but require the most careful biological investigation. The conditions, however, are such that we must demand in every case a clear differentiation among these three causes.

There is little doubt that in the modern eugenic movement the assumption of hereditary transmission as a cause of defects has been exaggerated. Although certain mental defects that occur among well-to-do families seem to be determined by heredity, the mental defects generally included in eugenic studies are of such a character that many of them may readily be recognized as due to social conditions rather than as expressing specific hereditary traits. A weakling who is economically well situated is protected from many of the dangers that beset an individual of similar characteristics whose economic condition is not so favorable, and it must be admitted that criminality in families that may be mentally weak and which are at the same time struggling for the barest subsistence is at least as much determined by social conditions as by heredity. Investigators of criminal families have succeeded in showing frequencies of occurrence of criminality which are analogous to frequencies which may be due to heredity, but they have failed to show that these frequencies may not as well be explained either wholly or in part by environmental conditions. We should be willing to admit that among the poor undernourished population, which is at the same time badly housed and suffers from other unfavorable conditions of life, congenital weakness may develop which lowers the resistance of the individual against all forms of delinquency. Whether this weakness is hereditary or congenital is, however, an entirely different question. Experiments made with generations of underfed rats [1] suggest that a strain of rats which has deteriorated by underfeeding can be fed up by a careful amelioration of conditions of life, and it may well be questioned whether delinquent strains in man may not be improved in a similar way. Certainly the history of the criminals deported to Australia and of their descendants is very much in favor of such a theory. In other words, it seems very likely that the condition of our subnormal population is not by any means solely determined by heredity, but that careful investigations are required to discriminate between environmental, congenital, and hereditary causes.

FORMULATION OF PROBLEM

From the preceding discussion, we may formulate the principal problems that must be taken up in a study of the population of the United States. We have to investigate first the degree of homogeneity of the population; second, the hereditary characteristics of the existing lines; third, the influence of environment; fourth, the influences of selection. On the basis of the data thus collected, we have to interpret the significance of the differences between various types, and investigate the bearing that our results may have upon public policies.

The study of the adult population alone would not give us adequate data to enable us to clear up the causes which determine the final development of the body—the events which take place during the period of growth must also be taken into consideration.

Familiarity with the bodily forms of children is necessary also from a morphological point of view. On the whole, the development of individuals is divergent, so that the most characteristic forms of each type are found in the adult male. The adult female forms are not quite so divergent, perhaps in part for the reason that the period of development of the female is shorter than that of the male, although it must be remembered that secondary sexual characteristics are present in childhood. The younger the human form that we investigate, the less clearly are racial characteristics expressed. We may, therefore, say that the most generalized forms of a racial type will be found in the infant or, even still more clearly, in prenatal stages, while the most highly specialized local forms will be found in the male adult. A knowledge of the specialized forms ought to include, therefore, a study of progressive differentiation. Particularly for the study of the influences of environment it is indispensable that the development of the body in childhood should be studied while the influences are still at

[1] Helen Dean King, *Studies on Inbreeding* (Wistar Institute, 1919).

work. We have to know the conditions which bring about retardation or acceleration in the development of various parts of the body, and their ultimate effects upon the human form. We must study other minute changes that may perhaps not be related to retardation or acceleration, but that may be due to a direct effect of environmental causes. In the adult these changes have been completed and can no longer be subjected to analysis, while in the growing child, their gradual development and unfolding may be observed.

The same is true with regard to selection. If selection is related to bodily form, it will probably act with particular intensity during the early years of childhood. It might be revealed by a comparison of the surviving and dying parts of the population of various ages.

These considerations make it quite necessary to include in the study of the population, not only adults, but also children.

One method of approach should consist, therefore, in the study of the growth and development of children, classified according to descent and geographical and social environment. If it were feasible to include records of the longevity of the individuals measured in childhood, the problem of selection could also be attacked. In the study of adults a careful classification according to descent and social position will be necessary.

The phenomena of homogeneity and of heredity make it necessary that the investigation should not be confined to studies of individuals, but that the anatomical characteristics of families should be made the subject of inquiry.

A considerable amount of work has been done by many investigators, throwing light upon a number of aspects of the problems here discussed. The earliest and most extensive series of observations was collected in connection with the War of the Rebellion and was published by Gould and Baxter.[1] Their well-known statistics, which have been quoted again and again, give data with regard to the stature of enlisted men according to their nativity, descent, and occupation, and reveal the facts that inhabitants of different parts of the United States differ in their physical development; that the differences between the various European nationalities are repeated here; but that in every single case, the members of a certain nationality exceed in bulk of body the corresponding European series; and, finally, that certain differences may be observed between groups of individuals following different occupations.

The next important inquiry relating to our subject was an investigation of school children of Boston by Henry P. Bowditch,[2] in which similar differences appeared. Bowditch also showed that the differences between various nationalities persisted throughout the period of growth, and that

[1] B. A. Gould, *Investigations in the Military and Anthropological Statistics of American Soldiers* (New York, 1869).

[2] H. P. Bowditch, "The Growth of Children," *8th Annual Report, Massachusetts Board of Health* (Boston, 1875), pp. 273-323; *10th Annual Report* (1879), pp. 33-62; *21st Annual Report* (1890), pp. 287-304; *22nd Annual Report* (1891), pp. 479-525.

marked differences are found according to social stratification. Classification of the population according to the occupation of the parents showed a better development among the commercial and professional classes than is found among unskilled labor. Soon after Bowditch's investigation similar inquiries were instituted by Peckham [1] in Milwaukee, and later on in a number of other cities—Worcester, Mass.; [2] St. Louis, Mo.; [3] Toronto, Canada; [4] Oakland, Cal., [5] etc. On the whole, the methods pursued were similar to those applied by Bowditch, and the results proved the occurrence of analogous phenomena. Porter, in his investigation in St. Louis, added to his inquiries the problem of the relative development of the children of varying mental achievement, and demonstrated a difference in the development of what he called precocious and dull children. Work of this type was gradually taken up by educational institutions and the effort was made to correlate physical development with school work, with a view to demonstrating a practical way of assigning a child to his proper developmental stage.

In similar investigations in Europe attention had been called to the fact that the measurement of children of different ages and the calculation of a growth curve on this basis does not give us adequate information with regard to the details of the phenomena of growth, and it was pointed out that repeated measurements of the same individual are necessary to obtain fuller records. In spite of numerous efforts that have been made to obtain such series, it has not been possible up to the present time to follow out the development of the same individual from childhood to adult life, at least not in numbers that are sufficient for a clear understanding of the phenomena involved in this process.

A certain amount of material bearing upon stature and weight has been collected by life insurance companies. This, however, is probably to a great extent so uncertain that it is only of slight use for scientific investigations. Military statistics taken in the United States since the War of the Rebellion are not numerous and not very extensive. A certain amount of work was done during the recent war, but the results have only now been made accessible. The only fairly extended investigation of families that has been undertaken in the United States was made in connection with the

---

[1] C. W. Peckham, "The Growth of Children," *6th Annual Report of the State Board of Health of Wisconsin* (1881), pp. 28–73.

[2] Franz Boas and Clark Wissler, "Statistics of Growth," *Report of the U. S. Commissioner of Education for 1904* (Washington, 1905), pp. 25–132.

[3] W. T. Porter in the *Transactions of the Academy of Sciences of St. Louis*, "The Physical Basis of Precocity and Dullness" (1893), pp. 161–181; "The Relation between the Growth of Children and their Deviation from the Physical Type of Their Sex and Age" (1893), pp. 263–280; "The Growth of St. Louis Children" (1894), pp. 263–380; also *Quarterly Publications of the American Statistical Association*, N. S., vol. 3 (1893), pp. 577–587; vol. 4 (1894), pp. 28–34.

[4] Franz Boas, "The Growth of Toronto Children," *Report of the U. S. Commissioner of Education for 1896–97* (Washington, 1898), pp. 1541–1599.

[5] Franz Boas, "The Growth of First-Born Children," *Science*, N. S., vol. 1 (1895), pp. 402–404.

work of the Immigration Commission, during which a fairly large number of Jewish, Bohemian, Italian, and Scotch families were studied in such a manner that the phenomena of heredity could be considered in some detail. We have practically no material whatever bearing upon the facts of racial mixture. It is particularly worth remembering that there are hardly any investigations to speak of that bear upon the physiological development of the Negro and Mulatto population. In view of the ever-repeated claim that the Mulatto is inferior in physical development to either the pure Negro or to the White, and considering the large number of Mulattoes in our population, it seems of fundamental importance that an investigation of this kind should be made.

Although less important from a practical point of view than the Negro problem, race mixture between Whites and Indians has received some attention. Material collected in 1892 shows that the half-blood, so far as fertility and stature are concerned, is superior to the full-blood Indians.[1] The observations relating to fertility were confirmed by the material collected in the census of 1910.[2] Recently an inquiry into the characteristics of the half-bloods of Minnesota was made by Professor Albert E. Jenks.[3] We are still lacking, however, full investigations into the anatomical and physiological characteristics of half-bloods.

The problem of the intermixture between Negro and White and Negro and Indian has hardly been touched at all. A few studies of Negro children and soldiers do not contribute much to our knowledge. A systematic study of the problem was made by Felix von Luschan in 1915, but the results of his observations are not yet available. Another important inquiry is that by Eugen Fischer on the Rehobother Bastards, the descendants mainly of Dutch settlers and Hottentots in South Africa. This is the only work in which the anthropological characteristics of the Mulattoes have been taken up in detail. The theoretical as well as the practical importance of the investigation of the Mulatto question can hardly be sufficiently emphasized. On the one hand, we may hope to obtain by this means an insight into the laws of heredity in man. On the other hand, the well-being of so many millions of citizens of our country is involved that the most painstaking inquiry should be demanded. This is the more urgent since many States have regulated race intermixture by laws which are based simply upon public prejudice without the shadow of knowledge of the underlying biological facts—without even the knowledge of the peculiar form of racial intermixture that characterizes the relations between Whites and Negroes in the United States. In by far the greater number of cases the

---

[1] Franz Boas, "The Half-Blood Indian, an Anthropometric Study," *Popular Science Monthly*, vol. 45 (1894), pp. 761–770 (see pp. 138 *et seq.* of this volume). Louis R. Sullivan, "Anthropometry of the Siouan Tribes," *Anthropological Papers of the American Museum of Natural History*, vol. 23, Part III (1920), p. 199.

[2] Roland B. Dixon, *Indian Population in the United States and Alaska,* 1910 (Washington, 1915), pp. 157–160.

[3] "Indian-White Amalgamation," *University of Minnesota Studies in Social Science,* No. 6 (Minneapolis, 1916).

mother is a Negress and the father a White man. This results in an infusion of White blood into the Negro race without affecting materially the White race. A searching analysis of the hereditary characteristics of the racial groups has not yet been made. It is true that the records of morbidity suggest typical physiological differences, but considering the fact that similar differences are found between different social groups of the same race, it is not possible without further investigation to distinguish definitely between the influences of heredity and of social environment.[1]

I refrain from giving a detailed bibliography and review of the anthropometric material collected in the United States in view of the very excellent collection of titles made by Professor Bird T. Baldwin, of the Bureau of Child Study of the University of Iowa.[2]

PROPOSED INVESTIGATIONS

The first and most fundamental inquiry that has to be made relates to a description of the various types constituting the population of the United States. As explained before, it will not be sufficient to describe the adult male and female forms, but it will also be necessary to determine the course of growth and development which is characteristic of each form. In order to carry through this inquiry it is necessary to obtain information with regard to the forms characteristic of each moment of the period of the development, and to determine the sequence of the characteristic developmental stages of each type. It is not admissible to assume that the physiological conditions which are found in a six-year-old Italian child must be the same as those of a six-year-old Scandinavian child. Furthermore, the individuals of each racial group will differ among themselves considerably with regard to the time when certain stages of physical development are reached, and it is therefore necessary to investigate fully the variability of physiological development characteristic of each group. It must be considered one of the most urgent aims of an investigation to determine the sequence of events and the racial and environmental conditions that influence them. There are indications that these problems may be found to be exceedingly intricate. An example may illustrate this point. The development of poor children is considerably retarded. Nevertheless, the second dentition among these children is accelerated. This may perhaps be due to less care given to the deciduous teeth and their earlier loss which stimulates the appearance of the permanent teeth—or it may be due to other causes. It is, however, an indication that the sequence of events indicating the physiological changes in the body are subject to quite diverse causes.

The determination of all phenomena of this kind is very difficult when the attempt is made to derive data by the so-called generalizing method, that is to say, if we merely collect information that children of a certain age show the stage of development in question so and so often, and if we

[1] See also E. B. Reuter, *The Mulatto in the United States* (Boston, 1918).

[2] "The Physical Growth of Children from Birth to Maturity," *Iowa Child Welfare Research Station Study,* vol. 1 (1921), No. 1.

try to derive the rate of development by subtracting the relative frequency of occurrence observed in one year from the relative frequency of occurrence in the next year. If we observe, for instance, that a certain tooth is present in 50 per cent of the children of one age and in 70 per cent of another set of children who are one year older, and conclude that in 20 per cent of the children the tooth in question will erupt in the course of that year, the different composition of the annual groups and the different numbers observed make it difficult to obtain reliable results. It is almost indispensable that for each individual there should be noted the moment of occurrence of the physiological change which is being studied. Material of this type is almost non-existent.

The movability of our modern city populations causes great practical difficulty in the organization of this work. It is not easy for an investigator to remain in touch for a sufficiently long time with the same children, and so many children change from one place to another that an initial number of, let us say one hundred, who are studied when five years old, will have dwindled down to an insignificant number at the time when the adult stage is reached. For this reason an elaborate organization is needed to carry through this work completely. To a greater or less extent, the work must be pieced together of fragments. For children of school age, roughly speaking from four or five years to fourteen years, the investigation might be organized. For older children of high-school age, it will also ordinarily be possible to carry through the inquiry, and in certain cases the transfer of a subject from high school to college may also be followed up. It is, however, obvious that the individuals who can be followed in this way are a group selected according to economic and social conditions. Those groups of the population which are well-to-do and which lay great stress upon the acquisition of a good education will be represented much more fully than other groups. The observations for different ages will therefore require a consideration of the different composition of the series. An organization like the Child Study Bureau of Chicago or the corresponding organizations in Iowa City and Detroit, or the Association for Improving the Condition of the Poor in New York, will be best able to control inquiries into these subjects.

The most difficult problem encountered in these investigations is the differentiation between hereditary differences and those due to retardation or acceleration. To give an example: A boy twelve years old may be tall because his hereditary characteristics are such that he belongs to a tall stock, or it may be that he is tall on account of an acceleration of his development. Since, furthermore, the adult stature of the individual will depend not only upon his hereditary characteristics, but also upon environmental conditions that have an effect upon the acceleration or retardation of his growth, it is difficult to determine directly how much is contributed by hereditary and how much by environmental causes. From a practical point of view the demand is always made that the anthropometric investigation of the individual shall differentiate between these two causes.

In most cases, however, it seems almost impossible to do so, except by a very detailed investigation of the physiological conditions of the body. Measurements are always subject to alternative explanations, as being due either to hereditary causes or to acceleration or retardation, while physiological changes are not so likely to be fundamentally different for different hereditary lines. If, for instance, in a certain individual the loss of healthy deciduous canines should be very much retarded, we should have the right to assume that, in whole or in part, his bodily development may be influenced by retardation. This, of course, presupposes a previous investigation which would show that the hereditary characteristics of different strains do not show very great differences in the time element of the loss of the first canine, provided the environmental conditions remain the same. Here, again, we are entirely lacking in material that would enable us to answer this question, and it is evident that a very considerable amount of information would have to be amassed in order to enable us to solve the problem. It does not seem a hopeless task to determine the contributory effect of retardation and acceleration in an individual child, but it presupposes a much more thorough knowledge of the sequence of the developmental stages than we now possess.

The description of racial types cannot be considered complete without an inquiry into the homogeneity or the heterogeneity of the series. It is clear from the remarks made on pages 32 et seq. that this problem can be solved only by an investigation of the forms represented in fraternities, because homogeneity can be proved only by showing that the types represented in different families are the same. In other words, the investigation of homogeneity must be based on an inquiry into the variations presented by different families. The small size of the human family makes it necessary to see to it that the proper weight is given to each fraternity in accordance with its numerical composition.[1] This investigation must be supplemented by an inquiry into each fraternity, the variability of which will depend upon the more or less composite character of its ancestry.

We are thus led to a consideration of the problem of how far it is possible to discover relative unity or multiplicity in the ancestry of a racial type. The method to be pursued will depend entirely upon the laws of heredity involved. In those cases in which we have some kind of Mendelian inheritance—that is to say, a tendency of certain traits of the offspring to revert to either parental type—we must obviously expect a higher degree of variability in the mixed types than the one found in the pure parental types. Attention has been called to the occurrence of such a phenomenon with regard to the head index of Italians.[2] The short-headed north Italians are, comparatively speaking, uniform in type, and the long-headed south Italians are also fairly uniform in type, while in the intermediate regions in which undoubtedly the two types have intermingled for a long period, the

[1] See footnotes on p. 32.
[2] Franz Boas and Helene M. Boas, "The Head Forms of the Italians as Influenced by Heredity and Environment," *American Anthropologist*, N. S., vol. 15 (1913), pp. 163 et seq.

variability of the head index is very much increased. In a similar way, we find that there is an increase of variability in Sweden in those regions in which there is an admixture of foreign types that are more short-headed than the Swedes.[1] It has also been shown that in those cases in which father and mother belong to the same racial group, but in which they represent extreme head forms, the one extremely short-headed, the other extremely long-headed, the variability of the children is greater than in those cases in which the parents represent nearly the same type.[2] We recognize, therefore, that when a Mendelian reversion occurs, increased variability may indicate composite descent.

There are, however, other cases in which the results of mixture have not the effect of increasing variability. Statistics of half-blood Indians have shown that the width of face, which is great in the Indian race and very small in the White race, has an intermediate value among the half-bloods, with a marked tendency, however, of reversion to a form that is narrower than the face of the pure Indian and wider than the face of the pure White, while the values for width of face which are half-way between the characteristic values of the Indians and of the Whites are not so frequent as the two other values previously mentioned. There is, therefore, a certain kind of reversion in this case. Nevertheless, the total variability of the width of the face of the half-bloods is almost the same as that of the pure parental types.[3] If we assume in this case a pure reversion to either type, we should find that the variability would be considerably more than that of the parental races. It appears, therefore, that we cannot generalize with regard to the phenomenon, and we have not the right to assume that mixture will always be accompanied by increased variability and that slight variability does not always indicate purity of descent.

Whenever the laws of heredity are of a still different type, the variability may be affected in a very different manner. Thus it has been shown that mixture between Europeans and Indians results in a stature which exceeds that of the pure Indians, which in turn is greater than that of the pure Whites. It is obviously quite impossible to predict in this case what the variability of the series may be.

Another method of investigating mixed descent of a race is by means of a study of the correlations of different measurements of the body. To give an instance: when two peoples intermingle, one of which has very long and very narrow heads, while the other has very short and very broad heads, and if, furthermore, reversion to parental forms obtains, then we

---

[1] Franz Boas, "Notes on the Anthropology of Sweden," *Amer. Jour. of Physical Anthropology,* vol. 1 (1918), pp. 415 *et seq.*

[2] Franz Boas, *Changes in Bodily Form of Descendants of Immigrants,* Columbia University Press (New York, 1912), pp. 76 *et seq.*

[3] Franz Boas, "Zur Anthropologie der nordamerikanischen Indianer," *Verhandlungen der Berliner Gesellschaft für Anthropologie, Ethnologie und Urgeschichte,* vol. 27 (1895), pp. 404 *et seq.*

Louis R. Sullivan, "Anthropometry of the Siouan tribes," *Anthropological Papers of the American Museum of Natural History,* vol. 23, Part III (1920) pp. 3, 136, 161.

must expect that among the individuals representing this population very broad heads are commonly associated with shortness, while very narrow heads are associated with greater length. We should, therefore, expect of such a population that the broader the head, the shorter it will be. In other cases, where we have a single line of descent, the condition is reversed. The size of the head depends upon the bulk of the body, and since in such a case broad heads are indicative of length of body, the length of head is also increased, and we find that a broad head is associated with greater length of head. In the case mentioned before, the reversion of the normal correlation is indicative of mixed descent.

Here again many variations may occur. If, for instance, we had two races intermingled with a tendency to reversion to parental forms in which the heads of one group are very high and at the same time narrow and short, while those in the other group are flat and at the same time broad and long, then the result would be that in the study of the correlation between length and breadth of head, the correlation would appear inordinately high, because all the shortest heads would belong to the high type and would, therefore, also be narrow, while all the longest heads would belong to the low type and would also therefore be broad.

A characteristic case in which heterogeneity of a series causes abnormal correlation between physical features is found in Italy. Normally there is practically no correlation between hair color and stature, but in Italy the tall Alpine type has lighter hair than the short Mediterranean type. In Piedmont where the Mediterranean type is practically absent we find the following distribution:

Stature	*Hair*			
	Red	Blond	Brown	Black
Less than 160	0.5	12.3	64.1	23.1
160–165	0.8	12.4	63.9	22.9
165–170	0.8	12.2	63.4	23.6
170 and more	0.8	12.9	64.3	22.0

In Sicily where the Alpine type is practically absent we find:

Stature	*Hair*			
	Red	Blond	Brown	Black
Less than 160	0.3	4.8	56.8	38.1
160–165	0.4	5.1	55.7	38.9
165–170	0.4	5.2	56.6	37.8
170 and more	0.5	5.0	56.6	37.9

In Venice and Latium, on the other hand, where mixed types occur, we find:

Stature	*Hair*							
	Venice				*Latium*			
	Red	Blond	Brown	Black	Red	Blond	Brown	Black
Less than 160	0.8	10.1	63.8	25.3	0.7	5.4	60.5	33.4
160–165	0.7	11.9	62.0	25.4	0.6	6.1	60.6	32.7
165–170	0.8	12.8	60.9	25.5	1.1	6.4	60.7	31.9
170 and more	0.8	14.0	61.2	23.6	0.6	8.2	62.4	28.8

and still more clearly for the whole Kingdom:

Stature		*Hair*		
	Red	Blond	Brown	Black
Less than 160	0.5	7.0	59.7	32.8
160–165	0.5	7.9	60.0	31.6
165–170	0.6	8.5	60.1	30.8
170 and more	0.6	9.5	61.0	28.8

On account of the greatly varying laws of heredity it is impossible to predict which method of inquiry will lead to a satisfactory result. By some of the means here described the problem of pure or mixed descent may be approached.

The study of any particular type will, therefore, require a multiplicity of investigations, the most important of which relate to the development of the racial type from childhood on, the homogeneity of the series, and the purity of the ancestry. For these purposes the investigations of children and of families are indispensable and must accompany a generalized investigation of the population as a whole.

For the study of the influence of environment the investigation of growing children is, if anything, more important than for the investigation of racial characteristics. After the adult stage has been reached environment will not exert any further influence. The earlier in life the investigation can begin, the more likely we are to obtain adequate results.

In this investigation the generalizing method of comparing local types or types presented in social strata is of little use, because in order to establish definitely an influence of environmental causes, we must be certain that the hereditary composition of the populations which we study is the same. For instance, when we compare a rural and an urban community, there is nothing that will guarantee to us that both populations are derived from the same ancestry. On the contrary, we may assume that the urban population is drawn from a wider group than the rural population. In the same way, when we compare the inhabitants of a long secluded valley and find differences in bodily form between the people living in the lower part and those living in the upper part, the question would arise whether the ancestry of the two groups is the same and whether the people in the upper regions have not been more isolated than those farther down. It is on the whole easier to exclude obvious environmental influences in an investigation of racial types than to exclude differences of racial descent in studies of the influence of environment. The only way to escape from these complications is by confining the studies strictly to a comparison between parents and children.

It has been explained before that in a number of cases we may find apparent hereditary traits which may be deduced from the similarity of parents and their own children, and which nevertheless are primarily due to environmental causes. If we should find, for instance, a low stature among individuals who have been undernourished as children, and if the next generation will also be undernourished, we may have an apparent similarity in stature which is not due primarily to heredity, but rather to the fact that the same environmental causes act upon the parental group and upon the group of children. In most cases these elements cannot be eliminated unless we have the opportunity to study the same racial type in different forms of environment.

It has been stated before that a modification of bodily form due to environment which is observed by comparing parents and their children does not contradict the phenomena of heredity. If we find, for instance, that the stature of Jewish immigrants into the United States is lower than that of their children, the hereditary stability of stature will nevertheless manifest itself. The children of an exceptionally tall couple who exceed the average stature of the immigrant Jew by a certain amount may be expected to show an excess of stature which is correlated to the excess of stature of the parents, which, however, has to be added to the increased average stature of the children of immigrants. In short, a change in type due to environmental influences simply means that the correlated deviations in the group of parents and of children must be reckoned from the point which is typical for the generation in question.

In some cases in which the environmental influences are very strong, a generalizing method may give adequate results. Bowditch, in his investigation of Boston children, was able to show that Irish children differ in their development according to the economic condition of the parents, and there is little reason to doubt the uniformity of the genetic composition of his various Irish groups. But whenever the differences involved are slight, and when they may be equally well explained on the basis of difference in genetic composition, the comparison between parents and children is indispensable. The data for the study of environmental influences must, therefore, be based on the comparison of the bodily forms of parents and their offspring. In this manner the doubt as to the difference in genetic composition may be eliminated, although it is at least conceivable even in this case that there may have been selective rather than environmental influences. It might be said, for instance, that when some parents have children in charitable institutions while other children stay at home, differences between the two groups of children might not be due to environmental influences only but also to selection. This example indicates that care must be taken to eliminate the influences of selection even when we are dealing with family groups in which diversity of genetic descent has been excluded.

At the present time it is unknown to what extent the influences of environment may determine bodily form. Notwithstanding the numerous claims of the fundamental effect of climate upon the body of man, we have no evidence whatever that will show that pigmentation undergoes fundamental changes under climatic conditions; that the White race would become darker in the tropics; or that the Negroes would become lighter in the north. Whatever statistics we have on this subject show rather a remarkable stability of pigmentation. We have not even any definite indication that the pigmentation of the hair undergoes changes under different climatic conditions, although in this case the change in color from the period of childhood until middle life is so great that we might very well expect environmental influences to express themselves. On the other hand, we know that the bulk of the body is very susceptible to environmental influences, and it is but natural that retardation or acceleration during the period of growth will also leave its effect upon those proportions of the body which depend upon bulk. Other changes which occur very early in life are not so easily explained. I think the evidence showing that the form of the head is susceptible to environmental influences is incontrovertible. I also believe that adequate proof has been given for modifications in the width of the face under changed conditions of life. The causes of these changes are still entirely obscure. It may well be, as suggested by Harvey Cushing, that chemical changes occur under new environmental conditions and unequally influence growth in different directions. This would agree with the changes in chemical constitution found in lower animals living in different types of environment. If it is true that changes of this kind do occur and modify the form of body so fundamentally that according to the ordinary schemes of classification a people might be removed from one group and placed in another one, then we have to consider the investigation of the instability of the body under varying environmental conditions as one of the most fundamental subjects to be considered in an anthropometric study of our population.

CHANGES IN BODILY FORM OF DESCENDANTS
OF IMMIGRANTS [1]

THE following is a brief summary of the principal results of a study of the anthropometric characteristics of immigrants and their descendants.

1. American-born descendants of immigrants differ in type from their foreign-born parents. The changes which occur among various European types are not all in the same direction. They develop in early childhood and persist throughout life.[2]

INCREASE (+) OR DECREASE (—) OF MEASUREMENTS OF CHILDREN OF IMMI-
GRANTS BORN IN THE UNITED STATES COMPARED WITH THOSE OF
IMMIGRANTS BORN IN EUROPE (p. 56 Final Report)

Nationality and Sex	Length of Head mm.	Width of Head mm.	Cephalic Index	Width of Face mm.	Stature cm.	Weight
Bohemians:						
Males	—0.7	—2.3	—1.0	—2.1	+2.9	170
Females	—0.6	—1.5	—0.6	—1.7	+2.2	180
Hebrews:						
Males	+2.2	—1.8	—2.0	—1.1	+1.7	654
Females	+1.9	—2.0	—2.0	—1.3	+1.5	259

[1] The following is the substance of "Changes in the Bodily Form of Descendants of Immigrants" *American Anthropologist*, N.S., vol. 14, no. 3 (1912); and "Veränderungen der Körperform der Nachkommen von Einwanderern in Amerika" *Zeitschrift für Ethnologie*, vol. 45, Heft 1 (1913). These papers contain a summary of the results of an investigation of the anthropometric characteristics of immigrants and their descendants, a work entrusted to me by the United States Immigration Commission. It is written as a reply to various criticisms of the results of the inquiry. A partial report was asked for by the Commission and submitted to Congress on December 16, 1909, and published about March, 1910. It was stated in the report (p. 6) that the investigation was not complete. An abstract of the complete report was submitted to Congress on December 3, 1910, and issued on March 17, 1911. The final report was presented on December 5, 1910, by the Secretary of the Commission, submitted to Congress on June 8, 1911, printed in September, 1911, and issued in May, 1912. It was reprinted and published by the Columbia University Press in New York in 1912.

[2] Partial Report, pp. 7–16; Abstract, pp. 11–28; Final Report, pp. 55–56, and tables, pp. 10–55.

Nationality and Sex	Length of Head mm.	Width of Head mm.	Cephalic Index	Width of Face mm.	Stature cm.	Weight
Sicilians:						
Males	—2.4	+0.7	+1.3	—1.2	—0.1	188
Females	—3.0	+0.8	+1.8	—2.0	—0.5	144
Neapolitans:						
Males	—0.9	+0.9	+0.9	—1.2	+0.6	248
Females	—1.7	+1.0	+1.4	—0.6	—1.8	126

2. The influence of American environment makes itself felt with increasing intensity, according to the time elapsed between the arrival of the mother and the birth of the child.[1]

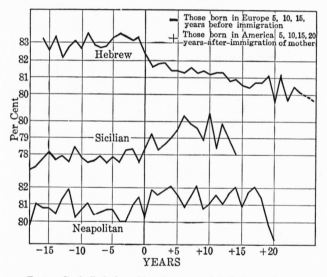

FIG. 1. Cephalic index of immigrants and their descendants.

The changes of the initial values for o years which are in the direction of the observed changes deserve attention.

Fig. 1 represents the average values of the cephalic index of the immigrants born in Europe and their descendants born in the United States according to the interval between immigration of mother and birth, respectively according to the age at the time of immigration.

The differences in cephalic index between parents and their own

[1] Partial Report, pp. 17–22; Abstract, pp. 29–37; Final Report, pp. 57–64, 99–115.

American-born children, 'born less than ten years after arrival of the mother, and of those born more than ten years after the arrival of the mother, are, —0.83 and —1.92 respectively.[1] Their difference is, there-

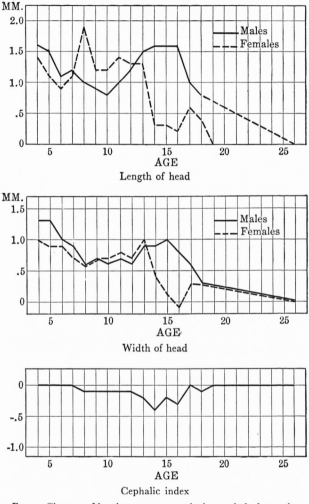

Fig. 2. Changes of head measurements during period of growth.

fore, 1.09 with an error of about ±0.22, so that the significance of this difference is also quite probable.

1 Recalculated from Table 47, p. 127, Final Report.

3. The observations on intraracial heredity show an increased variability of children of dissimilar parents, which proves a regression of the children to either parental type, not a regression to the midparental type.[1]

Difference between Cephalic Indices of Parents	Square of Variability of Children [a]	Cases
0 — 2.9	6.8	1102
3 — 5.9	6.7	736
6 — 8.9	8.3	317
9	13.0	108

[a] The ± in the Final Report are in error.

It is apparent that the variability increases rapidly for the greater differences between parents.

4. The head measurements show the same acceleration of growth during the prepubertal period as has long been known for measurements of the bulk of the body, i.e., stature and weight [2] (Fig. 2).

5. The average stature of children decreases with the size of the family [3] (Fig. 3).

Incidentally a number of problems were touched upon which are, however, of secondary importance in relation to the whole problem, and the investigation of which was necessary for the correct interpretation of the observations referred to before.

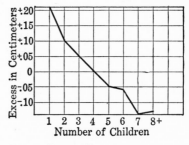

FIG. 3. Excess of stature over average stature for families of various sizes.

6. The comparison of immigrants and their descendants necessarily refers to groups which immigrated at different periods. For instance, 15-year-old American-born boys are children of parents who immigrated more than 15 years ago; while 15-year-old foreign-born boys

[1] Abstract, pp. 54-55; Final Report, pp. 76-78, 153-154 in regard to the cephalic index.

[2] Abstract, pp. 55-57; Final Report, pp. 78-79, 137-151.

[3] Partial Report, p. 28; Abstract, p. 57; Final Report, pp. 79-80, 161-166. It may be remarked here that this accounts for the apparent higher stature of first-born children because the low values of late-born children occur only in large families while first-born occur in all families. See "The Growth of First-Born Children," *Science*, N.S., vol. 1 (1895), p. 402.

are children of parents who immigrated less than 15 years ago. If, therefore, the constitution of the immigration representing a certain people changed, there would be an apparent change of type, which in reality would reflect only the differences in type of the immigrants of

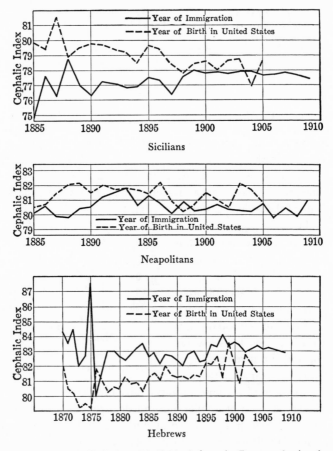

Fig. 4. Cephalic index of individuals born in Europe who immigrated in certain years compared with that of American-born descendants of mothers who immigrated in the corresponding years.

various periods. A comparison of individuals born in Europe in a certain year with American-born descendants of mothers who immigrated in the corresponding year showed that for each year the differences observed in the total series persist (Fig. 4).

7. The differences between immigrants and *their own* European-born children are always less than those between them and their own American - born children and the differences agree in direction and value with those obtained from the general population. (Partial Report, pp. 44-50; Abstract, p. 47; Final Report, pp. 69-70, 117-128). Thus the cephalic index of American-born children of Hebrew immigrants is by 1.60 units lower than that of their European born children.

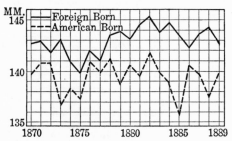

Fig. 5. Width of face of adult Bohemian males born in Europe who immigrated in certain years, compared with that of American-born descendants of mothers who immigrated in corresponding years.

For Sicilians it is 1.78 units higher than that of their European-born children. The following table gives the average differences between measurements of foreign-born immigrants and their own American-born descendants.

Measurements	Bohemians	Hebrews	Sicilians	Neapolitans
Weight of observations	416	515	338	367
Stature (mm.)	—5.60	—13.10	+2.60	—11.90
Length of head (mm.)	+0.74	—1.65	+2.91	+1.56
Width of head (mm.)	+1.31	+1.52	—1.05	—0.48
Cephalic index	+0.69	+1.60 [a]	—1.78	—0.97
Width of face (mm.)	+1.04	+2.10	+1.33	+1.55

[a] Erroneously in the Final Report p. 70, 1.50.

8. The width of face of American-born children of immigrants is decidedly narrower than that of the foreign-born (Fig. 5). Furthermore there is a decided decline of those born a considerable length of time after the immigration of the mother, so that we get the impression of a cumulative effect of American city environment (Fig. 6). The phenomenon is complicated by the fact that the width of face of the immigrants themselves has been declining, in so far as those born in early years, beginning with 1880, show a wider face than later immigrants.[1]

[1] Franz Boas, "Studies in Growth III," *Human Biology,* vol. 7 (1935), pp. 313 *et seq.*

9. When the Hebrew boys are classified according to their pubescence in groups of about equal physiological development, as I, II, III (pre-pubescent, beginning pubescence, completed pubescence), the same differences persist (Fig. 7).[1] This observation is important because it

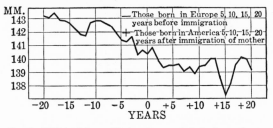

FIG. 6. Width of face of Bohemians and their descendants.

shows that the differences are not due to a retardation of development, for no appreciable differences have been found in the tempo of development of the two groups.

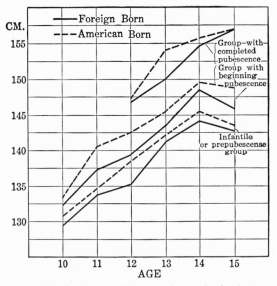

FIG. 7. Relation between stature and maturity for foreign-born and American-born boys.

10. Basing my inquiry on the assumption that the variations of hair color in any particular people follow the exponential law, I have shown

[1] Partial Report, pp. 25–28; Abstract, pp. 38–43; Final Report, pp. 129 *et seq.*

that numerical values for pigmentation can be obtained.[1] I have divided the whole series of pigmentation from black to ash-blond in 20 equidistant steps, excluding reds, o being black, 20 ash-blond, but not without pigment like the hair of albinos. In this manner the results given in the accompanying diagram showing the degree of darkening with increasing age were obtained (Fig. 8).

According to this table, in the rate the darkening amounts to nearly 5 units—one-fourth of the whole scale of colors. If the amount of darkening of females in the first two groups is less, we have to allow for the dyeing of hair, which is practised by many women, and also for the use of false hair by married Jewesses. For this reason I do not lay great stress upon the figures obtained from observations on adult females,

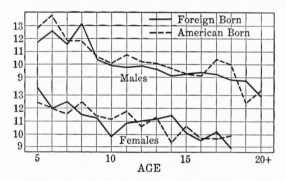

FIG. 8. Color of hair of foreign-born and American-born Hebrews, showing the increase of pigmentation with increasing age.

except among the Italians. It would seem as though among them the hair of women averages a little lighter than that of men. This apparent different may, however, be due to the lighter color of the tips of the long hair of women. The process of darkening progresses at least until the twenty-sixth year, if not longer. An attempt to calculate the annual amount of darkening for the Hebrews shows this very clearly. For dark-haired as well as for light-haired groups the darkening amounts to about 0.2 point a year.

It has been objected [2] that the number of observations on which these

[1] Final Report, pp. 93-98.
[2] Hans Fehlinger, *Politisch-anthropologische Revue,* vol. 10, no. 8 (Nov. 1911), pp. 416-418; Giuseppe Sergi, "Il preteso mutamento nelle forme fisiche dei discendenti degl' immigrati in America," *Rivista Italiana di Sociologia,* vol. 16 (1912), pp. 16-24.

results have been based are inadequate, but a comparison of the values of the observed differences and their errors proves that this criticism is not valid.[1]

It might perhaps have been said that a psychological cause existed in the minds of the observers, which produced one personal equation for foreign-born and another for American-born. It is well known that an expected result may influence an observation. The study of the personal equations of the observers disproves this assumption. Besides this, the results among various types lie in different directions; the observers did not know what to expect; in many cases the statistical information was recorded by one observer, the measurements by another; and constant changes between foreign-born and American-born occurred in practice. All these make such a psychological explanation highly improbable. Here it must be considered as particularly important that the results agree with the previous observations by Ammon in Baden and Livi in Italy, which are, therefore corroborative evidence of the accuracy of the results.

Other objections have been raised. Thus Fehlinger thinks that the individuals investigated are not of pure descent, but in part children of parents of mixed nationality. This is a misunderstanding of my work. His claim that measurements of stature and head form—which, he says, are exceedingly variable in almost all human types—lead more easily to errors than other measurements, I fail to understand.

Attempts have been made, either to deny that any changes occur, or to explain the observations as due to selection. The former attempt has been made by Sergi,[2] who interprets the continued occurrence of long, medium and round heads in New York by claiming that they continue to exist but that the relative frequency of their occurrence has changed. I discuss the arbitrary character of this explanation on p. 73 of this book.

I turn to the question of the interpretation of my observations and repeat, first of all, my own conclusions. Starting from the observation that changes in the values of the averages occur at all ages, that these are found among individuals born almost immediately after the arrival of their mothers, and that they increase with the length of time elapsed between the arrival of the mother and the birth of the child, I have

---

[1] See Final Report, p. 56; Abstract, p. 28.

[2] *Loc. cit.;* also C. Toldt, *Korrespondenz-Blatt der deutschen Gesellschaft für Anthropologie, Ethnologie und Urgeschichte,* vol. 43 (1912), p. 78.

tried to investigate various causes that might bring about such a phenomenon. I have, as I believe, disproved the possibility that the difference between the two groups of American-born and foreign-born may be due to differences in their ancestry. This objection has been raised by Professor Sergi.[1] As mentioned before, the comparison of parents and their own children, and the comparison between immigrants who came to America in one particular year and the descendants who came to America in the same year, seem to eliminate entirely this source of error, which has been considered by me in detail.

Less satisfactory is the attempted proof of the theory that the cradling of infants has no influence upon their head form. The fact remains that among the Hebrews there is a radical difference in the bedding and swathing of infants born abroad and of those born here. Against this fact may be adduced the other one that no such radical difference in the treatment of children exists among the Sicilians, and that, nevertheless, changes occur and that these are in a direction opposite to those observed among the Hebrews. Even more unfavorable to this theory are the changes in width of face among Bohemians which develop among immigrating children who are no longer subject to such mechanical influences. I consider a further investigation into the influences of the method of bedding children desirable.[2]

It also occurred to me that illegitimate births of children whose fathers were Americans might bring about changes. I have disproved this assumption by proving that the degree of similarity between American-born children and their reputed fathers is as great as that between foreign-born children and their fathers (Abstract, p. 51 ; Final Report, pp. 154 *et seq.*). Besides this the social conditions of the Hebrew, Italian, and Bohemian colonies are not at all favorable to such an assumption. This point has been raised again by an anonymous English critic,[3] without, however, referring to my discussion of the question and the answer given by me.

After disposing of these points which would give the phenomenon an accidental character, without deep biological significance, I have taken up the biological problem itself, and first of all have called attention to the parallel observations by Ammon and Livi and suggested that the changes observed by them as occurring between urban and rural

---

[1] *Loc. cit.,* largely reprinted by Radosavljevich in *Science* (May 24, 1912), pp. 821-824.

[2] See p. 74.

[3] *Edinburgh Review,* vol. 215 (1912), p. 374.

populations may be due to the same causes as those observed in the descendants of immigrants. If this be true, then Ammon's interpretation of the phenomenon as due to selection, and Livi's as due to the more varied descent of urban populations, which makes them deviate from excessive values to more median values, must be revised.

I have also referred to the possibility that the breaking of the more or less inbred lines of small European villages after arrival of the people in America and the consequent change in the line of descent may be a cause producing changes in type.

Finally, I have pointed out that the changes can be accounted for by a process of selection only, if an excessively complicated adjustment of cause and effect in regard to the correlation of mortality and bodily form were assumed—so intricate that the theory would become improbable on account of its complexity.

It will, therefore, be seen that my position is that I find myself unable to give an explanation of the phenomena, and that all I try to do is to prove that certain explanations are impossible. I think this position is not surprising, since what happens here happens in every purely statistical investigation. The resultant figures are merely descriptions of facts which in most cases cannot be discovered by any other means. These observations, however, merely set us a biological problem that can be solved only by biological methods. No statistics will tell us what may be the disturbing elements in intra-uterine or later growth that result in changes of form. It may be that new statistical investigations in other types of environment may give us a grouping of these phenomena which suggests certain groups of causes, clues that can then be followed up by biological methods—it is certainly asking too much to expect the solution of this problem from *one* series of observations. I at least am more inclined to ask for further material from other sources than to force a solution that must be speculative.

This defines my position toward the criticisms of Gaston Backman [1] and Giuseppe Sergi. The former claims that the explanations given by Ammon are adequate, and simply identifies my observations and his. He overlooks the all-important difference that I have compared parents and their own children, a method which introduces an entirely new point of view and practically disproves Ammon's claim that these changes are due to natural selection. I have always considered Livi's theory as the most plausible explanation of the European observations,

[1] *Ymer* (1911), pp. 184-186.

and still think that it must be a strong contributory cause, although it is not applicable to our series and for this reason can no longer be considered as explaining the whole phenomenon. Backman's views are, it seems, not in accord with the results of our inquiry. He states: "The causes underlying the alteration will then have to be sought in factors of selection that may be of the most divergent nature. When, nevertheless, Boas wants to maintain that he by his researches has proved the plasticity of human races, this conclusion seems to me to carry further than the facts in question will permit. It seems, on the contrary, to me to be quite plain that it is the change from country life to city life that has been the fact of real importance in the matter of the alterations which the descendants of the immigrants have undergone, and not the special American conditions. The point of weight must be sought in those conditions which the changes from country life to city life carry with them." I have shown that selection is extremely unlikely to bring about the results observed. That the essential causes may be the city conditions is possible, but not proven. I have not ventured to claim that I have discovered these causes. Besides, what would it help us if we assign the phenomena to city life, since the manner of its influence is as obscure as that of any other causes?" I may quote here from my "Abstract" (p. 52), which Mr. Backman reviews (also Final Report, p. 75). When speaking of the differences between urban and rural types, noted by Ammon and Livi, I say: "Our American observations show that there is also a direct influence at work" (in so far as the differences occur also between parents and their own children, in which case selection is highly improbable and mixture excluded). "Ammon's observations are in accord with those on our American city-born central Europeans; Livi's, with those on our American city-born Sicilians and Neapolitans. Parallel observations made in rural districts and in various climates in America, and others made in Europe, may solve the problem whether the changes that we have observed here are only those due to the change from rural life to urban life. From this point of view the slight changes among the Scotch are also most easily intelligible because among them there is no marked transition from one mode of life to another, most of those measured having been city-dwellers and skilled tradesmen in Scotland, and continuing the same life and occupations here."

As long, then, as we do not know the causes of the observed changes, we must speak of a plasticity (as opposed to permanence) of types, including in the term changes brought about by any cause whatever—by selection, by changes of prenatal or postnatal growth, or by changes in the hereditary constitution, as Mr. Backman seems to do. In order to avoid the impression of defining a particular course I have used expressly the term "instability or plasticity of types" (Abstract, p. 53).

Professor R. S. Steinmetz [1] suggests that the observed changes may be due to the elimination of degenerate types that develop under the unfavorable European conditions and are, therefore, a reversion to the better developed old types. I do not consider this likely, because the conditions under which the immigrants live are not favorable; but this suggestion is worth following up as one of the possible contributory causes.

It has also been suggested [2] that the lowering of the head index may be due to the increase in stature which occurs in America. I have myself pointed out that the cephalic index tends to decrease with increasing stature, because the correlation between all anteroposterior measurements—in this case length of head and stature—is closer than the correlation between these and transversal measurements. This relation, however, occurs only in a group which has been treated as a statistical unit. As soon as the groups are classified from distinct social or racial points of view, it ceases. This question has been treated by E. Tschepourkowsky.[3] It is clear that the same relation cannot be expected between stature and head measurements in a group which contains individuals of only one selected stature, as in a group in which all statures are increased owing to some cause that affects the whole group, and which may affect other measurements in peculiar ways. Furthermore, the absolute width of head of the Hebrews born in America decreases, the length of head increases. Among the Italians the reverse is the case.

Professor Sergi criticizes my views from the standpoint that he considers sudden changes in germ plasm in new surroundings impossible and tries to reduce the phenomenon entirely to one of varying composition of the series, that is, if we follow out his ideas, to a differing fertility or mortality of component types of the immigrants. If his remarks, as it may seem, should indicate that he considers brachycephalic, meso-

[1] "Het nieuwe Menschenras in Amerika," *Nederl. Tijdschrift voor Geneeskunde,* (1911), pp. 342-352.

[2] Elias Auerbach, *Archiv für Rassen-und Gesellschafts-Biologie,* vol. 9 (1912), p. 608; Schiff, *Korrespondenz-Blatt der deutschen Gesellschaft für Anthropologie, Ethnologie und Urgeschichte,* vol. 43 (1912), p. 94.

[3] *Biometrika,* vol. 4 (1905-6), pp. 286-312.

cephalic, and dolichocephalic individuals as distinct types, the criticisms made before hold for his view also. His is an attempt to explain the phenomena by natural selection, the success of which, as said before, I consider as extremely doubtful. The particular form in which it is presented by Professor Sergi is based on his method of analyzing the somatological types constituting a people. I cannot consider this method as fruitful, since the analysis which he demands is impossible. If we establish a number of arbitrary types it is always possible to analyze a series of observations accordingly, but this analysis does not prove the correctness of our subjective classification and the existence of the selected forms as types, but is due merely to the fact that the distribution of observations *can* be made according to any fitting theory ; but the correctness or incorrectness of the theory can be proved only in exceptional cases.

The greater the number of types that are to be segregated, the more arbitrary becomes the method, and almost any analysis according to a sufficient number of types *can* be made. There are, of course, distributions that demand an analysis—like von Luschan's bi-modal curves of Asia Minor, or my own for width of face of half-blood Indians, and others—but there must be strong internal evidence of a compound character, and even then the analysis will be arbitrary if the component types are not known. This is perfectly evident if we realize that each type must be defined by at least three constants—average, variability, and relative frequency—so that for two component elements five constants must be determined (one value of the relative frequencies being determined by the relative frequency of the constituent series), for three component elements eight, etc. The greater the number of constants to be determined, the better can the theoretical and observed series be made to coincide, regardless of the correctness of the theory which is expressed by the constants.

I conclude from this that the claim that the change must be explained by a different composition of the series of American-born is inadmissible, because it is an entirely arbitrary solution of the problem.

I repeat that I have no solution to offer, that I have only stated the results of my observations and considered the plausibilities of various explanations that suggest themselves, none of which were found satisfactory. Let us await further evidence before committing ourselves to theories that cannot be proven.

Finally, a few words on the opinion that has been expressed or implied, that our observations destroy the whole value of anthropometry, in particular that the study of the cephalic index has been shown to have no importance. It seems to me, on the contrary, that our investigations, like many other previous ones, have merely demonstrated that results of great value can be obtained by anthropometrical studies, and that the anthropometric method is a most important means of elucidating the early history of mankind and the effect of social and geographical environment upon man. The problem presented by the geographical distribution of head forms—for instance, of the cephalic index—has not been solved by our inquiry. All we have shown is that head forms may undergo certain changes in course of time, without change of descent. It seems to my mind that every result obtained by the use of anthropometric methods should strengthen our confidence in the possibility of putting them to good use for the advancement of anthropological science.

In regard to the question of the effect of cradling I have made a study of Armenians living in New York.[1] One of the most striking characteristics of the Armenian head form is the flatness of the occiput. Von Luschan and others consider this one of the principal characteristics of the type, while Chantre [2] assumed that the flatness was due to deformation.

Inquiries among the Armenians living in New York showed that according to their own opinion the plan-occipital form of the head is due to the position of the child in the cradle. Formerly the child was placed on a large diaper reaching up to the shoulders and covered thickly with a white clay found in the mountains. The diaper was pulled up between the legs and both ends folded firmly from right and left over the body. Another cloth was placed over the diaper and folded so as to press the arms firmly against the body. Then the child was placed on its back in the cradle. The pillow was often filled with wool. The child was kept permanently in this position. Immediately after birth the midwife pressed the head of the new-born infant so as to give it a round shape and compressed the nose from both sides. It does not seem probable that these manipulations had a permanent effect.

The question whether artificial deformation affects the form of the

[1] "Bemerkungen über die Anthropometrie der Armenier," *Zeitschrift für Ethnology*, vol. 56 (1924). Berlin, p. 74.

[2] Ernest Chantre, "Mission scientifique en Transcaucasie, Asie Mineur et Syrie," *Archives du Musée d'histoire naturelle de Lyon*, vol. 6 (Lyon, 1895), p. 50.

head can be solved only by comparing the head forms of individuals cradled in the old fashion with those who were not swaddled. The Armenians living in America do not swaddle their children. In the cities of the Orient, particularly among Armenians who are in close relation to missions, the custom is also disappearing, so that among the younger generation its influence is probably less than among the older Armenians.

In order to settle this question I measured a fairly adequate number of Armenians, partly born in Asia, partly in the United States or in western Europe. These measurements show a considerable difference between the two groups. Those born in the United States and western Europe have longer heads than those born in Asia. The length of head of those born in America exceeds by 6 mm. that of those born in Asia, while the width of head is 4 mm. less.

NEW EVIDENCE IN REGARD TO THE
INSTABILITY OF HUMAN TYPES[1]

A NUMBER of years ago I carried on, under the auspices of the United States Immigration Commission, an investigation on the physical types of immigrants and of their descendants. One of the results of this inquiry was the establishment of the fact that there is a difference in appearance between the immigrants and their descendants. So far as the bulk of the body is concerned, this information was not new. Analogous phenomena had been observed in 1877 by H. P. Bowditch in Boston, and by Peckham in Milwaukee. It was new, however, that there is also a change in such features as the cephalic index and the width of the face. It was found that on the average the heads of descendants of immigrants of East European types are more elongated, and those of the descendants of South Europeans more rounded, than those of their parents. The data were obtained partly by a generalizing method, partly by a comparison between parents and children.

The results of this inquiry have been attacked by many writers, on the basis that they decline to believe that such changes can occur. I have not found any actual criticism of my method and of the results, except by Corrado Gini, who doubts the inferences drawn in regard to the populations of Italian cities which also show a modification of the cephalic index.

I think the hesitation of many authors to accept the results is due largely to a misinterpretation of their significance. I may be allowed to state concisely here what I think has been proved, and what inferences seem justifiable.

The investigation has a direct bearing upon the question of the classification of human local types, more particularly of European types. Many attempts have been made to give a satisfactory classification of the divergent types that occur in Europe. Pigmentation, stature, form

[1] *Proceedings of the National Academy of Sciences*, vol. 2 (December, 1916), p. 713.

of the head, and form of the face, show material differences in various parts of Europe, notwithstanding the fundamental sameness of the whole race. Authors like Deniker, and many others, have carried out on this basis an elaborate classification of European types in a number of "races" and "sub-races."

In this classification the assumption is made that each race that we find at the present time in its particular environment is an hereditary type different from the others. In order to express this assumption, I should like to use the term that these races and sub-races represent, "genetic" types—genetic in the sense that their characteristics are determined by heredity alone. The question, however, has not been answered, whether these types are really genetic types, or whether they are what I might call "ecotypes," in so far as their appearance is determined by environment or ecological conditions. If we include in this term not only environmental conditions in a geographical and social sense, but also conditions that are determined by the organism itself, we might, perhaps, still better call them physiological types, in the same sense in which the biologist speaks of physiological races. My investigation then was directed to the question of how far a certain type of man may be considered a genetic type, of how far a physiological type. If there is any kind of environmental influence, it is obvious that we can never speak of a genetic type *per se,* but that every genetic type appears under certain environmental or physiological conditions, and that in this sense we are always dealing with the physiological form of a certain genetic type. The question, then, that demands an answer, is, in how far genetic types may be influenced by physiological changes.

I believe, that, on the basis of the material that I collected, we must maintain that the same genetic type may occur in various physiologically conditioned forms, and that so far as stature, head form, and width of face are concerned, the differences between the physiological forms of the same genetic type are of the same order as the differences between the races and sub-races which have been distinguished in Europe. I must add, however, that these remarks do not refer to pigmentation, for, contrary to a widespread belief, we have no proof of environmental influences upon pigmentation. For this reason the classification of European races cannot be considered as proving genetic differentiation.

The whole investigation which I carried on, and certain comparable observations obtained from older literature, do not indicate in any way to what physiological conditions the observed changes may be due.

The only physiological causes in regard to which evidence is available relate to the bulk of the body, and to a certain extent to the proportions of the limbs. The size of the body depends upon the conditions under which growth takes place. Growth depends upon nutrition, upon pathological conditions during childhood, and upon many other causes, all of which have an effect upon the bulk of the body of the adult. When these conditions are favorable, the physiological form of a certain genetic type will be large. If there is much retardation during early life, the physiological form of the same genetic type will be small. Retardation and acceleration of growth may also account for varying proportions of the limbs. On the other hand, we have no information whatever that would allow us to determine the cause of the physiological diminution in the size of the face that has been observed in America, nor for the change in the head index that occurs among the descendants of immigrants.

Furthermore, there is nothing to indicate that these changes are in any sense genetic changes; that is to say, that they influence the hereditary constitution of the germ. It may very well be that the same people, if carried back to their old environment, would revert to their former physiological types.

In fact, it can be shown that certain features are strictly hereditary, and that, although the physiological form of a genetic type may vary, nevertheless the genetic type as such will exert its influence. Professor von Luschan has repeatedly called attention to this fact as revealed in the modern populations of Asia Minor, where, notwithstanding the mixture which has continued for at least four thousand years, the characteristic Armenian, Northwest European, and Mediterranean types survive in the mixed population. Similar examples may be observed in Italy. I have calculated the variability of the head form that is found in different parts of Italy, based on the data collected by Ridolfo Livi. The head form of the North Italians is excessively short. The head form of the South Italians is decidedly elongated. In between we find intermediate forms. In the Apennines, we have, in addition to the mixture of these two Italian forms, a marked immigration from the Balkan Peninsula, which introduced another short-headed type. As a result of these long-continued mixtures, we observe low degrees of variability in northern and southern Italy, high degrees of variability in the central regions, particularly in the Abruzzi. These indicate permanence of the component types of the mixed population.

During the last few years some new data have been collected that confirm my previous observations. I have pointed out several times that changes of types have been observed in Europe wherever a careful comparison between city population and country population has been made. Generally the changes that occur there have been ascribed to selective influences; but the intensity of selection would have to be so great that it does not seem plausible that they can be explained by this cause.

In conjunction with Miss Helene M. Boas, I have made a comparison between the head forms of the city populations of Italy and of the rural population in the areas surrounding the cities, and compared these data with the information given in the Italian census in regard to the immigration into cities. I found throughout that the variability of head form in each city is smaller than would be found in a population in which all the constituent genetic types were present without physiological modification. This result has been criticized by Corrado Gini, on the basis that in former times migration was less than what it is now. I grant this point; but nevertheless it is quite obvious that, although no exact data are available, the mixture of population in a city like Rome or like Florence must be very great, since the political conditions for the conflux of Italians, and even of individuals from outside of Italy, have been favorable for a very long period. If this is true, we should expect a very high degree of variability in Rome, which, however, is not found.

Turning to new data, I may mention the observation made by Dr. Hrdlička, who, in a paper read before the Pan American Scientific Congress, has stated that he found the width of face of Americans of the fourth generation—that is to say, of descendants of Europeans who had no foreign-born ancestor after the fourth generation back—was materially decreased as compared to the width of face found among European types. This conforms strictly with what I found among the descendants of immigrants of all nationalities.

A year ago I had the opportunity to make an anthropometric investigation of a considerable number of natives of Puerto Rico. This work was carried on in connection with the Natural History Survey of Puerto Rico organized by the New York Academy of Sciences. The population of Puerto Rico is derived from three distinct sources—from people belonging to the Mediterranean type of Europe, from West Indian aborigines, and from Negroes. The Mediterranean ancestry of the Puerto Ricans leads back to all parts of Spain; but among the more recent immigrants, Catalans, people from the Balear Islands and from the Canary Islands prevail. There are also a fair number of Corsicans. The Spanish immigration has been quite strong even up to the present time. Among the individuals whom I measured, 14 per cent had Spanish-born fathers, some even Spanish-born mothers. From all we know about the history of the people of Puerto Rico, we must consider them essentially as descendants of male immigrants who intermarried with native women. It is evident that in early times this must have led to the development of a Mestizo population, in which, however, the amount of Indian blood must have decreased very rapidly owing to the continued influx of Spanish blood, and the elimination from the reproductive series of the male Mestizo element. The Negro population is settled particularly on the outer coast of the island; while the amount of Negro blood in the interior is apparently not very great, except near the principal routes of travel.

According to European observations, the Spanish ancestors of this population, while living in Spain, are long-headed. The Negro element is of mixed provenience, from many different parts of Africa, but, on the whole, the Negro in Africa is also long-headed. The West Indian element, judging from the few prehistoric crania that have been recovered, represents a very short-headed type. The modern Puerto Rican is short-headed to such a degree that even a heavy admixture of Indian blood could not account for the degree of short-headedness. If we apply the results of known instances of intermixture to our particular case, and assume stability of type, we find that, even if the population were one-half Indian and one-half Spanish and Negro, the head index would be considerably lower than what we actually observe. There is therefore no source that would account for the present head form as a genetic type; and we are compelled to assume that the form which we observe is due to a physiological modification that has occurred under the new environment. The head form of those individuals whose fathers were born in Spain is noticeably more elongated than that of the individuals whose parents are both Puerto Ricans. The head index of the Mulatto population is intermediate between the index of the native Puerto Ricans and that of those whose one parent is Spanish. The average index of the Puerto Rican is 82.5. The average index of the Spaniard in Spain is less than 77. We find, therefore, an increase of five units here, which can in no way be accounted for by genetic considerations.

I may mention in this connection that the average stature of the Puerto Ricans is apparently almost the same as that of the Sicilians in New York, and that throughout the period of growth the stature follows about the same curve as that represented by Sicilian children living in America. If anything, the stature is a little lower, and there is no indication of that acceleration of development which is so often claimed to be characteristic of a tropical environment. Undoubtedly poor nutrition, and probably also pathological causes, have a retarding influence here, which might easily be overcome by better hygienic conditions.

It is unfortunate that we have no accurate statistics of Puerto Rican immigration and emigration, which would enable us to state with much greater definiteness what genetic type should be expected here. There is a popular belief in Puerto Rico that in certain parts of the island, in the so-called "Indiera," Indian types have persisted to a greater extent than elsewhere. I have not been able to find any definite indication of a difference in type; but I have measured only a few individuals from these districts. The material that I have been able to study comes from all parts of the island, but principally from the western-central part. The phenomena here described occur with equal intensity in all parts of the island.

The question of the degree of instability of human types seems to my mind an exceedingly important one for a clear understanding of the problems of physical anthropology. It would be particularly desirable to study the problem among immigrants living in different rural communities of the United States, and it would be even more desirable to have information in regard to the types that develop among the East Europeans and South Europeans who return to Europe and settle in their old geographical environment.

INFLUENCE OF HEREDITY AND ENVIRONMENT
UPON GROWTH [1]

WE HAVE seen that among the individuals composing a population considerable differences in the rate and ultimate result of development are found and that these depend largely on external conditions under which growth and development take place. The question arises whether it is possible to separate the variability caused by environ-ment from hereditary conditions.

In an attempt to answer this question we have to investigate the relations between the bodily forms of parents and children and those between members of fraternities. The method by which these relations can be investigated may be explained by the example of the head index.

If in a given population fathers with unusually rounded heads are compared with their children, it is found that their children have also the tendency to have rounded heads, but less so than the selected group of fathers. For instance, if the average head index of a population is 80% and a sufficiently large number of fathers with an index of 86% is picked out, the average head index of the children of this group will be 82%, about one-third [2] of the deviation of the fathers from the norm of the selected group of fathers. In this way all the body parts may be investigated and a relation similar to the one just mentioned may be established. In populations which have lived for a long time in the same place and whose families have intermarried the "similarity" of fathers and children, as here defined, is about one-third. The same value has been found for the similarity of mothers and their children. The similarity among brothers and sisters is much greater. In a population like the one just referred to a group of men may be selected whose head-

---

[1] *Zeitschrift für Ethnologie*, vol. 45 (1913), pp. 622 *et seq.*

[2] I have used here a value lower than the one found by Karl Pearson (*Biometrika*, vol. 2 [1902–3], pp. 378, 379; see also E. Schuster, *Ibid.*, vol. 4 [1905–6], p. 478), since the following calculations are based on material which gives the value here adopted (Franz Boas, *Changes in Bodily Form*, p. 156). The low value of the regression is due to the character of the series which consists of Russian Jews, a population more homogeneous than Pearson's English material. See in regard to this matter Franz Boas, *The Mind of Primitive Man*, 1938, pp. 60 *et seq.*

form is characterized by the index 86%. Then the average index of their brothers will be 83%, in other words the difference between the norm and the average of the brothers of the selected group is about one-half of the difference between the norm and the value of the selected group. We may say that the similarity of the brothers is about one-half.

Observations regarding the similarities between parents and children and those between brothers and sisters are similar to those mentioned here: about one-third and one-half. Often the values are a little different. Much larger values have been found for twins, particularly for identical twins—that is, those developed from a single ovum. For the present the values given here may be considered as the norms for European populations.

In parts of the body which in the course of growth undergo marked individual changes, such similarities may be considered in the following way: Besides the hereditary similarities which are determined by the values just given each individual develops independently of all the others, with varying tempo and intensity, according to more or less favorable conditions of life. If these causes are of such a character that they are expressed in the bodily form of the adult, there must be, besides the hereditary causes, other accidental ones which are different for the different individuals. In this case a weakening of the similarities may be expected. Therefore, if the observed similarities are so arranged that the similarities of those forms which are permanently established shortly after birth are compared with those which take their permanent forms later in life, it may be expected that the latter group will show lower degrees of similarity.

I have carried through this inquiry for the statures of East European Jews measured in New York. The results show a considerable decrease for the degree of similarity as compared to that of the measurements of the head. The similarity between parents and children for length and width of head, which are established early in life, obtained from more than 2,300 observations is about .36, while that for stature referring to parents and their adult children is only .21. The similarity of siblings (brothers and sisters) in regard to stature is .33 as compared to .56, the similarity for head measures. We may conclude from this that the reduction of variability is essentially due to external differences under which the individuals develop.[1]

[1] Here follows an attempt to evaluate the relative contributions of hereditary and environmental determinants of variability which is here omitted.

If it is assumed that the hereditary part of the similarity is the same for all parts of the body—an assumption that needs proof—it is possible to determine the part of the variability to be ascribed to heredity and the other to be ascribed to environment.

I have assumed that every individual is advanced or held back in his development entirely independently of all the others. This hardly corresponds to actual conditions. Comparing poor and well-to-do families, all members of each family are obviously more or less exposed to similar conditions. The poor are less favorably developed than the rich, so that a secondary family resemblance develops not dependent upon heredity but upon sameness of environment. The same may be said of various parts of a population forming social strata or inhabiting different geographical localities.

At present the real amount of the environmental influences to which families are subjected cannot be determined.

We must furthermore remember that even those forms that reach their final form at an early age are exposed to outer influences, and that the values obtained by the assumption that the values observed for early completed forms are maximal values express only a minimum for the effects of environmental determinants. This is indicated by the increased similarity of heterozygous twins which must be explained as due to the sameness of their prenatal life.

It follows from these considerations that we may expect not only differences between individuals due to exogene causes, but that there will also be differences between populations due to the conditions under which they live. We may also conclude from available data that among individuals of the same descent such variations in stature may be measured by a standard variability of $\pm$ 3.5 cm., so that in the same population according to outer conditions differences in stature of several centimeters may be expected. This is quite in accord with the observation made both in Europe and America showing that stature has increased by about 3 cm. during the last fifty years.

I repeat that the maximal value for similarity obtained from head measurements must not be considered as an expression of hereditary influences only, but that a certain amount of external influences is contained in it. The same considerations that we made before may, therefore, be applied, and, as we found that the stature in populations must be variable according to environmental conditions although the hereditary character of the population remains constant, so we may say in general that modifications of type may result from environmental conditions without any fundamental, hereditary changes in the hereditary character of populations. It seems to me that this explanation of the changes observed in the United States is quite adequate and that it is, for the present at least, unnecessary to look for hereditary changes.

It should be emphasized again that I have assumed here that the degree of hereditary similarity for all characters is equal—an assumption that may not be taken for granted without further investigation. Thus it seems probable that in a mixed population, descendants of one population with high and another with low head index, while the hereditary element of stature is the same in either, the degree of similarity for head index and for stature would be quite different. Nevertheless the material used in this discussion seems to indicate that the method can be used in fairly homogeneous populations. Extended investigations on similarity are needed in order to show whether the suggested approach is admissible.

THE TEMPO OF GROWTH OF FRATERNITIES [1]

I HAVE shown that when the period of maximum rate of growth is early, the whole growth proceeds at a rapid rate from early years on, at least as far as our material permits us to follow it; the onset of the puberty spurt is early, its intensity great, its duration short. Conversely, when the period of maximum rate of growth is late its intensity is slight, its duration long. This is expressed by the values of the maximum rates of growth which are low for those who reach maturity late, high for those who reach it early.

It is a most important question to decide whether this unity of the tempo of development that prevails until maturity has been reached will extend over later life. As far as I am aware the only reliable material that shows an interrelation of phenomena of aging and of the life span is that discovered by Dr. Felix Bernstein, who has proved that early presbyopia indicates an early death by senile degeneration. All others are more or less impressions of medical practitioners who believe, for instance, that early calcification of the larynx indicates an early onset of arterial degeneration. It seems most important that by organized effort the life history of individuals should be followed up in order to show whether the rate at which physiological development and decay occur are constitutionally determined. Studies on longevity also suggest that this is the case, but they can never be quite convincing.

The observations here discussed refer to individual development. We had to investigate next whether the conditions that determine the speed of the life cycle are hereditary or determined by environment. If they are hereditary we may expect that members of fraternities are alike in their tempo, provided the social conditions of the whole community investigated are fairly uniform. The best material at my disposal is contained in the records of the Hebrew Orphan Asylum in New York, for here the conditions of nutrition, shelter and mode of life are as uniform as can be obtained. I have already shown that there is a fairly strong positive correlation between the dates of first menstruation

[1] *Proceedings of the National Academy of Sciences,* vol. 21 (1935), pp. 414-416.

of sisters.[1] Unfortunately it was not possible to classify the material relating to growth in the same manner as was done for other series because, on account of gaps in the series of observations, the moment of maximum rate of growth cannot be determined for all members of each family and the material would have been too scanty. On account of the asymmetries of the increment curve, particularly during adolescence, I did not use correlations, but classified the material in three groups, about equal in numbers—children tall, medium and short at a given age—and compared the curves of growth of their brothers and sisters.

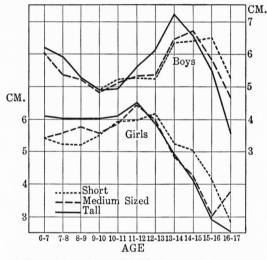

Fig. 1. Annual growth of brothers and sisters, tall, medium-sized and short, at the selected ages of 7, 9, 11, and 13 years. Continuous observations. Hebrew Orphan Asylum.

Then it appeared that the brothers and sisters of the tall ones, who include many of those with rapid tempo of development, will also have a rapid tempo, an early time for the maximum rate of growth, a rapid rate and an early termination of growth, while the brothers and sisters of the short ones, who include many of those with sluggish tempo of development, have a slow rate of growth of less intensity and longer duration (Fig. 1). Since the conditions under which these children live are unusually uniform, we may conclude that proof for the heredity of the tempo of growth has been given. This agrees with the results

[1] *Human Biology,* vol. 4, no. 3 (1932), p. 308.

obtained by Pearl by experimentation with animals and with observations on plants of short and long vegetative periods. An analogous study of children in the Horace Mann School gave the same result. In this case it might be suspected that similar home environment is a contributory cause to the similarity of the growth curve of members of each fraternity (Fig. 2).

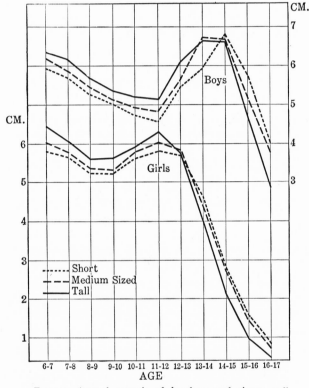

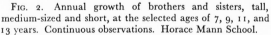

Fig. 2. Annual growth of brothers and sisters, tall, medium-sized and short, at the selected ages of 7, 9, 11, and 13 years. Continuous observations. Horace Mann School.

It is obvious that a phenomenon of such complexity as length of body and tempo of development must be governed by many hereditary factors and that we are dealing with a phenomenon of general organization of the body and that a search for genes would not be advisable. Is not there some danger anyway, that the number of genes will depend rather upon the number of investigators than upon their actual existence?

CONDITIONS CONTROLLING THE TEMPO
OF DEVELOPMENT AND DECAY [1]

I VENTURE to bring to your attention a number of observations regarding the life span which I hope may be of interest to you.

The life span is usually understood to be expressed by tables of expectation of life; but this is not what I mean to discuss. I wish to exclude all deaths due to infections, contagious diseases and accidents, and consider only the life span that we should find, if the strength of the organism were allowed to exhaust itself and death were to occur as a result of senility.

Even here certain allowances have to be made, for we may distinguish between an hereditary, purely biologically determined element and another one that depends upon conditions of life. Ample or deficient nutrition, more or less exhausting daily labor, abuse of the body, greater or lesser nervous strains are elements that modify the life span as it may be determined by heredity. Even geographical conditions may have their influence. Tropical or temperate climate, the degree of humidity, altitude, all have their influence upon the life span. It is, therefore, impossible to speak of the life span of an individual as determined absolutely by hereditary constitution. It must always be understood as the result of a hereditary constitution subject to a given set of environmental conditions. Therefore, even in a population of the same descent, the life span will depend upon social and economic conditions.

A closer examination of the problem shows that the simple statement that a certain length of life may be expected for an individual of known hereditary character and living in a known environment does not exhaust it. The life span is the result of physiological processes that go on throughout life and that have to be observed from the time of birth until death. When we study the distribution of moments of the occurrence of definite physiological changes, it appears that the variability of the time of occurrence increases with great rapidity during life. Meas-

[1] Read at the 46th Annual Meeting of the Association of Life Insurance Medical Directors of America, October 17-18, 1935.

ured by standard variations, the period of pregnancy has a variability of a few days, the appearance of the first teeth of a few weeks, the time when puberty is reached varies by more than a year, the time of menopause by several years, and death by arteriosclerosis by more than seven years. These rapid increases are not the same for different types of physiological phenomena. The teeth, for instance, behave quite differently from the skeleton. All, however, show the characteristic rapid increase in variability. This may be due to one of two causes. Either the increase of variability may be due to a high degree of variability of the changes which occur during a given interval without any relation to the time when a previous stage is reached, or the given interval may have a marked correlation with the time when the previous stage has been reached. If the former is the case, it would be impossible to predict the future, if the latter we may be able to predict the course of the life span. It is, therefore, of fundamental importance for the understanding of the life span to determine whether there is any correlation between the rapidity of physiological processes during life.

Unfortunately it is very difficult without a somewhat rigid organization to follow individuals from birth to death. Continuous observations on individuals are most easily obtained during school life, and I have asked myself the question whether during youth there is any evidence of a consistent speed of physiological changes. The observations show clearly that such consistency prevails. Following young children of six years up to maturity it may be observed that growth is completed earlier for tall ones than for short ones, both for boys and girls. During adolescence all children show a decided increase in the speed of development. Among girls this occurs earlier than among boys. This sudden spurt is followed by a rapid decrease in the rate of growth. Among young children, those who are tall have the spurt earlier than those who are short. Tall girls have their first menstruation, on the average, earlier than short ones. The criterion of size of young children is not as clear as might be desired, because some children are tall because they are accelerated in development, others are tall because by heredity they belong to a tall strain. It is, therefore, more instructive to compare all those who have the period of maximum rate of growth at the same time. Then it appears that the whole growth period for those who mature early is condensed.[1] The bodily growth occupies a short period and proceeds with great energy. The reverse is true of those with a late

[1] See p. 118.

spurt. They develop slowly and the whole period of growth is extended. The same observation may be made on girls arranged according to the time when they reach maturity, but it is not quite so clearly defined, because the relation between sexual maturity and bodily growth is more indirect. It is, however, evident from all the material collected that the period of bodily development is a unit which in some individuals proceeds rapidly, in others slowly.

The next important question to be decided is whether this unity of the rate at which the physiological life process runs on is determined by heredity or by the influence of outer conditions. The latter may be proved by a number of observations. Many investigators have shown that the average stature of European populations has increased considerably since the middle of the past century. Previous studies do not show us how this change comes about, whether it is a result of speeding the process of development and of an incidental final increase, or whether it is a general rise of the standards for each age. So far as the material collected to date allows us to judge, there is a speeding up of growth which brings about very great differences during the growth period. These differences decrease when growth begins to slow up, but result in a somewhat higher stature of the adult. The groups compared were measured, the one in 1909, the other in 1935. It would seem that the changed conditions result in a change of the tempo of development. In other words, we find here proof that the tempo of the life cycle in youth may be strongly modified by conditions of life. I do not venture to speculate on the causes that may underlie these changes, for it is not apparent that the social and economic conditions of the groups concerned have changed noticeably during the interval of twenty-five years. The only other series known to me is one of measurements of children in Jena [1] in Germany ; one taken from 1878–1880, the other in 1921. This shows also a considerable increase in stature among the children measured in 1921 notwithstanding the malnutrition of the preceding years. It is not convincing because during the interval Jena had become an industrial center which attracted people from a distance. Since the native Thuringian population is markedly short, that of the wider environment taller, I was inclined to ascribe the difference to the differing ancestry of the two series. The phenomenon observed here in New York in a more homogeneous group indicates, however, that con-

---

[1] Robert Rössle and Herta Böning, "Das Wachstum der Schulkinder," *Veröffentlichungen aus der Kriegs- und Konstitutions Pathologie*, vol. 4, part 1 (1924).

ditions similar to those prevailing here may have contributed to the increase in stature.

These observations conform with the experimental results of observations on rats. Between 1912 and 1919 Gudernatsch [1] administered dried endocrine glands to successive generations of white rats. He observed that the feeding of dried thymus gland brought it about that the animals treated were healthy, had numerous pregnancies, large litters and long life. Recent work by L. G. Rowntree, J. H. Clark, and A. M. Hanson [2] showed that injections of thymus extract (Hanson) accelerated the rate of growth and development, hastened the onset of adolescence in the offspring of the treated rats and increased the fertility of parent rats. It is still more interesting to note that the acceleration is much greater in later litters of the second generation and is more marked in each succeeding generation under treatment. Omission of the injection in one generation caused the loss of all these changes. Analogous observations were made by Dr. Otto Roth.[3] There is still some doubt as to the active principle that causes the acceleration. Both the experiments on rats and the observations on man show clearly that the tempo of development and the ultimate size may be influenced by outer conditions.

Nevertheless, the importance of hereditary determinants may not be neglected. Many attempts have been made to investigate the correlations between the ages at death of parents and children, and it has been found that a fairly marked positive correlation exists. The same is true for members of a fraternity. The material is not quite convincing because it is difficult to eliminate complex social causes and to confine the cases strictly to death due to senile degeneration. I have investigated the question in how far the tempo of development of one member of a fraternity may be repeated among other members of the same fraternity. The data prove that a child tall for its own age will have brothers and sisters who mature early, while others who are short for their own age will have such of a slow tempo of development. These data are from an orphan asylum, where all the children were under the same environmental conditions, so that external influences, if any, were very slight. This also agrees with observations made on animals. Pearl [4] par-

[1] Max Hirsch, *Handbuch der inneren Sekretion* (1930). Chapter: Entwicklung und Wachstum.
[2] *Archives of Internal Medicine*, vol. 56 (1935), no. 1, pp. 1–29.
[3] *Zeitschrift für Morphologie und Anthropologie*, vol. 33 (1935), pp. 409–439.
[4] See for instance "The Biology of Death VI," *The Scientific Monthly* (1921), pp. 143-162.

ticularly has raised from a mixed series strains differing materially in life span.

All these observations may be summarized in the statement that each individual has by heredity a certain tempo of development that may be modified by outer conditions. The gross, generalized observations available at the present time suggest that in a socially uniform group the tempo of development may be considered as an hereditary characteristic of individuals.

The data which we have at our disposal end with the completion of growth and the important question arises whether the characteristic tempo of the individual extends over later periods of life; whether a rapid tempo of growth will also be associated with rapid decay and earlier death, or whether other types of relation exist. Unfortunately it is quite impossible at the present time to obtain adequate data which, as you will readily observe, must be based on long continued observations of the same individual. If we can obtain the coöperation of the proper authorities such data might easily be secured from the officer corps of the Army and Navy and in similar organizations that require periodic health examinations.

We owe the knowledge of data in regard to later life to Dr. Felix Bernstein [1] who proved by means of life insurance records that an early onset of presbyopia is associated with other early degenerative processes which lead to an earlier death by arteriosclerosis. I do not doubt that many records of death in the archives of life insurance companies could by appropriate search be associated with the growth curves of individuals. Private schools which keep such records remain in touch with their graduates, and by means of proper organization, policyholders among them could be found in sufficient number to give the required information. Furthermore, since we know that the tempo of development is hereditary we might investigate the degree of presbyopia among the parents of children whose growth curve is known. This might also be secured with the help of private schools.

The general problem of the tempo of physiological processes in relation to the life span is certainly not only of theoretical interest, but may also enable us to predict with increased accuracy the expectation of life even in early years.

[1] *Zeitschrift für die gesammte Versicherungs-Wissenschaft*, vol. 31 (1931), p. 150.

REMARKS ON THE ANTHROPOLOGICAL
STUDY OF CHILDREN [1]

IF I venture to lay before you some brief remarks on the anthropological study of children, I do so for the reason that problems of hygiene are necessarily based on the consideration of the anatomical, physiological, and pathological conditions of masses of individuals, phenomena with which anthropological science is intimately concerned, for anthropology deals with the racial and social influences that determine form and function of the body, without reference to the peculiarities of the individual as such, although the range of variations in form and function in individuals who constitute a social group is a most important topic of our investigations. I wish to deprecate, therefore, at the outset all attempts at an individualistic interpretation of our results, which express only the general conditions that have to be considered in a study of the life of the individual, and which are modified in each individual by his peculiar life history and hereditary conditions that cannot be expressed in our generalized results. Nevertheless, the importance of these is great, for they express in a concise way the general effects of social and racial conditions that cannot be formulated in any other manner, and set definite problems to the student of hygiene as well as of anatomy and physiology.

The phenomena that interest us here are those of the development and growth of the child. The first attempt to study growth by metrical methods was made by Quetelet, in Belgium; but our first accurate knowledge is due to the investigations of Henry P. Bowditch, in Boston, and, later on, to those of Roberts, in England. These were followed by work on similar lines in America, Italy, Germany, France, Russia, and Japan. New lines of research were developed by the application of more rigid biometrical methods, the development of which we owe in large part to the influence of Francis Galton and to the work of Karl Pearson.

[1] *Transactions of the 15th International Congress on Hygiene and Demography, held at Washington, D. C., September 23-28, 1912,* (Washington, 1913).

The results of these studies and the present status of the problem may be summarized as follows: The rate of growth of the body, measured by weight and stature, increases very rapidly until the fifth month of fetal life. From that time on the rate of growth decreases, first rapidly, then more slowly, until about four years before the age of puberty. During adolescence the rate of growth is considerably accelerated, and decreases again rapidly after sexual maturity has been reached. Thus the curve of growth represents a line which possesses a very high maximum at about the fifth month of fetal life. It decreases rapidly, and has a second although much lower maximum shortly before sexual maturity is reached, and not long afterwards reaches the zero point. The increase in bulk of the body continues much longer than that of length. In the beginning the rates of growth of the two sexes are about equal, that of the male probably exceeding slightly that of the female. Since, however, sexual maturity begins to develop earlier in the female than in the male, the concomitant acceleration also sets in at an earlier time, with the result that for a few years girls have a larger bulk of body than boys.

Although the periods of most active growth of the parts of the body differ considerably, it would seem that the characteristics of the curve of growth as here outlined are repeated in many if not in all organs and parts of the body. For instance, although the head reaches nearly its full size at an early time, so that its rate of growth shows a much more rapid decrease with age than that of the bulk of the body, there is an acceleration of growth during the period of adolescence. The differences between the sexes are in this case quite marked in early life, the head of the girl being always considerably smaller than that of the boy. The early prepubertal acceleration of the girl is not sufficient to bring the head measurements of girls up to those of boys, even during the prepubertal period. The difference in the measurement of the sexes is, therefore, not by any means solely due to the shorter period of development of girls, as might be supposed from a study of stature and weight alone, but important secondary sexual characteristics exist in early childhood.

These prove that the difference in physiological development between the two sexes begins at a very early time, and that in the fifth year it has already reached a value of more than a year and a half.

I give here a tabular statement of the available observations:

| | *Age in Years* | | *Difference* |
	Boys	Girls	
Ossification of scaphoid	5.8	4.2	—1.6
Ossification of trapezoid	6.2	4.2	—2.0
Eruption of inner permanent incisors.....	7.5	7.0	—0.5
Eruption of outer permanent incisors.....	9.5	8.9	—0.6
Eruption of bicuspids	9.8	9.0	—0.8
Minimum increase of annual growth......	10.3	8.2	—2.1
Eruption of canines	11.2	11.3	+0.1
Maximum increase of annual growth......	13.2	11.2	—2.0
Eruption of second molars	13.2	12.8	—0.4
Maximum variability of stature..........	14.8	12.4	—2.4

These data are not very accurate and must be considered a first approximation only.

When we remember that growth depends upon physiological development, it will be recognized that we must not compare the stature of girls of a certain age with that of boys of the same age, but that from the fourth year on a girl of a certain age should be compared with a boy a year and a half older than she is.

If this view is correct, then it appears that the relation in size of the two sexes persists even in childhood.

I think no better proof can be given of the correctness of this view than the peculiar behavior of those parts of the body which complete their growth at a very early time; for instance, that of the head.[1] The total amount of the growth of the head from the second year on is slight. If, therefore, girls are ahead of boys in their development by about a year and a half or two years, the total amount of growth of the head in their favor will be the small amount of growth accomplished during this period of a year and a half or two years. If, then, there is a typical difference between the size of the body of male and female in childhood of the same character as found in adult life, then the head of the girl ought to be at all periods smaller than the head of the boy; and this is what actually happens. The phenomenon has been interpreted as indicating a less favorable development of the head of the woman; but the previous remarks show that it is obviously due solely to the different rate of physiological development of the two sexes. The results of physiological tests which show very generally that girls do better than boys of the same age may be another expression of the general acceleration of their development.

[1] See also p. 114.

While we may thus speak of a curve of growth and development of the whole body and its organs, which has characteristic values for each moment in the life of the totality of individuals that compose a social group, not all the individuals pass through these stages of development with equal rapidity. It is easiest to make these conditions clear to ourselves by stating the various ages at which certain points in the physiological development of the individual are reached. Data are available for the periods of pregnancy, eruption of teeth, pubescence, sexual maturity, and development of long bones. So far as these can be reduced according to fairly accurate methods, the following results have been obtained: The average period of pregnancy is 269.4 days. One-fourth of all the children observed have been born in the periods of pregnancy between 265 and 273 days, one-half, between 260 and 278 days, and three-fourths, between 254 and 285 days. According to the laws of large numbers, the ratio of children born between any other limits of time can be determined, if any one of the pairs of values here mentioned is known; for instance, the pair which indicates the limits in which the middle half of all the children are born. In our case these limits are, accurately speaking, 269.4 days (the average), plus and minus 9 days. We may, therefore, call 9 days the measure of the variability of the period of pregnancy. I repeat that this means that one-half of all the children are born within the period limited by 269.4 days (the average), minus 9 days (i.e., 260.4 days), and plus 9 days (i.e., 278.4 days). In this way the variabilities shown in table on page 98 [1] have been determined.

It appears, from this table, which may be represented in the form of a curve, that the variability of the physiological stages of development increases very rapidly, probably so that its logarithm is in a ratio approximately proportional to the actual age, or, to use the term applied by Dr. Crampton and Dr. Rotch, to the chronological age. The causes that lead to this rapidly increasing variability are so far entirely unknown. It is certain, however, that there must be definite causes at work which bring about this phenomenon; for, if the variability were due to accidental causes only, it would increase much more slowly than in a ratio proportional to the increasing age, namely, proportional to its square root. The study of the general curve indicating the increase of variability in physiological development points to an irregularity at

[1] Compare table on p. 112 in which the ages and standard variabilities for other features are given.

	Age (years).	Variability (years).
Pregnancy	0.0	±0.09
First incisors	.6	± .14
First molars	1.6	± .20
Inner permanent incisors, girls	7.0	±1.10
Inner permanent incisors, boys	7.5	± .90
Outer permanent incisors, girls	8.9	±1.40
Bicuspids, girls	9.0	±1.90
Outer permanent incisors, boys	9.5	±1.40
Bicuspids, boys	9.8	±1.10
Permanent canines, boys	11.2	± .90
Permanent canines, girls	11.3	± .70
Appearance of pubic hair, boys (Boas)	12.7	±1.60
Second molars, girls	12.8	±1.10
Second molars, boys	13.2	±1.30
Appearance of pubic hair, boys (Crampton)	13.4	±1.00
Full development of pubic hair, boys (Boas)	14.6	±1.10
Full development of pubic hair, boys (Crampton)	14.5	± .90
Puberty, girls	14.9	±1.30
Wisdom teeth, boys	19.3	±1.40
Wisdom teeth, girls	22.0	±1.20
Menopause	44.5	±3.90
Death due to arterial diseases, men	62.5	±8.80

the time of approaching maturity. At this period the variability seems to increase at an unusually rapid rate, and either to be stationary or to decrease again at a later time.

I have spoken here of the variability of the physiological development of the body as though this were a unit. In 1895, in a discussion of Porter's observations on the growth of school children in St. Louis, I pointed out the fact that a general variability in physiological development accounts for the close correlation between the distribution of children of the same age in school grades and the variations in the size of the body and its organs; and this problem was later on worked out by myself and Dr. Clark Wissler in regard to various measurements. These correlations have also been proved in a most interesting manner by Dr. Crampton's observations on pubescence, and by Dr. Rotch's study of the development of the epiphyses. It is true that a close correlation between the states of the physiological development of the various parts of the body exists, but there exists also a certain amount of variability in the development of one organ when another one has reached a certain definite stage. The correlation is so close that the condition of the bones, or that of pubescence, gives us a better insight into the physiological development of the individual than his actual chronological age, and may therefore be advantageously used for the regulation of child labor and school entrance, as Dr. Rotch and Dr. Crampton advocate; but we must not commit the error of identifying physiological development with physiological age, or of considering chronological age as irrelevant.

The clearest proof that is available is found in the data relating to increase of stature, and in observations on pubescence made according to Dr. Crampton's methods. Bowditch was the first to investigate the phenomenon of growth of individuals who are short or tall at a given age, but his method was based on a statistical error. Later on, I showed that retarded individuals possess a late acceleration of growth, and these results were amplified by studies made by Dr. Beyer and Dr. Wissler. Recently I had occasion to make a more detailed statistical analysis of the phenomenon of growth,[1] which shows that groups whose prepubertal accelerated growth begins late in life have rates of growth that exceed by far those of the normal individual; in other words, that, among the retarded groups, the whole energy required for growth is expended in a very brief period. In the case of stature, the phenomenon is complicated by the great differences in hereditary stature among the various parts of the population. It appears more clearly in observations on pubescence. Thus it can be shown that, if the first pubic hair appears in one group of boys at $11\frac{1}{2}$ years, and in another at $15\frac{1}{2}$ years, it will take the former much longer than the latter to attain the full development of pubic hair, and the rate of change found among them will be much greater than that of normally developed individuals. In other words, individuals who exhibit the same stages of physiological development are not the same, physiologically speaking, if their actual chronological ages differ; their past is not the same, and prospective physiological changes in their bodies will proceed in different ways. It is clear, therefore, that the greater the retardation or acceleration in any one particular respect, the greater also will be the disharmonies that develop in the body, since not all the other organs will follow the same rate of acceleration and retardation. The causes of these phenomena are unknown, but we may perhaps venture on the hypothetical explanation that all the cells of the body undergo certain progressive changes with increasing age, and that the internal secretions which become active

[1] These observations, so far as stature is concerned, are contradicted by the data given on p. 118. I have not had an opportunity to check the observations on pubescence on new material.

at the time of puberty exert a stimulus upon the cells which causes accelerated growth in the cells, which depends, however, also upon the state of development of these cells. This may refer to the whole body, as well as to the glands that have a direct influence upon the rate of growth. In retarded individuals many of the cells have advanced in their development more nearly normally than the groups of cells involved in sexual maturity; and when their action sets in the cells of the body are stimulated much more vigorously than the less developed ones of an individual that reaches maturity at an earlier time. This hypothesis, however, would have to be tested experimentally. It is intended only to bring nearer to our understanding the complicated phenomena of retarded and accelerated growth.

It seems very likely that the abnormally large amount of energy expended upon rapid growth during a short period is an unfavorable element in the individual development. A study of the phenomena of growth of various groups of the same population has shown that early development is a concomitant of economic well-being, and that for the poor the general retardation in early childhood and the later accelerated growth are characteristic. It follows from this that there is a corresponding, although not equal, retardation in early mental development, and a crowding of developmental processes later on that probably places a considerable burden on the body and mind of the poor which the well fed and cared for do not suffer.[1] The general laws of growth also show that a retardation kept up for an unduly long period cannot be made up in the short period of rapid growth; so that it would seem that, on the whole, excessive retardation is an unfavorable element in the growth and development of the individual. Whether there are similar disadvantages in a considerable amount of early acceleration is not so clear.

A word may also be said in regard to the evident increase in the general statures of the people of Europe, which has been proved by the study of military statistics. I presume this is partly due to better nutrition and earlier development, but it seems likely that much of it may be due to the better control of infantile diseases, which exert a long retarding influence upon the growth during the earlier years of childhood.

When we turn from the more general phenomena of growth to a consideration of their controlling causes, particularly of the influences

---

[1] This paragraph has to be revised in view of the contradictory observations mentioned in note 1, p. 99, and the discussions of tempo of growth pp. 86 *et seq.*

of heredity and of environment, we have to confess our ignorance of the most elementary facts. While there is no doubt that the bodily size of the parents determines to a certain extent the growth of the bulk of the body of the children, it is not by any means clear in how far part of this may be due to the controlling effect of environmental causes to which parents and their children are equally subject. It is quite obvious that the earlier in fetal life certain traits are formed, and the earlier they reach their full development, the stronger will be the hereditary influence; while the later in life the full development is attained the greater will be the influence of environment, not only on account of the longer time of its action but also owing to the greater diversity of its form. Thus, if the anterior part of the palate has very nearly reached its final form and size in the sixth year no amount of subsequent change of food or use will materially influence its form; while weight and stature, and, even more, mental development, will be modified by the influences to which the individual is subject during the first two or three decades of his life. The problem of growth must, therefore, be studied for every organ independently.

Some observations have been made that illustrate the influence of environment, not only upon growth of the bulk of the body but also upon some of the forms that develop very early in life. Thus, it has been shown that urban and rural populations in Europe exhibit characteristic differences in size and form of the head. These differences are slight, and the attempt has been made to explain them as due to selection or mixture; but reasons can be brought forward that suggest other causes for the modification of the bodily forms. It has also been observed that a fairly homogeneous people like the East European Jews develop distinctive forms in the different parts of Europe that they inhabit, and that Italians, Bohemians, and Jews who come to America develop distinctive characteristics. Whatever the causes of these changes may be, whether due to selection or to internal changes brought about by the new environment, they indicate that heredity is not the sole factor that determines the development of the body.

The few observations which we possess on the growth of children of different races seem to show that there are definite characteristics of the growth curve for each group. Thus, Indian children seem to be shorter than European children, while the adult Indian is as tall as or taller than the European; but it is impossible to tell in how far this is due to the mode of life and how far to the influences of heredity. It is not too much to say that all the work on these problems remains to be done. Our ignorance of these facts should make us hesitate to judge rashly of the mental and bodily inferiority or superiority of races, since the data for forming a judgment are entirely lacking, and since most of the features on which we are accustomed to form our judgment develop late in life, and are therefore, as explained before, to a great extent subject to the influence of environment.

Related to these questions is the problem of the period of development of racial traits. At a very early stage of development children of all races are much alike, and many of the most characteristic traits do not develop until maturity is reached. Traces of these racial traits may be observed at an early time, but their accentuation occurs comparatively late. Here we have undoubtedly traits that are determined by a long line of ancestors, not by environment. Thus, parts of the body that are alike in childhood are subject to a more active growth in one race than in another. For instance, the elevation of the nose of the European, the prominence of the face of the Negro, the great length of the leg of the Negro, the great width of face of the Mongol and Indian are due to a marked growth of these features. Others, on the other hand, lag behind. Thus we are confronted with the ontogenetic problem of the origin of the diversity of human types, and of the oft-claimed but never-proved phenomena of early arrest of development in certain groups.

On the whole, what little we know would indicate that the periods of growth are the same everywhere, but that the rate of growth of various parts of the body is greater in one group than in another, and that in this manner the racial characteristics are developed. Too little is known, however, to express any definite opinion on this important subject.

The subject is one that, in its general aspects, as well as in the questions relating to the influence of heredity and environment, has a direct bearing upon questions of social well-being and upon our estimate of racial characteristics, and for this reason deserves systematic study, not only for the sake of its scientific interest but also on account of its practical importance.

GROWTH

EARLY studies of growth have proved that from birth on the rate of the absolute value of growth of the body as a whole is decreasing until shortly before adolescence, and that at this time a rapid increase of the rate of growth develops which lasts for a few years. It is followed by a decrease which continues until the maximum stature is attained. Bowditch,[1] Peckham[2] and Roberts,[3] who made these early studies also showed that the distribution of statures and weights were asymmetrically distributed. In 1892 I investigated these asymmetries and showed that they were probably due to the changing rate of growth. I assumed that the physiological development of children did not proceed at the same rate, that some might be retarded, others accelerated and that their physiological status would be distributed symmetrically according to the laws of chance. This would result in an asymmetrical distribution of statures.[4]

William Townsend Porter's[5] measurements of St. Louis children showed that children of a certain age in higher school grades were taller and heavier than those of the same age in lower grades, and concluded

[1] See footnote 2, p. 49.
[2] Geo. W. Peckham, "The Growth of Children," *6th Annual Report of the State Board of Health of Wisconsin* (1881) pp. 28–73.
[3] Charles Roberts, *A Manual of Anthropometry* (London, 1878).
[4] Franz Boas, "The Growth of Children," *Science,* vol. 19 (May 6 and 20, 1892), pp. 256, 257, 281, 282; vol. 20 (December 23, 1892), pp. 351, 352.
[5] a. "The Physical Basis of Precocity and Dullness," *Transactions of the Academy of St. Louis,* vol. 6, no. 7 (March 23, 1893).
   b. "The Relation between the Growth of Children and Their Deviation from the Physical Type of Their Sex and Age," *Ibid.,* vol. 6, no. 10 (November 14, 1893).
   c. "Untersuchungen der Schulkinder in Bezug auf die physischen Grundlagen ihrer geistigen Entwicklung," *Verh. d. Berliner Gesellschaft für Anthropologie* (1893), pp. 337–354.
   d. "The Growth of St. Louis Children," *Transactions of the Academy of Science of St. Louis,* vol. 6, no. 12 (April 14, 1894), pp. 263–380; republished in *The Quarterly Publications of the American Statistical Association,* N.S., vol. 3, no. 24 (December, 1893), pp. 577–587.
   e. "The Growth of St. Louis Children," *Ibid.,* vol. 6, nos. 25, 26 (March–June, 1894), pp. 28–34.

that bright children grow more rapidly than dull ones. In reviewing his results I wrote as follows.[1]

I should prefer to call the less favorably developed grade of children retarded, not dull; these terms are by no means equivalent, as a retarded child may develop and become quite bright. In fact, an investigation which I had carried on in Toronto with the same object in view, but according to a different method, gives just the reverse result. The data were compiled by Dr. G. M. West, who found that the children pronounced by the teacher as bright were less favorably developed than those called dull. Furthermore, I do not believe it is correct to say that the facts found by Dr. Porter establish a basis of precocity and dullness, but only that precocious children are at the same time better developed physically; that is to say, the interesting facts presented by Dr. Porter prove only that children of the same age who are found in higher grades are more advanced in their general development than those found in lower grades. Dr. Porter has shown that mental and physical growth are correlated, or depend upon common causes; not that mental development depends upon physical growth.

This brings me back to the question of the cause of the asymmetries of the observed curves. According to the above interpretation of Dr. Porter's results (which is merely a statement of the observed facts), we must expect to find children of a certain age to be at different stages of development. Some will stand on the point corresponding exactly to their age, while others deviate from it. This was the assumption which I made in the paper quoted above, when trying to explain the asymmetries of the curves, and I consider Dr. Porter's observations a strong argument in favor of my theory, which may be briefly summarized as follows:

When we consider children of a certain age we may say that they will not all be at the same stage of development. Some will have reached a point just corresponding to their age, while others will be behind, and still others in advance of their age. Consequently the values of their measurements will not exactly correspond to those of their ages. We may assume that the difference between their stage of development and that belonging to their exact age is due to accidental causes, so that just

---

[1] "On Dr. William Townsend Porter's Investigation of the Growth of the School Children of St. Louis," *Science*, N.S., vol. 1 (1895), pp. 227 *et seq.*

"Dr. William Townsend Porter's Untersuchungen über das Wachsthum der Kinder von St. Louis," *Korrespondenz-Blatt der Deutschen anthropologischen Gesellschaft,* vol. 26 (1895), pp. 41–46.

as many will be less developed as further developed from the average child of a particular age. Or, there will be as many children at a stage of development corresponding to that of their age plus a certain length of time as corresponding to that of their age minus a certain length of time.

The number of children who have a certain amount of deviation in time may be assumed to be arranged in a probability curve, so that the average of all the children will be exactly at the stage of development belonging to their age.

At a period when the rate of growth is decreasing rapidly, those children whose growth is retarded will be further remote from the value belonging to their age than those whose growth is accelerated. As the number of children above and below the average of development is equal, those with retarded growth will have a greater influence upon the average measurement than those whose growth is accelerated, therefore the average value of the measurement of all the children of a certain age will be lower than the typical value, when the rate of growth is decreasing ; higher than the typical value when the rate of growth is increasing. This shows that the averages and means of such curves have no meaning as types. I have shown in the place quoted above, how the typical values can be computed and also that for stature they differ from the average up to the amount of 17 mm.

These considerations also show clearly that the curves must be asymmetrical. Supposing we consider the weights of girls of thirteen years of age, the individuals composing this group will consist of the following elements : girls at their normal stage whose weight is that of the group considered, advanced girls, and retarded girls. In each of these groups which are represented in the total group in varying numbers, the weights of the individuals are probably distributed according to the laws of chance, or according to the distribution of weights in the adult population. What, however, will be the general distribution? As the rate of increase of weight is decreasing, there will be crowding in those parts of the curves which represent the girls in an advanced stage of development, and this must cause an asymmetry of the resultant general curve, which will depend upon the composition of the series. This asymmetry does actually exist at the period when the theory demands it, and this coincidence of theory and observation is the best argument in favor of the opinion that advance and retardation of development are general and do not refer to any single measurement.

Furthermore, the increase in variability until the time when growth begins to decrease, and its subsequent decrease, are entirely in accord with this theory. I have given a mathematical proof of this phenomenon in the paper quoted above (p. 103, note 4). . . . Dr. Porter's formulation of the phenomenon, namely that "the physiological difference between the individual children in an anthropometric series and the physical type of the series is directly related to the quickness of growth" does not quite cover the phenomenon.

It will be seen from these arguments that the very natural supposition that some children develop more slowly than others is in accord with all the observed facts. It was necessary to prove this in some detail because the further interpretations made by Dr. Porter largely hinge upon this point.

These conclusions are based on the assumption that "the type at a certain deviation from the mean of an age will show the same degree of deviation from the mean at any subsequent age; for example, a type boy in the 75 percentile grade at age 6 will throughout his growth be heavier than 75 per cent of boys of his own age." This assumption which I have criticised on a former occasion [1] is incorrect.

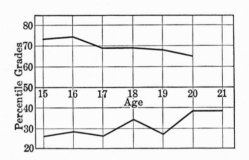

Fig. 1. Change in percentile position of individuals starting at 15 years with the percentile grades of 27 and 73 respectively. U. S. Naval Cadets.

The criticism made in this paper against the assumption that children will always remain on the same percentile grade, as assumed by Bowditch and Porter was empirically supported by Henry G. Beyer.[2] In reviewing his paper [3] I said:

"The most important part of the investigation is the discussion of individual growth which proves beyond a doubt that the assumption

[1] "The Growth of Children," *Science,* 20 (December 23, 1892), p. 351.

[2] "The Growth of United States Naval Cadets," *Proceedings of the United States Naval Institute,* vol. 21, no. 2, whole series no. 74.

[3] Review of Henry G. Beyer's "The Growth of U. S. Naval Cadets," *Science,* N.S., vol. 2 (1895), pp. 344 *et seq.*

made by Bowditch and Porter, namely, that on the average individuals of a certain percentile rank retain this rank through life does not hold good . . ." (Fig. 1).

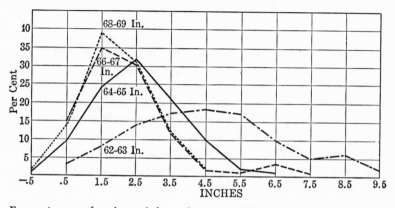

FIG. 2. Amount of total growth from 16 years to adult of males of various statures.

Another important phenomenon brought out in this paper is that tall boys of 16 years grow much less than short boys, because they are nearer the adult stage (Fig. 2).

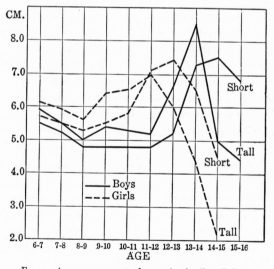

FIG. 3. Average amount of growth of tall and short children. Worcester, Mass.

From data collected in Worcester, Mass.,[1] I proved that in early years short children grow more slowly than tall children [2] (Fig. 3); that is to say, their general development continues to be slow. Later on, during the period of adolescence, they continue to grow, while tall children have more nearly reached their full development. Small children are throughout their period of growth retarded in development, and smallness at any given period as compared to the average must in most cases be interpreted as due to slowness of development. During early life slowness of development which has manifested itself is likely to continue, while some of the effects of retardation will be made good during the period of adolescence, which is liable to be longer than in children who develop rapidly in early life.

On account of these intricate relations between the amounts of growth and stature attained at a given moment the percentile position of individuals or of groups of individuals does not remain the same, but approaches the average.

The results of this investigation suggest that the differences of growth observed in children of different nationalities and of parents of different occupations may also be partly due to retardation or acceleration of growth, partly to differences in heredity.

In order to decide this question we may assume that in the averages obtained for all the series representing various social groups only accidental deviations from the general average occurred. Then it is possible to calculate the average deviation which would result under these conditions. When the actual differences that have been found by observation are taken into consideration another average deviation results. If the latter nearly equals the former, then the constant causes that affect each social group are few and of slight importance. If it is much larger than the former, then the causes are many and powerful. The ratio between the theoretical value of the deviation and the one obtained by observation is therefore a measure of the number and value of the causes influencing each series.

I have applied these considerations to the measurements of Boston school children obtained by Dr. H. P. Bowditch. I have used thirteen different classes in my calculations, namely, five nationalities: American, Irish, American and Irish mixed, German and English; and eight

---

[1] "The Growth of Toronto Children," *Report of the U. S. Commissioner of Education for 1896–97* (Washington, 1898), p. 1549.
[2] "The Growth of Children," *Science,* N.S., vol. 5 (1897), p. 571.

classes grouped according to nationalities and occupations: American professional, mercantile, skilled labor and unskilled labor, and the same classes among the Irish.

The observed and theoretical values are indicated in the following diagram (Fig. 4).

The values obtained by actual observation are always greater than those obtained under the assumption that only accidental causes influence the averages for each class. These causes reach a maximum during the period of growth and decrease as the adult stage is reached. The maximum is found in the fourteenth year in the case of girls, i.e., in those years in which the effects of acceleration and retardation of growth are strongest. Although the values given here cannot claim any very great weight on account of the small number of classes, this phenomenon is brought out most clearly.

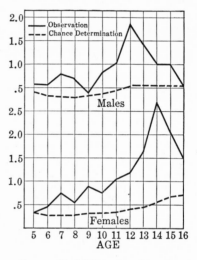

The figures prove, therefore that the differences in development between various social classes are, to a great extent, results of acceleration and retardation of growth which act in such a way that the social groups which show higher values of measurements do so on account of accelerated growth, and that they cease to grow earlier than those whose growth is in the beginning less rapid, so that there is

Fig. 4. Variability of social and national groups as observed and as expected, if only chance determined the variability.

a tendency to decreasing differences between these groups during the last years of growth.

The interpretation here given explains the simultaneous advance of stature, weight, and school achievement. The question is of sufficient importance to demand further corroboration. If the general development affects all the traits of the body, being dependent upon physiological age, we may expect that the correlation of measures during the period of rapid growth is increased, because all are affected at the same time in the same way. This was shown to be the case for school children of Worcester, Mass., and for selected years for those of Milwaukee and Toronto [1] (Fig. 5).

The theory is further corroborated by the observation of those chil-

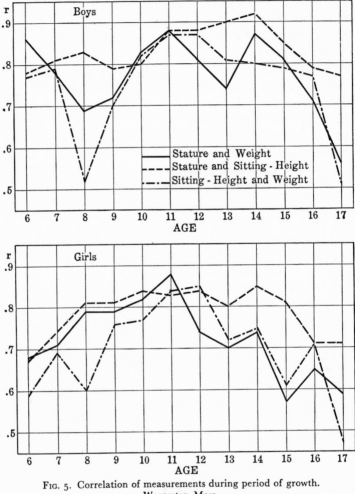

FIG. 5. Correlation of measurements during period of growth.
Worcester, Mass.

dren who have their maximum rate of growth during a given annual interval and who may be supposed to be nearly at the same stage of physiological development. The typical increase of variability which is

[1] "Statistics of Growth," Chapter II, from the *Report of the U. S. Commissioner of Education for 1904* (Washington, 1905), p. 27.

found in the total series and which is due to the combination of individuals who differ in the stage of physiological development disappears almost completely in many of these selected, uniform groups [1] (Fig. 6).

Considering that on account of the inaccuracy of measurements the period of maximum growth is not exactly determined, it seems plausible that if the classifications were made more rigidly the ill defined maxima would disappear entirely.[2] The reduction in variability and the weakening of the maximum prove again that the great increase in variability of the total series at the period of adolescence is solely an effect of the

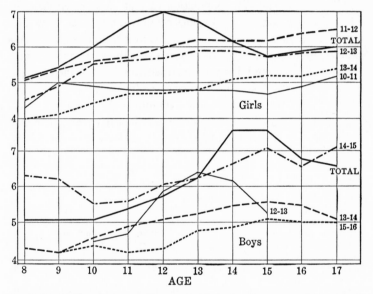

FIG. 6. Variability of stature of boys and girls having the same periods of maximum growth, compared with variability of total series. Horace Mann School.

retardation and acceleration of different individuals, for during the period of rapid growth those who are retarded will be much shorter than those who are accelerated.[3]

[1] "Studies in Growth," *Human Biology,* vol. 4, no. 3 (September, 1932), pp. 319 *et seq.;* "Studies in Growth II," *Human Biology,* vol. 5, no. 3 (1933), pp. 432 *et seq.*

[2] *Ibid.,* vol. 4 (1932), p. 326.

[3] Recently the same question has been discussed by Dahlberg in his observations on correlations of stature during the period of growth. It also agrees with observations on the development of girls with premature first menstruation. Gunnar Dahlberg, "Korrelationserscheinungen bei nicht erwachsenen Individuen, etc.," *Zeitschrift für Morphologie und Anthropologie,* vol. 29 (1931), pp. 288 *et seq.,* particularly, p. 302.

The theory is finally proved by the determination of the tempo of development as shown in the moments when certain physiological stages are reached and by their variability.[1]

As might be expected individual differences in the tempo of development occur. Even children of the same family do not all develop at the same rate. Some of these differences are hereditary, but others due to outer conditions are at least equally important. Satisfactory nutrition and absence of pathological processes accelerate growth. Poor nutrition and frequent diseases retard it. Therefore we have to investigate in how far individuals of the same population vary at various periods of life; for instance, at what age the canines of individuals of the same group erupt. The investigation of various events in the life of man which are characteristic of certain age classes shows that the variability of the age in which such an event takes place increases rapidly with increasing age. For example, the period of pregnancy varies by a few days, the eruption of the first deciduous tooth by a few months, puberty by more than a year, and death by arteriosclerosis by more than ten years. The degree of variability is expressed by the mean square deviation from the average age.[2]

	Male	Female	Difference
Pregnancy		±.04	
Eruption of deciduous teeth			
Lower central incisor	1.01±.25	.89±.28	—.12
Lower molar 1	1.70±.25	1.68±.32	—.02
Loss of deciduous teeth			
Lower central incisor	6.4±1.0	6.1±.9	—.3
Upper lateral incisor	7.4±1.3	7.0±.9	—.4
Lower canine	10.6±1.4	9.7±1.3	—.9
Eruption of lower molar 2	12.5±1.1	12.1±1.7	—.4
Ossification of hand			
Presence of triquetrum	2.6	1.2	—1.4
Presence of naviculare	5.8	4.7	—1.1
Presence of pisiforme	11.2	9.8	—1.4
Maximum rate of growth	14.4±1.1	12.0±1.2	—2.4
Calcification of first rib 60%	36.0±8.6	38.0±8.6	+2.0
Menopause		44.5±5.3	

An increase in variability occurs also in the grouping of children according to mental maturity as expressed by their standing in school

[1] See also tables on pp. 97, 98 in which the variability is expressed by the value of the probable variability.

[2] "Einfluss von Erblichkeit und Umwelt auf das Wachstum," *Zeitschrift für Ethnologie*, vol. 45 (1913), pp. 618–620. In part translated on pp. 82 *et seq.* of this volume.

grades.[1] Thus girls in Worcester, Mass., in 1890 were distributed as follows:

Age	Average grade
9	3.8± .9
10	4.8±1.0
11	5.4±1.1
12	6.4±1.3
13	7.1±1.4

It appears from these data that the increase in variability of physiological age is rapid until the fifth or sixth year. From the sixth to the twentieth year it increases slowly. At a later age the increase is very rapid.

I have described here the variability of the physiological development as though the whole body were a unit. There are, however, differences in the speed of development of various organs. This is brought out most clearly by a comparison of the dates for eruption of teeth of boys and girls. While in all other traits girls of a given age are much more mature than boys of the same age, there are very slight differences only in the eruption of teeth, proof that these are subject to influences different from those acting upon the skeleton.

It is not admissible to assume with Crampton that physiological development is equal to physiological age.

This appears in a comparison between growth and menarche. The earlier the age of maximum growth, the longer is the interval between this moment and the date of menarche.[2]

Age of Maximum Growth Years	Average Interval between Date of Maximum Growth and Menarche Months
9–10	+27.3
10–11	+18.7
11–12	+13.2
12–13	+12.6
13–14	+11.7

A general comparison between the data for males and females shows that the whole development of the female is more rapid than that of the male. This brings about a curious relation between the measures of the

[1] "Statistics of Growth," *Report of the United States Commissioner of Education for 1904* (Washington, 1905), p. 38.

[2] "Studies in Growth," *Human Biology*, vol. 4, no. 3 (1932), p. 311.

two sexes.[1] It has been assumed that the sexes develop at approximately the same rate until the prepubertal spurt of the girls sets in, about two years before that of the boys. During this period stature and weight of girls exceed those of boys and this lasts until the prepubertal spurt of the boys begins while the girls are concluding their period of growth.

When we remember that growth depends upon the physiological state of the body, we recognize that from four years on girls should be compared with boys who are about a year and a half older than they themselves. If this view is correct it will be seen that the relation of size of the sexes found in the adult is also present in childhood.

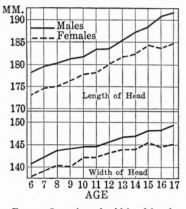

FIG. 7. Length and width of head of boys and girls.

The best proof of the correctness of this view is given by the peculiar relation of the measures which complete the principal part of their growth at an early time. The growth of the head offers a good example. The total amount of increment from the second year on is slight. Therefore, if girls are ahead of boys by one year and a half the increment of growth corresponding to this period is slight. If the typical difference between the sizes of the sexes should be present during early childhood the heads of girls ought to be smaller than those of the boys of the same age. This is actually the case. The length of head of the adult woman is about 96% of that of men. In childhood the length of head of girls is about 97.4% of that of boys of the same age (Fig. 7). The ratio of 96% would be found among girls chronologically three years younger than boys.[2] For stature the normal relation of sizes of adult men and women is found for girls chronologically one and a half years younger than boys which corresponds to their physiological acceleration. The results of psychological tests also show better results for girls than for boys of the same age, which may also be due to a greater speed of development of girls.

[1] "Einfluss von Erblichkeit und Umwelt auf das Wachstum," *Zeitschrift für Ethnologie*, vol. 45 (1913), p. 618.
[2] The same has been shown by Ruth Sawtell Wallis for the diaphysis of radius and tibia ("How Children Grow," University of Iowa Studies in Child Welfare, vol. 5 (1931), pp. 86, 117).

The general growth curve, being composed of individuals of mark-edly different physiological stages becomes clearer when those having the same physiological stage at some moment of their development are segregated. I chose for this moment the time when the maximum rate of growth of stature occurs, since this moment is in all probability most closely related to the development of stature. The following curve shows the growth of the various groups (Fig. 8).

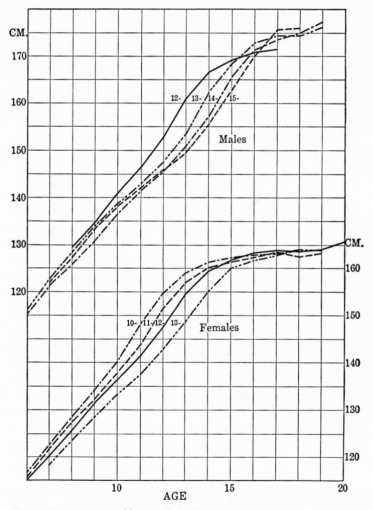

FIG. 8. Growth curves of boys and girls for those having maximum rate of growth at the same time. Horace Mann School.

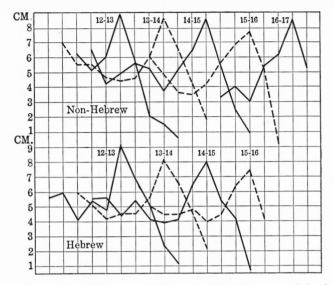

Fɪɢ. 9. Annual increments for boys who have the same periods of maximum rate of growth. Annual intervals to be read from apex of each curve. Horace Mann School.

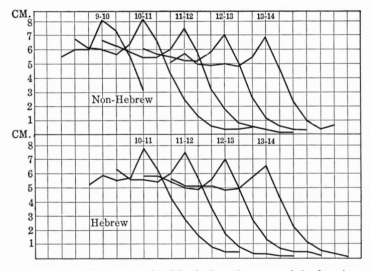

Fɪɢ. 10. Annual increments for girls who have the same periods of maximum rate of growth. Annual intervals to be read from apex of each curve. Horace Mann School.

It has been shown before that in these groups the increase in variability which coincides approximately with the period of maximum growth all but disappears.

A comparison of the rates of annual growth for those who have the maximum rate of growth at the same time, during the periods preceding and following that moment, show that development proceeds the more rapidly the earlier it sets in (Figs. 9, 10).

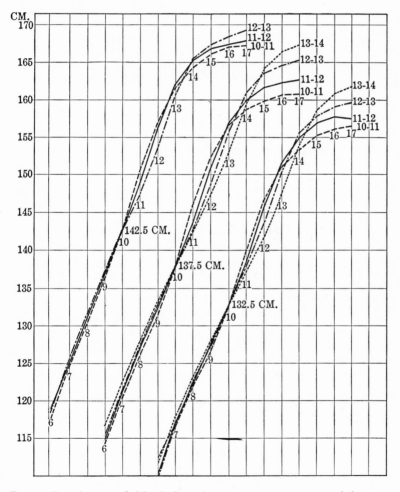

FIG. 11. Growth curves of girls who have the same stature at 10 years and the same period of maximum rate of growth. Horace Mann School.

This is also indicated by the total amount of increment during longer periods preceding and following the moment of maximum rate of growth, for example, during a period of 4½ years before and 4½ years after this moment.

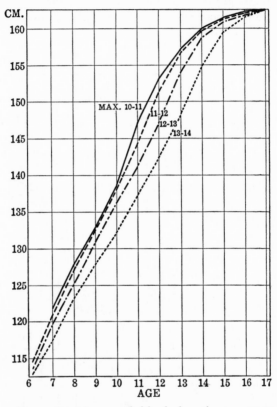

Fig. 12. Growth curves of girls who have the same stature at 17 years and the same periods of maximum rate of growth. Horace Mann School.

During this period, girls [1] who have their maximum rate of growth between

$$
\begin{array}{rll}
9 \text{ and } 10 & \text{grow} & 50.4 \text{ cm.} \\
10 \text{ " } 11 & \text{"} & 46.6 \\
11 \text{ " } 12 & \text{"} & 41.6 \\
12 \text{ " } 13 & \text{"} & 38.2 \\
13 \text{ " } 14 & \text{"} & 35.4 \\
\end{array}
$$

[1] Franz Boas, "Studies in Growth," *Human Biology,* vol. 4, no. 3 (1932), p. 333.

The character of the growth curve may be analyzed still further by considering those children who have the maximum rate of growth and the same stature at a given time. We may then expect that accelerated individuals will have attained the selected stature on account of their acceleration, and since they are nearer the end of their growth period the remaining amount of growth will be less, so that genetically they belong to a short type while the retarded individuals would have the same stature because they are tall by heredity. An examination of the growth curves compiled in this manner shows that the later the time of maximum rate of growth for a selected stature, the greater is the adult stature; also that the higher the selected stature for individuals with the same time of maximum rate of growth the greater is the adult stature. Conversely during the years preceding the selected stature for a given year those who are accelerated are taller than those retarded. This is clearest in the later years of growth (Figs. 11, 12).

Unfortunately the available data do not permit us to follow the observation

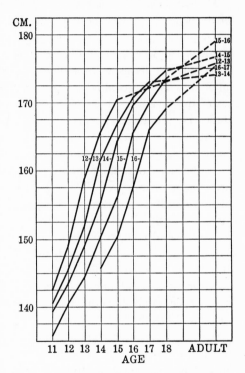

FIG. 13. Growth of boys in the Newark Academy with the same period of maximum rate of growth.

up to absolutely completed growth. Some scanty data on boys of the same social stratum who have been followed up to the completed adult stage (Fig. 13) do not indicate that acceleration has any result on the final stature, while the observations on girls followed up to 17 years on which the data discussed above refer would indicate a slight effect. It is exceedingly difficult to obtain data containing an adequate number of continuous observations up to the adult stage.

The observations for 8-year-old girls[1] may be represented by the equation

$$\text{Adult stature} = 161.35 + .99x + .96y$$

x representing the deviation from the average stature at 8 years in centimeters, y the deviation in years from the average moment of maximum rate of growth. The variability of menarche is $\pm$ 1.6 years. According to this, girls whose menarche is twice the variability, i.e., 3.2 years before the average age, would be 3.2 $\times$ .96, or about 3 cm. shorter than those of average physiological development. On the other hand stature in young years, on account of its great variability, will have a much more marked influence. The variability is approximately $\pm$5.5 cm. Consequently retarded individuals whose deviation from the norm is twice the variability, i.e., 11 cm. too low, will be as adults 10.9 cm. shorter than the average girl. In other words, what is presumably hereditary stature has a much stronger influence than tempo of development.

At the same time the tempo of development does not depend entirely upon environment. This has been demonstrated by our discussion on pp. 86 *et seq.*, which showed that familial traits influence the rates of growth of brothers and sisters.

The general increase in stature which has been observed in every part of Europe proves that non-hereditary influences affect the growth of the body. Various studies have shown that children of parents living under modern conditions exceed their parents in stature. The recent study of the stature and other bodily measurements of Harvard students compared with those of their own fathers[2] demonstrates this definitely.

A study of growing children of each age shows that those born in recent years are taller than those born earlier. In order to avoid possible errors I investigated the statures of the parents of immigrant children contained in my report on Changes in Bodily Form of Immigrants.[3] These measurements were taken in 1909. The ages of the adults give, therefore, at the same time the year of birth.

Figure 14 indicates merely the gradual decrease of stature with increasing age. If there should be any increase with time of birth it would be very slight. I think we may safely say that the stature of Hebrew

[1] Franz Boas, "Studies in Growth," *op. cit.* p. 339.

[2] G. F. Bowles, *New Type of Old Americans at Harvard* (Cambridge, 1932).

[3] *Changes in Bodily Form of Descendants of Immigrants* (Washington, Government Printing Office, 1911, 61st Congress, 2d Session. Senate Document 208). The original data are contained in *Materials for the Study of Inheritance in Man,* Columbia University Contributions to Anthropology, vol. 6 (1928).

immigrants has remained the same from 1845 to 1890. This corresponds to the stability of their economic and social condition in Europe during this period.

The condition of the children admitted to the Hebrew Orphan Asylum and the Hebrew Shelter and Guardian Society shows, on the contrary, a very considerable increase in stature according to their dates of birth. Only observations at the time of admittance were used in the diagrams (Fig. 15) which give the average differences between the stature of the entering child and the general average for quinquennial periods of data of birth. The observations in Horace Mann School

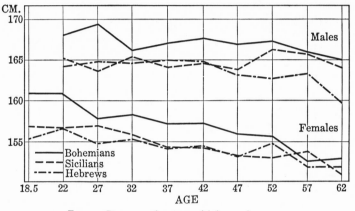

FIG. 14. Decrease of stature with increasing age.

which are contained in the same diagram show similar results. The increase for the population consisting of children of American-born parents, represented here by the Non-Hebrew population of Horace Mann School, is less than that of children of more recent immigrants, represented by the other groups. The increase is most marked for the Negro population of the Riverdale Orphan Asylum.

A comparison of a number of measures of adult Hebrews living in America, mostly born in the United States, taken in 1909 and in 1937 shows also increases in all measures although not in equal proportional amounts.

Increase of Measures in Percent

	Male	Female
Stature	6.5	2.6
Length of head.........	2.3	1.6
Width of head	1.3	1.2
Width of face	3.8	2.4

The tempo of development has also become quicker during this period. Girls in the Hebrew Orphan Asylum born in the quinquennial period 1905–1909 had their first menstruation at the average age of 14.8 years, those born in the quinquennial period 1915–1919 at the

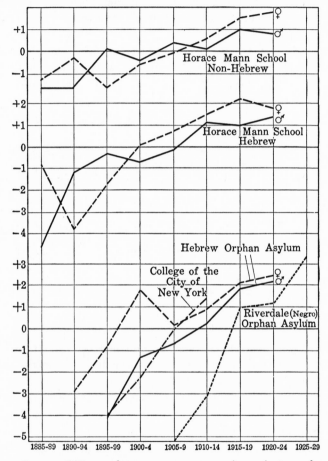

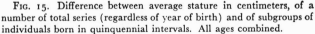

FIG. 15. Difference between average stature in centimeters, of a number of total series (regardless of year of birth) and of subgroups of individuals born in quinquennial intervals. All ages combined.

average age of 13.1 years. Negro girls in the Riverdale Orphanage reached maturity in the period 1910–1914 at the age of 14.3 years, in the period 1920–1924 at the age of 13.3 years. For Horace Mann School the acceleration between 1886 and 1918 amounts to about five months. The acceleration for the period of maximum rate of growth for the same period is approximately 6.5 months.

The influence of outer conditions upon growth may also be studied by a comparison of various social strata. As an example I give the statures of Hebrew children in an expensive private school compared with the general East Side population of Hebrews, both series belonging to the same period (Fig. 16).

The importance of environmental influences appears also in the development of Hebrew infants in a well conducted orphan asylum. It

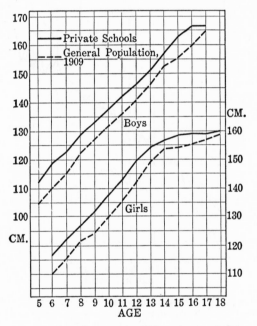

FIG. 16. Growth curves for Hebrew boys and girls.

seems that the children at the time of their admission are in a very poor condition. Under the excellent medical care they enjoy, their weight increases favorably (Fig. 17). When they enter they are much lighter than the average American children,[1] but the older they are and, therefore, the longer they have been in charge of the Institution, the heavier they are, and after 29 months they begin to exceed children of the gen-

[1] R. M. Woodbury, "Statures and Weights of Children under Six Years of Age," *Department of Labor, Children's Bureau* (Washington, D. C., 1921).

eral population. At the same time the eruption of their deciduous teeth remains much retarded.

A study of the effect of institutional life upon children has given further evidence of the effect of environment on growth. This investigation was made in the Hebrew Orphan Asylum in New York City, first in 1918, and repeated in 1928 on children entering after 1918. The former investigation had shown that life in the Orphan Asylum affected growth during the first few years unfavorably, and that it took a long

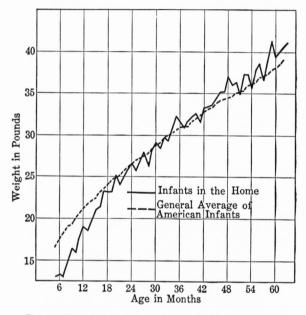

FIG. 17. Weights of Hebrew infants in an orphan asylum compared with the weights of infants of the general American population.

time before the loss could be made up. In 1918 the general policy of the administration changed. There was a change in diet, less regimentation, more outdoor exercise and an effort to meet the needs of individual children.

The results of the measurements of children at entrance are given in Figure 18.

It will be seen that the children placed in charge of the Hebrew Orphan Asylum before 1918 were, at the time of admission, shorter than those admitted after 1918.

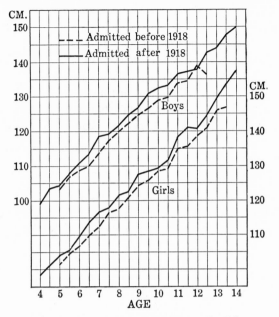

Fig. 18. Statures of children admitted to the Hebrew
Orphan Asylum before and after 1918.

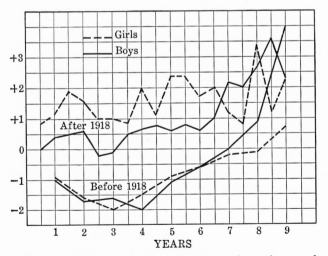

Fig. 19. Difference between average statures in centimeters of
children of all ages at time of admission to the Hebrew Orphan
Asylum, and statures after from 1-9 years of residence.

According to the statement of Mr. Simmonds, the director of the asylum, the selection of families before and after 1918 has remained the same. The larger value in the columns after 1918 must, therefore, be due to the larger statures of those born in later years. In Figure 19 the effect of residence in the Orphan Asylum is indicated. For children in the Asylum before 1918 we find first a deficit of stature during the first few years of residence. It reaches its maximum after about four years of residence. After almost seven or eight years normal growth is

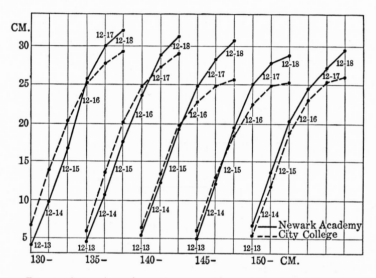

FIG. 20. Comparison of growth curves of boys of the same stature at 12 years of age in Newark Academy and in the College of the City of New York. The curves show the amount of growth from 12 years on for boys of statures from 130-150 cm. in 5 cm. groups.

attained. For children admitted after 1918 there is an increasing improvement over the norm with increasing time of residence.

Racial determinants of growth curves are difficult to determine on account of the strong environmental influences that affect growth. The tempo of growth seems to be little affected by racial descent, but depends rather upon environment. The average time of maturity of girls in New York is practically the same for North Europeans and Hebrews.[1]

[1] These values are obtained by allowing a correction of crude values. This correction is necessary, because many children were observed before they had reached maturity.

Horace Mann School		Hebrew Orphan Asylum	Italian Public School	Negro Orphan Asylum Girls
Non-Hebrew	Hebrew			
13.5±1.3	13.4±1.2	13.6±1.2	13.2±1.1	13.6±1.2

A larger number of cases observed in the Abraham Lincoln High School gave an average of 13.1 ± 1.0 for 1714 Jewish girls. The period of maximum rate of growth of girls in Horace Mann School is 12.0 ± 1.2 for Non-Hebrews, 12.1 ± 1.2 for Hebrews; for North European

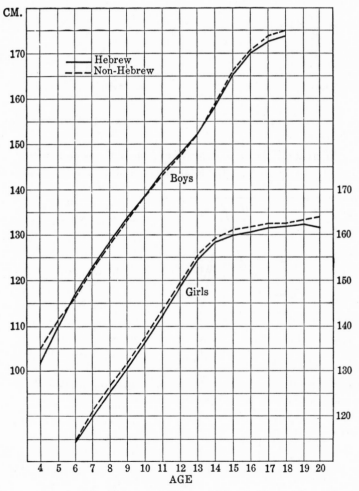

FIG. 21. Growth of Non-Hebrew and Hebrew children in Horace Mann School.

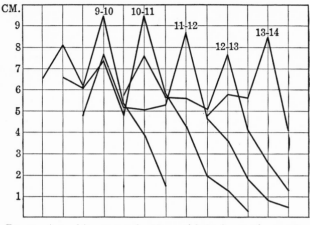

FIG. 22. Annual increments for Negro girls having maximum rates
of growth at various periods.

boys of Newark Academy 14.4 ± 1.1, for boys of City College (almost
all Hebrew) [1] 14.7 ± 1.1.

A difference in the growth curves of Non-Hebrews and Hebrews appears in a comparison of the total amounts of growth for boys of the

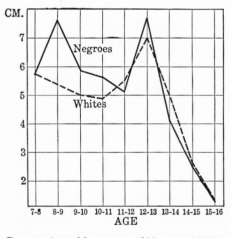

FIG. 23. Annual increments of Negro and White
girls.

same statures at 12, 13, and
14 years observed respec-
tively in Newark Academy
and City College. The short
boys of City College, largely
Hebrew, grow up to a cer-
tain point more rapidly
than the Newark Academy
boys who after this time
grow more rapidly than the
City College boys (Fig.
20). The diagram shows
that the decline of the rapidity of growth sets in
earlier in the short Hebrew
boys than in the short Non-
Hebrew boys. The greater

stature of young Hebrew children appears also in a comparison of
Hebrew and Non-Hebrew children in private schools. Still, it is doubt-

[1] This value is probably too high because the series begins with 12-year-old
boys.

ful whether this is mainly a racial characteristic, for when the same comparison is made for children of the Horace Mann School whose economic conditions are more strictly comparable, the Hebrew children are very little shorter than the Non-Hebrew ones (Fig. 21). For boys in the same school the statures of the children of these two groups are practically the same. In most of the series the adult statures of Hebrews is considerably below that of Non-Hebrews, but in this respect also the

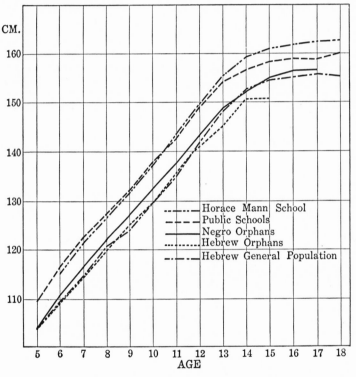

CM.

160

150

140

130

———— Horace Mann School
———— Public Schools
———— Negro Orphans
———— Hebrew Orphans
———— Hebrew General Population

120

110

5   6   7   8   9   10   11   12   13   14   15   16   17   18
AGE

FIG. 24. Comparative growth curves of girls.

results are not consistent, for the statures of Hebrew and Non-Hebrew males at 17 and 18 years are almost equal. The results are not such that we can infer with certainty an effect of racial descent. It seems most plausible for adult stature, but even there it is not certain.

A comparison of Negro and White in New York shows that the time of adolescence and of the period of maximum rate of growth coincide, or at least, that the difference in period is very slight. As among the Whites, the earlier the period of maturation the more intense is the growth (Fig. 22).[1] Besides this we find that on the average the intensity of growth among the Negroes is greater than among the Whites. It is not possible to decide whether this is a racial characteristic or due to environmental factors (Fig. 23).

The total growth curve of Negro orphan girls agrees with that of other groups growing up under unfavorable conditions (Fig. 24).

[1] The cases where maximum rate of growth occurs between 13 and 14, and 14 and 15 apparently deviate, but the amount of available material is insufficient to draw safe conclusions.

STATISTICAL STUDY OF ANTHROPOMETRY[1]

DURING the last few decades a vast amount of anthropometrical material has been collected. By far the greatest part of this material and the most valuable has been collected by the directors of gymnasia connected with colleges, schools, and associations of young people, so that the average anthropometric type of the young American may be said to be fairly well known.

The material has been collected largely from a practical point of view. The main object of the measurements is to determine how the physical development of a given individual compares with the average physical development of the group to which he belongs. The observed deficiencies in his development determine the selection of gymnastic exercises by which the physical development of the subject may be improved. The application of anthropometry to practical work in the gymnasium is founded on two fundamental assumptions: First, that the average measurement represents an ideal type; and, secondly, that small variations from the type may be considered as physiological variations. I wish to discuss these two fundamental assumptions in some detail.

It has often been pointed out that the average type obtained by a series of anthropometrical examinations includes not only those individuals who are perfectly healthy and normally developed, but also others who are deficient in one or the other respect. If abnormality had an equal tendency to increase or to decrease the normal measurement, this cause of variation might be disregarded. It would seem, however, that most of the causes of abnormalities bring about a retardation of development with the result of a final diminution of the value of the measurement. Malnutrition causes decrease of stature. Deficient development of the lungs results in small thoracic circumference and capacity. Disuse of muscles results in lacking development of muscular parts. We may therefore conclude that the types, as obtained from miscellaneous measurements, represent a somewhat pathological type, not by any means the ideal that would be observed if the type were constructed

[1] *American Physical Education Review*, vol. 4 (1902).

from measurements of individuals of absolutely perfect health record. Since the general sanitary conditions improve with increasing wealth, i is probably safe to assume that the differences observed between the physical development of the poor and those of the wealthier portions of our communities are due largely to the elimination of unfavorable influences.

From this point of view it would seem desirable to subdivide the subjects measured in a number of classes according to their health records. Such classification must be founded partly on the history of each case, partly on the observations of the gymnasium director. The metrical results obtained from the best class would be most likely to give us an insight into the form of the normal individual. As defined in this way, the normal individual would not be the one whose form is the most frequent, but the one whose form would be most frequent if conditions were as favorable as possible during the period of development.

A second important question which arises in this connection is whether it is justifiable to assume that there is one and only one ideal type, which all the individuals of our community approach. If different classes of our community represent different types, it would evidently be incorrect to measure the abnormality of an individual by comparison with one single ideal type.

As a matter of fact the individuals measured in our gymnasia differ in regard to their ages, their descent, and the environments in which they live, and it is necessary to decide whether it is justifiable to disregard all these influences. Our American population embraces descendants of practically all European nationalities, and, therefore, includes representatives of all the different types inhabiting Europe. Speaking in a general way we may say that we must distinguish at least three types among the European populations: the blond, tall, long-headed type of Northern Europe; the dark, tall, short-headed type of Central Europe; and the short, dark, long-headed type of Southern Europe. These three types must have been distinct for exceedingly long periods, and possibly the present distribution of European types may be considered as a resultant of their intermixture. I do not mean to say that the three types enumerated here are the only fundamental European types. The views of anthropologists on this point vary to a certain extent, but it is sufficient for our purpose to recognize that in our population the three types enumerated here are represented with a rather strong preponderance of the North European type.

If we happen to measure an individual belonging to the Central European type, we must compare his measurements with the ideal Central European type. It would, evidently, be wrong to compare him with the standard obtained from measurements of North Europeans. For this reason the method of judging the physical development of an individual belonging to a population of mixed descent by comparing him to the general type does not seem free of objection.

The same is true in regard to the effect of age, which factor becomes of the greatest importance in work among growing children. When we measure a sixteen-year-old boy we are by no means certain how near the particular boy is to the adult stage, how nearly he has completed his development. The most superficial examination of the physical and mental development of children and of adults brings out the fact that the physiological development of the individual cannot be measured by years only. We observe children who are precocious; who are in every respect in advance of their age. We observe others who are physically and mentally retarded; while later on the same children will overtake those who previously were far ahead of them. The same phenomenon may be observed when we compare the physical development of older people. With some, the period of decadence begins before the fortieth year is reached, while others retain their full vigor until much later times. The distinct signs of old age also appear in different individuals at widely differing times. It is, therefore, evident that the whole current of life must not be measured by years alone, and that individuals vary, if we may use the expression, in regard to the tempo with which they run through their life's course.

This way of considering the phenomena of growth, development and decay gives a sufficient explanation of all the peculiarities observed in anthropometrical statistics of children, and for this reason I regard this mode of considering the course of human life as fully consistent with observation.

Bearing in view this fact, it is evidently not sufficient to classify individuals according to their ages, but we must also bear in mind the acceleration and retardation of individual development.

But, it may be asked, how is it possible to determine in each and every case the type with which the individual must be classed, and the period of development which he represents?

It would seem that at the present time neither of these questions can be definitely answered. The correlations of the series of measurements characterizing the various European types have never been determined, and the correlations characteristic of various periods of development are also unknown. It would therefore, in the present stage of our knowledge, be largely a matter of judgment on the part of the gymnasium director how to classify each individual according to his general characteristics; or it would be necessary to establish a number of tentative classes in which the individuals might be arranged.

It appears, however, from these considerations, that it is highly desirable to subdivide the anthropometrical material collected in gymnasia in a most minute and painstaking way in order to investigate in how far it will be feasible to class any individual with a definite type. I do not wish to convey the impression that I consider it feasible even after the most extended statistical investigation of anthropometrical material to establish a number of clearly distinct types, the variability of each of which would be so small as to allow us to class any individual with a definite type. I only desire to point out the necessity of classifying our material from various points of view, and of placing each individual in the class to which he most probably belongs.

A diversity of types manifests itself in a series of measurements. It is one of the fundamental laws of correlation that in a homogeneous series deviations from any typical measurement are proportionate to the excess or deficiency of any other measurement. Taking, for instance, stature as a standard, the following condition would be found : If one man is, let us say, ten centimeters in excess of the ordinary stature, another man twenty centimeters in excess of the ordinary stature, then the excess of chest circumference of the second man will be twice as large as the excess of chest circumference of the first man. If, however, the tall individuals should happen to belong to a type different from that to which the majority of short individuals belong, then this law would no longer hold good. We have, therefore, a means of discovering in our extensive anthropometrical series a mixture of divergent types. This investigation is an important one and should be taken up at an early date.

I wish to bring to your attention another point which seems to me of vital importance. We are accustomed to consider the types represented in our tables as constant. We speak, for instance, of the typical measurements of an entering class, and of those of a graduating class. There is a change in the values obtained from these two classes. This change is due to a gradual development. Our point of view is, therefore, only a rough approximation to the actual conditions. The anthropometrical problem is not a statical one, but a dynamical one, and we should take into consideration the rates of changes characteristic of various individuals and their effect upon the distribution of measurements. If we include this problem in our plan of researches it becomes vastly more complex, but at the same time vastly more interesting, because the physiological changes in the individual and the types and variabilities of these changes become accessible to investigation.

For these purposes we need repeated measurements of the same individuals. We must not confine ourselves to comparisons of general anthropometric tables, but we must compare individual measurements with individual increments. The study is still in its infancy, but its importance is far-reaching. It makes it incumbent on our observers to use the most painstaking care in their measurements, and to avoid all rounding off. The increments are in most cases so small that errors introduced by the process of rounding off may be larger than the values which must be investigated. If, for instance, measurements of statures of boys of 16 or 17 years are made, it will be seen that the small average increase may be completely obscured by the inaccuracy of measurement and by the process of rounding off to the nearest full or even half centimeter. If we wish to make progress in this important branch of our inquiry, the very highest accuracy of method of measurement must be demanded.

It is important to bear in mind that questions of this character are not merely of theoretical value, but will also lead to a new point of view in the practical application of anthropometrical results.

The second question which I desire to discuss relates to the scope of physiological variation. We know that no two organisms are absolutely alike, and that various processes lead to slight differences of form in different individuals belonging to the same type. It is only when these variations assume excessive values that we are justified in speaking of pathological cases in so far as the combination of measurements observed is a rare one, and therefore likely to be due to abnormal causes. What, then, is the range of physiological variation? When we are dealing with single measurements we may, perhaps, assume that all those individuals are normal which represent the middle half of the total series of measurements. The lowest measurements and the highest measurements, both of which combined constitute the other half of the series, might be considered as abnormal. When we consider two measurements of the same individual, the question becomes somewhat more complicated. If the two measurements are not correlated at all, if the one changes without influencing in the least the other, we might say again that that series is normal which embraces the middle half of the two measurements. Evidently we should measure the normality or abnormality of a certain combination by the frequency of its occurrence. The average type in regard to both measurements will be the most frequent one, and slight deviations in both directions will have comparatively high probabilities. In the particular case which we are discussing here, namely, when both measurements are entirely independent of each other, it is evident that an individual who has a small deviation in one respect and no deviation at all in regard to the second measurement, will be more frequent than an individual who stands, as we are accustomed to say, in both respects on the same percentile grade. Supposing that stature and transversal diameter of the head were entirely independent of each other, it would be more probable to find a tall man with the average transversal diameter of the head than a tall man with a correspondingly large transversal diameter of the head.

As a matter of fact, there are hardly two measurements that do not influence each other to a certain extent. This fact is easily seen when we tabulate the measurements of tall people and of short people. It will be found that on the whole the measurements of tall people are larger than those of short people, although the proportional increase of the average measurement is not the same for all measures. In all these cases that combination is most probable for which the second measurement bears a certain characteristic relation to the first measurement, which is determined by what we call the coefficient of regression.

It appears from these considerations that a type which is characterized by a series of measurements, all of which represent the same percentile grade, and which, on our anthropometrical charts, would be represented by a number of points standing very nearly on the same level, is *not* as probable as a type which in one of its measurements deviates considerably from the average type, while in all other respects it has only a comparatively small deviation from the average type. This considerable deviation may occur in any of the numerous measurements which we are in the habit of taking. And for many combinations of deviations, one of which is large while the others are small, the frequency of the type will remain the same. We find, therefore, as a result of these considerations, that the most frequent types, and for this reason the types which we must consider as inside the limits of physiological variations, are not by any means those which in all respects are enlarged or reduced replicas of the average type, but such that deviate more or less from this type in regard to their correlated measurements.

I have tried to point out in these remarks a few directions in which it would seem that our anthropometrical material may be made more useful and more significant than it is at the present time. I am fully aware of the difficulties and of the vast amount of labor involved in carrying out any of the suggestions here outlined, but I fully believe that any labor devoted to this matter will be repaid by results interesting from a scientific point of view and valuable for the gymnasium director. Much can be attained by hearty co-operation, and I hope that our deliberations may lead to a way of making the vast amount of anthropometric work that we are doing more useful in scientific and practical lines.

THE HALF-BLOOD INDIAN[1]

THERE are few countries in which the effects of intermixture of races and of change of environment upon the physical characteristics of man can be studied as advantageously as in America, where a process of slow amalgamation between three distinct races is taking place. Migration and intermarriage have been a fruitful source of intermixture in the Old World, and have had the effect of effacing strong contrasts in adjoining countries. While the contrasts between European, Negro, and Mongol are striking, their territories are connected by broad stretches of land which are occupied by intermediate types. For this reason there are only few places in the Old World in which the component elements of a mixed race can be traced to their sources by historical methods. In America, on the other hand, we have a native race which, although far from being uniform in itself, offers a marked contrast to all other races. Its affiliations are closest toward the races of Eastern Asia, remotest to the European and Negro races. Extensive intermixture with these foreign races has commenced in recent times. Furthermore, the European and African have been transferred to new surroundings on this continent, and have produced a numerous hybrid race the history of which can also be traced with considerable accuracy. We find, therefore, two races in new surroundings and three hybrid races which offer a promising subject for investigation: the Indian-White, the Indian-Negro, and the Negro-White. The following study is devoted to a comparison of the Indian race with the Indian-White hybrid race.

It is generally supposed that hybrid races show a decrease in fertility, and are therefore not likely to survive. This view is not borne out by statistics of the number of children of Indian women and of half-blood women. The average number of children of five hundred and seventy-seven Indian women and of one hundred and forty-one half-blood women more than forty years old is 5.9 children for the former and 7.9 children for the latter. It is instructive to compare the number of children for each woman in the two groups. While about ten per cent

[1] *Popular Science Monthly* (October, 1894).

138

of the Indian women have no children, only 3.5 per cent of the half-bloods are childless. The proportionate number of half-bloods who have one, two, three, four, or five children is smaller than the corresponding number of Indian women, while many more half-blood women than full-blood women have had from six to thirteen children. This distribution is shown clearly in Figure 1, which represents how many among each one hundred women have a certain number of children. The facts disclosed by this tabulation show that the mixed race is more fertile than the pure stock. This cannot be explained by a difference of social environment, as both groups live practically under the same conditions. It also appears that the small increase of the Indian population is almost entirely due to a high infant mortality, as under better hygienic surroundings an average of nearly six children would result in a rapid

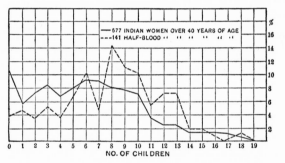

FIG. 1. Number of children of Indian women and half-blood women.

increase. It is true, however, that a decrease of infant mortality might result in a decreased birth rate.

Among the Indians of the Pacific Coast the infant mortality is also very great, but we find at the same time a still larger proportion of women who bear no children.

It is of some interest to note the average number of children of women of different ages as indicating the growth of families. Among the Indians there is an average interval of four years and a half—as shown in the following table—which, however, must not be confounded with an average interval between births:

Indian women	20	years of age have on the average	1	child.
" "	25	" " " "	2	children.
" "	28	" " " "	3	"
" "	33	" " " "	4	"
" "	38	" " " "	5	"

Among the half-bloods the interval is shorter, but the number of available observations is insufficient for carrying out the comparison in detail.

The statures of Indians and half-bloods show differences which are also in favor of the half-bloods. The latter are almost invariably taller than the former, the difference being more pronounced among men than among women. The White parents of the mixed race are mostly of French extraction, and their statures are on an average shorter than those of the Indians. We find, therefore, the rather unexpected result that the offspring exceeds both parental forms in size. This curious phenomenon shows that size is not inherited in such a manner that the size of the descendant is intermediate between those of the parents, but that size is inherited according to more intricate laws.

From investigations carried on among Whites we know that stature increases under more favorable surroundings. As there is no appreciable difference between the social or geographical surroundings of the Indians and of the half-bloods, it seems to follow that the intermixture has a favorable effect upon the race.

The difference in favor of the half-blood is a most persistent phenomenon, as may be seen by a glance at the following table:

DIFFERENCES OF AVERAGE STATURES OF INDIANS AND HALF-BLOODS

Tribes	Men, Centimeters	Women, Centimeters
Eastern Ojibwa	—0.1	0.0
Omaha	0.0	— 0.7
Blackfeet	+0.1	.....
Micmac	+0.6	— 0.2
Sioux	+1.0	+ 0.9
Delaware	+1.6	+ 0.4
Ottawa	+1.7	+ 0.4
Cree	+2.0	+ 2.8
Eastern Cherokee	+3.2	.....
Western Ojibwa	+3.2	+ 0.7
Chickasaw	+4.5	.....
Choctaw	+7.0	.....
Tribes of medium stature (165 to 169 centimeters)	+3.3	+ 2.5
Shortest tribes (less than 165 centimeters)	+8.3	+14.8

The last two entries in this table embrace mainly the Indians of the Southwest and of the Pacific Coast.

The facts which appear so clearly in the preceding table may be brought out in a different manner by grouping all the Indian tribes in three classes according to their statures: those measuring more than 169 centimeters, or tall tribes; those measuring from 165 to 169 centimeters, or tribes of medium stature; and those measuring less than 165 centimeters, or short tribes. The frequencies of various statures in each

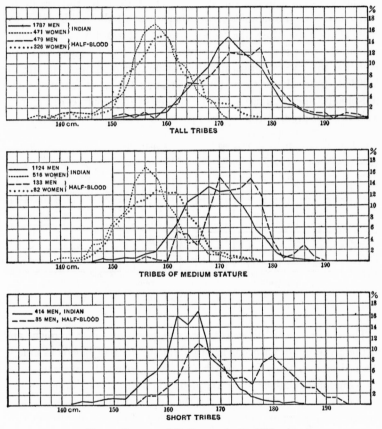

FIG. 2. Statures of Indians and of half-bloods.

of these classes have been plotted in Figure 2. The horizontal line represents the individual statures from the lowest to the highest. The vertical distance of the curves from any point of the horizontal line shows how many among each one hundred individuals have the stature represented by that particular point. Thus it will be seen that 14.4 per cent of the full-blood men of the tallest class have a stature of 172 centimeters, while only 12.3 per cent of the half-blood of the same class have the most frequent stature belonging to them—namely, 178 centimeters. Among the Indian women of the tall, full-blood tribes 16.8 per cent have a stature of 158 centimeters, while only 14.4 per cent of the half-bloods have their most frequent stature—namely, 160 centimeters.

This tabulation brings out the peculiarity that the statures of the half-bloods are throughout higher than those of the full-bloods; and that, at the same time, the most frequent statures are more frequent among the pure race than in the mixed race. This is expressed by the fact that the curves illustrating the distribution of statures among the half-bloods are flatter than those illustrating the same feature among full-bloods. This peculiarity may be noticed in all the curves of Figure 2, with the exception of that of the men of the second group.

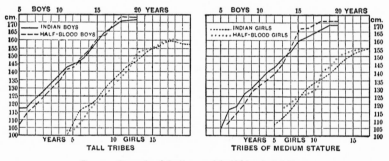

Fig. 3. Growth of Indian and half-blood children.

The statures near the average of each group are most frequent and as these values do not occur as often among the half-bloods as among the full-bloods, the values which are remote from the average are at the same time relatively more frequent. Thus it becomes apparent that the mixed race is less homogeneous than the Indian race.

Another important phenomenon is revealed by a comparison of the growth of Indians and half-bloods (Figure 3). When the average statures of children of both races are compared, it appears that during the early years of childhood the Indian is taller than the half-blood, and that this relation is reversed later on. This is found in both the groups for tall tribes and for tribes of medium stature. It is to be regretted that this comparison cannot be carried on for Whites also. The social surroundings of the White child are, however, so entirely different from those of the Indian and of the half-blood children that no satisfactory conclusions can be drawn from a comparison. It is difficult to see why the laws of growth of the Indian and half-blood should differ in this manner; why the Indian child at the age of three years should be taller than the half-blood child, and then develop more slowly than the latter.[1] This peculiarity is most striking in the growth of the tribes of medium stature, as in this case the difference in the statures of adults is so con-siderable. Unfortunately, we do not know if the same difference pre-vails at the time of birth; but even if this were the case the difference in the rate of growth would remain mysterious. The various phe-nomena described here merely emphasize the fact that the effect of intermixture is a most complicated one, and that it acts upon physio-logical and anatomical qualities alike. We observe in the mixed race that the fertility and the laws of growth are affected, that the variability of the race is increased, and that the resultant stature of the mixed race exceeds that of both parents.

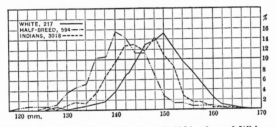

FIG. 4. Breadth of face of Indians, half-bloods, and Whites.

One of the most striking characteristics of the Indian face is its great breadth as compared with that of the Whites. It is therefore of peculiar interest to compare this measurement among the full-blood Indian, the half-bloods, and the Whites. The curves on Figure 4 show the result of this inquiry. Among adult students of American colleges we find an average breadth of face (between the zygomatic arches) of 140 mil-limeters, while the average value among Indians is nearly 150 milli-meters. The facial measurements of the half-bloods are intermediate, the average value being near the typical Indian measurement and remote from the White measurement. We find in these curves also the peculiarity observed before—that the half-blood is more variable than the pure race. This fact is expressed in the greater flatness of the curve.

[1] According to the data given on pp. 117–119, this may indicate a more rapid development of the young Indian.

It will be noticed that the central portion of the curve illustrating the distribution of the measurements of breadth of face of half-bloods is markedly irregular, particularly that it shows a depression in its central portion. This might seem accidental, but it will be seen that in Figures 5 and 6, where the same measurements for the Sioux and Ojibwa are given, the same phenomenon appears. We see in all these curves that the measurements which are near those of the parental races appear more frequently in the mixed race than the intermediate measurements. It is true that the number of observed cases may seem rather small to

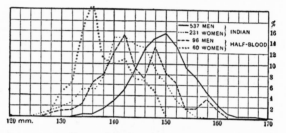

FIG. 5. Breadth of face, Sioux.

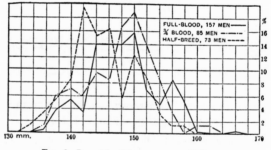

FIG. 6. Breadth of face, eastern Ojibwas.

draw this deduction with absolute certainty; but I have noticed that all tabulations of face and head measurements which include more than five hundred individuals give very regular curves except in the case of half-bloods, so that I believe I am justified in interpreting the phenomenon illustrated in Figure 4 as a real one, and that it is not due to the small number of measurements. The correctness of this view can be proved definitely by an appropriate grouping of the available material according to the following point of view: The breadth of face and the breadth of head of man are closely correlated. The broader the head, the broader the face. Irregularities in the distribution of the measurement of the face will, therefore, appear more distinctly when individuals who have the same breadth of head are grouped together. I have grouped the material in four classes, with the result that the double maximum of frequency, corresponding to the breadth of face of the parental types, appears more strongly marked in every class. Therefore we must draw the important inference that the face of the offspring has a tendency to reproduce one of the ancestral types—not an intermediate type. The effect of intermixture in this case differs, therefore, fundamentally from the effect observed in the measurements of stature.

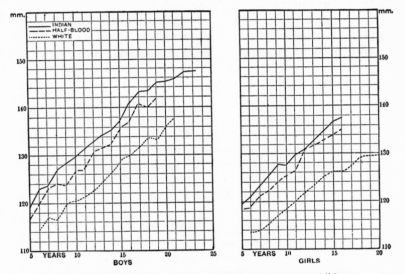

FIG. 7. Breadth of face of Indian, half-blood and White children.

When comparing the average breadth of face for Indians, half-bloods, and Whites, another interesting phenomenon may be seen. The average breadth of face of the half-blood stands between that of the Indian and that of the White, but nearer the former. When computing this average from year to year, it is found that the same relation prevails throughout from the fourth year to the adult stage, and in men as well as in women (Fig. 7). The relation of the three groups remains unchanged throughout life. The amount of White and Indian blood in the mixed race is very nearly the same. We find, therefore, that the Indian type has a stronger influence upon the offspring than the White type. The same fact is expressed in the great frequency of dark hair and of dark eyes among half-bloods.

Two reasons may be assigned for this fact. It rҩay be that the dark hair and the wide face are more primitive characteristics of man than the narrow face and light eyes of the Whites. Then it might be said that the characteristics of the Indian are inherited with greater strength because they are older. It must, however, also be considered that half-bloods are almost always descendants of Indian mothers and of White fathers, and this may have had an influence upon the race, although there is no proof that children resemble their mothers more than they resemble their fathers.[1]

In carrying out the comparison of breadths of face it would be better to study the curves of distribution for each year, but the number of observations is insufficient for applying this method. As stated before,

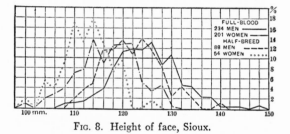

FIG. 8. Height of face, Sioux.

the distribution of measurements is such that the parental types are more frequent than the average; for this reason the latter has no real biological significance. It must be considered merely as a convenient index of the general distribution.

Among the eastern Ojibwa I was able to make a classification into three groups: Indians, three-quarter bloods, and half-bloods. In this case (Fig. 6) it will be noticed that the influence of the white admixture is very slight in the three-quarter bloods. The maximum frequency of the breadth of face remains at 150 millimeters, and we observe that a small increase in frequency takes place at 140 millimeters.

From the breadth of face I turn to the consideration of the height of face—i.e., the distance from the chin to the suture between the nasal bones and the frontal bone (Fig. 8). This measurement is subject to considerable variations, on account of the difficulty of determining the

[1] This would be expressed now-a-days by saying that the Indian type contains dominant elements.

initial points of the measurement with sufficient accuracy. This accounts for the irregularity of the curves. It appears clearly that the face of the half-blood is shorter than that of the White. I am not able to say whether this phenomenon is due to a general shortening, or whether the nose, the jaw, or the teeth contribute most to this effect. The difference between full-blood and half-blood is much smaller than in the case of the breadth of face.

The two measurements combined show that the Indian face is considerably larger than the face of the half-blood, while the latter is in turn larger than the face of the White. As the head measurements of the tribes which have contributed to these statistics prove that there is no appreciable difference between these races regarding the size of the head, we are led to the conclusion that the Indian face is also relatively larger than that of the half-blood and of the White.

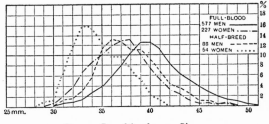

FIG. 9. Breadth of nose, Sioux.

Another characteristic difference between Indians and half-bloods will be found by comparing the breadth of nose of both races. It is well known that the nostril of the Indian is round, and that it is bordered by thick alæ, while the nostril of the White is elongated and has fine alæ. Unfortunately, there are no measurements of the nose of the White available, but a comparison of the transversal breadths of the nose of Indian and half-blood (Fig. 9) makes it clear at once that intermixture has the effect of making the nostril narrower and the alæ thinner, thus producing a much narrower nose. It appears at once that the nose of the half-blood man is not wider than that of the full-blood woman. The three-quarter bloods of the Ojibwa (Fig. 10) are found to take an intermediate position between full-bloods and half-bloods.

We will finally consider the effect of intermixture upon the length of head from the point between the eyebrows (the glabella) to the occiput among a tribe with a head that is shorter than that of the

American White. The Ojibwa has a head which measures about 191 millimeters, while that of the White measures about 195 millimeters. A comparison of the three classes (Fig. 11) shows a gradual increase in length from the full-blood, through the three-quarter blood, to the half-blood.

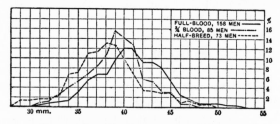

FIG. 10. Breadth of nose, eastern Ojibwas.

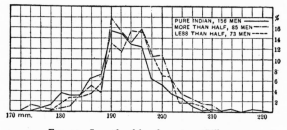

FIG. 11. Length of head, eastern Ojibwas.

We find, therefore, that the laws of heredity in the forms of the head and face are uniform, in so far as intermediate forms are produced. I presume, however, that in all these cases the middle forms are not found as frequently as forms resembling the two parental types.

REVIEW OF PAUL EHRENREICH,
"ANTHROPOLOGISCHE STUDIEN
UEBER DIE UREINWOHNER BRASILIENS," 1897[1]

THE present volume is of great importance, not only on account of the detailed information given in the special part of the work, but also on account of a critical examination of the methods of somatology. The following lines are intended as a review of this general part of the work.

Dr. Ehrenreich is one of the few anthropologists who have an equal command of somatological, ethnological and linguistic methods. His criticism of modern somatology is directed mainly against the excessive weight given to measurements as compared to morphological description and to the loose use of the terms race and type.

He would reserve the term "race" for the principal divisions of mankind, while he would call the varieties of these main divisions "types." He objects strongly to the application of the term "race" to closely affiliated varieties which differ in regard to a few measurements, while their fundamental morphological features are much alike. He justly attributes much of the confusion prevailing in anthropological literature to a lack of clear distinction between the main groups and their subdivisions, and particularly to the tendency which has developed in recent years to consider a few anthropometrical criteria as a sufficient basis for the establishment of a new race.

In determining the "races," or the main divisions of mankind, Ehrenreich demands the consideration of three principal phenomena. He claims that each race is characterized by similarity of anatomical traits, geographical continuity of habitat, and similarity of the structure of the languages spoken by the people constituting the race. The first two points are well taken. They refer, of course, to conditions prevailing before the modern migrations of races. I doubt, however, if it is admissible to introduce the last point of view in the definition of the principal

[1] *Science,* N.S., vol. 6 (December 10, 1897), pp. 880–883.

divisions of mankind. Ehrenreich is led to include languages in the characterization of races by three considerations. He says: (1) Every race has developed a greater or lesser number of characteristic linguistic stocks. (2) These stocks are not found outside the limits of each race, excepting a few instances which are explained by certain peculiar conditions. (3) There are fundamental differences between the structures of the languages spoken by the different races, and no connecting links between them exist. Based on these arguments he distinguishes six races, leaving the position of the Papuas and of the black peoples of Asia doubtful. I will not lay great stress upon the fact that these principles of classification lose their applicability among the last-named people, as in their case peculiar conditions prevail. But there are other cases which show that these principles do not help us to establish a definite number of races. The linguistic considerations would make it impossible to include the pre-Aryan peoples of Europe and western Asia, in what Ehrenreich terms the Caucasian or Mediterranean race, although the anatomical characteristics of these peoples are identical with those of the Mediterranean race. On the other hand, the American race shows considerable anatomical uniformity as compared to other races, and, nevertheless, there is no unity of structure of language in Ehrenreich's sense of the word. It is no less possible to imagine a connecting link between the principles of structure of the Algonquin and Eskimo than between the Eskimo and Ural-Altaic languages. If we are willing to consider American languages as a unit, and include only those principles in the general characterization of American languages that hold good in all of them, there is nothing to prevent us from including Ural-Altaic languages in the same group. Ehrenreich agrees in these opinions with the views expressed by Brinton in his discussion of the characteristics of American languages. (*Essays of an Americanist*, pp. 350 *et seq.*)

Dr. Ehrenreich's second criticism of modern anthropology is directed against the excessive weight given to measurements as compared to morphological descriptions. He expresses the opinion that the classification according to cephalic indices which has held sway since the days of Retzius has greatly hampered the development of somatology and has made efforts at classification futile, since these were based on measurements, particularly on indices, alone, while they must be based on morphological descriptions. These latter, he holds, cannot be replaced by numerical values. While heartily agreeing with this view, particularly with the objection to the exaggerated value given to the length-breadth index of the head, I do not think that Dr. Ehrenreich's condemnation of anthropometry is quite justified. He defines the object of somatology as the somatic investigation, description, and if possible explanation of racial characteristics. With this, I believe, all anthropologists will agree. The only question is what methods are best adapted to these ends. A broad view of the history of anthropology shows that measurements were originally introduced in order to give precision to certain descriptive features which could not be expressed satisfactorily in words. This appears to have been the leading view of Daubenton and Camper, who were the first to introduce measurements in discussions referring to comparative anatomy. The nearer alike the types which we compare, the more difficult it is to describe in words their nice distinctions. Anthropology was the first branch of descriptive biology to deal with closely allied varieties, and for this reason the need of substituting exact numerical values for vague descriptions was soonest felt. Since zoology, more particularly the study of mammals and of birds, has begun to take into consideration the geographical races of the same species we observe the same tendency of adding measurements to verbal descriptions.

In so far as Dr. Ehrenreich's criticism is directed against the substitution of measurements for descriptions that they should supplement, it is most timely and ought to be taken to heart by investigators. The terms dolichocephalic and brachycephalic as indicating two groups of head forms determined by measurements have by some investigators been raised almost to the rank of specific characters, although, as Ehrenreich justly emphasizes—and in this he has the support of Sergi, Harrison Allen and others—the sameness of the index does not by any means signify sameness of morphological type. He disclaims the significance of these characters when not supported by general morphological agreement. In all this the author is certainly right. But he overlooks entirely the principal and fundamental value of numerical measures as illustrating the range of variability of types which cannot be given by any verbal descriptions. The type inhabiting a certain region cannot be defined satisfactorily by a substitution of descriptive features selected by even the closest observation. It is not possible, as Ehrenreich says, to represent a type by a typical individual. The description must include all the individuals in order to illustrate the composition of the group that is being studied. In order to give an adequate description it is necessary to illustrate the frequency of different types composing the group. While the types found in two adjoining areas may be almost identical their distribution may differ. The attempts to treat the same subject by means of composite photographs or composite drawings, which from a purely theoretical point seem very promising, offer serious practical obstacles which make it difficult to use these methods. The variability of a type can, therefore, be expressed only by means of carefully selected measurements. Dr. Ehrenreich states with great clearness that none of the proposed series of measurements are satisfactory, but we must add that a way exists of discovering such measurements. This way is shown in Professor Karl Pearson's admirable investigation on correlations which was suggested by Galton's important work on heredity. By its means laws of correlation may be discovered which express morphological laws. It seems to me, therefore, that the author's condemnation of anthropometrical methods for determining geographical varieties is too sweeping.

The skepticism with which the author regards the results of anthropometry leads him also to the conclusion that sameness of type is not a sufficient proof of common descent; that the latter is only proved if supported by historical and linguistic evidence. This opinion is open to serious objections. It is certainly true that it is impossible to determine by anatomical characteristics alone to what people a single individual belongs. But it is perfectly feasible to identify a series of individuals belonging to a certain people or district, if the series is sufficiently large. Dr. Ehrenreich, it would seem, has been misled by the fact that all types are variable and cannot be represented by a single typical individual to consider the whole task a hopeless one. Even though it is not possible to establish for a people a single anatomical type to which all individuals conform and which is characteristic of that people and no other, this does not prove that we cannot trace its genesis by means of a study of the various types constituting the people and their distribution among the people itself and its neighbors. The author acknowledges this fact to a certain extent, saying: "Whoever tries to rely in these investigations on physical characters alone will certainly be led astray. A consideration of the geographical point of view and of historical evidence will give much greater certainty to his conclusions." Here, as in the discussion of the races of man, the author strongly emphasizes the geographical point of view, and in this he agrees with F. Ratzel. He urges the necessity of considering the geographical probability of blood-relationship before generalizing from anatomical similarities. The considerations of this point of view, on which the reviewer has also repeatedly insisted, will certainly prevent anthropologists from forming rash conclusions and propounding extravagant theories.

But I do not believe that the introduction of linguistic considerations in the somatological problem will be found to be of advantage. It is true that wherever we find two tribes speaking affiliated languages there must have existed blood-relationship; but we have abundant proof showing that by infusion of foreign blood the anatomical types have changed to such an extent that the original type has been practically swamped by the intruders. Such is the case in North America among the Athapascan tribes of the Southwest, among the widely scattered Shoshonean tribes, and in many other cases. The laws according to which anatomical types are preserved are not the same as those according to which languages are preserved, and for this reason we must not expect to find the results of classifications based on these two considerations to coincide. Dr. Ehrenreich seems to think that types are too variable to give any satisfactory basis for deductions of this character. But, notwithstanding the fact that certain anatomical features are easily affected by the influence of environment, I cannot acknowledge that any proof of the transformation of the fundamental features of types exists.

In our investigations on the early history of mankind three methods are available, each directed to a certain series of phenomena—physical type, language, customs. These are not transmitted and do not develop in the same manner. The one persists when the other changes, but all may be made to contribute to the solution of the general problem. The study of the distribution of languages permits us to make nicer divisions and to follow historical changes in greater detail than that of the distribution of physical types. But often the latter give evidence in regard to phenomena which cannot be approached by linguistic methods. The distribution of the Alpine type of man in Europe, or that of the Sonoran type in North America, may be mentioned as instances of this kind. It would be absurd to state that in these cases similarity of type does not prove blood-relationship because there is no linguistic evidence to support it. On the contrary, the physical investigation supplies evidence that cannot be gained by linguistic facts. The three methods mentioned above are all equally valuable, but since they do not refer to the same classes of facts it must not be expected that they will clear up the same incidents in the early history of mankind, but all may be utilized with equal advantage in the study of this subject.

In regard to the affinities of the American race to other races Dr. Ehrenreich seems to be inclined to consider it as equally closely related to the Asiatic and to the European races. He lays particular stress upon the proportions of the body and the form of the hair as distinguishing the Americans from the Asiatics. In this opinion he agrees to a certain extent with Brinton. It would seem to me that in determining the position of a race we should be guided by the morphology of its most generalized forms, namely of women and children. The far-reaching similarity between American and Asiatic children and women is striking. They have in common the wide and rather low nose, the form of the eye and of the maxilla. The physiognomic similarity is so great that it would seem to be of greater weight than the variable proportions of the body which are much more subject to influences of environment.

REVIEW OF WILLIAM Z. RIPLEY,
"THE RACES OF EUROPE"[1]

THE primary object of Professor Ripley's studies is the explanation of the present distribution of human types in Europe. Four factors determine the same: heredity, environment, chance variation and selection.

It is a difficult task to ascribe to each of these its proper sphere of influence in the development of the human types inhabiting a continent whose people have undergone so many changes of location as those of Europe. Professor Ripley agrees with most authors in recognizing three fundamental types in Europe: the long-headed, dark Mediterranean; the short-headed, brunet Alpine; and the long-headed, blond Teutonic type. The author rightly dwells on the fact that, on the whole, human types are comparatively stable in given areas, and for this reason prefers to give to the types geographical names (p. 128). He suggests that it would have been desirable to designate the type of northwestern Europe also by a geographical term—such as Deniker's "Nordic"—rather than by a national term, such as "Teutonic," which he uses throughout. The prevalent types of various regions he explains largely as due to mixtures of these fundamental types, and as modifications due to environment, chance variation and selection.

The multiplicity of these causes and our lack of knowledge of the mode of their action make all conclusions based on them very doubtful. The causes may be combined in various manners to explain a given phenomenon. The lower stature of mountaineers is explained by less favorable influence of the highest region and said to be counterbalanced by its selective influence, which eliminates the less vigorous elements of the population. When the obscure effects of social or geographical environments are insufficient to explain existing conditions, heredity as expressed by mixture, and selection or chance variation, enter as

[1] *Science,* N.S., vol. 10 (September 1, 1899), pp. 292–296.

convenient factors which enable us to find a plausible explanation. The ease with which the extremely complex phenomena can be explained by various combinations of these causes seems to me a reason of weakness of the conclusions set forth by Professor Ripley. Our ignorance of the conditions which influence modification of inherited form suggest that before accepting a given theory we should seek for historical corroboration of the same. This has been given in a few cases, as in the discussion of the types of Britanny (p. 101) ; but sufficient historical and archaeological evidence is not available or has not been given to raise many conclusions beyond serious doubt. It would seem that combinations of causes such as are brought forward to explain the conditions in Burgundy (p. 144) are so uncertain that they cannot be considered more than a very risky hypothesis. The uncertainty of this method is also well illustrated in the discussion of the characteristics of the types of the Alps. The author is led to explain in many places the permanence of the Alpine types by the remoteness and unattractiveness of Alpine valleys, while in others the high variability of the Alpine population is explained by the assumption that the valleys contain the "ethnological sweepings of the plains" (p. 106). Historical evidence is just as much necessary in the study of physical types as it is in that of geographical names, which are very liable to lead to erroneous results, unless studied in their oldest accessible forms. Only when our knowledge of the causes influencing human types is much more definite than it is now may we hope to reconstruct the details of their history without the corroboration of historical evidence. Many of the explanations contained in the book are certainly plausible, and add much to its attractiveness; but I should be inclined to emphasize the elements of uncertainty much more than the author does.

On the whole, Professor Ripley considers economic attractiveness as one of the principal causes that regulate the distribution of types. According to his theory the fertile plains were always subject to foreign invasion, while the less fertile hills contain the most ancient types. While in historic times, when population had reached a considerable density, this cause must have been very effective, we may doubt if it acted in the same manner in early times, when the continent was sparsely settled, when agriculture was not the only means of subsistence and when dense forests and swamps, difficult of access, or steppes that are now fertile covered the plains. The author calls attention to the fact that the invasion of the Alpine type cannot be explained in this manner.

I feel least in accord with Professor Ripley's ready resort to mixture as an explanation of peculiarities of type. This view is closely connected with the interpretation of what constitutes a type or a race. I do not think the term "Races of Europe" a fortunate one, but, with Gerland and Ehrenreich, I am inclined to reserve the term for the largest divisions of mankind. The differences between the three European types are certainly not equal in value to the differences between Europeans, Africans and Mongols; but they are subordinate to these. The term "type" appears most appropriate for the subdivisions of each race.

It would seem that if the author had given us in his work not only an analysis of what differentiates the various types of Europe, but also a description of what is common to them—a subject that would seem eminently proper in a discussion of European man—his views might have been somewhat modified. The important anatomical characteristics of the race as a whole have found no place in his work; in the chapter on European origins (pp. 457 et seq.), in which he deals with the general question of race, only the anthropometric evidence and pigmentation are treated. Considering the most generalized form of the European race as it reveals itself in the child, we should be inclined to consider it a highly specialized form of the Mongoloid type from which it departs principally, by the peculiar development of the nose and adjoining parts of the face and by a general decrease of pigmentation. On account of the high degree of variability; of the originally limited distribution of this type, and of the apparent tendency of hybrids with other races to revert to the other parental race rather than to the European race, I should be inclined to consider the European one of the latest human types. In early times this race was probably slightly specialized in a number of areas, each area exhibiting a considerable degree of variability. The loss of pigmentation, and change in facial form, were not equally pronounced everywhere, so that one region would be darker colored or broader faced than another, although not by any means uniform in itself. For this reason the occurrence of blonds or of narrow-faced and elongated heads in an otherwise dark, broad-faced and short-haired region does not necessarily prove mixture. At present we have no means of telling how stable these types had become before the extensive mixture which certainly has taken place throughout Europe. For this reason it seems a vain endeavor to seek for individuals representing the "pure type," even if there had been no mixture. In his discussion of the "Three European Races" (Chap. VI) Professor Ripley acknowledges the variability without, however, discovering that it makes conclusions as to mixture exceedingly doubtful, except in very pronounced cases.

It does not seem to me justifiable to consider all the individuals that are short-headed and brunet, although living in an area which, on the average, is long-headed and blond, as belonging to the Alpine type, and to explain their presence as due to mixture between the two types. They may simply represent the remoter variations from the long-headed blond type. This question has a most important bearing upon the explanation of facts of social selection (pp. 537 *et seq.*) by the assumption of different tendencies in the two types.

The problem can hardly be solved satisfactorily until we have acquired a much better knowledge than we now possess of the variabilities of the various types and of the degrees of correlation between the features that characterize each type. This information is not yet available. No method has yet been devised for measuring the variability of pigmentation. The military selection, which vitiates so many anthropometric results, unfortunately often obscures the actual variability entirely. Thus all curves of stature in Livi's great work on Italy are asymmetrical on account of the elimination of all individuals below 155 cm. and the decreasing frequency of rejection correlated with increasing stature. This selection increases all the averages, and lessens the variabilities the more, the shorter the average of the type. Neither is it quite safe to take the irregularities of curves of distribution as evidence of mixture, unless they are subjected to a very careful analysis.

The author considers as the most valuable anthropometric characteristic the form of the head as expressed by the cephalic index, and deprecates the value of facial proportions and of absolute measurements. We cannot quite agree with this view. The cephalic index is often a most valuable means of distinguishing the types composing a race, but not by any means the only one. Our selection of characteristic measurements must always be guided by existing differences, whatever these may be. Two types may have the same cephalic index and still differ in the general form of the skull and of the face to such a degree as to require separate treatment. Neither must we disregard the absolute values of the diameters of the head. The great length of the Negro cranium as compared to its small capacity has a meaning quite different from the same length of the European cranium of large capacity. For this reason we cannot accept the daring map of the distribution of the

cephalic index the world over (p. 42) as signifying any racial relationships. Cephalic index alone cannot be considered a primary principle
of classification.

Neither are cephalic index and pigmentation alone a sufficiently
broad basis for the characterization of racial types. The consideration
of these two features leads the author to designate the European race
as intermediate between the African and Asiatic races, without considering the objections to this theory which are founded in the form of
the face, the size and form of the brain, the proportions of the extremities. Neither do we feel it safe to explain the fine, wavy hair of the
European as due to a mixture between the frizzly African and the
straight Asiatic hair.

We most heartily concur with the author's emphatic demand for
treating physical, ethnographical, and linguistic methods separately.
The misconception of what constitutes a racial type, a cultural group,
and a linguistic stock has caused a vast amount of futile speculation.
The three methods may be used, each in its particular domain, for reconstructing part of the history of mankind, and each may be used, to
a limited extent, as a check on the two others. When two groups of
people speak closely related languages the inference may be drawn that
they are in part related in blood, although the strain of common blood
may be so slight as to escape anthropometrical methods entirely. Cultural similarity is no proof of blood-relationship, since culture may be
easily disseminated among tribes of different descent.

REVIEW OF ROLAND B. DIXON,
"THE RACIAL HISTORY OF MAN" [1]

DURING the last quarter of a century, particularly since the development of studies on heredity, the attempts to unravel the history of human types have been based more and more on the investigation of morphological forms. The more mechanical classifications according to metrical features which dominated anthropological inquiry during the end of the past century do not play as important a part as they used to do. An excellent instance of this kind is the detailed investigation of the history of the Melanesian-Australian type given by Sarasin in his study of New Caledonia.[2] The same tendencies manifest themselves in the study of the ancient remains of man, particularly of those belonging to the paleolithic period. It is recognized more and more clearly that metrical values must be considered merely as a means of a quantitative statement of descriptive features.

Professor Dixon's attempt to unravel the racial history of man runs counter to this whole development. His book is based on the thesis that three measurements of the head—length, breadth and height—and two measurements of the nose—height and breadth—have remained stable since paleolithic times. The second hypothesis on which his analysis is based is the assumption that all those human types which are characterized by the extreme forms of the length-breadth and length-height index of the head and the height-breadth index of the nose are primary forms and that all intermediate forms are due to intermixture between these primary forms. In this way he obtains necessarily eight fundamental races, representing the eight possible combinations of three independent features.

From a biological point of view it is difficult to see how these two fundamental hypotheses could be maintained. First of all, we have no

[1] *Science*, N.S., vol. 57 (May 18, 1923), pp. 587–590.
[2] Fritz Sarasin, *Anthropologie der Neu-Caledonier und Loyalty-Insulaner* (Berlin, 1916–1922).

evidence that human types may be considered as absolutely stable. It is true that not all types of organisms react equally energetically to environmental influences, but there is no evidence that would permit us to assume that man is absolutely resistant to them. We have the best possible evidence that the size of the body and proportions of the limbs are strongly influenced by environment and, so far as I can see, no observations have been made that would contradict my own observations on the changes of head and face form of immigrants in the United States and of the descendants of Spaniards living in Puerto Rico. The proof may not have been given that the differences between town population and country population observed in Europe is due to direct environmental influences, but even if we assume with Ammon [1] that it is due to selection, it would show that the constitution of a group of people may be materially changed.

The strongest argument in favor of the plasticity of skeletal form is shown in observations of domesticated animals. Changes in head form and in size of the skull have been noted not only in many domesticated animals, but also among animals born in captivity. Differences have been observed between wild lions and lions born in zoological parks and between wild rats and rats raised in cages. Attention has been called by Eduard Hahn and by the writer to the fact that men must be considered a domesticated form and this thesis has been most fully worked out by Eugen Fischer and recently by Berthold Klatt.[2] With these observations in mind, the thesis of the absolute stability of human forms from paleolithic times to the present would require proof before it could be accepted. This view is practically a restatement of the thesis of J. Kollmann, who considered the modern human types as "Dauer-formen."

In order to maintain the second hypothesis, Professor Dixon has assumed (p. 17) that the three features which he discusses are not subject to Mendelian inheritance. While we do not know in detail how the three features are inherited, there is fairly conclusive evidence that there is a tendency towards reversion to parental types. A study of the data collected by Walter Scheidt [3] shows that the formation of middle types as a result of crossings is not probable.

It would seem to the reviewer that an attempt to establish the ex-

[1] O. Ammon, *Zur Anthropologie der Badener* (Jena, 1899).

[2] "Mendelismus, Domestikation und Kraniologie," *Archiv für Anthropologie,* vol. 18 (1921), p. 225.

[3] *Familienkunde* (Munich, 1923), pp. 75-109.

tremes of a variable series as fundamental types is based on a misconception of the meaning of variability. We know from the studies of inbreeding carried out by Miss King [1] on rats and by Johannsen [2] on beans that even in extreme cases of long continued inbreeding there will always remain a considerable amount of variability. This is not surprising, considering the complexity of the organism and the many ways in which it is subject to formative influences which can never be fully controlled. We are fairly familiar with the variability of the two head indices and of the nasal index. If we assume for a moment that we have a human type which, in regard to the three classes established by Professor Dixon, occupies exactly a middle position and if we assume furthermore the variability in this group to be equal to one-half of the space occupied according to his definition by the middle group and if, furthermore, we disregard the correlations between the various measurements, we should find that in a group of this kind all the extreme groups would be represented by 0.5 per cent of the whole series; all the groups containing two extreme forms and one middle form would be represented by 1.8 per cent; those reprsenting one extreme and two middle forms each by 7.6 per cent and those representing three middle forms by 28.7 per cent. As a matter of fact, the variability here assumed for the three ratios considered by Professor Dixon is lower than the normal variability that occurs in any given type and we would have to say, therefore, that in a group of people of this kind all the extreme forms would be represented. Professor Dixon would go on to say that all the middle forms are mixed and he would thus obtain 12.5 per cent for each one of his primary types as the ancestry of the group. The assumption that the variability of a series of this kind is due to mixture is entirely arbitrary. In short, the proof is not given that the extreme forms are actually fundamental forms. On the contrary we should rather be inclined to assume that the extreme forms are due to certain excessive conditions that determine the particular form of the individual in question.

It seems, therefore, that the theoretical basis of the whole investigation would require proof of the two fundamental hypotheses and this the author fails to give, and it is my belief that it cannot possibly be given.

It is, of course, true that the human races have intermarried to such

---

[1] *Studies on Inbreeding* (Philadelphia, 1919).

[2] W. Johannsen, *Elemente der exakten Erblichkeitslehre* (Jena, 1909).

an extent that the attempt to find a pure race anywhere is futile. Notwithstanding this fact, we ought not to overlook the similarity of the phenomenon to the analogous variability of plants and animals which occur over extended areas. Exactly the same method might be applied to forms of bears or to forms of mice. Here also extreme forms might be established and all the intermediate forms might then be explained as due to mixture. This simplification of the problem would, however, hardly appear justifiable because here, also, the dogmatic assumption would be made that the forms are permanent and not in any way subject to environmental influences.

The difficulties of these hypotheses made by the author appear very clearly when he compares his fundamental types as occurring in different parts of the world. As might be expected he does not find any kind of correlation between the ratios which he studies and other anatomical traits, such as pigmentation, hair form and so on. It is quite obvious that when we compare long-headed, high-headed, flat-nosed individuals living in the Alps of Europe with similarly proportioned individuals from Australia and West Africa, there must be serious differences in regard to other traits. Because Professor Dixon assumes that these three values are fundamental, he is compelled to assume that none of the other traits are permanent and are all subject to change. No attempt it made to prove this conclusion, which is merely an inference drawn from the assumed permanence of the given traits. It is, of course, true that there is a possibility that features like kinky hair may have developed independently in different races, as Sarasin assumes, but this assumption does not overcome the objections based on the failure to consider any other bodily features.

On account of our fundamental disagreement with the general position of the author it does not seem advantageous to enter into a detailed discussion of the distribution of the various types which is given in a number of maps. It must be understood, of course, that the maps are analogous in character to the usual maps showing the distribution of, for instance, short statures and tall statures, or low cephalic index and high cephalic index and that all of these are only fragmentary reproductions, because the plotted values depend upon two factors, the average and the variability of the measurements. The author's maps ought to be labeled as expressing approximately the frequency of occurrence of certain combinations of features. The maps certainly do not prove that these are fundamental races.

It is quite impossible to check up the data contained in the book because the general tables are not given. This is obviously impossible in a book which evidently is intended to appeal not only to the specialist but also to the general reader, but furthermore, the summary tables given on page 22 and those contained in the conclusion do not agree and the numbers are so small that any general inferences drawn from them seem rather risky.

In the final chapter Professor Dixon tries to prove that those groups which agree in regard to the selected ratios also agree in regard to other metric features. He uses for this purpose a series of fourteen measurements, eight of which are the length, breadth and height of the head and length and breadth of nose and the three ratios on which his whole system is built up. He tries to show that the six remaining measurements agree. One of these is the breadth-height index which is derived from the same material as the length-breadth and length-height indices. The others and the bizygomatic diameter, two facial indices, the gnathic index and the capacity of the skull. It is not surprising that the measurements on which his classification is based should agree fairly well. However, in my judgment, the rest do not show any satisfactory agreement, particularly considering the small number of individuals upon which the comparisons are based.

A word should be said also in regard to Professor Dixon's general attitude towards the question of the relation between racial ability and anatomical form. In one place he expresses himself as quite convinced that achievement proves hereditary ability (p. 518). I cannot consider this argument conclusive. If it were valid, then at different periods it would justify entirely different views. It is not very long since Russia would have seemed in cultural achievement very much inferior to western Europe. The conclusion as to racial inferiority is in this case contradicted by the considerable number of eminent scientists and artists produced by Russia since social conditions have changed. If the ancient Greeks or still earlier the Egyptians or Chinese had used the same argument, they would have classified the northern Europeans as belonging to an inferior race, incapable of ever attaining cultural eminence. The proof of racial superiority certainly has to be based on other evidence. It is curious to note that when it suits the author's emotional attitude he changes his argument completely and indulges in flings at the assumed claim of racial pre-eminence on the part of the Germans—an attitude which hardly helps to make convincing a treatise that attempts to be scientific.

SOME RECENT CRITICISMS OF PHYSICAL
ANTHROPOLOGY [1]

D URING recent years a number of severe attacks against the methods of physical anthropology have been made, which are directed
mainly against two points—(1) the possibility of classifying mankind
according to anatomical characteristics, and (2) the practicability of
description of types by means of measurements.

Before we attempt to reply to these criticisms, it may be well to make
a few brief remarks on the development of the methods of physical
anthropology. The living representatives of the various races of man
were originally described according to their general appearance—the
color of the skin, the form and color of the hair, the form of the face,
etc. Later this general description was supplemented by the study of
the skeletons of various races, and a number of apparently characteristic
differences were noted. One of the principal reasons that led to a more
detailed study of the skeleton and to a tendency to lay the greatest stress
upon characteristics of the skeleton, was the ease with which material
of this kind could be obtained. Visitors to distant countries are likely
to bring home skeletons and parts of skeletons, while not much opportunity is given for a thorough examination of a considerable number
of individuals of foreign races. The difficulty of obtaining material
relating to the anatomy of the soft parts of the body has had the effect
that this portion of the description of the anatomy of man has received
very slight attention. In comparatively few cases have we had opportunity to make a thorough study of the characteristics of the soft parts
of the body of individuals belonging to foreign races. The desire to find
good specific characters in the skeleton has also been stimulated by the
necessity of studying extinct races. The conditions in these cases are
the same as those found in paleontological studies, where the osseous
remains alone of extinct species are available. Researches into the
earliest history of man must be based on studies of the skeleton.

[1] *American Anthropologist*, N.S., vol. 1 (January, 1899).

Studies of the human skeleton had not been carried very far when it was found to be not quite easy to determine racial characteristics with sufficient accuracy by mere verbal description. This led to the introduction of measurements as a substitute for verbal description. With the increase of the material, the necessity of accurate description became more and more apparent, because intermediate links between existing forms were found with increasing frequency. These conditions have led to a most extensive application of the metric method in the study of the human skeleton and also in the study of the external form of the living.

The results of the minute studies that have been carried on in this manner appear discouraging to many students, because we have not been able to find any criterion by which an individual skeleton of any one race can be distinguished with certainty from a skeleton belonging to another race, except in a very general way. A typical full-blood Negro may be distinguished from a White man, and an Indian of Florida from an Eskimo; but it would be difficult to distinguish the skeleton of a Chinaman from that of certain North American Indians.

This lack of definite individual descriptive features has led many investigators to conclude that the method is at fault, and that the skeleton cannot be used as a satisfactory basis for a classification of mankind. This view has been strengthened by the belief, frequently expressed, that the characteristic features of each race are not stable, but that they are influenced to a great extent by environment, geographical as well as social.

It seems to me that these views are not borne out by the observations that are available. The first objection, which is based on the lack of typical characteristics in the individual, does not take into consideration the fact that anthropological study is not a study of individuals, but of local or social varieties. While it may be impossible to classify any one individual satisfactorily, any local group existing at a certain given period can clearly be characterized by the distribution of forms occurring in that group. I do not hesitate to say that, provided we had satisfactory statistics of the distribution of human forms over the whole globe, an exhaustive description of the physical characteristics of any group of individuals belonging to one locality would enable us to identify the same without any difficulty. This clearly emphasizes the fact that anthropological classification must be considered as a statistical study of local or social varieties. But it will be asked, How does this help in classifying individual forms? The problem must be considered in the following way:

Each social unit consists of a series of individuals whose bodily forms depend on their ancestry and on their environment. If the opinion of the critics of physical anthropology regarding the predominant effect of environment is correct, then we cannot hope to make any discoveries as to ancestry of local or social groups by means of anatomical investigations. If, on the other hand, it can be shown that heredity is the predominant factor, then the prospects of important discoveries bearing on the early history of mankind are very bright indeed. It seems to the writer that a biological consideration makes it very probable that the influence of heredity should prevail, and thus far he has failed to find conclusive proof to the contrary.

The critics of the method of physical anthropology will of course concede that a Negro child must be a Negro, and that an Indian child must be an Indian. Their criticism is directed against the permanence of types within the race; for instance, against the permanence of short or tall statures, or against the permanence of forms of the head. It must be conceded that muscular development may exert an important influence on the form of bones, but it does not seem likely that it can bring about an entire change of form. The insufficiency of the influence of environment appears in cases where populations of quite distinct types inhabit the same area and live under identical conditions. Such is the case on the North Pacific coast of our continent; such was the case in successive populations of southern California and of Utah.

While this may be considered good evidence in favor of the theory of predominance of the effect of heredity, the actual proof must be looked for in comparisons between parent and offspring. If it can be shown that there is a strong tendency on the part of the offspring to resemble the parent, we must assume that the effect of heredity is stronger than that of environment. The method of this investigation has been developed by Francis Galton and Karl Pearson, who have given us the means of measuring the degree of similarity between parent and child. Wherever this method has been applied, it has been shown that the effect of heredity is the strongest factor in determining the form of the descendant. It is true that thus far this method has not been applied to series of generations, and under conditions in which a considerable change of environment has taken place, and we look forward to a definite solution of the problem of the effect of heredity and of environment through the application of this method. In the study of past generations we cannot, on the whole, compare directly parent and offspring, but we have to confine ourselves to a comparison between the occurrence of types during successive periods. The best available evidence on this subject is found in the populations of Europe. It does not seem likely that the present distribution of types in Europe can be explained in any other way than by the assumption that heredity had a predominant influence. Much has been made of the apparent change of type that takes place in the cities of Europe in order to show that natural selection may have played an important part in making certain types of man predominant in one region or another. Ammon has shown that the city population of southwestern Germany is more short-headed than the country population, and concludes that this is due to natural selection. All the phenomena of this character that have been described can be explained satisfactorily by the assumption that the city population is more mixed than the country population. This point has been brought out most clearly by Livi's investigations in Italy. He has proved that in regions where long-headed forms prevail in the country, in the city the population is more short-headed; while in regions in the country in which short-headed forms prevail, in the city the population is more long-headed.

Under present conditions, it seems best not to start the study of the anatomical characteristics of man from far-reaching assumptions in regard to the question of the effect of heredity and environment, but first of all to ascertain the distribution of types of man. This is a definite problem that requires treatment and investigation just as much as the study of languages or the study of the customs of various tribes. At the present time we are far from being familiar with the distribution of types on the various continents. No matter what the ultimate explanation of the distribution of types may be, we cannot evade the task of investigating their present distribution and of seeking for the explanation of the reasons for such distribution.

Before entering into this subject more fully, it may be well to take up the second criticism of the method of physical anthropology, which has been made with increasing frequency of late years. A number of investigators object to the metric method of anthropology, and desire to bring about a substitution of description for measurements. This proposition is based on a misunderstanding of the function of measurements. The necessity of making measurements developed when it was found that the local varieties of mankind were very much alike—so much so that a verbal description failed to make their characteristics sufficiently clear. The process by means of which measurements have been selected has been a purely empirical one. It has been found that certain measurements differ considerably in various races, and are for this reason good classificatory criteria. The function of measurements is therefore solely that of giving greater accuracy to the vague verbal description. It is true that in the course of time a tendency has developed of considering as the sole available criteria of race the measurements which by experience have been found to be useful. This is true particularly of the so-called cephalic index; that is, the ratio of width to length of head. There are anthropologists who have subordinated everything else to the study of the cephalic index, leaving out of consideration altogether the forms of the skull and of the skeleton as expressed by their metric relations or as expressed by means of drawings or diagrams. It has frequently been pointed out that the same cephalic index may belong to forms that anatomically cannot be considered as equivalent. We find, for instance, that the same cephalic index belongs to the Eskimo, to the prehistoric inhabitant of southern California, and to the Negro. Still these three types must be considered as fundamentally different. Anthropologists who limit their work to the mechanical application of measurements, particularly of single measurements, and who try to trace the relationships of races by such means, do not apply the metric method in a correct way. It must be borne in mind that measurements serve the purpose only of sharper definition of certain peculiarities, and that a selection of measurements must be adapted to the purpose in view. I believe the tendency of developing a cast-iron system of measurements, to be applied to all problems of physical anthropology, is a movement in the wrong direction. Measurements must be selected in accordance with the problem that we are trying to investigate. The ratio of length and breadth of head may be a very desirable measurement in one case, while in another case it may be of no value whatever. Measurements should always have a biological significance. As soon as they lose their significance they lose also their descriptive value.

The great value of the measurement lies in the fact that it gives us the means of a comprehensive description of the varieties contained in a geographic or social group. A table that informs us of the frequency of various forms as expressed by measurements that occur in a group gives us a comprehensive view of the variability of the group that we are studying. We can then investigate the distribution of forms according to statistical methods; we can determine the prevalent type and the character of its variation. The application of rigid statistical methods gives us an excellent means of determining the homogeneity and the permanence of the type that is being studied. If a group of individuals who present a homogeneous type is not subject to changes, we must expect to find the types arranged according to the law of probabilities; that is to say, the average type will be the most frequent one, and positive and negative variations will be of equal frequency. If, on the other hand, the homogeneous type is undergoing changes, the symmetry of arrangement will be disturbed, and if the type is heterogeneous we must expect irregularities in the whole distribution. Investigations of this character require the measurement of very extensive series of individuals in order to establish the results in a satisfactory manner. But the character of the distributions that may thus be obtained will furnish material for deciding a number of the most fundamental questions of physical anthropology.

I may now revert to the question previously under discussion. I have tried to show that the metric method may furnish us material proving the homogeneity or heterogeneity of groups of certain individuals. This test has been applied to a number of cases. I have examined from this point of view the North American half-bloods, that is, individuals of mixed Indian and White descent. I have shown that the transverse development of the face, which is the most distinctive difference between Indian and White, shows a tendency in the mixed race to revert to either of the parental races, and that there is no tendency toward the development of an intermediate form. Bertillon has shown similar irregularities to exist in France. On the other hand, extensive series of measurements of enlisted soldiers of Italy show in many parts of the kingdom a comparatively homogeneous series. Hand in hand with this phenomenon go remarkable differences of variability. In places where we have reason to believe that distinct types have intermingled, we find a great increase in variability, while in regions occupied by homogeneous populations the variability seems to decrease. These facts are strong arguments for the assumption of a great permanence of human types. It is necessary that the analysis of distributions of measurements be carried much further than it has proceeded up to the present time; this done, I believe we shall obtain a means of determining with considerable accuracy the blood-relationships of the geographical varieties of man.

I wish to say a word here in regard to the question of the relationship between the earliest prehistoric races and the present races. In so far as the reconstruction of the characteristics of prehistoric races can be based on extensive material, there will be a certain justification for a reconstruction of the soft parts, if a detailed comparison of the osteological remains of prehistoric types and of present types proves them to be conformable. Where, however, the similarity is based on a few isolated specimens, no such reconstruction is admissible, because the attempt presupposes the identity of the prehistoric race with the present. Since remains of the earliest man are very few in number, it is hardly possible to gain an adequate idea of what the characteristics of the soft parts of his body may have been except in so far as the forms of muscular attachments allow us to infer the size and form of muscles.

When we base our conclusions on the considerations presented in this paper, we must believe that the problem of physical anthropology is as definite as that of other branches of anthropology. It is the determination and explanation of the occurrence of different types of man in different countries. The fact that individuals cannot be classified as belonging to a certain type shows that physical anthropology cannot possibly lead to a classification of mankind as detailed as does the classification based on language. The statistical study of types will, however, lead to an understanding of the blood-relationship between different types. It will consequently be a means of reconstructing the history of the mixture of human types. It is probable that it will lead also to the establishment of a number of good types which have remained permanent through long periods. It will be seen that that part of human history which manifests itself in the phenomena that are the subject of physical anthropology is by no means identical with that part of history which manifests itself in the phenomena of ethnology and of language. Therefore we must not expect that classifications obtained by means of these three methods will be in any way identical. Neither is it a proof of the incorrectness of the physical method if the limits of its types overlap the limits of linguistic groups. The three branches of anthropology must proceed each according to its own method; but all equally contribute to the solution of the problem of the early history of mankind.

THE RELATIONS BETWEEN PHYSICAL AND
SOCIAL ANTHROPOLOGY [1]

DURING the last decades physical anthropology and social anthropology have drifted more and more apart. This seems unavoidable on account of the difference in subject matter and the
necessity of a thorough biological training for the one branch, while the
other requires a knowledge of ethnological methods. With the wide
extent of either field it is hardly possible to combine the two adequately.

Nevertheless some method must be found, if the important borderland between the two is not to be neglected—much to the detriment of
either.

It may be conceded that the purely morphological study of early
forms of man and of races is a matter that should be treated by the
morphologist. It is more doubtful whether the study of living races can
be left entirely to him. He must include in his study the determining
factors that stabilize or differentiate racial types: heredity, environment, and selection as well as the occurrence of mutations. The social
anthropologist is interested in the history of society and for this reason
he has to know the origin and history of each type. Its distribution may
throw important light upon historic events. The physical anthropologist
has to answer many questions asked by the student of society. Is the
similarity of types living in remote countries due to genetic relationship or to parallel mutations? Is, for instance, the type of the Ainu due
to an old genetic relationship with Europeans, or is it a spontaneous
mutation in the Mongoloid race? What rôle has domestication played in
the development of races? In how far have anthropometric measures a
taxonomic value showing genetic relationship, or in how far are they
determined by environment or selection? When the biologist—for so
we may call the physical anthropologist—wants to answer these questions, he must be familiar with ethnic data. The attempts of certain
anthropologists to analyze on the basis of measurements and observa-

[1] *Essays in Anthropology in Honor of Alfred Louis Kroeber* (University of California Press, 1936).

tions a population and to discover the constituent races is, at present at least, a hopeless task. Without the most detailed knowledge of the laws of heredity of each feature considered, as well as of the effects of environment, the task is like that of a mathematician who tries to solve without any further data a single equation with a large number of unknown quantities. If anything is to be done on these lines the historical composition of the population has to be known in detail.

Any attempt at a morphological classification of races, excepting the very largest groups, like Negroes, Mongoloids, Australians, does not lead to satisfactory results without knowledge of the conditions that have made the type what it is. A purely taxonomic description of local types determined by means of those traits that strike the observer as most frequently occurring in the population in question, or that may be proved to be so, do not clear up the history of the population. We might claim that the frequency of various values of the head index in southern Italy indicates descent from distinct hereditary groups and state that a certain percentage of "Alpine" types have intermingled with the "pure" Mediterranean strain; or we might claim that the frequency of blue eyes in Sicily corresponds to the amount of Norman blood. These conclusions are valueless if it cannot be shown that the cephalic index is solely determined by heredity and that in a "pure" race its variations do not exceed very narrow limits, and that blue eyes may not originate by mutation, as they certainly must have done at one time, and that this mutation may not occur again in any one of the strongly depigmented European populations.

Added to these difficulties is that of an adequate definition of type. Actually the type of a population is always an abstraction of the striking peculiarities of the mass of individuals which are assumed to be represented combined in a single individual. What the striking peculiarities are depends largely upon the previous experiences of the observer, not upon the morphological value of the observed traits. This explains the diversities of opinion in taxonomic classification. They all contain so many subjective elements without necessary morphological checks that conclusions based on them have slight value. A result of historical significance can be obtained only by a study of the many genetic lines constituting the population, not selected from the arbitrary point of view of which is "typical," but with due consideration of the variety of forms that occur, of their frequencies in succeeding generations, and of their response to varying environmental influences.

Classifications made on the basis of a selected number of traits, like those of Deniker and many others, have an interest from a purely statistical point of view, showing how certain traits are distributed, but they do not give us any right to differentiate between racial strains.

These difficulties are the greater the less marked the difference between two populations, either on account of their genetic relationship or on account of intermingling of types. They disappear only in those cases in which no overlapping of types occurs.

A purely subjective selection of racial types according to their local distribution, and even more so the attempts to select by subjective judgments typical forms as constituent elements of a population, will never give us a true picture of racial history.

Where it can be proved historically that a population is mixed, such as the American Mulattoes, the half-blood Indians, or the half-castes of the Orient, biological questions arise that require a thorough knowledge of social conditions. If it were true, as has been claimed so often, that mixed bloods are inferior in physique to their parents of pure stock, or that disharmonies of forms will develop that have detrimental effects, it must still be asked who were the parents? Were they of normal value, or of inferior strains in the race to which they belong, and are the conditions under which the mixed population live equal to those of the two parental stocks? Without an answer to these questions, which require sociological knowledge, the biological inferences have little value. Data like those available on American Negroes show the strong influence of unfavorable social conditions, while those obtained from Pitcairn Island, from the South African Bastards, from Kisar, or from North American Indians show that mixed populations may preserve full vigor.

The considerations relating to the significance of taxonomic differences are the more important the greater the environmental influences upon the feature studied. Among bodily traits this is true, for instance, of stature and weight, which are quite variable under varying conditions. Still more significant is this variability in the study of physiological and psychological functions.

While the physical anthropologist is liable to look at functional phenomena as expressions of structure, the ethnologist will bear in mind the varying conditions influencing functions. Undoubtedly these are, to a certain extent, determined by structure, but they vary in the same individual according to conditions, so that in a large population, containing many distinct hereditary lines, similar outer conditions may produce functional similarities that may give the impression of being determined by racial descent, while actually they are due to similar conditioning. The interpretation of such phenomena requires the greatest caution, on account of the constant danger of considering as causally related anatomical and functional characteristics that are only accidentally related. This is particularly true of the attempts to correlate mental characteristics of populations and bodily form. It may be that differences in personality exist in races fundamentally distinct, but no convincing proof has been given so far that the observed differences are actually structurally determined, while the modification of various aspects of personality of members of the same race who live under changed conditions has been proved.

In this field particularly a clear understanding of the meaning of social conditions is essential if the grossest errors are to be avoided. Sameness of conditions is altogether too readily either assumed or overlooked. If Davenport and Steggerda assume equality of all social groups in Jamaica they overlook group differences which can be evaluated only by those intimately familiar with the social life of the people. On the other hand the experimentally determined similarities in very simple reactions of identical twins are overvalued when applied to complex activities dependent upon cultural situations.

THE ANALYSIS OF ANTHROPOMETRICAL SERIES [1]

THE criticisms of my investigations relating to the bodily forms of descendants of immigrants in New York in comparison with those of their European-born parents are based largely upon the current method of subdividing anthropometric series in a number of arbitrary groups and to describe the whole series by the percentual frequencies of these groups. For instance, it is said that a certain population contains such and such percentages of short, medium and tall individuals, or such and such percentages of individuals with elongated, medium and rounded head forms; or a larger number of groups are distinguished or characterized by various combinations of forms.

Since the applicability of this method, particularly the interpretation of the frequencies of these groups, is of fundamental importance for the formulation of many problems a consideration of the theoretical basis of this procedure seems desirable.

In support of this method the statement is always made that averages have no meaning, that it is necessary to determine the distributions of individual values. That is true. Two series may have the same average and still be quite distinct; but two series cannot have different averages and be nevertheless identical. The average is of great value as a discriminating criterion, particularly because it can be determined with greater accuracy than any other value that depends upon the distribution of individual values of the series. For this purpose it is indispensable. Although we ascribe to the average no more than this discriminating value, it should not be neglected.

The average of the series may be the same but the distribution of individual values may be quite different. The attempt is made to overcome this difficulty by the establishment of groups and the determination of their percentual frequencies. In this manner we learn more about the series than by a statement of the average.

The solution offered by this method is not satisfactory, because it gives a very inadequate picture of the distribution of frequencies. It

[1] *Archiv für Rassen- und Gesellschafts-Biologie,* vol. 10 (1913), pp. 290 *et seq.*

may be asked whether a better method may not be found. This problem has been solved by the introduction of the mean square variability as a measure of the scattering of individuals in the series. Experience has shown that in many series average and mean square variability permit us to determine with an adequate degree of accuracy the frequency of any selected group. As an example I give Livi's observations on the cephalic index of 7,760 enlisted soldiers from Palermo. The average and its mean square variability are 79.1 $\pm$ 3.66. The distribution of cephalic indices according to observation and theory is as follows:

Index	Observation	Theory
67–69	.2	.4
70–74	8.1	9.5
75–79	46.6	43.7
80–84	38.2	39.2
85–89	6.2	6.9
90–94	.8	.2

The theoretical values may be obtained from any table of the probability integral.[1]

In a short series we must be satisfied with the mean square variability as the best attainable index of the character of the series because the distribution of the individual values is too much affected by chance.

In order to explain the reasons that compel us to adopt this method of presentation a more fundamental consideration of the character of variable quantities seems desirable.

We must define the difference between a constant and a variable. An example will illustrate this. It is obvious that the two statements: a cubic centimeter of pure water at greatest density at a given place weighs 1 gram; and the stature of Scotchmen is 175 cm., do not mean the same formally. If I should extend the term "water" to include water of any temperature and any kind of impurity the two statements would be formally of the same kind. The essential difference in the first case is that the term "water" is assumed to be completely defined, as opposed to the incomplete definition of what is a Scotchman or what is impure water. A constant is the measure of a completely defined object, a variable the series of measures of all the incompletely defined individuals composing a class. Only if we know all the influences that determine each member of the class completely could they also become constants. The class itself is completely defined, not the individual representatives of the class. Variability is not a specifically

[1] See for example W. F. Sheppard, *Biometrika*, vol. 2 (1902–1903), pp. 174 *et seq.*

biological problem but an expression of the fact that the individuals of a class are subject to unknown influences.

This point of view is of the greatest importance for a logical treatment of variables. It shows that every member of a class has all the *essential* traits that characterize the *class,* but modified by unknown factors. Therefore, if I want to describe the class—in our case an anthropometric series—I must try to express both the essential class character and the influence of the unknown factors. When we segregate a particular group characterized by certain metric values out of the whole class, we do not only unnecessarily restrict the material that is being discussed, but—and this is more important—we segregate certain combinations of unknown factors and thus introduce a subjective element that has no relation whatever to the series itself. The series is a unit that cannot be broken and that must be described as a unit. The average and mean square variability fulfil these conditions because they consider each individual of the series as of equal value. They have the added advantage that in many cases they describe the distribution of individuals with sufficient accuracy. We have seen that two series having different averages cannot be equal. Two series with different mean square variabilities also cannot be equal. When two series have the same average and variabilities they may be equal, but this does not follow necessarily.

It follows from what has been said that when two averages are different and the variability remains the same, changes in the percentual frequencies of selected groups will follow. If the variabilities are also different the same frequencies for selected groups may result, although the series are distinct.

I will now turn to the fundamental question as to what may be inferred from the description of a series by means of average and mean square variability. A comparison between the description of constants and variables shows that the distribution of variants, however they may be expressed, are solely a description of the class. From the fact that a cubic centimeter of pure water of greatest density weighs 1 gram I cannot infer why this is the case; so also in a variable the observed values have solely a descriptive value. The fact that water and mercury have different specific weights does not tell me why they differ in specific weight. In the same way, if I have one variable expressed by the measure 183 ± 3 and another expressed by 184 ± 4, I know only that they are different, and, if the distribution of individual values is of the usual type, the numerical values would not tell me why they are different.

It may be that each corresponding individual grew on the average by one unit and that the growth itself was variable. This would give the observed result. It might also be that each value was somehow changed in its frequency of occurrence, which would also account for the observed changes. It might also be that new elements were introduced so that the two series would not be comparable. Even the most intense study of the observed numerical values will throw no light upon the causal factors that bring about the change in both average and variability. The constantly repeated attempts to interpret descriptive features without further data do not prove that this method is acceptable.

As an example I chose a discussion by Hans Fehlinger [1] of the gradual decrease of the average cephalic index with increasing age, from birth until the adult stage is reached. Fehlinger concludes that the only possible explanation of this phenomenon is selective mortality, because in the series of children of various ages the frequency of round-headed individuals gradually decreases. If it were not the cephalic index, but stature that is under consideration, nobody would imagine that the gradual disappearance of those of short stature is due to selection, for we know that it is due to individual growth. The changes of head index are also due to growth. The development of the frontal sinuses and of the muscular attachments at the occiput bring it about that the antero-posterior diameter of the head increases more rapidly than the transversal one. Therefore the cephalic index decreases with increasing age, not on account of an elimination of the round heads. It seems hardly plausible that very few children who have a certain cephalic index should die, let us say, between 8 and 11 years of age, while of those who have another index, one-third would die. Still, this would be required as a general phenomenon of the development of population if the universal decrease of the number of round-headed individuals in all populations were to be explained by selection.

I have discussed the whole subject somewhat fully, in order to show that the statistical data are purely descriptive, that the interpretation must be based on biological considerations. It follows that all attempts to derive conclusions solely from the statistical data are futile.[2]

[1] *Petermann's Mitteilungen*, vol. 59 (1913), pp. 19 *et seq.*

[2] Exceptions are certain forms of distribution which imply the presence of disturbing factors. Such are unusually high or low variability, presence of decided multiple maxima, forms of asymmetry. Additional observations or the study of interrelations between series may supply materials for further analysis. The point made here shows only that the ordinary descriptive features of a normal series gives no clue that allows us to interpret its origin.

We have to return to our previous remarks which showed that every individual belonging to a series or class has the essential characteristics of the class modified by unknown causes. From this point of view a fundamental error made in the comparison of subgroups determined by selected measurements becomes apparent. It consists in the grouping together of individuals that happen to have the same measurements but belong to different classes. Thus Fehlinger equates the long-headed boys of from 4 to 6 years with adults with long heads, although they are from a biological point of view not equivalent and belong to different classes.

It is easy to show that the critique of these concepts is not unnecessary dialectic refinement, for real differences in such cases are the rule, not exceptions. Thus I found that, when in two populations individuals whose head index is 80 are selected the head forms of the children of this part of the population are not determined by the selected index of the parents alone, but also by the average index of the population to which the parents belong. If the average index of the population is 76 the children of the group with index 80 will have an index of about 78.4; if the average index of the population is 84, the index of the children of the group with index 80 would be 81.6.

Therefore it is wrong to speak of the "blond," "round-headed" or "tall" groups in various parts of Europe as though they were identical from a biological point of view. Blond Italians are Italians, tall Sicilians, Sicilians, and round-headed Swedes, Swedes. Maps showing the distribution of long-headedness, tallness, etc., do not give trustworthy information regarding the distribution of types.

It follows, that, if we wish to understand the character of a variable which is defined by certain known characteristics of the class and by many unknown factors influencing the individuals, we must not segregate a small part of the class and assume that we have segregated a factor or factors causing the variability. All we have done is to segregate individuals who have the same measure which, however, may be due to the most diverse unknown influences. No conclusion can be drawn from such a procedure. The class has to be treated as a whole and every attempted analysis must be based on the study of single factors within the whole series.

THE MEASUREMENT OF DIFFERENCES BETWEEN
VARIABLE QUANTITIES[1]

IN biological statistics it is often necessary to study the differences between two variable types. The problem may be exemplified by a consideration of the differences between the types represented by populations of various countries, as, for instance, between the populations of Sweden, Switzerland, and Central Africa. It is obvious that the type of Sweden differs less from that of Switzerland than the latter differs from the type of Central Africa. Nevertheless, it is difficult to say just what is meant by greater or lesser difference in type. The attempt to establish and describe varieties of races according to characteristic features that are considered as significant from a morphological point of view suffers, therefore, from a lack of clarity of concept.

The differences between the averages of types have been utilized for the purpose of segregating subtypes of human races, as, for instance, in the classification of the local types into which the European race may be divided. Pigmentation, stature, form of hair, head, face, and nose have been so utilized. For example, local types have been described by Deniker[2] by assigning to each group peoples among whom certain average values of measurements are found. All those that have average statures, head indices, facial forms, nose forms, and pigmentation falling within certain limits that may be expressed numerically were assigned by him to a certain subrace. Although it is possible to give in this manner a definite description of local types, the biological significance of the observed differences remains undetermined. Obviously the classification obtained by the method here indicated will vary according to the limits set for each division. If we call tall those populations whose average stature is more than 170 cm., their assignment to a subdivision will not be the same as the one obtained when we call those tall whose average stature is more than 172 cm. If no valid reason can be given for

[1] *Quarterly Publication of the American Statistical Association* (December, 1922), pp. 425–445.
[2] *The Races of Man* (London, 1900).

the choice of one or the other limit, then the subtype so established can have only a conventional descriptive meaning. If we wish to establish a biologically significant classification we should have to prove that the descriptive features selected are morphologically significant. Furthermore, it would be necessary to distinguish between environmental and hereditary influences that determine the particular features which are made the basis of the classification. As a matter of fact, this study has never been made; and since the lines of demarcation between classes are arbitrary, these classes will be only a convenient schematic review of the distribution of certain selected combinations of descriptive features.[1]

In the following pages I wish to discuss the question whether a valid method of comparing closely allied forms can be found, so that arbitrary classifications may be avoided and measurable differences between two types established.

It may seem that maps showing the distribution of a single feature or of combined features would give this information. Retzius' maps of Sweden, Livi's maps of Italy, Virchow's map of hair color in Germany, anthropological maps of France, England, and Spain, all illustrate the distribution of forms of the body, either by showing the areas in which the same average value of a measurement occurs or by showing areas in which certain selected values occur with equal frequency. The maps are intended to convey the impression that sameness of average values or of frequencies indicates the occurrence of the same racial forms. They also indicate that the differences between types are equivalent whenever the differences between averages or between frequencies of occurrence of selected values are the same. This has often led to the interpretation that the values whose frequency is shown represent separate racial types. Thus, the frequency of long-headedness in an area is often said to mean that a long-headed race forms a certain proportion of the population, although no biological basis can be given for the claim that the arbitrarily selected values represent a separate racial type.

The essential difficulty of our problem may be made clearer by the following considerations. Each racial type is variable. When we study the distribution of any particular feature, let us say of the cephalic index among European types, we find that the forms which occur in each

---

[1] See also St. Poniatowski, "Ueber den Wert der Index Klassifikation," *Archiv für Anthropologie*, N.F. voi. 10 (1911), p. 50.

area are variable, and the individuals composing the populations of different areas show in part the same numerical values of the measurement. The distribution of forms in each population is such that the types overlap. The average cephalic index in Sweden may be 77; in Bavaria 85. Nevertheless, there will be many individuals that have the index 81, both in Bavaria and in Sweden; and according to this particular feature individuals may belong to either group. We know that if two regions are not too far apart, in most cases it is quite impossible to assign with certainty a single individual to either of them.

If we should assume for the moment the variability found both in Sweden and in Bavaria to be very low, so that the highest cephalic index occurring among Swedes would be not more than 80 and the lowest occurring in Bavaria not less than 82, then the two series would appear to us entirely distinct. It would be quite inadmissible to claim that the differences between the pair of groups were the same in the cases of greater variability (which has actually been observed) and the lesser variability (which has here been assumed), although in both cases the averages show the same differences. In the latter case we judge that the difference is greater, or perhaps better, more fundamental.

Obviously our judgment is influenced by the degree of variability; still more, by the degree of overlapping of the two series. Only if we assume quite arbitrarily that the individuals that show the average values of the measurement in question—or some other selected value— were the true representatives of the whole population, and that all others were present only as foreign, intrusive elements, or if their occurrence represented modifications of the typical form due to extraneous causes —only under these conditions could we say that the difference between the selected values represents the difference between the types. A concept of variability like the one involved in these assumptions is, however, quite inadmissible. The group must be considered as a *class* and its variability determined by the definition of the class in question. Our detailed study of the class will always be directed toward the discovery of new principles of classification by means of which subclasses are formed whose variability will be less than that of the original class. In this way we try to define the newly formed subclasses more sharply than the original class, and the advance in our knowledge consists in the discovery of the factors that make the subclass more determinate. It would be quite arbitrary to select one particular individual as the type, and to claim either that all others are not really members of the class or that they are modified forms of the type. This method of procedure would contravene the fundamental concept of variability, for a variable comprises all the representatives of a class, the individual components of which are only defined in so far as they are members of the class—this in contradistinction to constants which are assumed to be completely defined and must therefore be the same in every case.

As soon as these principles are held clearly in mind, it appears that the ordinary definition of arithmetical difference is not applicable in our case. The term "difference" as applied to variables does not mean the same as the term "difference" applied to constants. Variables cannot be brought into a measurable series by the same means that we use for constants which may be compared by means of an arbitrary standard that is also constant.

The problem before us is how to overcome these difficulties—how to give a definite meaning to the differences between variables and make these differences measurable.

The question has been treated by G. H. Mollison [1] and by J. Czekanowski.[2] Mollison has discussed particularly the problem of differences between two types, and he gives an arbitrary formula which later on was modified by St. Poniatowski.[3]

In the following pages I shall discuss some possible approaches to the problem.

What we call difference in this case is not by any means an arithmetical difference; it is a judgment of the degree of dissimilarity of two series. If two series are so far apart that notwithstanding their variability they do not overlap, they are entirely dissimilar. If they do overlap they will be the more dissimilar, the less the amount of overlapping. In this sense we may say that two pairs of series in which the amount and character of overlapping are equal will be equally dissimilar. While we may thus determine equality of dissimilarity we are not in a position to determine quantitatively the degree of dissimilarity.

In treating this problem we may first of all explain the meaning of similarity and dissimilarity by means of a few examples. Let us assume that a pure Negro and a pure White population are to be compared. The types are so distinct in all their features that in comparing them we should emphasize simply their dissimilarities. Now let us assume

[1] *Morphologisches Jahrbuch,* vol. 42, p. 79.
[2] *Korrespondenz-Blatt der Deutschen anthropologischen Gesellschaft,* vol. 40.
[3] *Archiv für Anthropologie,* N.F. vol. 10 (1911), p. 274.

that a third community is added, consisting perhaps of baboons. It appears at once that our point of view would be shifted from a consideration of dissimilarities between Negroes and Whites to the similarities which they have in common as compared with the baboon, and their similarities will appear to us now under a new angle and as of different value.

When we compare a group of blond, blue-eyed North Europeans with dark complexioned, brown-eyed South Europeans, their dissimilarities are the most striking feature. If we add a Negro community to these two groups the similarities between the North and South Europeans would be much more prominently in our minds. We may observe the same changing attitude when we speak of family resemblances, or similarities. When we consider the children of a family, entirely by themselves, without any reference to any other family, they will appear to us as dissimilar. If the family has a particular characteristic feature, let us say, for instance, a long narrow nose, which all the children have to a greater or less extent, this will become the feature which makes them similar as compared to the rest of the population.

It is, therefore, clear that the concept of the degree of similarity depends upon the characteristics of all the groups that are under consideration and will change with the groups that are being compared.

In investigations on heredity it has been customary to determine the degree of similarity by means of the coefficient of correlation. When, for instance, parents and offspring are compared, the coefficient of correlation between the two will indicate the degree of their similarity. There is a biological relation between parent and offspring. The average form of the offspring is determined by the degree to which the parent differs from the average of the population to which he belongs. In marriage we may have selective mating through which the forms of two parents may be correlated. When the husband differs from the average of the population by a certain amount his wife may differ by a correlated amount. In both of these cases there is a functional relation between the two values. The distinguishing feature of fraternal correlation is that we are dealing with a natural group in which there is no true functional relation between the members. In a very large fraternity, disregarding the fraternity as part of a population, the bodily form of one member does not influence in any way either the average body form of the rest of the fraternity or the distribution of the individual forms. This is due to the fact that the members of the fraternity are all members of the same variable class, while in all the other cases previously noted we are dealing with relations between different classes. Fraternal correlation originates only in a population in which the fraternities represent different types. If all the families had the same average value there would be no correlation and no similarity between brothers. The greater the heterogeneity of the family lines, the greater will be the correlation and similarity between members of a fraternity.

Exactly the same considerations may be made for racial types. A local variety may be considered as a fraternal group. The coefficient of correlations between the local groups will then be a measure of their heterogeneity or of their dissimilarity.

The problem of the definition of similarities has been treated fully in experimental psychology. Weber's law is actually based on the observation that the differences between two pairs of sensations are judged to be equal. In this case the basis of empirical determination of similarity is the probability of mistaking one difference for another. It is not, as was originally assumed, a measure of quantitative value of the sensation itself. This concept of similarity holds good not only in the case of simple sensations but also in the field of more complex experience. We may speak of similarity, or of the probability of failing to differentiate, for the most diverse kinds and the most complex forms of mental experience. The problem that we are discussing here has suggested itself in every comparative study of mental processes.

In an analogous manner we may define the degree of similarity as the probability of mistaking an individual who belongs to one group for a member of any of the other groups concerned. The degree of dissimilarity may then be determined by the probability of recognizing an individual as belonging to his own group.

The same measurement will occur with varying frequency in the groups forming the aggregate of groups that is being investigated. Each individual may belong to any one of these groups and the probability of his belonging to a particular group will be determined by the ratio between the frequency of the measurement identifying the individual as a member of his group and of its frequency in the aggregate. Thus the probability of the correct assignment of a single individual or of all individuals of the group having the trait in question can be determined. When each series is compared with the aggregate of all the series and the degrees of diversity are established these may be subtracted from one another, and in this manner differences in the degree of similarity may be determined.

When three series are compared in this manner in pairs, the resultant values are not additive. If only series (1) and series (2), then series (1) and (3), then series (2) and (3) are considered, the sum of the difference between (1) and (2) plus that between (2) and (3) will not be equal to the difference between (1) and (3). This is another expression of the observation made before that the meaning of similarity changes with the aggregate of the series that is being considered.

It might also seem possible to arrange the single series in the order of their averages and to determine their dissimilarities step by step. Here the difficulty may arise that two succeeding averages may be nearly the same, while their variabilities may be quite different. Whenever this occurs quite an erroneous impression of the differences will be given. The reason for this difficulty lies in the fact that the difference as here defined depends upon the averages and variabilities of the single series, and that certain combinations of these two values result in the same degree of dissimilarity.

In the case treated here the various series enter into the aggregate according to the number of individuals representing each series. It might be, for instance, that a large mass of material has been accumulated for one group and that another group is known through the study of a very few individuals only. Our expression contains, therefore, a weighting according to number which obscures the more general theoretical question. If the groups were known perfectly, then all would have equal weight, i.e., we should have to assume them to be represented by equal numbers.

Whether this point of view or the other should be taken depends upon the clarity of our concept of the characteristics of each group. If we assume each group as thoroughly studied and therefore known in all its characteristics, then equal numbers will represent the conditions adequately. On the other hand, if we are impressed by the unclassified series as a whole, without detailed study of each group, and if we try to determine the similarities and dissimilarities on this basis, the actual numerical frequency of each group will correspond to the conditions of the investigation. If subjective elements are to be eliminated as far as possible, we must try to adjust conditions so that equal numbers can be applied. As a matter of fact, our judgment of similarity in all cases of this type is fluctuating; sometimes one group, sometimes another, is most prominently in our minds, and the actual assignments are therefore different from the two extreme forms discussed here and may lie somewhere in between, or they may change with changing mental conditions. The more thorough our knowledge of each series, the closer will be the approach to the treatment of all classes as equal in number.

The method here discussed presents the inconvenience that the values obtained for similarity are the smaller, the larger the number of series forming the aggregate, so that when the number of similar series is very great the values of their similarities will be exceedingly small.

In the final results it may appear that some of these series have the same degree of dissimilarity. If the averages and variabilities of these series are also indicative of identity, the series should be combined.

It must be remembered that it is possible for a number of different distributions to result in the same amount of dissimilarity. Since every distribution depends at least upon two constants, average and standard deviation, there are whole sets of functions which will give us the same value for the total probability of mistaking a member of one series for a member of the rest of the aggregate. However, owing to the general likeness of forms of distribution, the occurrence of this event is improbable. On the other hand, dissimilarity can occur only when distributions are unlike. The minimum amount of dissimilarity is found when all the series are identical. If there are n series, the value of dissimilarity, in other words the probability of assigning any one individual to its proper series, will be $1/n$.

In applying the fundamental thought underlying our considerations to the classification of mankind, we might ask ourselves which are the series for which the similarity or the probability of a misjudgment becomes zero, and these might be considered as the present fundamental human types. A satisfactory solution of this problem must not be based on the consideration of a few standardized measurements, but the features to be studied must be selected after a careful investigation of what is most characteristic of each group.

It is also feasible to find in this manner outstanding types of a definite area and to arrange them according to the degrees of their similarity. The interpretation of the similarity, whether due to mixture, environment, or other causes, is of course a purely biological problem for which the statistical inquiry furnishes the material but which cannot be solved by statistical methods.

We have seen that, in an attempt to analyze a mixed series according to types, the individuals of a definite bodily form are not all assigned by us to the group to which they belong. The impression which we receive of characteristic forms of a particular series depends upon the distribution and the forms of individuals whom we assign to it, and for this reason our impression of the general characteristic form of the series is expressed by the average of individuals whom we assign to it. This value is obtained by averaging all those individuals who, according to our judgment, are assigned to the local type, leaving out the others that are placed erroneously. This consideration shows that we receive an exaggerated impression of the characteristics of a series, because individuals that are similar to other series are assigned to them according to their appearance and are merged in the general background represented by the aggregate. Our impression, however, does not correspond to an actual type. This proves that the attempts to analyze a series into a number of subtypes according to similarities of individuals is methodologically not admissible, and that all subdivisions must be based on the study of the series as a whole, not upon selected types.

The chief difficulty in the practical application of the method outlined in the preceding pages is due to the facts that the degree of similarity depends upon the aggregate treated, and that there is no relation between the numerical values obtained for different aggregates. Not even the equality of differences between several given series need persist if new members are added to the aggregate or are taken away from it.

In cases of continuous changes of a type from one extreme form to another, an artificial classification of the aggregate is unavoidable. By means of repeated adjustment equal degrees of similarity might be found according to the method outlined here, but the actual carrying out of such a plan offers serious difficulties. In such cases each series might be considered as a specialized form of the general aggregate and compared with it. The aggregate itself may, however, be established in two different ways. We may disregard the number of existing individuals, considering each morphological type contained in the aggregate as a unit. The units would then be given equal weight (i.e., equal numbers of cases). Or we may take the whole series as it exists at the present time, counting the total number of individuals that it contains, regardless of local types that may represent the same morphological form. By either of these methods we ascertain how dissimilar each morphological type is from the aggregate, but these values cannot be used to determine the mutual dissimilarities of the single series contained in the aggregate. When the types are combined according to the present actual number of individuals representing them, the most numerous type will appear least distinct from the average, merely on account of the large number of its members. This difficulty can hardly be avoided by comparing each series with the aggregate of the remaining series, because by this method the standard of comparison is changing. On the other hand, the formation of the aggregate by giving equal weight to each morphological type entails the difficulty that we tried to avoid, namely, an arbitrary classification of the groups as a number of morphological types.

The problem may be approached in another manner. We may determine the frequency distribution of the differences between individuals belonging to one series and those belonging to all the series of the aggregate including the one selected for study. In this inquiry we have to determine the average difference between the representatives of one series and those of all the series, and the variability of this difference. When the series are arranged in pairs, the differences between the averages are additive, but the variabilities are not comparable. The interrelations between the series can be determined only when we consider any one series in relation to the whole series.

The problems take a slightly different form when populations are compared with regard to features that occur in a certain percentage of individuals and are absent in the rest. If, for instance, one population consists of 15 per cent Negroes and 85 per cent Whites, another one of 30 per cent Negroes and 70 per cent Whites, it might seem that the difference could be stated simply as a difference of 15 per cent, but obviously the dissimilarity of these two types of population would not be the same as in another pair in which we have 40 per cent Negroes and 60 per cent Whites in one and 55 per cent Negroes and 45 per cent Whites in the other. In the latter case the populations would seem more alike to us than in the former case. The difficulty is still more pronounced if there are present not merely two types but a larger number in varying proportions. In all these cases we may apply the same methods which we used for the determination of similarity of measurable quantities.

RACE AND CHARACTER [1]

AT THE present time so much is being written on the relations between race and character that it is worth while to examine with
some care the line of thought that leads investigators to the conclusion that racial descent is the determining cause for the character of a
people.

It is a matter of observation that peoples located in different areas
are different both in bodily form and mental traits; and also that different social strata differ in bodily build and in behavior. Using the
favorite terminology of modern literature we may also say that there
is a correlation between the bodily build and mental characteristics of
geographically or socially arranged groups of people. However, not
every correlation signifies a causal relation.

I may be allowed to illustrate this by means of a few examples. We
know that in a homogeneous population all anteroposterior measures
are more closely related among themselves than to transverse ones. For
this reason with increasing stature of adults the length of head increases
more rapidly than the width of head and in consequence the cephalic
index decreases with increasing stature. Every homogeneous population
shows a negative correlation between stature and head index which is
causally explained by the intimate interrelation between longitudinal
measures as over their loose relation to transverse measures. In this
sense the correlation expresses a causal relation.

If we examine the population of Italy from the same point of view
it is found to be locally strongly differentiated. There is a geographical
arrangement of fairly homogeneous groups of various types. In northern Italy we find tall, round-headed types, in southern Italy short, long-
headed ones. If we compare the groups as such we find that the taller
the average stature of the group, the larger is its cephalic index; but we
may not conclude that this relation is determined organically. It is due
to the heterogeneous character of the material and the distribution of
various types. If the whole Italian population were investigated without

[1] *Anthropologischer Anzeiger,* vol. 8 (1932), pp. 280–284.

reference to their location we should probably find a very weak positive correlation, or perhaps no correlation whatever between these two measures.

This observation may perhaps be made still clearer by an artificial example. I imagine a series of sticks of equal length, placed parallel, side by side, so that their ends from left to right form a straight line at right angles to the length of the sticks. Then I cut the other ends off obliquely so that the length of the sticks decreases from left to right. Next another person paints these sticks so that the larger ones, to the left, are darkest and the intensity of color decreases towards the right. Now there is an intimate relation between length and intensity of color, but length and intensity are not causally connected. The correlation is a result of the position of the sticks and of two unrelated actions. I may not say: the intensity of color is determined by the length of the sticks, but it is due to the fact that the sticks were in a certain order when they were painted. If I had changed the position of the sticks before painting them in the same way a different kind of correlation would have resulted; if I should have shaken them, so that they lay in chance order there would have been no correlation between length and intensity of color.

Matters would have been different, if knife and brush had been firmly tied together. The position of the sticks would still have been decisive, but every stick would have had a color and length which belonged together even without consideration of position. A study of the length and color would not clear up this point. It would require an examination of knife and brush.

Now let us consider instead of the sticks lying in order, a number of populations according to their geographical position; instead of length of stick, bodily form; instead of color, mental character. We will also imagine a continuous change in regard to both in a straight line. Then a correlation will become apparent. Every people in a certain geographical position has a characteristic bodily form combined with a characteristic mental behavior. This, however, does not prove that both are causally related, unless it can be proved by biological and psychological methods that bodily form determines mental character.

The same consideration is valid when the distribution of populations is discontinuous and irregular. In this case the relation cannot be expressed numerically, but the phenomenon remains the same. The population of each locality or every social group has certain traits of bodily form and mental behavior peculiar to itself, but this does not prove that the two are causally related.

Bodily form and mental characteristics change each according to its own laws and each in its own tempo, so that it is justifiable to ask whether the population placed in another geographical location may not retain its bodily form and change its mental character, analogous to the change of the location of sticks of decreasing length before the paint had been applied.

I repeat, the essential question, whether bodily form and mental character are causally connected cannot be answered by means of the observation that populations in different geographical location or in differing social strata are different in both respects. The proof has to be given by biological and psychological methods. We have here one of the numerous cases in which the uncritical use of the concept of correlation leads to unjustifiable conclusions.

It might be objected that the study of heredity and constitution has proved the existence of partial, biologically determined relation between bodily form and mental character which is not due to location in a given order. This may be admitted. If behaviorists deny such relations in the individual their claim is contradicted by the most elementary facts of pathology. In how far there may be, nevertheless, room for individual differences in mental character among individuals of the same bodily form does not need to be discussed here.

On the other hand it is essential for our problem to differentiate between individual character and the character of a population. I may illustrate this problem also by the example of our sticks. We assume that a large number of series, let us say each of one hundred sticks, are cut obliquely, as indicated before, but in such a manner that there are a few only of the longest and shortest ones, while in the center of the series the length changes slowly so that in this region there are many of almost equal length. The absolute lengths of the sticks of the first group extend from 1 to 80, that of the second from 2 to 81, and so on; those of the last from 21 to 100. Next each series is painted separately, as before. Knife and brush are supposed to be firmly connected so that there is a causal relation between color and length. Now the dark colors appear solely in the first few series, the light ones solely in the last series, but all of them contain numerous sticks of middle length and color. As groups the series will differ only slightly, although we have assumed a causal relation between length and color. The degree of differences in color will depend upon the number of occurrence of sticks of the same length in each series.

Let us transfer this to the question of relation between form of body and mental traits. Length corresponds to bodily form, color to mental traits, each series to a population. Now the populations differ slightly, in regard to form of body and mental characteristics, although we assume that individually mental characteristics are conditioned by form of body. Since the relation between form of body and mental characteristics is not absolute, their relation is still further weakened, even if the overlapping of the series in regard to bodily form were less. The questions to be answered are the following: How strong is the correlation between bodily form and mental characteristics? And secondly, how are the bodily characteristics which are important for the determination of mental characteristics distributed between various groups of people, and to what extent are the same bodily characteristics found among various people? All these questions have to be treated without reference to geographical or social position.

Let us return once more to the series of sticks which I have used as an example. After they have been cut and painted we arrange bundles, the first one is to contain sticks of the length 1 to 80, the second, those of the length 2 to 81 and so on, the last one to contain sticks of the length 21 to 100. Now we place the bundles in a series and paint as before the whole bundles from left to right, let us say, in twenty degrees of intensity, dark to the left, light to the right. Then every bundle will have a different color. After this the sticks of equal length taken from all the bundles are placed together and it will be found that the distribution of colors for each length shows very slight differences. Only the first length has the color 1, only the two first ones contain the colors 1 and 2. For the length 20 to 80 distribution of the colors is alike. In the lengths from 81 to 100 the dark colors disappear gradually until finally the last one remains with the lightest color. Since the very short and very long sticks are few in number they do not influence the general picture very much and the result is that the relation between length and color is very weak.

Transferring this as before to form of body and mental characteristics we find that populations arranged geographically or socially are different like the bundles. It is impossible to determine from observation of the distribution whether the differences are due to causal relations or to the arrangement of the bundles. Individuals are so distributed that the relation between form of body and mental characteristics in the whole mass is very slight. In the most numerous groups, all kinds of bodily form and mental characteristics occur, providing the types are as similar as those of Europe. This does not preclude the possibility of the hereditary determination of the relation between bodily build and mental characteristics in family lines, since the whole population consists of numerous different lines.

In many cases in populations of similar bodily build and also among different generations of the same people, mental characteristics of considerable difference occur. For this reason it seems more likely that differences between populations are rather due to position than to immediate causal relations.

This may also be expressed in a simpler way. Assuming for the sake of simplicity that position, bodily form and mental characteristics each are distributed according to chance so that the ordinary method of determining correlations can be used, then observations will show high correlations between position and bodily build and between position and mental characteristics. From this fact we may not infer how high may be the correlation between bodily build and mental characteristics unless this is determined by an investigation which does not take into consideration position. According to the simple factual observation they may be non-existent or may be very high. Or, stated in a still more general form, a series of phenomena may be placed in a definite order, then exposed to two causes, each of which has a certain influence upon it. According to their character these two causes are entirely independent of the principle of arrangement. Then every member of the series will have two definite characteristics. Whether they are related or not can only be determined by an investigation of the relation between the two causes without any regard to the arrangement.

LANGUAGE

INTRODUCTION INTERNATIONAL JOURNAL OF AMERICAN LINGUISTICS [1]

THE International Journal of American Linguistics will be devoted to the study of American aboriginal languages. It seems fitting to state briefly a few of the problems that confront us in this field of research.

It is not necessary to set forth the fragmentary character of our knowledge of the languages spoken by the American aborigines. This has been well done for North America by Dr. Pliny Earle Goddard,[2] and it is not saying too much if we claim that for most of the native languages of Central and South America the field is practically *terra incognita.* We have vocabularies; but, excepting the old missionary grammars, there is very little systematic work. Even where we have grammars, we have no bodies of aboriginal texts.

The methods of collection have been considerably improved of late years, but nevertheless much remains to be done. While until about 1880 investigators confined themselves to the collection of vocabularies and brief grammatical notes, it has become more and more evident that large masses of texts are needed in order to elucidate the structure of the languages.

The labors of Stephen R. Riggs, James Owen Dorsey, and Albert S. Gatschet marked a new era in the development of linguistic work. Besides these should be mentioned the "Library of Aboriginal Literature," edited and published by Daniel G. Brinton, which contains largely older material of a similar character. During the following decades, texts were published on a quite extended scale, but largely brought together by the same methods. They were obtained by dictation from a few informants, and taken down verbatim by the recorder. In later years the example of James Owen Dorsey, who published texts written by natives, has been adapted to the recording of aboriginal literature; and quite a number of collections of folk lore have been published in Indian

[1] *International Journal of American Linguistics,* vol. 1 (1917), p. 1.
[2] *Anthropology in North America* (New York, 1915), pp. 182 *et seq.*

languages, the originals of which have been written by the natives themselves.

Marked differences in stylistic character exist between tales thus recorded and those written by investigators who are not in perfect command of the language, who often have to acquire it by means of the collected text material. The slowness of dictation that is necessary for recording texts makes it difficult for the narrator to employ that freedom of diction that belongs to the well-told tale, and consequently an unnatural simplicity of syntax prevails in most of the dictated texts. When, on the other hand, a native has once acquired ease in the use of the written language, the stylistic form becomes more natural, and refinements of expression are found that are often lost in slow dictation.

Nevertheless the writing of single individuals cannot replace the dictated record, because the individual characteristics of the writer become too prominent, and may give a false impression in regard to syntactic and stylistic traits; even the variability of grammatical form may be obscured by the one-sidedness of such records. Whenever it is possible to train several writers, many of these difficulties may be overcome. Where a native alphabet exists, as among the Cherokee, Fox, and Cree, and where for this reason many persons write with ease, a serviceable variety of stylistic and syntactic expression may be secured. Excellent examples of native texts recorded naïvely by natives are contained in the Eskimo publications printed in Greenland, which are devoted both to topics of daily interest and to ancient folk lore. Similar conditions prevail in the Cherokee material collected by James Mooney, and in some of the daily papers printed in aboriginal languages. Even when good written records are available, control by means of the spoken language is necessary, because the expression of the written language may differ considerably from the spoken form.

Up to this time too little attention has been paid to the variety of expression and to the careful preservation of diction. We have rather been interested in the preservation of fundamental forms. Fortunately, many of the recorded texts contain, at least to some extent, stereotyped conversation and other formulas, as well as poetical parts, which give a certain insight into stylistic peculiarities, although they can seldom be taken as examples of the spoken language.

An added difficulty in the use of texts written by natives is that most are written by Indians who have had a modern school education. It may be observed in all parts of America that the native languages are being modified by the influence of European languages, not only in vocabulary, but also in phonetics and grammar. The far-reaching influence of these causes may be observed in a most striking manner in modern Mexican and other Central American languages that have been under Spanish influence for centuries, and which not only have lost large parts of their vocabularies that have disappeared with the ancient ideas, but which have also developed a new syntax, and, in part at least, new morphological forms. Modifications of this type are common in those regions where the intercourse between Indian and White is intimate, and particularly where the children are segregated from the parents. On the Pacific Coast, for instance, the articulation of the glottalized consonant loses much of its strength, old words disappear, and new syntactical forms develop. Even the old facility of composition of stems tends to disappear. It is therefore necessary to obtain text material also from the older generation, because it is required for the study of the recent development of the languages.

On account of the difficulties and expense involved in the collection of texts, collectors have not only hesitated to obtain similar material from different individuals, but they have also confined themselves largely to the collections of native traditions. In some cases, native poetry has been included in the collections. Albert Gatschet recognized the need of varied material and collected texts on diverse topics in his studies of the Klamath, and J. Owen Dorsey published a collection of letters. The contents of the Eskimo publications and the native newspapers previously referred to also form a notable exception to this rule. Among later collectors, Drs. Goddard and Sapir have given particular attention to the collection of texts of varied contents. On the whole, however, the available material gives a one-sided presentation of linguistic data, because we have hardly any records of daily occurrences, everyday conversation, descriptions of industries, customs, and the like. For these reasons the vocabularies yielded by texts are one-sided and incomplete.

Notwithstanding the progress that during the last few decades has been made in the character of the material recorded, both as regards the accuracy of phonetic transcription and the character of the matter recorded, there is ample room for improvements of method.

With the extent of our knowledge of native languages, the problems of our inquiry have also assumed wider and greater interest. It is quite natural that the first task of the investigator was the registering and the rough classification of languages. It appeared very soon that languages are more or less closely related, and that comparison of brief vocabularies was sufficient to bring out the most striking relationships. The classification of North American languages, that we owe to Major J. W. Powell, which will form the basis of all future work, was made by this method. Further progress on these lines is beset with great difficulties that are common to America and to those continents in which we cannot trace the development of languages by means of historical documents. The results of the historical and comparative studies of Indo-European languages show very clearly that languages that have sprung from the same source may become so distinct that, without documents illustrating their historical development, relationships are difficult to discover; so much so, that in some cases this task might even be impossible. We are therefore permitted to assume that similar divergences have developed in American languages, and that quite a number of languages that appear distinct may in a remote period have had a common origin.

Here lies one of the most difficult problems of research, and one in which the greatest critical caution is necessary, if we wish to avoid the pitfalls that are besetting the path of scientific inquiry. The method of investigation has to take into account possibilities of linguistic growth, in regard to which generalized data are not available. Modern languages have developed by differentiation. In so far as this is true, the establishment of a genealogical series must be the aim of inquiry. On the other hand, languages may influence one another to such an extent that, beyond a certain point, the genealogical question has no meaning, because it would lead back to several sources and to an arbitrary selection of one or another as the single ancestral type. Our knowledge of linguistic processes is sufficiently wide to show that lexicographic borrowing may proceed to such an extent that the substance of a language may be materially changed. As long, however, as the inner form remains unchanged, our judgment is determined, not by the provenience of the vocabulary, but by that of the form. In most Indian languages etymological processes are so transparent that borrowing of whole words will be easily detected; and, on the whole, the diffusion of words over diverse groups does not present serious difficulties, provided the borrowed material does not undergo radical phonetic changes.

The matter is different when we ask ourselves in how far phonetics and morphological features may have been borrowed. In these cases our experience does not permit us to give a definite answer. The system of sounds of a language is certainly unstable; but in how far inner forces and in how far foreign influence mould its forms is a question not always easy to answer. In America we can discern various areas that have common phonetic characteristics; like the areas of prevalence of nasalization of vowels, of glottalization, of superabundant development of laterals, of absence of bi-labials or of labio-dental spirants, or of trills. These areas do not coincide with any morphological groupings, and are apparently geographically well defined. If we are dealing here with phenomena of late assimilation, a disturbing element is introduced that will make it more difficult to assign a language to a definite genealogical line, much more so than is the case in the borrowing of words. The conditions favoring such phonetic influence must have been much more frequent in primitive America than they were in the later development of European languages. The number of individuals speaking any given American dialect is small. Many women of foreign parentage lived in each tribe, and their speech influenced the pronunciation of the young; so that phonetic changes may have come about easily.

Still more difficult is the problem presented by the distribution of morphological traits. Even with our imperfect knowledge of American languages, it may be recognized that certain morphological types have a wide continuous distribution. This is true of morphological processes as well as of particular psychological aspects of American languages. Thus the incorporation of the nominal object, which in former times was considered one of the most characteristic features of American languages, is confined to certain areas, while it is foreign to others. The tendency to qualify generalized verbal terms by means of elements which express instrumentality is characteristic of some areas. The occurrence of various specific elements that define locality of an action, as affecting objects like "hand," "house," "water," "fire," or other special nominal concepts, is characteristic of other regions. Classification of actions or of nouns according to the form of the actor or of the object also belong to several groups of languages. Nominal cases are present in some languages, absent in others. In a similar way we find present in some regions, absent in others, processes like that of reduplication or of vocalic or consonantic modification of stems.

Attempts to classify languages from these distinct points of view do not lead to very satisfactory results. Not only would the purely morphological classifications be contradictory, but in many cases where a close morphological agreement exists, it remains highly unsatisfactory to co-ordinate vocabularies and the phonetic equivalents of similar morphological ideas. On the basis of Indo-European experience, we should be inclined to seek for a common origin for all those languages that have a far-reaching morphological similarity; but it must be acknowledged that, when the results of classifications based on different linguistic phenomena conflict, we must recognize the possibility of the occurrence of morphological assimilation. The problem is analogous to that of the relation between Finnish and Indo-European languages, which Sweet assumed as established, while the observed relations may also be due to other causes.

Owing to the fundamental importance of these questions for the solution of the problem of the historical relationship between American languages, it seems particularly important to attempt to carry through these classifications without prejudging the question as to the genealogical position of the various groups. It is quite inconceivable that similarities such as exist between Quileute, Kwakiutl, and Salish, should be due to a mere accident, or that the morphological similarities of Californian languages, which Kroeber and Dixon have pointed out, should not be due to a definite cause. The experience of Aryan studies might induce us to agree that these must be members of single linguistic stocks; but this assumption leaves fundamental differences unaccounted for, and neglects the possibility of morphological assimilation, so that at the present time the conclusion does not seem convincing. We ought to inquire, first of all, into the possibility of mutual influences, which will be revealed, in part at least, by lack of correspondence between lexicographic, phonetic, and detailed morphological classifications.

We do not mean to say that the investigation may not satisfactorily prove certain genealogical relationships; but what should be emphasized is that, in the present state of our knowledge of primitive languages, it is not safe to disregard the possibility of a complex origin of linguistic groups, which would limit the applicability of the term "linguistic family" in the sense in which we are accustomed to use it. It is certainly desirable, and necessary, to investigate minutely and carefully all suggestive analogies. The proof of genetic relationship, however, can be considered as given, only when the number of unexplained distinct elements is not over-large, and when the contradictory classifications, to which reference has been made before, have been satisfactorily accounted for.

It is quite evident that, owing to the lack of knowledge of the historical development of American languages, convincing proof of genealogical relationship may be impossible to obtain, even where such relation exists; so that, from both a practical and a theoretical point of view, the solution of the problems of genetic relationship presents a large number of attractive problems.

Considering the complexity of this question, and the doubts that we entertain in regard to some of the principles to be followed in our inquiry, it seems probable that a safer basis will be reached by following out dialectic studies. Very little work of this kind has been done on our continent. James Owen Dorsey was able to point out a few phenomena pertaining to the interrelation of Siouan dialects. Similar points have been made in regard to the Salish languages and in a few other cases, but no penetrating systematic attempt has been made to clear up the processes of differentiation by which modern American dialects have developed. It is fortunate for the prosecution of this study that quite a number of linguistic families in America are broken up into numerous strongly divergent dialects, the study of which will help us the more in the investigation of the relations between distinct languages, the more markedly they are differentiated. Siouan, Algonquian, Muskhogean, Salishan, Shoshonean, Wakashan, Caddoan, are languages of this type. They present examples of divergence of phonetic character, of differences in structure and vocabulary, that will bring us face to face with the problem of the origin of these divergent elements.

The more detailed study of American languages promises rich returns in the fields of the mechanical processes of linguistic development and of the psychological problems presented by languages of different types. In many American languages the etymological processes are so transparent that the mechanism of phonetic adaptation stands out with great clearness. Contact-phenomena, and types of sound-harmony that affect more remote parts of words, occur with great frequency. Phonetic shifts between related dialects are easily observed, so that we can accumulate a large mass of material which will help to solve the question in how far certain phonetic processes may be of more or less universal occurrence.

Remotely related to this problem is the question that was touched upon by Gatschet, in how far the frequent occurrence of similar sounds for expressing related ideas (like the personal pronouns) may be due to obscure psychological causes rather than to genetic relationship. Undoubtedly, many hitherto unexpected types of processes will reveal themselves in the pursuit of these studies.

The variety of American languages is so great that they will be of high value for the solution of many fundamental psychological problems.

The unconsciously formed categories found in human speech have not been sufficiently exploited for the investigation of the categories into which the whole range of human experience is forced. Here, again, the clearness of etymological processes in many American languages is a great help to our investigation.

The isolation of formal elements and of stems, or of co-ordinate stems —whichever the case may be—is easily performed, and the meaning of every part of an expression is determined much more readily than in the innumerable fossilized forms of Indo-European languages.

Lexicographic differentiation corresponds to the morphological differentiation of languages. Where ideas are expressed by means of separate stems or by subordinate elements, generalized stems will be found that express a certain action regardless of the instrument with which it has been performed; while, in languages that are not provided with these formal elements, a number of separate words will take the place of the modified general stem. In languages that possess a full equipment of adverbial and locative formative elements, generalized words of motion may be qualified by their use; while, wherever these elements are absent, new stems must take their place. The same is true of grammatical elements that designate form or substance. Where these occur, the languages may lack words expressing predicative ideas relating to objects of different form and consisting of different substances (like our words "to lie," "to sit," "to stand," "to tear," "to break").

A lexicographic analysis based on these principles of classification promises important results, but requires a much more accurate knowledge of the meaning of stems than is available in most cases.

No less interesting are the categories of thought that find expression in grammatical form. The older grammars, although many of them contain excellent material, do not clearly present these points of difference, because they are modelled strictly on the Latin scheme, which obscures the characteristic psychological categories of Indian languages. Thus the idea of plurality is not often developed in the same sense as in Latin, but expresses rather the idea of distribution or of collectivity. The category of gender is rare, and nominal cases are not common. In the pronoun we find often a much more rigid adherence to the series of three persons than the one that we apply, in so far as the distinction is carried through in the pronominal plural and in the demonstrative. Furthermore, new ideas—such as visibility, or position in regard to the speaker in the six principal directions (up, down, right, left, front, back), or tense—are added to the concept of the demonstrative pronouns. In the numeral the varied bases of numeral systems find expression. In the verb the category of tense may be almost suppressed or may be exuberantly developed. Modes may include many ideas that we express by means of adverbs, or they may be absent. The distinction between verb and noun may be different from ours. In short, an enormous variety of forms illustrates the multifarious ways in which language seizes upon one or another feature as an essential of expression of thought.

Besides the greater or lesser development of categories that are parallel to our own, many new ones appear. The groups of ideas selected for expression by formative elements are quite distinctive, and they belong to the most important features in the characterization of each language. In some cases they are poorly developed, but most American languages possess an astonishing number of formative elements of this type.

In some cases their number is so great that the very idea of subordination of one element of a word under another one loses its significance; and we are in doubt whether we shall designate one group as subordinate elements, or whether we shall speak of the composition of co-ordinate elements. While in some languages, as in Algonquian or Kutenai, this may be a matter of arbitrary definition, it involves a problem of great theoretical interest; namely, the question whether formative elements have developed from independent words, as has been proved to be the case with many formal suffixes of European languages.

The objectivating tendency of our mind makes the thought congenial, that part of a word the significance of which we can determine by analysis must also have objectively an independent existence; but there is certainly no *a priori* reason that compels us to make this assumption. It must be proved to be true by empirical evidence. Although the history of American languages is not known, and therefore cannot furnish any direct evidence for or against this theory, the study of the etymological processes will throw light upon this problem, because in many cases the very phonetic weakness of the constituent elements, their internal changes, and the transparency of the method of composition, make it clear that we are performing here an analytical process that does not need to have as its counterpart the synthesis of independent elements. The same question may also be raised in regard to phonetic modifications of the stem, which may be secondary, and due to the influence of changing accents in composition or to vanished component elements, while they may also be primary phenomena.

This problem is in a way identical with the whole question of the relation between word and sentence. Here also American languages may furnish us with much important material that emphasizes the view that the unit of human speech as we know it is the sentence, not the word.

The problems treated in a linguistic journal must include also the literary forms of native production. Indian oratory has long been famous, but the number of recorded speeches from which we can judge their oratorical devices is exceedingly small. There is no doubt whatever that definite stylistic forms exist that are utilized to impress the hearer; but we do not know what they are. As yet, nobody has attempted a careful analysis of the style of narrative art as practiced by the various tribes. The crudeness of most records presents a serious obstacle for this study, which, however, should be taken up seriously. We can study the general structure of the narrative, the style of composition, of motives, their character and sequence; but the formal stylistic devices for obtaining effects are not so easily determined.

Notwithstanding the unsatisfactory character of the available material, we do find cases in which we may at least obtain a glimpse of the intent of the narrator. In many cases metaphorical expressions occur that indicate a vigorous imagination. Not much material of this character is available, but what little we have demonstrates that the type of metaphor used in different parts of the continent shows characteristic differences. It would be interesting to know in how far these expressions have become purely formal without actual meaning, and in how far they reflect an active imagination.

Evidence is not missing which shows that the sentence is built up with a view of stressing certain ideas or words by means of position, repetition, or other devices for securing emphasis. There are curious differences in the tendency to fill the discourse with brief allusions to current ideas difficult to understand for anyone who is not versed in the whole culture of the people, and the enjoyment of diffuse, detailed description. Collectors of texts are fully aware that in the art of narrative there are artists and bunglers in every primitive tribe, as well as among ourselves.

At present there is hardly any material available that will allow us to characterize the tribal characteristics of the art of narrative.

The most promising material for the study of certain aspects of artistic expression are the formal elements that appear with great frequency in the tales of all tribes. Most of these are stereotyped to such an extent that little individual variation is found. Even in poorly recorded tales, written down in translation only, and obtained with the help of inadequate interpreters, the sameness of stereotyped formulas may sometimes be recognized. Conversation in animal tales and in other types of narrative, prayers and incantations, are probably the most important material of this character.

Attention should also be paid to the existing forms of literature. The narrative is of universal occurrence, but other forms show a much more irregular distribution. The psychological basis of the trivial American anecdote is not easily understood. The connotation of meaningless syllables that occur in songs, the frequent use of distorted words in poetry, and the fondness for a secret language, including obsolete, symbolic, or arbitrary terms, deserve the most careful attention. Here belong also the peculiar modes of speech of various personages, that are recorded in many tales, and which Dr. Sapir has found so fully developed among the Nootka, and Dr. Frachtenberg among the Quileute. The fixity of form of the recitative used by certain animals, to which Dr. Sapir has called attention in his studies of the Paiute, also suggests an interesting line of inquiry.

Equally important is the absence of certain literary forms with which we are familiar. The great dearth of proverbs, of popular snatches, and of riddles, among American aborigines, in contrast to their strong development in Africa and other parts of the Old World, requires attentive study. The general lack of epic poetry, the germs of which are found in a very few regions only, is another feature that promises to clear up certain problems of the early development of literary art. We are able to observe lyric poetry in its simplest forms among all tribes. Indeed, we may say that, even where the slightest vestiges of epic poetry are missing, lyric poetry of one form or another is always present. It may consist of the musical use of meaningless syllables that sustain the song; or it may consist largely of such syllables, with a few interspersed words suggesting certain ideas and certain feelings; or it may rise to the expression of emotions connected with warlike deeds, with religious feeling, love, or even to the praise of the beauties of nature. The records which have been accumulated during the last few years, particularly by students of primitive music, contain a mass of material that can be utilized from this point of view.

Undoubtedly the problems of native poetry have to be taken up in connection with the study of native music, because there is practically no poetry that is not at the same time song. The literary aspects of this subject, however, fall entirely within the scope of a linguistic journal.

Let us hope that the new journal may be able to contribute its share to the solution of all these problems!

THE CLASSIFICATION OF AMERICAN LANGUAGES [1]

E VER since Major Powell completed his classification of American languages, which was published in the seventh volume of the Annual Reports of the Bureau of (American) Ethnology, and a revised edition of which is contained in the first volume of the Handbook of North American Indians, students of American languages have paid more attention to a better understanding and a more thorough knowledge of the single languages than to classification. Much of the material on which Major Powell's work is based is exceedingly scanty, and it is obvious that more accurate studies will show relationships between linguistic stocks which at the time could not be safely inferred. The classification is largely based on vocabularies. Many of these were contained in old literature and are very inadequate. Others were hastily collected in accordance with the exigencies of the situation and neither Major Powell nor any of his collaborators, like Albert S. Gatschet and James Owen Dorsey, would have claimed that their classification and the map of distribution of languages could be considered as final.

Of late years, largely through the influence of Dr. Edward Sapir, the attempts have been revived to compare, on the basis of vocabularies, languages which apparently are very distinct, and Drs. Sapir, Kroeber, Dixon, and particularly Radin, have attempted to prove far-reaching relationships.

Since for many years I have taken the position that comparison between American languages should proceed from the study of fairly closely related dialects towards the study of more diverse forms, it seems desirable to state briefly the theoretical points of view upon which my own attitude has been and is still based. As early as 1893 I pointed out that the study of the grammar of American languages has demonstrated the occurrence of a number of striking morphological similarities be-

[1] *American Anthropologist*, N.S., vol. 22 (1920), pp. 367–376.

tween neighboring stocks which, however, are not accompanied by appreciable similarities in vocabulary. At that time I was inclined to consider these similarities as a proof of relationship of the same order as that of languages belonging, for instance, to the Indo-European family. While further studies, particularly in California, have shown that we may generalize the observations which I made based on the languages of the North Pacific Coast, I doubt whether the interpretation given at that time is tenable.

When we consider the history of human languages as it is revealed by their present distribution and by what little we know about their history during the last few thousand years, it appears fairly clearly that the present wide distribution of a few linguistic stocks is a late phenomenon, and that in earlier times the area occupied by each linguistic family was small. It seems reasonable to suppose that the number of languages that have disappeared is very large. Taking our American conditions as an example, we may observe at the present time that many languages are spoken by small communities, and while there is no proof of the recent development of any new very divergent language, there are numerous proofs showing the extinction of some languages and the gradual extension of others. As the area occupied by the Indo-European family has gradually extended and as foreign languages have become extinct owing to its expansion, so we find that Chinese has gradually expanded its area. In Siberia, Turkish and other native languages have superseded the ancient local languages. In Africa the large expansion of Bantu is rather recent. Arabic is superseding the native speech in North Africa. In America the expansion of Algonquian speech has been continuing during the historic period, and several of the isolated languages of the Southeast have been superseded by Creek and related languages. I have discussed this question in another place and have explained my view that probably at a very early time the diversity of languages among people of the same physical type was much greater than it is now. I do not mean to imply by this that all the languages must have developed entirely independently, but rather that, if there was an ancient common source of several modern languages, they have become so much differentiated that without historical knowledge of their growth, the attempts to prove their interrelation cannot succeed.

It should be borne in mind that the problem of the study of languages is not one of classification but that our task is to trace the history of the development of human speech. Therefore, classification is only a means to an end. Our aim is to unravel the history of the growth of human language, and, if possible, to discover its underlying psychological and physiological causes. From this point of view the linguistic phenomena cannot be treated as a unit, but the manifestations of linguistic activity must be studied first each by itself, then in their relations to other linguistic phenomena.

The three fundamental aspects of human speech are phonetics, grammar, and vocabulary. When we turn to their consideration separately, we find, at least in America, a curious condition. The study of phonetics indicates that certain features have a limited and well-defined distribution which, on the whole, is continuous. To give an example: the extraordinary development of the series of *k* sounds and of laterals (*l* sounds) is common to the most diverse languages of the North Pacific Coast, while in California and east of the Rocky Mountains this characteristic feature disappears. In a similar way nasalization of vowels is absent in the northwest part of America, but it is very strongly developed on the central and eastern plains. The labialization of *k* sounds following an *o* or *u* is widely spread in the extreme Northwest, and infrequent outside of that territory. The study of the phonetics of America is not sufficiently developed to describe in detail areas of distribution of characteristic sounds or sound groups, but it may safely be stated from what we know that similar phonetic traits often belong to languages which are morphologically entirely distinct; and that on the other hand, very great phonetic differences develop in the same linguistic stock.

The study of the morphology of American languages illustrates also definite areas of characterization. It is, for instance, most striking that reduplication as a morphological process occurs extensively on the Great Plains and in the Eastern Woodlands, as well as in that part of the Pacific Coast south of the boundary between British Columbia and Alaska. Among the great families of the north it is entirely unknown. Incorporation, which in earlier times was considered as one of the most characteristic traits of American languages, is also confined to certain definite groups. It is characteristically developed in the Shoshonean group, Pawnee, Kutenai, and Iroquois, while north of this region it is either absent in its characteristic form, or only weakly developed. The use of instrumentals, which indicate the manner of action as performed with parts of the body, or by other instruments, shows also on the whole a continuous distribution. It is a fundamental trait of Kutenai, Shoshonean, and Sioux, and in all of them it is expressed in a similar manner. The use of true cases and of locative and similar noun forms occur among the Shoshonean and some of their neighbors, while in other regions it is rather rare. Of even greater importance is the differentiation between nominal and verbal concepts, and between neutral and active verbs, the distribution of which is somewhat irregular.

Although our knowledge of these phenomena is not by any means adequate, it appears fairly clearly that, when the various features are studied in detail, the areas of their distribution do not coincide.

The study of the vocabulary presents similar conditions. It would seem that the number of loan words in American languages is not as great as in European languages. At least, it is difficult to recognize loan words in large numbers. It is, however, striking that the word categories which appear in neighboring languages are sometimes quite similar. This appears, for instance, in the case of terms of relationship. The remarkable extent to which the use of reciprocal terms of relationship is found on the western plateaus is a characteristic example. It is intelligible that nomenclature and cultural states are closely related, and, therefore, it seems plausible that similarities in underlying categories of vocabularies will occur where cultural conditions are the same or nearly the same.

This remark has no direct bearing upon the stems that underlie word formation. To a certain extent they are dependent upon morphological characteristics, at least in so far that nonexistent grammatical categories must be supplied in other ways. When, for instance, some languages, like the Eskimo, lack those adverbial elements which correspond to our prepositions (in, out of, up, down, etc.), these must be supplied by special verbs which do not need to exist in languages that abound in locative verbal elements. On the whole, a certain correlation may be observed between the lexicographical and morphological aspects of a language. The more frequently "material" concepts (in Steinthal's sense) are expressed by morphological devices, the more generalized are, on the whole, the word stems, and words are generally formed by limitation of these stems. When we find similar structure, we find, therefore, also a tendency towards the development of similar categories of stems. There are, however, others that are not so determined. It is, for instance, characteristic of many American languages that verbal ideas are expressed by different stems according to the form of the object in regard to which the verb predicates. This feature occurs particularly in verbs of existence and of motion, so that existence or motion of round, long, flat, etc., objects, are differentiated. This feature is prominent, among others, in Athapascan, Tlingit, Kwakiutl, and Sioux.

While I am not inclined to state categorically that the areas of distribution of phonetic phenomena, of morphological characteristics, and of groups based on similarities in vocabularies are absolutely distinct, I believe this question must be answered empirically before we can undertake to solve the general problem of the history of modern American languages. If it should prove true, as I believe it will, that all these different areas do not coincide, then the conclusion seems inevitable that the different languages must have exerted a far-reaching influence upon one another. If this point of view is correct, then we have to ask ourselves in how far the phenomena of acculturation extend also over the domain of languages.

Considering the conditions of life in primitive society, it is intelligible how the phonetics of one language may influence those of another one. Many of the American tribes are very small, and intertribal marriages are, comparatively speaking, frequent, either owing to peaceful intercourse, or to the abduction and enslavement of women after warlike raids. There must always have been a considerable number of alien women in each tribe who acquired the foreign language late in life and who, therefore, transmitted the foreign pronunciation to their children. It is true that we cannot give definite observations which prove the occurrence of this phenomenon, but it can hardly be doubted that these processes were operative in all those cases where the number of alien women was considerable in proportion to the number of native women. The objective study of languages also shows that phonetic influences do spread from one people to another. The most characteristic example probably is that of the southern Bantu who have adopted the clicks of the Bushmen and Hottentots, notwithstanding the hostility that prevails between these groups.

It is not so easy to understand the development of similar categories of words in neighboring languages. It is undoubtedly true that forms of social and political organization, as well as religious life, have become alike among neighboring tribes owing to a process of acculturation. The similarity in forms of life creates the necessity of developing terms expressing these forms, and will thus bring about indirectly similarity in those ideas that are expressed by words. When we apply this assumption to such concepts as terms of relationship, in which we remain in doubt as to whether the term creates the feeling accompanying the subsummation of an individual under a category, or whether the feeling creates the term, it seems difficult to understand the psychological process that led to the similarity of classification, although the facts of distribution make it perfectly clear that the similarities are due to diffusion. This difficulty is still greater when we deal with the fundamental concepts contained in the ancient stems that underlie the modern words. How, for instance, should the habit of mind to classify all motion according to form spread from one language to another?

Equally difficult to understand is the spread of morphological traits from one language to another. Nevertheless, I am very much inclined to believe that such transfers do occur, and I even consider it possible that they may modify fundamental structural characteristics. An example of this kind is the intrusion of nominal cases into the upper Chinook dialects, presumably due to Sahaptin influence. I believe that the peculiar development of the second third person in Kutenai, which is so characteristic of Algonquian, is also due to a contact phenomenon, because we find hardly anywhere else a similar development of this tendency. Still another case of peculiar parallelism is found among the Eskimo and Chukchee. Notwithstanding the fundamental differences between the two languages, the modern development of the verb with its numerous semi-participial forms, shows a peculiar parallelism. The traits in question are entirely absent in neighboring languages, and for this reason it is difficult to abstain from the conclusion that these similarities must be due to historical reasons.

The distribution of these phenomena the world over is so irregular that it would be entirely unwarranted to claim that all similarities of phonetics, classification of concepts, or of morphology, must be due to borrowing. On the contrary, their distribution shows that they must be considered as due to psychological causes such as the unavoidable necessity of classification of experience in speech, which can lead to a limited number of categories only, or the physiological possibilities of articulation that also limit the range of possible sounds which are sufficiently distinct to the ear for clear understanding.

To give a few examples: it would hardly be possible to claim that the numerous instrumental prefixes of the Haida and those of Shoshonean, Kutenai, and Sioux, are historically related. It is true that Shoshonean, Kutenai, and Sioux form a continuous group to which might be added many of the Californian languages. Considering the continuity of this area and the absence of analogous forms outside, I am strongly inclined to believe that some historical reason must have led to their peculiar development, but it would be difficult to connect historically the Haida with this district. In the same way, it would be rash to associate the strong development of glottalized sounds in Chile with the analogous sounds on the Northwest Coast of America; the distinction between neutral and active verbs among the Maya, Sioux, and Tlingit; or the occurrence of three genders in Indo-European and in Chinook.

Our experience in Indo-European and Semitic languages shows clearly that extended borrowing of words may occur and that borrowed words may undergo such changes that their origin can be understood only by historical study. That similar phenomena have occurred in American languages is indicated by the distribution of such words as names of animals and of plants which are in some cases borrowed. Other classes of nominal concepts are not so subject to borrowing on account of the extensive use in many American languages of descriptive terms. Nevertheless, in mixed settlements considerable numbers of borrowed words may be found. An example of this kind is presented by the Comox of Vancouver Island who speak a Salish language with a strong admixture of Kwakiutl words, or by the Bella Coola, another Salish people, who have borrowed many Kwakiutl and Athapascan terms. There is no particular difficulty in understanding the process which leads to the borrowing of words. Intertribal contact must act in this respect in a similar way as international contact does in modern times.

If these observations regarding the influence of acculturation upon language should be correct, then the whole history of American languages must not be treated on the assumption that all languages which show similarities must be considered as branches of the same linguistic family. We should rather find a phenomenon which is parallel to the features characteristic of other ethnological phenomena—namely, a development from diverse sources which are gradually worked into a single cultural unit. We should have to reckon with the tendency of languages to absorb so many foreign traits that we can no longer speak of a single origin, and that it would be arbitrary whether we associate a language with one or the other of the contributing stocks. In other words, the whole theory of an "Ursprache" for every group of modern languages must be held in abeyance until we can prove that these languages go back to a single stock and that they have not originated, to a large extent, by the process of acculturation.

It is true enough that in a comparison of modern Indo-European languages, without any knowledge of their previous history, it might be very difficult to prove releationship—let us say, between Armenian and English—and we might be compelled to adopt a conclusion similar to the one suggested here. Partially this inference would be correct, because our modern Indo-European languages contain much material that is not Indo-European by origin. The fundamental question is whether this material may become so extensive and influence the morphology so deeply that the inclusion of a language in one group or another might become arbitrary.

To sum up, it seems to my mind that a critical attitude towards our problem makes it necessary to approach our task from three points of view. Firstly, we must study the differentiation of dialects like those of the Siouan, Muskhogean, Algonquian, Shoshonean, Salishan, and Athapascan. Secondly, we must make a detailed study of the distribution of phonetic, grammatical, and lexicographical phenomena, the latter including also particularly the principles on which the grouping of concepts is based. Finally, our study ought to be directed not only to an investigation of the similarities of languages, but equally intensively towards their dissimilarities. Only on this basis can we hope to solve the general historical problem.

CLASSIFICATION OF AMERICAN INDIAN LANGUAGES [1]

[The author points out cases in which contiguous languages, though different in structure and vocabulary, exhibit in common striking morphological peculiarities that must have spread by borrowing from language to language. A simple genealogical classification cannot therefore adequately represent the development, but "hybridization" must also be taken into account.]

IN A paper published in 1920 [2] I discussed the problem of the interrelation of American Indian languages. I pointed out that morphological types are distributed over large areas and that in these morphological groups differences representing the character of the vocabulary occur which make it difficult to assume that the languages, as now spoken, are derived from the same "Ursprache." I pointed out that in the small linguistic units of early times, the conditions of mixture were quite different from those found in languages spoken over large areas and by many individuals. A further consideration of the problem led to the conclusion that an answer to the fundamental question must be sought through an investigation of mutual influences and the extent to which they may modify languages; particularly, in how far one linguistic type may influence the morphology of another.

I believe everybody will agree that words may be borrowed and may modify the vocabulary of a language; perhaps also that the phonetic character of one language may influence that of its neighbors. I have given a few general instances in the paper mentioned before, and today I will add one example that seems to be particularly instructive. The Nez Percé, an eastern Sahaptin language, has rigid rules of vocalic harmony according to which vowels may be divided into two classes: *a* and *o* as one group; all the others as a second group. In the system of consonants occurs an *s* with raised margin of the tongue and the dental *t* series. Another characteristic sound is a voiced affricative, something

[1] *Language,* vol. 5, No. 1 (1929).

[2] "Classification of American Languages," *American Anthropologist,* N.S., vol. 22 (1920), pp. 367–76, pp. 211 *et seq.* of this volume.

like *dl*. During the eighteenth century a large group of the Sahaptin penetrated into the State of Washington and some of them crossed the Cascade Mountains where they intermarried with the Salishan tribes resident there. The phonetic elements of the present dialect of this region are practically identical with those of the neighboring Salishan tribes. The vocalic system is the same. There is no trace of vocalic harmony.

We recognize that a comparison of vocabularies of languages the history of which is unknown offers serious difficulties, and that the changes brought about by the shifting of sounds, by semantic modification, and by new formations, may be so numerous that identification becomes possible in exceptional cases only. Languages behave differently in these respects. Some, like the Eskimo, are so conservative that even now the differentiation between Alaskan and Greenland dialects is slight, although the two groups have been separated for more than a thousand years. The more striking is the divergence of the vocabulary of the probably related Aleutian. Aztekan has changed in so far as the higher literary style has disappeared and as old ideas have vanished and new ones have been introduced with concomitant change of vocabulary. The syntactic subordination and co-ordination of phrases have yielded to Spanish types. In all other respects the modern language has not changed. It seems even possible to recognize the dialectic differences of various areas which may be reconstructed from the grammars of the early sixteenth century. On the other hand, the Salishan languages of British Columbia and Washington illustrate a great instability in morphology and lexicography. We can only guess what the causes of the difference in behavior of different languages may be. The often expressed opinion that "primitive languages" undergo very rapid changes is true to a very limited extent only.

There is no doubt that in many cases languages sprung from the same source and changing by internal forces only may have become so different that without historical data their relation cannot be established.

Nevertheless the question remains whether hybridization of languages, not only in phonetics and vocabulary, but also in morphology, may have occurred.

So far as I know the actual process of a transfer of grammatical categories from one language to another has never been observed, although minor changes, like the adoption of a form here and there, and syntactic influences are known to occur. The syntactic modification of

American languages under Spanish influence offers a good example of the latter type of change. The proof of the diffusion of morphological forms can be only indirect, based on facts of distribution and partial conformity by the side of fundamental differences.

In some cases of far-reaching similarity of morphology, like that of Athapascan and Tlingit, we may feel that an assimilation of the structure of an older language by Athapascan is quite unlikely; and that, if no safer correspondence of vocabulary can be found than has been presented up to this time, we may suspect that an older vocabulary has been taken over by the invading Athapascan. Until definite phonetic shifts can be proven by a sufficient number of parallel forms, and until an exhaustive comparison of vocabularies has been made, we have to admit that a vast array of stems in the two languages cannot be identified, including pronouns, numerals, and most other stems; and we must leave open the question whether all, or most of the lexicographic material can be derived from a common source.

More difficult are those cases in which a partial agreement in morphological traits exists between neighboring and apparently distinct languages, and disagreement in the dialects of obviously related languages. I may give an example of this kind. I mentioned before the vocalic harmony of the Nez Percé. So far as I am aware only the Coos of Oregon exhibit a similar, consistent phenomenon. It is not known whether the neighboring Molala and Kalapuya have it. Other Sahaptin dialects do not show it.

Chinook possesses pronominal gender. There are not only pronouns of three genders—or more strictly speaking five nominal categories, for dual and plural belong to the same system—but every noun has prefixed one of the five pronouns. None of the languages of the adjoining groups have sex gender except a number of dialects located in close proximity to the Chinook, particularly all the dialects of Salish tribes that live along the coast northward and southward, and the Quileute. In the Salish dialects of the interior, gender does not occur. If the Quileute should prove to be related to Wakashan, to which it shows morphological resemblances, it will be the only language of this group which has gender. In all these dialects gender is confined to the pronoun.

Chinook expresses diminutives by consonantic changes. Voiced and unvoiced consonants become glottalized and š changes to s. Velar fricatives become midpalatal fricatives. The neighboring Sahaptin groups, which differ fundamentally from Chinook, use consonantic changes for the same purpose. Some of the changes are the same as in Chinook; š changes to s, velars to midpalatals, and besides these a change from n to l occurs.

We find sporadic, fossilized use of the same process in the Salish dialect spoken just north of the Chinook area, in Coos on the coast of Oregon,[1] and as a living feature in Wiyot in Northern California. Geographical contiguity for the last example cannot be established.

It will be noticed that while gender exists in a coastwise direction north and south, the formation of the diminutive by consonantic changes occurs in a territory extending eastward.

Another curious resemblance may be traced between Quileute, Kwakiutl, and Tsimshian, which are spoken in an area extending from the State of Washington to the Alaskan boundary. In these three languages the pronominal representation of the noun (or article) is treated differently for proper names and for common nouns. These form throughout two distinct classes. In Quileute and Kwakiutl a further correspondence is found in so far as the article used with proper names is also used for indefinite, that is unknown objects. For instance, "I look for a whale", indefinite; "I found a whale", definite.

Many American languages draw a clear distinction between possession by the subject and possession by another person, like the Latin suus and ejus. A small group, including the Eskimo, Algonquian, and Kutenai, express these relations by special verbal forms, the so-called obviative of the missionaries who wrote on Algonquian, the fourth person of Thalbitzer. The phenomenon is most pronounced in Kutenai, for even in the case of the simple transitive verb with third person subject and nominal object the presence of the two third persons is indicated by the obviative suffix following the nominal object. It is interesting to note that the western Sahaptin languages, which as a whole group adjoin the Kutenai, make the same distinction for the subject of the sentence for sentences containing only one third person and those in which the sentence contains two third persons. In both Kutenai and western Sahaptin there is a differentiation between the forms in a sentence like, "the man saw me," and "the man saw the woman." In Kutenai the difference is found in the object, in Sahaptin in the subject. In some of the Sahaptin dialects this trait is found only in the pronoun, not in the noun. The general usage, in the group of languages just discussed, is alike notwithstanding the difference of devices used.

[1] *Handbook of American Indian Languages,* part 2 (Washington, 1922), p. 383.

Another interesting feature may be observed in the languages of the North Pacific Coast. Demonstrative pronouns are often very elaborate. They not only distinguish between the person near the speaker, near the person addressed, and near the person spoken of, but more exact locations are often added. The Tlingit of Alaska differentiate between what is near him but nearer than you, and what is near him but farther than you; or positions in front, behind, above, or below the speaker may be designated. Among the tribes extending from Columbia River northward to Alaska—the same group which differentiates between proper names and common nouns—a different demonstrative concept is introduced, namely that of visibility and invisibility. The Chinook has demonstratives designating, for instance, "near the speaker, visible." The same occurs in Quileute and Coast Salish, but not in the Salish dialects of the interior. It is a characteristic feature of Kwakiutl. I do not know of its occurrence in any other group of neighboring languages.

Still another feature characteristic of part of the same group is the separation of pronominal subject and object in transitive verbs. The verb unaccompanied by what we should call an adverb, takes a suffix consisting of pronominal subject and object combined. When a qualifying adverb accompanies the verb, the subject is attached to this qualifier which takes the form of an intransitive verb, while the object remains attached to the primary verb. "I did not see him" would be expressed by "not-I see-him." This tendency occurs in exactly the same form in Quileute, Coast Salish, and Wakashan. In Tsimshian it is less fully developed, in so far as in subjunctive forms the pronominal subject precedes the verb and is phonetically united with the preceding adverb. The analogy, however, is not strict.

Another interesting comparison may be made between Chukchee and Eskimo. In regard to the general form, these two languages are quite distinct. Chukchee employs terminal reduplication, prefixes, suffixes, and vocalic harmony. Besides this there are rigid rules regarding initial consonantic clusters which bring about important modifications of stem form. Eskimo has nothing of the kind. There is no reduplication, no prefixes whatever, no trace of vocalic harmony. Whatever changes occur in the stem are due to the influence of suffixes. On the other hand, a number of categories occur which are common to these two neighboring languages. The plural forms are alike; both Eskimo and Chukchee form the plural by a suffix *t*. The nominal subject in Eskimo is treated differently in the case of transitive and intransitive verbs. The subject of the transitive verb has what might be called a relational form, common to both the genitive and the transitive subject. The subject of the intransitive verb has the same form as the object of the transitive verb. This feature occurs also in other languages, as in Sahaptin, and it is found in the pronominal forms of many other languages. But in the circumpolar area only the Chukchee and Eskimo have this differentiation of the nominal forms. The processes by means of which this differentiation is made in Eskimo and Chukchee are quite distinct, for the object in Chukchee is formed by terminal reduplication; in Eskimo the subject is differentiated by a suffix. Furthermore we find in both languages a considerable number of postpositions which express local relationships, such as "at," "towards," "from," and so on. The analogy in the modal development of the verb is also quite striking. A remarkable variety of participial forms occur which may take personal pronouns and the group of concepts expressed by the modalities shows marked similarity.

Considering these data as a whole, we may say that in a considerable number of native languages of the North Pacific Coast we find, notwithstanding fundamental differences in structure and vocabulary, similarities in particular grammatical features distributed in such a way that neighboring languages show striking similarities. The areas in which similar features are found do not coincide in regard to the various traits compared.

It seems to me almost impossible to explain this phenomenon without assuming the diffusion of grammatical processes over contiguous areas.

Stress must be laid here upon the contiguity of distribution, because comparative grammar shows clearly that similar features may develop independently in different parts of the world. Sex categories, phonetic similarity between the Northwest Coast and Chile, the application of reduplication, and many other traits appear in such distribution that historical connection is excluded. On the other hand the distribution of the same particular grouping of concepts, or of the same methods of expression over contiguous areas can hardly be explained on the basis of independent origin.

So far as I can see an attempt to bring together the different languages of contiguous areas which have similar processes is not feasible on account of the fundamental differences in conceptualization, in grammatical processes, and in vocabulary.

The phenomena here discussed lead to a result analogous to that reached by Lepsius in his study of African languages. He concluded that a large number of mixed languages occur in Africa. His conclusions are largely corroborated by more recent investigations, particularly of the Sudanese languages. It is also parallel to the results obtained by von der Gabelentz in his study of the languages of New Guinea and Melanesia, and his inferences are substantiated by the recent investigations of Dempwolff. The problem has been well formulated by Professor Prokosch, who demands a detailed comparison of the European languages with all their neighbors, no matter to what linguistic stock they may belong. It also agrees with the view of Schuchardt, who points out that there is a gradation beginning with a slight amount of borrowing and extending through more intensive intermingling, to a complete change of language. The question in which we are interested is not that of the theoretical definition of relation of languages as defined by Meillet, but merely a question of historical development.

If the view expressed here is correct, then it is not possible to group American languages rigidly in a genealogical scheme in which each linguistic family is shown to have developed to modern forms, but we have to recognize that many of the languages have multiple roots.

SOME TRAITS OF THE DAKOTA LANGUAGE[1]

IN THE following I will discuss a few features of the language of the Dakota Indians which seem to have a wider linguistic interest.

First of all I shall discuss the classification of verbs. There are two types of verbs, active and static. Active verbs take active pronouns, static verbs take static pronouns. "I am sick" is static, and the form for "I" is the static pronoun which is identical with the object of the transitive verb. This is a frequent feature of American languages. It is peculiar to Dakota that only stems expressing activities performed by living beings can be active, all others are static. Static verbs may be made active by instrumental, sometimes by locative prefixes, but the stem itself is static. Thus the term "to break" is formed from the static verb "to be in a broken condition," and might be translated "to cause by means of pressure to be in a broken condition." The static terms are differentiated according to the form and character of the substance to which they refer, such as long, or flat, and liquid, soft, brittle, etc. Many of the static stems are obsolete and occur only with activating prefixes.

The second refers to the phonetic rendering of a close association of ideas. The initial vowel of Dakota words is preceded by a glottal closure. When, therefore, a word with terminal consonant precedes a word with initial vowel there is a decided break following the consonant. The consonant does not become glottalized but the glottal closure follows it. When two such words become intimately associated and form a unit concept the break disappears: *napo'g.na* [2] 'a handful', for *nap-'o'g.na* ; *wali'top'e* 'an oar', from *wa'l-'i-top'a'* (boat-rowing-instrument) ; *hǫ'pap'a'-'ec'ų'pi* 'moccasin game', for *hǫp-'ap'a'* 'moccasin striking', *'ec'ų'pi* 'they do'.

A distinction is made between verbs that take the prefix *wa-* which expresses an indefinite object and nouns which contain the same prefix.

[1] *Language*, vol. 13, no. 2 (1937), pp. 137–141.

[2] According to the customary orthography of Dakota *ǫ, į, ų* are nasalized vowels; *ž, š* correspond to French *j* and English *sh*; *č* to English *ch*, medial; *ġ, ħ* are velar spirants.

The latter are unit concepts, the former express an indefinite object for which a definite object may be substituted: *waa'wąyaka* 'he stands guard', *wa·'wąyaka* 'a guard'. When verbs of this type assume a special meaning they may also be contracted: *waa'gli* 'he brings something back home', *wa·'gli* 'he comes back successful from a hunt'; *wayu'ġa* 'he separates something from its covering'; *wo·'ġa* 'he husks corn'. The same phenomenon occurs in the possessive pronoun, intimate possession being expressed by contraction: *tᶜao'wį* 'his earrings', *i.e.,* those he made, or those he happens to wear; *tᶜo·'wį* 'earrings he always wears and that nobody else has a right to wear'; *tᶜawo'wašte* 'his occasional good acts', *tᶜo·'wašte* 'his goodness' as a permanent quality.

These examples show a close parallelism between the concept of psychological and phonetic unity. According to a communication of Dr. Gladys Reichard similar phenomena occur in Navaho: *hoɣan caɣan* [1] 'my home'; *ca'aɣan* 'house in which I am living, not my property'; *cit'a'* 'my wing' (a bird speaking), *ca'at'a'* 'my feather' i.e., the feather I use.

A third point is a curious contradiction between the ease of forming new words by means of affixes and composition and the frequent failure to treat such words according to their etymological structure. It must not, of course, be assumed that new words are consciously built up with an understanding of the meaning of the constituent elements, nor that these are present in the mind of the speaker; but, so far as my knowledge goes, their grammatical treatment follows the general rules of the language. A question regarding the meaning of the compound may elicit a folk etymology. Nevertheless in use the words are generally easily understood. Contractions or abbreviations of words frequently used do not seem unusual. Thus we have *wičᶜa'* 'raccoon', understood as an abbreviation for *wičᶜi'te g.le'ġa* 'striped face'; *pᶜežu'ta* 'medicine', from *pᶜeži'-hu'te* herbs-butt-end'; *pᶜetą'l* 'on the fire', from *pᶜe'ta aką'l* 'fire-on-top-of'. More remarkable are cases of metathesis like *hąkpᶜa'* 'moccasin strings', for *hąpkᶜa'*; *wąsma'hi* 'iron arrow head' from *mas-* 'iron', *wą* 'arrow', *hi* 'tooth'.

Sometimes the grammatical forms show a complete misunderstanding, the phonetic form being more suggestive than etymology. Thus *ana'ġoptą* 'to obey', stands evidently for *ano'ġoptą* (*a* 'on'; *no'ġe* 'ear'; *o'ptą* 'to turn toward'); *na* is taken for a prefix and the first person *wa*

[1] *c = sh* English.

is inserted after *na*: *ana'wagoptą* 'I obey'. In the same way *ina'piskąyą* is treated as though *na* were a prefix, the pronoun *wa* preceding the *p*. Still the derivation is *i-nap-i-ską-ya* 'against-hand-by-means-of-move-cause'.

A fourth trait of Dakota is its old consonantic sound symbolism. The sets, *s, š, h* and *z, ž, ġ* represent gradations, the *s* and *z* being the lowest, *š* and *ž* the middle, and *h* and *ġ* the highest grades. I have given many examples in a previous paper.[1] A few of these will suffice to make the essential point clear. *sle'ča, šle'ča, hle'ča* 'to split things'; *m.nų'za, m.nų'ža, m.nų'ġa* 'to crunch'. With *s* or *z* it is done easily, with *š* or *ž* with greater difficulty, with *h* or *ġ* with great difficulty. The grades of intensity are not always quite so clear. Sometimes the *š* series expresses wetness: *ska'pa* 'to slap', *ška'pa* 'to slap wet surfaces'; *ski'ca* 'to compress dry things', *škica* 'to compress wet things'. A few examples in addition to the list mentioned are: *ze'zeya* 'dangling', *ap'a'žežeya* 'right on the edge, almost falling over'; *ġe'ġeya* 'hanging down'; *wašte'* 'peculiar, good', *wahte'šni* 'bad (not good)'; *šloka* 'to take out of a hole', *hlo'ka* 'to break a hole'; *b.laska'* 'flat and hard', *b.laška'* 'flat and flabby'. *zi* 'yellow', *ži* 'tawny', *ġi* 'brown'. It may well be that the three stages have reference rather to the consistency of material than to intensity. A good many examples can be interpreted more easily in that way.

E. Kennard[2] has found a number of pairs of similar character in Mandan: *dusa'p* 'to pull a little', *duha'p* 'to tear'; *sɛ'ro* 'to jingle', *hɛ'ro* 'to rattle', etc.

Lipkind has discovered a considerable number in Winnebago.[3] Examples are: *sąwą* 'to be melted', *šąwą* 'to be softened,' *hąwą* 'to be moistened' (Dakota *spa, špą, hpą*); *siri* 'to be squeezed out', *hiri* 'to be mashed' (Dakota *šli, hli*); *k'es* 'to be scraped bare', *k'eh* 'to be scraped'.

This consonantic symbolism is similar to the diminutive and consonantic shifts of some of the Pacific Coast languages. In Chinook we have changes from sonants to glottalized sounds to express diminutives[4] and also changes in the place of articulation of palatal affricatives. In Kwakiutl we find a limited number of words in which glottalization

---

[1] "Notes on the Dakota, Teton Dialect," *International Journal of American Linguistics*, vol. 7, nos. 3–4 (1932), p. 112.

[2] "Mandan Grammar," *International Journal of American Linguistics*, vol. 9, no. 1 (1936), p. 32.

[3] Personal communication.

[4] Edward Sapir in F. Boas, *Handbook of American Indian Languages*, part 2 (Washington, 1911), p. 638.

indicates smallness, e.g. *kyɔpa'* to embrace, *ky'ɔpa'* to take up with tongs; *qɔ'mkwa* to snap together, *q'ɔ'mkwa* to bite off. Quite similar changes occur in diminutive forms in Sahaptin.[1] The velar consonants become mid-palatal and *n* changes to *l*. In Wiyot, a Californian language, the following changes are found in the diminutive: *d* becomes *ts*, *t* > *ts* or *tc*, *s* > *c*, *l* > *r*.[2] In Coos[3] traces of a similar process are found. It also seems to be a live process in Tillamook, a Salishan dialect.[4]

The fifth point refers to the demonstrative pronoun. It is a feature that is not particularly characteristic of Dakota, but appears in many North American languages. We are accustomed to a development of the demonstrative pronoun parallel to position "near me" and "away from me," or to position "near one of the three personal pronouns." Many American languages have a strong feeling for localization, and add to the fundamental ideas of position "near one of the three personal pronouns" reference to the concept of visibility and invisibility.

This makes the exact definition of demonstratives particularly difficult, because it is always necessary to reconstruct the position in which the speaker images himself to be. In Dakota we have the fundamental forms *le, he, ka, to* which express 'near me', 'away from me', 'away from me visible', 'somewhere'. The concepts 'near thee' and 'near him' are not distinguished. The particular place in reference to two persons is expressed by the suffix -*k'i* (after *e* > *c'i*). Thus *le'c'i* means 'here and away from you or him', *he'c'i* 'there and away from me', *ka'k'i* 'yonder visible, away from me'. With the ending *ya* these forms express a region rather than a spot.

The distinction of visibility and invisibility is made in a number of languages. In Kwakiutl the glottal stop added to demonstrative forms expresses invisibility *t'e'sɔmgya* 'this stone visible' (-*gya* indicates 'near me'), *t'e'sɔmgya'* 'this stone invisible'. In Quileute[5] the independent demonstrative pronouns for visibility and invisibility are distinct.

[1] Melville Jacobs, *A Sketch of Northern Sahaptin Grammar,* University of Washington Publications in Anthropology, vol. 4 (1931), pp. 136, 139.

[2] Gladys Reichard, *Wiyot Grammar and Texts,* University of California Publications in Anthropology and Ethnology, vol. 22 (1925), p. 29.

[3] Leo J. Frachtenberg, Coos, in F. Boas, *Handbook of American Indian Languages,* part 2 (Washington, 1922), p. 383.

[4] May Edel, The Tillamook Language, *International Journal of American Linguistics,* vol. 10 (1939), p. 16.

[5] Manuel J. Andrade, "Quileute," in *Handbook of American Indian Languages,* part 3 (J. J. Augustin, 1933-38), p. 246.

Kutenai [1] has three positions: indefinite, here or previously referred to, and absent. Each of these has one form for visible, one for invisible, the latter distinguished by the insertion of an *a, e.g.* the prefix *sn-* means 'here visible standing', *san-* 'here invisible standing'. In Chinook also the independent demonstratives are divided into the classes visible and invisible.[2]

Reference to a third person is highly developed in Tlingit. We find *yá* 'this near me', *wé* 'that near thee', *hé* 'that near him and nearer than you', *yú* 'that near him and farther away than you.' [3]

In Coeur d'Alêne [4] all expressions regarding movements are expressed by means of prefixes. If only a speaker and the person addressed are involved the terms hither and thither are sufficient. When a third place is involved a definite position of reference must be included. If this point is termed 'there', the expressions would mean: (1) from beyond there hither and to beyond there, (2) from beyond there hither, to there or this side of there, (3) from there or this side of there hither, (4) from this side of there thither to beyond there, (5) from this side of there thither to there or to this side of there, (6) from beyond there thither to farther beyond there.

In movement Dakota distinguishes between thither and hither, completion of movement thither and hither, movement thither and hither to a place formerly occupied (*i.e.*, return); completion of movement thither and hither to a place previously occupied (*i.e.*, arrival returning). The combinations of the verbs of arrival and motion express the concept of starting, *e.g.*, he went to arrive there, *i.e.*, he started going thither, etc.[5]

Dakota is also remarkable for the tendency to express by means of particles, conjunctions, and adverbs the general emotional state accompanying the statement. Thus, *ki, k'ų* and *wą* (definite present, definite past, and indefinite) at the end of the sentence express respectively

---

[1] Pater Philippo Canestrelli, S.J., annotated by Franz Boas, "Grammar of the Kutenai Language," *International Journal of American Linguistics,* vol. 4 (1927), p. 57.

[2] Franz Boas, "Chinook," *Handbook of American Indian Languages,* part 1 (Washington, 1911), p. 617.

[3] Franz Boas, "Grammatical Notes on the Language of the Tlingit Indians," *University of Pennsylvania, The University Museum Anthropological Publications,* vol. 8, no. 1 (1917), p. 113.

[4] Gladys Reichard, "Grammar of Coeur d'Alene," in *Handbook of American Indian Languages,* part 3 (1933-38), pp. 597 *et seq.*

[5] Franz Boas and Ella Deloria, "Notes on the Dakota, Teton Dialect," *International Journal of American Linguistics,* vol. 7, nos. 3-4 (1932), p. 117.

annoyance, the feeling that a statement is unnecessary because known to the person addressed, and pleasant agreement. Thus in a sentence meaning 'I'll finish this first' the addition of *kį* implies the speaker's annoyance at being interrupted; with *k'ų* the implication is that the person addresses knows that the speaker wishes to finish first; with *wą* that there is pleasant agreement. Similarly in 'I gave it to him, but he did not take it' : if for 'but' *yesą* is used, the implication is that he ought to have taken it; if *tk'aš*, that the offer ought not to have been made; if *k'eyaš*, an indifferent attitude is implied. Similar implications can be made by varying the translation of 'instead' (*eha'*, *k'eš*, *iye'š*, *e'e'*) in sentences such as 'he gave me a stone instead of bread', 'bread instead of meat', 'meat instead of bread'.

METAPHORICAL EXPRESSION IN THE LANGUAGE OF THE KWAKIUTL INDIANS[1]

IN THE language of the Kwakiutl[2] Indians of Vancouver Island metaphorical expressions referring to unhappy events are of euphemistic character. Instead of "to die" (*łEla'*) words are used signifying "to grow weak" (*wäL!emasᵉid* R 710.6 [3]) ; "to be nothing" (*wä'la* R 707.55) ; "to perish without reaching the end" (*wibā'lisEm*). These terms are derived from the negation *wī-*. From the same stem are derived "to become nothing in mind" (*wīk·!exᵉid* R 710.13 and *wuyᴇ'm-sᵉid*. *Wä'nEm* may be derived from a stem *wān-* "deserving of pity". Often the term is used "it tears off" (viz. the breath) (*ăłᵉᴇ'ls* R 708.69 'to tear off on the ground, outside of the house'; *ăłᵉ ā'lił* 'to tear off in

[1] *Verzameling van Opstellen door Oud-Leerlingen en Bevriende Vakgenooten Opgedragen aan Mgr. Prof. Dr. Jos. Schrijnen, 3 Mei 1929* (Chartres, France), pp. 147–153.

[2] ᴇ a very weak vowel, probably derived from a weakened ă
ä the German umlaut ä
â as in English "law"
! glottalizes the preceding consonant
ᵉ glottal stop
g·, k·, x· palatized, similar to gy, ky, and German *ch* in "ich"
g, q, x velar g, k, and German *ch* in "Bach"
ᵘ expresses labialization of the preceding *g, k, x̣, g, q, x*
ł voiceless *l*
L affricative *tl*
ʟ affricative *dl*
x̣ᵘ medial labialized spirant

[3] Quotations refer to pages and line of the following publications:

R	"Ethnology of the Kwakiutl," *35th Annual Report of the Bureau of American Ethnology* (1921).
J III, X	"Kwakiutl Texts," *Publications of the Jesup North Pacific Expedition*, vols. 3, 10 (Leiden, 1902, 1905)
C II	*Kwakiutl Tales*, Columbia University Contributions to Anthropology, vol. 2 (1910).
C III	*Contributions to the Ethnology of the Kwakiutl*, Columbia University Contributions to Anthropology, vol. 3 (1925).
M	"The Social Organization and the Secret Societies of the Kwakiutl Indians," *Report of the U. S. National Museum for 1895* (Washington, 1897).

the house'). In speeches we find "to have gone to rest" (*x·oyoxwā'lis* C III 74.7) ; "to lie down" (*qElyax·ᵉā'lis* C III 78.26) ; "to disappear from this world" *k·!ēaxᵉwid lā'xwa ᵉnā'lax* C III 96.25). For the death of many it is said "all are (ended)" (German "alle werden" *ᵉwī'ᵉwEla* R 1147.67), and for the slaughter of man "to cause all (to end)" (German "alle machen", *ᵉwī'wEᵉlā'mas* R 1224.38). To kill is also expressed by "to cause to reach the end" (*hēbaᵉyā'mas*). To take revenge on an enemy is "to eat meat" (*q!Esa'* J III 136.33).

Instead of "to be sick" they say "to lie abed" (*qE'lgwil*).

Misfortune is called "it goes wrong" (*ō'dzEg·ila* C II 16.13) ; a widow "the one who spoils good luck" (*aă'msila* R 604.27).

Many metaphorical expressions and actions are used on ceremonial occasions. To invite to a feast is called simply "to walk" (*qā'sa* C III 120.16) and the messenger is "the one who serves as walker" (*qā'sElg·Es* C III 120.19). It is not customary to follow an invitation at once, and the messengers go a second and third time to call. This is termed "to (go) around again" (*ē'tseᵉsta* C III 126.26) and the messengers "those who serve (going) around again" (*ētseᵉstElg·Es* C III 128.8). Then the guests come in, except the principal one for whose sake the ceremonial act is performed. The messengers go a last time "to look for a face" (*dā'doqwEm* R 752.37). This last term is used only in the sacred winter ceremonial (R 752.41). A single invitation is also called "to walk around" (*qā'tseᵉsta* C III 136.23).

Speeches are called "breath" (*haseᵉ* C III 182.1) of the speaker. A good speech has "a sweet taste" (*ē'x·p!a* C III 182.9). A speech is called "equal in weight" (*gwa'ᵉyokᵘ* J III 449.26) to another one.

The speech after a meal "pushes it down into the stomach" (*Lā'gwEns* R 791.76). And the words of the speech "strike" (*sEpa'* C III 182.15) the guests, as a spear strikes the game or as the rays of the sun strike the earth. A messenger who invites the tribe standing in the doorway of the house reports that "our words have gone out of the house" (*laᵉmē' lā'g·aᵉElsEnts wā'ldEma* C III 220.24). The words of the host's speaker addressed to his guests "go to the floor of the house" (*lā'g·aᵉlil* R 789.24). The speaker "vomits" (*hō'qwa* J III 449.1) all he has in his mind.

Instead of "to sing" the metaphoric expression "the breath rises" (*hasō'stâ* C III 183.3) or "it goes rising" (*lā'g·ustâ* C III 176.23) is used. Singers and messengers "tell the world" (*nē'laxa ᵉnā'la* R 789.22) what is being done. In the sacred winter ceremonial a special messenger is sent out of the house to tell the world that the ceremonial is beginning. The words of the song are its "place of walking" (qā'yas C III 136.21).

Guests who arrive by canoe are invited to come in to "warm themselves" (tE'lts!a C III 142.21) or "to warm their faces in the house" (ts!E'lqwEmg·aᵉlił C III 160.17). In a formal feast two courses are given and the second one is called "doing the right thing afterwards" (hē'leg·End C III 108.21).

The guests of a person as well as wealth that he acquires are called his "salmon" (k·!ō'tEla C III 172.13, mEyâ' C III 174.1); a great many guests "a school of salmon" (wayō'qwax·iweᵉ C III 172.14), and the house or village of the host his "salmon weir" (Ḷā'wayu C III 152.14) into which he hauls (wa't!ed C III 152.17) his guests.

The valuable copper plates (L!ā'qwa), the symbols of wealth, particularly, are called "salmon," and the host expecting a copper plate called "War", says in regard to it, "heavy is this salmon caught in my weir here" (gwE'nt!aᵉEmg·ada k·!ō'tElak· mä'ts!âsg·En Ḷā'wayukᵘ C III 152.21). The invitation to a potlatch in which host and guests rival in prodigality is likened to war. The messengers who carry the invitation are called warriors (wī'na C III 164.20) and the arriving guests sing war songs (wī'nak·!ala C III 172.1). The copper plate is also called the "citadelle" of the chief. The orator says: "Behold, now we stand on War (name of a copper plate), the citadelle of our chief" (laᵉE'mxōḷEnts g·ēxtodEx wīnäxa x̣wEsEläsEn g·ī'gEmaᵉyex C III 146.26). To give a present in return for services rendered is called "making a soft layer" (tE'lqwa C III 140.22), and the blankets that are given away "are danced on" (yū'dzEᵉwesoᵉ C III 174.22) by the host's daughter who performs a ceremonial dance on that occasion. The giving away of blankets on a small scale is called "spreading out" (LEpa' C III 124.1).

The large amount of property given away "stands a mountain of blankets, reaching through the world" (Ḷaxᵘsâlis lā'xEnts ᵉnālag·ada nEg·ä'k· p!E'lxElasgEm J III 455.2).

The chief is designated by laudatory terms. He is the "post of our world" (qE'ldEmsEnts ᵉnā'lax J III 449.30), "the only long one standing in the world" (ᵉnE'mts!aqe lā'xwa ᵉnā'lax J III 449.29), "great mountains standing on edge" (k·!ō'xk!egwidze naE'ng·adze R 1284.40) "an overhanging cliff" (k·!ē'k·!EsLEn J III 449.31, Lā'qwanux̣ᵘdze M 669.8), "the one to whom no one can climb up" (hē wīyag·Elidze M 668.1, wits!eg·ustoᵉ J III 449.31), "loaded canoe" (mō'gwEmeᵉ

M 668.5), "the (cedar) that canont be spanned" (*wawe^εstalax^udze* C III 196.8), "the thick root of the tribe" (*ʟEgwā'nEwe^ε* R 1290.10), "the one farthest ahead" (*k·!ē's^εoyak·Elis* R 1285.6), the *Dzōnoq!wa* (a fabulous being which is much feared J III 455.18). He is called "the head" (*x·ōms* C III 108.26), his speaker "the mouth (piece)" (*sEms* C III 160.30). Of the death of one chief it is said "the moon went down in the waters" (*k·!ō'gwEnsâlag·iʟa^εyaxa* *^εmEkŭlak·as^εox^udä* R 1292.2). Those who are the first to receive presents are the "eagles" (*kwēk^u*) who, in the potlatch, stand outside of the recognized divisions of the tribe and take precedence of them.

The chief's eldest daughter says, "copper is my seat in the house" (*ʟ!ā'qwag·En k!wadzâlil* R 1315.2).

Of the Kwakiutl it is said, that "like a great, high mountain they have a steep (high) face" (*g·ada* *^εnEmā'x·EsEk·* *ʟō^ε* *ē'k·agEm* *^εwā'las* *nEg·ä'* J III 455.16).

In speaking of rival chiefs derogatory terms are used. They are called "little sparrows" (*ts!E'sqwanaō'^ε* C III 122.9), "little flies" (*gag·adē'-namE^εnē'x^u* C III 128.24), "little horseflies" (*sā'dEk!wamEnē'x^u* C III 128.27), "little mosquitoes" (*ʟ!ē'sʟEnamE^εnē'x^u* C III 128.30), "old broken (coppers)" (*lElaxs^εamot* M 667.18, *q!Elq!atisot* M 667.18), "spider woman" (*yā'yaqet!eneğa* M 669.21), "old dog" (*^εwayoł* M 670.7), leavings of food (*ha'^εyamota* R 1284.25).

Rivals are ridiculed by saying that they "decorate" (*ămō'sa* M 670.1) their speeches by claiming privileges that do not belong to them. Their tongues loll (*E'l^εElqwEla* R 1288.8) ; they are losing their tails (like old salmon) (*xwāk·!axsdala* R 1291.11) ; (the chief) throws them across his back (like the wolf a deer) (*xwē'leg·End* R 1293.12). When they try to rival the chief, "they talk through their noses" (*x·E'ndzasâla* R 1280.33). They "walk zigzag" (*wailē'qa* M 670.1) ; of one rival it is said that "he holds a canoe in his throat" (*xwā'gwiʟ!Exâla* M 670.2), and that "he holds giving-away-canoes in his throat" (*sag·iʟ!Exâla* M 670.2), meaning that he promises to give away a canoe, but that he will never do it. The guests "cry like the bluejay" (*kwā'^εyala* R 1282.65). One who has never given a great feast (a "grease" feast in which fish oil is poured on the fire) is called "dry face" (*lE'mlEm-xwEmlis* M 670.4), or "mouldy face" (*qwēqwExlEmlis* M 670.4). Of one who is called an old dog it is said that he "spreads his legs before (the host)" (*yāqaʟalg·iwe^ε* M 670.7).

A young woman whose father has not repaid his son-in-law adequately is called "slim wristed" ($hē'wägEmx·ts!ane^ε$), because her wrist is not compressed by the wearing of bracelets.

Chiefs praise their own strength. They "burn to ashes (the tribes)" ($q!wā'lo^εso$ J III 483.1), they "make the world smoky (by the fire of their feasts)" ($kwa'nesEla'mas$ R 669.18), the great one whose smoke of the fire is meeting ($kwā'kwExâladze$ R 669.19) ; he makes people run away ($q!wE'mx·^εidamas$ J III 483.2). When a guest outdoes the host in prodigality his "fire is extinguished" ($k·!E'lx·^εideda lEgwi'l$ R 774.28) ; he has chiefs as his servants ($ā'łanok^u$ J III 482.16) or as his speakers ($a^εyE'lgwad$ J III 482.16).

A warrior says, "I am the double-headed serpent in my world" ($yEn sī'sEyuL laxg·En ^εnā'lak·$). Warriors are called "hellebore" ($ăx^usō'le$ R 1311.2), a term also applied to people of violent character. Warriors say, "for we are the great thunderbirds and we avenge (bite) our late ancestors" ($yE'ntsaxg·Ents ^εwā'lasEk· kwE'nkwEnxwElig·a^εya qEnts q!Es^εē'de qaE'nts wiwompdäEnts$ J III 468) ; "we shall soar and grasp with our talons the Bella Coola" [1] ($q!ā'nex·^εidEL qEnts lē'LEns xap!ē'dEł lax BE'lxwElax·de$ J III 468.11). The warriors say that they are no longer men, "we are now killerwhales" ($lEnts la maE'mx^εenox^u la$ J III 470.18. Men killed in war are "eaten" ($hă'mk·!ăes$ J III 469.29) by the enemy, and when they are avenged they say, "our late tribe fellows have been vomited up (by the enemy)" ($hō'x^εwitsEnts g·ō'kulotaEnts$ J III 469.30).

Many metaphorical expressions are used in connection with the purchase of copper plates and with marriage ceremonies. These are accompanied by symbolic acts. In the purchase of a copper the preliminary payment is called "the pillow" ($qē'nulił$) ; the "soft layer" ($tE'lqwa$) ; the harpoon line ($dō'x^usEm$) by which the copper is held like a seal ; or "what results in the lifting (of the copper) from the floor" ($dā'g·ElelEm$). The purchase itself is called "pushing" ($Lā'sa$), viz., pushing the purchase money under the name of the purchaser whose rank is raised by the purchase. To offer a copper plate "which groans in the house" ($gwāLElag·Elił$ J III 448.32) for sale is called to let it "lie dead by the side of the fire" ($yā'gwEnwa^εlis$ J III 448.32). The purchaser must "take it up from the floor" ($dā'g·Elił$ C III 282.4).

The knife used for cutting a copper plate that is to be broken is called "crazy edged" ($nā'nulx·ä$ C III 216.25), and the copper is "killed" ($hă'łxwa$, a word belonging to the Bella Bella dialect C III 218.4).

---

[1] An enemy tribe.

For marrying they use the term "walking into the house" (*qa'dzeL* C III 238.26); the blankets paid to the bride's father are "what results in a marriage" (*qā'dzeɭEm* C III 242.11, or "the means of marrying" (*qǎ'dzeɭayu* C III 248.8). The word *qā'dzeL* means that the property given to the bride's father walks into his house.

Marriages between the eldest children of chiefs are very elaborate. They are called "taking-care-of-the great-bringing-out-of-the-crests marriage" (*ᵉwā ᵉwalatsila k·!ēsᵉoɬt!End qā'dzeLa* C III 240.9), that means that the chiefs who act as messengers have to use their crests in proposing to the bride's father. A number of chiefs make the first proposal. They receive for this message from the bride's father each a blanket. This is rolled up and carried in arms like a child. They return carrying it to the groom's father and say in regard to it "it is great, we come carrying in our arms your future wife" (*g·āxdzeᵉmEnuᵉxᵘ q!ElElqālaxg·as gEnE'mɭg·os* C III 238.22). After the first proposal they go back "to shake (the bride) from the floor of the house" (*tEmsx·Eg·Eliɬ* C III 246.13). One chief after another gives a mimic representation of his family myth, which means "he tries to lift (the bride) from the floor" (*wā'wixEliᵉla* C III 250.4), or "to lift from the floor" (*wī'xEliɬ* J III 464.1), or "to handle a heavy weight" (*gwāgwEntseliɬ* J III 464.2). One of them, for instance, has the family myth according to which his ancestor was given the power to become a whaler. He appears carrying a whaling harpoon which he throws into the house, thus harpooning the bride whom he calls "a whale" (*gwEᵉyE'm* C III 252.13). By these performances they induce the bride to move on the floor (*qwEnēqwEliɬ* C III 252.20; *k!wēmg·Eliɬ* C III 256.19; *k·!aniᵉlälag·Eliɬ* C III 256.24; *k!wäg·Eliɬ ɭē'qwEliɬ* C III 264.30) and finally "to come right off the floor" (*hē'lq!Eg·Eliɬ* C III 260.7) and "to come to the door" (*g·āxstoliɬ* C III 268.13), and "to approach the door" (*ē'x·astoliɬ* C III 268.4). Finally she is "off the floor" (*Lā'g·Eliɬ* C III 272.19). Then blankets to be paid to the bride's father are given as "a means of calling (the bride)" (*Lē'ᵉlalayu* C III 272.30) and the girl comes out "dressed" (*q!wälEnkᵘ* C III 274.17) in (that is, carrying) a copper plate. The bride's father gives her blankets as "a tump line" (*ǎō'xɭäas* C III 276.16). These are distributed "to be used as belts" (*wEsē'x·ᵉid* C III 278.28) by the groom's tribe.

A year or more after the marriage the bride's father repays the property received. This is called *qotē'x·a*, a word that in the Bella Bella dialect signifies "to dress." He arrives symbolically in a canoe which is represented by a square of ceremonial box-covers. In it stands a copper plate "the mast" of the canoe (*Ḷāk·Eᵉyala* C III 280.10) ; blankets represent "the mat" (*ḷE'ᵉweᵉ* C III 294.16) on which the bride sits. The marriage is also called "to make war on the princesses" (*wī'nax k·!ē'sk·!edeła* J III 463.18). Other forms of marriage are called "to try to get a slave" (*q!ā'q!ak!wa* C III 280.4), "to take hold of the foot" (*dā'x·sidzEnd* C III 280.4) and "sham marriage" (*xwē'sa*). A union without formal marriage is called "sticking behind (like dogs)" (*k!wEt!Exsda'* R 1105.26), a child born of such a union, "obtained by sticking behind" (*k!wEt!Exsdā'nEm* R 1099.27).

In all purchases as well as in marriages, the blankets which are the standard of value are designated by what they represent. After the price has been paid, blankets are given as "boxes" to store the blankets, as "canoes" to carry them away ; or a canoe worth so and so many blankets is given as "a dress" for the recipient. The carrying strap for blankets ; the belt for travelling ; all these are represented by blankets. Split sticks represent canoes or the values of canoes measured in blankets that are given away (J III 457–458). Carpenters who are hired receive blankets to protect their hands (*tE'lxts!ane* C III 316.10).

In all speeches reference is made to the adherence to old customs. They "walk the road made by the creator of chiefs" (*qā'sa lax t!ExE'-läsa g·ī'gEmēg·ilä* R 790.62) ; they walk in "that what results as the groove of the world" (*xwE'lt!alidzEm* R 789.25). The chief says, "I follow the road made by my late ancestors" (*lEn nEgEłtEwē'x t!Ex·ī'laᵉ-yasEn wiwō'mpᵉwŭła* C III 124.22) ; or "what is laid down by our ancestors" (*k·!ā'taᵉyasEnts g·ā'lEmg·a'lisa* C III 146.10). Progress in social rank is "walking along on flat (blankets)" (*qä'dzo* C III 130.22), or "walking along" (*qäᵉna'kwEla* R 791.71). Customs are also called "the support of the tribe" (*qa'dad* C III 884.10).

In talking to children or to intimate friends, people use terms of self-effacement. The most frequently used term is "master" literally "the one who owns (me) as a slave" (*q!ā'gwid*) ; children are addressed as "the one who owns (me) as a dog" (*ᵉwā'dzid*). The grandfather calls himself "old dog" (*ᵉwa'yoł* R 1313.3). Parents also call themselves "slaves" (*q!ā'k·o* R 712.45) ; and they call the children "treasures" (*ḷō'gweᵉ* R 712.44). The chief speaks of his wife as "receptacle of wisdom" (*nâ'gats!e* C III 158.19), because she manages the property needed for potlatches.

A name given during a potlatch is fastened (*E'lg·ăaLElod* C III 130.5) to its owner. A person who is ashamed "wipes off (the shame) from his body" (*dēg·it* C III 132.19) by giving a potlatch.

Love is called "sickness, pain" (*ts!Ex·Ela* R 1309.2). The lover wishes to be the bed (*ts!ā'g·it* R 1310.15) or pillow (*qē'not* R 1310.16) of the beloved. To be downcast is called "to be withered" (*xwE'lsa* R 186.2) ; to ridicule "to nettle" (*dzE'nk·a* JX 67.6).

CULTURE

THE AIMS OF ANTHROPOLOGICAL RESEARCH [1]

THE science of anthropology has grown up from many distinct beginnings. At an early time men were interested in foreign countries and in the lives of their inhabitants. Herodotus reported to the Greeks what he had seen in many lands. Caesar and Tacitus wrote on the customs of the Gauls and Germans. In the middle ages Marco Polo, the Venetian, and Ibn Batuta, the Arab, told of the strange peoples of the Far East and of Africa. Later on, Cook's journeys excited the interest of the world. From these reports arose gradually a desire to find a general significance in the multifarious ways of living of strange peoples. In the eighteenth century Rousseau, Schiller and Herder tried to form, out of the reports of travelers, a picture of the history of mankind. More solid attempts were made about the middle of the nineteenth century, when the comprehensive works of Klemm and Waitz were written.

Biologists directed their studies towards an understanding of the varieties of human forms. Linnaeus, Blumenbach, Camper are a few of the names that stand out as early investigators of these problems, which received an entirely new stimulus when Darwin's views of the instability of species were accepted by the scientific world. The problem of man's origin and his place in the animal kingdom became the prime subject of interest. Darwin, Huxley and Haeckel are outstanding names representing this period. Still more recently the intensive study of heredity and mutation has given a new aspect to inquiries into the origin and meaning of race.

The development of psychology led to new problems presented by the diversity of the racial and social groups of mankind. The question of mental characteristics of races, which at an earlier period had become a subject of discussion with entirely inadequate methods—largely stimulated by the desire to justify slavery—was taken up again with the more

[1] Address of the president of the American Association for the Advancement of Science, Atlantic City, December, 1932. *Science* N.S., vol. 76 (1932), pp. 605–613.

243

refined technique of experimental psychology, and particular attention is now being paid to the mental status of primitive man and of mental life under pathological conditions. The methods of comparative psychology are not confined to man alone, and much light may be thrown on human behavior by the study of animals. The attempt is being made to develop a genetic psychology.

Finally sociology, economics, political science, history and philosophy have found it worth while to study conditions found among alien peoples in order to throw light upon our modern social processes.

With this bewildering variety of approaches, all dealing with racial and cultural forms, it seems necessary to formulate clearly what the objects are that we try to attain by the study of mankind.

We may perhaps best define our objective as the attempt to understand the steps by which man has come to be what he is, biologically, psychologically and culturally. Thus it appears at once that our material must necessarily be historical material, historical in the widest sense of the term. It must include the history of the development of the bodily form of man, his physiological functions, mind and culture. We need a knowledge of the chronological succession of forms and an insight into the conditions under which changes occur. Without such data progress seems impossible and the fundamental question arises as to how such data can be obtained.

Ever since Lamarck's and Darwin's time the biologist has been struggling with this problem. The complete paleontological record of the development of plant and animal forms is not available. Even in favorable cases gaps remain that cannot be filled on account of the lack of intermediate forms. For this reason indirect proofs must be resorted to. These are based partly on similarities revealed by morphology and interpreted as proof of genetic relationship, partly on morphological traits observed in prenatal life, which suggest relationship between forms that as adults appear quite distinct.

Caution in the use of morphological similarities is required, because there are cases in which similar forms develop in genetically unrelated groups, as in the marsupials of Australia, which show remarkable parallelism with higher mammal forms, or in the white-haired forms of the Arctic and of high altitudes, which occur independently in many genera and species, or in the blondness and other abnormal hair forms of domesticated mammals which develop regardless of their genetic relations.

As long as the paleontological record is incomplete we have no way of reconstructing the history of animals and plants except through morphology and embryology.

This is equally true of man, and for this reason the eager search for early human and prehuman forms is justified. The finds of the remains of the Pithecanthropus in Java, the Sinanthropus in China, of the Heidelberg jaw and of the later types of the glacial period are so many steps advancing our knowledge. It requires the labors of the enthusiastic explorer to furnish us with the material that must be interpreted by careful morphological study. The material available at the present time is sadly fragmentary. It is encouraging to see that it is richest in all those countries in which the interest in the paleontology of man has been keenest, so that we may hope that with the increase of interest in new fields the material on which to build the evolutionary history of man will be considerably increased.

It is natural that with our more extended knowledge of the evolutionary history of the higher mammals certain points stand out that will direct the labors of the explorer. Thus on the basis of our knowledge of the distribution of ape forms, nobody would search for the ancestors of humanity in the New World, although the question when the earliest migration of man into America took place is still one of the problems that is prominent in researches on the paleontology of the glacial period of America.

The skeletal material of later periods is more abundant. Still it is difficult to establish definitely the relation of early skeletal remains and of modern races, because many of their most characteristic traits are found in the soft parts of the body that have not been preserved. Furthermore, the transitions from one race to another are so gradual that only extreme forms can be determined with any degree of definiteness.

On account of the absence of material elucidating the history of modern races, it is not surprising that for many years anthropologists have endeavored to classify races, basing their attempts on a variety of traits, and that only too often the results of these classifications have been assumed as expressions of genetic relationship, while actually they have no more than a descriptive value, unless their genetic significance can be established. If the same metric proportions of the head recur in all races they cannot be a significant criterion of fundamental racial types, although they may be valuable indications of the development of local strains within a racial group. If, on the other hand, a particular hair form is a trait well-nigh universal in extensive groups of mankind, and one that does not recur in other groups, it will in all probability represent an ancient hereditary racial trait, the more so, if it occurs in a geographically continuous area. It is the task of the anthropologist to search out these outstanding traits and to remember that the exact measurement of features which are not exclusive racial characteristics will not answer the problems of the evolution of fundamental types, but can be taken only as an indication of independent, special modifications of late origin within the large racial groups.

From this point of view the general question of the occurrence of parallel development in genetically unrelated lines assumes particular importance. We have sufficient evidence to show that morphological form is subject to environmental influences that in some cases will have similar effects upon unrelated forms. Even the most skeptical would admit this for size of the body.

Changes due to environment that occur under our eyes, such as minute changes in size and proportion of the body, are probably not hereditary, but merely expressions of the reaction of the body to external conditions and subject to new adjustments under new conditions.

However, one series of changes, brought about by external conditions, are undoubtedly hereditary. I mean those developing in domestication. No matter whether they are due to survival of aberrant forms or directly conditioned by domestication, they are found in similar ways in all domesticated animals, and because man possesses all these characteristics he proves to be a domesticated form. Eduard Hahn was probably the first to point out that man lives like a domesticated animal; the morphological points were emphasized by Eugen Fischer, B. Klatt and myself.

The solution of the problem of the origin of races must rest not only on classificatory studies and on those of the development of parallel forms, but also on the consideration of the distribution of races, of early migrations and consequent intermingling or isolation.

On account of the occurrence of independent development of parallel forms it seems important to know the range of variant local forms that originate in each race, and it might seem plausible that races producing local variants of similar types are closely related. Thus Mongoloids and Europeans occasionally produce similar forms in regions so wide apart that it would be difficult to interpret them as effects of intermingling.

The biological foundations of conclusions based on this type of evidence are, to a great extent, necessarily speculative. Scientific proof would require a knowledge of the earliest movements of mankind, an intimate acquaintance with the conditions under which racial types may throw of variants and the character and extent of variations that may develop as mutants.

The solution of these problems must extend beyond morphological description of the race as a whole. Since we are dealing to a great extent with forms determined by heredity, it seems indispensable to found the study of the race as a whole on that of the component genetic lines and of their variants, and on inquiries into the influence of environment and selection upon bodily form and function. The race must be studied not as a whole but in its genotypical lines as developing under varying conditions.

In the study of racial forms we are too much inclined to consider the importance of races according to the number of their representatives. This is obviously an error, for the important phenomenon is the occurrence of stable morphological types, not the number of individuals representing each. The numerical strength of races has changed enormously in historic times, and it would be quite erroneous to attribute an undue importance to the White race or to the East Asiatics, merely because they have outgrown in numbers all other racial types. Still, in descriptive classifications the local types of a large race are given undue prominence over the less striking subdivisions of lesser groups. As an example, I might mention Huxley's divisions of the White race as against his divisions of other races.

We are interested not only in the bodily form of races but equally in the functioning of the body, physiologically as well as mentally. The problems presented by this class of phenomena present particular difficulties on account of the adjustability of function to external demands, so that it is an exceedingly precarious task to distinguish between what is determined by the biological make-up of the body and what depends upon external conditions. Observations made on masses of individuals in different localities may be explained equally well by the assumption of hereditary racial characteristics and by that of changes due to environmental influences. A mere description of these phenomena will never lead to a result. Different types, areas, social strata and cultures exhibit marked differences in physiological and mental function. A dogmatic assertion that racial type alone is responsible for these differences is a pseudo-science. An adequate treatment requires a weighing of the diverse factors.

Investigators are easily misled by the fact that the hereditary, biologically determined endowment of an individual is intimately associated with the functioning of his body. This appears most clearly in cases of bodily deficiency or of unusually favorable bodily development. It is quite a different matter to extend this observation over whole populations or racial groups in which are represented a great variety of hereditary lines and individuals, for the many forms of bodily make-up found in each group allow a great variety of functioning. Hereditary characteristics are pronounced in genetic lines, but a population—or to use the technical term, a phenotype—is not a genetic line and the great variety of genotypes within a race forbids the application of results obtained from a single hereditary line to a whole population in which the diversity of the constituent lines is bound to equalize the distribution of diverse genetic types in the populations considered. I have spoken so often on this subject that you will permit me to pass on to other questions.

While paleontological evidence may give us a clue to the evolution of human forms, only the most superficial evidence can be obtained for the development of function. A little may be inferred from size and form of the brain cavity and that of the jaw, in so far as it indicates the possibility of articulate speech. We may obtain some information on the development of erect posture, but the physiological processes that occurred in past generations are not accessible to observation. All the conclusions that we may arrive at are based on very indirect evidence.

The mental life of man also can be studied experimentally only among living races. It is, however, possible to infer some of its aspects by what past generations have done. Historical data permit us to study the culture of past times, in a few localities, as in the eastern Mediterranean area, India, China as far back as a few thousand years—and a limited amount of information on the mental life of man may be obtained from these data. We may even go farther back and extend our studies over the early remains of human activities. Objects of varied character, made by man and belonging to periods as early as the Quaternary, have been found in great quantities, and their study reveals at least certain aspects of what man has been able to do during these times.

The data of prehistoric archeology reveal with progress of time a decided branching out of human activities. While from earliest periods nothing remains but a few simple stone implements, we see an increasing differentiation of form of implements used by man. During the Quaternary the use of fire had been discovered, artistic work of high esthetic value had been achieved, and painted records of human activities had been made. Soon after the beginning of the recent geological period the beginnings of agriculture appear and the products of human labor take on new forms at a rapidly accelerating rate. While in early Quaternary times we do not observe any change for thousands of years, so that the observer might imagine that the products of human hands were made according to an innate instinct, like the cells of a beehive, the rapidity of change becomes the greater the nearer we approach our time, and at an early period we recognize that the arts of man cannot be instinctively determined, but are the cumulative result of experience.

It has often been claimed that the very primitiveness of human handiwork of early times proves organic mental inferiority. This argument is certainly not tenable, for we find in modern times isolated tribes living in a way that may very well be paralleled with early conditions. A comparison of the psychic life of these groups does not justify the belief that their industrial backwardness is due to a difference in the types of organism, for we find numbers of closely related races on the most diverse levels of cultural status. This is perhaps clearest in the Mongoloid race, where by the side of the civilized Chinese are found the most primitive Siberian tribes, or in the American group, where the highly developed Maya of Yucatan and the Aztecs of Mexico may be compared with the primitive tribes of our western plateaus. Evidently historic and prehistoric data give us little or no information on the biological development of the human mind.

How little the biological, organic determinants of culture can be inferred from the state of culture appears clearly if we try to realize how different the judgment of racial ability would have been at various periods of history. When Egypt flourished, northern Europe was in primitive conditions, comparable to those of American Indians or African Negroes, and yet northern Europe of our day has far outdistanced those people, who at an earlier time were the leaders of mankind. An attempt to find biological reasons for these changes would necessitate innumerable unprovable hypotheses regarding changes of the biological make-up of these peoples, hypotheses that could be invented only for the purpose of sustaining an unproved assumption.

A safer mode of approaching the problems at issue would seem to lie in the application of experimental psychology which might enable us to determine the psychophysical and also some of the mental characteristics of various races. As in the case of biological inquiry it would be equally necessary in this study to examine genotypical lines rather than populations, because so many different lines are contained in the mass.

A serious difficulty is presented by the dependence of the results of all psychophysical or mental tests upon the experiences of the individual who is the subject of the tests. His experiences are largely determined by the culture in which he lives. I am of the opinion that no method can be devised by which this all-important element is eliminated, but that we always obtain a result which is a mixed impression of culturally determined influences and of bodily build. For this reason I quite agree with those critical psychologists who acknowledge that for most mental phenomena we know only European psychology and no other.

In the few cases in which the influence of culture upon mental reaction of populations has been investigated it can be shown that culture is a much more important determinant than bodily build. I repeat that in individuals a somewhat close relation between mental reaction and bodily build may be found, which is all but absent in populations. Under these circumstances it is necessary to base the investigation of the mental life of man upon a study of the history of cultural forms and of the interrelations between individual mental life and culture.

This is the subject-matter of cultural anthropology. It is safe to say that the results of the extensive materials amassed during the last fifty years do not justify the assumption of any close relation between biological types and form of culture.

As in the realm of biology our inferences must be based on historical data, so it is in the investigation of cultures. Unless we know how the culture of each group of man came to be what it is, we cannot expect to reach any conclusions in regard to the conditions controlling the general history of culture.

The material needed for the reconstruction of the biological history of mankind is insufficient on account of the paucity of remains and the disappearance of all soft, perishable parts. The material for the reconstruction of culture is ever so much more fragmentary because the largest and most important aspects of culture leave no trace in the soil; language, social organization, religion—in short, everything that is not material—vanishes with the life of each generation. Historical information is available only for the most recent phases of cultural life and is confined to those peoples who had the art of writing and whose records we can read. Even this information is insufficient because many aspects of culture find no expression in literature. Is it then necessary to resign ourselves and to consider the problem as insoluble?

In biology we supplement the fragmentary paleontological record with data obtained from comparative anatomy and embryology. Perhaps an analogous procedure may enable us to unravel some of the threads of cultural history.

There is one fundamental difference between biological and cultural data which makes it impossible to transfer the methods of the one science to the other. Animal forms develop in divergent directions, and an intermingling of species that have once become distinct is negligible in the whole developmental history. It is otherwise in the domain of culture. Human thoughts, institutions, activities may spread from one social unit to another. As soon as two groups come into close contact their cultural traits will be disseminated from the one to the other.

Undoubtedly there are dynamic conditions that mould in similar forms certain aspects of the morphology of social units. Still we may expect that these will be overlaid by extraneous elements that have no organic relation to the dynamics of inner change.

This makes the reconstruction of cultural history easier than that of biological history, but it puts the most serious obstacles in the way of discovering the inner dynamic conditions of change. Before morphological comparison can be attempted the extraneous elements due to cultural diffusion must be eliminated.

When certain traits are diffused over a limited area and absent outside of it, it seems safe to assume that their distribution is due to diffusion. In some rare cases even the direction of diffusion may be determined. If Indian corn is derived from a Mexican wild form and is cultivated over the larger part of the two Americas we must conclude that its cultivation spread from Mexico north and south ; if the ancestors of African cattle are not found in Africa, they must have been introduced into that continent. In the majority of cases it is impossible to determine with certainty the direction of diffusion. It would be an error to assume that a cultural trait had its original home in the area in which it is now most strongly developed. Christianity did not originate in Europe or America. The manufacture of iron did not originate in America or northern Europe. It was the same in early times. We may be certain that the use of milk did not originate in Africa, nor the cultivation of wheat in Europe.

For these reasons it is well-nigh impossible to base a chronology of the development of specific cultures on the observed phenomena of diffusion. In a few cases it seems justifiable to infer from the worldwide diffusion of a particular cultural achievement its great antiquity. This is true when we can prove by archeological evidence its early occurrence. Thus, fire was used by man in early Quaternary times. At that period man was already widely scattered over the world and we may infer that either the use of fire was carried along by him when he migrated to new regions or that it spread rapidly from tribe to tribe and soon became the property of mankind. This method cannot be generalized, for we know of other inventions of ideas that spread with incredible rapidity over vast areas. An example is the spread of tobacco over Africa, as soon as it was introduced on the coast.

In smaller areas attempts at chronological reconstruction are much more uncertain. From a cultural center in which complex forms have developed, elements may radiate and impress themselves upon neighboring tribes, or the more complex forms may develop on an old, less differentiated basis. It is seldom possible to decide which one of these alternatives offers the correct interpretation.

Notwithstanding all these difficulties, the study of geographical distribution of cultural phenomena offers a means of determining their diffusion. The outstanding result of these studies has been the proof of the intricate interrelation of people of all parts of the world. Africa, Europe and the greater part of Asia appear to us as a cultural unit in which one area cannot be entirely separated from the rest. America appears as another unit, but even the New World and the Old are not entirely independent of each other, for lines of contact have been discovered that connect northeastern Asia and America.

As in biological investigations the problem of parallel independent development of homologous forms obscures that of genetic relationship, so it is in cultural inquiry. If it is possible that analogous anatomical forms develop independently in genetically distinct lines, it is ever so much more probable that analogous cultural forms develop independently. It may be admitted that it is exceedingly difficult to give absolutely indisputable proof of the independent origin of analogous cultural data. Nevertheless, the distribution of isolated customs in regions far apart hardly admits of the argument that they were transmitted from tribe to tribe and lost in intervening territory. It is well known that in our civilization current scientific ideas give rise to independent and synchronous inventions. In an analogous way primitive social life contains elements that lead to somewhat similar forms in many parts of the world. Thus the dependence of the infant upon the mother necessitates at least a temporary difference in the mode of life of the sexes and makes woman less movable than man. The long dependence of children on their elders leaves also an inevitable impress upon social form. Just what these effects will be depends upon circumstances. Their fundamental cause will be the same in every case.

The number of individuals in a social unit, the necessity or undesirability of communal action for obtaining the necessary food supply constitute dynamic conditions that are active everywhere and that are germs from which analogous cultural behavior may spring.

Besides these, there are individual cases of inventions or ideas in lands far apart that cannot be proved to be historically connected. The fork was used in Fiji and invented comparatively recently in Europe; the spear, projected by a thong wound spirally about the shaft, was used on the Admiralty Islands and in ancient Rome. In some cases the difference in time makes the theory of a transfer all but unthinkable. This is the case, for instance, with the domestication of mammals in Peru, the invention of bronze in Peru and Yucatan and that of the zero in Yucatan.

Some anthropologists assume that, if a number of cultural phenomena agree in regions far apart, these must be due to the presence of an exceedingly ancient substratum that has been preserved notwithstanding all the cultural changes that have occurred. This view is not admissible without proof that the phenomena in question remain stable not only for thousands of years, but even so far back that they have been carried by wandering hordes from Asia to the extreme southern end of South America. Notwithstanding the great tenacity of cultural traits, there is no proof that such extreme conservatism ever existed. The apparent stability of primitive types of culture is due to our lack of historical perspective. They change much more slowly than our modern civilization, but wherever archeological evidence is available we do find changes in time and space. A careful investigation shows that those features that are assumed as almost absolutely stable are constantly undergoing changes. Some details may remain for a long time, but the general complex of culture cannot be assumed to retain its character for a very long span of time. We see people who were agricultural become hunters, others change their mode of life in the opposite direction. People who had totemic organization give it up, while others take it over from their neighbors.

It is not a safe method to assume that all analogous cultural phenomena must be historically related. It is necessary to demand in every case proof of historical relation, which should be the more rigid the less evidence there is of actual recent or early contact.

In the attempt to reconstruct the history of modern races we are trying to discover the earlier forms preceding modern forms. An analogous attempt has been demanded of cultural history. To a limited extent it has succeeded. The history of inventions and the history of science show to us in course of time constant additions to the range of inventions, and a gradual increase of empirical knowledge. On this basis we might be inclined to look for a single line of development of culture, a thought that was pre-eminent in anthropological work of the end of the past century.

The fuller knowledge of to-day makes such a view untenable. Cultures differ like so many species, perhaps genera, of animals, and their common basis is lost forever. It seems impossible, if we disregard invention and knowledge, the two elements just referred to, to bring cultures into any kind of continuous series. Sometimes we find simple, sometimes complex, social organizations associated with crude inventions and knowledge. Moral behavior, except in so far as it is checked by increased understanding of social needs, does not seem to fall into any order.

It is evident that certain social conditions are incompatible. A hunting people, in which every family requires an extended territory to insure the needed food supply, cannot form large communities, although it may have intricate rules governing marriage. Life that requires constant moving about on foot is incompatible with the development of a large amount of personal property. Seasonal food supply requires a mode of life different from a regular, uninterrupted food supply.

The interdependence of cultural phenomena must be one of the objects of anthropological inquiry, for which material may be obtained through the study of existing societies.

Here we are compelled to consider culture as a whole, in all its manifestations, while in the study of diffusion and of parallel development the character and distribution of single traits are more commonly the objects of inquiry. Inventions, economic life, social structure, art, religion, morals are all interrelated. We ask in how far are they determined by environment, by the biological character of the people, by psychological conditions, by historical events or by general laws of interrelation.

It is obvious that we are dealing here with a different problem. This is most clearly seen in our use of language. Even the fullest knowledge of the history of language does not help us to understand how we use language and what influence language has upon our thought. It is the same in other phases of life. The dynamic reactions to cultural environment are not determined by its history, although they are a result of historical development. Historical data do give us certain clues that may not be found in the experience of a single generation. Still, the psychological problem must be studied in living societies.

It would be an error to claim, as some anthropologists do, that for this reason historical study is irrelevant. The two sides of our problem require equal attention, for we desire to know not only the dynamics of existing societies, but also how they came to be what they are. For an intelligent understanding of historical processes a knowledge of living processes is as necessary as the knowledge of life processes for the understanding of the evolution of life forms.

The dynamics of existing societies are one of the most hotly contested fields of anthropological theory. They may be looked at from two points of view, the one, the interrelations between various aspects of cultural form and between culture and natural environment; the other the interrelation between individual and society.

Biologists are liable to insist on a relation between bodily build and culture. We have seen that evidence for such an interrelation has never been established by proofs that will stand serious criticism. It may not be amiss to dwell here again on the difference between races and individuals. The hereditary make-up of an individual has a certain influence upon his mental behavior. Pathological cases are the clearest proof of this. On the other hand, every race contains so many individuals of different hereditary make-up that the average differences between races freed of elements determined by history cannot readily be ascertained, but appear as insignificant. It is more than doubtful whether differences free of these historic elements can ever be established.

Geographers try to derive all forms of human culture from the geographical environment in which man lives. Important though this may be, we have no evidence of a creative force of environment. All we know is that every culture is strongly influenced by its environment, that some elements of culture cannot develop in an unfavorable geographical setting, while others may be advanced. It is sufficient to see the fundamental differences of culture that thrive one after another in the same environment, to make us understand the limitations of environmental influences. The aborigines of Australia live in the same environment in which the White invaders live. The nature and location of Australia have remained the same during human history, but they have influenced different cultures. Environment can affect only an existing culture, and it is worth while to study its influence in detail. This has been clearly recognized by critical geographers, such as Hettner.

Economists believe that economic conditions control cultural forms. Economic determinism is proposed as against geographic determinism. Undoubtedly the interrelation between economics and other aspects of culture is much more immediate than that between geographical environment and culture. Still it is not possible to explain every feature of cultural life as determined by economic status. We do not see how art styles, the form of ritual or the special form of religious belief could possibly be derived from economic forces. On the contrary, we see that economics and the rest of culture interact as cause and effect, as effect and cause.

Every attempt to deduce cultural forms from a single cause is doomed to failure, for the various expressions of culture are closely interrelated and one cannot be altered without having an effect upon all the others. Culture is integrated. It is true that the degree of integration is not always the same. There are cultures which we might describe by a single term, that of modern democracies as individualistic-mechanical; or that of a Melanesian island as individualization by mutual distrust; or that of our Plains Indians as overvaluation of intertribal warfare. Such terms may be misleading, because they overemphasize certain features, still they indicate certain dominating attitudes.

Integration is not often so complete that all contradictory elements are eliminated. We rather find in the same culture curious breaks in the attitudes of different individuals, and, in the case of varying situations, even in the behavior of the same individual.

The lack of necessary correlations between various aspects of culture may be illustrated by the cultural significance of a truly scientific study of the heavenly bodies by the Babylonians, Maya and by Europeans during the Middle Ages. For us the necessary correlation of astronomical observations is with physical and chemical phenomena; for them the essential point was their astrological significance, i.e., their relation to the fate of man, an attitude based on the general historically conditioned culture of their times.

These brief remarks may be sufficient to indicate the complexity of the phenomena we are studying, and it seems justifiable to question whether any generalized conclusions may be expected that will be applicable everywhere and that will reduce the data of anthropology to a formula which may be applied to every case, explaining its past and predicting its future.

I believe that it would be idle to entertain such hopes. The phenomena of our science are so individualized, so exposed to outer accident that no set of laws could explain them. It is as in any other science dealing with the actual world surrounding us. For each individual case we can arrive at an understanding of its determination by inner and outer forces, but we cannot explain its individuality in the form of laws. The astronomer reduces the movement of stars to laws, but unless given an unexplainable original arrangement in space, he cannot account for their present location. The biologist may know all the laws of ontogenesis, but he cannot explain by their means the accidental forms they have taken in an individual species, much less those found in an individual.

Physical and biological laws differ in character on account of the complexity of the objects of their study. Biological laws can refer only to biological forms, as geological laws can refer only to the forms of geological formations. The more complex the phenomena, the more special will be the laws expressed by them.

Cultural phenomena are of such complexity that it seems to me doubtful whether valid cultural laws can be found. The causal conditions of cultural happenings lie always in the interaction between individual and society, and no classificatory study of societies will solve this problem. The morphological classification of societies may call to our attention many problems. It will not solve them. In every case it is reducible to the same source, namely, the interaction between individual and society.

It is true that some valid interrelations between general aspects of cultural life may be found, such as between density and size of the population constituting a community and industrial occupations; or solidarity and isolation of a small population and their conservatism. These are interesting as static descriptions of cultural facts. Dynamic processes also may be recognized, such as the tendency of customs to change their significance according to changes in culture. Their meaning can be understood only by a penetrating analysis of the human elements that enter into each case.

In short, the material of anthropology is such that it needs must be a historical science, one of the sciences the interest of which centers in the attempt to understand the individual phenomena rather than in the establishment of general laws which, on account of the complexity of the material, will be necessarily vague and, we might almost say, so self-evident that they are of little help to a real understanding.

The attempt has been made too often to formulate a genetic problem as defined by a term taken from our own civilization, either based on analogy with forms known to us or contrasted to those with which we are familiar. Thus concepts, like war, the idea of immortality, marriage regulations, have been considered as units and general conclusions have been derived from their forms and distributions. It should be recognized that the subordination of all such forms, under a category with which we are familiar on account of our own cultural experience, does not prove the historical or sociological unity of the phenomenon. The ideas of immortality differ so fundamentally in content and significance that they can hardly be treated as a unit and valid conclusions based on their occurrence cannot be drawn without detailed analysis.

A critical investigation rather shows that forms of thought and action which we are inclined to consider as based on human nature are not generally valid, but characteristic of our specific culture. If this were not so, we could not understand why certain aspects of mental life that are characteristic of the Old World should be entirely or almost entirely absent in aboriginal America. An example is the contrast between the fundamental idea of judicial procedure in Africa and America; the emphasis on oath and ordeal as parts of judicial procedure in the Old World, their absence in the New World.

The problems of the relation of the individual to his culture, to the society in which he lives have received too little attention. The standardized anthropological data that inform us of customary behavior, give no clue to the reaction of the individual to his culture, nor to an understanding of his influence upon it. Still, here lie the sources of a true interpretation of human behavior. It seems a vain effort to search for sociological laws disregarding what should be called social psychology, namely, the reaction of the individual to culture. They can be no more than empty formulas that can be imbued with life only by taking account of individual behavior in cultural settings.

Society embraces many individuals varying in mental character, partly on account of their biological make-up, partly due to the special social conditions under which they have grown up. Nevertheless, many of them react in similar ways, and there are numerous cases in which we can find a definite impress of culture upon the behavior of the great mass of individuals, expressed by the same mentality. Deviations from such a type result in abnormal social behavior and, although throwing light upon the iron hold of culture upon the average individual, are rather subject-matter for the study of individual psychology than of social psychology.

If we once grasp the meaning of foreign cultures in this manner, we shall also be able to see how many of our lines of behavior that we believe to be founded deep in human nature are actually expressions of our culture and subject to modification with changing culture. Not all our standards are categorically determined by our quality as human beings, but may change with changing circumstances. It is our task to discover among all the varieties of human behavior those that are common to all humanity. By a study of the universality and variety of cultures anthropology may help us to shape the future course of mankind.

SOME PROBLEMS OF METHODOLOGY IN THE
SOCIAL SCIENCES [1]

I INTEND to speak on some problems of methodology in the social sciences. You will permit me to confine myself to those aspects with which I have to deal as an anthropologist.

As Simmel justly remarks, the development of the social sciences is largely due to the general tendency of our times to stress the interrelations between the phenomena of nature, and also to the social stresses that have developed in our civilization. We have recognized that the individual can be understood only as part of the society to which he belongs, and that society can be understood only on the basis of the interrelations of the constituent individuals. In earlier times experimental psychology was based on the assumption that the individual exists *in vacuo,* that mental activities are based essentially on the organically determined functioning of the structure of the individual. This attitude presents the most striking contrast to the more modern view, which requires an understanding of the individual, even the youngest as reacting to its general, particularly its social, environment. The problems of the social sciences are thus easily defined. They relate to forms of reactions of individuals, singly and in groups, to outer stimuli, to their interactions among themselves, and to the social forms produced by these processes.

It is possible to isolate a number of apparently generally valid social tendencies and to study as well the forms in which they express themselves as their psychological basis. Thus co-ordination and subordination of human beings, solidarity of the social groups and antagonism against the outsider, imitation of foreign forms and resistance to outside influences may be studied. The results give rise to a representation which may take the form of a system of forms developed under these stresses, or of a social psychology in which the forms are analyzed on the basis of their psychological motivation.

[1] *The New Social Science,* edited by Leonard D. White (University of Chicago Press, 1930), pp. 84-98.

These attempts are based on the assumption of generally valid social tendencies. There is a question, however, that must be answered before this synthesis is attempted, namely, Which are the social tendencies that are general human characteristics? It is easy to be misled in this respect. Much of our social behavior is automatic. Some may be instinctive, that is, organically determined. Much more is based on conditioned responses, that is, determined by situations so persistently and early impressed upon us that we are no longer aware of the character of the behavior and also ordinarily unaware of the existence or possibility of a different behavior. Thus a critical examination of what is generally valid for all humanity and what is specifically valid for different cultural types comes to be a matter of great concern to students of society. This is one of the problems that induces us to lay particular stress upon the study of cultures that are historically as little as possible related to our own. Their study enables us to determine those tendencies that are common to all mankind and those belonging to specific human societies only.

Another vista opens if we ask ourselves whether the characteristics of human society are even more widely distributed and found also in the animal world. Relations of individuals or of groups of individuals may be looked at from three points of view; relations to the organic and inorganic outer world, relations among members of the same social group, and what, for lack of a better term, may be designated as subjectively conditioned relations. I mean by this term those attitudes that arise gradually by giving values and meanings to activities, as good or bad, right or wrong, beautiful or ugly, purposive or causally determined. Relations with the organic and inorganic outer world are established primarily by the obtaining of sustenance, protection against rigor of the climate, and geographical limitations of varied kinds. The relations of members among the same social group include the relation of sexes, habits of forming social groups and their forms. Obviously, these phases of human life are shared by animals. Their food requirements are biologically determined and adjusted to the geographical environment in which they live. Acquisition and storage of food are found among animals as well as in man. The need of protection against climate and enemies is also operative in animal society, and adjustment to these needs in the form of nests or dens is common. No less are the relations between members of social groups present in animal life, for animal societies of varied structure occur. It appears, therefore, that a considerable field of social phenomena does not by any means belong to man alone but is shared by the animal world, and the question must be asked, What traits are common to human and animal societies?

The wide gulf between the social behavior of animal and of man appears only in what we call subjectively conditioned relations. Even here the gulf is not absolute. Parental love, subordination of the individual to social needs, protection of individual or social property may be observed in the behavior of animals, and it does not seem possible to distinguish clearly between the psychological basis of animal and human behavior in regard to these traits. Even what we designate in human society as inventions, and enjoyment of beauty may not be entirely absent in animals.

If we say that animal behavior is largely instinctive, we mean that much of it is organically determined, not learned. Nevertheless, we do know that animals learn and certain patterns of their behavior are expressions of acquired adjustments.

The difference between human culture and animal behavior is based largely on the enormously increased number of learned adjustments, and these depend on what we have called subjectively conditioned relations. It is well to make it clear to ourselves that the objective appearance of the industries of man during the Paleolithic period gives the impression of stability through untold generations. We may infer from this that the subjectively determined attitudes were weak, that the relations to the outer world and the fixed form of social contact swayed life almost completely. The ever-increasing rapidity in the rate of change that prehistoric research and knowledge of human history teach us is an expression of the increasing importance of subjectively conditioned reactions. On account of the great variety of forms that have developed in the course of time under these stresses, the problem of what is generally human and what is characteristic of specific societies stands out as one of the greatest importance and one that requires close study.

We may observe that certain attitudes are universally human, but that in each society they take specific forms, or that even in some societies social pressure may be so strong that the general attitude may seem to be suppressed. A serious danger lies in the methodological error of conceiving the form as indissolubly tied to the attitude. An example is presented by modesty. Certain forms of modesty occur everywhere, but they differ enormously in character. The most frequent forms of modesty relate to behavior toward bodily functions, eating, excreting, and sexual acts. It is hardly possible at the present time to determine what is the generally human basis of modesty and in how far it is a learned characteristic. There is no doubt that specific forms are culturally acquired, but there remains a generally human residue that has not yet been adequately defined. While attempts have been made in this field to separate the specific cultural from the generally human, there are many other fields in which the specific cultural character of the phenomenon is not recognized with sufficient clarity. The method of research must be based on comparisons and analogies of the phenomena in question as they appear in separate cultures.

In these investigations we must guard against a particular danger. We may find objective similarities that give a deceptive impression of identity, while actually we may have been dealing with quite distinctive phenomena. An example of this kind is presented by the widely spread adolescence ceremonies, particularly of boys, which we are apt to associate with the disturbed mental state that we know as accompanying approaching maturity. There is little doubt in my mind that the rites have nothing to do with those mental attitudes that are familiar to us in our civilization. They are rather determined by the increasing participation of the maturing individual in tribal affairs, and that in the most varying ways. It seems quite probable that the origin of these rites must be accounted for by a great variety of social conditions. This also accounts for the great variations of age at which the rites take place, and which are not by any means always coincident with the period of approaching sexual maturity.

Attention has often been called to the danger inherent in the identification of social phenomena that we happen to classify under a single term. Goldenweiser's investigation of totemism is an example in point. The varieties of forms of maternal descent also show the possibility of the origin of analogous customs from diverse sources.

Thus the problem is often shifted from that of discovering the fundamental psychological causes of the most generalized form of behavior to another one, namely, to that of understanding why diverse psychological drives tend to develop forms that are objectively similar, or why similar forms are liable to be explained by a variety of psychic motivations.

The problems which I have treated here may seem to be rather those of social psychology and of sociology than of anthropology, but they can be solved only by the use of anthropological material.

I will turn to another question that concerns anthropology particularly, although it is not foreign to other social sciences. Sociology, if I understand its history aright, has developed through the growing recognition of the integration of culture. We have had economics, politics, pedagogy, and linguistics as individual branches of knowledge, but we had no scientific viewpoint that treats what is common to all of them, no way of determining the interaction of these varied aspects of culture. Anthropology is still confronted by a similar difficulty. Most anthropological literature gives us information on the economic life, inventions, social structure, religious beliefs, and art of certain tribal groups as though these were so many independent units that do not influence one another. Where fuller information is available we may learn of the historic growth of all these phases of social life, of their inner development, and of outer influences that have contributed to their growth in a particular culture.

Understanding of a foreign culture can be reached only by analysis, and we are compelled to take up its various aspects successively. Furthermore, each element contains clear traces of changes that it has undergone in time. These may be due to inner forces or to the influence of foreign cultures. The full analysis must necessarily include the phases that led to its present form. I do not intend to discuss here the methods by which a partial reconstruction can be made of the history of primitive cultures that belong to people without written records and without reliable oral tradition. I will merely mention that our principal approach has been through prehistoric archaeology, through the study of geographical distribution, and through methods analogous to those so successfully applied in the study of prehistory and history of European languages. As the last-named example shows, the analytic study of historic sequences in culture gives us first of all a history of each aspect separately: of language, of invention, economic life, social system, and religion.

This leaves us with little information regarding the interplay of all these aspects of primitive culture, although it is obvious that relations between them must exist. The unremitting demands made upon the Eskimo hunter occupy his time so fully that no possibility exists for prolonged periods given over to festive occasions; and the necessity of moving about without other than human means of transportation restricts the amount and bulk of household property of the Bushman and

Australian. A synthesis of the elements of culture must be undertaken that will give us a deeper insight into its nature.

Certain lines of inquiry have been instituted intended to explain the intricacies of cultural life as dependent upon one single set of conditions. Just as present great stress is being laid upon race as a determinant of culture. Since the ambitious attempt of Gobineau to explain national characteristics as due to racial descent, and since the recognition of the importance of heredity as determining the characteristics of each individual, the belief in hereditary, racial characteristics has gained many adherents. I do not believe that any convincing proof has ever been given of a direct relation between race and culture. It is true enough that human cultures and racial types are so distributed that every area has its own type and its own culture, but this does not prove that the one determines the form of the other. It is equally true that every geographical area has its own geological formation and its own flora and fauna, but the geological strata do not determine directly the species of plants and animals that live there. The error of the modern theories is due largely to a faulty extension of the concept of individual heredity to that of racial heredity. Heredity acts only in lines of direct descent. There is no unity of descent in any of the existing races, and we have no right to assume that the mental characteristics of a few selected family lines are shared by all the members of a race. On the contrary, all large races are so variable and the functional characteristics of the component hereditary lines are so diverse that similar family lines may be found in all races, particularly in all closely related local types, divisions of the same race. Hereditary characteristics when *socially* significant *have* a cultural value as in all cases of race discrimination or in those cultural conditions in which a specially gifted line is given the opportunity to impress itself upon the general culture. Any attempt to explain cultural forms on a purely biological basis is doomed to failure.

Another line of inquiry by which the attempt has been made to explain cultural forms is that of studying their relation to geographical conditions. Karl Ritter, Guyot, Ratzel, De la Blache, Jean Brunhes have devoted themselves to this problem. To the anthropologist the attempts that have been made must remain unsatisfactory. There is no doubt that the cultural life of man is in many and important ways limited by geographical conditions. The lack of vegetable products in the Arctic, the absence of stone in extended parts of South America, the dearth of water in the desert, to mention only a few outstanding facts, limit the activities of man in definite ways. On the other hand, it can also be shown that in a given culture the presence of favorable geographical conditions may serve to develop existing cultural traits. This is most clearly evident in modern civilization, in which the utilization of natural resources has been raised to a much higher degree of perfection than in primitive life; but even in our civilization we may see that geographical conditions become operative only when cultural conditions make their utilization important. The discovery of the use of coal, the possibility of reducing low grade ores, the discovery of applications for rare metals, the invention of paper made of wood pulp, all of these have modified our relations to our environment. No wonder that with the more limited uses to which primitive man puts the resources of nature and the greater diversity of his limited inventions, the determining influence of environment upon culture is less than it is in modern life. Environmental conditions may stimulate existing cultural activities, but they have no creative force. The most fertile soil will not create agriculture; navigable water will not create navigation; a plentiful supply of wood will not create wooden buildings; but where agriculture, the art of navigation and architecture exist they will be stimulated and in part moulded by geographical conditions. According to the cultural possessions of peoples, the same environment will influence culture in diverse ways. The western plains of our country influenced the Indian in one way before he had the horse, in another way after he had acquired the horse; and again different is their influence upon the life of the modern agricultural, pastoral, or industrial settler.

Thus it is fruitless to try to explain culture in geographical terms, for we do not know of any culture that has sprung from the immediate response to geographical conditions; we know only of cultures' influenced by geographical conditions. Undoubtedly the location of a people, whether placed in easy and many-sided contact with neighbors of varying culture, or whether placed in inaccessible areas, has an important bearing upon the development of its culture; for the response to foreign stimuli, the knowledge of new ways of acting and thinking are important elements in bringing about cultural change. However, the spatial relations give only the opportunity for contact; the processes are cultural and cannot be reduced to geographical terms.

Not very different are the attempts to interpret the development of human culture in terms of economics. The early attempts of Morgan to associate social organization and economic conditions have proved to be fallacious, but more recent attempts to interpret forms of culture as due to purely economic conditions have been equally unsuccessful. The interrelations between economic conditions and culture are undoubtedly closer than those between geographical conditions and culture. One reason is that economic conditions form part of cultural life. But they are not the only determinants, they are rather both determined and determinants. Nothing in economic life will make man an agriculturist or a herder. These arts develop from experience gained in the contact between man and plants and animals that in themselves are only indirectly related to economic conditions. Still less is it possible to explain intricate social forms, religious ideas, or art styles as brought forth by economic needs. Mental attitudes of a different order are determinants in these phases of social life. It is true, economic conditions determine the medium in which these attitudes come into play; their action may be furthered or hindered by favorable or unfavorable economic conditions; but their forms will not be so determined. When economic conditions give no leisure for industrial pursuits, artistic industry cannot flourish; a roving life enforced by economic needs and without means of transportation forbids the accumulation of bulky property. Conversely, leisure and stability of location favor the increase of industrial production and the development of artistic industry, but they do not create the particular kind of industry nor an artistic style.

It is our general experience that attempts to develop general laws of integration of culture do not lead to significant results. We might think that religion and art are closely associated, but comparative study merely shows that art forms may be used to express religious ideas; a result that is of no particular value. In some cases the religious significance of the art product will act as a stimulant toward the development of a higher style; in other cases it will induce slovenly execution, perhaps due to the short-lived usefulness of the object. In still other cases artistic representation of religious ideas may be forbidden. Nevertheless in every specific case the particular kind of integration of art and of religion may be recognized as an important social feature. Similar observations may be made in regard to social organization and industrial activities. There is no significant law that would cover all the phases of their relations. We have simple industries and complex organization, or diverse industries and simple organization; we have occupational divisions in tribes with diverse industries. All that can be claimed is that, with a certain amount of diversification and the necessity of production in large quantities, division of occupations becomes necessary. In short, the danger is ever present that the widest generalizations that may be obtained by the study of cultural integration are commonplaces.

This is due to the character of the social sciences, particularly of anthropology, as historical sciences. It is often claimed as a characteristic of the *Geisteswissenschaften* that the center of investigation must be the individual case, and that the analysis of the many threads that enter into the individual case are the primary aims of research. The existence of generally valid laws can be ascertained only when all the independent series of happenings show common characteristics, and the validity of the law is always confined to the group that shows these common characteristics. As a matter of fact, this is true not only of the *Geisteswissenschaften* but of any science that deals with specific forms. The astronomer's interest lies in the actual distribution, movements, and constitution of stars, not in generalized physical and chemical laws. The geologist is concerned with the strata and movements of the earth's crust, and may recognize certain laws that are tied up with the recurrence of similar forms. No matter how much he may generalize, his generalizations will cling to certain specific forms. It is the same with the social sciences. The analysis of the phenomena is our prime object. Generalizations will be the more significant the closer we adhere to definite forms. The attempts to reduce all social phenomena to a closed system of laws applicable to every society and explaining its structure and history do not seem a promising undertaking.

These considerations lead us to another methodological problem. The attempts to correlate various aspects of culture imply the necessity of a study of the dynamics of their interrelation. The material at our disposal is the analytic description of cultural forms. This and the practical difficulties of ethnological inquiry bring it about that most of the available material is over-standardized. It is given to us as a list of inventions, institutions, and ideas, but we learn little or nothing about the way in which the individual lives under these institutions and with these inventions and ideas, nor do we know how his activities affect the cultural groups of which he is a member. Information on these points is sorely needed, for the dynamics of social life can be understood only on the basis of the reaction of the individual to the culture in which he lives and of his influence upon society. Many aspects of the problem of change of culture can be interpreted only on this basis.

It should be clearly understood that historical analysis does not help us in the solution of these questions. We may know the history of a language in greatest detail—this knowledge does not explain how the speaker who uses the language in its present form, the only one known to him, will react to its use. Knowledge of the history of Mohammedanism in Africa and its influence in the Sudan does not add a particle to an understanding of the behavior of the Negro who lives in the present culture. The existing conditions may be objectively known to us in their whole historic setting. They affect the individual who lives under them, and he affects them only as they exist today. We may gain objectively a better understanding through a knowledge of their history, but this does not concern the individual who has absorbed all the elements of his culture. If we knew the whole biological, geographical, and cultural setting of a society completely, and if we understood in detail the ways of reacting of the members of the society and of society as a whole to these conditions, we should not need historical knowledge of the origin of the society to understand its behavior. The error of the earlier anthropology consisted in utilizing material of this kind, garnered without critical examination, for historical reconstructions. For these it has no value. An error of modern anthropology, as I see it, lies in the overemphasis on historical reconstruction, the importance of which should not be minimized, as against a penetrating study of the individual under the stress of the culture in which he lives.

THE LIMITATIONS OF THE COMPARATIVE
METHOD OF ANTHROPOLOGY [1]

MODERN anthropology has discovered the fact that human society has grown and developed everywhere in such a manner that its forms, its opinions and its actions have many fundamental traits in common. This momentous discovery implies that laws exist which govern the development of society, that they are applicable to our society as well as to those of past times and of distant lands; that their knowledge will be a means of understanding the causes furthering and retarding civilization; and that, guided by this knowledge, we may hope to govern our actions so that the greatest benefit to mankind will accrue from them. Since this discovery has been clearly formulated, anthropology has begun to receive that liberal share of public interest which was withheld from it as long as it was believed that it could do no more than record the curious customs and beliefs of strange peoples; or, at best, trace their relationships, and thus elucidate the early migrations of the races of man and the affinities of peoples.

While early investigators concentrated their attention upon this purely historical problem, the tide has now completely turned, so that there are even anthropologists who declare that such investigations belong to the historian, and that anthropological studies must be confined to researches on the laws that govern the growth of society.

A radical change of method has accompanied this change of views. While formerly identities or similarities of culture were considered incontrovertible proof of historical connection, or even of common origin, the new school declines to consider them as such, but interprets them as results of the uniform working of the human mind. The most pronounced adherent of this view in our country is Dr. D. G. Brinton, in Germany the majority of the followers of Bastian, who in this respect go much farther than Bastian himself. Others, while not denying the occurrence of historical connections, regard them as insignificant in re-

[1] Paper read at the meeting of the A. A. A. S. at Buffalo. *Science,* N.S., vol. 4 (1896), pp. 901–908.

sults and in theoretical importance as compared to the working of the uniform laws governing the human mind. This is the view of by far the greater number of living anthropologists.

This modern view is founded on the observation that the same ethnical phenomena occur among the most diverse peoples, or, as Bastian says, on the appalling monotony of the fundamental ideas of mankind all over the globe. The metaphysical notions of man may be reduced to a few types which are of universal distribution; the same is the case in regard to the forms of society, laws and inventions. Furthermore, the most intricate and apparently illogical ideas and the most curious and complex customs appear among a few tribes here and there in such a manner that the assumption of a common historical origin is excluded. When studying the culture of any one tribe, more or less close analoga of single traits of such a culture may be found among a great diversity of peoples. Instances of such analoga have been collected to a vast extent by Tylor, Spencer, Bastian, Andree, Post and many others, so that it is not necessary to give here any detailed proof of this fact. The idea of a future life; the one underlying shamanism; inventions such as fire and the bow; certain elementary features of grammatical structure—these will suggest the classes of phenomena to which I refer. It follows from these observations that when we find analogous single traits of culture among distant peoples, the presumption is not that there has been a common historical source, but that they have arisen independently.

But the discovery of these universal ideas is only the beginning of the work of the anthropologist. Scientific inquiry must answer two questions in regard to them: First, what is their origin? and second, how do they assert themselves in various cultures?

The second question is the easier one to answer. The ideas do not exist everywhere in identical form, but they vary. Sufficient material has been accumulated to show that the causes of these variations are either external, that is founded on environment—taking the term environment in its widest sense—or internal, that is founded on psychological conditions. The influence of external and internal factors upon elementary ideas embodies one group of laws governing the growth of culture. Therefore, our endeavors must be directed to showing how such factors modify elementary ideas.

The first method that suggests itself and which has been generally adopted by modern anthropologists is to isolate and classify causes by grouping the variants of certain ethnological phenomena according to external conditions under which the people live, among whom they are found, or to internal causes which influence their minds; or conversely, by grouping these variants according to their similarities. Then the correlated conditions of life may be found.

By this method we begin to recognize even now with imperfect knowledge of the facts what causes may have been at work in shaping the culture of mankind. Friedrich Ratzel and W J McGee have investigated the influence of geographical environment on a broader basis of facts than Ritter and Guyot were able to do at their time. Sociologists have made important studies on the effects of the density of population and of other simple social causes. Thus the influence of external factors upon the growth of society is becoming clearer.

The effects of psychical factors are also being studied in the same manner. Stoll has tried to isolate the phenomena of suggestion and of hypnotism and to study the effects of their presence in the cultures of various peoples. Inquiries into the mutual relations of tribes and peoples begin to show that certain cultural elements are easily assimilated while others are rejected, and the time-worn phrases of the imposition of culture by a more highly civilized people upon one of lower culture that has been conquered are giving way to more thorough views on the subject of exchange of cultural achievements. In all these investigations we are using sound, inductive methods in order to isolate the causes of observed phenomena.

The other question in regard to the universal ideas, namely that of their origin, is much more difficult to treat. Many attempts have been made to discover the causes which have led to the formation of ideas 'that develop with iron necessity wherever man lives.' This is the most difficult problem of anthropology and we may expect that it will baffle our attempts for a long time to come. Bastian denies that it is possible to discover the ultimate sources of inventions, ideas, customs and beliefs which are of universal occurrence. They may be indigenous, they may be imported, they may have arisen from a variety of sources, but they are there. The human mind is so formed that it invents them spontaneously or accepts them whenever they are offered to it. This is the much misunderstood elementary idea of Bastian.

To a certain extent the clear enunciation of the elementary idea gives us the psychological reason for its existence. To exemplify: the fact that the land of the shadows is so often placed in the west suggests the endeavor to localize it at the place where the sun and the stars vanish.

The mere statement that primitive man considers animals as gifted with all the qualities of man shows that the analogy between many of the qualities of animals and of human beings has led to the generalization that all the qualities of animals are human. In other cases the causes are not so self-evident. Thus the question why all languages distinguish between the self, the person addressed and the person spoken of, and why most languages do not carry out this sharp, logical distinction in the plural is difficult to answer. The principle when carried out consistently requires that in the plural there should be a distinction between the 'we' expressing the self and the person addressed and the 'we' expressing the self and the person spoken of, which distinction is found in comparatively few languages only. The lesser liability to misunderstandings in the plural explains this phenomenon partly but hardly adequately. Still more obscure is the psychological basis in other cases, for instance, in that of widely spread marriage customs. Proof of the difficulty of this problem is the multitude of hypotheses that have been invented to explain it in all its varied phases.

In treating this, the most difficult problem of anthropology, the point of view is taken that if an ethnological phenomenon has developed independently in a number of places its development has been the same everywhere; or, expressed in a different form, that the same ethnological phenomena are always due to the same causes. This leads to the still wider generalization that the sameness of ethnological phenomena found in diverse regions is proof that the human mind obeys the same laws everywhere. It is obvious that if different historical developments could lead to the same results, that then this generalization would not be tenable. Their existence would present to us an entirely different problem, namely, how it is that the developments of culture so often lead to the same results. It must, therefore, be clearly understood that anthropological research which compares similar cultural phenomena from various parts of the world, in order to discover the uniform history of their development, makes the assumption that the same ethnological phenomenon has everywhere developed in the same manner. Here lies the flaw in the argument of the new method, for no such proof can be given. Even the most cursory review shows that the same phenomena may develop in a multitude of ways.

I will give a few examples: Primitive tribes are almost universally divided into clans which have totems. There can be no doubt that this form of social organization has arisen independently over and over again. The conclusion is certainly justified that the psychical conditions of man favor the existence of a totemic organization of society, but it does not follow that totemic society has developed everywhere in the same manner. Dr. Washington Matthews believes that the totems of the Navaho have arisen by association of independent clans. Capt. Bourke assumes that similar occurrences gave origin to the Apache clans, and Dr. Fewkes has reached the same conclusion in regard to some of the Pueblo tribes. On the other hand, we have proof that clans may originate by division. I have shown that such events took place among the Indians of the North Pacific coast. Association of small tribes, on the one hand, and disintegration of increasing tribes, on the other, has led to results which appear identical to all intents and purposes.

To give another example: Recent investigations have shown that geometrical designs in primitive art have originated sometimes from naturalistic forms which were gradually conventionalized, sometimes from technical motives, that in still other cases they were geometrical by origin or that they were derived from symbols. From all these sources the same forms have developed. Out of designs representing diverse objects grew in course of time frets, meanders, crosses and the like. Therefore the frequent occurrence of these forms proves neither common origin nor that they have always developed according to the same psychical laws. On the contrary, the identical result may have been reached on four different lines of development and from an infinite number of starting points.

Another example may not be amiss: The use of masks is found among a great number of peoples. The origin of the custom of wearing masks is by no means clear in all cases, but a few typical forms of their use may easily be distinguished. They are used for deceiving spirits as to the identity of the wearer. The spirit of a disease who intends to attack the person does not recognize him when he wears a mask, and the mask serves in this manner as a protection. In other cases the mask represents a spirit which is personified by the wearer, who in this shape frightens away other hostile spirits. Still other masks are commemorative. The wearer personifies a deceased person whose memory is to be recalled. Masks are also used in theatrical performances illustrating mythological incidents.[1]

These few data suffice to show that the same ethnical phenomenon

---

[1] See Richard Andree. *Ethnographische Parallelen und Vergleiche.* Neue Folge (Leipzig, 1889), pp. 107 ff.

may develop from different sources. The simpler the observed fact, the more likely it is that it may have developed from one source here, from another there.

Thus we recognize that the fundamental assumption which is so often made by modern anthropologists cannot be accepted as true in all cases. We cannot say that the occurrence of the same phenomenon is always due to the same causes, and that thus it is proved that the human mind obeys the same laws everywhere. We must demand that the causes from which it developed be investigated and that comparisons be restricted to those phenomena which have been proved to be effects of the same causes. We must insist that this investigation be made a preliminary to all extended comparative studies. In researches on tribal societies those which have developed through association must be treated separately from those that have developed through disintegration. Geometrical designs which have arisen from conventionalized representations of natural objects must be treated separately from those that have arisen from technical motives. In short, before extended comparisons are made, the comparability of the material must be proved.

The comparative studies of which I am speaking here attempt to explain customs and ideas of remarkable similarity which are found here and there. But they pursue also the more ambitious scheme of discovering the laws and the history of the evolution of human society. The fact that many fundamental features of culture are universal, or at least occur in many isolated places, interpreted by the assumption that the same features must always have developed from the same causes, leads to the conclusion that there is one grand system according to which mankind has developed everywhere; that all the occurring variations are no more than minor details in this grand uniform evolution. It is clear that this theory has for its logical basis the assumption that the same phenomena are always due to the same causes. To give an instance: We find many types of structure of family. It can be proved that paternal families have often developed from maternal ones. Therefore, it is said, all paternal families have developed from maternal ones. If we do not make the assumption that the same phenomena have everywhere developed from the same causes, then we may just as well conclude that paternal families have in some cases arisen from maternal institutions; in other cases in other ways. To give another example: Many conceptions of the future life have evidently developed from dreams and hallucinations. Consequently, it is said, all notions of this character have had the same origin. This is also true only if no other causes could possibly lead to the same ideas.

We have seen that the facts do not favor at all the assumption of which we are speaking; that they much rather point in the opposite direction. Therefore we must also consider all the ingenious attempts at constructions of a grand system of the evolution of society as of very doubtful value, unless at the same time proof is given that the same phenomena must always have had the same origin. Until this is done, the presumption is always in favor of a variety of courses which historical growth may have taken.

It will be well to restate at this place one of the principal aims of anthropological research. We agreed that certain laws exist which govern the growth of human culture, and it is our endeavor to discover these laws. The object of our investigation is to find the *processes* by which certain stages of culture have developed. The customs and beliefs themselves are not the ultimate objects of research. We desire to learn the reasons why such customs and beliefs exist—in other words, we wish to discover the history of their development. The method which is at present most frequently applied in investigations of this character compares the variations under which the customs or beliefs occur and endeavors to find the common psychological cause that underlies all of them. I have stated that this method is open to a very fundamental objection.

We have another method, which in many respects is much safer. A detailed study of customs in their relation to the total culture of the tribe practicing them, in connection with an investigation of their geographical distribution among neighboring tribes, affords us almost always a means of determining with considerable accuracy the historical causes that led to the formation of the customs in question and to the psychological processes that were at work in their development. The results of inquiries conducted by this method may be three-fold. They may reveal the environmental conditions which have created or modified cultural elements; they may clear up psychological factors which are at work in shaping the culture; or they may bring before our eyes the effects that historical connections have had upon the growth of the culture.

We have in this method a means of reconstructing the history of the growth of ideas with much greater accuracy than the generalizations of the comparative method will permit. The latter must always proceed from a hypothetical mode of development, the probability of which may be weighed more or less accurately by means of observed data. But so far I have not yet seen any extended attempt to prove the correctness of a theory by testing it at the hand of developments with whose histories we are familiar. Forcing phenomena into the strait-jacket of a theory is opposed to the inductive process by which the actual relations of definite phenomena may be derived. The latter is no other than the much ridiculed historical method. Its way of proceeding is, of course, no longer that of former times when slight similarities of culture were considered proofs of relationships, but it duly recognizes the results obtained by comparative studies. Its application is based, first of all, on a well-defined, small geographical territory, and its comparisons are not extended beyond the limits of the cultural area that forms the basis of the study. Only when definite results have been obtained in regard to this area is it permissible to extend the horizon beyond its limits, but the greatest care must be taken not to proceed too hastily in this, as otherwise the fundamental proposition which I formulated before might be overlooked, viz: that when we find an analogy of single traits of culture among distant peoples the presumption is not that there has been a common historical source, but that they have arisen independently. Therefore the investigation must always demand continuity of distribution as one of the essential conditions for proving historical connection, and the assumption of lost connecting links must be applied most sparingly. This clear distinction between the new and the old historical methods is still often overlooked by the passionate defenders of the comparative method. They do not appreciate the difference between the indiscriminate use of similarities of culture for proving historical connection and the careful and slow detailed study of local phenomena. We no longer believe that the slight similarities between the cultures of Central America and of eastern Asia are sufficient and satisfactory proof of a historical connection. On the other hand, no unbiased observer will deny that there are very strong reasons for believing that a limited number of cultural elements found in Alaska and in Siberia have a common origin. The similarities of inventions, customs and beliefs, together with the continuity of their distribution through a limited area, are satisfactory proof of the correctness of this opinion. But it is not possible to extend this area safely beyond the limits of Columbia River in America and northern Japan in Asia. This method of anthropological research is represented in our country by

F. W. Putnam and Otis T. Mason; in England by E. B. Tylor; in Germany by Friedrich Ratzel and his followers.

It seems necessary to say a word here in regard to an objection to my arguments that will be raised by investigators who claim that similarity of geographical environment is a sufficient cause for similarity of culture, that is to say, that, for instance, the geographical conditions of the plains of the Mississippi basin necessitate the development of a certain culture. Horatio Hale would even go so far as to believe that similarity of form of language may be due to environmental causes. Environment has a certain limited effect upon the culture of man, but I do not see how the view that it is the primary moulder of culture can be supported by any facts. A hasty review of the tribes and peoples of our globe shows that people most diverse in culture and language live under the same geographical conditions, as proof of which may be mentioned the ethnography of East Africa or of New Guinea. In both these regions we find a great diversity of customs in small areas. But much more important is this: Not one observed fact can be brought forward in support of this hypothesis which cannot be much better explained by the well known facts of diffusion of culture; for archæology as well as ethnography teach us that intercourse between neighboring tribes has always existed and has extended over enormous areas. In the Old World the products of the Baltic found their way to the Mediterranean and the works of art of the eastern Mediterranean reached Sweden. In America the shells of the ocean found their way into the innermost parts of the continent and the obsidians of the West were carried to Ohio. Intermarriages, war, slavery, trade, have been so many sources of constant introduction of foreign cultural elements, so that an assimilation of culture must have taken place over continuous areas. Therefore, it seems to my mind that where among neighboring tribes an immediate influence of environment cannot be shown to exist, the presumption must always be in favor of historical connection. There has been a time of isolation during which the principal traits of diverse cultures developed according to the previous culture and the environment of the tribes. But the stages of culture representing this period have been covered with so much that is new and that is due to contact with foreign tribes that they cannot be discovered without the most painstaking isolation of foreign elements.

The immediate results of the historical method are, therefore, histories of the cultures of diverse tribes which have been the subject of study. I fully agree with those anthropologists who claim that this is not the ultimate aim of our science, because the general laws, although implied in such a description, cannot be clearly formulated nor their relative value appreciated without a thorough comparison of the manner in which they become manifest in different cultures. But I insist that the application of this method is the indispensable condition of sound progress. The psychological problem is contained in the results of the historical inquiry. When we have cleared up the history of a single culture and understand the effects of environment and the psychological conditions that are reflected in it we have made a step forward, as we can then investigate in how far the same causes or other causes were at work in the development of other cultures. Thus by comparing histories of growth general laws may be found. This method is much safer than the comparative method, as it is usually practiced, because instead of a hypothesis on the mode of development actual history forms the basis of our deductions.

The historical inquiry must be considered the critical test that science must require before admitting facts as evidence. By its means the comparability of the collected material must be tested, and uniformity of processes must be demanded as proof of comparability. Furthermore, when historical connection between two phenomena can be proved, they must not be admitted as independent evidence.

In a few cases the immediate results of this method are of so wide a scope that they rank with the best results that can be attained by comparative studies. Some phenomena have so immense a distribution that the discovery of their occurrence over very large continuous areas proves at once that certain phases of the culture in these areas have sprung from one source. Thus are illuminated vast portions of the early history of mankind. When Edward S. Morse showed that certain methods of arrow release are peculiar to whole continents it became clear at once that the common practice found over a vast area must have had a common origin. When the Polynesians employ a method of fire making consisting in rubbing a stick along a groove, while almost all other peoples use the fire drill, it shows their art of fire making has a single origin. When we notice that the ordeal is found all over Africa in certin peculiar forms, while in those parts of the inhabited world that are remote from Africa it is found not at all or in rudimentary forms only, it shows that the idea as practiced in Africa had one single origin.

The great and important function of the historical method of anthropology is thus seen to lie in its ability to discover the processes which in definite cases led to the development of certain customs. If anthropology desires to establish the laws governing the growth of culture it must not confine itself to comparing the results of the growth alone, but whenever such is feasible it must compare the processes of growth, and these can be discovered by means of studies of the cultures of small geographical areas.

Thus we have seen that the comparative method can hope to reach the results for which it is striving only when it bases its investigations on the historical results of researches which are devoted to laying clear the complex relations of each individual culture. The comparative method and the historical method, if I may use these terms, have been struggling for supremacy for a long time, but we may hope that each will soon find its appropriate place and function. The historical method has reached a sounder basis by abandoning the misleading principle of assuming connections wherever similarities of culture were found. The comparative method, notwithstanding all that has been said and written in its praise, has been remarkably barren of definite results, and I believe it will not become fruitful until we renounce the vain endeavor to construct a uniform systematic history of the evolution of culture, and until we begin to make our comparisons on the broader and sounder basis which I ventured to outline. Up to this time we have too much reveled in more or less ingenious vagaries. The solid work is still all before us.

THE METHODS OF ETHNOLOGY [1]

D URING the last ten years the methods of inquiry into the historical development of civilization have undergone remarkable changes. During the second half of the last century evolutionary thought held almost complete sway and investigators like Spencer, Morgan, Tylor, Lubbock, to mention only a few, were under the spell of the idea of a general, uniform evolution of culture in which all parts of mankind participated. The newer development goes back in part to the influence of Ratzel whose geographical training impressed him with the importance of diffusion and migration. The problem of diffusion was taken up in detail particularly in America, but was applied in a much wider sense by Foy and Graebner, and finally seized upon in a still wider application by Elliot Smith and Rivers, so that at the present time, at least among certain groups of investigators in England and also in Germany, ethnological research is based on the concept of migration and dissemination rather than upon that of evolution.

A critical study of these two directions of inquiry shows that each is founded on the application of one fundamental hypothesis. The evolutionary point of view presupposes that the course of historical changes in the cultural life of mankind follows definite laws which are applicable everywhere, and which bring it about that cultural development is, in its main lines, the same among all races and all peoples. This idea is clearly expressed by Tylor in the introductory pages of his classic work "Primitive Culture." As soon as we admit that the hypothesis of a uniform evolution has to be proved before it can be accepted, the whole structure loses its foundation. It is true that there are indications of parallelism of development in different parts of the world, and that similar customs are found in the most diverse and widely separated.parts of the globe. The occurrence of these similarities which are distributed so irregularly that they cannot readily be explained on the basis of diffusion, is one of the foundations of the evolutionary hypothesis, as it was the foundation of Bastian's psychologizing treatment of cultural

[1] *American Anthropologist*, N.S., vol. 22 (1920), pp. 311–322.

phenomena. On the other hand, it may be recognized that the hypothesis implies the thought that our modern Western European civilization represents the highest cultural development towards which all other more primitive cultural types tend, and that, therefore, retrospectively, we construct an orthogenetic development towards our own modern civilization. It is clear that if we admit that there may be different ultimate and co-existing types of civilization, the hypothesis of one single general line of development cannot be maintained.

Opposed to these assumptions is the modern tendency to deny the existence of a general evolutionary scheme which would represent the history of the cultural development the world over. The hypothesis that there are inner causes which bring about similarities of development in remote parts of the globe is rejected and in its place it is assumed that identity of development in two different parts of the globe must always be due to migration and diffusion. On this basis historical contact is demanded for enormously large areas. The theory demands a high degree of stability of cultural traits such as is apparently observed in many primitive tribes, and it is furthermore based on the supposed co-existence of a number of diverse and mutually independent cultural traits which reappear in the same combinations in distant parts of the world. In this sense, modern investigation takes up anew Gerland's theory of the persistence of a number of cultural traits which were developed in one center and carried by man in his migrations from continent to continent.

It seems to me that if the hypothetical foundations of these two extreme forms of ethnological research are broadly stated as I have tried to do here, it is at once clear that the correctness of the assumptions has not been demonstrated, but that arbitrarily the one or the other has been selected for the purpose of obtaining a consistent picture of cultural development. These methods are essentially forms of classification of the static phenomena of culture according to two distinct principles, and interpretations of these classifications as of historical significance, without, however, any attempt to prove that this interpretation is justifiable. To give an example : It is observed that in most parts of the world there are resemblances between decorative forms that are representative and others that are more or less geometrical. According to the evolutionary point of view, their development is explained by arranging the decorative forms in such order that the most representative forms are placed at the beginning, the others being so placed that they show a gradual transition from representative to purely conventional geometric forms.

This order is then interpreted as meaning that geometric designs originated from representative designs which gradually degenerated. This method has been pursued, for instance, by Putnam, Stolpe, Balfour, and Haddon, and by Verworn and, in his earlier writings, by von den Steinen. While I do not mean to deny that this development may have occurred, it would be rash to generalize and to claim that in every case the classification which has been made according to a definite principle represents an historical development. The order might as well be reversed and we might begin with a simple geometric element which, by the addition of new traits, might be developed into a representative design, and we might claim that this order represents an historical sequence. Both of these possibilities were considered by Holmes as early as 1885. Neither the one nor the other theory can be established without actual historical proof.

The opposite attitude, namely, origin through diffusion, is exhibited in Heinrich Schurtz's attempt to connect the decorative art of Northwest America with that of Melanesia. The simple fact that in these areas elements occur that may be interpreted as eyes, induced him to assume that both have a common origin, without allowing for the possibility that the pattern in the two areas—each of which shows highly distinctive characteristics—may have developed from independent sources. In this attempt Schurtz followed Ratzel who had already tried to establish connections between Melanesia and Northwest America on the basis of other cultural features.

While ethnographical research based on these two fundamental hypotheses seems to characterize the general tendency of European thought, a different method is at present pursued by the majority of American anthropologists. The difference between the two directions of study may perhaps best be summarized by the statement that American scholars are primarily interested in the dynamic phenomena of cultural change, and try to elucidate cultural history by the application of the results of their studies; and that they relegate the solution of the ultimate question of the relative importance of parallelism of cultural development in distant areas, as against worldwide diffusion, and stability of cultural traits over long periods to a future time when the actual conditions of cultural change are better known. The American ethnological methods are analogous to those of European, particularly of Scandinavian, archaeology, and of the researches into the prehistoric period of the eastern Mediterranean area.

It may seem to the distant observer that American students are engaged in a mass of detailed investigations without much bearing upon the solution of the ultimate problems of a philosophic history of human civilization. I think this interpretation of the American attitude would be unjust because the ultimate questions are as near to our hearts as they are to those of other scholars, only we do not hope to be able to solve an intricate historical problem by a formula.

First of all, the whole problem of cultural history appears to us as an historical problem. In order to understand history it is necessary to know not only how things are, but how they have come to be. In the domain of ethnology, where, for most parts of the world, no historical facts are available except those that may be revealed by archaeological study, all evidence of change can be inferred only by indirect methods. Their character is represented in the researches of students of comparative philology. The method is based on the comparison of static phenomena combined with the study of their distribution. What can be done by this method is well illustrated by Lowie's investigations of the military societies of the Plains Indians, or by the modern investigation of American mythology. It is, of course, true that we can never hope to obtain incontrovertible data relating to the chronological sequence of events, but certain general broad outlines can be ascertained with a high degree of probability, even of certainty.

As soon as these methods are applied, primitive society loses the appearance of absolute stability which is conveyed to the student who sees a certain people only at a certain given time. All cultural forms rather appear in a constant state of flux and subject to fundamental modifications.

It is intelligible why in our studies the problem of dissemination should take a prominent position. It is much easier to prove dissemination than to follow up developments due to inner forces, and the data for such a study are obtained with much greater difficulty. They may, however, be observed in every phenomenon of acculturation in which foreign elements are remodeled according to the patterns prevalent in their new environment, and they may be found in the peculiar local developments of widely spread ideas and activities. The reason why the study of inner development has not been taken up energetically, is not due to the fact that from a theoretical point of view it is unimportant, it is rather due to the inherent methodological difficulties. It may perhaps be recognized that in recent years attention has been drawn to this problem, as is manifested by the investigations on the processes of acculturation and of the interdependence of cultural activities which are attracting the attention of many investigators.

The further pursuit of these inquiries emphasizes the importance of a feature which is common to all historic phenomena. While in natural sciences we are accustomed to consider a given number of causes and to study their effects, in historical happenings we are compelled to consider every phenomenon not only as effect but also as cause. This is true even in the particular application of the laws of physical nature, as, for instance, in the study of astronomy in which the position of certain heavenly bodies at a given moment may be considered as the effect of gravitation, while, at the same time, their particular arrangement in space determines future changes. This relation appears much more clearly in the history of human civilization. To give an example: a surplus of food supply is liable to bring about an increase of population and an increase of leisure, which gives opportunity for occupations that are not absolutely necessary for the needs of every day life. In turn the increase of population and of leisure, which may be applied to new inventions, give rise to a greater food supply and to a further increase in the amount of leisure, so that a cumulative effect results.

Similar considerations may be made in regard to the important problem of the relation of the individual to society, a problem that has to be considered whenever we study the dynamic conditions of change. The activities of the individual are determined to a great extent by his social environment, but in turn his own activities influence the society in which he lives, and may bring about modifications in its form. Obviously, this problem is one of the most important ones to be taken up in a study of cultural changes. It is also beginning to attract the attention of students who are no longer satisfied with the systematic enumeration of standardized beliefs and customs of a tribe, but who begin to be interested in the question of the way in which the individual reacts to his whole social environment, and to the differences of opinion and of mode of action that occur in primitive society and which are the causes of far-reaching changes.

In short then, the method which we try to develop is based on a study of the dynamic changes in society that may be observed at the present time. We refrain from the attempt to solve the fundamental problem of the general development of civilization until we have been able to unravel the processes that are going on under our eyes.

Certain general conclusions may be drawn from this study even now.

First of all, the history of human civilization does not appear to us as determined entirely by psychological necessity that leads to a uniform evolution the world over. We rather see that each cultural group has its own unique history, dependent partly upon the peculiar inner development of the social group, and partly upon the foreign influences to which it has been subjected. There have been processes of gradual differentiation as well as processes of leveling down differences between nighboring cultural centers, but it would be quite impossible to understand, on the basis of a single evolutionary scheme, what happened to any particular people. An example of the contrast between the two points of view is clearly indicated by a comparison of the treatment of Zuñi civilization by Frank Hamilton Cushing on the one hand, on the other by modern students, particularly by Elsie Clews Parsons, Leslie Spier, Ruth Benedict and Ruth Bunzel. Cushing believed that it was possible to explain Zuñi culture entirely on the basis of the reaction of the Zuñi mind to its geographical environment, and that the whole of Zuñi culture could be explained as the development which followed necessarily from the position in which the people were placed. Cushing's keen insight into the Indian mind and his thorough knowledge of the most intimate life of the people gave great plausibility to his interpretations. On the other hand, Dr. Parsons' studies prove conclusively the deep influence which Spanish ideas have had upon Zuñi culture, and, together with Professor Kroeber's investigations, give us one of the best examples of acculturation that have come to our notice. The psychological explanation is entirely misleading, notwithstanding its plausibility, and the historical study shows us an entirely different picture, in which the unique combination of ancient traits (which in themselves are undoubtedly complex) and of European influences, have brought about the present condition.

Studies of the dynamics of primitive life also show that an assumption of long-continued stability such as is demanded by Elliot Smith is without any foundation in fact. Wherever primitive conditions have been studied in detail, they can be proved to be in a state of flux, and it would seem that there is a close parallelism between the history of language and the history of general cultural development. Periods of stability are followed by periods of rapid change. It is exceedingly improbable that any customs of primitive people should be preserved unchanged for thousands of years. Furthermore, the phenomena of acculturation prove that a transfer of customs from one region into another without concomitant changes due to acculturation, are very rare. It is, therefore, very unlikely that ancient Mediterranean customs could be found at the present time practically unchanged in different parts of the globe, as Elliot Smith's theory demands.

While on the whole the unique historical character of cultural growth in each area stands out as a salient element in the history of cultural development, we may recognize at the same time that certain typical parallelisms do occur. We are, however, not so much inclined to look for these similarities in detailed customs as rather in certain dynamic conditions which are due to social or psychological causes that are liable to lead to similar results. The example of the relation between food supply and population to which I referred before may serve as an example. Another type of example is presented in those cases in which a certain problem confronting man may be solved by a limited number of methods only. When we find, for instance, marriage as a universal institution, it may be recognized that marriage is possible only between a number of men and a number of women; a number of men and one woman; a number of women and one man; or one man and one woman. As a matter of fact, all these forms are found the world over and it is, therefore, not surprising that analogous forms should have been adopted quite independently in different parts of the world, and, considering both the general economic conditions of mankind and the character of sexual instinct in the higher animals, it also does not seem surprising that group marriage and polyandrous marriages should be comparatively speaking rare. Similar considerations may also be made in regard to the philosophical views held by mankind. In short, if we look for laws, the laws relate to the effects of physiological, psychological, and social conditions, not to sequences of cultural achievement.

In some cases a regular sequence of these may accompany the development of the psychological or social status. This is illustrated by the sequence of industrial inventions in the Old World and in America, which I consider as independent. A period of food gathering and of the use of stone was followed by the invention of agriculture, of pottery and finally of the use of metals. Obviously, this order is based on the increased amount of time given by mankind to the use of natural products, of tools and utensils, and to the variations that developed with it. Although in this case parallelism seems to exist on the two continents, it would be futile to try to follow out the order in detail. As a matter of fact, it does not apply to other inventions. The domestication of animals, which, in the Old World must have been an early achievement, was very late in the New World, where domesticated animals, except the dog, hardly existed at all at the time of discovery. A slight beginning had been made in Peru with the taming of the llama, and birds were kept in various parts of the continent.

A similar consideration may be made in regard to the development of rationalism. It seems to be one of the fundamental characteristics of the development of mankind that activities which have developed unconsciously are gradually made the subject of reasoning. We may observe this process everywhere. It appears, perhaps, most clearly in the history of science which has gradually extended the scope of its inquiry over an ever-widening field and which has raised into consciousness human activities that are automatically performed in the life of the individual and of society.

I have not heretofore referred to another aspect of modern ethnology which is connected with the growth of psycho-analysis. Sigmund Freud has attempted to show that primitive thought is in many respects analogous to those forms of individual psychic activity which he has explored by his psycho-analytical methods. In many respects his attempts are similar to the interpretation of mythology by symbolists like Stucken. Rivers has taken hold of Freud's suggestion as well as of the interpretations of Graebner and Elliot Smith, and we find, therefore, in his new writings a peculiar disconnected application of psychologizing attitude and the application of the theory of ancient transmission.

While I believe some of the ideas underlying Freud's psycho-analytic studies may be fruitfully applied to ethnological problems, it does not seem to me that the one-sided exploitation of this method will advance our understanding of the development of human society. It is certainly true that the influence of impressions received during the first few years of life have been entirely underestimated and that the social behavior of man depends to a great extent upon the earliest habits which are established before the time when connected memory begins, and that many so-called racial or hereditary traits are to be considered rather as a result of early exposure to certain forms of social conditions. Most of these habits do not rise into consciousness and are, therefore, broken with difficulty only. Much of the difference in the behavior of adult male and female may go back to this cause. If, however, we try to apply the whole theory of the influence of suppressed desires to the activities of man living under different social forms, I think we extend beyond their legitimate limits the inferences that may be drawn from the observation of normal and abnormal individual psychology. Many other factors are of greater importance. To give an example: The phenomena of language show clearly that conditions quite different from those to which psycho-analysts direct their attention determine the mental behavior of man. The general concepts underlying language are entirely unknown to most people. They do not rise into consciousness until the scientific study of grammar begins. Nevertheless, the categories of language compel us to see the world arranged in certain definite conceptual groups which, on account of our lack of knowledge of linguistic processes, are taken as objective categories and which, therefore, impose themselves upon the form of our thoughts. It is not known what the origin of these categories may be, but it seems quite certain that they have nothing to do with the phenomena which are the subject of psycho-analytic study.

The applicability of the psycho-analytic theory of symbolism is also open to the greatest doubt. We should remember that symbolic interpretation has occupied a prominent position in the philosophy of all times. It is present not only in primitive life, but the history of philosophy and of theology abounds in examples of a high development of symbolism, the type of which depends upon the general mental attitude of the philosopher who develops it. The theologians who interpreted the Bible on the basis of religious symbolism were no less certain of the correctness of their views, than the psycho-analysts are of their interpretations of thought and conduct based on sexual symbolism. The results of a symbolic interpretation depend primarily upon the subjective attitude of the investigator who arranges phenomena according to his leading concept. In order to prove the applicability of the symbolism of psycho-analysis, it would be necessary to show that a symbolic interpretation from other entirely different points of view would not be equally plausible, and that explanations that leave out symbolic significance or reduce it to a minimum, would not be adequate.

While, therefore, we may welcome the application of every advance in the method of psychological investigation, we cannot accept as an advance in ethnological.method the crude transfer of a novel, one-sided method of psychological investigation of the individual to social phenomena the origin of which can be shown to be historically determined and to be subject to influences that are not at all comparable to those that control the psychology of the individual.

EVOLUTION OR DIFFUSION? [1]

IN a paper on Tewa kin, clan, and moiety by Elsie Clews Parsons [2] and another on the social organizations of the tribes of the North Pacific Coast by myself [3] the distribution of clans and related social phenomena in two regions has been discussed. The inference must be drawn that in geographically extreme areas in these districts distinctive types of social organization occur, the intermediate regions showing transitional types.

This phenomenon is by no means confined to these regions or to social organization, but may be observed to a greater or less extent in all other cultural phenomena and in other parts of the world. The component elements of folktales common to two areas decrease in number the greater the distance, and while in intermediate regions we may find much that reminds us of the extreme types, that are being compared, the extremes themselves may be fundamentally distinct. This condition may be observed in the folklore of the North Pacific Coast when comparing Alaskan tribes with those of Oregon, or the Coast tribes with those of the interior, or when comparing the folklore of the Plateau tribes with that of the Pueblos. The same condition may be observed also in material culture and is found when we compare the tribes of the Plateaus with those of the Plains, or the Eskimo and the Northwest Coast tribes. It may be seen in the distribution of art styles. All this does not preclude the possibility of a unified stylistic pattern originating in the intermediate areas, and it does not imply necessarily a greater purity of the extreme, and a more mixed character of the intermediate forms.

It does, however, prove, in our opinion, that all special cultural forms are the products of historical growth, and that unless considerations entirely foreign to the observed distribution are introduced, no proof can be given that one of the extreme forms is more ancient than the other.

[1] *American Anthropologist*, N.S., vol. 26 (1924), pp. 340–344.
[2] *Ibid.*, pp. 333–339.
[3] *Ibid.*, pp. 323–332; pp. 370 *et seq.* of this volume.

If we adopt the theory that matrilineal clans must be older than patrilineal or bilateral organization, we might be tempted to say that in the southern part of British Columbia and the eastern Pueblo district the clan organization has broken down, the more so the farther we move away from the centers in which this type of organization is still flourishing. The distribution itself does not lead to such an assumption. On the contrary, we see merely the intermingling of two distinctive types, the combination of which leads to new forms and new ideas.

The importance of diffusion has been so firmly established by the investigation of American material culture, ceremonies, art and mythology, as well as by the study of African cultural forms and by that of the prehistory of Europe, that we cannot deny its existence in the development of any local cultural type. It has not only been proved objectively by comparative studies, but the field student has also ample evidence showing the ways in which diffusion works. We know of cases in which a single individual has introduced a whole set of important myths. As an instance we might mention the tale of the origin of the Raven which is found in one single tribe on the northern part of Vancouver Island. It is still known to a few individuals that this tale was introduced by a man who had for many years been a slave in Alaska, and who was ultimately ransomed by his friends. Nevertheless, the myth is regularly told as part of the Raven cycle, although it is repudiated by all the neighboring tribes. Another example is the introduction of the Badger clan in Laguna by a Zuñi woman. Her husband, also from Zuñi, introduced to Laguna Zuñi kachina rituals and Zuñi stories which are now flourishing in their new environment. In earlier times the carrying away of women after raids, adoptions of foreigners, and other similar phenomena must have been a fruitful source of introduction of foreign ideas, the more so the smaller in numbers the tribe, and the more efficacious the influence of a single person. The introduction of new ideas must by no means be considered as resulting purely mechanically in additions to the cultural pattern, but also as an important stimulus to new inner developments.

A purely inductive study of ethnic phenomena leads to the conclusion that mixed cultural types that are geographically or historically intermediate between two extremes, give evidence of diffusion.

The question then arises as to how the extreme and most divergent forms must be considered. In our particular examples, the North Pacific clan organization with a small number of clans and many local groups possessing definite privileges must be compared with the bilateral organization of the south with numerous independent local units practically without privileges. In the Southwest, the matrilineal clan organization of the western Pueblos, almost entirely devoid of moieties, must be compared with the paternal moieties of the east without clans.

If it can be shown inductively that one of these types is the older one and that there are inherent dynamic conditions that tend to bring about transition from the older condition to the newer one, and that these conditions work in such a way that their potency decreases from the center to the periphery, the theory of a uniform development might be maintained. We require, therefore, in this case proof of three historical conditions: First, proof that one type is older than the other; second, that the younger type develops necessarily from the older one—in other words, that the dynamic conditions for a change in this direction are ever present; and thirdly that these conditions act with increasing intensity from the periphery towards the center.

As against these hypotheses the theory of diffusion takes the two distinctive types as given, and accepts as proven the presence of diffusion.

It should be borne in mind that the assumption of the antiquity of one particular type is essentially due to a classification in which the form that appears as the simplest from any one point of view is considered at the same time as historically the oldest. Nobody has felt the weakness of this assumption more clearly than Tylor who tried to support the general thesis by the study of survivals which indicate the character of earlier developmental stages. It cannot be claimed that a systematic attempt has ever been made to substantiate the theory of a definite evolutionary sequence on the basis of the study of survivals. All that can be said is that fragments of earlier historical stages are bound to exist and are found. We can, perhaps, best illustrate this by the example of matrilineal institutions. Whenever these are connected with the holding of social prerogatives in the hands of men, and where, nevertheless, the family in our sense is an important social feature, there is a constant cause of conflict because the matrilineal descent requires that property or position must pass out of the family into another family group. This entails an element of weakness, because the allegiance of the individual is divided between two conflicting groups. It is, therefore, plausible, that, in this case, matrilineal society contains elements of instability, and may, owing to inner dynamic conditions, develop into a patrilineal or bilateral system. Then we may find examples of the survival of matrilineal forms in patrilineal society. This, however, does not by any means prove that everywhere matrilineal society must have been the earlier form. It merely proves the instability of matrilineal society of a certain type.

To us the assumption of a unique form of cultural beginnings does not seem plausible. Setting aside the question of what form of social life may have existed at the time when our ancestors first developed speech and the use of tools, we find everywhere phenomena that point to very early differentiations from which even the simplest cultural forms developed. Language and art are perhaps the best proof of this contention. Even if we should accept with Trombetti the unity of the origin of human speech, or with Marty, the conscious invention of language for the purpose of communication, we must concede that in the early development of language fundamental categories of grammar and lexicography have arisen that cannot be reduced to common principles, excepting those general forms that are determined logically or by the fact that language is a means of communication. The same is true in regard to stylistic forms of art which cannot be reduced to a single source. What is true of language and art, which do not become a subject of retrospective reasoning, seems to us no less true of those aspects of life which are subject to remodeling by rationalizing processes. To this class belong the forms of social organization. The theory of the priority of maternal organization implies necessarily that the original economic and social unit consisted of a first generation of mothers and their brothers and of a second generation of children, and that the fathers of the children and the grandchildren were only temporary visitors to the family unit. It implies, therefore, a cohesion of this group long after the children had become independent adults, and a group consciousness in which no relations between father and children existed. The continued cohesion between mother and adult children is, to say the least, doubtful. According to the usual division of labor, such an organization rigidly carried through in a sparsely occupied territory and among a tribe dependent on hunting, would have doomed to extinction all groups without brothers and adult sons. While groups of this type may result from nonmarital sexual relations, we do not know of any cases where relations between men and women remain temporary throughout life, but marital relations continuing over a more or less extended period are the norm, and the social group includes the father.[1] It is, therefore, to us equally likely that primary units existed which consisted of families in our sense, and that adult children separated from the original groups and formed new family groups. Unless it can be proved that in an overwhelming number of cases the bilateral family retains evidences of a prior maternal stage, we have no right to assume that all the ancient types of groups of kin would conform to the same pattern, without any regard to the economic and other conditions that determine the size and character of the social unit.

It seems to us that the uniformity of early patterns cannot be proved. By analogy to the phenomena recently mentioned, we may rather infer diversity of early patterns.

We believe, therefore, that the great mass of observed facts bears out the theory that in the regions under consideration two fundamentally distinct forms came into contact, that the one is not derived from the other, but that through the mingling of the two forms new types arose in the intermediate districts.

---

[1] For a full discussion of this matter see R. H. Lowie, *Primitive Society* (New York, 1920), pp. 63 *et seq.*

REVIEW OF GRAEBNER,
"METHODE DER ETHNOLOGIE" [1]

MR. GRAEBNER is one of the serious and broad-minded students who are not satisfied with an accumulation of facts, but who are carrying through their own investigations according to a well-considered plan, and who try to contribute to science in a certain well-defined line of research and look for results that have a definite bearing upon the whole field of their inquiries. In the present book Mr. Graebner gives us a statement of the method that he is following and which will interest all ethnologists. If, however, Mr. Graebner calls his method *the* method of ethnology, we cannot agree with him. He must not expect that all ethnologists will limit the field of their researches in the way set forth in these "Methods." It appears from Mr. Foy's, the editor's, preface, that in this respect his own views and Graebner's coincide; in fact, in outlining the program of the whole series, Mr. Foy excludes expressly "alle geschichtsphilosophischen und völkerpsychologischen Betrachtungen" (p. v). This exclusion of the psychological field seems to me to give to the whole "Method" a mechanical character, and to be the essential cause of differences of opinion between the author and myself which I shall briefly characterize in the following pages.

The book is divided into three chapters: critique of sources, interpretation of data and combination of data. I do not quite share Mr. Graebner's unfavorable view in regard to the lack of critique of all writers on ethnological subjects, and in regard to the feeling that we are confronted by an appalling lack of all method; a feeling that, according to the author, the historian experiences who takes up the study of ethnology. It is true that much that has been written is based on inadequate evidence, and that particularly the so-called "comparative" ethnologists do not weigh their evidence well. Spencer, Frazer and Westermarck, not to mention others, have been criticized again and again by experts from this point of view. However, the whole modern method of ethnology, at least as developed in the United States, is a continuous struggle

[1] *Science,* N.S., vol. 34 (1911), pp. 804–810.

for gaining a critical viewpoint in regard to data collected by earlier authors who did not understand the objects and problems of modern anthropology. We believe that a safe interpretation of the older observed data must be based on careful archeological, ethnological and somatological field work. While I see a perfectly sound tendency in these studies, sounder than Mr. Graebner believes it to be, I still recognize the usefulness of the first chapter in which the author expresses the experiences of the historian in a form interesting and important to the unexperienced ethnologist. On the whole, the training given nowadays to students in universities and museums will impress upon them the safeguards on which the author insists, and which are too often forgotten by the amateur.

Our interest centers in the following two chapters : Interpretation and Combination of Data. The fundamental difference of opinion between the author and myself appears in the chapter on Interpretation. He defines interpretation as the determination of the purpose, meaning and significance of ethnic phenomena (p. 55) ; but he does not devote a single word to the question how these are to be discovered. He accepts, without any attempt at a methodical investigation, myths as interpretations of celestial phenomena (pp. 56, 57), as, for instance, the Jona theme as signifying the temporary disappearance of a heavenly body ; a conclusion which I for one am not by any means ready to accept. At this place the complete omission of all psychological considerations makes itself keenly felt. The significance of an ethnic phenomenon is not by any means identical with its distribution in space and time, and with its more or less regular associations with other ethnic phenomena. Its historical source may perhaps be determined by geographic-historical considerations, but its gradual development and ethnic significance in a psychological sense, as it occurs in each area, must be studied by means of psychological investigations in which the different interpretations and attitudes of the people themselves toward the phenomenon present the principal material. In the case of mythology, by means of which Mr. Graebner exemplifies his considerations, I should demand first of all an investigation of the question : why, and in how far are tales explanatory or related to ritualistic forms ? The very existence of these questions and the possibility of approaching them has been entirely overlooked by the author. On the whole, he seems to assume that the psychological interpretation is self-evident in most cases, but that by migrations and by dissemination combinations may be brought about which may lead to misinterpretations in so far as several groups that were originally distinct may be considered as one by origin (p. 64). Related to this disregard of the psychological problem is Mr. Graebner's claim, that no objective criteria have been found that can prove relations other than those due to historical connection; that the evolutionary investigation can do no more than answer the question: "How can I best and with the least number of contradictions imagine the course of human development in accordance with my general, fundamental views?" (p. 82). Against this method he claims that transfer has been proved to exist everywhere, while the presence of parallel development cannot be proved by objective criteria (p. 107). I think, we must say, that certain types of changes due to internal forces have been observed everywhere, and that, therefore, the question of similar or dissimilar evolution through internal forces does not rest on a more hypothetical basis than changes due to transmission.

Another fundamental difference of opinion between Graebner and myself relates to the phenomenon of "convergence," and here again the conclusions reached by the author seem to me due to a narrow, mechanical definition of the term "convergence." He ascribes this idea to Thilenius and Ehrenreich. I may, perhaps, point out that I have raised the essential point in an essay "The Limitations of the Comparative Method of Anthropology," [1] and again in my essay "The Mind of Primitive Man." [2] Graebner's first error in regard to this phenomenon is one which he shares with almost all other students of anthropogeography. I quote from p. 94: "Gleichartige Erscheinungen können auch durch Angleichung ursprünglich verschiedener Erscheinungen unter dem Einfluss gleicher Natur- oder Kulturumgebung zustande kommen. Da eine spezifisch gleiche Kulturumgebung ausser durch Kulturverwandtschaft aber ihrerseits nur als durch gleiche Naturumgebung hervorgerufen denkbar ist, bleibt diese allein als primäre Ursache von Konvergenzen übrig." This presupposes an existence of a mankind without any individual differences, or an absolute identity of the psychical conditions that are affected by geographical environment. As soon as the cultural basis is distinct, even the most absolute identity of environment cannot be assumed to lead to the same result. It is a curious view that is so often held, that when we speak of the influence of environment upon the human mind, only the enrivonment need be consid-

---

[1] *Science*, N.S., vol. 4 (1896), pp. 901–908; pp. 270 *et seq.* of this volume.
[2] *Journal of American Folk-Lore*, vol. 14 (1901), pp. 1–11.

ered. Is not in every problem of interaction the character of each of the interacting phenomena of equal importance? In the particular case here discussed we may say that our whole experience does not exhibit a single case in which two distinct tribal groups are so much alike in their mental characteristics that, when they are subjected to the same modifying causes, these mental differences could be disregarded, and it is an entirely hypothetical and improbable assumption that in earlier periods absolute mental uniformity as expressed in culture ever existed in distinct groups.

The idea that in cases of independent origin of the same cultural phenomena identity of environment can give the only satisfactory explanation is deeply rooted in Mr. Graebner's mind, for he repeats, on p. 112: "Gleiche Kulturbedingungen bei selbständiger Entstehung können ihrerseits wieder nur auf die Naturbedingungen zurückgehen."

The phenomenon of convergence is next considered as non-existent for two reasons: a theoretical one and an empirical one. The former is based on the consideration that convergence can occur only under identical cultural conditions, and that, therefore, heterogeneous cultural conditions such as are found in cultures not genetically related, cannot possibly lead to the same result. The empirical argument is based on a consideration of conditions found in Europe (pp. 113–114). A consideration of the same data leads me to results diametrically opposed to those observed by Graebner. The very fact that in modern civilization a new idea is frequently discovered independently by several individuals seems to me a proof of parallel lines of thought; and Mr. Graebner's statement that the thought of only one man becomes socially active, *i.e.*, is adopted, seems to me to demonstrate just the reverse of what he claims. For an idea expressed at a time that is not ready for it remains barren of results; pronounced at a period when many think on similar, convergent lines, it is fruitful and may revolutionize human thought. May I point out that Graebner's own book may be taken as an example of this tendency? For it expresses the same fundamental idea that is so potent at present in all lines of biological research, that of the permanence of unit characters. An idea may become effective whenever the ethnic conditions are favorable to its adoption and development, no matter what the historical origin of the present general status may have been.

The questions of independent origin and convergence cannot be entirely separated, and some of the previous remarks may perhaps rather relate to the probability of independent origin which Graebner practically denies. One aspect of the theory of convergence relates more specifically to the question whether two ethnic groups that are genetically distinct, which are confronted by the same problem, will solve it in a similar manner. The theory of convergence claims that similar ways *may* (not *must*) be found. This would be a truism, if there existed only one way of solving this problem, and convergence is obviously the more probable the fewer the possible solutions of the problem. This, however, is not what we ordinarily understand by convergence. Ethnic phenomena are, on the whole, exceedingly complex, and apparently similar ones may embrace quite distinct complexes of ideas and may be due to distinct causes. To take a definite example : Taboos may be arbitrarily forbidden actions ; they may be actions that are not performed because they are not customary, or those that are not performed because associated with religious or other concepts. Thus a trail may be forbidden because the owner does not allow trespassing, or it may have a sacred character, or it may be feared. All ethnic units, separated from their cultural setting, are artificial units, and we always omit in our comparisons certain groups of distinctive characteristics—no matter whether the comparisons are made from the point of view of cultural transmission, or of evolutionary series. Thus, in our case, the forbidden action stands out clearly as a unit, that of the taboo, although its psychological sources are entirely distinct—and this is one of the essential features of convergence. Nobody claims that convergence means an absolute identity of phenomena derived from heterogeneous sources ; but we think we have ample proof to show that the most diverse ethnic phenomena, when subject to similar psychical conditions, or when referring to similar activities, will give similar results (not equal results), which we group naturally under the same category when viewed not from an historical standpoint, but from that of psychology, technology or other similar standpoints. The problem of convergence lies in the correct interpretation of the significance of ethnic phenomena that are apparently identical, but in many respects distinct ; and also in the tendency of distinct phenomena to become psychologically similar, due to the shifting of some of their concomitant elements—as when the reason for a taboo shifts from the ground of religious avoidance to that of mere custom.

In the foregoing remarks I have tried to show why Mr. Graebner's negative critique of parallelism and convergence does not seem to me conclusive. Just as little convincing appear to me the arguments on which he bases his method of determining cultural relationships. Here, also, the fundamental error seems to me based on the complete disregard of mental phenomena. Mr. Graebner lays down the following methodological principle: Two or more phenomena are comparable, and the one may be used to interpret the other, if it can be shown that they belong, if not to the same local cultural complex, at least to the same cultural group" (p. 64). It seems to me an entirely arbitrary hypothesis to assume *a priori* the homogeneity of similar phenomena belonging to the same cultural group. Mr. Graebner explains his standpoint by the example of the discussion of agricultural rites in Frazer's "Golden Bough," and accepts the discussion on account of the homogeneity of the cultural groups of Europe and western Asia, from which the examples have been taken. This part of Frazer's deductions seems to me just as unmethodical as the others which are based on examples taken from a wider series of cultural groups. The concepts of comparability and homogeneity, as I understand them, have to deal not only with historical relationship, but to a much higher degree with psychological similarity, for only as elements of the mental make-up of society do ideas or actions become potent and determining elements of further development. To give an instance of what I mean: If the aged are killed by one people for economic reasons, by another to insure them a happy future life, then the two customs are not comparable, even if they should have their origin in the same historical sources. Graebner's idea appears clearly in the following statement: "If in different parts of the earth peoples are found that are closely related in their ways of thinking and feeling, evidently the same question arises, that has been treated before in regard to cultural forms, viz., whether these similarities are not based on community of descent or on early cultural contact" (p. 112). Such a view can be maintained only if we disregard the action of inner forces, that may lead two people of like cultural possessions after their separation to entirely distinct conditions. In short it is based on the view of a very limited action of internal forces.

Through the restriction of comparability and interpretation exclusively to the phenomena of transmission and original unity—a definition that I do not find given, but that is everywhere implied—and by the hypothesis, that ethnic phenomena that occur in two areas due to transmission or to original unity will always remain comparable and can be mutually interpreted, the author is necessarily led to his conclusions, which are merely a restatement of his incomplete definitions and of his hypothesis; for, if we call comparable exclusively phenomena that are historically related, naturally then there can be no other kind of comparability, and psychological ethnology does not exist.

Exactly the same criticism must be made against the sense in which the term "causal connection" is used. Here also the psychological connections are intentionally excluded, because the psychological argument, its method and validity, are not congenial to the author; and "causal connection" is simply identified with historical connection. On this basis only can I understand the statement that in literary tradition causal relations are directly given (p. 73). This is not meant to refer to modern historical science, but to the literary sources of Asia and Europe. Is not literary tradition on the whole proof of the misunderstanding of causal relations, rather than the reverse—provided we understand under causal nexus not the simple mechanical aspect of transmission, but the complex social conditions that admit transmission and that bring about internal changes.

A correlate of the assumption that ethnic elements that are genetically related remain always comparable plays a most important part in Mr. Graebner's method of proving cultural relations: "Whenever a phenomenon appears as an inorganic element in its ethnic surroundings, its presence is due to transmission." This might be true if primitive cultures were homogeneous units; which, however, is not the case. The more we learn of primitive culture, the clearer it becomes that not only is the participation of each individual in the culture of his tribe of an individual character, or determined by the social grouping of the tribe, but that also in the same mind the most heterogeneous complexes of habits, thoughts and actions may lie side by side, without ever coming into conflict. The opinion expressed by Mr. Graebner seems to me so little true, that I rather incline toward the reverse opinion. It seems at least plausible, although it has never been proved, that on the whole only such ethnic features are transmitted that in some way conform to the character of some feature of the life of the people that adopt them. The criterion in question seems to me, therefore, not acceptable, until it can be sustained by observed facts.

This idea is probably related to the author's conception of the transmission of cultural elements in the form of complexes. He says: "A migration of single cultural elements, also of tales, over wide distances, without the spread of other cultural possessions at the same time, may be designated without hesitation as a 'kulturgeschichtliches' nonsense"

(p. 116). I should like to see the proof of this daring proposition. It is, of course, not the question whether one cultural group owes much or little to another one, but whether cultural elements are necessarily transmitted in groups. To take only a few examples. Is not the gradual introduction of cultivated plants and domesticated animals a case in kind? Does not the irregular distribution of tales show that they are carried from tribe to tribe without relation to other transmissions? It seems to me that the more the problem of cultural contact is studied, the more amazing becomes the independence of far-reaching influences in one respect, from the spread of other cultural possessions. The example of language used by Mr. Graebner (p. 111) presents facts entirely different from those which he imagines. Thus we find phonetic influences without corresponding lexical or morphological influences and *vice versa*. The serious defect of the "Method" is here clearly seen. Instead of operating with the purely mechanical concepts of transmission and conservatism relating to the most ancient types of culture, we must investigate the innumerable cases of transmission that happen under our very eyes and try to understand how transmission is brought about and what are the conditions that favor the grouping of certain new elements in an older culture.

I think I have shown that not only the psychological and evolutionary standpoints contain hypothetical elements that must be subject to a rigid criticism, but that the restriction of all ethnic happenings to mechanical transmission or preservation contains many hypotheses the validity of which is open to most serious doubt. Mr. Graebner has failed in his attempt, because he does not apply the same rigorous standard to his own favorite views, that he applies so successfully to a discussion of the evolutionary theory (pp. 77 *et seq.*) Here he is at his best, and his criticism of the many hypothetical assumptions contained in all theories of the evolution of culture are well taken and should be read and minded by all students of ethnology. In a few cases, particularly in the discussion of correlated ethnic phenomena, he does not seem to do quite justice to the force of the argument, because he prefers spatial interpretation of these correlations to a sequential one; but both are certainly equally possible and probable.

It is, however, curious to note that, notwithstanding his uncompromising negative position, the author tacitly re-introduces some of the most fundamental concepts of cultural evolution. Thus he speaks on p. 63 of the "well-known tendency of degeneration and disintegration, ac-

cording to which myths become legends and fairy-tales, significant institutions formal traits"; and again on p. 152: "Undoubtedly sound
points of view are, that the beginnings of every phenomenon must be
simple and in a way grow naturally, and that the development must be
intelligible by the most simple psychological process." My criticism of
these assumptions would be much more far-reaching than that of Mr.
Graebner.

Thus it seems to me that the methods of Mr. Graebner are subject to
the same strictures as those of the other schools, and the "Ferninterpretation," "Kulturkreise" and "Kulturschichten" must be considered as no
less hypothetical than the "Stufenbau" of Breysig or the sequences of
Lamprecht.

In the development of science it is, however, useful to carry through
a hypothesis to its limits and to investigate the ultimate conclusions to
which it will lead. From this point of view pages 104–151, in which
the principle of conservatism and transmission are strained to the utmost
with an absolute disregard of all other possibilities, will be helpful for
a gradual clearing of our views. Perhaps even more helpful is the actual
application that Mr. Graebner has made of these principles in his
chosen field of Melanesia in its relations to the whole rest of the world.

My own opinions in regard to the value of a single evolutionary series,
the importance of very old cultural elements that survive in many parts
of the world, and the occurrence of transmission over enormous areas
coincide to a great extent with those of Mr. Graebner. I also hold the
opinion that the discovery of a really new idea is much more difficult
than is generally admitted, and therefore a manifold spontaneous origin
quite unlikely. Nevertheless, I cannot acknowledge that he has given
us *any* safe criterion that would enable us to tell that in any given case
transmission can be definitely proved against independent origin, and
I am just as skeptical as before reading his book in regard to the advis-
ability of accepting Ratzel's "Ferninterpretation." I rather repeat once
more the warning that I have given again and again for twenty years:
rather to be overcautious in admitting transmission as the cause of
analogies in cases of the sporadic occurrence of similar phenomena,
than to operate with the concept of lost links of a chain of cultural
intercourse.

That through the exaggerated application of a single principle, when
several must be admitted as acting, new viewpoints may be discovered
—that much I willingly admit, and I enjoy to follow the daring gener-

alizations to which Mr. Graebner is led. I may, however, be pardoned if I cannot accept this as the method of ethnology. I see safe progress essentially in the patient unraveling of the mental processes that may be observed among primitive and civilized peoples, and that express the actual conditions under which cultural forms develop. When we begin to know these, we shall also be able to proceed gradually to the more difficult problems of the cultural relations between isolated areas that exhibit peculiar similarities.

HISTORY AND SCIENCE IN ANTHROPOLOGY:
A REPLY[1]

IT was interesting to me to read Dr. Kroeber's analysis not only of my scientific work but also of my personality.[2] I may perhaps misinterpret both. Nevertheless I wish to express my complete disagreement with his interpretation. It is quite true that as a young man I devoted my time to the study of physics and geography. In 1887 I tried to define my position in regard to these subjects,[3] giving expression to my consciousness of the diversity of their fundamental viewpoints. I aligned myself clearly with those who are motivated by the affective appeal of a phenomenon that impresses us as a unit, although its elements may be irreducible to a common cause. In other words the problem that attracted me primarily was the intelligent understanding of a complex phenomenon. When from geography my interest was directed to ethnology, the same interest prevailed. To understand a phenomenon we have to know not only what it is, but also how it came into being. Our problem is historical. Dr. Kroeber suggests as

the distinctive feature of the historical approach, in any field, not the dealing with time sequences, though that almost inevitably crops out when historical impulses are genuine and strong; but an endeavor at descriptive integration. . . . Process in history is a nexus among phenomena treated as phenomena, not a thing to be sought out and extracted from phenomena.

I confess that to me this does not give any sense. We have descriptions of culture more or less adequately understood. These are valuable material. They yield, if well done, most illuminating material in regard to the working of the culture, by which I mean the life of the individual as controlled by culture and the effect of the individual upon culture. But they are not history. For historical interpretation the descriptive material has to be handled in other ways. For this work archaeological,

[1] *American Anthropologist*, N.S., vol. 38 (1936), pp. 137–141.
[2] *Ibid.*, vol. 37 (1935), pp. 539–569.
[3] "The Study of Geography," *Science*, vol. 9 (1887), pp. 137–141; pp. 639 *et seq.* of this volume.

biological, linguistic, and ethnographic comparisons furnish more or less adequate leads.

If Dr. Kroeber calls my first piece of ethnological work, "The Central Eskimo," (written in 1885), historical, I fail to understand him. It is a description based on intimate knowledge of the daily life of the people, with bad gaps, due to my ignorance of problems. The only historical points made are based on a comparison of the tribe studied with other Eskimo tribes and with the Indians of the Mackenzie basin, on a careful study of evidences of earlier habitations of the Eskimo, and a guess as to the course of their early migrations. The rest is description pure and simple. If in later writings I did not stress geographical conditions the reason must be sought in an exaggerated belief in the importance of geographical determinants with which I started on my expedition in 1883–84 and the thorough disillusionment in regard to their significance as creative elements in cultural life. I shall always continue to consider them as relevant in limiting and modifying existing cultures, but it so happened that in my later field work this question has never come to the fore as particularly enlightening.

May I remind Dr. Kroeber of one little incident that illustrates my interest in the sociological or psychological interpretation of cultures, an aspect that is now-a-days called by the new term functionalism. I had asked him to collect Arapaho traditions without regard to the "true" forms of ancient tales and customs, the discovery of which dominated, at that time, the ideas of many ethnologists. The result was a collection of stories some of which were extremely gross. This excited the wrath of Alice C. Fletcher who wanted to know only the ideal Indian, and hated what she called the "stable boy" manners of an inferior social group. Since she tried to discredit Dr. Kroeber's work on this basis I wrote a little article on "The Ethnological Significance of Esoteric Doctrines" [1] in which I tried to show the "functional" interrelation between exoteric and esoteric knowledge, and emphasized the necessity of knowing the habits of thought of the common people as expressed in story telling. Similar considerations regarding the inner structural relations between various cultural phenomena are contained in a contribution on the secret societies of the Kwakiutl in the Anniversary Volume for Adolf Bastian (1896) and from another angle in a discussion of the same subject in the reports on the Fourteenth Congress of Americanists, 1904 (published 1906); the latter more from the angle of the establishment

[1] *Science*, N.S., vol. 16 (1902), pp. 872–874, pp. 312 *et seq.* of this volume.

of a pattern of cultural behavior. These I should call contributions to cultural history dealing with the ways in which the whole of an indigenous culture in its setting among neighboring cultures builds up its own fabric.

In an attempt to follow the history of a culture back into earlier times we are confined to indirect evidence and it is our duty to use it with greatest circumspection. Dr. Kroeber accuses me of not being interested in these questions. I do not know, then, why I should have used years of my life in trying to unravel the historical development of social organization, secret societies, the spread of art forms, of folktales on the Northwest Coast of America. I think that such a detailed study is worth while not only for its own sake but because it illuminates also general aspects of the history of mankind, for here we see the totality of cultural phenomena reflected in the individual culture. Is it that painstaking work of this kind does not seem to Dr. Kroeber worth while, but that it requires the flight of an unbridled imagination to have his approval? I cannot understand in any other way his praise of a public lecture which I gave as President of the New York Academy of Sciences on "The History of the American Race," [1] guarding my statement, however, at the very beginning by saying that I should give my fancy freer rein than I ordinarily permit myself. When as early as 1895 [2] I made a careful analysis of the then available material, showing the relations of Northwest Coast mythologies among themselves and to other American and Old World areas, the object was to demonstrate historical relations. Perhaps I did not go far enough for Dr. Kroeber in establishing the center of origin of each element; but there I balk, because I believe this can be done in exceptional cases only. The fact that a phenomenon has its highest development at a certain point does not prove that it had its origin there. The belief in this, which I consider an unjustified assumption, and a more light-hearted weighing of evidence differentiates our methods. In a conversation Dr. Kroeber admitted that I wanted a high degree of probability for a conclusion, while he was satisfied with much less. That is an Epicurean position, not that of a modern scientist.

I am sorry that I cannot acknowledge as fair the summary of my work. It is true that I have done little archaeological work myself. My own only contribution was the establishment of the sequence of archaic,

---

[1] *Annals of the New York Academy of Sciences,* vol. 21 (1912, pp. 177–183, pp. 324 *et seq.* of this volume.
[2] *Indianische Sagen von der Nord-Pacifischen Küste Amerikas* (Berlin, 1895).

Teotihuacan type and Aztec in Mexico, I believe—except Dall's work on the Aleutian Islands—the first stratigraphic work in North America; but in the plan of the Jesup Expedition I assigned an important part to archaeological work which in the careful hands of Harlan I. Smith gave important results on Fraser River showing the invasion of inland culture. If farther north it did not give any results the cause was not lack of interest but failure to find significant material. I may also claim to have kept before our scientific public year after year the necessity of careful archaeological work in northern Alaska, which has unfortunately been deviated from its main object by sensational artistic finds, although the main problem remains that of the occurrence or non-occurrence of pre-Eskimo types in the Bering Sea region.

In regard to linguistic work Dr. Kroeber's criticism does not seem to me to hit the mark at all. Relationship of languages is a powerful means of historical research. It remains equally valid, whether we assume purely genetic relationship or whether we ask ourselves whether by contact languages may exert far-reaching mutual influences. This question is important for the interpretation of relationships but has absolutely nothing to do with an historic or non-historic approach. If it can be settled we shall know how to interpret historically the linguistic data. That I am here as elsewhere opposed to ill substantiated guesses, goes without saying, but has nothing to do with the case. Here also a 40% possibility is no satisfactory proof for me.

Dr. Kroeber's strictures on my book on "Primitive Art" are entirely unintelligible to me. He says style has not been treated. There is a whole chapter on style and one specific one on Northwest Coast style intended as a sample of treatment of the problem. Maybe Dr. Kroeber has an idea of his own of what style is, as he has an idea of his own of what history is. He reproaches me for not having written on the history of Northwest Coast style. Unfortunately there are no data that throw any light on its development. It appears in full bloom and disappears under the onslaught of White contact. The slight local differences and the relation between the arts of the Eskimo and other neighboring tribes do not seem to me to throw any light on the subject. Does he want me to write its history without such data? Am I to repeat the wild guesses of Schurtz?

I have never made the statement that history is legitimate and proper, but historical reconstruction unsound and sterile. As a matter of fact, all the history of primitive people that any ethnologist has ever developed is reconstruction and cannot be anything else. There is, however, a difference between cautious reconstruction based on ascertained data and sweeping generalizations that must remain more or less fanciful. I do recognize quite a number of very fundamental general historical problems in regard to which I have more or less decided opinions, such as the distribution and relationships of races, the relation of America to the Old World, that of Africa to Asia, and so on. It depends entirely upon the evidence how strongly I hold to these opinions. It has happened to me too often that a suggestion cautiously made has been repeated by others as though I had pronounced it as a set dogma.

Now as to the use of statistics in ethnology as a tool of research. Being somewhat familiar with the difficulties of statistical work I do not believe that it is a safe guide in ethnological inquiry. I believe I was the first after Tylor's discussion of 1888 [1] to try it on the field of mythology, and if at that time the correlation method had been as much abused as it is now, and since I had not yet understood its dangers, I might have established some nice coefficients of correlation for elements of mythology.[2] The data of ethnology are not of such character that they can be expressed by mathematical formulas so that results are obtained which are in any way more convincing than those secured by simpler ways of numerical comparison. Behind these always loom the unanswered questions in how far the materials enumerated are really comparable, or in other types of problems, like Tylor's, in how far they are independent.

I regret that Dr. Kroeber also does not see the aim I have in mind in physical anthropology. We talk all the time glibly of races and nobody can give us a definite answer to the question what constitutes a race. The first stimulus to my active participation in work in physical anthropology was due to G. Stanley Hall and to the atmosphere of Clark University, and had little to do with racial questions, rather with the influences of environment upon growth. When I turned to the consideration of racial problems I was shocked by the formalism of the work. Nobody had tried to answer the questions why certain measurements were taken, why they were considered significant, whether they were subject to outer influences; and my interest has since remained centered on these problems which must be solved before the data of

[1] *Journal, Royal Anthropological Institute of Great Britain and Ireland,* vol. 18 (1889), pp. 245–272.
[2] *Indianische Sagen,* pp. 341 *et seq.*

physical anthropology can be used for the elucidation of historical problems. Equally important seems to me the question in how far the functioning of the body is dependent upon bodily structure. The answer to
this problem is the necessary basis for any intelligent discussion of racial
physiology and psychology.

Dr. Kroeber refers to the discussion on anthropological methods at
the time of the Americanist Congress held in New York in 1928. He
does not quite completely tell the story of this incident. The discussion
had centered entirely around Kulturkreise and other attempts at historical reconstruction. Finally I said that I had all through my life
tried to understand the culture I was studying as the result of historical
growth, but since the whole discussion had been devoted to historic
sequences I had to arise as the *advocatus diaboli* and defend those who
sought to understand the processes by which historical changes came
about, knowledge of which is needed to give a deeper meaning to
the picture. This was no new position of mine, as I think has become
sufficiently clear from the preceding. It is true enough that in general
the participants in the discussion did not want to have anything to do
with the investigation of "processes" which seemed anathema but pre-
ferred to stick to their pet theories.

Robert Redfield, in the introduction to "Social Anthropology of
North American Tribes" (Chicago, 1937) takes up Kroeber's argument. He accepts Kroeber's definition of history : "a historian is he who
confines himself to 'functional' ethnographic accounts—definitions of
unique societies, without comparison, but each presented as an organic
whole composed of functionally interrelated and integrating organs."
Others would call this a good ethnographic description and I do not
believe that any historian would accept this as history. Redfield's
criticism of my work is summed up in the words: "he does not write
histories, and he does not prepare scientific systems." The latter point
agrees fully with my views. The history of any selected group or of mankind—history taken both in the ordinary sense of the term and in the
abnormal sense given to it by Kroeber—including biological, linguistic
and general cultural phenomena, is so complex that all systems that can
be devised will be subjective and unrevealing. Classification, which is
a necessary element of every system, is misleading, as I tried to illustrate
in the discussion of totemism (pp. 316 *et seq.* of this volume). What
Kroeber and Redfield call the "history" of a tribe appears to me as a
penetrating analysis of a unique culture describing its form, the dynamic

reactions of the individual to the culture and of the culture to the individual. It obtains its full meaning only when the historical development of the present form is known. Unfortunately we are compelled to reconstruct the historical development of primitive cultures from very inadequate material, but part of it at least can be inferred. I think that Radcliffe-Brown's indifference to these reconstructions is based on an overestimation of the certainty of documentary history, particularly of history of culture. Some of our results obtained by means of archaeological or distributional studies are no less certain than those obtained by documentary history. The difficulties encountered in the attempts to give an adequate picture of the dynamism and integration of culture have often been pointed out. To introduce the analogy between an organism and society—one of the early speculative theories—as Radcliffe-Brown seems to do in his emphasis on function—is no help.

Redfield objects to what he calls ambiguity of methodological approach, that is to say "a reluctance to classify the historical and social anthropological ('scientific') approach." This seems to indicate that he considers these approaches as mutually exclusive. An unbiased investigator will utilize every method that can be devised to contribute to the solution of his problem. In my opinion a system of social anthropology and "laws" of cultural development as rigid as those of physics are supposed to be are unattainable in the present stage of our knowledge, and more important than this: on account of the uniqueness of cultural phenomena and their complexity nothing will ever be found that deserves the name of a law excepting those psychological, biologically determined characteristics which are common to all cultures and appear in a multitude of forms according to the particular culture in which they manifest themselves.

The confusion in regard to my own point of view is perhaps largely due to the fact that in my early teaching, when I fought "the old speculative theories," as I am now fighting the new speculative theories based on the imposition of categories derived from our culture upon foreign cultures, I stressed the necessity of the study of acculturation (1895, see p. 425) and dissemination. When I thought that these *historical* methods were firmly established I began to stress, about 1910, the problems of cultural dynamics, of integration of culture and of the interaction between individual and society.

Absolute systems of phenomena as complex as those of culture are impossible. They will always be reflections of our own culture.

THE ETHNOLOGICAL SIGNIFICANCE
OF ESOTERIC DOCTRINES [1]

IN recent years the study of the esoteric teachings found in American tribal society has become one of the favorite subjects of research of ethnologists. The symbolic significance of complex rites, and the philosophic views of nature which they reveal, have come to us as a surprise, suggesting a higher development of Indian culture than is ordinarily assumed. The study of these doctrines conveys the impression that the reasoning of the Indian is profound, his emotions deep, his ethical ideals of a high quality.

It seems worth while to consider briefly the conditions under which these esoteric doctrines may have developed. Two theories regarding their origin suggest themselves: the esoteric doctrine may have originated among a select social group, and the exoteric doctrine may represent that part of it that leaked out and became known, or was made known, to the rest of the community; but it may also be that the esoteric doctrine developed among a select social group from the current beliefs of the tribe.

It seems to my mind that the second theory is the more plausible one, principally for the reason that the contents of the teachings among different tribes are often alike, no matter how much the systems may differ. Almost all the rituals that are the outward expression of esoteric doctrines appear to be old, and many have probably existed, almost in their present form for considerable periods. Nevertheless, there is ample evidence of frequent borrowing and changes of sacred rites. Examples are the Sun Dance, various forms of the Ghost Dance, and the Mescal ceremonials. Miss Fletcher has called attention to the fact that Pawnee rituals have influenced the development of the rites of many tribes of the Plains. I might add similar examples from the Pacific coast, such as the transmission of Kwakiutl rituals to neighboring tribes.

There is also abundant proof showing that the mythologies of all tribes, notwithstanding the sacredness of some of the myths, contain

[1] *Science,* N.S., vol. 16 (1902), pp. 872–874.

many elements that can be proved to be of foreign origin. It seems very likely that similar conditions prevailed in the past, because the wide distribution of many cultural features can be understood only as the effect of a long-continued process of borrowing and dissemination.

Since the esoteric teaching refers to the rituals, and is often largely based on mythological concepts, it seems plausible that it should have developed as a more or less conscious attempt at systematizing the heterogeneous mass of beliefs and practices current in the tribe. Whenever a certain ceremonial came to be placed in charge of a small social group, were they chiefs, priests or simply men of influence, the conditions must have been favorable for the development of an esoteric doctrine. The thoughts of the men charged with the keeping of sacred rites must have dwelt on philosophical or religious questions, and it would seem natural that in the succession of generations the sacredness of the rite grew, and its philosophical significance increased in depth.

If this view is correct, the esoteric doctrine must have been evolved on the foundation of the general culture of the tribe, and must be considered as a secondary phenomenon the character of which depends upon the exoteric doctrine.

The opposite view, that the exoteric doctrine is a degenerate form of esoteric teaching, does not seem to me equally plausible, because it presupposes a highly complex system of actions and opinions originating spontaneously in a selected group of individuals. It is difficult to conceive how, in tribal society, conditions could have prevailed that would make such a development possible. This theory would seem to presuppose the occurrence of a general decay of culture. There is no reason that compels us to assume that such a decay has taken place, although it may have occurred in exceptional cases. If, on the other hand, we assume that the esoteric doctrine developed from popular beliefs, we do not need to assume any cultural conditions materially different from those found at the present time. It is quite evident that the esoteric doctrine, after it was once established, influenced, in its turn, popular belief, and that, therefore, there is a mutual and probably inextricable interrelation between the two doctrines.

If these considerations are correct, then the esoteric doctrine must, to a great extent, be considered as the product of individual thought. It expresses the reaction of the best minds in the community to the general cultural environment. It is their attempt to systematize the knowledge that underlies the culture of the community. In other words, this doctrine must be treated like any other system of philosophy, and its study has the same aims as the study of the history of philosophy.

Two characteristics of esoteric doctrine are quite striking. The first is that at the bottom of each doctrine there seems to be a certain pattern of thought which is applied to the whole domain of knowledge, and which gives the whole doctrine its essential character. This line of thought depends upon the general character of the culture of the tribe, but nevertheless has a high degree of individuality in each tribe. The theory of the universe seems to be based on its schematic application. The second characteristic is that, notwithstanding this systematization of knowledge, there remain many ideas that are not coordinated with the general system, and that may be quite out of accord with it. In such cases the contradiction between the general scheme and special ideas often escapes entirely the notice of the native philosophers. This phenomenon is quite analogous to the well-known characteristics of philosophic systems which bear the stamp of the thought of their time. The philosopher does not analyze each and every conclusion, but un-consciously adopts much of the current thought of his environment ready-made.

The theories regarding the origin of esoteric doctrine may be proved or disproved by a careful study of its relations to popular beliefs and to esoteric doctrines found among neighboring tribes. It is evident that the material needed for the solution of the problem includes both the esoteric teaching and the popular forms of belief.

What has been said before shows that, to the ethnologist, the prob-lem of the genesis of exotery is of no less importance than that of esotery. However we may consider the origin of the latter, it must be admitted that it is the expression of thought of the exceptional mind. It is not the expression of thought of the masses. Ethnology, however, does not deal with the exceptional man; it deals with the masses, and with the characteristic forms of their thoughts. The extremes of the forms of thought of the most highly developed and of the lowest mind in the community are of interest only as special varieties, and in so far as they influence the further development of the thought of the people. It may, therefore, be said that the exoteric doctrine is the more general ethnic phenomenon, the investigation of which is a necessary foundation for the study of the problems of esoteric teaching.

It is, therefore, evident that we must not, in our study of Indian life, seek for the highest form of thought only, which is held by the priest, the chief, the leader. Interesting and attractive as this field of research may be, it is supplementary only to the study of the thoughts, emotional life, and ethical standards of the common people, whose interests center in other fields of thought and of whom the select class forms only a special type.

It has taken many years for the study of the culture of civilized peoples to broaden out so as to take in not only the activities of the great, but also the homely life of the masses. The appreciation of the fact that the actions of every individual have their roots in the society in which he lives, has developed only recently, and has led to the intensive study of folk-lore and folk-customs that is characteristic of our times. It seems peculiar that, with increasing knowledge of the more complex forms of Indian culture, we seem to be losing interest in the popular belief; that we look for the "true" inward significance of customs among the select few, and become inclined to consider as superficial the study of the simpler and cruder ideas and ideals of the common folk. If it is true that for a full understanding of civilized society the knowledge of the popular mind is a necessity, it is doubly true in more primitive forms of society, where the isolation of social groups is very slight, and where each and every individual is connected by a thousand ties with the majority of the members of the tribe to which he belongs.

Far be it from me to deprecate the importance of studies of the philosophies developed by the Indian mind. Only let us not lose sight of their intimate relation to the popular beliefs, of the necessity of studying the two in connection with each other, and of the error that we should commit if we should consider the esoteric doctrine, and the whole system of thought and of ethical ideals which it represents, as the only true form of the inner life of the Indian.

THE ORIGIN OF TOTEMISM [1]

IN the numerous discussions of totemism published during the last few years much has been said about the "American theory" of totemism—a theory for which I have been held responsible conjointly with Miss Alice C. Fletcher and Mr. Charles Hill-Tout. This theory is based on the idea that the clan totem has developed from the individual manitou by extension over a kinship group. It is true that I have pointed out the analogy between totem legend and the guardian-spirit tale among the Kwakiutl, and that I have suggested that *among this tribe* there is a likelihood that under the pressure of totemistic ideas the guardian-spirit concept has taken this particular line of development.[2] Later on Mr. Hill-Tout [3] took up my suggestion and based on it a theory of totemism by generalizing the specific phenomena of British Columbia. About the same time Miss Fletcher [4] gave a wider interpretation to her observations among the Omaha. Mr. J. G. Frazer [5] and Emile Durkheim [6] both discuss my arguments from this point of view. Their interpretation of my remarks is undoubtedly founded on their method of research, which has for its object an exhaustive interpretation of ethnic phenomena as the result of a single psychic process.

My own point of view—and I should like to state this with some emphasis—is a quite different one.[7] I do believe in the existence of

---

[1] Expanded from *Tsimshian Mythology,* 31st Annual Report of the Bureau of American Ethnology (1916), pp. 515–518. *American Anthropologist,* N.S., vol. 18 (1916), pp. 319–326.

[2] *Bastian-Festschrift* (Berlin, 1896), p. 439; "12th and Final Report of the North-Western Tribes of Canada," *British Association for the Advancement of Science,* 1898, Reprint p. 48; see also Fifth Report on the North-Western Tribes of Canada, 1889, Reprint pp. 24 *et seq.;* "The Social Organization and the Secret Societies of the Kwakiutl Indians," *Report U. S. National Museum for 1895,* (Washington, 1897), pp. 332, 336, 662.

[3] *Transactions of the Royal Society of Canada,* vol. 7 (1901–1902), Section II, pp. 6 *et seq.*

[4] *The Import of the Totem, a Study from the Omaha Tribe* (Salem, Mass., 1897).

[5] *Totemism and Exogamy* (London, 1910), vol. 4, p. 48.

[6] *Les formes élémentaires de la vie réligieuse* (Paris, 1912), pp. 246 *et seq.*

[7] "The Origin of Totemism," *Journal of American Folk-Lore,* vol. 23 (1910), p. 392; "Some Traits of Primitive Culture," *ibid.,* vol. 17 (1904), p. 251; *Psycholog-*

analogous psychical processes among all races wherever analogous social conditions prevail; but I do not believe that ethnic phenomena are simply expressions of these psychological laws. On the contrary, it seems to my mind that the actual processes are immensely diversified, and that similar types of ethnic thought may develop in quite different ways. Therefore it is entirely opposed to the methodological principles to which I hold to generalize from the phenomenon found among the Kwakiutl and to interpret by its means all totemic phenomena. I will state these principles briefly.

First of all it must be borne in mind that ethnic phenomena which we compare are seldom really alike. The fact that we designate certain tales as myths, that we group certain activities together as rituals, or that we consider certain forms of industrial products from an esthetic point of view, does not prove that these phenomena, wherever they occur, have the same history or spring from the same mental activities. On the contrary, it is quite obvious that the selection of the material assembled for the purpose of comparison is wholly determined by the subjective point of view according to which we arrange diverse mental phenomena. In order to justify our inference that these phenomena are the same, their comparability has to be proved by other means. This has never been done. The phenomena themselves contain no indication whatever that would compel us to assume a common origin. On the contrary, wherever an analysis has been attempted we are led to the conclusion that we are dealing with heterogeneous material. Thus myths may be in part interpretations of nature that have originated as results of naïvely considered impressions (Naturanschauung); they may be artistic productions in which the mythic element is rather a poetic form than a religious concept; they may be the result of philosophic interpretation, or they may have grown out of linguistic forms that have risen into consciousness. To explain all these forms as members of one series would be entirely unjustifiable.

What is true of wider fields of inquiry is equally true of narrower fields. Decorative art as applied by an artist who devotes much time and an inventive genius to the making of a single beautiful object, and decorative art as applied in factory production, which occurs in certain

---

ical *Problems in Anthropology,* Lectures and Addresses delivered before the Department of Psychology and Pedagogy in celebration of the Twentieth Anniversary of Clark University (Worcester, 1910), pp. 125 *et seq.;* see also *The Mind of Primitive Man* (1938), pp. 177 *et seq.*

primitive industries as well as in modern industries, are not comparable, for the mental processes applied in these two cases are not alike. Neither are the free invention of design in a familiar technique and the transfer of foreign designs from an unfamiliar technique to another familiar one comparable. To disregard these differences and to treat decorative art as though the psychological processes involved were all of the same character means to obscure the problem.

The phenomenon of totemism presents a problem of this kind. A careful analysis shows that the unity of this concept is a subjective, not an objective one.

I quite agree with the view of Doctor Goldenweiser,[1] who holds that the specific contents of totemism are quite distinct in character in different totemic areas. Common to totemism in the narrower sense of the term is the view that sections of a tribal unit composed of relatives or supposed relatives possess each certain definite customs which differ in content from those of other similar sections of the same tribal unit, but agree with them in form or pattern. These customs may refer to taboos, naming, symbols, or religious practices of various kinds, and are in their special forms quite distinctive for different totemic areas. There is no proof that all these customs belong together and are necessary elements of what Doctor Goldenweiser calls a "totemic complex." Since the contents of totemism as found in various parts of the world show such important differences, I do not believe that all totemic phenomena can be derived from the same psychological or historical sources. Totemism is an artificial unit, not a natural one.

I am inclined to go a step farther than Doctor Goldenweiser does in his later publications. I consider it inadvisable to draw a rigid line between totemic phenomena in a still more limited sense,—namely, in so far as the characteristics of tribal exogamic sections deal with the relations of man to animals and plants,—but believe that we should study all the customs connectedly, in their weaker form as well as in their most marked totemic forms.

Although we must lay stress upon the subjective character of the groups that we isolate and make the subject of our studies, it is important to bear in mind that the processes by which extended groups of mental activities are systematized by retrospective thought (that is by reason), occur also as an ethnic phenomenon in each social unit, so that

---

[1] "Totemism, an Analytical Study," *Journal of American Folk-Lore,* vol. 23 (1910), pp. 179 *et seq.*

the unification of heterogeneous material that we attempt as an ill-founded scientific method, is only one aspect of a wide range of ethnic phenomena, the essential feature of which is the remodeling of activities, thoughts, and emotions under the stress of a dominant idea. Thus, in the case of totemism the dominant idea of exogamic division has attracted the most varied activities of most diverse origin which now appear to the people themselves as a unit, and to us as a problem that we are tempted to solve as though it were the result of a single historical process, and as though it had its historical origin in a single psychological condition. I have discussed associations of this type in one of the essays to which I referred before.[1]

It follows from this consideration, that under the stress of a uniform dominant idea analogous forms may develop from distinct sources. Thus I do not feel convinced that the substratum of the totemism of the tribes of northern British Columbia and southern Alaska must have been the same. On the contrary, there seems to be evidence showing that their beginnings may have been quite different. Still, historical contact, and the effect of the idea of privilege attached to position, seem to have modeled the totemic customs of these tribes and of their southern neighbors, so that they have assumed similar forms. We call this development from distinct sources "convergence," no matter whether the assimilation is brought about by internal psychic or by external historical causes.

In order to state my position in regard to the theoretical problem definitely, I have to add a third point. Wundt [2] and Durkheim [3] use the term "totemic viewpoint" in a sense quite different from the one that I am accustomed to connect with it. While they do not disregard the connection between social group and totemic ideas, they lay stress upon the identification of man and animals; that is, a characteristic feature of totemism in the most restricted sense of the term. This idea occurs in many other aspects of the mental life of man,—in his magic, art, etc. Neither is this view an essential part of the totemic complex in its widest sense. It seems to me that if we call this the basis of totemic phenomena, one trait is singled out quite arbitrarily, and undue stress is laid upon its totemic association. It appears to me, therefore, an

[1] "Some Traits of Primitive Culture," *Journal of American Folk-Lore,* vol. 17 (1904), pp. 243-254.
[2] *Völkerpsychologie,* vol. 2, Part 2 (1906), pp. 238 *et seq.: Elemente der Völkerpsychologie* (1912), pp. 116 *et seq.*
[3] *Les formes élémentaires de la vie réligieuse* (Paris, 1912).

entirely different problem that is treated by these authors,—a problem interesting and important in itself, but one which has little bearing upon the question of totemism as a social institution. Their problem deals with the development of the concepts referring to the relation of man to nature, which is obviously quite distinct from that of the characterization of kinship groups. The only connection between the two problems is that the concepts referring to the relation of man to nature are applied for the purpose of characterizing social, more particularly kinship groups.

I am inclined to look at the totemic problem as defined before in a quite different manner. Its essential feature appears to me the association between certain types of ethnic activities and kinship groups (in the widest sense of the term), in other cases also a similar association with groups embracing members of the same generation or of the same locality. Since, furthermore, exogamy is characteristic of kinship groups, endogamy of generation groups or local groups, it comes to be the association of varying types of ethnic activities with exogamy or endogamy. The problem is, how these conditions arose.

The recognition of kinship groups, and with it of exogamy, is a universal phenomenon. Totemism is not. It is admissible to judge the antiquity of an ethnic phenomenon by its universality. The use of stone, fire, language, is exceedingly old, and it is now universal. On this basis it is justifiable to assume that exogamy also is very old. The alternative assumption, that a phenomenon of universal occurrence is due to a psychic necessity that leads to it regularly, can be made for the kinship group, not for the other cases. We may, therefore, consider exogamy as the condition on which totemism arose.

When exogamy existed in a small community, certain conditions must have arisen with the enlargement of the group. The size of the incest group may either have expanded with the enlargement of the group, or individuals may have passed out of it, so that the group itself remained small. In those cases in which, perhaps owing to the ever-recurring breaking-up of the tribes into smaller units, cohesion was very slight, the exogamic group may always have remained restricted to the kinship group in the narrow sense of the term, so that there must always have been a large number of small co-ordinate independent family groups. A condition of this type, which is exemplified by the Eskimo, could never lead to totemism.

On the other hand, when the tribe had greater cohesion, the consciousness of blood relationship may well have extended over a longer period; and if the idea of incest remained associated with the whole group, a certain pressure must soon have resulted from the desire to recognize at once an individual as belonging to the incest group. This may be accomplished by the extension of the significance of terms of relationship, by means of which the members of the incest group may be distinguished from the rest of the tribe. Many systems of relationship include such a classification of relatives; but with increasing size of habitat or tribe, this form must also ultimately lead to the passing of individuals of unknown relationship out of the incest group.

The assignment of an individual to the incest group is easiest when the whole group is given some mark of recognition. As soon as this existed, it became possible to retain the incest or exogamic group, even when the family relationship of each individual was no longer traceable. It is not necessary that such an assignment should be made by naming the group. Common characteristics, like a ritual or symbols belonging to the whole group, would have the same result.

It is obvious that this characterization of an incest group presupposes the development of the concept of the unilateral family. Where this concept does not prevail, permanent differentiation of subgroups of the tribe can hardly develop. The origin of the unilateral family must probably also be looked for in the conditions of life of the primitive economic group. Where permanent marital relations prevailed, and both maternal and paternal lines were represented in the economic group, conditions for the development of a unilateral family were absent. A case of this kind is presented by the Eskimo. Where, however, marital conditions were unstable and the women remained members of the parental economic group, maternal descent was the only one possible. Where in the case of more permanent marital relations either husband or wife separated from his or her parental group and joined the opposite parental group, conditions favored the growth of unilateral families. Such changes of domicile may have been determined by a variety of considerations. They would result even in primitive conditions where property right in the man's hunting territory existed, and in which, therefore, the strange woman would join the economic group of the man. We might expect in this case the development of paternal families. When, on the other hand, property right in agricultural land prevailed, the man may have joined the woman's group and a maternal family would have developed. Possibly this may be related to the prevalence of maternal descent among the agricultural tribes of North America.

It is not my aim to follow out here the development of the unilateral family. I merely wish to point out that a varied development may be expected under varying primitive conditions.

It will readily be seen that the elements of totemic organization are given wherever a unilateral family is designated by some characteristic feature.

Furthermore, wherever unilateral descent prevails, either paternal or maternal, there must be a tendency towards a decrease of the number of lines that constitute the exogamic units. This must be the case the more, the smaller the number of individuals constituting the tribal unit and the slower the rate of increase of population. If we assume as initial point a number of women, all representing distinct lines, then all those men (or women) whose descendants do not reach maturity and those who have only sons (or daughters, as the case may be) will not become originators of lines, and obviously the number of lines will decrease with the progress of generations, unless this tendency is counteracted by new accessions or by subdivision into new lines. In small social units the reduction would continue until only two exogamic units are left. Historical evidence of the extinction of unilateral families is represented in the disappearance of families of the European nobility.[1]

The three lines of development, namely the restriction of the incest group to the family without the occurrence of large exogamic groups, the extension of terms of relationship over larger groups, and the naming or other characterization of exogamic groups are all represented in the ethnological data that have been collected.

If the theory outlined here is correct, we must expect to find a great variety of devices used for the purpose of characterizing exogamic groups, which must develop according to the general cultural type to which the people belong. It is obvious that in such cases, when the characterization of the group is due to the tendency to develop a distinguishing mark, all these marks must be of the same type, but different in contents. It does not seem plausible that distinguishing traits should belong to entirely distinct domains of thought; that one group might be recognized by a name, another one by a ritual, a third one by crests

[1] Fahbleck, Pontus E., *Der Adel Schwedens,* Jena, 1903, 361 pp.

or emblems. The fundamental principle of classification as manifested in the mental life of man shows that the basis of classification must always be founded on the same fundamental concepts. We may conclude, conversely, that the homology of distinguishing marks of social divisions of a tribe is a proof that they are due to a classificatory tendency.

THE HISTORY OF THE AMERICAN RACE [1]

THE custom which demands that your President address you at the time of the annual meeting—not when the Academy is in formal session, but when seated around the hospitable board—lays upon him a difficult duty. You expect from him the best that he can give in his science; and still what he gives should be appropriate to the hour, when in pleasant personal intercourse thoughts find expression as they arise, and the stimulated imagination carries us away to more daring flights than those we venture on when our thoughts are given to serious work. Permit me, therefore, to join in the imaginative mood and to lay aside the scruples and doubts of the study and to tell you how in my dreams the stones that we are shaping with arduous labor, and that may in time form a solid structure, but none of which is finished as yet, seem to fit together; and let me sketch before your eyes the airy picture of a history of the American race as it appears before me in dim outlines.

Man had arisen from his animal ancestors. His upright posture, his large brain, the beginnings of articulate and organized language and the use of tools marked the contrast between him and animals. Already a differentiation of human types had set in. From an unknown ancestral type, that may have been related to the Australoid type, two fundamentally distinct forms had developed—the Negroid type and the Mongoloid type. The former spread all around the Indian Ocean; the latter found his habitat in northern and central Asia, and also reached Europe and the New World. The uniformity of these types ceased with their wide spread over the continents, and the isolation of small communities. Bushmen, Negroes and Papuans mark some divergent developments of the one type; Americans, East Asiatics and Malays, some of the other. The development of varieties in each group showed similarities in all regions where the type occurred. The races located on both sides of the Pacific Ocean exhibited the tendency to loss of pigmentation of skin,

[1] Address of the retiring President, read at the annual meeting of the Academy, 18 December, 1911. *Annals of the New York Academy of Sciences*, vol. 21 (1912), pp. 177–183.

eyes and hair; to a strong development of the nose, and to a reduction of the size of the face. Thus types like the Europeans, the Ainu of Japan and some Indian tribes of the Pacific coast exhibit certain striking similarities in form. This tendency to parallel modification of the type indicates early relationship.

After these conditions had developed, one of the last ice ages set in. The members of the race that lived in America were cut off from their congeners in the Old World, and during a long period of isolation an independent development of types occurred. Still the time was not long enough to wipe out the family resemblance between the Asiatics and Americans, which persists up to this day; but numerous new lines of growth developed. The face assumed a distinct form, principally through the increase of size of the nose and of the cheek-bones. The wide spread of the race over the whole territory of the two Americas that was free of ice, and the isolation and small number of individuals in each community, gave rise to long-continued inbreeding, and, with it, to a sharp individualization of local types. This was emphasized by the subtle influences of natural and social environment. With the slow increase in numbers, these types came into contact; and through mixture and migration a new distribution of typical forms developed. Thus the American race came to represent the picture of a rather irregular distribution of distinct types and colors, spread over the whole continent. The color of the skin varied from light to almost chocolate brown; the form of the head, from rounded to elongated; the form of the face, from very wide to rather narrow; the color of the hair, from black to dark brown and even blond, its form from straight to wavy; the lips were on the whole moderately full; the nose varied from the eagle nose of the Mississippi Indian to the concave nose of some South Americans and northwest Americans. Notwithstanding the wider distribution of these types, each area presented a fairly homogeneous picture.

Gradually the great ice-cap retired. Communication between America and Asia became possible, while Europe was cut off by the wide expanse of the Atlantic Ocean. Man followed the ice-cap northward. Members of the American race crossed over to Asiatic soil and occupied parts of Siberia, where finally they came into contact with the Asiatic group, which had also spread northward with the retreat of the ice.

Even at this early time, when the tribes were small in number and weak, human migration was only halted by impassable barriers; and thus contact of members of one group with those of another was not rare, and was always accompanied by the exchange of inventions and other cultural possessions.

We must revert once more to the earlier period, when man first entered our continent. The step from animal to man had long been made. Man brought with him a language, the use of fire, the art of making fire, the use of tools for breaking and cutting and his companionship with the dog. No other animal had yet become the associate of man. Whether he was acquainted with the bow and arrow, the lance and other more complex tools, is doubtful.

What the languages of the earliest Americans may have been we cannot tell. There is no reason to believe that there was only one language, for the slow infiltration of scattered communities may have brought groups possessing entirely different forms of linguistic expression into the continent. Certain it is, that, when man began to increase in numbers, the number of languages spoken were legion. Complexity of form characterized all of them. Sprung from the same root, some became so much differentiated, that their genetic relationship can hardly be recognized. By mutual influences, the articulations of some were so changed as to agree with those of their neighbors. Forms of thought as expressed in one language influenced others, and thus heterogeneous elements were cast in similar forms. As the race increased in numbers, some tribes became more powerful than others, and in intertribal wars many communities were exterminated. With them died their languages and sometimes also their types, although it is likely that in most cases these persist in the descendants of captured women. Thus a gradual elimination of the older stocks occurred, which were replaced by newer dialects of a few groups in which, for this reason, genetic relationship can still easily be traced. Only in those regions where no tribe gained the ascendancy does the old multiplicity of stocks persist. Hence the confusion of languages in California, in many parts of Central and South America, and the comparative homogeneity on the Great Plains, on the plateau of Mexico, and in eastern South America. The diversity of sound and grammatical form which pertains to the old stocks is so great that it is hardly possible to find one feature that is common to the languages of America and that does not belong also to other continents. Certainly all the most prominent characteristics of many American languages are found to the same extent among the tribes of Siberia.

When the contact between Asia and America was re-established, the culture of the whole continent was very simple. Some new inventions had been added to the old stock; weapons had been perfected; the beginnings of decorative art had been laid, and the ideas of the race had advanced in many directions. At this period, the Central Americans made the important step from the gathering of roots, berries and grains to the permanent cultivation of plants near their homes. The development of the cultivated Indian corn occurred. With it the food-supply of the people became more stable, and the population increased at a much more rapid rate than before. Other plants, like the bean, were taken into cultivation; and the more certain the food-supply, the more rapid became the increase in population. The process that began in the Old World with the cultivation of millet and other grains was paralleled here; and step by step the new art spread over new territories, until it had reached the area now occupied by the Argentine Republic in the south, and the Great Lakes in the north. Only the extreme south of South America and the extreme north and northwest of this continent remained outside of this zone, partly due to climatic reasons, partly due to their remote geographical position.

The cultivation of plants and the concurrent increase in population revolutionized the ethnological conditions of the continent; for, owing to their large numbers, the agricultural people also gained the ascendancy over others who did not conform to their habits and remained fewer in numbers.

About this time, perhaps even before the perfected cultivation of plants, a marvelous industrial development set in. Basketry, pottery and weaving were some of the important industries that originated in this period. It is not likely that their origin can be traced in the same way to one restricted area, as in the case of the cultivation of Indian corn, but the many beginnings were more or less moulded in one form, and cultural stimuli probably flowed in many different directions, giving rise to technical forms that, notwithstanding their great diversity, bear the impress of one continental development. Nothing shows this process of assimilation more impressively than the decorative art of the continent. Forms exuberantly developed in Mexico or western South America recur in simpler form in the United States and in the Argentine Republic—not identical, to be sure, but still betraying their family resemblance. The marginal people of the continent alone have learned nothing of these arts. Pottery reached neither the Pacific Northwest nor the extreme south of South America, and the art forms of the North

Pacific coast and of the Arctic coast show no affiliation with those of the middle portions of the continent. These districts remained almost excluded from the general flow of American culture, as it developed in the agricultural areas of the middle parts of the two Americas. Here we may perhaps still find something similar to what existed in our continent before the period of rapid cultural advance set in.

The religious life of the race grew with its other cultural achievements. A strong ceremonialism pervaded the whole life and attained its culminating point in the most complex and populous communities. The fundamental ideas were disseminated from tribe to tribe and found an echo wherever they reached. Thus from many distinct beginnings grew up a peculiar type of ritualism that preserves a similar character almost wherever it exists at all. The thinkers among all these tribes were moved by one fundamental set of ideas, and hence all developed on somewhat similar lines; but the harder the conditions of life, the less is the number of independent thinkers, and the diversity and individuality of tribal ritualism decrease, therefore, as the agricultural resources of the tribes dwindle. In the extreme Northwest and South, only weak traces of the middle American ceremonialism are found.

Thus presents itself to our minds the picture of American civilization developing in the favored middle parts of the continents and spreading by a continuous flowing to and fro of ideas and inventions which stimulated continued growth. In contrast to these, the marginal areas of the extreme South and of the North and Northwest remained in a more stable condition.

Neither history nor archæology nor ethnology allows us at present to follow this complex development in any detail. On the contrary, there seem to be yawning gaps between the various centers that sometimes seem as though they could not be bridged; and still the conviction grows stronger and stronger that this whole culture represents as much an inner unity as that of the Old World.

Somewhat aside from the general current stands eastern South America, which, although not uninfluenced by the stream of Western culture, followed in a halting way·only, and in many respects went its own way. The isolation of the dense forests, the smallness of the tribes and their position aside from the great current of events that had their seat in the plateaus of the west may have contributed to this condition of affairs. Sufficient vigor, however, existed here to allow an energetic expansion northward, which built a cultural bridge between the Atlantic slopes of North and South America that brought about a certain degree of individualization of the East as compared to the West.

I will not follow the higher civilizations that were built up on the basis of the western culture in Mexico, Yucatan and on the western plateaus of South America. When these civilizations arose, their foundations were probably those that I described before as pertaining to a large portion of middle America, extending from some parts of the United States well south into South America. On this basis, however, they built up a promising structure: they laid the foundation of the sciences, developed the art of writing, learned how to work precious metals and copper and advanced in the arts of architecture and engineering. When the advent of the Spaniards cut short this growth, it had attained a stage that might easily have led to accelerated advances.

We must now turn to the northern marginal area, which did not take part to any considerable extent in the cultural work of the people of middle America. Notwithstanding this, the area was not isolated but received stimuli from another direction. The Old World lies near at hand, and from here flowed the sources of new cultural achievements.

As in the New World the early growth of culture in Central America had stimulated the neighboring tribes, and as inventions and ideas had been carried to and fro, so it happened in the Old World. A constant exchange of cultural achievements may be observed from the coasts of the Mediterranean Sea to China and Japan. What wonder, then, if the waves of this movement struck the shores of our world where it is nearest Asia, not with a strong impact but as the last ripples of the spreading circle. The Siberians and Americans were closely affiliated before the introduction of domesticated animals gave a new character to Siberian life; and at this time the Asiatic house, bow, armor and Asiatic tales found their way to America and spread over the whole northwestern portion of the North American continent, reaching even the tribes of our western prairies.

The southern marginal area, the extreme south of South America and parts of Brazil present a different set of conditions—an isolation that is probably equaled in no other part of the world excepting, perhaps, in Tasmania. Unfortunately, our knowledge of these regions is so imperfect that almost nothing can be said in regard to the type of culture of the tribes inhabiting this area. May I point out that here lies the most important problem for the investigation of the earliest ethnic history of the American Continent, because here alone may we hope to recover remains of the earliest types of American mental development. The investigation of this problem, of the ethnology of the Fuegians and Ghes tribes according to modern thorough methods, may therefore urgently be recommended to the Carnegie Institution, that furthers so many lines of research, or to other institutions that are devoted to the advancement of knowledge.

Here halts my fancy, which has taken me in rapid flight over thousands of years, over endless changes of types and peoples. I do not venture to speculate about the question of a cultural relation between the islands of Polynesia and South America; for the suggestions are too slight, and the improbability of relations seems at present too great.

We may, however, cast a glance at the forms that America presents when compared with the Old World. If our picture contains any truth, the independence of American achievements from Old World achievements stands out prominently. The industrial arts were discovered in two large areas independently—the Afro-Asiatic and the American. They spread over continents but remained separated until the period of European colonization. To a great extent, the discoveries made were analogous—basketry, weaving, pottery, work in metals, agriculture. The important step that the Asiatic or European hunter made to the domestication of animals had hardly begun in America, where the Peruvians had developed the use of the llama. Much less had the still more far-reaching discovery been made of agriculture with the help of animals and the invention of the wheel. The use of smelted iron for tools was not known. Important differences may also be traced in fundamental forms of social institutions, arts and religious beliefs. Thus some of the most important advances of the races of the Old World were not known in America, although in other respects the work of civilization had far advanced.

In concluding, I beg to remind you once more that the sketch that I have given, although based on the accumulation of observed data, must not be taken as more than a lightly woven fabric of hypothesis. At every step, there are lacunae of our knowledge which our imagination may temporarily bridge to serve as a guide for further inquiries but which have to be filled by solid, careful work to reach results that will be acceptable before the forum of science.

ETHNOLOGICAL PROBLEMS IN CANADA [1]

A T the meeting of the International Congress of Americanists, held at Quebec in 1906, I called attention to a number of unsolved problems relating to the ethnology of Canada. If on the present occasion I venture to speak again on this subject, I am prompted by its urgency. With the energetic economic progress of Canada, primitive life is disappearing with ever-increasing rapidity; and, unless work is taken up at once and thoroughly, information on the earliest history of this country, which has at the same time a most important bearing upon the general problems of anthropology, will never be obtained.

During the last three years, comparatively speaking, very little anthropological work has been done in the Dominion. The Archæological Institute of Ontario has continued its work. Mr. Teit is still carrying on his valuable researches on the Salish tribes of British Columbia. Dr. Lowie has obtained some information on the tribes of the southern Mackenzie region; but the most important investigation has been the study of the Ojibwa by the lamented William Jones, who lost his life in the service of science. Under the auspices of the Carnegie Institution, he made a profound study of the tribes of Lake Superior. Some work has also been conducted by Mr. Hill-Tout, under the auspices of the Committee of your Association [2] appointed to conduct an ethnological survey of Canada. Some valuable information, collected by Scotch and American whalers in the northern waters of the Dominion, has also been accumulated since 1906.

I do not propose to discuss today in detail the various special problems that invite investigation. I may be allowed merely to point out again that the interior of Labrador, the eastern part of the Mackenzie Basin, the northern interior of British Columbia, the Kootenay valley, and southern and western Vancouver Island require intensive study.

During the last twenty years a general reconnaissance of the ethnological conditions of the Dominion has been made, largely stimulated by your Association; and it seems to my mind that the time has passed

[1] *Journal of the Royal Anthropological Institute,* vol. 40 (1910), pp. 529–539.
[2] British Association for the Advancement of Science.

when superficial reports on the various tribes and on the archæological remains of various districts are of great value. Collections of miscellaneous data hastily gathered can no longer take the place of a thorough study of the many important anthropological problems that await solution. Brief reports on local conditions were well enough when even the rough outlines of our subject had not come into view. Since these have been laid bare a different method is needed. Not even exhaustive descriptions of single tribes or sites fulfil the requirement of our time. We must concentrate our energies upon the systematic study of the great problems of each area. The fruitfulness of such inquiries following general surveys has been demonstrated by the scientific success of the work of the Cambridge Torres Strait Expedition, and by the many points cleared up by the systematic inquiries of the Jesup North Pacific Expedition, which dealt with the ethnology of the coasts of British Columbia, Alaska, and north-eastern Asia.

I may be allowed to formulate today a few problems that seem to me of great magnitude, and which must be solved by the labors of an ethnological survey of Canada. In doing so, I may omit mention of the importance of all anthropological and ethnological research for the purpose of clearing up the earliest history of the country. I will rather call attention to a few problems relating to the whole continent, the solution of which rests on a thorough study of the tribes of Canada.

In a general survey of the ethnic conditions of the American Continent a peculiar uniformity of culture may be observed among the Indians living around the Gulf of Mexico and the Caribbean Sea, on the Great Plains, in the eastern United States and in a considerable part of South America. All these tribes, notwithstanding far-reaching differences among themselves, have so much in common, that their culture appears to us as specifically American. The extended use of Indian corn, of the bean and the squash, the peculiar type of ritualistic development, their social institutions, their peculiar angular decorative art, are among the most characteristic features common to this area. When we compare this culture with the cultures of Polynesia, Australia, Africa, or Siberia, the similarities appear clearly by contrast with the non-American types of culture, and the common American traits stand out quite markedly.

There are, however, a number of American tribes that differ in their culture from that of the large area just mentioned. In South America many tribes of the extreme south and of the Atlantic coast, far into the interior of Brazil, exhibit marked differences from their north-western neighbors. On the northern continent the tribes of the Arctic coast, of the Mackenzie basin, of the Western Plateaus, and of California, do not participate in the type of culture referred to before. Looking at the distribution of these phenomena from a wide geographical stand-point, it appears that the tribes inhabiting the extreme north and north-west and those inhabiting the extreme south and south-east, have ethnic characteristics of their own.

This observation gives rise to two important lines of inquiry : the one relating to the origin of the similarities in what may be called in a wider sense the middle part of America, the other relating to the interpreta-tion of the characteristics of the marginal areas : the one in the extreme south-east of South America, the other in the extreme north-west of North America. The unity of culture in the former area suggests mutual influences among the tribes of this vast territory. The solution of this problem must be attempted by a searching study of the tribes concerned, beginning in the Argentine Republic and reaching north-ward to the Great Lakes and the Western Prairies, and including the continental bridge between North and South America formed by Cen-tral America, as well as the insular bridge formed by the West Indies.

The isolation of the tribes of the extreme south-east and of the extreme north-west suggests that these districts may have preserved an older type of American culture that has not been exposed, or that has at least not been deeply impressed by the influences that swept over the middle parts of the continent and left their impress everywhere. If our point of view is correct, we might expect to find a gradual decrease of the typical middle American elements as we go northward and southward ; and we might expect that on the whole the tribes least affected were also the latest to come under the dominating influences of middle American culture. From what I have said it appears that the bulk of the Canadian aborigines belong to the northern marginal area. The important prob-lem of the significance of the type of culture here found is therefore specifically a Canadian problem.

Its solution must be attempted by means of a painstaking analysis of the physical characteristics, languages, and forms of culture of the various tribes of the Dominion, with a view to segregating the charac-teristics of the older aboriginal type of culture from those elements that may have been imported from the south. Some general considerations relating to this subject may here be given.

In the east the Iroquois seem to be closely allied to tribes of the south. Although historical evidence shows that at the time of the discovery the Iroquois were located along the lower St. Lawrence River, where they were met by Champlain, I have reasons to believe that the previous seats of this tribe were somewhere in the southern part of the United States, perhaps near the Mississippi River.

The Cherokee, who are linguistically related to the Iroquois, have resided in the Southern Appalachian area ever since they have been known, thus forming a link between the Iroquois and the Southern tribes. Other tribes, still more closely related to the Iroquois, lived near them. What appears to me as more important is the fact that the morphological structure of the Iroquois language has nothing in common with the structure of Eskimo, Algonquian, and Siouan tribes, whose neighbors they are in the north, and with whom they have been in contact during the last few centuries; but that it must be classed with the highly incorporating languages of the south-west, which embody the nominal object in the verb—a peculiarity which was formerly believed to be characteristic of all American languages.

Although the relationship between the Iroquois and the tribes of the south, if it really exists, may well be so old that none of the cultural elements belonging to the one area exist in the other, the linguistic observations here referred to necessitate inquiries in this direction. As a matter of fact, it is easy to show that the Iroquois have absorbed or retained many of the most characteristic features of middle American culture; and we may even venture to point out that some of their inventions, like the blow-gun, connect them directly with the tribes of the Gulf of Mexico and of South America. I am inclined to lay great stress upon the peculiar development of the clan system of the Iroquois and upon the type of their tribal organization, which exhibits the very common American trait that social divisions are assigned definite political functions.

If these views should prove to be true, the Iroquois would have to be considered as not belonging to the northern marginal area.

The conditions among the Algonquian are quite different. The Algonquian tribes have changed their habitat so extensively during the last few centuries that it seems necessary, first of all, to reconstruct their earlier distribution. In comparatively speaking recent times the two important western tribes of Canada—the Ojibwa and Cree—resided north and north-east of the Great Lakes. They have gradually migrated westward, and their territory extends at present to the foot-hills of the Rocky Mountains. We even know of Cree warriors who reached a point near Kamloops on the Thompson River in British Columbia. A comparison between the culture of the Algonquian and that of their neighbors of the prairies shows even at the present time a peculiar contrast. The Algonquian appear as the typical inhabitants of the north-eastern woodlands. They were essentially food-gatherers, and agriculture played a very unimportant *rôle* in their life. They carried with them the peculiar mide ceremonies which have been adopted by their nearest Siouan neighbours, particularly by the Winnebago. The most western offshoots of the Algonquian are highly differentiated. The Cheyenne and Arapaho, as well as the Blackfoot who belong in part to the Dominion of Canada, have come to be prairie tribes. It has been shown, however, that the Cheyenne and Arapaho, who resided formerly upon the eastern borders of the Prairie, practised agriculture; while the Blackfoot seem to have come from the Saskatchewan, where they may have lived in a way similar to the present Central Algonquian tribes north of the Great Lakes. From these considerations I am inclined to infer that the Algonquian were at one time a north-eastern tribe; that the most southern branches—namely those extending through the Middle Atlantic States, and south of the Iroquois towards Lake Michigan—have by contact been assimilated to the tribes of the south-east; while the most western offshoots, then living on the upper Mississippi, were influenced by the agricultural tribes of the Lower Mississippi. If this view be correct, we may expect to find the earlier type of Algonquian culture north of the Great Lakes and in the interior of Labrador, which for this reason are particularly inviting to the student. From what little I know of the unpublished results of Dr. Jones's study of the Ojibwa, north of Lake Superior, the views here expressed seem to be fairly well supported, and are certainly worthy of further investigation. On the whole, the organization of the northern Algonquian seems to be so loose, their social structure so simple, that the impression of a strong contrast between the tribe and those of the south is conveyed. The conditions in Nova Scotia and the Atlantic provinces, where related though distinct tribes reside, are also in accord with the views here expressed.

Still clearer are these conditions in the vast area extending from Hudson Bay north-west to the Arctic Ocean, and westward into the interior of Alaska and to the Coast Range of British Columbia. This is the home of the Athapascan tribes. Their migrations and adaptations to different social conditions secure to them a peculiar place among the tribes of North America.

Isolated Athapascan tribes are found all along the Pacific Ocean, in British Columbia, in Washington, Oregon, and California; and two of the most important tribes of the South—the Apache and Navaho, who occupy the borderland between the United States and Mexico—belong to this stock. All the isolated bands in Oregon share the Oregonian culture, and are indistinguishable in their physical type from their neighbors speaking other languages. The Athapascans in California are Californians in type and culture; and those of the southwest are a typical south-western tribe in appearance as well as in their industrial arts and their beliefs. What is true of the isolated bands is also true of the large body of Athapascans of the north. Wherever they come into contact with neighboring tribes they have readily adopted their customs. Thus the Athapascan tribes of the lower Yukon are to all intents and purposes Eskimo; those of the upper course of the Skeena River in British Columbia have adopted much of the coast culture; and those of the coast of Alaska have learned many of the arts and beliefs of their neighbors. The most southern groups of the Mackenzie Basin proper have adopted the customs of the Algonquian tribes. I do not think that this adaptability should be considered as a characteristic racial trait. It seems much more an effect of the lack of intensity of the old Athapascan culture. The same phenomenon is repeated among other tribes whose culture resembles that of the Athapascan. The Salishan tribes of British Columbia and Washington and the Shoshonean tribes of the Western Plateaus of the United States have been affected by their neighbors in exactly the same manner. It would seem, from reports of older travellers, that Athapascan culture, comparatively speaking, uninfluenced by neighboring tribes, may be found in the district west of Hudson Bay, and perhaps also on the upper courses of the western tributaries of the Mackenzie River.

Investigation of this simple culture must be considered as one of the most important problems of Canadian ethnology. Its importance lies in the probability that we may recognize in it an older type of American culture than the cultures observed on the prairies and in the eastern part of the United States.

From what little we know about this district, it seems likely that its culture may be similar to that of the Salishan tribes of the interior of

British Columbia, which are being thoroughly investigated by Mr. James Teit. A simple social organization, simplicity of industrial life, and what may perhaps be called a general individualistic tendency, seem to be common to both groups of tribes. This tendency, combined with sparsity of population, with lack of great rituals which bring people together, and accompanied by a lack of strong artistic proclivities, seems to make these tribes susceptible to foreign influence.

There is little doubt that the Eskimo, whose life as sea-hunters has left a deep impression upon all of their doings, must probably be classed with the same group of peoples. The much-discussed theory of the Asiatic origin of the Eskimo must be entirely abandoned. The investigations of the Jesup North Pacific Expedition, which it was my privilege to conduct, seem to show that the Eskimo must be considered as, comparatively speaking, new arrivals in Alaska, which they reached coming from the east.

I must not leave the discussion of the significance of the culture of this whole district without referring, at least, to the important question of the relation between America and Asia. The Jesup North Pacific Expedition, the plans for which I suggested in 1897, was intended to contribute to the solution of this problem, and I think our investigators have succeeded in showing that there has been close contact between Siberia and the northern marginal area of America. I may be permitted to mention a few of the points which prove the existence of diffusion of culture throughout this territory. Many traditions have been found that are common to Siberia and the north-western part of the American Continent, reaching as far as northern California, the northern Prairies, and Hudson Bay. The treatment of birch-bark, the method of embroidering with reindeer and moose-hair, the forms of houses—all suggest long-continued intercourse. A consideration of the distribution, and the characteristics of languages and human types in America and Siberia, have led me to suggest the possibility that the so-called Palae-Asiatic tribes of Siberia must be considered as an offshoot of the American race, which may have migrated back to the Old World after the retreat of the Arctic glaciers.

I have so far left entirely out of consideration one of the most difficult problems of Canadian ethnology—that of British Columbia. Nowhere in the Dominion is a like number of types and languages met within so small an area; nowhere is found a culture of such strong individuality as in this region.

The fundamental features of the material culture of the fishing tribes of the coast of north-eastern Asia, of north-west America, and of the Arctic coast of America, are so much alike that the assumption of an old unity of this culture seems justifiable, particularly since the beliefs and customs of this large continuous area show many similarities. These have been pointed out by Mr. Jochelson in his descriptions of the Koryak of the Okhotsk Sea. On this common basis a strongly individualized culture has originated on the coast of British Columbia, particularly among the Haida, Tsimshian, and Kwakiutl, which presents a number of most remarkable features, and is best exemplified by the style of art of this region, that has no parallel in any other part of our continent. At the same time some of the customs and beliefs of these people recall so strongly customs that are found only east of the Rocky Mountains, and again customs of the Melanesians that a highly interesting and difficult problem arises, which has so far baffled a complete interpretation, notwithstanding the detailed investigations that have been conducted.

Let us turn now from the consideration of these geographical and historical problems to that of their bearing upon fundamental theoretical questions. In our previous discussions we made the tacit assumption, with which perhaps not all of you agree, that the culture of the tribes of our continent is a complex historical growth, in which by careful analysis the component elements may be segregated, and which in this way becomes historically intelligible. We started with the hypothesis that the ideas of a people depend upon the cultural elements handed down to them by their ancestors, upon additions to their knowledge based on their own experience and upon ideas that they have acquired from their neighbors. Our hypothesis implies that ideas and activities of a people undergo fundamental changes due to complex causes.

We must recognize that this hypothesis does not exhaust the field of anthropological experience. Besides similarities due to obvious cases of borrowing, there are others that cannot be thus explained—similarities sometimes extending to minute details, which occur in regions widely separated. We believe that their occurrence is due to a psychological necessity, which brings about the appearance of certain groups of ideas and activities on certain stages of culture.

The phenomena here referred to have, however, given rise to the further hypothesis that these peculiar similar phenomena, which are not historically connected, arise by necessity whenever a tribe lives in the corresponding cultural conditions; and, furthermore, that these phenomena show us the sequence of all early cultural development the world over. So far as the theory assumes a psychological basis for similarities of ethnic phenomena in regions far apart, it seems to me incontrovertible; in so far as it assumes the necessary occurrence of this whole group of phenomena and their fixed sequence, I believe it is open to grave doubt.

An example will make clear the difference between these points of view. One of the striking features found among primitive people are the customs and beliefs which we are used to combine under the term "totemism." Totemism is found among many American tribes. In Canada it occurs among some Algonquian tribes, the Iroquois, and on the Pacific coast. It is often combined with maternal descent—with the custom of reckoning the child as a member of the mother's family, not as a member of the father's family. Totemism and maternal descent have existed in earlier times among many people where they have now disappeared, and a complete recurrence to these customs, after they have once been given up, is rare, and has never been observed in the history of the civilized world. From this it is inferred that totemism and maternal descent belong to an earlier period in the evolution of civilization, and have gradually been superseded by other forms of social organization and belief. While we may grant that this is the general course of events, the conclusion that totemism and maternal descent precede everywhere paternal descent and family organization does not seem to me necessary. The tendency to their disappearance may exist everywhere; but this does not prove that they are a necessary stage in human development. In many parts of the world they may never have existed. The conditions in America are not at all favorable to the assumption of their omnipresence. The tribes which have the least complex culture, like those of the Mackenzie Basin, and which therefore would appear to be less developed, have paternal descent and no trace of totemism. Those that are socially and politically highly organized, like the tribes of the eastern part of the United States, have maternal descent and highly developed totemism. This has been proved by the investigations of Dr. John R. Swanton. Furthermore, I have tried to show that totemism and maternal descent have been adopted by tribes of British Columbia that were apparently in former times on a paternal stage. Mr. Hill-Tout later on confirmed some of my conclusions, and similar observations were made by Father Morice in the interior of

British Columbia. The attempts to give a different interpretation to these facts, which have been made, for instance, by Breisig, do not seem convincing to me, because they start from the assumption that the unusual sequence of cultural forms is against the hypothetical general scheme of evolution.

It would seem that an acceptable general theory of the development of civilization must meet the demand that the historical happenings in any particular region conform to it. So far as I can see, the various theories of totemism all fail to do so, because they try to explain too much. To the student who delves into the depths of the thought of primitive man, without paying attention to theories, it becomes very soon apparent that the convenient term "totemism" covers a wide range of the most diverse ideas and customs, which are psychologically not at all comparable, but which have in common certain ideas in regard to incest groups—groups in which marriage is forbidden—and peculiar types of religious ideas. Where these ideas occur they tend to associate themselves, and are called "totemism." Where only the one or the other prevails, no totemism can develop. Therefore it seems that totemism may be viewed as a product of peculiar combinations of cultural traits that develop here and there.

I do not wish, however, to add a new theory to the many already existing. I merely wish to point out that, as long as the hypothetical sequence of events does not fit actual cases, the evolutionary scheme cannot be proved to represent the line followed by the whole of mankind.

On the other hand, the proof of dissemination of cultural elements seems to be incontrovertible. The sameness of Algonquin and Iroquois mythology, which Brinton derived from the psychic unity of their minds, is obviously due to borrowing. During the last fifteen years the process and extent of borrowing of myths has been studied in such detail in America, that no reasonable doubt can exist in regard to the gradual dissemination of tales from the Pacific Ocean to the Atlantic Ocean, from the Plateaus of Mexico to the Mackenzie River, and from the heart of Asia to Hudson Bay. No less convincing is the proof derived from the study of American decorative art, with its uniformity of style and its multiplicity of interpretation. In short, it seems to my mind that the fact can no longer be ignored, that the ethnic life of even the most primitive tribe is a complex historical growth. With this, the necessity arises of making the attempt to unravel the historic process, and to verify our general theories by application to the history of each culture.

I wish to state once more that, in advocating this procedure, I do not mean to imply that no general laws of development exist. On the contrary, the analogies that do occur in regions far apart show that the human mind tends to reach the same results, not under similar, but under varying circumstances. The association of decorative art with symbolic interpretation, that of social classification and religious belief, of material actions and magic results, of novelistic happenings and interpretations of nature, are among the fundamental tendencies common to humanity in the earlier stages of civilization. The problem that we have to solve is, on the one hand, the psychological one, how these fundamental tendencies come into existence, and the more specifically ethnological one, why they manifest themselves in various ways at different stages of culture.

I believe this is the anthropological problem that our time is called upon to solve. It has the most far-reaching influence upon the whole treatment of our science, and its investigation must be based on observations made in a region where dissemination can easily be traced. Conditions for this study are favorable wherever a number of distinct types of culture are in close contact, and still sufficiently distinct to allow us to recognize the peculiar traits of each. These conditions are remarkably well fulfilled in Canada. The Arctic coast, the Eastern Woodlands, the Prairies, the Plateau and Mackenzie area, and the Pacific coast, are so many districts sharply individualized, and still not segregated by insuperable barriers from the others. Therefore attempts to carry through a comparative analysis of neighboring tribes is promising. I have referred briefly to some facts that seem suggestive, but the method of research here advocated may perhaps be further elucidated.

The Eskimo, who appear, on the whole, sharply differentiated from their neighbors, have nevertheless many traits in common with them. With the Chukchee and Koryak of north-eastern Asia they share almost all the fundamental inventions relating to the sea-hunt—the kayak, the boat, the harpoon, household utensils. Their pictographic art and their realistic carvings have the same style, which reaches its highest perfection among the Koryak. Certain rituals of the Eskimo and of these tribes are alike. Their hero-tales show similarities in type, and, to some extent, in detail. With their Athapascan neighbors the Eskimo have in common looseness of social organization; with both Athapascan and Iroquois, the concept of confession as a means of warding off the results of sin; that is, of the breaking of customary behavior. With the Athapascan and northern Algonquian they share the occurrence of a peculiar type of animal fable, that, so far as I am aware, has not its like in any other part of America. A number of specific tales can be traced from southern British Columbia to East Greenland and from Lake Superior to Smith Sound. To the former group belongs the tale of the blind man who recovered his eyesight by diving with a loon, and who then took revenge on his mother, who had maltreated him while he was blind; and the story of the being that robbed graves, and was overcome by a courageous youth, who, feigning death, had himself buried, was carried away by the monster, and finally escaped by the incidents known as "the magic flight." The characteristic feature of all these phenomena is their occurrence over continuous areas and their absence outside of this area. Indeed, the study of the component features in the culture of any given tribe must lay the greatest stress upon geographical continuity of occurrence; for, as soon as we admit in our proof the possibility of loss in intermediate districts, we might prove connection between all parts of the world. Continuity of distribution and a sufficient number of analogous elements in neighboring cultures, seem, however, to justify the assumption of borrowing and mutual influences. Ample opportunity for such relations is given in the wars, trading relations and intermarriages of tribes.

I may perhaps now be allowed to enumerate a few of the most obvious gaps in our knowledge of Canadian ethnology, which should be filled to enable us to conduct the searching analysis suggested. Among tribal monographs, those of the Athapascan tribes of the Mackenzie, between Great Slave Lake and Hudson Bay, and that of the Algonquin tribes in the northern part of the Labrador Peninsula, seem to me the most urgently needed, because, as explained before, they are presumably the least affected types of northern marginal culture. In the west, the Kootenay are only little known, and the relation of the Tsimshian to their neighbors requires an exhaustive study. The Coast Salish and the Nootka of the west coast of Vancouver Island still offer important fields for detailed investigation.

In the field of Algonquian research we require a full record of the gentile system of the tribes and of their rituals, particularly an inquiry into the essential characteristics of the mide ceremonies; in the Athapascan group, a detailed study of the complicated customs of avoidance and of the correlated intimacy, which, both in America and Siberia, always seem to go hand in hand, but have until recently escaped the attention of observers, because they are not as striking as the customs of avoidance.

In archæology one of our most important tasks must be the accurate determination of the most north-western extent of ancient pottery and of the relations between the prehistoric types of the Great Lake area and the present population of the same district. I may also point out here the need of an investigation of the shell heaps of Alaska in regard to the question whether a short-headed type preceded the present Eskimo, the only link that is lacking in closing the proof of the eastern origin of the Eskimo.

Most important appears a thorough and systematic study of Canadian languages, based on modern phonetic systems. While we suspect a relationship between Tlingit, Haida, and Athapascan, and again between Salishan and Wakashan, this has not been proved yet. The relationship between these languages is a problem of fundamental importance.

I might go on with my enumeration, but enough has been said.

After the analysis of individual types of civilization, here suggested, has been made, the problem of what constitutes the individuality of the culture of each tribe stands out with great clearness. The tenacious conservatism of the Eskimo, his inventiveness, his good nature, his peculiar views of nature, cannot be explained as resultants of borrowing, but appear as the outgrowth of his mode of life, and of the way in which he has remodelled the cultural materials transmitted to him by his forbears and by his neighbors.

I have dwelt so fully on this question, which is of fundamental importance for a right interpretation of ethnic phenomena, because Canada offers an exceptionally favorable field for their discussion. An exhaustive study of the types of culture and of their relations will show in how far we may be allowed to consider them as representatives of evolutionary types, or in how far the present conditions are the outgrowth of complicated historical happenings, in how far the widest generalisations of anthropology may be expressed in the form of sequences of beliefs and customs, or in how far they are rather psychological laws relating to the mental activities of mankind under conditions determined by the traditional views and attitudes found in different types of culture. Whatever our views may be in regard to these questions, their importance will be recognized by all. The opportunity to solve these theoretical questions, as well as the historical ones propounded before, is given. May we not hope that it may be seized upon, and that the aborigines of the Dominion may be studied before it is too late?

RELATIONSHIPS BETWEEN NORTH-WEST AMERICA AND NORTH-EAST ASIA [1]

RELATION OF AMERICAN RACE TO OLD WORLD RACES

THE relation of the American race to the races of the Old World is one of the important problems of anthropology. It involves the question of the origin of the American race, of the cultural status of the earliest American, and of the later relations between America and the Old World.

The present status of palæontological knowledge leaves us no doubt that the American race cannot have originated on this continent. No indications have been found of any form that could be considered an immediate predecessor of man, no form that could have been the immediate ancestor of anthropoid apes. The gaps that yawn between man and lower forms are infinitely wider in America than in the Old World. There is nothing in America that corresponds to the various anthropoids, to Pithecanthropus, to the Mauer, or to the Neandertal race. The origin of man must be looked for in the Old World.

The physical relationship of the American native to the east Asiatic is closer than that to any other race. Straight, dark hair; wide, rather flat face; heavy nose; tendency to a Mongoloid eye are common to both of them. Locally, types are found that are so much alike that it would be rather difficult to say whether an individual is an Asiatic or an American.

The American race has marked local varieties. In the wide stretch extending from the Arctic Ocean to Tierra del Fuego a considerable number of local types may be distinguished. The hair is sometimes not straight, but wavy; in a few localities lighter colors occur, as for instance in northern British Columbia; the iris is not always dark brown, but may show lighter shades. The skin color varies around a medium yellowish tinge from very light to very dark. The nose is in some regions very prominent and broad, in others narrow and elevated, in still

<hr>

[1] *The American Aborigines, Their Origin and Antiquity,* edited by Diamond Jenness (University of Toronto Press, 1933).

others rather flat and broad, like similar Asiatic forms. The prominence of the cheek-bones, one of the most persistent characteristics of the east Asiatic race, is always present, in some regions excessive, in others so moderate that the face recalls east European forms. As among the east Asiatics the body hair is almost always scanty ; here and there a little fuller, but probably never as full as that of the European. The American race appears most closely affiliated with the large group that includes the peoples of the Malay Archipelago, and of the whole of eastern and central Asia, but excludes the Negroid and Australoid types which occur in the southern part of that area.

While we are not in a position to state definitely at what time the Mongoloid race was specialized we may assume that this occurred some time during the middle-Quaternary.

The early-Quaternary remains of Europe do not suggest the presence of a Mongoloid type on that continent. The only European specimen that has been claimed to be of an American-like type is the Chancelade skull of the Magdalenian period which Testut considered as analogous to the modern Eskimo. Other investigators assign it to the regular Cro-Magnon type.

At the period of the Pleistocene, connection between America and the Old World across the Atlantic was broken. During the Tertiary, when a possible connection existed, the Mongoloid race certainly did not exist. The immigrant ancestors of the modern Indian must, therefore, have come to America from the Pacific side. There are no indications, so far, of any pre-Indian non-Mongoloid race existing on our continent.

The same arguments must be brought forward against the theory of Mendes Correa, who suggests an immigration of Tertiary man from Australia by way of the Antarctic to South America.

Admitting this, the question arises, how did man come to America? If we assume a very early period for his immigration he may have been without means of navigation, and Bering Strait, notwithstanding its narrowness, would have been an impossible barrier. It is more than likely that the configuration of Bering Sea has undergone considerable changes during and since the Quaternary period. Collins has found evidence of changes of shore-line during the habitation of the coast by the Eskimo, and ample geological evidence of raised shore-lines is available. It is not so easy to demonstrate subsidence, because the old shore-lines are submerged, but the configuration of the coast-line with its numerous inlets and small bays, is characteristic of recent submergence. The whole of Bering Sea is shallow and it is plausible, considering the evidence of changes of level, that at one time or several times, there may have been land connections between Asia and America. It is necessary to assume such connection on account of the migration of large land mammals from Siberia to America or *vice versa*.

Immigration across the Pacific Ocean would compel us to assume that it occurred at a time when navigation was highly developed. Since the settling of the islands of the South Pacific must be an event of recent times, it would mean that man came to America at a very late period, a theory contradicted by the conservative time limits of about 7000 years set for the oldest remains found so far in North America.

Since the theory of a direct relation between America and Melanesia has recently been advocated by a number of investigators, it seems well to state that, in my opinion, no valid proof has been given. It seems quite conceivable that in later times Polynesian or even Melanesian canoes may have strayed to the coast of South America, even that a few cultural achievements may have found their way to our continent; but this is not equivalent to deriving the whole Indian race or part of it from this source.

The attempts made by de Quatrefages, ten Kate, Rivet, Søren Hansen, Sergi, Sullivan, and Hellman, who emphasize the similarity of the type of Lagoa-Santa and related forms in South and Central America to those of Australians and Melanesians, are worthy of attention but do not carry the conviction of any genetic relation. I am not as ready as Hrdlička to deny the existence of certain analogies, but I hesitate to accept them as proof of a genetic affiliation, except in so far as I consider a very remote relation between the European and Mongoloid, perhaps also the Australian races as conceivable.

Still less convincing are the attempts to prove a relation between Melanesia, Australia, and America by means of linguistic evidence. We might say that the defenders of this theory prove too much. It is not possible to conceive of a recent close contact between the speakers of these languages, and still we are asked to accept as proof of relationship close similarities of sound and meaning selected from a wide range of languages. Without a reconstruction of the history of words, without the proof of definite phonetic shifts, such attempts are vain, and I do not believe that a single identification of American languages and languages of the west Pacific will hold good.

Most of the ethnological parallels that have been adduced as proving relations between America and the western islands of the Pacific Ocean may be considered as possibly due to dissemination. It should, however, be recognized that all of them consist of minor aspects of cultural life. Imbelloni has dwelt on the striking similarities of certain Polynesian and American clubs; the featherwork of South America and that of Polynesia shows similarities. Most significant seems von Hornbostel's discovery of the sameness of the absolute pitch of South American and East Asiatic musical instruments. His observations are based on a few specimens only, and it remains to be seen whether the examination of a larger number of instruments will corroborate his results.

Opposed to these observations are a number of fundamental differences between the cultures of America and of the Old World. Indian corn, beans, and squashes are the basis of North and South American agriculture; manioc and potato, yam, beans, and chile pepper of eastern South America have no early parallels in the Old World, and none of the cultivated plants of the Old World like wheat, barley, and millet have found their way here.[1] Nor have any of the domesticated animals

[1] Imbelloni, in a paper published in the *Mitteilungen der Anthropologischen Gesellschaft, Wien,* vol. 58 (1928) p. 301, claims that a number of American cultivated plants were introduced from the Old World. Professor E. D. Merrill, director of the New York Botanical Garden, had the kindness to answer as follows to my inquiry: *"Batatas edulis (Ipomoea batatas)* is absolutely a native of tropical America and was introduced into Old World tropics and into Europe after the discovery of America by Columbus; there is, however, some evidence that this, the sweet potato, may have reached some parts of Polynesia in ·pre-Columbian times. The genus *Dioscorea* is pan-tropic in distribution, but there are no species common to the tropics of both hemispheres. Some of the Old World species yield edible tubers, and the same is true of some of the American species. There is no evidence whatever that any Old World species reached America, or *vice versa,* before Magellan's voyage. Certainly, the more important Old World species, particularly *Dioscorea alata,* were introduced into America from the Old World tropics after Magellan's voyage.

"There are no edible *Aroideae* common to the two hemispheres, and I have never seen any evidence that would lead me to believe that any of the few cultivated species had reached both hemispheres before the time of Columbus. The important one in the Old World is the Taro *(Colocasia),* and while this was widely distributed in the Indo-Malayan region and throughout Polynesia at an early date, there is no evidence for considering that it reached America until some time after 1520. The important American representatives of this family are several species of *Xanthosoma,* but these were all confined to America until very recent times. Within the past century some of the species have been introduced into the Old World tropics.

"Apparently a single representative of the *Cucurbitaceae,* the common gourd *(Lagendaria),* attained pan-tropic distribution long before the time of Columbus; but whether this was actually introduced by man, or whether it was naturally distributed, is a problem that I cannot answer. The plant is, of course, a relatively unimportant one from the standpoint of food production.

"*Spondias dulcis* is Polynesian, with two *varieties* credited to Mexico and South America. I am not at all sure that they are correctly named. I suspect confusion here with the indigenous American *S. lutea.*"

been carried to the New World. At a previous time I have pointed out a number of other traits that set off American cultural life fundamentally from Old World life. All this makes it justifiable to say that if there has been any ethnic influence of Oceania upon the New World it has never had an important influence upon American life, and whatever it has been, it can have occurred only in recent times after the invention and perfection of navigation. An ancient immigration in the south seems very unlikely, if not impossible.

We infer from all this that our principal problem relates to the question of the time of the migration of man to the American Continent by way of the region now occupied by Bering Sea and Bering Strait.

The final answer to this question must be based on the geological age of human remains found in America. Search for these has continued for a long time, but we are not yet in a position to state definitely the period to which the oldest remains belong. It is a question of geological age, not of cultural type, with which we are concerned, for it is not admissible to assume that the types of implements belonging to a certain geological period must have been the same all over the world.

So far as I can judge we have no finds in America that with absolute certainty can be ascribed to the Quaternary. We have conclusive evidence that man lived on our continent at a time when a number of animals, now extinct, still roamed over the country. The finds at Folsom and Gypsum Cave are the most conclusive evidence of this kind. The remains of Folsom prove that man used beautifully shaped stone weapons in hunting the extinct bison; those of Gypsum Cave show that man was contemporaneous with the extinct ground sloth. The state of preservation of the sloth remains shows also that the time elapsed since the extinction of the animals cannot be very long. The finds of cave habitations on Promontory Point in Utah may also be significant, because they seem to indicate that man lived in them at a time when Lake Bonneville was much larger than its present remains. Further studies of these sites may give us a clearer insight. The only safe statement that can be made at the present time is that we have no incontestable evidence of man's presence in America before the close of the Ice Age, let us say 10,000 years ago.

From a theoretical point of view it seems difficult to accept this as a final judgment. If man came to America by way of what is now Bering Sea, he travelled from the extreme northern climate through the Tropics to the extreme south. Even admitting climatic changes during this period the physical and cultural acclimatization required time. [According to recent archæological investigations in Tierra del Fuego human remains of the region date back at least 3000 years, probably more.[1]] The present Indian race, notwithstanding its fundamental unity, represents many decidedly distinct local types. Even in North America the Eskimo, north-west coast, Mississippi valley, California types—to mention only a few—are each quite well characterized. We must assume that either these types were differentiated within the short period available, or that a number of distinct types, one after another, came to our continent.

The same difficulty presents itself in regard to American languages. These are so different among themselves that it seems doubtful whether the period of 10,000 years is sufficient for their differentiation. The assumption of many waves of immigrants who represented many types and many languages is an arbitrary solution of the dilemma.

All we can say, therefore, is that the search for early remains must continue. If ultimately nothing should be found that indicates a greater age of man on our continent, we shall have to make sure whether it is possible to assume many waves of migration, or whether we have to revise our opinions in regard to the stability of types and of fundamental grammatical forms.

At the time of his first arrival in America man must have had a certain number of cultural achievements. Prehistoric archæology proves that the art of making chipped stone implements had advanced considerably and that the use of fire was known. The use of clothing, ornaments, and the custom of burial also prevailed. It seems reasonable to suppose that these were brought to America. We may also infer that the dog, if not domesticated, at least followed man in his migrations.

What else man had can be discovered only by an analysis of the basic elements of American cultural forms, in so far as they are common to the whole continent, and by a comparison of these with fundamental traits of Old World culture.

Such reconstruction involves many difficulties, for what is common to the two Americas may be due as well to diffusion as to antiquity. Furthermore the most generalized traits of culture may have developed

---

[1] Junius Bird, "Antiquity and Migrations of the Early Inhabitants of Patagonia," *The Geographical Review*, vol. 28 (1938), pp. 250–275. Later addition to the original essay.)

independently in most areas. For these reasons I do not believe that we can discover much that is necessarily ancient beyond what is found by archæological research.

In order to utilize cultural forms for establishing their antiquity it would be necessary to prove their stability. Certain motor habits; in a sense, language; general mental attitudes may be stable over long periods.

I have pointed out repeatedly that American culture is set off by many traits from that of the Old World. I may repeat some of their fundamental differences: agriculture in most parts of America based on Indian corn, beans, and squashes; lack of wheat, barley, millet, and rice; lack of the domesticated animals used in the Old World except the dog and, locally, turkey and llama, and lack of their use for agricultural purposes; the narrow localization and late use of bronze; weakness of executive organs in political structure combined with the absence of judicial procedure, except in Mexico and the Andean plateaus; the lack of the use of evidence, the oath, and the ordeal for judicial purposes; the weakness of the belief in the evil eye and in obsession (if such existed at all in the strict sense of the word); the almost complete absence of the riddle and proverb in native literature, and the rarity of the use of decorative designs for protective purposes. In addition to all this we must consider that the cultivation of Indian corn must have originated in Mexico, because the ancestral wild plant belongs to that area, so that American agriculture based on Indian corn must have developed independently.

These American traits are overlaid by others due to modern contact, which may be divided into two groups. The one contains the features common to the circumpolar area of the Old and New Worlds; the other consists of traits which extend farther to the south.

CIRCUMPOLAR CULTURE TRAITS

The characteristics of the circumpolar culture are only in part explained by the similarity of geographical environment. The climate does not permit agriculture, and all the people rely essentially upon animal food—fish, sea-mammals, and land animals. The domestication of the dog is well-nigh universal. It is, however, characteristic of the circumpolar region alone that the dog is used as a draft animal. It is not unlikely that the dog cart which has been used up to the present in northern Europe is a survival of this use of the dog. In Asia and Arctic

America the dog is used as a draft animal in connection with a sledge. In America its use has spread southward from the Arctic region, but the Indian tribes of the plains use it in a peculiar manner. Instead of the sledge or toboggan, they use a frame resting on two poles which are tied to each side of the dog and are dragged over the ground. This contrivance, the so-called *travois,* was used both in summer and winter.

Another characteristic trait of the circumpolar region is the use of birch bark for making vessels and canoes and for building houses. The Indian birch-bark wigwam is well known. The construction of the Siberian tent is, in principle, the same. A framework of poles is erected and covered over with sheets of birch-bark. The bark canoes are also of similar structure.

It might be said that the use of skins and bark for covering framework is dictated by the availability of these materials, but this point of view is hardly tenable when we consider also the similarity of the birch-bark vessels which are used on both continents. Baskets and vessels of various kinds are formed by cutting and folding birch-bark in appropriate ways, and many of the ideas of treatment are practically identical. The strengthening of the rim and the decoration of the sides are characteristic for Siberia and for America, but they do not seem to occur in other parts of the world.

Common to Siberia and America also is the characteristic flat drum consisting of a hoop covered by a single head, sometimes with a handle consisting of crossed thongs or wire or similar material. In practically all other regions where drums with a single head occur, the shell is high, as, for instance, in the large drums of Africa. The only other form similar to the American and Siberian drum is the tambourine, which seems to be confined to the Mediterranean and to southern Asia. The tambourine, however, is much smaller and is characterized by the additional jingles.

I do not feel convinced that the use of tailored fur clothing and the methods of fishing can be added as a proof of ancient, historical relationship, because they are dependent upon climatic and geographic conditions. Still an inhospitable climate does not produce adequately protective clothing, as is shown by the scanty covering of the north-west coast and of Tierra del Fuego.

Another feature common to the north-western part of America and to Asia is the use of slat armor, consisting of cuirasses and other protective devices made of rods or slats, of wood, bone, or ivory, securely lashed together. If this type of armor should have developed from Chinese and Japanese patterns it would be proof of long-continued cultural influence that extended northward and south-eastward. Of similar character is the use of the sinew-backed bow which is widely used in the Old World and occurs in an extensive area of north-west America.

Similarities in religious ceremonials, beliefs, and traditions prove an intimate relation between Asia and America. Recently Dr. Hallowell has published a detailed study of the bear ceremonial in the Old and New Worlds and proved its wide distribution over the whole extent of the circumpolar area and the adjoining districts farther to the south. It is hardly admissible to assume that the cult of the bear has developed independently all over this country on account of the fear inspired by this animal, for form and content are too much alike. At the same time these particular ceremonials are not found in regard to other dangerous animals.

Attention might also be called to the peculiar use of wood-shavings, grasses, and shredded bark as religious symbols which characterize the ceremonials of the Ainu, Koryak, Chukchee, and of the coast tribes of British Columbia and southern Alaska.

It is not unlikely that some of these traits have spread far to the south, even to South America. Ehrenreich's comparisons of North and South American mythologies suggest a number of similar traits that are presumably due to transfer, and among these are typical Asiatic traits.

It seems important to point out how rapidly details of culture may be grafted upon foreign cultures even when there is no direct contact between the carrier of the new cultural trait and those who adopt it. Proof of this is, for instance, the spread of tobacco and Indian corn almost all over the world. In America Spanish and Negro customs and ideas have influenced distant native tribes. The occurrence of the musical bow in California can hardly be an independent invention, since no stringed instruments were known in aboriginal America. The picture writing of the Cuna and the invention of syllabic writing are also cases in point. Still more interesting is the complete assimilation of a number of European or African tales which reached this continent only a few hundred years ago. I will not refer to the innumerable rabbit tales which are found even in the remotest parts of South America, for these are not in any way assimilated. More interesting is the tale of the ascent of the tree, fully treated by Dr. Parsons, which in most cases is thoroughly integrated in the mythology of the Indians; or the tale of the turtle's war party which ends with the well-known trick of Bre'r Rabbit who, when captured, begs his enemies not to kill him by throwing him into the briar bushes, the place where he always lives. Rapidity of integration is also illustrated by the various religious movements that originated among the Indians.

Considering these phenomena the modern transfer of cultural elements from Siberia to America does not seem surprising, and does not necessitate the assumption of very great antiquity of this connection.

LANGUAGES OF SIBERIA AND AMERICA

Finally we have to discuss the problem of a possible genetic relationship between the languages of Siberia and of America. The answer to this problem depends upon a number of fundamental theoretical questions. As stated before, the languages of America that cannot be safely reduced to common origins are very numerous. The attempts that have been made to combine them into a very few related stocks are dictated rather by the wish to unify them than by satisfactory evidence. There are a number of languages that are split up into divergent dialects and that are spoken over extended territories, such as Athapascan, Algonquian, Shoshone, Siouan, Caribbean, Arawak. Others are confined to very small territories and are spoken by small communities. In North America such regions are found on the Pacific coast and in Texas; farther south all through Central America; in South America in the Andean region. It has often been claimed that such diversity of languages in restricted areas is a condition due to the extinction of earlier forms of speech spoken in wider contiguous areas. This view is based on observations in Europe, where we see the Basque gradually retreating before French and Spanish, languages of the Lithuanian groups giving way to German, Polish, and Russian; and Finnish-speaking tribes adopting Russian. I believe the essential point to be observed is that all languages which have a wide distribution now-a-days have attained it in, anthropologically speaking, recent times. Indo-European, Turkish, Chinese, Bantu, Malayo-Polynesian, Algonquian, Athapascan, Carib, Arawak, can be proved or inferred to have extended their territories not so very long ago. The assumption that single, widely-spread languages occurred in the regions now occupied by them cannot be proved. There is rather evidence that many different languages have been superseded by them. The ancient conditions in Asia Minor and in Italy certainly indicate such a development. Whether this occurred also in Africa and America must be decided by a more detailed study of native languages. The general history of languages shows that many forms of speech have disappeared, generally distinct, as far as we can see, from those surviving. There is no reason to believe that this is a new process. We are, therefore, led to the conclusion that in early times each language was spoken in a restricted territory and that the multiplicity of languages which we find at present on the Pacific coast of America, in Siberia, in the Caucasus, and in the Sudan was at one time characteristic of the whole world.

If this view is correct we may see in the whole area in which Palæ-Asiatic languages are spoken, together with western America, a district in which very ancient conditions survive. The Turkish and Tungus languages which have superseded the ancient Siberian languages do not belong to this group.

It may be asked whether there is any indication that the Palæ-Asiatic languages are related to American languages more closely than other languages of the Old World. So far as genetic relationship is concerned no proof has been given that any one of the Palæ-Asiatic languages and any American language are derived from the same stock.

American languages differ among themselves so fundamentally that a common characteristic cannot be given. They have been called poly-synthetic and incorporating, but by no means are these characteristic of all American languages, and similar forms occur outside of America.

The classification of experience which is the foundation of linguistic expression does not follow the same principles in all American languages. On the contrary, many different forms are found. The content of nouns and of verbs depends upon cultural conditions. What for a people of temperate zone is simply "ice," has many shades of meaning for an Arctic people like the Eskimo, "salt water ice, fresh water ice, drifting ice, ice several years old." Terms of relationship and those relating to social structure vary in their contents; classifications occur such as animate and inanimate; long, flat, or round; female and non-female. In verbs modalities of action, forms of object acting or acted upon, or local ideas may be expressed. In short, the variety of linguistic content is very great.

So are the linguistic processes. Prefixing, suffixing, stem modification, stem expansion, vocalic harmony are found in endless variation.

For this reason it would be difficult to find a language that might not fit into the American scheme. Especially the Siberian languages possess many traits that are found in American languages and which structurally might just as well be American as not. However, this might be claimed for the agglutinating languages too, for their fundamental processes are repeated in fairly parallel form in Eskimo, except that Eskimo does not use vocalic harmony in the word unit. Other American languages have laws of vocalic harmony, such as Sahaptin (Nez Percé) and partly Chinook.

An early unity of Palæ-Asiatic and American languages has not been established. In fact the two languages which at present are nearest neighbors, Chukchee and Eskimo, differ fundamentally in structure, vocabulary, and phonetic principles. It is interesting to note that, notwithstanding their fundamental differences, there is a similarity in the mode of analyzing experience. In other words, the ideas expressed by linguistic devices are somewhat alike, although the methods of expression are quite different. "Cases" of the noun, the multitude of demonstrative pronouns, and modes of the verb express quite similar ideas. The different treatment of transitive and intransitive verbs follows the same pattern. These similarities are so striking, particularly on account of their absence outside of the Aleut-Eskimo-Chukchee-Koryak-Kamchadal territory, that we must assume a common cause.

It would seem most likely that this must be looked for in a later mutual morphological influence which molded structural forms to such an extent that the psychological structures of the languages acquired to a certain degree a common type.

It is possible that in the intercourse between neighboring tribes, this process may have occurred often, and that it may account for many curious similarities of structure. This type of cultural contact between Siberia and America would also not demand great antiquity.

THE SOCIAL ORGANIZATION OF THE
KWAKIUTL[1]

IN THE Annual Report of the United States National Museum for 1895 I have given a description of the social organization and secret societies of the Kwakiutl based on observations and inquiries made prior to 1895. Further information relating to the social organization of the Kwakiutl collected on my last visit to Vancouver island, and since that time obtained through correspondence with Mr. George Hunt clears up a number of points of this difficult problem.

One of the greatest obstacles to a clear understanding of the social organization of the Kwakiutl is the general confusion caused by the reduction in numbers of the tribe. I have tried to clear up the situation by recording the histories of a number of families in all possible detail. In the following I shall give the principal results that may be derived from my collection of data.

I will begin with the discussion of what constitutes a tribe. There is a very fundamental difficulty in the definition of the tribal unit and of its subdivisions. I do not know of a single Kwakiutl tribe that is at present an undivided unit. All those studied consist of well-recognized subdivisions.

Furthermore, a single locality is claimed as the place of origin of each division of the tribe. In the consciousness of the people these divisions are fundamental units. The development of the concept of a tribal unit is not, by any means clear, except in so far as it appears as an effect of the congregation at one place of a number of local units. Recent tradition, the historical truth of which cannot well be doubted, shows clearly that such a congregation has occurred repeatedly. Units may also have broken up, owing to inner dissensions or to other accidents.

On the other hand, each tribe consists of units that claim as their places of origin, localities not far apart. In a few cases only, may one or the other division of the tribe claim as the place of its origin a locality removed quite a long distance from the traditional home of the other divisions. This is the case for instance with the "Rich Side" group of the

[1] *American Anthropologist*, N.S., vol. 22 (1920), pp. 111–126.

Kwakiutl. Some of the tribal names are purely geographical terms and indicate that we are dealing with communities that live in close proximity, including perhaps groups that moved to the territory in question. Other types of names, however, occur. The translations given by the natives for some of them are folk-etymologies and cannot be taken as authoritative. Thus the name Kwakiutl is derived from a stem $kwak^u$- of unknown significance, but is considered by the natives as a derived form of $kwax\cdot$—which means "smoke." [1] The name $^\varepsilon n\bar{a}'k'wax\cdot da^\varepsilon x^u$ is explained by them as derived from nEq-, "ten," philologically an impossible etymology. In previous writings, I accepted some of these etymologies, but I am certain that they must be rejected.

In a number of cases the relations between the divisions of a tribe are explained by tradition. Thus two divisions of one sept [2] of the Kwakiutl which are assumed to be descended from two brothers and whose names are found among many tribal groups, were scattered among the different tribes. Since their names are honorific names ("The First Ones" and "Chief's Group"), it may be doubted whether any historic meaning attaches to this tradition. This is more plausible for the division "Real Kwakiutl" ($KwEkw\bar{a}'k'wEm$) which is found among two septs of the Kwakiutl, which, according to tradition, are assumed to be derived from the same place of origin. In some cases we find in a tribe a subdivision which has for its name the stem of the tribal name with the ending -Em, as in the division just mentioned, the $S\bar{e}ntl'Em$ and $dl\bar{e}'q'Em$ [3] and outside of the Kwakiutl proper, the $Mamaleleq'am$. The meaning of this ending is "the real ones." According to the statement of the Indians there was, in former times, in almost each division a noble family that bore a name of this type, while the rest of the people were designated by the ordinary name of the division. Mythologically this is explained as meaning that the select group, called "the real" members of the division, were descended from the ancestor, while the other families at an early time became associated with the ancestor without being descended from him.

On the other hand, according to tradition, several pairs of subdivisions of one sept of the Kwakiutl are considered as the descendants of two brothers, one of the elder, the other of the younger one. In another

---

[1] $x\cdot$ is pronounced like *ch* in German *ich;* x like *ch* in German *ach.*

[2] The Kwakiutl proper consist of four septs or subtribes, each being divided into a number of subdivisions which are the fundamental social units.

[3] q is a k pronounced at the soft palate; the apostrophe indicates a break; E is a weak vowel, like *e* in flower.

case, the divisions of the tribe are considered each as descended from one of four brothers. When I inquired later on why in one of these pairs the one division was considered of lower rank, the following information was obtained. In the generation *I* the ancestor of the division *a* of one sept *A* had a slave whom we may call *IAa*1. He married the woman slave of the ancestor of another division *b* of another sept *B* whom we may call *IBb*2. Their eldest son (Generation *II*, designated *IIBb'*3), married the daughter (*IIAc*7) of the chief (*IAc*6) of the division *c* of the sept *A*, assumed a chief's name and became the ancestor of the division *b'*, of the sept *B*, or of the line *Bb'*, which is up to this time associated with *Bb*. At a former time this line was described to me as descended from the younger brother of the ancestor of *Bb*. The daughter of *IAa*1

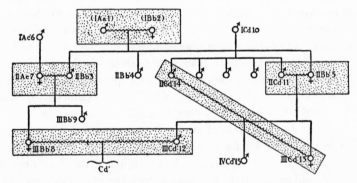

Fig. 1. *I, II, III*, first, second, third generations; *A, B, C*, tribal divisions; *a, b, c, d*, subdivisions of *A, B, C; b', c', d'*, subdivisions affiliated with *b, c*, and *d*.

and *IBb*2, whom we may call *IIBb'*5 married the fifth son (*IICd*11) of the chief of the division *d* of the sept *C*, whom we may call *IICd*10. Their daughter (*IIICd'*13) married her father's eldest brother *IICd*14, without letting him know of her descent. Therefore her descendants were not accepted by her husband's division *Cd*, but assigned to *Cd'*. The elder son (*IIICd'*12) of this couple married the daughter (*IIIBb'*8) of the couple who had established the line *Bb'*, and their children also belong to the line *Cd'*. Their descendants are the division *Cd'*, which is up to this day associated with the line *Cd*. These relations are illustrated by the diagram above (fig. 1).[1] This is an example of

[1] The details of this genealogy are given in Franz Boas, "Ethnology of the Kwakiutl," *Thirty-fifth Annual Report of the Bureau of American Ethnology*, Washington (1921), pp. 1093 *et seq.*

the intricate mythological interrelations between the divisions that belong to a single tribe.

We may therefore say that in the concept of the Indians, the tribe consists of a number of divisions, each of which is derived from one ancestor, but which includes also individuals of different descent who at an early time joined the ancestor. In a number of cases, the ancestors of the various divisions are brothers and the divisions represent elder and younger lines. In other cases there is no such relation, the lines representing disconnected local groups.

Although in the present period the concept of the tribe is very clear in the minds of the Indians, there seems to be little doubt that the tribes have undergone many changes in number and composition. There are some indications of this process even at the present time. Thus one sept of the Kwakiutl proper (the "Rich Side") are generally grouped with the "Great Kwakiutl," and the tendency is such that within a short time the consciousness of their separate existence might well disappear. The union of the Tl'a'tl'asiqwala and NaqwE'mgilisala in one village has not yet led to their fusion, but externally at least they form a single tribe. The stability of tribes is primarily due to the fact that the tribal units have fairly definite functions distinct from the functions of the tribal divisions. These appear particularly in formal gatherings in which the tribes are arranged in rank and in which, furthermore, definite tribes are matched. Thus in northern Vancouver island, we find the following parallel arrangement of Kwakiutl tribes and of the tribes further to the east.

"Northerners ($Gw\bar{e}'t\varepsilon la$) matched with Mamaleleqala

"Rich-in-Middle" ($Q'\bar{o}'moy\hat{a}^\varepsilon ye$) matched with "Far Siders" ($Qw\bar{e}'qsot'enox^u$)

"Great Kwakiutl" ($^\varepsilon w\bar{a}'las Kw\bar{a}'g\cdot ul$) matched with Nimkish

"Rich Side" ($Q'\bar{o}'mk\cdot'ut\varepsilon s$) matched with "Angry Ones" ($\unicode{0x141}\bar{a}'wits'es$)

Notwithstanding the relative stability of the tribes, the tribal divisions must be considered as the fundamental units. In previous writings I have used the terms "gens" and "clan" according to the varying impression of prevalence of maternal and paternal descent, both of which are important. After much hesitation I have decided to use the native term *numaym* ($^\varepsilon nE^\varepsilon m\bar{e}'m$) because the characteristics of the unit are so peculiar that the terms "gens" or "clan" or even "sib" [1] would be mis-leading. We have to recognize first of all that positions in a *numaym,* or at least the ranking positions must be filled and that their disappear-ance, according to the ideas of the Indians, would be a misfortune. A position is defined by the name attaching to it and by a number of privileges $(k''\bar{e}'s'o)$. I prefer the term "privilege" to the term "crest," because the privileges are quite varied in character, although not so much varied in form as among the Nootka.

A clear understanding of the constitution of the *numaym* is made very difficult by the fact that the number of positions is at present greater than the number of members of the tribe, so that many individuals hold more than one position in more than one *numaym.* It may be that even in early times, important personages had the right to do so, but the present extension of this right is, no doubt, due to the reduction in the number of members of the tribe. As a matter of fact, the Indians them-selves are not by any means clear as to the rights of each individual, and quarrels regarding rank and position are of common occurrence. In these each party tries to defend its rights by facts based on descent. The fundamental principle seems to be that primogeniture, regardless of sex, entitles the first-born child to the highest rank held by one of its parents. Rank is, on the whole, determined by the order of birth, and the noblest line is the line of the first-born. The lowest in rank that of the youngest born. Hence when a father and mother are of equally high rank, the first-born child may be assigned to one *numaym,* the following to an-other *numaym.* In cases of equal rank of both parents the father's *numaym* has preference and to it the first-born child is assigned. I have never been able to learn definitely whether a child that is assigned to another *numaym,*—not his mother's—retains, nevertheless, the right to membership in his father's *numaym* or not. In some cases it seems that way, in others it seems that a person either has no position in the father's *numaym,* or that he definitely severs his relations with it and gives up his place in it. The Indians emphasize again and again the rule that the "house name" and the attached position and privileges can never go out of the line of primogeniture and may not be given away in mar-riage. The first-born child must take them no matter whether it is male or female. It is not clear, however, even from the genealogies at my dis-posal, what was done in former times if the parents did not hold enough

---

[1] See Robert H. Lowie, "The Matrilineal Complex," *University of California Pub-lications in American Archaeology and Ethnology,* vol. 16 (1919), pp. 29 *et seq.*

seats and names to go around among their children, unless in these cases the children received names from the mother's father. At present and for about seventy years past, this condition has probably never arisen. The inference from the general point of view of the modern Indian is that the younger lines had names of inferior rank and formed the lower classes.

It seems to me that the conditions among the Kwakiutl and the Nootka must have been quite similar in so far as a sharp line between nobility and common people did not exist, that rank was rather determined by the seniority of the lines of descent. In one Kwakiutl tale, it is even stated that the youngest of five brothers "was not taken care of by his father and was like a slave or a dog." [1]

In case of the death of the eldest child, the younger brothers and sisters rank in order of their birth regardless of sex. Where there are no children, the younger brothers and sisters of the deceased in order of birth would be the successors to his position. When there are no brothers or sisters, a father's (or mother's as the case may be) brother and sister and their descendants would be the successors.

Among some of the noble families, we find a strong desire to retain the privileges in the narrowest limits of the

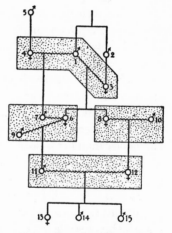

FIG. 2. Genealogy illustrating endogamous marriages.

family. This is done by means of endogamous marriages. Marriages are permitted between half-brother and half-sister, *i.e.*, between children of one father, but of two mothers, not *vice-versa;* or, marriages between a man and his younger brother's daughter, but not with his elder brother's daughter, who is, of course, of higher rank, being in the line of primo-geniture or at least nearer to it. An excellent example is the genealogy represented in fig. 2.[2] We have here first a marriage between a man 1 and his younger brother's daughter 3. Then a marriage between half-brother and sister 6 and 7 and finally between the

[1] Franz Boas, "Ethnology of the Kwakiutl," *Thirty-fifth Annual Report of the Bureau of American Ethnology* (1921), p. 1097.

[2] *l. c.,* p. 781.

son 11 and daughter 12 of two full sisters 6 and 8. It is expressly stated that these marriages were intended to prevent the privileges from going out of the family. In other genealogies I have found practically no cases of endogamy. On the contrary, we find, so far as I can see, only exogamous marriages.

We may say that the *numayms* are based on descent with a preference for the paternal line; the highest positions in the *numaym* which form the nobility are the senior lines, at the head of which stands the first-born line. There are, therefore, a series of noble names in each *numaym* that may be considered as similar to offices which must be filled. The occupants of these positions must have the hereditary right to occupy their places, but their positions are actually determined by assignment, each occupant of a position having the right to determine his successor provided the laws of descent give him a title to the position.

The peculiar transfer of name, position and privileges from the woman's father to his son-in-law has been described by me before.[1] The complex rules of this transfer have given rise to much discussion. Ordinarily name and position are given by a man to his son-in-law's children. This does not entail any difficulties when the woman is a first-born child and nobler than her husband, or when younger children are concerned. When the husband is the nobler, it would however, contradict the rules of primogeniture previously described.

I have said in earlier publications that the son-in-law holds the name and privileges which he receives from his father-in-law on behalf of his son who becomes the real owner when he grows up. I believe this does not quite correspond to the actual conditions. In return for the marriage presents given by the young man, the father-in-law promises to give names, positions and privileges to any member of the son-in-law's family, to the son-in-law himself, his father, brother or sister, and for his prospective children.

The transmission from individual to individual through marriage is most arbitrary. Thus we have one case in which a man (1) obtains his name and position (a) from his sister's husband (2), who had obtained it from his own father (3), who in turn obtained it through a former marriage—not with the mother of the individual (2)—from his former wife's father. Diagrammatically this may be expressed as follows (fig. 3). In another case the father of a man was given a name and position

---

[1] "The Social Organization and the Secret Societies of the Kwakiutl Indians," *Report of the U. S. National Museum for 1895,* Washington (1897), p. 334.

by his daughter-in-law's father. In these cases the person who paid the marriage price to the bride's father receives the gifts returned by the father-in-law.

These names and positions, of course, cannot be actually taken until the son-in-law gives a feast at which the gifts are formally bestowed and at which the presents received from the father-in-law are distributed among the numayms of the son-in-law's tribe, excluding his own numaym. Practically the son-in-law is the recipient of these names, but they are given to him to be bestowed upon certain designated persons. In most cases the son-in-law, who already holds a noble position, uses the new name and position that he himself received from his father-in-law only at the festival at which he distributes the marriage presents which he has received from his father-in-law, and then he "puts away" the name until he in turn gives it to his son-in-law or to some member of his son-in-law's family. There, are however, cases in which this is not done. Thus a noble chief of the Kwakiutl gave up his position

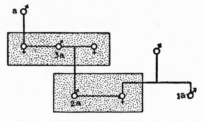

Fig. 3. Transfer of position a through marriage.

and took the place of his father-in-law who was a Mamaleleqala. The Kwakiutl were dissatisfied with this arrangement and in order to adjust matters, he sent his second and third children to take his places in the numaym to which he belonged, while he himself, his wife, eldest and youngest sons took their places among the Mamaleleqala. Such a transfer of a son-in-law to his wife's numaym and tribe does not seem to be frequent, although it is permitted.

The actual position of the first born child is, therefore, that by birth it belongs to a certain numaym and that under normal conditions it will remain there and receive additional names and positions from its father-in-law. These will be given up when his or her daughter marries and ordinarily descend to her son, although this is not absolutely necessary. Later born children are liable to attain high rank through marriage and will be more readily transferred through marriage to a new numaym. That the son-in-law has the free disposal of names given to him personally is brought out clearly by the fact that he can transmit them even after a divorce and a new marriage to the descendants of relatives of his new wife, or that he may bestow names received from his second wife to descendants or relatives of his former wife.   It is also interesting to note that in some cases names and privileges received in marriage are split and become the property of different individuals.

The most common arrangement is that a man places his daughter's husband in one of the positions at his disposal, either his own or one belonging to him in some other way.   The positions acquired by marriage are retransmitted in the same way, so that the holders will always be the husbands of a succession of daughters.   The names and privileges are held by the men, although they descend throughout through the line of daughters.   In the genealogies at my disposal I have not found cases of such continued transmission, neither do I find a continued transmission from maternal grandfather to grandson.   There is rather a tendency for the lines transmitted through marriage to disappear.   It is not safe, however, to infer from this that continued transmission through marriage does not occur, because the genealogies are naturally so arranged that the privileges of a certain noble person now living are accounted for.   Owing to the fact that the record of transmission of positions and privileges in younger lines is incomplete, that the positions accounted for are generally in the line of primogeniture, the disappearance of privileges obtained by marriage may be rather apparent than real.   Transmission through the mother, *i.e.,* from the maternal grandfather to the grandson is found very frequently in the genealogies at my disposal, but it is not as frequent as direct transmission from father to son.   In one genealogy, transmission from maternal grandfather to child appears fourteen times, from father to child, twenty-nine times.

Evidently the individual wish of a dying person regarding the disposition of his name, position, and privileges is one of the decisive elements in the assignment of social position.   As long as any right can be construed that justifies the desired transfer, the *numaym* will abide by the wish of the deceased.   If, however, selection can in no way be justified by the laws of descent, the *numaym* may not permit the proposed transfer.

In those cases in which the disgrace of illegitimate descent, *i.e.,* descent from a couple who did not go through all the formalities of a marriage, attaches to the proposed successor, he may not be admitted to the positions bequeathed to him.   The effect of such a disgrace is illustrated by the following example.   A man, who belonged to the *numaym* mentioned before, which is considered as descended from slaves who were not married according to the customary form, was considered as of lower rank because he belonged to this *numaym*. Furthermore, his parents were not properly married and he himself lived with a woman of high rank without performing the proper marriage ceremonies. He became very wealthy and inherited a number of high positions. The *numayms,* however, will not allow his children to take his place. His name is to die and the children will be assigned to positions in the mother's *numaym*.[1] Although they will assume high positions, their descent will always be felt as a blemish. I presume in early times, when other individuals of pure descent were available, they would not have been permitted to occupy these positions.

The wish of the dying person may also be vetoed by a member of his family who has a nearer right to succession than the designated successor.

According to the ideas of the Indians, the two categories of names and privileges, those in the line of primogeniture and those that may be transferred by marriage, are quite distinct. Nevertheless, the law of preventing the transfer of the inalienable family names and privileges to another family is broken every now and then, in accordance with the wish of the holder of the place expressed on his death-bed. I do not doubt that in early times, when the claims of the individual could be maintained by force, a usurped position could be held, provided the holder had sufficient strength to withstand his rivals and enemies. The law may also be broken when a tribe or *numaym* demands that one of the descendants of a chief be made his successor.

The names and privileges belonging to the line of primogeniture and those that may be transferred by marriage are of the same character, excepting only a number of offices like that of the Keeper of the Order of Seats in a *numaym*. There is no reason that would compel us to assume that the two sets have distinct origins. It may rather be assumed that certain privileges and names that have been transmitted in a family for a long time, were considered as the inalienable property of the family. There is an unsurmountable contradiction involved because the Indian theory requires that from the very beginning there must have been these two classes of privileges, a condition that does not seem tenable. If, however, we project modern conditions into the past and assume as an early custom, the arbitrary assignment of a child to one place or another according to the wish of the parents, and according to the right which the child holds by reason of his descent, then the present order is quite intel-

---

[1] Nevertheless, in 1930 the eldest son had taken his mother's position and name as head of a *numaym*.

ligible. We must assume that certain privileges were given away, while others which were considered more valuable were retained in the line of direct descent. In this manner, a division between the two groups of names and privileges may have developed. We may perhaps compare the conditions to the European Majorate and to the transmission of family heirlooms as against free disposal of other property. The law is not so rigid that we could speak of an entailment of certain names and privileges because it is sometimes broken. The transfer by marriage may be compared to those cases in which jewelry is handed down in a family to be worn by the eldest son's wife.

I do not see any reason for a change of my opinion in regard to the relative antiquity of the transfer of names and privileges through the male or the female line. It is, of course, impossible to obtain historical data that would prove the actual development and we can only discuss the probable course of events. I base my argument largely upon the general cultural assimilation between the Bella Coola and the Kwakiutl tribes and the Nootka on the one hand, and their northern neighbors on the other hand. Linguistically, the Bella Coola are closely associated with the Coast Salish. Vocabulary and structure prove that at one time the two groups must have been one and must have lived on the seacoast. All the Coast Salish tribes, with the exception of the Bella Coola, are organized in simple village communities with preponderant patrilineal descent. Village communities may still be recognized as the funda-mental divisions of the Bella Coola, but the organization is overlaid by the use of crests and privileges which are characteristic of the Tsimshian and of the northern Kwakiutl. The forms and names of privileges and the names of individuals using the privileges prove the most intimate association with the neighboring tribes. Similar conditions, only less developed, may be traced among the northern Coast Salish, who have adopted privileges for a few social units while other social units have no such privileges. On Fraser river these ideas have even penetrated to the Lower Thompson tribes and northward to the Lillooet. The Kwakiutl are so thoroughly saturated with the use of privileges that no essential differences can be discovered in the various groups. Unfortunately, we do not know enough about the northern Kwakiutl tribes to state defi-nitely the conditions prevailing among them. The observations among the southern tribes, however, make it clear that among the southern Kwakiutl, as well as among the Nootka and the Coast Salish, the village community is conceived as a closed group and forms the basis of modern social organization. The exogamous lines, which are superimposed upon the village communities and embrace all of them, and which are an essential feature of the social system of the northern tribes, do not occur. The fragmentary archaeological evidence which we possess from the Kwakiutl territory suggests that the whole elaborate artistic development of the crest is not very old. Even the remains from graves that belong approximately to the middle of the last century indicate that the complete crowding out of geometrical ornament by conventional animal representations occurred quite recently.

It appears to me largely as a psychological question how the highly specialized use of privileges may have been superimposed upon an older simple organization which has a rather wide distribution on the coast. There is nothing to indicate that the simpler form should have been developed from a totemic organization. The evidence appears to me rather the other way. If Dr. Farrand's and my own observations are correct, namely, that the prevailing line of descent among the northern Kwakiutl tribes is matrilineal, then it seems to me plausible to assume that in marriages between men of these tribes and Tsimshian or Haida women, privileges were imported which the foreign born women could transmit according to the customs of their own tribes only to their own children and through their daughters to their grandchildren, but not to the children of their sons. The conditions of life on the coast indicate that the possession of such privileges was felt as a great social advantage to which the owners would cling. Since the Kwakiutl do not permit transfer from a man to his sister's sons, it would seem natural that the characteristic method found in mythological tales of the acquisition of Tsimshian privileges and which is even nowadays practised in the potlatch, should be adopted. This method is the transfer of privileges by gift from the husband's family to the wife's family. When a northern woman marries a Kwakiutl man, her son would be entitled to her crests. Since according to the property rights of the Kwakiutl, he could not transmit them to his sister's children, the possibility presented itself, to transmit them as a present to the family of his daughter's husband and to secure in this way the transmission to her children. As stated before, the mythological data indicate that this custom must have prevailed among the northern tribes.[1] Perhaps I have myself unwittingly con-

---

[1] Leonhard Adam has called attention to the discrepancy between tradition and modern customs to which I referred above. *Ztschr. f. vergl. Rechtswissenschaft,* vol. 30 (1913), p. 193; also Boas, "Tsimshian Mythology," *Thirty-first Annual Report of the Bureau of American Ethnology* (1916), p. 528.

tributed to the disagreement of opinion in regard to the historical development of the social organization of this area. When I stated that in my opinion maternal descent was later than paternal, I did not point out specifically the difference between the type of maternal descent as usually conceived and that prevailing on the Northwest coast, because it seemed to me obvious that we have no trace of the characteristic succession from uncle to sister's son, but only a somewhat cumbersome transmission of privileges from daughter to daughter in which the husband is the bearer of name and privileges.

The fundamental difference between the organization of the Kwakiutl and the northern tribes appears also in the terminology of relationship. Their terms are throughout the same for the paternal and maternal lines; uncle and aunt, nephew and niece are terms used indiscriminately for father's and mother's brothers and sisters and for brother's and sister's children without regard to the sex of the speaker. There is no trace of the recognition of clan or gentile relationship. The terms correspond to a loose organization in which relationship is counted equally on both sides.[1] The terminology by which individuals are called members of tribes indicates decidedly a preference to the father's side. The child of a father belonging to one tribe and of a mother belonging to another tribe is designated by the name of the father's tribe or *numaym* with the ending *-ts!Edze, i.e.,* offspring of such and such a tribe or *numaym.* The mother's tribe is indicated by her tribal name and the ending *-ky!otEm, i.e.,* one side of face such and such a tribe. Furthermore, in a marriage between two members of different tribes, the wife is called "married far outside." This agrees with the custom that in by far the majority of cases the woman goes to live with her husband, as well when both belong to the same village as when they belong to different villages.

It appears from all that has been said that the privileges are individual property, not property of the whole *numaym,* so that the social divisions are not in any sense properly speaking totemic groups. The relation to a very generalized form of the clan crest which belongs to every member of the clan, which is characteristic of the northern tribes is absent here. Common to all the northern tribes and to the Kwakiutl is the personal privilege of persons of high rank to certain specific crests and privileges.

---

[1] Franz Boas, "Tsimshian Mythology," *Thirty-first Annual Report, Bureau of American Ethnology* (1916), p. 494. The term 'nEmwot which is given at that place as relating only to members of the family, is used very often as applying not only to the *numaym* but also to outsiders, friends.

Among the Kwakiutl a new-born child has no crest and no definite position until it is given to him by his parent or another relative and there is no association between all the members of the *numaym* and the "totem." It is true that the nobility believe that they are descended from an ancestor who had the form of an animal, a whale, killer-whale, or supernatural bird, "who took off his mask and became secular." As stated repeatedly, this does not refer to persons of low rank and not even to all *numayms*. Individually the belief may arise that a person is helped by his crest animal. Thus a ⁼nāk·wax·da⁼x" chief of the *numaym* "Great-One" sacrificed to the killer-whales and was believed to be helped by them, but this was felt by the Indians as something quite unusual. In regard to other animals the evidence is contradictory. I have been told that a *numaym* which has the bear for a crest will be helped by the bear, but others flatly contradict such an idea. The statement that the Thunderbird, the ancestor of the "First-Ones" of the Nimkish, thunders whenever one of the *numaym* (probably one of the chiefs) dies may also be mentioned here.[1]

The essential feature of the relationship of the whole *numaym* to an animal is either entirely missing, or at least very weakly developed.

There is nothing to indicate that these forms are broken down remains of an older true totemic organization. The close relationship between Kwakiutl organization and that of the Coast Salish and the ideas clustering around the crests make it much more plausible that these semi-totemic notions may spring up every now and then without ever having been characteristic of the organization as a whole. I feel quite certain that the case of the relation of an individual to the killer-whale to which I referred just now, was developed by that particular person on the basis of the general beliefs of the tribe. Neither do I consider it a proof of older totemic ideas if a chief in a formal speech identifies himself with his animal ancestor who became "secular." This must be taken as no more than a metaphorical expression similar to those in which he calls himself the "Pillar of Heaven" or "Rockslide" or "River of Wealth." We must not interpret an oratorical metaphor as having a deeper religious significance, although it may stimulate thought in directions that may lead to religious tenets.

[1] Franz Boas, *Kwakiutl Tales,* Columbia University Contributions to Anthropology, vol. 2 (1910), p. 85.

THE SOCIAL ORGANIZATION OF THE TRIBES
OF THE NORTH PACIFIC COAST[1]

THE variety of forms of social organization found among the tribes of the coasts of Alaska and British Columbia has given rise to extended discussion which relates to fundamental questions regarding the theory of the growth of social institutions.[2] In the extreme north we find a purely matrilineal clan organization, while in the extreme south we find village communities with a loose family organization with bilateral descent in which, however, preference is given to paternal descent. In the central regions a mixed type is found in which descent in the female line is obtained by the transfer of privileges from a man to his son-in-law.

[1] *American Anthropologist*, N.S., vol. 26 (1924), pp. 323–332.

[2] I mention here a few of the more important publications containing data and discussion:

Leonhard Adam, "Stammesorganisation und Häuptlingstum der Tlinkit Indianer," *Zeitschrift für vergleichende Rechtswissenschaft*, vol. 29 (1912), pp. 86 *et seq.*

"Stammesorganisation und Häuptlingstum der Haida und Tsimshian," *Ibid.*, vol. 30 (1913), pp. 161–268.

"Stammesorganisation und Häuptlingstum der Wakashstämme," *Ibid.*, vol. 35 (1918), pp. 105–430.

C. M. Barbeau, "Growth and Federation in the Tsimshian Phratries," *Proceedings of the 19th International Congress of Americanists* (Washington, 1917), pp. 402–408.

Franz Boas, "The Social Organization and the Secret Societies of the Kwakiutl Indians," *Report of the United States National Museum for 1895* (1897), pp. 311–737.

"Der Einfluss der sozialen Gliederung der Kwakiutl auf deren Kultur," *Internationaler Amerikanisten-Kongress, 14 Tagung* (Stuttgart, 1904), pp. 141–148.

"Tsimshian Mythology," *31st Annual Report of the Bureau of American Ethnology* (1916), pp. 22–1037.

"The Social Organization of the Kwakiutl," *American Anthropologist*, N.S., vol. 22 (1920), pp. 111–126, pp. 356–369 of this volume.

"Ethnology of the Kwakiutl," *35th Annual Report of the Bureau of American Ethnology* (1921), pp. 43–1481.

Edward Sapir, "The Social Organization of the West Coast Tribes," *Transactions of the Royal Society of Canada*, Series 3, vol. 9 (1915), pp. 355–374.

John R. Swanton, (a) "Social Conditions, Beliefs and Linguistic Relationship of the Tlingit Indians," *26th Annual Report of the Bureau of American Ethnology* (1908), pp. 391–485.

(b) "Contributions to the Ethnology of the Haida," *Jesup North Pacific Expedition*, vol. 5 (1905).

During the past winter I had an opportunity to study the little-known coast tribes of the central part of British Columbia. The conditions found among them throw additional light upon the probable historical development of the cultural life of this area.

The matrilineal organization of the northern tribes has been described by Swanton, Barbeau and myself. The Tlingit and Haida are divided into two exogamic groups each of which embraces a large number of localized sibs. It seems probable that the number of these exogamic groups was larger at an earlier time. Among the neighboring Athapascan tribes a three-group division has been recorded,[1] and among the Tlingit Swanton furnishes definite information of the existence of a small group which may intermarry with the two main divisions,[2]—in other words, of a group which forms a third unit. Swanton suspects the existence in past times of a similar group among the Haida.[3] One of the chief differences in the Tsimshian organization, as compared to that of the Haida and Tlingit, is that we have here four exogamic groups instead of the apparent dual division among their northern and western neighbors. As among them, the exogamic division does not form a unit, but consists of a number of well localized sibs.

The fundamental idea of exogamy of the matrilineal divisions underlies the organization of all these tribes.

There are, however, evidences that the fundamental concept of sib relationship is not the same in all these groups. These differences are expressed in the systems of terms of relationship, in regard to which the Tsimshian differ very much from the Tlingit and Haida. The terminology of all three, however, has in common the trait that parallel cousins are considered as brothers and sisters, while cross-cousins belong to the group into which one may marry, and are designated by a separate term. In the paternal generation different terms are used for the individuals on the father's side as against individuals on the mother's side. In the generation of grandparents, and that of grandchildren, no distinction is made according to the divisional affiliations of individuals. The Tsimshian system is characterized by a prevalence of reciprocal terms in one's own generation.

South of the Tsimshian live the tribes of Gardiner Inlet and Douglas Channel, which speak a Kwakiutl dialect closely akin to the Bella Bella.

---

[1] See discussion and literature in Franz Boas, *Tsimshian Mythology*, pp. 478–480.
[2] See Swanton (*a*), 309, 409.
[3] Swanton (*b*), 90.

My information in regard to these tribes is very fragmentary. It is based on information obtained from two individuals whom I happened to meet at Bella Bella. They have five divisions, four of which correspond to the Tsimshian divisions, namely, Eagle, Raven, Wolf and Killer Whale. The last of these corresponds to the Gispawaduweda of the Tsimshian. Besides these they have the Beaver, which among the Tsimshian and Haida is an important crest in the Eagle group. The existence and the number of these five divisions were corroborated by Bella Bella informants. I was told that the five divisions are exogamic and that the child belongs to the mother's side. One of my informants, however, told me that her own children, as they were growing up, had been placed in different divisions by being given names belonging to the sides of one or the other of the four grandparents. Nevertheless she claimed that even after changing the position of the child the laws of exogamy continued, and that the children counted as members of the division in which they had been placed. I cannot give a definite statement in regard to this point.

The conditions among the Bella Bella have been described by Farrand and myself. In a previous statement I said that the Bella Bella have three divisions, Eagle, Raven, and Killer Whale. Farrand adds to these the Wolf. My inquiries during the past winter brought out the fact that, of old, the northern Bella Bella had actually only three division and that the southern Bella Bella represent the Wolf group. The idea that these four sides as such are localized appears here very much more clearly than among the three northern tribes. According to the concept of the Bella Bella, the ancestor of any local unit descended from the sky or sprang up from the ground, and the ancestral tradition shows to which one of the divisions he belonged. If he came down in the form of an eagle, or had some other association with an eagle, he would belong to the Eagle clan, and so on. The Wolf clan is definitely associated with the village Hauyad. A woman who plays a most important part in Bella Bella mythology married a wolf and her descendants form the Wolf clan. The eldest of her children assumed the rôle of transformer and culture hero. The tradition is important for all the divisions of the Bella Bella. The song of the wolf children is the marriage song, and the mourning song of the mother is the funeral song in the ceremonies of all the divisions of the Bella Bella tribe.

There is no rule of exogamy connected with the fourfold division of the tribe. We find intermarriages between individuals of the same divisions not only at the present time, but also in descriptions of occurrences of an earlier period. Some elderly Bella Bella expressed themselves very clearly in regard to their concept. They said: "The northern tribes make a great mistake. Who has ever seen a wolf mating with an eagle? It is right that an eagle should mate with an eagle." Although they are perfectly familiar with the customs of the northern tribes, the idea of exogamy is entirely foreign to them. They favor local endogamy among the nobility in about the same way as is done by the Bella Coola, and as is also found exceptionally among the Kwakiutl. In speaking about the relations of these divisions they merely say that all members of one particular division visiting a distant village will be welcomed by their "friends," that is to say, by members of the division that bears the same name, no matter whether these are Bella Bella or Tsimshian or other northern tribes. I did not hear that they were aware of the absence of the fourfold division among the northern tribes.

Since these divisions do not form exogamic units, and since, furthermore, endogamy is only favored, not by any means enforced, the divisions are fairly evenly distributed over the whole territory. Nevertheless, the opinion is general that the Wolves belong to the southern Bella Bella tribe.

The primary position of an individual is definitely with his mother's division. However, position is not by any means permanent, but in the same way as among the Kwakiutl a person may take his father's or his grandfather's position. For this reason the affiliations of an individual may change as he rises in rank.

It is interesting to note that the terminology of relationship which underlies the social system of the Bella Bella and of the more northern Kwakiutl tribes is the same as that of the Kwakiutl proper. In this system no distinction is made between collateral relatives in maternal and paternal lines. Father's and mother's brothers and father's and mother's sisters are designated by the same terms, and the same is true in regard to brother's and sister's children. While in general the terms of relationship are the same among all the tribes of Kwakiutl lineage, two terms show considerable variation according to dialect. These are the terms for uncle, (both maternal and paternal,) and for brother-in-law, (both wife's brother and sister's husband).

It seems that farther to the south the system of matrilineal descent with a small number of divisions never exceeding five, disappears completely. The tribe of Rivers Inlet speaks the Bella Bella dialect, but so far as I have been able to discover from indirect reports, there is no trace of matrilineal clan organization found among them. From Rivers Inlet southward we find throughout tribes composed of small units, and derived through descent from a single ancestor and from other individuals who at an early period associated themselves with him. The number of these units in each tribe is quite large. Preference is given to paternal descent.

The general condition on the North Pacific Coast may be described as follows : In the north we have a group of tribes in which maternal and paternal lines are clearly distinguished and where we find a small number of divisions, from two to five, with definite functions regulating marriage, the matrilineal clans being exogamic. The most southern group of these tribes, the Tsimshian, have four clans, the Eagle, Raven, Wolf, and Bear (Killer Whale). Further to the south, the Bella Bella have the same clans that are found among the Tsimshian, but they lack entirely the function of regulating marriage, and the idea that intermarriage between two members of the same clan is incestuous is entirely foreign to the thoughts of the people. The clans have a political function determining friendship or enmity between groups. We find also that maternal descent prevails, although it is not rigidly adhered to in so far as there is great freedom in assigning to an individual in later life a position in any one of the clans to which his ancestors belonged. The contrast between the terminology of the systems of relationship and the clan organization with preference of the maternal line is quite striking.

When we direct our attention primarily to the village communities of the Bella Bella, the organization is decidedly similar to that of the Kwakiutl. The whole tribe is found to consist of a great many local units, each of which claims certain privileges on account of its descent from an ancestor who came down from the sky or appeared in some other supernatural way. The same is true of the northern matrilineal tribes, except that the character of the traditions of the local units stresses the encounter of the ancestor with a supernatural being.

I have pointed out that the organization of the Kwakiutl is identical with that of the northern coast Salish tribes. However, the idea that local units have certain privileges, is much less developed among the coast Salish tribes.

We might, therefore, describe the whole situation in the following way : As we go northward from the State of Washington, the idea of the unity of the village community becomes more and more intimately associated with certain privileges which may be described as crests. When we reach Bella Bella we find overlying this system a system of a small number of clans which are identical in name with the clans of the northern matrilineal tribes. The sameness of the clan names can be due only to historical connection. The four clans are almost functionless as compared to the functioning of the village communities. Connected with the occurrence of the clans, the idea of maternal descent prevails. The emphasis on matrilineal descent is quite contrary to the linguistic forms used among these tribes. Still farther to the north the emphasis laid upon local units or village communities persists, but the communities are strictly subordinated to the exogamic clan and the position of the individual is absolutely fixed, both in regard to the local unit and to the clan to which he belongs. Changes occur rarely, and then only by formal adoption.

We might consider in the same way the clan system of the north, and follow its characteristics southward. The characteristic exogamy of the large tribal divisions dwindles down and disappears as we reach the most southern tribes. In some regions it gives way to a marked tendency to endogamy. In the north the local units are definitely assigned to one or the other of the larger divisions; in the south they form units that are the more independent the farther south we go.

The general conditions among the Bella Coola fit in well with the distribution just described. They represent an isolated branch of the Coast Salish tribes, which are organized in village communities. Among the Bella Coola we have village communities with privileges quite analogous to those of the Bella Bella, and with a prevalence of paternal descent. There is no grouping of these units in larger divisions and, as among the Bella Bella, a tendency to endogamy among the nobility occurs.

From my earlier studies of the distribution of types of social organization, on the North Pacific Coast, I have concluded that the transmission of social position to the daughter's son which is found among the Kwakiutl has developed through the influence of the northern tribes, from whom the Kwakiutl obtained the concept of crest privileges, and that the stimulus to this development lay in marriages between the men of the southern tribes and women of the northern tribes. This conclusion is strongly corroborated by the conditions found among the Bella Bella, who show a type intermediate between that of the Vancouver Island Kwakiutl and the Tsimshian.

The matrilineal clan is fully developed among the tribes of northern British Columbia and of the coast of Alaska. As we go southward it loses more and more in significance until it finally disappears entirely. On the other hand the village community with bilateral descent but with an inclination to favor the paternal line is most fully developed in the southern part of the North Pacific Coast. Although it continues to be an important element in the north, but with matrilineal descent, it is subordinated to the matrilineal clan organization.

The following table shows these conditions at a glance.

	Coast Salish	Kwakiutl	Bella Bella	Northern Tribes
Kinship terms		Bilateral		Unilateral
Descent	Patrilineal	Patrilineal with transfer of privileges to daughter's son. Privilege of change to other ancestral lines	Matrilineal with privilege of change to other ancestral lines	Matrilineal
Marriage	Preference to village exogamy among nobility	Exogamy for obtaining new privileges. Endogamy for retaining highly valued privileges in family		Exogamy
Privileges of local units	Family tradition of chief's family. In the north sporadically weak crests	Crests and traditions		
Matrilineal clans	Absent	Absent	Present, from two to five	

I may add here notes on some of the characteristic traits of the political and religious organization of the Bella Bella. The tribe is divided according to rank into a number of classes. At the head of the local community are two head-chiefs of equal rank who are considered the descendants of the mythical ancestor of the local unit. They are called *gyā'laxa*, which may be translated as "the first down." According to the explanation given to me by several Bella Bella, this is not now interpreted as the first ancestor to come down from the sky, but as "the first to receive presents in a potlatch." The existence of two head chiefs explains a peculiar institution among the Kwakiutl for which I have never before been able to obtain an adequate explanation. There are in each tribe a small number of individuals who are the first to receive in a potlatch. They are called $kwēk^u$, that is eagle, or $g\cdot ā'laxa$,[1] first to receive. They are not considered chiefs, and the Kwakiutl are unable to explain the origin of their privilege except by the reference to a myth in which it is told that the ancestors of certain units received their gifts in order. These positions may be survivals of an older head chieftaincy which has been superseded by a class of *nouveau riche*, who now form the aristocracy of the tribes and claim the highest rank and heavenly descent.

The second class among the Bella Bella are the chiefs ($hē'^\varepsilon mas$). Next to these are the nobility ($ō'^\varepsilon ma$). The common term for chief which is used by the Kwakiutl ($g\cdot ī'găme^\varepsilon$, stem $g\cdot īg$) [1] is not known to the Bella Bella. (Another word $g\cdot īgăme^\varepsilon$ occurs in Bella Bella and in Kwakiutl, but is derived from the stem $g\cdot ī$- to be in a certain position; $g\cdot ī'$-$găme^\varepsilon$, standing in front.) The term $ō'^\varepsilon ma$ is used by the Kwakiutl for a chief's wife, who is designated by the Bella Bella as $k\cdot a'niɫ$. The Kwakiutl, however, use the term $ō'^\varepsilon mayu$ to indicate high social position, greatness in a social sense, so that it would seem that this term also had in former times a more general meaning among the southern Kwakiutl tribes. The fourth class among the Bella Bella are the $g\cdot a'lgEm$, and the lowest group are the $xā'mala$. In Kwakiutl this word means orphan, and is used as an opprobrium, for orphans are of low rank because they are not helped by their parents to rise according to the regular scale of advancement.

This organization is, to a certain extent, connected with the organization of the tribe during the winter ceremonial. Only the two head chiefs can become cannibal dancers. A number of the more important dances of the winter ceremonial belong to the chiefs and to the nobility. In the winter ceremonial the seats of the two head chiefs are in the middle of each side of the house. The management of the winter ceremonial is not in the hands of the head chiefs, but is controlled by eight members of the nobility who form a council, and who arrange the winter ceremonial for each year.

The enormous complexity and confusion in the arrangement of the winter ceremonial at Fort Rupert seems to have arisen through a confusion between the family ceremonials of the Bella Bella and the winter

---

[1] $g\cdot$, $k\cdot$ are pronounced somewhat like gy, ky; g is a g pronounced at the **soft** palate. See note [1] on p. 232.

ceremonial. Although we do find among the Kwakiutl a distinction between the family ceremonial and the winter ceremonial, many traits of the former have been transferred to the winter ceremonial. The number of ceremonies (or dances) among the Bella Bella is limited. There are essentially only four groups of the winter ceremonial. These are from the lowest to the highest : the ō' lala, the q!ō'minoqs, the tā'nis, and finally the nō'nɫtsista. These are mutually exclusive, and the dance house used by one group is taboo for members of the lower groups. Besides this, all the families have their family ceremonials, the ʟɛwɛ'laxa. Initiation into one of these is entirely distinct from initiation into the winter ceremonial.

THE GROWTH OF THE SECRET SOCIETIES
OF THE KWAKIUTL[1]

THE secret societies of the Kwakiutl, as we know them nowadays, are undoubtedly a complex growth. The history of their development may be elucidated, in part at least, by means of a study of the present organization, its geographical distribution, and the component elements of the rituals and their explanatory myths.

A comparison of the ceremonials of the various tribes of the North Pacific Coast does not leave any doubt that they are in the main derived from the same source. Not only are the ceremonials much alike; even their names are identical. Among all the tribes the badges of the ceremonials are made of cedar bark, which is dyed red in the juice of the alder. Head rings, neck rings, and masks are worn by the dancers. The performances themselves are essentially the same from Alaska to Juan de Fuca Strait. But the most certain proof of their common origin lies in the identity of name among the various tribes. Among the Haida, Tlingit, and Tsimshian we find the names *ōlala, mē'iLa,* and *nō'nlEm,* which belong to the ceremonial of the Kwakiutl as well. Among the Bella Coola the names cannot be derived from the same words as among the other tribes, but there the ceremonial itself is almost identical with that of the Kwakiutl. It certainly does not differ more from the ceremonial as described here than that of other tribes of Kwakiutl lineage differs from the ceremonial of the Kwakiutl proper. Besides this, the names of the dancers, if not those of their dances, are often borrowed from the Kwakiutl. Turning to the south, we find the Nootka as well as the Salishan tribes who practice the ceremonial, terming it by the two names *Ḷō'gwala* and *nō'nlEm,* both of which are names used for portions of the ceremonial of the Kwakiutl.

The following table exhibits the terms that are used to designate parts of the ceremonial among various tribes:

[1] With slight modifications from pp. 660–664, of the "The Social Organization and the Secret Societies of the Kwakiutl Indians," *Report of the U. S. National Museum for 1895* (Washington, 1897).

Kwakiutl	Haida and Tsimshian	Nootka	Salish
ts'ā'eqa	ts'ē'ik	tsā'yeq	
ʟō'gwala		ʟō'gwala	ʟō'gwala
ō'lala	ōlala'		
nō'nlɛm	lōlɛ'm, nōlɛ'm	nōnlɛ'm	nōnlɛ'm
mē'iʟa	mēiʟa'		mē'iʟa

As all the words here enumerated belong to the Kwakiutl language, there can be no doubt that the ceremonial of the Kwakiutl has influenced to a very great extent those of the neighboring tribes. It does not follow necessarily that no secret societies existed before the Kwakiutl exerted their influence over the people of the coast, for the wide distribution of secret societies and the general similarity of the underlying principle all over North America make it probable that such societies did exist. But there can be no doubt that their present character was attained among the Kwakiutl, from whom the societies in their present form spread over a vast territory.[1]

The question then arises, How did the societies acquire their peculiar characteristics among the Kwakiutl? I may refer at this place to the growth of the clan system of the Kwakiutl tribes. This system probably attained its present development under the impetus of the clan system of the northern tribes. The social distinction connected with the possession of a clan legend gave a sufficient suggestion to the mind of the Indian to turn his imagination in this direction.

The close similarity between the clan legends and those of the acquisition of spirits presiding over secret societies, as well as the intimate relation between these and the social organization of the tribes, allow us to apply the same argument to the consideration of the growth of the secret societies. This leads us to the conclusion that the same psychical factor that molded the clans into their present shape molded the secret societies.

If this argument is correct, we must expect that the legends of the secret societies, although belonging to the most sacred myths of the tribes, show indications of foreign influences, as these must have offered the material for the suggestions which gave rise to the myths. I will not at this place enter into a detailed discussion of these traditions as I have done so in another publication.[2] I have shown that all legends of this

[1] It cannot be proved that any connection exists between the torture ceremonies of the Kwakiutl (hawi'nalaʟ) and the sun-dance ceremonies of the Sioux and Blackfoot, but their analogy is quite striking.

[2] Indianische Sagen von der Nord-Pacifischen Küste Amerikas (Berlin, 1895), p. 329.

region are of complex origin, and that they must have been carried over enormous distances from tribe to tribe. This is true of the more insignificant tales as well as of the most important myths, such as creation legends, and the legends of the origin of the secret societies. To give only one or two examples: In the tale of the origin of the cannibal society of the Bella Bella, it is told how a woman gave birth to a number of dogs, who attained the secrets of the cannibal society. This tale is found over the whole of the northwestern portion of North America, among all the Athapascan tribes, among the Eskimo, and all along the North Pacific Coast. Only in this single instance is it connected with the origin of the secret societies, and I conclude, therefore, that a foreign story has been embodied in this myth.

While here the foreign portion of the myth forms only a slightly connected incident of the tale, foreign material is much more closely interwoven with the whole fabric in the most important one of all the legends of secret societies, viz., the tale of $Bax^ubakwālanux^usī'we^\varepsilon$. When we compare this myth with the creation myth of the Chinook we find a remarkable resemblance in certain parts of the legends. The grandmother of the divinity of the Chinook,[1] when a child, was carried away by a monster. Their child became the mother of the culture hero, and by her help the monster was slain. Among the Kwakiutl, the cannibal spirit carries away a girl, and is finally slain. In one version their child becomes the new cannibal spirit. There exist several stories on the west coast of Vancouver Island which form probably the connecting links between these two legends.[2] Furthermore, the important incident of the magic flight which figures in the Kwakiutl legend has so wide a distribution, not only on the Pacific Coast but also in the Old World, that we must consider it a foreign element in this myth.

These instances show that the myths referring to the ceremonial are of complex origin.

I will point out another peculiarity of these traditions: When we compare the legends as told by the various tribes of the coast, we find that the ceremonial is derived from a variety of myths. Some men obtained it from $Bax^ubakwālanux^usī'we^\varepsilon$, others from the wolves, still others brought it down from heaven. The legend of the Tsimshian tells that a hunter obtained it from a bear who took him into his lodge in the interior

---

[1] Chinook Texts, *Bulletin 20 of the Bureau of Ethnology* (1894), p. 9.

[2] For a remarkable analogue of this tradition collected among the Golds of Amoor River, see *Globus*, vol. 71 (1897), p. 92.

of a rock. Traditions which are entirely distinct in character and origin are brought forward to explain the origin of the same ceremonial.

What does this prove? We have seen that none of the tales referred to can be considered as a growth of the genius of any of these tribes uninfluenced by any foreign sources. All the traditions are full of foreign elements which can be traced, step by step, to distant regions. When we see, therefore, that the same ritual is explained by a variety of traditions, we must conclude that in this region at least the ritual is older than the tradition referring to the ritual; that the former must be considered as primary, the latter as secondary.

I believe the source of the ritual, as well as of the legends which are connected with it, must be looked for in the advantages and the prerogatives which the membership of secret societies gives. This must have caused a desire to possess such membership, which either led the men to acquire memberships in existing societies, or, where these were not sufficient, for the people to invent new ones. Of course, I do not mean to say that the Indian invented traditions consciously and intentionally, but that the desire excited his fancy and his whole state of mind, and that in this manner, after appropriate fasting, the opportunity was given for hallucinations, the material for which was necessarily taken from the existing ideas, or from the ideas of neighboring tribes. These are the peculiar phenomena which were set forth by Stoll in his book on Suggestion, and I think in a deeper manner by Tarde in his book on the Laws of Imitation.

It is easily understood how the exciting aspect of the ceremonial of the cannibal society caused a young man who had gone fasting to believe that he saw in his hallucinations the same spirit under new conditions, and to tell of his experience after his return. As the notion had become established that the spirit, after having been seen, had a tendency to reappear to the descendants, an opportunity was given for the formation of a new place in the secret society. We may therefore assume that the psychological explanation for the development of the complicated system of the membership in secret societies lies in the combined action of the social system and the method of acquiring guardian spirits.

While these considerations explain the variety of forms of the secret societies and prove that the myths on which the ritual is apparently founded are probably secondary in character, they do not give a clue to the origin of the secret societies and of the peculiar customs connected with them. There are, however, indications which allow us to conclude that these customs had their origin in methods of warfare. First of all, the deity *Wina'lag'ilis* is considered the bringer of the ceremonial. The name means "the one who makes war in the whole world," and he rules the mind of man at the time of war as well as during the period of activity of the secret societies. For this reason, also, the secret societies are in action during times of war, in winter as well as in summer. All the oldest songs of these societies have reference to war; the cannibal, the bear dancer, and the fool dancer, are considered as chief warriors, and fall into ecstasies as soon as they have killed an enemy. All this seems to indicate that the origin of secret societies has a close connection with warfare.

But one thing more must be considered. The customs which we observe nowadays are evidently a modern development of more ancient forms. The ceremonial of cannibalism, which nowadays is the most important part of the whole ceremonial, is known to have been introduced among the various tribes recently, although its foundation, the idea of the existence of a spirit who is killing people, is present among all the tribes. The Kwakiutl state uniformly that the custom of devouring men was introduced among their tribe about 1830, and that it was derived from the Bella Bella. We also have conclusive evidence that the custom was acquired by the Tsimshian not before 1820 approximately, and that they also obtained it from the Bella Bella. Therefore there is no doubt that the custom originally was confined to the small territory of the Bella Bella. Among the southern tribes the action of the cannibal was confined to his taking hold with his teeth of the heads of enemies, which were cut off in war.

The form in which the ceremony of cannibalism of the Bella Bella appeared first was the following: A slave was killed by his owner, and then was torn and eaten by the cannibals, or pieces of flesh were torn with the teeth from the arms or the chests of people, or finally, corpses which were prepared in a particular manner were devoured by the cannibal. The first of these customs shows clearly its close connection with warfare. The slave is the booty of the cannibal, or of his relatives, and by slaying him the victory is once more brought before the eyes of his admiring friends. It is hardly possible to prove definitely that the secret societies have developed exclusively from customs relating to warfare, but I believe my remarks have made clear the close connection between the two phenomena.

THE RELATIONSHIP SYSTEM OF THE
VANDAU [1]

THE system of relationship terms of the Vandau of Portuguese South-east Africa is founded on the following principles:

1. Within the family position is determined in such a way that all those counted as members of one generation take precedence over those of the following generation.

2. In the family consisting of parents and children both parents have equal position, and siblings of both sexes also have equal position.

3. When a girl marries her position in reference to her brother is lowered by one step so that she counts as a member of the next lower generation. For convenience's sake these steps in position may be designated by the term generation.

4. When referring to collateral relatives the rank of the speaker is determined by the relation of the intermediate relative to the person referred to; for instance, in talking to a mother's brother his position is determined by the relation of the mother to her brother.

5. Siblings of the same sex, and children of the same sex of siblings of the same sex are designated by the same terms.

6. For a man parents and brothers of his wife, and the wife of his son-in-law (these terms understood in Vandau sense) occupy an exceptional position; for the woman the parents, grandfathers, and sisters of the parents of her husband, excepting however the sisters of his father; for both man and woman the daughter-in-law occupies an exceptionally high position.

In the following the numbers in parentheses added to the names refer to the schematic genealogies; number without a prime to the man's genealogy (A), those with a prime to a woman's genealogy (B). The individuals are so arranged that, as far as possible, all those relatives who are designated by the same term are placed together. Instead of placing individuals according to their biological position they are placed according to their social position.

[1] *Zeitschrift für Ethnologie,* vol. 54 (1922), pp. 41–51.

The principal difficulty for a clear understanding of this system lies in the correct appreciation of the relations between brother and sister. When she marries her brother controls her choice and according to the third principle she loses one step. Her children are, therefore, two steps under her brother and equal in position to his grandchildren. Therefore they are also called by the same term that is used for the man's grandchildren. In the same way a man's father's sister loses one step when she marries and becomes equal to the speaker's sister and as his sister she loses another step compared to him on account of her marriage, so that she drops to the same position as the speaker's children. In other words, all the women, as "sisters" of all the men in the successive ascendant male generations are in a lower position. In Fig. 1 are repre-

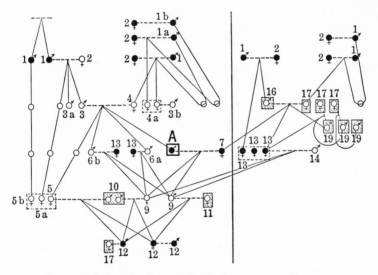

Fig. 1. Relationship system of the Vandau; terms used by man.

sented the relations between the male speaker A, his sister (5) and her children (12); his paternal aunt (5) and her children (12), and so on in ascending generations. For the sake of clarity the biological generations are indicated by circles. They are not valid from a Vandau point of view.

On the other hand the brother of a married woman (B fig. 2) is one step above his sister. Therefore his children are equal in position to that of the woman speaking. Since the son of her brother is her "brother" he also moves one step up when the woman speaking marries and his daughters are "sisters" of the speaker, his sons "brothers" who again move up one step. Thus all the male descendants of a man in the male line are "brothers" of his sister. In fig. 2 this is indicated by the recurving line which brings back the son of 6′ to the same point.

As a result of this the mother's brother (1) who is one step above the mother, his son and their sons and son's sons throughout all the descend-

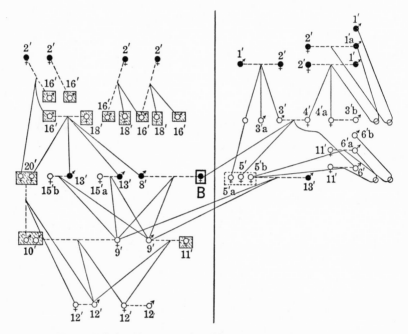

Fig. 2. Relationship system of the Vandau; terms used by woman.

ing generation are in the position of the mother's father and are called "grandfather". In the same way the "sister's" child, no matter whether this is the own sister, the father's or grandfather's sister will be two steps below the male speaker and is called "grandchild" (12).

Following is a list of the terms in use [1]:

(1) t'et'egulu   pl. vat'et'egulu, madjit'et'egulu, vadjit'et'egulu
(2) mbiya   pl. madjimbiya, vadjimbiya
(3) baba   pl. vababa, madjibaba, vadjibaba
(4) ma.i   pl. vama.i, madjima.i, vadjima.i
(5) t'et'adji   pl. madjit'et'adji, vadjit'et'adji

[1] ẓ, ṣ are strongly labialized.

(6a) *nyevanši*[1] pl. *madjinyevanši, vadjinyevanši*
(6b) *munuk'una* pl. *vanuk'una, vadjinuk'una*
 (7) *muk'adji* pl. *vak'adji*
 (8) *mulume* pl. *valume, vadjilume*
 (9) *myana* pl. *vana, mazana, madjivana* (the last two having a slightly discourteous meaning)
(10) *mukwambo* pl. *vakwambo, madjikwambo* (the latter, impolite)
(11) *nyamyana*[1] pl. *vanyamyana, madjinyamyana, vadjinyamyana*
(12) *muzuk'ulu* pl. *vazuk'ulu, madjizuk'ulu* (the latter, impolite)
(13) *myalamu* pl. *vamyalamu, madjimyalamu, vadjimyalamu*
(14) *mulovozi* pl. *valovozi;* also *vamulovozi, madjilovozi*
(15a) *vatšano*[2] pl. *vatšano, madjitšano*
(15b) *mp'ele* pl. *mp'ele, madjimp'ele*
(16) *vat'ežala*[2] pl. *vat'ezala, madjit'ezala, vadjit'ezala*
(17) *vambiya*[2] pl. *vambiya, madjimbiya, vadjimbiya*
(18) *nyešala*[1] pl. *vanyešala, madjinyešala, vadjinyešala*
(19) *važele*[2] pl. *važele, madjinžele, vadjižele*
(20) *myanavene* pl. *vanavene, madjimyanavene, vadjimyanavene*
(21) *vap'oŋgozi* pl. *vap'oŋgozi, vamup'oŋgozi, madjip'oŋgozi, vadji-p'oŋgozi*

To avoid confusion I use in the following only singular forms:

(1) *t'et'egulu or tšegulu* (great father; the Bantu stem *t'a* "father" is not used in Chindau); paternal and maternal grandfather. Since my (man's) mother (4) after her marriage is one step below her brother (1a), her brother, i.e. my maternal uncle (1a) is also two steps above myself, therefore, my *t'et'egulu* and so on through the whole series of ascending generations. This does not occur on the paternal side, because the father and his brother are on the same level. Since my wife calls her grandfathers (1') and her mother's brother (1'a) *t'et'egulu* I use the same term. This is different for the woman in relation to her husband's grandfathers and mother's brother. (See under 16.)

(2) *mbiya;* paternal and maternal grandmother. Since the mother's brother (1) is called *t'et'egulu* his wife is called *mbiya.* Man and woman call all the women whom their mate calls *mbiya* by the same term.

(3) *baba;* father (3) and all his brothers (3a), also the sons of the brothers of the paternal grandfather; husbands of the mother's sisters (3b) and of all those called *ma.i* (see no. 4). The father's elder brother is also called *baba muk'ulu* (great father), the father's younger brother *baba mdok'o* (little father).

(4) *ma.i* mother (4) and her sisters (4a); the daughters of the sisters

---

[1] *nye* head.
[2] *va* singular, expressing respect.

of the maternal grandmother. Since the mother's brother is a step higher than the mother, and since she calls her brother's daughter *t'et'adji* (no. 5) the latter is also called *ma.i*. The wives of all the men called *baba* (3) are also *ma.i*. In other words, the wives of all the *baba* and the *t'et'adji* of the mother are called *ma.i*. The mother's elder sister is also called *ma.i muk'ulu* (great mother), the mother's younger sister *ma.i mdok'o* (little mother).

(5) *t'et'adji* (Bantu *t'a* father, *γali* female). Sisters without regard of relative age. Since the father's sister (5a) on marrying moves one step down she is on the same level as my (a man's) sister (5) who also moves down one step when she marries. Therefore both are on the same level as my own children and I call them *t'et'adji* and my own children, both boys and girls, call them by the same term. Conversely: since the woman on marrying moves down one step in relation to her brother, her brother's (6') daughter (5') and she herself are on the same level, that is she is her *t'et'adji*, which, therefore signifies,

> for the man: sister (5), father's sister (5a), father's father's sister (5b), etc.

> for the woman besides these: brother's daughter (5'b).

(6) *nyevanši;* elder brothter (6a); *munuk'una* younger brother (6b); also, elder viz. younger son of father's brother, or mother's sister. Age is determined by the age of the speaker, not by that of his parents. The woman calls all her brothers and her father's brother's sons *nyevanši* (6'). Since after marriage she moves one step down in relation to her brother, his son (6'a) is also her *nyevanši* and so on through all generations. Therefore *nyevanši* signifies

> for the man: elder brother (6a).

> for the woman: brother (6'), brother's son (6'), brother's son's son, etc.

munuk'una younger brother (6b) is a term used only by men.

(7) *muk'adji* wife.

(8) *mulume* husband.

(9) *myana* own children and those of the *nyevanši* and *munuk'una* of the man; and for a woman those of the *t'et'adji*. Therefore the term signifies

> for the man: child, brother's child, child of wife's sister, child of sister of wife's father, child of daughter of wife's brother.

> for the woman: child, sister's child, child of husband's brother, child of father's sister, child of brother's daughter.

(10) *mukwambo* a man married to a woman of the next lower level,
for the man : husbands of all *t'et'adji* (5), or *mɣana* (9).

for the woman : husbands of *mɣana* (9') and *mɣanavene* (20'),
i.e., the husband's sister who is one step below her brother (6').
A contradiction is involved in this in so far as the *mɣanavene*
is at the same time a person to be treated with respect (see
sixth principle).

Instead of *mukwambo* the term *mɣalamu* (13) may be used.

(11) *nyamɣana* (=head child) ; wife of the *mɣana ;* for the woman
besides this the brother's wife. The man may also use this term for the
wife of his *muzuk'ulu* (12) whom he ordinarily calls *vambiya* (17).

(12) *muzuk'ulu* (=great *muzu*) ; for both, man and woman, child
of the *mɣana* (9).

> For the man also children of his *t'et'adji* (5) ; also husband of the
> *muzuk'ulu.*

> For the woman also the children of the *t'et'adji* of her husband, be-
> cause she herself in her marriage has been placed on her hus-
> band's level. Also the husband or the wife of the *muzuk'ulu.*
> The wife of the *muzuk'ulu* is called by the man *vambiya* (17).

(13) *mɣalamu*

> For the man, all his wife's *t'et'adji,* including the daughter of his
> wife's brother, the sisters of his wife's father, and the wives
> of his *nyevanši* (6) and *munuk'una* (6b).

> For the woman, all the *nyevanši* and *munuk'una* of her husband,
> and the husbands of her own *t'et'adji.*

The term *mɣalamu* may also be used in place of *mukwambo* (10) although the relation of the speaker to the *mukwambo* is quite different
from that to his *mɣalamu*. The term *mɣalamu* may also be used instead
of *vazele* (19).

(14) *mulovozi* husband of wife's *t'et'adji ;* perhaps better ; husband
of a *mɣalamu* (13) who is wife's *t'et'adji* (5). Used only by men.

(15') *vatšano* (15'a) and *mp'ele* (15'b) ; wife of husband's elder
brother (15'a), viz. of his younger brother (15'b) ; also wives of the
mɣalamu who are her husband's *nyevanši* or *munuk'una*. Used only by
women.

(16) *vat'ezala* husband's viz. wife's father and their "brothers." For
the woman also husband's grandfathers. The term *vat'ezala* or *vazele*
is also used for the father of the *nyamɣana* (11), although he is usually
called *mup'oŋgozi* (21).

(17) *vambiya* (=honorable grandmother) ; wife's mother, wife's brother's wife; for the man also the wife of the *muzuk'ulu* (12) (who, however is called *muzuk'ulu* by the woman). The term may also be used for the mother of the *nyamɣana* (11) instead of the usual *mup'oŋgozi* (21). A man may also use the term *vambiya* for his *nyamɣana*. The woman never uses the term *vambiya* for the women of her husband's family or of those of her children. She employs it only for the *vambiya* of her brother whose terms of address or reference she adopts.

(18) *nyeśala* (=head *śala*) husband's mother.

(19) *važele* wife's brother. Since the wife's brother's son is her *nyevanśi*, his son, his son's son, etc., are also *važele*.

(20′) *mɣanavene*, husband's *t'et'adji*.

(21) *mup'oŋgozi* reciprocal term used by parents of a married couple. It is most commonly used by women.

The reciprocal terms used by relatives are accordingly as follows:

$$
\begin{array}{ll}
\left.\begin{array}{l} t'et'egulu~(1) \\ mbiya~(2) \end{array}\right\} & muzuk'ulu~(12) \\[2ex]
\left.\begin{array}{l} baba~(3) \\ ma.i~(4) \end{array}\right\} & m\gamma ana~(9) \\[2ex]
nyevanśi~(6a)~\left\{\begin{array}{l} munuk'una~(6b) \\ t'et'adji~(5) \end{array}\right. \\[2ex]
mulume~(8) \qquad\qquad muk'adji~(7) \\[2ex]
\left.\begin{array}{l} važele~(19) \\ vat'ežala~(16) \\ vambiya~(17) \end{array}\right\} mukwambo~(10) \\[2ex]
\left.\begin{array}{l} vat'ežala~(16) \\ m\gamma anavene~(20) \\ nyeśala~(18) \end{array}\right\} nyam\gamma ana~(11) \\[2ex]
vatśano~(15'a) \qquad mp'ele~(15'b)
\end{array}
$$

Reciprocal terms are:

> *mɣalamu* (13)
> *mulovozi* (14)
> *mup'oŋgozi* (21)

and for women *t'et'adji*.

The schematic drawings, Figures 1 and 2, represent these conditions. Broken lines indicate marriages, straight lines descent. When the son of a person is designated the same way as his father, this is indicated by a returning loop in which a circle on the level of the generation indicates the passage through that generation. Thus the son of the *t'et'egulu* (1) on his mother's side is also *t'et'egulu* (1a, b). Also when a woman of one generation is designated in the same way as a woman of the following descending generation, the line of descent is carried on to that generation and the passage through the biological generation is indicated by a circle. In Figure 1, *A* is speaking, in Figure 2, *B*. The rectangles enclosing certain groups of individuals indicate that the same conditions of marriage prevail for all of them. The rank is also expressed in the mutual use of forms of address. Persons who are respected belonging to a higher rank are addressed by "you" (*imɣimɣi*), and with the prefix of respect *va* preceding the name. Conversely all those of lower rank are called "thou" (*iwewe*).

The man calls "thou"	*The woman calls "thou"*
his wife and all the *mɣalamu*	————
his sisters	her brothers
his father's sisters, except those older than the speaker	her father's sisters, except when they are older than the speaker
his younger brothers	her younger sisters
————	her brothers' wives
————	the wives of her husband's younger brothers
his children	her children
his *muzuk'ulu,* except when they are older than the speaker	her *muzuk'ulu,* except those older than the speaker

The man calls "you"	*The woman calls "you"*
his grandparents	her grandparents
his parents	her parents
his older brothers	her older sisters and her father's sisters in case they are older than the speaker
his sisters' husbands	————
his wife's brothers	her husband's sisters
————	her husband
————	her *mɣalamu*
————	the wife of her husband's elder brother, except when she is younger than the speaker
his *mukwambo*	her *mukwambo*
his parents-in-law	her parents-in-law
his daughter-in-law	————
the wife of his *muzuk'ulu*	————

The *mup'oŋgozi* call one another "you." Comparing this with the schematic presentation, it will be seen that the individuals corresponding to the first six terms on the right use the term "you" speaking to all those on the left. The next group (Nos. 16, 17, 19) and the *mukwambo* (10) call one another "you", also the *mup'oŋgozi* (21) among themselves. Among the women the *myanavene* (20) and the younger *nyamyana* (11) use "thou," while the *nyesala* (18), *vatezala* (16), and *nyamyana* (11) use "you." The male *myalamu* (13) calls the female "thou." The female calls the male *myalamu* (13) "you." The distinction between elder and younger brothers and elder and younger sisters is carried through more strictly in so far as the elder ones call the younger ones "thou", the younger ones the elder ones "you".

The mutual behavior of relatives is strictly regulated. In certain groups a joking relationship is permitted. I have indicated this by black circles for all those who are allowed to joke. With others there is a respect relationship which is extreme for the *vambiya*, mother-in-law, for whom avoidance (*k'upfava*) is prescribed. I have indicated the groups which are in a respect relationship by hachure. For others there is no prescribed behavior. It depends upon personal relations in how far joking is permitted. There is a certain degree of constraint between brothers and sisters, and between children and parents. Children are instructed in sexual matters by their grandparents.

Respect is also expressed in another manner. It is considered improper to accept anything from an older person with one hand, particularly with the left hand. It must be accepted with both hands cupped and held together. If this should be impossible, the one hand, either left or right, must grasp the wrist of the receiving hand.

Young men in the presence of older persons must sit with knees drawn up and feet crossed. They are not permitted to squat so that the heels stand up on the side of the thighs. Women may squat but the feet must be placed to one side. It is improper to sit with legs stretched out in the presence of older people.

Older people are given a mat to sit on.

Before the meal the older people wash their hands first and begin, the younger ones follow. The younger ones are not allowed to stop until the older people have stopped eating.

It is improper to smack one's lips while eating, particularly in the presence of older persons.

Young people should not contradict older ones in a loud voice.

When a man has to talk to his mother-in-law he has to clap his hands while speaking, the hands being cupped. He must also clap his hands when his mother-in-law is speaking. In the presence of his mother-in-law he must sit with closed fists, thumbs bent under, and knuckles upward. To stretch out the thumbs is considered a serious insult.

When a son-in-law wishes to enter the house of his mother-in-law he claps his hands to announce his arrival. The same is done with strangers before entering the house. People well known to the visitors knock at the door. When a man meets a respected woman—seldom one of his own family—he stands still and claps his hands. She bends her knees and crosses her arms over her breast. When meeting his mother-in-law a man bends his knees and claps hands. The mother-in-law also kneels and bends forward. Then the man steps aside and allows his mother-in-law to pass. She walks on the opposite side of the road in order to avoid him.

When two relatives or neighbors meet, men or women, they clap the right hand on the left side of the chest and cup their hands. People who do not know each other pass without greeting.

A person meeting the chief claps his hands about eight times and then stops with two short clappings with long pauses.

A visitor who happens to come in at mealtime is invited to share. It is customary not to accept such an invitation too often.

The children are counted as members of the father's family. The tribe is divided in septs (*mut'up'o*), every one of which has a certain taboo. The septs are divided in sibs (*bvumbo*), which are named according to the part of the country they inhabit. Marriages within the sib are strictly forbidden, also those among maternal relatives, so far as they are known. Therefore the whole group of consanguineous relatives may not marry among themselves. Among those related by affinity the man can never marry a *vambiya* or a *nyamɣana*, the women no *mukwambo* or *vat'eẓala*. Among the "grandmothers" "and grandchildren" (that is, *mbiya* and *muẓuk'ulu*) there are a whole series who are not consanguineous, also among "fathers" (*baba*) and "mothers" (*ma.i*). A man may marry his *ma.i* who is not consanguineous with him. The informant is not certain whether this is an old custom or due to Zulu influence. At present such marriages are not approved of but not forbidden. In past generations a man married his father's widows, except his own mother, or the widows of his own brothers because he inherited them. Therefore a man may marry his *ma.i*, but the woman can never

marry her *baba.* Conversely a woman may marry her *mɣana,* but a
man can never marry his *mɣana.* Also a man can never marry his
muzuk'ulu, and a woman cannot marry her *t'et'egulu.* In other words
the man marries only into his own or higher steps, the woman her own
or lower steps. When attempting to explain the marriage regulations
my informant first of all refers to a disinclination to certain types of
marriages. Discussing the matter further it occurs to him that all the
t'et'egulu and *muzuk'ulu* are consanguineous and are therefore forbidden to marry. When his attention is called to it that this does not hold
good for the *baba* and *ma.i* he discusses economic conditions. Marriage
is arranged on the basis of a payment made by the man's family to the
wife's family which is represented by her brother who conducts the
negotiations. Through the marriage the woman becomes part of her
husband's family, so that after her husband's death she is taken over by
other men of her husband's family. On the other hand the man has on
account of the payment claim for her replacement in case she should
die, but only from her own rank, that is to say, among the *t'et'adji* of his
wife. According to this the widow would be first of all inherited by the
mɣalamu. Here, however, is a contradiction in so far as the *muzuk'ulu*
may claim her first. In previous generations also his claim would have
preceded that of the son of the deceased and that of the *mɣalamu.* It
seems to me that this cannot be explained on a purely economic basis.
My informant explained it in the following manner: When a girl (2)
marries a boy (1), the payment is made to her brother (3). He uses it
in order to buy a wife (4) for himself. If he should die the payment that
the man (1) made for his wife (2) has gone to the family of the
woman (4) and therefore the man (1) claims the woman (4) for whom
the last payment was made, for himself. He himself may not marry her
because she is his *vambiya,* but his *muzuk'ulu* has a claim to the widow.
Evidently this argument is not valid when the brother (3) of the widow
(2) marries first and it also does not explain why the son of the daughter
of (1) may claim the widow since a payment has been made for the
daughter. Evidently these economic considerations are of later origin
and do not explain the principle that the man must marry in the same or
higher rank group whenever relatives by affinity are concerned.

It may be that the customs of the Thonga [1] throw light on the situation. Among them a widower can compel the brother of his deceased

[1] Henry A. Junod, *The Life of a South African Tribe* (Neuchatel, 1913), vol. 1,
pp. 217 *et seq.*

wife to divorce his wife and make her over to the widower. Then the earlier marriage has to be dissolved ceremonially.

According to the present custom the man can only marry in his own or in the second older rank group, the woman only in her own and the second younger group. It might be suggested that this custom is related to the position of the sister's daughters who so far as the man is concerned are considered two steps under him, while the mother's brothers are two steps above him. The relation between the man and his *mγalamu* (13) is simple. He can marry all of them, and he inherits them after the death of his wife or his brothers. This is the ordinary levirate which refers to all the *t'et'adji* of the woman, and of the wives of all the *nevanši* and *munuk'una* of the man.

The principal difference between the system of the Vandau and that of the Zulu and the Thonga consists in the following: Among the latter the mother's brother is one step higher than the mother but is not called by the same term as the grandfather, but *malume*. His son is also *malume;* his daughter, *mame,* among the Zulu; *mamana* (=mother) among the Thonga. Among the Zulu, the father's sister is called *babakazi,* among the Thonga, *rarana.* The former means "female father," as among the Vandau, the latter "little father". Among the northern Thonga the uncle is also called by the same term as the grandfather.

Among the Thonga we find one important feature, the younger brother and the younger sister (?) move one step down. Only the wife of the old brother is the *namu* (corresponding to *mγalamu*) of the man. The wife of the younger brother is *mukoŋwana* (corresponding to *nyamγana*). The grandson is called *mupyana* (phonetically corresponding to a Vandau form *mušyana* which, however, does not occur), while the granddaughter is called *ntukulu* (corresponding to *muzuk'ulu*). In the north the grandson is also called *ntukulu.* It is not possible to carry through the comparison in detail since Junod's description is not sufficiently exhaustive.

The principal interest in the system of the Vandau lies in the fact that we have here a clear case of the avunculate in a tribe of paternal descent and that this system may be explained without difficulty based on the ranking of the generations. I am far from maintaining that the present explanation corresponds to the historical development of the system but it seems interesting to see that psychologically and sociologically considered the avunculate may develop without any trace of maternal succession. Because the sister of the man when she marries is moved one step down and her husband is placed in equal position with her, the woman's brother becomes the head of the family. Particularly owing to the fact that he directs the negotiations of the marriage, his position develops in such a way that he has control over his sister's children and can interfere in all the family affairs of his sister.

THE DEVELOPMENT OF FOLK-TALES
AND MYTHS [1]

THE collections of folk-tales and myths of all continents, but particularly of North America, that have been accumulated during the last few decades have yielded the definite results that the incidents of tales have a very wide distribution, that they have been carried from tribe to tribe, even from continent to continent, and have been assimilated to such an extent that rarely only is there any internal evidence that would indicate what is of native and what of foreign origin.

Although these incidents have a wide distribution, they have developed characteristic peculiarities in restricted parts of the territory in which they occur. I will illustrate this by means of some examples selected from among the folk-tales of the North Pacific coast of America.

An excellent illustration is presented by the North American tale of the Bungling Host. The fundamental idea of the story, the failure of the attempt to imitate magical methods of procuring food, is common to the whole North American continent, apparently with the sole exception of California and of the Arctic coast. The incidents, however, show considerable variation. Confined to the North Pacific coast are the tricks of letting oil drip from the hands, of obtaining fishroe by striking the ankle, and of letting berries ripen by the song of a bird. The widely spread trick of cutting or digging meat out of the host's body is practically unknown on the North Pacific coast. The host's trick of killing his children, who revive, which forms part of the Bungling Host tale in the State of Washington and on the Plateaus is well known on the North Pacific coast. However, it does not occur as part of this story. It is entirely confined to stories of visits to the countries of supernatural beings.

Similar observations may be made in regard to the prolific test theme. The dangerous entrance to the house of the supernatural beings is rep-

[1] *The Scientific Monthly,* vol. 3 (1916), pp. 335–343. See also Tsimshian Mythology, *31st Annual Report of the Bureau of American Ethnology* (1916), pp. 872 *et seq.*

resented among the northern tribes of the North Pacific coast by the closing cave or by the closing horizon; among the tribes farther to the south, by a snapping door; on the western plateaus, by animals that watch the door of the house. Heat tests occur frequently, but in some regions the heat is applied by baking the youth in an oven or boiling him in a kettle; in others by sending him into an overheated sweat-lodge or placing him near a large fire. More important differences may be observed in the general setting of the test tales, which in some areas are tests of the son-in-law; in others, matches between the inhabitants of a village and their visitors.

Other examples of the local development of the plot of a story by the introduction of specific incidents occur, as in the North Pacific coast story of raven killing the deer, whom, according to the Alaskan tale, he strikes with a hammer, while in the more southern form he pushes him over a precipice. Similarly, in a story of a rejected lover who is made beautiful by a supernatural being the magic transformation is accomplished in the northern versions by bathing the youth in the bathtub of the supernatural being, while in the south he is given a new head.

In other cases the geographical differentiation of the tales is not quite so evident, because different types of stories overlap. This is the case in the widely spread story of the deserted child. Tales in which a youth gives offense by being lazy or by wasting food belong to Alaska. Another type, in which a girl is deserted because she has married a dog, belongs to British Columbia; but the two types overlap in distribution. This particular theme occurs in a much wider area on the American Continent, and other types may easily be recognized in the stories of the Plains Indians.

Tales of marriages with supernatural beings or animals are often found in the form of the abduction of a girl who has unwittingly offended an animal. This type seems to belong primarily to Alaska, while the theme of helpful animals that succor unfortunate and innocent sufferers is much more frequent among the tribes of British Columbia.

All these examples illustrate that there are a number of simple plots, which have a wide distribution, and which are elaborated by a number of incidents that must be interpreted as literary devices peculiar to each area. In all these cases the incidents obtain their peculiar significance by being worked into different plots.

On the other hand, we find also certain incidents that have a very wide distribution and occur in a variety of plots. Many examples of these are given in the annotations to all the more important recent collections of folk-tales. The local character of folk-tales is largely determined by typical associations between incidents and definite plots.

In most of the cases here discussed the plot has a general human character, so that the processes of invention and diffusion of plots must be looked at from a point of view entirely different from that to be applied in the study of invention and diffusion of incidents. The latter are, on the whole, fantastic modifications of every-day experiences, and not likely to develop independently with a frequency sufficient to explain their numerous occurrences over a large area. On the other hand, the stories of a deserted child, of contests between two villages, of a rejected lover, and other similar ones, are so closely related to every-day experiences, and conform to them so strictly, that the conditions for the rise of such a framework of literary composition are readily given. Nevertheless the plots that are characteristic of various areas should be studied from the point of view of their literary characteristics and of their relation to the actual life of the people.

An attempt of this kind has been made by Dr. John R. Swanton,[1] who enumerates a number of formulas of tales of the North Pacific coast. In this area the following plots occur a number of times :

1. A woman marries an animal, is maltreated by it, and escapes.

2. A woman marries an animal, who pities and helps her ; she returns with gifts.

3. Men or women marry animals and receive gifts ; crest stories.

4. Men obtain crests through adventures in hunting or traveling.

5. Parents lose their children ; a new child is born owing to the help of some supernatural being ; adventures of this child.

6. A man maltreats his wife, who receives help from supernatural beings.

7. The adventures of hunters ; they meet dangers, which the youngest or oldest one overcomes.

8. War between two tribes, due to the seduction of a woman and the murder of her lover.

All these stories show a unity of the underlying idea. They are built up on some simple event that is characteristic of the social life of the people and that stirs the emotion of the hearers. Some tales of this type are elaborated in great detail, and therefore conform to our own literary

---

[1] John R. Swanton, "Types of Haida and Tlingit Myths," *American Anthropologist,* N.S., vol. 7 (1905), p. 94.

standards. To this class belongs, for instance, the tale of a deserted prince. It is told that a prince fed eagles instead of catching salmon. In winter when food was scarce he was deserted by his relatives, but was helped by the eagles, who gave him food. It is told in great detail how larger and larger animals were sent to him. When the prince had become rich he sent some food to the only person who had taken pity on him. By chance his good luck was discovered and he rescued the tribe that was starving and married the chief's daughter.

Another tale of this kind is "Growing-up-like-one-who-has-a-grandmother." This is a tale of another boy who is helped by a supernatural being, overcomes all the young men of the village in various contests, and thus obtains the right to marry the chief's daughter. The chief feels humiliated, deserts him, and the youth kills a lake monster. When wearing its skin he is able to kill sea game, but finally being unable to take off the skin he must remain in the sea.

Besides these, there are a large number of complex tales of fixed form, which are put together very loosely. There is no unity of plot, but the story consists of the adventures of a single person. I do not refer here to the disconnected anecdotes that are told of some favorite hero, such as we find in the Raven legend or in the Transformer tales, but of adventures that form a fixed sequence and are always told as one story. Examples of this kind are quite numerous.

It is noticeable that only a few of the complex tales of the last-named type are known to several tribes. Although enough versions have been recorded to show that in each area the connection between the component parts of the story is firm, the whole complex does not migrate over any considerable distance. It is rather that the parts of the tale have the tendency to appear in different connections. This point is illustrated, for instance, by the story of a man who is deserted on a sea-lion rock and is taken into the house of the wounded sealions whom he cures. This story appears in quite different connections in various regions. Other examples of similar kind are quite numerous.

The literary device that holds together each one of these tales consists in the use of the interest in the hero that has been created by the introductory story, and that makes the audience desirous of knowing about his further deeds and adventures. The greater the personal interest in the hero, the more marked is the desire to attach to his name some of the favorite exploits that form the subject of folk-tales. I presume this is the reason why in so many cases the introductory tales differ enormously, while the adventures and exploits themselves show a much greater degree of uniformity. This happens particularly in the case of tales of culture heroes. When a large number of the same exploits is thus ascribed to the heroes of different tribes, it seems to happen easily that the heroes are identified. Therefore I imagine that the steps in the development of a culture-hero myth may have been in many cases the following: An interesting story told of some personage; striking and important exploits ascribed to him; similar tales of these personages occurring among various tribes; identification of the heroes of different tribes. While I do not assume that this line of development has occurred every single time—and it seems to me rather plausible that in other cases the introductory story and the adventures may have come to be associated in other ways—it may be considered as proved that introduction and adventures do not belong together by origin, but are the results of later association. The great diversity of associations of this type compels us to take this point of view.

On the whole, in many forms of primitive literature, the interest in the personality of the hero is a sufficient means of establishing and maintaining these connections. Nevertheless there are a few cases at least in which the adventures conform to a certain definite character of the hero. This is the case in northwestern America in the Raven, Mink and Coyote tales, in which greed, amorous propensities and vaingloriousness are the chief characteristics of the three heroes. In tales that have a more human background these tendencies are hardly ever developed.

The recorded material shows also that the imagination of primitive man revels in the development of certain definite themes, that are determined by the character of the hero, or that lend themselves in other ways to variation. Thus in Alaskan tales Raven's voraciousness, that induces him to cheat people and to steal their provisions, is an ever-recurring theme, the point of which is regularly the attempt to induce the people to run away and leave their property. Mink's amorousness has led to the development of a long series of tales referring to his marriages, all of which are of the same type. The strong influence of a pattern of thought on the imagination of the people is also illustrated by tales of marriages between animals and men or women and a few other types to which I referred before.

The artistic impulses of a people are not always satisfied with the loose connections of stories, brought about by the individuality of the hero, or strengthened by the selection of certain traits of his character illustrated by the component anecdotes. We find a number of cases in which a psychological connection of the elements of the complex story is sought. An example of this kind is found in the Raven legend of British Columbia, in which a number of unrelated incidents are welded into the form of an articulate whole. The adventures of the Steelhead Salmon, the Grizzly Bear, and Cormorant, are thus worked into a connected series. Raven kills Steelhead Salmon because he wants to use it to deceive Grizzly Bear. He holds part of the salmon in front of his body, so as to make the Bear believe that he has cut himself. Thus he induces the Bear to imitate him and to kill himself. Finally he tears out the tongue of Cormorant, who had witnessed the procedure, so that he may not tell. Another excellent case from the same region is the story of Raven's son and Thunderbird. Raven has seduced a girl, and their son is stolen by Thunderbird. In order to take revenge, he makes a whale of wood, then kills Pitch in order to calk the whale, and by its means drowns the Thunderbird. Among other tribes the same tale occurs in another connection. The animals have a game, and Thunderbird wins. The defeated guests are invited, and the host's wife produces berries by her song. Then the Thunderbird abducts her, and the revenge of the animals by means of the whale follows. In the former group of tales the incident describing the death of Pitch is brought in, which ordinarily occurs as an independent story.

In these cases we find the same incidents in various connections, and this makes it clear that it would be quite arbitrary to assume that the incident developed as part of one story and was transferred to another one. We must infer that the elements were independent and have been combined in various ways. There certainly is nothing to prove that the connection in which an incident occurs in one story is older and nearer to the original form than one in which it occurs in another story.

The distribution of plots and incidents of North American folklore presents a strong contrast when compared to that found in Europe. European folk-tales, while differing in diction and local coloring, exhibit remarkable uniformity of contents. Incidents, plots, and arrangement are very much alike over a wide territory. The incidents of American lore are hardly less widely distributed; but the make-up of the stories exhibits much wider divergence, corresponding to the greater diversification of cultural types. It is evident that the integration of European cultural types has progressed much further during the last two or three thousand years than that of the American types. Cultural contrasts like those between the Northwest coast and the Plateaus, or between the Great Plains and the arid Southwest, are not easily found in Europe. Excepting a few of the most outlying regions, there is a great underlying uniformity in material culture, social organization, and beliefs, that permeates the whole European continent, and that is strongly expressed in the comparative uniformity of folk-tales.

For this reason European folk-lore creates the impression that the whole stories are units, that their cohesion is strong, and the whole complex very old. The analysis of American material, on the other hand, demonstrates that complex stories are new, that there is little cohesion between the component elements, and that the really old parts of tales are the incidents and a few simple plots.

Only a few stories form an exception to this rule—such as the complex Magic Flight or Obstacle myth—which are in themselves complex, the parts having no inner connection, and which have nevertheless a wide distribution.

From a study of the distribution and composition of tales we must then infer that the imagination of the natives has played with a few plots, which were expanded by means of a number of motives that have a wide distribution, and that there is comparatively little material that seems to belong to any one region exclusively, so that it might be considered as of autochthonous origin. The character of the folk-tales of each region lies rather in the selection of preponderant themes, in the style of plots, and in their literary development.

The supernatural element in tales shows a peculiar degree of variability. In a study of the varying details it appears a number of times that stories which in one region contain fantastic elements are given a much more matter-of-fact setting in others. I take my examples again from the North Pacific coast. In the tale of Raven's battle with South Wind we find in most cases an incident of an animal flying into the enemy's stomach, starting a fire, and thus compelling him to cough. In the Tsimshian version he simply starts a smudge in his house. In most tales of the liberation of the Sun the magical birth of Raven plays an important part, but among the Alaskan Eskimo he invades the house by force or by ordinary fraud. In the Tsimshian tale of the origin of Raven a dead woman's child flies up to the sky, while the Tlingit tell the same tale without any supernatural element attached to it. Another case of this kind is presented by the wedge test as recorded among the Lower Thompson Indians. In most versions of this tale a boy who is sent into the open crack of a tree and whom his enemy tries to kill by knocking out the spreading-sticks, escapes miraculously when the tree closes. In the more rationalistic form of the tale he finds a hollow which he keeps open by means of supports given to him. The available material gives me the impression that the loss of supernatural elements occurs, on the whole, near the border of the area in which the tales are known, so that it might be a concomitant of the fragmentary character of the tales. That loss of supernatural elements occurs under these conditions, appears clearly from the character of the Masset and Tlingit tales recorded by Swanton. In some of the Tlingit tales the supernatural elements are omitted, or weakened by saying that the person who had an incredible experience was out of his head. In the Masset series there are many cases in which the supernatural element is simply omitted. I am not prepared to say in how far this tendency may be due to conflicts between the tales and Christian teaching or in how far it may be due simply to the break with the past. The fact remains that the stories lost part of their supernatural character when they were told in a new environment.

I think it would be wrong to generalize and to assume that such loss of supernatural elements is throughout the fate of tales, for the distribution of explanatory tales shows very clearly that it is counterbalanced by another tendency of tales to take on new supernatural significance.

An additional word on the general theory of mythology. I presume I shall be accused of an entire lack of imagination and of failure to realize the poetic power of the primitive mind if I insist that the attempt to interpret mythology as a direct reflex of the contemplation of nature is not sustained by the facts.

Students of mythology have been accustomed to inquire into the origin of myths without much regard to the modern history of myths. Still we have no reason to believe that the myth-forming processes of the last ten thousand years differed materially from modern myth-making processes. The artifacts of man that date back to the end of the glacial period are so entirely of the same character as those left by the modern races, that I do not see any reason why we should suppose any change of mentality during this period. Neither is there any reason that would countenance the belief that during any part of this period intertribal contact has been materially different from what it is now. It seems reasonable to my mind therefore to base our opinions on the origin of mythology on a study of the growth of mythology as it occurs under our own eyes.

The facts that are brought out most clearly from a careful analysis of myths and folk-tales of an area like the northwest coast of America are that the contents of folk-tales and myths are largely the same, that the data show a continual flow of material from mythology to folk-tale and *vice-versa,* and that neither group can claim priority. We furthermore observe that contents and form of mythology and folk-tales are determined by the conditions that determined early literary art.

The formulas of myths and folk-tales, if we disregard the particular incidents that form the substance with which the framework is filled in, are almost exclusively events that reflect the occurrences of human life, particularly those that stir the emotions of the people. If we once recognize that mythology has no claim to priority over novelistic folk-lore, then there is no reason why we should not be satisfied with explaining the origin of these tales as due to the play of imagination with the events of human life.

It is somewhat different with the incidents of tales and myths, with the substance that gives to the tales and myths their highly imaginative character. It is true enough that these are not directly taken from every-day experience; that they are rather contradictory to it. Revival of the dead, disappearance of wounds, magical treasures, and plentiful food obtained without labor, are not every-day occurrences, but they are every-day wishes; and is it not one of the main characteristics of the imagination that it gives reality to wishes? Others are exaggerations of our experiences; as the power of speech given to animals, the enormous size of giants, or the diminutive stature of dwarfs. Or they are the materialization of the objects of fear; as the imaginative difficulties and dangers of war and the hunt or the monsters besetting the steps of the unwary traveler. Still other elements of folk-lore represent ideas contrary to daily experiences; such as the numerous stories that deal with the absence of certain features of daily life, as fire, water, etc., or those in which birth or death are brought about by unusual means. Practically all the supernatural occurrences of mythology may be interpreted by these exaggerations of imagination.

So far as our knowledge of mythology and folk-lore of modern peoples goes, we are justified in the opinion that the power of imagination of man is rather limited, that people much rather operate with the old stock of imaginative happenings than invent new ones.

There is only one point, and a fundamental one, that is not fully covered by the characteristic activity of imagination. It is the fact that everywhere tales attach themselves to phenomena of nature; that they become sometimes animal tales, sometimes tales dealing with the heavenly bodies. The distribution of these tales demonstrates clearly that the more thought is bestowed upon them by individuals deeply interested in these matters—by chiefs, priests, or poets—the more complex do they become, and the more definite are the local characteristics that they develop. The facts, however, do not show that the elements of which these tales are composed have any immediate connection with the phenomena of nature, for most of them retain the imaginative character just described.

The problem of mythology must therefore rather be looked for in the tendency of the mind to associate single tales with phenomena of nature and to give them an interpretative meaning. I do not doubt that when the anthropomorphization of sun and moon, of mountains and animals, had attracted stories of various kinds to them, then the moment set in when the observation of these bodies and of the animals still further stimulated the imagination and led to new forms of tales, that are the expressions of the contemplation of nature. I am, however, not prepared to admit that the present condition of myths indicates that these form any important part of primitive mythology.

That European myths happen to have developed in this direction—presumably by long-continued reinterpretation and systematization at the hands of poets and priests—does not prove that we must look for a poetic interpretation of nature as the primary background of all mythologies.

The mythological material collected in recent years, if examined in its relation to folk-tales and in its probable historical development, shows nothing that would necessitate the assumption that it originated from the contemplation of natural phenomena. It rather emphasizes the fact that its origin must be looked for in the imaginative tales dealing with the social life of the people.

INTRODUCTION TO JAMES TEIT, "TRADITIONS OF THE THOMPSON INDIANS OF BRITISH COLUMBIA" [1]

THE Thompson Indians, whose mythology has been recorded by Mr. James Teit, form a branch of the Salishan tribes which inhabit large portions of the states of Washington, Idaho, Montana, and of the Province of British Columbia. They live on Fraser and Thompson rivers a little above and below their confluence.

The following is a discussion of some of the important features of their mythology and folk-lore.

About one half of the collection is taken up by myths referring to transformers. While in most American mythologies there is only one transformer who is, at the same time, the culture hero, we find here several personages to whose actions the present shape of our world is due. These are: the Coyote, three brothers Hogfennel, [2] and the Old Man. The first and the second of these are decidedly the most influential and important personages in the whole mythology of the tribe.

The Coyote as well as the three brothers are in a way the culture heroes of the tribe, and the general characteristics of the legends referring to these beings are very similar to legends of this class as found among other American tribes. The story of the so-called "Culture Hero," who gave the world its present shape, who killed monsters that infested the land, and gave man the arts that make life worth living, is one of the most widely distributed Indian myths. In what we might call the prehistoric era there was no clear distinction between man and animals. At last the culture hero appeared, and transformed some of the beings of those times into animals, others into men. He taught the latter how to kill animals, how to make fire, and how to clothe themselves. He is the great benevolent being, the helper of mankind. But the same great culture hero appears in other groups of tales as a sly trickster, who vaingloriously thinks himself superior to all other beings, whom he

[1] *Memoirs of the American Folk-Lore Society*, vol. 6 (1898), pp. 1–18.
[2] *Peucedanum macrocarpum*, Nutt.

tries to deceive, and who is often punished for his presumption by the superior powers of his intended victims. No method of warfare is too mean for him, if it promises to lead to victory; no trick is too low to be resorted to, if it helps him to reach his end. Neither is the end sought one that we might consider worthy of this great being. It is selfish to the extreme, the possession of riches or that of beautiful women being his chief aim. It is difficult to harmonize these two aspects of the myths of the culture hero. Some investigators, prominently D. G. Brinton, and also Walter Hoffman,[1] have held that the explanation is to be sought for in a gradual deterioration of a purer and more primitive form of the myth, and that the more vulgar tales are later additions to the old cycle of myths. If this were so, the problem would still remain, why there is such a general tendency of making the ancient culture hero the principal figure in these tales. But it seems to my mind that the frequent occurrence of this phenomenon requires a different explanation. It does not seem likely that all mythologies collected while still in more or less vigorous life should have undergone the same kind of deterioration. I am rather inclined to think that we have to deal here with a most important characteristic of all primitive religion.

The main features of the transformer legend appear very clearly in the Raven tales of the Tlingit and Tsimshian.[2] The tale begins with the miraculous birth of the Raven. The faithless wife of a chief was killed and buried by her husband. After her death she gave birth to a child who was eventually found and raised by a chief. The boy made a blanket of birdskins, by means of which he flew up to the sky, where he married the Sun's daughter. They had a son who owing to an accident fell down from heaven and was found drifting in the sea. He was taken to an old chief, who loved him very much and worried because the child would not eat. By the advice of two old men who appeared in a miraculous manner, he was given a certain kind of food. As soon as he tasted it he became so voracious that he ate all the accumulated winter provisions of the tribe. Then the people deserted him. Now he assumed the shape of the raven and began to traverse the world in search of food. He came to the mouth of a large river, where he met

---

[1] D. G. Brinton, *The Myths of the New World*, third edition (1896), p. 194; Walter J. Hoffman, "The Menomini Indians," *14th Annual Report of the Bureau of Ethnology*, Part 1 (1896), p. 162.

[2] F. Boas, *Indianische Sagen von der Nord-Pacifischen Küste Amerikas* (Berlin, 1895), pp. 272ff., 311ff. A fuller version of the Raven legend of the Tsimshian has since been obtained, which has been utilized here.

some fishermen whom he asked to give him fish. They scorned him and refused his request. The fishermen was fishing in the dark, for at that time the sun did not shine on our world. He threatened them, saying that he would make the sun unless they would give him some fish, but they merely said: "We know you, Raven, you liar!" He flew away enraged, and went straight to the house of the chief who owned the daylight. Here he transformed himself into the spike of a hemlock-tree, in which form he was swallowed by the chief's daughter. In course of time she gave birth to a child who was no other than Raven. The old chief dearly loved his grandson, and was unable to refuse any of his requests. One day the boy asked to be allowed to play with the box containing the daylight. As soon as he had obtained it, he resumed the shape of the raven and flew away. He returned to the place where he had left the fishermen, liberated the sun, and then saw that the fishermen were the ghosts. They fled frightened, leaving their fish for Raven. He ate as much as he desired, and became very thirsty. But at that time there was no fresh water in the world. Therefore he set out to obtain the water, and deceived the old chief who held it in his possession. On being pursued he spilled the water, and for this reason we find water all over the world. At another time, when he was hungry, he set out to obtain the herring, which he obtained by fraud. He also cheated the cormorant, tearing out his tongue and thus depriving him of the faculty of speech. For that reason the cormorant says *wulewule-wule* up to this day.

It is not necessary to go into any further details. It will be seen that the main characteristic of these tales is the fact that the Raven gave the world its present shape while trying to satisfy his own wants, and that he employed fair means and foul to reach his own selfish ends. While his actions benefit mankind, he is not prompted by altruistic motives, but only by the desire to satisfy his own needs. I find that in most tales of the transformer, or of the culture hero, the prime motive is, as in this particular case, a purely egotistical one, and that the changes which actually benefit mankind are only incidentally beneficial. They are primarily designed by the transformer to reach his own selfish ends.

It will be well to illustrate the peculiar mental attitude of the transformer by giving a few other examples. Among the Chinook [1] we find

---

[1] F. Boas, "Chinook Texts," Bureau of Ethnology, Bulletin 20 (1894), pp. 92 *et seq.*

the Coyote as the principal transformer or culture hero. He was the first to catch salmon with nets. He was hungry and tried to learn the art of catching salmon. He made a little man of dirt, whom he asked about the method of obtaining salmon. This artificial adviser told him how to make a net, and informed him regarding all the numerous regulations referring to the capture of salmon. He obeyed only partially, and consequently was not as successful as he had hoped to be. He became angry, and said: "Future generations of man shall always regard many regulations, and shall make their nets with great labor, because even I had to work, even I had to observe numerous regulations." He used to drive his baskets filled with dry salmon to his winter quarters, but one day they all ran away and jumped into the river. Since he had failed in this attempt at making life easy, he cursed all future generations, condemning them to carry all loads on their backs and taking away their powers of making the loads go by themselves.

The Tillamook,[1] a Salishan tribe, tell the following story of the transformer: In the beginning there were two animals in each mussel, and one day the transformer overate. This annoyed him, and he threw away one of these animals, so that each mussel should not have too much meat. It will be seen from this that all the changes that these transformers made were in a way changes for the worse, and that they made them in anger at some disappointment that they had had, or at some discomfort that they had suffered, not with a view of benefiting mankind. While the Raven was regardless of man, the Coyote of the Chinook made most of the changes to spite him.

Among the Athapascan tribes of northwestern America we find also most inventions made and transformations accomplished by a being who tries to reach his own selfish ends. Thus Petitot [2] tells of Kunyan, who made the first arrows for defending himself. Later on he killed the people, and when the deluge was threatening he built a raft to save himself. It seems that on it he collected the animals for his future use. He then brought up the mud from the bottom of the sea, from which a new earth was created. Later on he found that there was no water in the world and he obtained it for his own use.

The Klamath myths of the "Old Man," recorded by Gatschet, seem to partake of the same character. The "Old Man" is the creator, but in ridding the country of malevolent beings he only tries to overcome his

---

[1] *Journal of American Folk-Lore*, vol. 11, no. 41 (1898).
[2] E. Petitot, *Traditions indiennes du Canada nord-ouest* (Paris, 1886), p. 141ff.

own enemies. He kills North Wind and South Wind in revenge for their having killed his brother.

I might add many more examples of this character, almost all from the tribes of the northwestern parts of America, but it may be well to add an example taken from another region. The god Kutka of the Kamchadal, according to the description given by Steller, corresponded exactly to the Raven creator of the Alaskan Indians.

It seems, therefore, that in this region at least, the being who gave to the world its present shape and to man his arts was not prompted by altruistic motives. He did so in the course of his personal adventures, often with the direct aim of harming his enemies. He is not what we ordinarily understand by the term "culture hero," a benevolent being of great power whose object it is to advance the interests of mankind, but he is simply one of many more or less powerful beings who gave the world its present shape. With this conception of the so-called culture hero the difficulty disappears of uniting in one person the benevolent being and the trickster. He helps man only incidentally by advancing his own interests. This he tries to do by fair means or foul, just as the Indian will treat his enemy. When he overcomes his enemies, the result of his labors must accrue to the benefit of his fellow beings or of later generations, while wherever he fails, he necessarily often appears as a foolish trickster. We have a condition corresponding almost exactly to the attitude of mediæval Christendom to the devil. The latter was considered as a powerful being, always intent to advance his own interests. Often he succeeds, but often his triumph is defeated by the cleverness of his adversaries. The difference between these two series of myths lies mainly in the fact that the devil in all his adventures had only one object in view, namely, the acquisition of souls, while the Indian transformer struggled with a great variety of enemies who infested the country.

This aspect of the transformer myths makes it also intelligible why failures as well as successes should be ascribed to the hero. There was no psychological reason which made it more difficult to ascribe failure to him than success; and since he was one of the most important figures of Indian mythology, it is quite reasonable to suppose that gradually more and more tales clustered around him.

It may be asked why, if the hero of these tales is not intentionally a benefactor of mankind, do his acts so often result in advantages to man. I believe the explanation of this phenomenon must be looked for largely in the circumstance that the human mind has a tendency to consider existing conditions as the results of changes. The world has not always been what it is now. It has developed, either for better or for worse. On the whole, the progress of invention among a more primitive people is not so rapid that man is induced to speculate on the possible future achievements of his race. There is rather a tendency to consider the present accomplishments as the stationary result of a previous development. Therefore it is hardly likely that Indian traditions should speak of lost arts; they will rather refer to the introduction of new arts, and consequently the introducer must appear as the culture hero. The only exceptions that seem at all possible are such that the native imagines the existence of previous races which were able to accomplish certain feats by means of magical powers, which in course of time were lost. These ideas are embodied in many animal stories, and appear very clearly in the Coyote tales of the Chinook to which I referred before.

It is the same when we consider the relation of man to animals and plants. Everywhere he has succeeded fairly well in conquering ferocious animals and making others useful to himself. There is hardly any being that he is not able to overcome in some manner or the other. But still the difficulties are often so great, that we can easily understand how his fancy will create stories of animals that man was not able to subjugate, or conditions under which he was not able to conquer the animals that furnish food and clothing. His fancy cannot as easily invent conditions under which it would be possible to conquer the animal world more easily by natural means, than is done now, because he cannot foresee possible improvements in weapons of attack and defense. Therefore it seems intelligible why so many stories describing the primitive status of our world refer to the extinction of monsters by heroes.

It seems to me that the tales described heretofore do not contain the peculiar psychological discrepancy which is so puzzling, if we bear only in mind that the so-called culture hero is not considered by the Indian as an altruistic being but as an egotist pure and simple.

But there are many cases in which the natives have advanced to a higher point of view, and ascribe to the hero at least partially the desire to benefit his friends. With the development of this point of view the incongruity of the various parts of the transformer myth becomes more and more striking. When the Algonquin, for instance, tell that Manibozhoo instituted all the secret societies for the benefit of mankind, that he is a great and benevolent being, and at the same time relate the most absurd stories of their hero, the psychological discrepancy of the two groups of myths becomes very evident.

It is important to note that we find a gradual transition from the purely egotistical transformer legends, if I may use this term, to the clearly altruistic series. The transformer legend of the Kwakiutl of Vancouver Island [1] is instructive in this respect. The transformer meets a number of enemies who are planning his death. They do not recognize him and tell him of their plans. Then he transforms them into animals, and ordains that they shall be the food of man. He is thirsty, and in order to obtain water, he slays a monster that has killed a whole tribe. In all these cases he acts from egotistical motives. Later on he gives the laws governing the religious ceremonials of the tribe. This he does in the following manner: he meets the ancestors of the various clans, and they test their powers. Sometimes he is vanquished, and then his adversary obtains certain privileges as the fruit of his victory. In other cases he proves to be the stronger. Then he takes pity on his rival, and gives him certain ceremonials as a present. In all these adventures he appears as a powerful chief who is travelling all over the world, not with a view of making man happier, but doing so incidentally in the course of his adventures. Still the Kwakiutl look at him distinctly as the culture hero, and in this I see a fundamental difference from the manner in which the Tsimshian look at the Raven. They recognize the Raven as the creator, but his actions were so little dictated by considerations of the needs of man that they owe him no thanks for what he has done. The Kamchadal express this attitude accurately when they say that the god Kutka was very foolish, that he might have arranged things much better when he was creating the world. The transformer of the Kwakiutl, on the other hand, gave his gifts to the ancestors of the various clans, and these gifts were naturally intended for the benefit of their families, although they were not prompted by clearly altruistic motives. Therefore the Kwakiutl revere their transformer. The mental attitude has entirely changed.[2]

Another instructive example is that of the transformer of the Blackfeet.[3] It is stated that he taught many arts to man because he pitied him.

---

[1] F. Boas, *Indianische Sagen von der Nord-Pacifischen Küste Amerikas*, p. 194ff.

[2] As a matter of fact, there are contradictory attitudes among the Kwakiutl. The group to which the transformer "belongs" have respect for his deeds, while others consider him as malevolent because he transformed men into animals (see F. Boas, *Religion of the Kwakiutl Indians*, Columbia University Contributions to Anthropology, vol. 10, Part 2, p. 177).

[3] George B. Grinnell, *Blackfoot Lodge Tales* (London, 1893), p. 137 *et seq.*

But other important changes of nature and similar events came about without any such intention on his part. Death was the result of a bet between him and a woman. Animals obtained their fat in a feast given to them by the transformer.

In short, we find that among various tribes the altruistic side is developed very unequally.

It seems quite intelligible that with the progress of society there should develop a tendency of substituting for the coarse motives of the primitive transformer higher ones. With the consciousness that the changes effected by the transformer were useful to man may have developed the idea that they were made with the view of benefiting mankind. The traditions of the Kwakiutl may be taken to indicate a transitional point in the ethical aspect of these myths, the changes being made not for the good of mankind, but for the benefit of a particular friend of the transformer. The less the altruistic idea is developed, the less will be the consciousness of a discrepancy between the tales representing the transformer as a benefactor and as a trickster. The higher it is developed, the greater will be the friction between the two groups of tales. Hence we find that wherever this idea is brought out most clearly, the tales of the trickster are ascribed to a different being. The personage of the transformer is split in two or more parts; the one representing the true culture hero, the other retaining the features of the trickster. This has been done in the mythology of the Micmac and Penobscot,[1] where Glooskap retains almost exclusively the features becoming to the benefactor of mankind. Still I think that in a few of his adventures the more primitive conception of the transformer may be recognized. The more sophisticated the tribe, the more sharply, it seems, is the line drawn between the culture hero and the trickster.

I am well aware that the theory here proposed does not clear up all the difficult questions connected with this subject, but I think that it at least does away with the troublesome psychological discrepancy between the two aspects of the transformer. I venture to suggest that perhaps this theory would appear better established if all the Indian mythologies were recorded just as told by the Indian uninfluenced by contact with civilization. As a matter of fact, many were recorded by missionaries, who would naturally introduce in all tales of a culture hero

---

[1] S. T. Rand, *Legends of the Micmac* (New York, 1894), *passim;* and Charles G. Leland, *The Algonquin Legends of New England* (Boston, 1885), pp. 15 *et seq.* and pp. 140 *et seq.*

the altruistic element much more strongly than intended by the Indian. Their whole training would tend to introduce this bias. The same is true to a certain extent of all White collectors, unless the traditions are recorded verbatim. I have examined the available literature quite closely, and find that very few collectors actually give the motive which led the transformer to carry out certain actions, although the latter is often implied by the incidents of the story. I think that in all probability if Indian mythologies were available in their pure original form, the egotistic character of the transformer would appear much more strongly than is the case at present.

Such criticism must, however, be applied most sparingly, because the plausibility of our theory may induce us to reject evidence on account of its incongruity with the theory. It seems, however, justifiable to suggest to collectors of myths the desirability of paying particular attention to the motives ascribed to the culture hero and to investigate if his character is that of a pure egotist in other regions and among other tribes than those mentioned before. If this should prove to be the case, I should be inclined to consider the theory that has been suggested here as well established.

The traditions of the Thompson Indians, as recorded by Mr. James Teit, show a peculiar development of the transformer myths. There are at least four distinct personages who may be considered as culture heroes or transformers. The most important one among them is the Coyote, around whom a great many traditions cluster. In his case the peculiar mixture of characteristics described on the preceding pages is well marked. He is a being of great power; he performed many feats in consequence of which the world assumed its present shape. A great many striking local features of the country inhabited by the Thompson Indians originated through his agency. In many of his actions he appears as the trickster, and all his methods are based on sly cunning. The series of Coyote legends of this tribe resembles the Coyote tales with which we are familiar from a number of points on the western plateaus of our continent, and I do not doubt that they belong to this series. In all these tales he appears as a transformer and a culture hero, but he is not moved by the desire of benefiting mankind; he accomplishes all transformations of the world in the pursuit of his own ends.

The second series of transformer myths refer to the three brothers. I do not think that we can interpret the differentiation of transformers in the legends of the Thompson Indians as solely due to the developing desire of differentiating the altruistic and egotistic side of this being, because the tales of the Brothers do not by any means bring out an altruistic point of view more clearly than those of the Coyote. It seems much more likely that the latter group of legends are simply new traditions introduced from the lower course of Fraser River. A comparison between these tales and the transformer legends of the tribes living at the delta of Fraser River and on southeastern Vancouver Island show that these two series are practically identical, except that the latter series is very much more elaborate.[1]

It is not so easy to explain the origin of the legend of the transformer Hog Fennel. This being is the son of the hog fennel (*Peucedanum*), a plant which plays a most important part in the ceremonials of the tribes of lower Fraser River, but which, so far as I am aware, is not personified to any extent among them. I have not found any analogon of this legend among the neighboring tribes.

The fourth transformer is called "The Old Man," but it does not seem that there are many elaborate myths referring to him. The whole concept of the Old Man is so much like that of the Kootenay and Blackfeet, that I am rather inclined to consider these groups of tales as having a common origin. In order to establish this point, it will be necessary to investigate the transformer tales of the Shuswap and Okanagon, which are, however, only imperfectly known.

If the legends of the Brothers and those of the Old Man are really of foreign origin, the numerous instances of contests between these beings may be explained quite naturally as a result of comparisons of their powers. Numerous examples of this kind are known from the mediæval epics, in which the heroes of most heterogeneous groups of legends are made to struggle against each other. This is the leading idea of the tradition of the "Rosegarden," in which all the heroes of the old German tales appear, and compete against one another.

This theory is acceptable only if it is possible to prove that the tales of the Thompson Indians really contain foreign elements. It may be well to discuss at least one of their legends rather fully with a view of establishing this important point. I select the Coyote tradition for this purpose.

We will begin our analysis with the story of Coyote's son.[2] It is not certain that the beginning of the story, in which it is told how the Coyote

---

[1] F. Boas, *Indianische Sagen*, etc., pp. 19 *et seq.*, pp. 45, 63; also pp. 66, 201.

[2] Teit, *Traditions, etc.,* p. 21.

made boys out of clay, gum, and stone, has any analogue among the neighboring tribes. It is true that among the coast tribes a myth occurs in which the gum is presented as a man who is made to melt in the sun; but it occurs in entirely different connections, and it is doubtful if this incident in the Coyote tradition is directly related to the corresponding tale of the coast. The latter refers to the attempt of the Raven to obtain gum. He induces the gum-man to go fishing with him. He exposes him to the hot sun until he is melted.

The next incident of our tale, however, can be traced among many of the neighboring tribes. Coyote makes a tree, which he induces his son to climb. Then he makes the tree grow until it reaches the sky. The inducement held out to the boy is a nest of eagles on the top of the tree. The Ponca [1] tell the same incident. They relate, how Ishtinike makes a tree, and induces his friend to climb it in order to recover his arrows. Petitot tells the identical story from the Hare Indians and from the Chippewayan.[2] Livingston Farrand has found the story of an ascent of the sky by means of a growing tree among the Chilcotin, who live northwest of the Thompson Indians. The boy reaches the sky and travels over an extensive prairie. After a while he reaches houses in which baskets and other household utensils are living, and when he tries to carry away one of them, he is beaten by the others, and finds that they are the inhabitants of the house. This last incident has no close analogue among the other tribes, although it reminds us forcibly of the visit to the house of the shadows, told by the Chinook, Tsimshian, and Tlingit.[3] In these tales the traveller reaches a house inhabited by shadows, by whom he is beaten whenever he tries to take away some of their provisions or their household utensils.

Coyote travels on, and meets two blind women, whom he makes quarrel by taking away their food. They recognize him by his scent and are transformed into birds. This tale is found extensively along the Pacific coast. The tribes of lower Fraser River tell of a boy who reached the sky, and met two blind sisters. He takes away their food and makes them quarrel. Then they advise him in regard to the dangers that he is going to encounter on his way to the house of the sun.[4] The same incident occurs in the traditions of the Coast Salish, referring to a

---

[1] J. O. Dorsey, "The Cegiha Language," *Contributions to North American Ethnology,* vol. 6 (1890), p. 607.

[2] Petitot, *Traditions indiennes du Canada nord-ouest* (Paris, 1886).

[3] F. Boas, *Indianische Sagen,* etc., p. 316; Chinook Texts, p. 181.

[4] *Indianische Sagen,* etc., p. 38.

man who tried to recover his wife, who was carried away by a finback whale. He descended to the bottom of the sea, and met a number of blind old women, one of whom was distributing food among the others. He took it away, opened their eyes, and in return was given advice by the women.[1] The Comox tell of a young man who visited the sky, where he met the Snail-women, whose food he took away. He restored their eyesight, and they advised him in regard to the dangers he would meet.[2] The Kwakiutl have the tradition of a man who wanted to marry the daughter of a chief. On his journey he met a number of old women, and the same incident occurred as told before.[3] In Nahwitti the same story is told of a great transformer who met four blind girls, whom he made quarrel in the same manner. He transformed them into ducks.[4] The Bella Coola tell of a boy who reached the sky, and restored the eyesight of a number of blind women. He transformed them into ducks. All these incidents are identical with those recorded among the Thompson Indians. Far to the east, in the collection of tales of the Ponca made by Dorsey, a similar incident occurs, which, however, bears only slight resemblance to the one discussed here, and which may be of quite independent origin. It is told how an invisible visitor burns the cheek of the Thunderers, and thus makes them quarrel.[5]

The following incident, in which it is told how the boy visited the spiders and how they let him down from the sky, does not exhibit any striking similarities with the tales of the neighboring tribes, although the occurrence of a descent from heaven by help of a spider is an exceedingly frequent feature of North American mythologies. The descent from the sky is remarkably similar to a descent told by the tribes of lower Fraser River, in which two spiders let the visitor down in a basket tied to a long rope. When he reaches the tops of the trees, he shakes the rope, whereupon the spiders continue to let him down until he reaches the ground.[6] In a Chippewayan story [7] a person is let down from the sky by means of a rope.

The following incidents of the tale do not give any occasion for remarks, although they remind us in a general way of the tales of the

[1] *Ibid.,* p. 55.
[2] *Ibid.,* p. 118.
[3] *Ibid.,* p. 136.
[4] *Ibid.,* p. 202.
[5] Dorsey, *The Cegiha Language,* p. 204.
[6] Boas, *Indianische Sagen,* etc., p. 40.
[7] Petitot, *Traditions indiennes du Canada nord-ouest,* p. 358.

neighboring tribes. When we confine ourselves to more complicated incidents, we are again struck by those told on p. 26. Raven is given deer-fat by a person whom he had helped before; he took the fat home and gave it secretly to his children. The attention of the people was called to this fact by the noise the children were making when being fed by Raven. A person made one of the children disgorge the fat, and thus discovered that Raven was well provided for, while the other people were starving. This incident occurs in the traditions of the Coast Salish, where a boy sends fish to his grandmother, who hides them until dark. The fish are discovered when she begins to eat them. The same tale is told by the Kwakiutl. The boy sends his grandmother whale blubber, which is discovered when she is eating it. The incident is also told at Nahwitti. Farther north the traditions agree with that of the Thompson Indians, in that a child is made to disgorge the food. We find this tale among the Bella Coola and among the Tsimshian.[1] Farrand has recorded the same tale among the Chilcotin.

The following parts of the tradition have close analoga on the coast; more particularly with the mink tales of the tribes on lower Fraser River and with the transformer tradition of the Tillamook.[2]

Among the other Coyote tales the fourth and the last are rather remarkable on account of their distribution. Coyote meets a cannibal. He proposes that they shall close their eyes and vomit into two dishes, in order to see what kind of food they eat. Coyote exchanges the dishes before the cannibal opens his eyes, thus making him believe that he himself is a cannibal. The Shuswap ascribe this incident to the Coyote and the Cannibal Owl, while far to the south the Navaho tell the same of Coyote and the Brown Giant.[3]

The last story tells of the unsuccessful attempts of Coyote to imitate his hosts who produced food by magical means. We may compare with this tale that of the Chinook, who tell how Blue Jay tried to imitate his hosts;[4] that of the Comox, Nootka, and Kwakiutl of Vancouver Island, and of the Bella Coola and Tsimshian of northern British Columbia.[5] who tell the same story of the Raven. Farrand found the tale among the Chilcotin. Dorsey has recorded it among the Ponca, who tell of

[1] Boas, *Indianische Sagen*, etc., pp. 53, 133, 180, 264, 303.

[2] *Journal of American Folk-Lore*, vol. 11, no. 41 (1898), p. 140.

[3] Washington Matthews, *Navaho Legends* (Boston, 1897), p. 227; Boas, *Indianische Sagen*, p. 9.

[4] *Chinook Texts*, p. 178.

[5] Boas, *Indianische Sagen*, pp. 76, 106, 177, 245.

Ishtinike's vain attempts to imitate his hosts,[1] and Rand tells it from the Micmac, among whom the Rabbit is the hero of the tale.[2] Finally we find it told of the Coyote among the Navaho, although among this tribe the incidents are materially changed.[3]

The distribution of the various parts of the Coyote legend as described here is conclusive proof of its complex origin. It is quite inconceivable that all these complex parts of the tradition should have originated independently among the tribes among which we find them now. This view is strengthened by the fact that the incidents are most nearly alike among neighboring tribes. In the Thompson tales recorded by Mr. Teit are found numerous additional instances of close resemblances to those of their neighbors which corroborate the evidence brought forward in the preceding remarks.

It appears, therefore, that there is ample proof of transmission of tales to the Thompson Indians from foreign sources and *vice versa*. It was suggested before (p. 416), that if such proof can be given, we may assume that the transformer myths originated from different sources, and have not had time to amalgamate. The similarity of the series of Coyote tales with the Coyote tales of the south and east, and with the animal tales of the coast, and of the legend of the Brothers with the transformer tales of the delta of Fraser River, point to the sources from which the various series of transformer tales sprang.

I doubt if it will ever be possible to determine the origin of all the parts of the tales of this tribe that have been woven into their structure. It may be that we shall better understand the history of their development when we shall have fuller collections than are now available from the tribes of Washington, Oregon, and Idaho. Their relation to the legendary lore of the coast tribes of British Columbia, however, seems well established. It appears that a considerable number of tales were borrowed bodily from the coast tribes, and were incorporated ready-made in the tales of the Thompson tribe. It is, therefore, certain that these importations when interwoven with mythical tales never have had any symbolic significance among the people whose property they are now. They are not nature myths, in the generally adopted sense of the term. While dealing with phenomena of nature and with the peculiarities of animals, they are not the result of tribal thought; they are

---

[1] Dorsey, *loc. cit.*, pp. 557.
[2] Rand, *loc. cit.*, pp. 300, 302.
[3] Matthews, *loc. cit.*, p. 87.

at best adaptations of foreign thought, but much more frequently importations that have undergone little if any change. The present character of Indian mythologies can be understood only by historical studies regarding their origin. How much is due to independent thought or to gradual adaptation, under the influences of environment and of new social conditions, remains to be determined by detailed comparative studies.

We may trace the influence of environment in the modifications that the tales undergo, owing to differences in the mode of life of various tribes. Thus the tales of the fishermen of the seacoast who spend most of their time in their canoes, and whose villages are located near the shore, differ in many respects from the tales of the Thompson Indians, who hunt part of the year in the mountains. The animals who are the heroes of the tales also change from one locality to the other. In northern British Columbia Raven takes the place of Coyote; on Vancouver Island Mink takes his place, while still farther south, among the Chinook, Blue Jay assumes many of his functions.

But much more striking than the influence of geographical environment is that of the social status of the tribe. The clan organization of the coast tribes pervades their whole mythology and all their traditions, while the loose social organizations of the tribes of the interior gives their tales a peculiar character. This difference is brought out strongly in the myths of the transformer as found among a number of coast tribes and those of the interior. Every clan[1] has a legend expounding the events that took place at the time of meeting between the transformer and the ancestor of the clan, while there is no such personal relation between the Indians and the transformer in the interior. The rivalry between clans is one of the mainsprings of action. It is evident that in many cases tales which originally had no totemic bearing were appropriated by a clan and changed so as to become clan traditions. I have described a number of such changes in a fuller discussion of the social system of the Kwakiutl.[2] Other tales developed numerous variants among various clans, the more elaborate social organization acting as a stimulus for the development of traditions. The same is true in the case of ritualistic myths. They are all part and parcel of the complicated rituals of the coast tribes and some of them are made to explain the ritual. Con-

---

[1] In regard to the use of the term clan see p. 359 of this volume.
[2] "The Social Organization and the Secret Societies of the Kwakiutl Indians," *Report of the U. S. National Museum for 1895* (1897), p. 328ff.

clusions founded on observation of the tribes of British Columbia and on that of the Pueblo tribes of the southwest agree, in that they tend to show that the ritual and, we may say in a more general way, the social system, have been foisted upon the myths, thus producing variations, which tend to establish harmony between mythology and social phenomena.

The Salish tribes, to which the Thompson Indians belong, owing to their wide distribution and diversity of culture, offer an interesting example of the influence of social organization upon mythology. The great body of the people have the same loose organization that we find among the Thompson tribe; but among the tribes living on the coast more complex conditions prevail. They have been under the influence of the tribes of the coast of British Columbia for so long a time, that their customs and beliefs have undergone material changes. The loose village community has been replaced by one claiming common descent from one mythical ancestor.

This transition may be observed among the tribes of the Delta of Fraser River, which are closely allied to the Thompson Indians. Each village has a mythical ancestor, and some of these are described as animals. It may be well to make clearer the peculiar character of these tales by means of a few abstracts of myths.

The ancestor of one tribe whose village is close to the mouth of Fraser River, was Beaver-Man. When the transformer visited his village they had a contest, in the course of which they tried to transform each other. Finally the transformer proved to be the stronger of the two. He transformed the man into a beaver. It seems that in a few cases these traditions contain memories of historical events. Such seems to be the case in the tradition of the origin of a tribe living on Harrison River. One of the descendants of their ancestor is said to have invited the ancestor of another tribe, who was descended from the marten and the mountain goat, to descend from the mountains and to live with him. Since that time the descendants of these two chiefs are said to have formed one tribe.[1] I think the occurrence of these traditions must be explained in the following way: The coast tribes north of Fraser River are divided into totemic clans, each of which has a clan tradition. All the privileges of the clans are explained by the clan traditions, which, for this reason, are considered a most valuable property. That this is so is indicated by the jealousy with which the property right to certain

[1] Boas, *Indianische Sagen*, pp. 24 *et seq.*

traditions is guarded by the families of the coast tribes. When the Salish tribes began to be thrown into contact with the coast tribes, the lack of family traditions must have been felt as a great disadvantage. Their lack made the tribe, in a way, inferior to their neighbors on the coast, and for this reason the tendency and the desire of evolving myths of this character becomes intelligible. But the tribe was organized on a different basis from that of the coast people. While the latter were divided into clans, the idea that was present to the minds of the Salish people was that of the village community; and it is clear, therefore, that the traditions which developed would be of such a character that each village would have one mythical ancestor.

The same change has taken place among the Bella Coola, whose mythology is much more thoroughly modified by the coast tribes than that of the Salish tribes of Fraser River.

These considerations have an important bearing upon the interpretation of the myths of primitive people. I have tried to show that the material of which they are built up is of heterogeneous origin, and that much of it is adopted ready-made. The peculiar manner in which foreign and indigenous material is interwoven and worked into a somewhat homogeneous fabric depends to a great extent upon the social conditions and habits of the people. Oft-repeated actions which are the expression of social laws, and which constitute the habits and customs of the people, may be expected to be more stable than traditions that are not repeated in a prescribed form or ritual, and have thus become intimately associated with habitual actions. This is probably the reason why we find that ritual moulds the explanatory myth, and why, in a more general way, the myth is made to conform with the social status of the people. Discrepancies between the two, in a general way at least, belong to the class of phenomena that are called "survivals." The discrepancy may consist in the preservation of earlier customs in traditions, or in fragments of early traditions under modified social conditions. The survivals themselves are proof of the gradual process of assimilation between social conditions and traditions which has wrought fundamental changes in the lore of mankind.

Both factors, dissemination and modification on account of social causes, must tend to obscure the original significance of the myth. The contents of mythology prove that attempts at the explanation of nature are the primary source of myths.[1] But we must bear in mind that, owing

---

[1] Compare my later views, pp. 446 *et seq.* of this volume.

to the modifications they have undergone, we cannot hope to gain an insight into their earliest form by comparisons and interpretations, unless they are based on a thorough inquiry into the historical changes that have given to myths their present forms. It would seem that mythological worlds have been built up, only to be shattered again, and that new worlds were built from the fragments.

THE GROWTH OF INDIAN MYTHOLOGIES [1]

A STUDY BASED UPON THE GROWTH OF THE MYTHOLOGIES OF THE NORTH PACIFIC COAST

IN a collection of Indian traditions recently published,[2] I have discussed the development of the mythologies of the Indians of the North Pacific coast. In the following I will briefly sum up the results at which I arrived in my investigation, and try to formulate a number of principles which, it seems to me, may be derived from it, and which, I believe, ought to be observed in all work on mythologies and customs of primitive people.

The region with which I deal, the North Pacific coast of our continent, is inhabited by people diverse in language but alike in culture.

The arts of the tribes of a large portion of the territory are so uniform that it is almost impossible to discover the origin of even the most specialized forms of their productions inside of a wide expanse of territory. Acculturation of the various tribes has had the effect that the plane and the character of the culture of most of them is the same; in consequence of this we find also that myths have travelled from tribe to tribe, and that a large body of legends belongs to many in common.

As we depart from the area where the peculiar culture of the North Pacific coast has reached its highest development, a gradual change in arts and customs takes place, and, together with it, we find a gradual diminution in the number of myths which the distant tribe has in common with the people of the North Pacific coast. At the same time, a gradual change in the incidents and general character of the legends takes place.

We can in this manner trace what we might call a dwindling down of an elaborate cycle of myths to mere adventures, or even to incidents of adventures, and we can follow the process step by step. Wherever

[1] Paper read at the Seventh Annual Meeting of the American Folk-Lore Society, Philadelphia, December 27, 1895. *Journal of American Folk-Lore,* vol. 9 (1896), pp. 1–11.
[2] *Indianische Sagen von der Nord-Pacifischen Küste Amerikas,* Berlin, 1895.

this distribution can be traced, we have a clear and undoubted example of the gradual dissemination of a myth over neighboring tribes. The phenomena of distribution can be explained only by the theory that the tales have been carried from one tribe to its neighbors, and by the tribe which has newly acquired them in turn to its own neighbors. It is not necessary that this dissemination should always follow one direction; it may have proceeded either way. In this manner a complex tale may dwindle down by gradual dissemination, but also new elements may be embodied in it.

It may be well to give an example of this phenomenon. The most popular tradition of the North Pacific coast is that of the raven. Its most characteristic form is found among the Tlingit, Tsimshian, and Haida. As we go southward, the connection between the adventurers becomes looser and their number less. It appears that the traditions are preserved quite fully as far south as the north end of Vancouver Island. Farther south the number of tales which are known to the Indians diminishes rapidly. At Nahwittee, near the north point of Vancouver Island, thirteen tales out of a whole of eighteen exist. The Comox have only eight, the Nootka six, and the Coast Salish only three. Furthermore, the traditions are found at Nahwittee in the same connection as farther north, while farther south they are very much modified. The tale of the origin of daylight, which was liberated by the raven, may serve as an instance. He had taken the shape of the spike of a cedar, was swallowed by the daughter of the owner of the daylight, and then born again; afterwards he broke the box in which the daylight was kept. Among the Nootka, only the transformation into the spike of a cedar, which is swallowed by a girl and then born again, remains. Among the Coast Salish the more important passages survive, telling how the raven by a ruse compelled the owner of the daylight to let it out of the box in which he kept it. The same story is found as far south as Grey's Harbor in Washington. The adventure of the pitch, which the raven kills by exposing it to the sunshine, intending to use it for calking his canoe, is found far south, but in an entirely new connection, embodied in the tradition of the origin of sun and moon.

But there are also certain adventures embodied in the raven myths of the north which probably had their origin in other parts of America. Among these I mention the story of the raven who was invited and reciprocated. The seal puts his hands near the fire, and grease drips out of them into a dish which he gives to the raven. Then the latter tries to imitate him, but burns his hands, etc. This tale is found, in one or the other form, all over North America, and there is no proof that it originally belonged to the raven myth of Alaska.

I believe the proposition that dissemination has taken place among neighboring tribes will not encounter any opposition. Starting from this point, we will make the following considerations:—

If we have a full collection of the tales and myths of all the tribes of a certain region, and then tabulate the number of incidents which all the collections from each tribe have in common with any selected tribe, the number of common incidents will be the larger the more intimate the relation of the two tribes and the nearer they live together. This is what we observe in a tabulation of the material collected on the North Pacific coast. On the whole, the nearer the people, the greater the number of common elements; the farther apart, the less the number.

But it is not the geographical location alone which influences the distribution of tales. In some cases, numerous tales which are common to a territory stop short at a certain point, and are found beyond it in slight fragments only. These limits do not by any means coincide with linguistic divisions. An example of this kind is the raven legend, to which I referred before. It is found in substantially the same form from Alaska to northern Vancouver Island; then it suddenly disappears almost entirely, and is not found among the southern tribes of Kwakiutl lineage, nor on the west coast of Vancouver Island, although the northern tribes, who speak the Kwakiutl language, have it. Only fragments of these legends have strayed farther south, and their number diminishes with increasing distance. There must be a cause for such a remarkable break. A statistical inquiry shows that the northern traditions are in close contact with the tales of the tribes as far south as the central part of Vancouver Island, where a tribe of Salish lineage is found; but farther they do not go. The closely allied tribes immediately south do not possess them. Only one explanation of this fact is possible, viz., lack of acculturation, which may be due to a difference of character, to long continued hostilities, or to recent changes in the location of the tribes, which has not allowed the slow process of acculturation to exert its deep-going influence. I consider the last the most probable cause. My reason for holding this opinion is that the Bella Coola, another Salish tribe, which has become separated from the people speaking related languages and live in the far north, still show in their mythologies the closest relations to the southern Salish tribes, with whom they have many more traits in common than their neighbors to the north and to the south. If their removal were a very ancient one, this similarity in mythologies would probably not have persisted, but they would have been quite amalgamated by their new neighbors.

We may also extend our comparisons beyond the immediate neighbors of the tribes under consideration by comparing the mythologies of the tribes of the plateaus in the interior, and even of those farther to the east with those of the coast. Unfortunately, the available material from these regions is very scanty. Fairly good collections exist from the Athapascan, from the tribes of Columbia River and east of the mountains, from the Omaha, and from some Algonquin tribes. When comparing the mythologies and traditions which belong to far-distant regions, we find that the number of incidents which they have in common is greater than might have been expected; but some of those incidents are so general that we may assume that they have no connection, and may have arisen independently. There is, however, one very characteristic feature which proves beyond cavil that this is not the sole cause of the similarity of tales and incidents. We know that in the region under discussion two important trade routes reached the Pacific coast, one along the Columbia River, which connected the region inhabited by Shoshonean tribes with the coast and indirectly led to territories occupied by Siouan and Algonquin tribes; another one which led from Athapascan territory to the country of the Bella Coola. A trail of minor importance led down Fraser River. A study of the traditions shows that along these routes the points of contact of mythologies are strongest, and rapidly diminish with increasing distances from these routes. On Columbia River, the points of contact are with the Algonquin and Sioux; among the Bella Coola with the Athapascan. I believe this phenomenon cannot be explained in any other way but that the myths followed the lines of travel, and that there has been dissemination of tales all over the continent. My tabulations include the Micmac of Nova Scotia, the Eskimo of Greenland, the Ponca of the Mississippi Basin, and the Athapascan of the Mackenzie River, and the results give the clearest evidence of extensive borrowing.

The identity of a great many tales in geographically contiguous areas has led me to the point of view of assuming that wherever considerable similarity between two tales is found in North America, it is more likely to be due to dissemination than to independent origin.

But without extending these theories beyond the clearly demonstrated truths of transmission of tales between neighboring tribes, we may reach some further conclusions. When we compare, for instance, the tales of the culture hero of the Chinook and that of the origin of the whole religious ceremonial of the Kwakiutl Indians, we find a far-reaching resemblance in certain parts of the legends which make it certain that these parts are derived from the same source. The grandmother of the divinity of the Chinook, when a child, was carried away by a monster. Their child became the mother of the culture hero, and by her help the monster was slain. In a legend from Vancouver Island, a monster, the cannibal spirit, carries away a girl, and is finally slain by her help. Their child becomes later on the new cannibal spirit. There are certain intermediate stages of these stories which prove their identity beyond doubt. The important point in this case is that the myths in question are perhaps the most fundamental ones in the mythologies of these two tribes. Nevertheless, they are not of native growth, but, partly at least, borrowed. A great many other important legends prove to be of foreign origin, being grafted upon more ancient mythologies. This being the case, I draw the conclusion that the mythologies as we find them now are not organic growths, but have gradually developed and obtained their present form by accretion of foreign material. Much of this material must have been adopted ready-made, and has been adapted and changed in form according to the genius of the people who borrowed it. The proofs of this process are so ample that there is no reason to doubt the fact. We are, therefore, led to the conclusion that from mythologies in their present form it is impossible to derive the conclusion that they are mythological explanations of phenomena of nature observed by the people to whom the myths belong, but that many of them, at the place where we find them now, never had such a meaning. If we acknowledge this conclusion as correct, we must give up the attempts at off-hand explanation of myths as fanciful, and we must also admit that explanations given by the Indians themselves are often secondary, and do not reflect the true origin of the myths.

I do not wish to be misunderstood in what I said. Certainly, the phenomena of nature are at the bottom of numerous myths, else we should not find sun, moon, clouds, thunder-storm, the sea and the land playing so important a part in all mythologies. What I maintain is only that the specific myth cannot be simply interpreted as the result of observation of natural phenomena. Its growth is much too complex. In most cases, the present form has undergone material change by disintegration and by accretion of foreign material, so that the original underlying idea is, at best, much obscured.

Perhaps the objection might be raised to my argument that the similarities of mythologies are not only due to borrowing, but also to the fact that, under similar conditions which prevail in a limited area, the human mind creates similar products. While there is a certain truth in this argument so far as elementary forms of human thought are concerned, it seems quite incredible that the same complex tale should originate twice in a limited territory. The very complexity of the tales and their gradual dwindling down to which I have referred before, cannot possibly be explained by any other method than by dissemination. Wherever geographical continuity of the area of distribution of a complex ethnographical phenomenon is found, the laws of probability exclude the theory that in this continuous area the complex phenomenon has arisen independently in various places, but compel us to assume that in its present complex form its distribution is due to dissemination, while its composing elements may have originated here and there.

It may be well to dwell on the difference between that comparative method which I have pursued in my inquiry and that applied by many investigators of ethnographical phenomena. I have strictly confined my comparisons to contiguous areas in which we know intercourse to have taken place. I have shown that this area extends from the Pacific coast to considerable distances. It is true that the mythologies of the far east and the extreme northeast are not as well connected with those of the Pacific coast by intermediate links as they might be, and I consider it essential that a fuller amount of material from intermediate points be collected in order that the investigation which I have begun may be carried out in detail. But a comparison of the fragmentary notes which we possess from intermediate points proves that most of those tales which I have enumerated as common to the east, to the north, and to the west, will be found covering the whole area continuously. Starting from this fact, we may be allowed to argue that those complex tales which are now known only from isolated portions of our continent are actually continuous but have not been recorded from intermediate points; or that they have become extinct in intermediate territory; or, finally, that they were carried over certain areas accidentally, without touching the intermediate field. This last phenomenon may happen, although probably not to a very great extent. I observed one example of this kind on the Pacific coast, where a tale which has its home in

Alaska is found only in one small group of tribes on northern Vancouver Island, where, as can be proved, it has been carried either by visitors or by slaves.

The fundamental condition, that all comparisons must be based on material collected in contiguous areas, differentiates our methods from that of investigators like Petitot and many others, who see a proof of dissemination or even of blood relationship in every similarity that is found between a certain tribe and any other tribe of the globe. It is clear that the greater the number of tribes which are brought forward for the purposes of such comparisons, the greater also the chance of finding similarities. It is impossible to derive from such comparisons sound conclusions, however extensive the knowledge of literature that the investigator may possess, for the very reason that the complex phenomenon found in one particular region is compared to fragmentary evidence from all over the world. By means of such comparisons, we can expect to find resemblances which are founded in the laws of the development of the human mind, but they can never be proofs of transmission of customs or ideas.

In the Old World, wherever investigations on mythologies of neighboring tribes have been made, the philological proof has been considered the weightiest, *i. e.,* when, together with the stories, the names of the actors have been borrowed, this has been considered the most satisfactory proof of borrowing. We cannot expect to find such borrowing of names to prevail to a great extent in America. Even in Asia, the borrowed names are often translated from one language into the other, so that their phonetic resemblance is entirely destroyed. The same phenomenon is observed in America. In many cases, the heroes of myths are animals, whose names are introduced in the myth. In other cases, names are translated, or so much changed according to the phonetic laws of various languages, that they can hardly be recognized. Cases of transmission of names are, however, by no means rare. I will give only a few examples from the North Pacific coast.

Almost all the names of Bella Coola mythology are borrowed from the Kwakiutl language. A portion of the great religious ceremony of the Kwakiutl has the name "dlo′gwala." This name, which is also closely connected with a certain series of myths, has spread northward and southward over a considerable distance. Southward we find it as far as Columbia River, while to the north it ceases with the Tsimshian; but still farther north another name of a part of the ceremonial of the

Kwakiutl is substituted, viz., "nontlem." This name, as designating a ceremonial, is found far away, in Alaska. But these are exceptions; on the whole, the custom of translating names and of introducing names of animals excludes the application of the linguistic method of investigating the borrowing of myths and customs.

We will consider for a moment the method by which traditions spread over contiguous areas, and I believe this consideration will show that the standpoint which I am taking, viz., that similarity of traditions in a continuous area is always due to dissemination, not to independent origin, is correctly taken. I will exemplify this also by means of the traditions of the North Pacific coast, more particularly by those of the Kwakiutl Indians.

It seems that the Kwakiutl at one time consisted of a number of village communities. Numbers of these village communities combined and formed tribes; then each village community formed a division of the new tribe. Owing probably to the influence of the clan system of the northern tribes, crests were adopted, and with these came the necessity of acquiring a crest legend. The social customs of the tribe are based entirely upon the divisions of the tribe, and the ranking of each individual is the higher—at least to a certain extent—the more important the crest legend. This led to a tendency of building up such legends. Investigation shows that there are two classes of these legends: the first telling how the ancestor of the division came down from heaven, out of the earth, or out of the ocean; the second telling how he encountered certain spirits and by their help became powerful. The latter class particularly bear the clearest evidence of being of recent origin; they are based entirely on the custom of the Indians of acquiring a guardian spirit after long-continued fasting and bathing. The guardian spirit thus acquired by the ancestor became hereditary, and is to a certain extent the crest of the division,—and there is no doubt that these traditions, which rank now with the fundamental myths of the tribe, are based on the actual fastings and acquisitions of guardian spirits of ancestors of the present division. If that is so, we must conclude that the origin of the myth is identical with the origin of the hallucination of the fasting Indian, and this is due to suggestion, the material for which is furnished by the tales of other Indians, and traditions referring to the spiritual world which the fasting Indian has heard. There is, therefore, in this case a strong psychological reason for involuntary borrowing from legends which the individual may have heard, no matter from what source they may have been derived. The incorporation in the mythology of the tribe is due to the peculiar social organization which favors the introduction of any myth of this character if it promises to enhance the social position of the division concerned.

The same kind of suggestion to which I referred here has evidently moulded the beliefs in a future life. All myths describing the future life set forth how a certain individual died, how his soul went to the world of the ghosts, but returned for one reason or another. The experiences which the man told after his recovery are the basis of the belief in a future life. Evidently, the visions of the sick person are caused entirely by the tales which he had heard of the world of the ghosts, and the general similarity of the character of this tale along the Pacific coast proves that one vision was always suggested by another.

Furthermore, the customs of the tribe are such that by means of a marriage the young husband acquires the crest legends of his wife, and the warrior who slays an enemy those of the person whom he has slain. By this means a large number of traditions of the neighboring tribes have been incorporated in the mythology of the Kwakiutl.

The psychological reason for the borrowing of myths which do not refer to crest legends, but to the heavenly orbs and to the phenomena of nature, are not so easily found. There can be no doubt that the impression made by the grandeur of nature upon the mind of primitive man is the ultimate cause from which these myths spring, but, nevertheless, the form in which we find these traditions is largely influenced by borrowing. It is also due to its effects that in many cases the ideas regarding the heavenly orbs are entirely inconsistent. Thus the Nahwittee have the whole northern legend of the raven liberating the sun, but, at the same time, the sun is considered the father of the mink, and we find a tradition of the visit of the mink in heaven, where he carries the sun in his father's place. Other inconsistencies, as great as this one, are frequent. They are an additional proof that one or the other of such tales which are also found among neighboring tribes,—and there sometimes in a more consistent form,—have been borrowed.

These considerations lead me to the following conclusion, upon which I desire to lay stress. The analysis of one definite mythology of North America shows that in it are embodied elements from all over the continent, the greater number belonging to neighboring districts, while many others belong to distant areas, or, in other words, that dissemination of tales has taken place all over the continent. In most cases, we can discover the channels through which the tale flowed, and we recognize that in each and every mythology of North America we must expect to find numerous foreign elements. And this leads us to the conclusion that similarities of culture on our continent are always more likely to be due to diffusion than to independent development. When we turn to the Old World, we know that there also diffusion has taken place through the whole area from western Europe to the islands of Japan, and from Indonesia to Siberia, and to northern and eastern Africa. In the light of the similarities of inventions and of myths, we must even extend this area along the North Pacific coast of America as far south as Columbia River. These are facts that cannot be disputed.

If it is true that dissemination of cultural elements has taken place in these vast areas, we must pause before accepting the sweeping assertion that sameness of ethnical phenomena is *always* due to the sameness of the working of the human mind, and I take issue clearly and expressly with the view of those modern anthropologists who go so far as to say that he who looks for acculturation as a cause of similarity of culture has not grasped the true spirit of anthropology.

In making this statement, I wish to make my position perfectly clear. I am, of course, well aware that there are many phenomena of social life seemingly based on the most peculiar and most intricate reasoning, which we have good cause to believe have developed independently over and over again. There are others, particularly such as are more closely connected with the emotional life of man, which are undoubtedly due to the organization of the human mind. Their domain is large and of high importance. Furthermore, the similarities in cultures which may or may not be due to acculturation indicate that the same sort of distinct ideas will originate independently in different minds, modified to a greater or less extent by the character of environment. Proof of this are the ideas and inventions which even in our highly specialized civilization are "in the air" at certain periods, and are pronounced independently by more than one individual, until they combine in a flow which carries on the thought of man in a certain direction. All this I know and grant.

But I do take the position that this enticing idea is apt to carry us too far. Formerly, anthropologists saw acculturation or even common descent wherever two similar phenomena were observed. The discovery that this conclusion is erroneous, that many similarities are due to the psychical laws underlying human development, has carried us beyond its legitimate aim, and we start now with the presumption that all similarities are due to these causes, and that their investigation is the legitimate field of anthropological research. I believe this position is just as erroneous as the former one. We must not accuse the investigator who suspects a connection between American and Asiatic cultures as deficient in his understanding of the true principles of anthropology. Nobody has proven that the psychologic explanation holds good in all cases. On the contrary, we know many cases of diffusion of customs over enormous areas. The reaction against the uncritical use of similarities for the purpose of proving relationship and historical connections is overreaching its aim. Instead of demanding a critical examination of the causes of similarities, we say now *a priori*, they are due to psychical causes, and in this we err in method just as much as the old school did. If we want to make progress on the desired line, we must insist upon critical methods, based not on generalities but on each individual case. In many cases, the final decision will be in favor of independent origin; in others in favor of dissemination. But I insist that nobody has as yet proven where the limit between these two modes of origin lies, and not until this is done can a fruitful psychological analysis be made. We do not even know if the critical examination may not lead us to assume a persistence of cultural elements which were diffused at the time when man first spread over the globe.

It will be necessary to define clearly what Bastian terms the elementary ideas, the existence of which we know to be universal, and the origin of which is not accessible to ethnological methods. The forms which these ideas take among primitive people of different parts of the world, the "Völker-Gedanken," are due partly to the geographical environment and partly to the peculiar culture of the people, and to a large extent to their history. In order to understand the growth of psychical life, the historical growth of customs must be investigated most closely, and the only method by which the history can be investigated is by means of a detailed comparison of the tribe with its neighbors. This is the method which is necessary in order to make progress towards a better understanding of the development of mankind. This investigation will also lead us to inquire into the interesting psychological problems of acculturation, viz., what conditions govern the selection of foreign material embodied in the culture of the people, and the mutual transformation of the old culture and the newly acquired material.

To sum up, I maintain that the whole question is decided only in so far as we know that independent development as well as diffusion has made each culture what it is. It is still *sub judice* in how far these two causes contributed to its growth. The aspects from which we may look at the problem have been admirably set forth by Otis T. Mason in his address on similarities in culture.[1] In order to investigate the psychical laws of the human mind which we are seeing now indistinctly because our material is crude and unsifted, we must treat the culture of primitive people by strict historical methods. We must understand the process by which the individual culture grew before we can undertake to lay down the laws by which the culture of all mankind grew.

The end for which we are working is farther away than the methods which are now in greatest favor seem to indicate, but it is worth our struggles.

[1] *American Anthropologist,* vol. 8 (1895), p. 101.

DISSEMINATION OF TALES AMONG THE
NATIVES OF NORTH AMERICA[1]

THE study of the folk-lore of the Old World has proved the fact that dissemination of tales was almost unlimited. They were carried from east to west, and from south to north, from books to the folk, and from the folk to books. Since this fact has become understood, the explanation of tales does not seem so simple and easy a matter as it formerly appeared to be.

We will apply this experience to the folk-lore and mythologies of the New World, and we shall find that certain well-defined features are common to the folk-lore of many tribes. This will lead us to the conclusion that diffusion of tales was just as frequent and just as widespread in America as it has been in the Old World.

But in attempting a study of the diffusion of tales in America we are deprived of the valuable literary means which are at our disposal in carrying on similar researches on the folk-lore of the Old World. With few exceptions, only the present folk-lore of each tribe is known to us. We are not acquainted with its growth and development. Therefore the only method open to us is that of comparison. This method, however, is beset with many difficulties. There exist certain features of tales and myths that are well-nigh universal. The ideas underlying them seem to suggest themselves easily to the mind of primitive man, and it is considered probable that they originated independently in regions widely apart. To exemplify : The tale of the man swallowed by the fish, or by some other animal, which has been treated by Dr. E. B. Tylor [2] is so simple that we may doubt whether it is due to dissemination. The German child tells of Tom Thumb swallowed by the cow; the Ojibwa, of Nanabozhoo swallowed by the fish; the Negro of the Bahamas, according to Dr. Edwards, of the rabbit swallowed by the cow; the Hindoo, of the prince swallowed by the whale; the Bible, of the prophet

[1] Journal of American Folk-Lore, vol. 4 (1891), pp. 13-20.
[2] Early History of Mankind (London, 1878), p. 345; Primitive Culture (London, 1891), vol. 1, pp. 328 et seq.

Jonah; the Micronesian, of two men inclosed in a bamboo and sent adrift. Are these stories of independent origin, or have they been derived from one source? This vexed question will embarrass us in all our studies of the folk-lore of primitive people.

Then, we may ask, is there no criterion which we may use for deciding the question whether a tale is of independent origin, or whether its occurrence at a certain place is due to diffusion? I believe we may safely assume that, wherever a story which consists of the same combination of several elements is found in two regions, we must conclude that its occurrence in both is due to diffusion. The more complex the story which the countries under consideration have in common, the more this conclusion will be justified. I will give an example which will make this clearer. Petitot [1] tells a story of the Dog-Rib Indians of Great Slave Lake: A woman was married to a dog and bore six pups. She was deserted by her tribe, and went out daily procuring food for her family. When she returned she found tracks of children around her lodge, but did not see any one besides her pups. Finally she discovered from a hiding-place that the dogs threw off their skins as soon as she left them. She surprised them, took away the skins, and the dogs became children, —a number of boys and one girl. These became the ancestors of the Dog-Rib Indians. We may analyze this story as follows: 1. A woman mated with a dog. 2. Bears pups. 3. Deserted by her tribe. 4. Sees tracks of children. 5. Surprises them. 6. Takes their skins. 7. They become a number of boys and one girl. 8. They become the ancestors of a tribe of Indians. These eight elements have been combined into a story in the same way on Vancouver Island, where a tribe of Indians derives its origin from dogs. The single "elements" of this tale occur in other combinations in other tales. The elements may have arisen independently in various places, but the sameness of their combination proves most conclusively that the whole combination, that is, the story, has been carried from Arctic America to Vancouver Island, or *vice versa*.

It is, however, necessary to apply this method judiciously, and the logical connection of what I have called "elements" must be taken into account. A single element may consist of a number of incidents which are very closely connected and still form one idea. There is, for instance, an Ainu tale of a rascal who, on account of his numerous misdeeds, was put into a mat to be thrown into a river. He induced the carriers to go

[1] *Traditions indiennes du Canada nord-ouest*, p. 311.

to look for a treasure which he claimed to possess, and meanwhile induced an old blind man to take his place by promising him that his eyes
would be opened. Then the old man was thrown into the river, and the
rascal took possession of his property. We find this identical tale in
Andersen's fairy tales, and are also reminded of Sir John Falstaff.
While it is quite probable that these tales have a common root, still they
are so consistent in themselves that the same idea might have arisen
independently on several occasions. In cases like this we have to look
for corroborating evidence.

This may be found either in an increase of the number of analogous
tales, or in their geographical distribution. Whenever we find a tale
spread over a continuous area, we must assume that it spread over this
territory from a single center. If, besides this, we should know that it
does not occur outside the limits of this territory, our conclusion will be
considerably strengthened. This argument will be justified even should
our tale be a very simple one. Should it be complex, both our first and
second methods may be applied, and our conclusion will be the more
firmly established.

I will give an example of this kind. Around the Great Lakes we find
a deluge legend : A number of animals escaped in a canoe or on a raft,
and several of them dived to the bottom of the water in order to bring
up the land. The first attempts were in vain, but finally the muskrat
succeeded in bringing up a little mud, which was expanded by magic
and formed the earth. Petitot recorded several versions of this tale
from the Mackenzie Basin. It is known to the various branches of the
Ojibwa and to the Ottawa. Mr. Dorsey recorded it among tribes of
the Siouan stock, and kindly sent me an Iowa myth, related by the Rev.
W. Hamilton, which belongs to the same group. On the Atlantic coast
the legend has been recorded by Zeisberger, who obtained it from the
Delaware, and Mr. Mooney heard it told by the Cherokee in a slightly
varied form.

They say that in the beginning all animals were up above, and that
there was nothing below but a wide expanse of water. Finally, a small
water-beetle and the water-spider came down from above, and, diving
to the bottom of the water, brought up some mud, from which the earth
was made. The buzzard flew down while the land was still soft, and by
the flapping of its wings made the mountains. The Iroquois have a
closely related myth, according to which a woman fell down from
heaven into the boundless waters. A turtle arose from the flood, and

she rested on its back until an animal brought up some mud, from which the earth was formed. I have not found any version of this legend from New England or the Atlantic Provinces of Canada, although the incident of the turtle forming the earth occurs. We do not find any trace of this legend in the South, but on turning to the Pacific coast we find it recorded in three different places. The Yocut in California say that at a time when the earth was covered with water there existed a hawk, a crow, and a duck. The latter, after diving to the bottom and bringing up a beakful of mud, died. Whereupon the crow and the hawk took each one half of the mud, and set to work to make the mountains. This tale resembles in some respects the Cherokee tale. Farther north I found the tale of the muskrat bringing up the mud among the Molalla, the Chinook, and the Bella Coola, while all around these places it is unknown. As, besides, these are the places where intercourse with the interior takes place, we must conclude that the tale has been carried to the coast from the interior. Thus we obtain the result that the tale of the bringing up of the earth from the bottom of the water is told all over an enormous area, embracing the Mackenzie Basin, the watershed of the Great Lakes, the Middle and South Atlantic coasts, and a few isolated spots on the Pacific coast which it reached by overflowing through the mountain passes.

We will now once more take up the legend of the woman and her pups. I mentioned that two almost identical versions are known to exist, one from Great Slave Lake, the other from Vancouver Island. The legend is found in many other places. On the Pacific coast it extends from southern Oregon to southern Alaska, but in the north and south slight variations are found. Petitot recorded a somewhat similar tale among the Hare Indians of Great Bear Lake, so that we find it to occupy a continuous area from the Mackenzie to the Pacific coast, with the exception of the interior of Alaska. Among the Eskimo of Greenland and of Hudson Bay we find a legend which closely resembles the one we are considering here. A woman married a dog and had ten pups. She was deserted by her father, who killed the dog. Five of her children she sent inland, where they became the ancestors of a fabulous tribe half dog, half man. The other five she sent across the ocean, where they became the ancestors of the Europeans. The Greenland version varies slightly from the one given here, but is identical with it in all its main features. Fragments of the same story have been recorded by Mr. James Murdoch at Point Barrow. We may analyze this tale as follows: 1. A woman married a dog. 2. She had pups. 3. Was deserted by her father. 4. The pups became ancestors of a tribe. Here we have four of the elements of our first story combined in the same way and forming a new story. Besides this, the geographical distribution of the two tales is such that they are told in a continuous area. From these two facts we conclude that they must have been derived from the same source. The legend of the half-human beings with dog legs forms an important element in Eskimo lore, and according to Petitot is also found among the Loucheux and Hare Indians. This increases the sweep of our story to that part of North America lying northwest of a line drawn from southern Oregon to Cape Farewell, the southernmost point of Greenland. It is worth remarking that in Baffin Land the mother of the dogs is, at the same time, the most important deity of the Eskimo. These arguments hardly need being strengthened.

We may find, however, additional reasons for our opinion in the fact that there are other stories common to Greenland and Oregon. One of the most remarkable among these is the story of the man who recovered his eyesight. The tale runs about as follows: A boy lost his eyesight, and ever since that time his mother let him starve. His sister, who loved him dearly, fed him whenever she was able to do so. One day a bear attacked their hut, and the mother gave the boy his bow and arrow, levelled it, and the boy shot the bear. His flesh served the mother and sister for food all through the winter, while she had told the boy that he had missed the bear and that it had made its escape. In spring a wild goose flew over the hut and asked the boy to follow it. The bird took the boy to a pond, dived with him several times, and thus restored his eyesight. The boy then took revenge on his mother. I recorded this story once on the shores of Baffin Bay, once in Rivers Inlet in British Columbia. Rink tells the same story from Greenland. Here we have an excellent example of a very complex story in two widely separated regions. We cannot doubt for a moment that it is actually the same story which is told by the Eskimo and by the Indian. Besides this story there are quite a number of others which are common to the Eskimo and to tribes of the North Pacific coast.

From these facts we conclude that diffusion of tales between the Eskimo and the Indian tribes of the western half of our continent has been quite extensive. On the other hand, notwithstanding many assertions to the contrary, there are hardly any close relations between the tales of the Algonquin and the Eskimo. In Leland's collection of New

England tales,[1] for instance, I found only one or possibly two elements that belong to Eskimo lore,—the capture of a bathing girl by taking away her clothing, and the killing of birds which were enticed to come into a lodge. Both of these appear, however, in combinations which differ entirely from those in which they occur in the Eskimo tales.

There are, however, very close relations between the tales of the Algonquin and those of the Pacific coast. I will select one of the most striking examples. Leland, in his collection of Algonquin legends,[2] tells of two sisters who slept in a forest, and, on seeing stars, wished them to become their husbands. On the following morning they found themselves in heaven, one the wife of a man with beautiful eyes, the other the wife of a man with red twinkling eyes,—both the stars whom they had desired for their husbands. Then they peeped down through a hole in the ground and perceived the earth, to which they eventually returned. This abstract may stand for another story which I collected at Victoria, B. C. There are quite a number of other Algonquin tales which are found also on the Pacific coast. I select some more examples from Leland's book because the distance between the tribes he studied and those of the Pacific coast is the greatest. He tells of the rabbit which tried to rival in a variety of ways a number of animals. The same tales are told of Hiawatha and Nanabozhoo; in Alaska they are told of the raven. In a Passamaquoddy legend it is stated [3] that a witch asked a man to free her from vermin which consisted of toads and porcupines. When she asked the man to crush the poisonous vermin he deceived her by crushing cranberries which he had brought along instead. I collected the same tale in a number of places on the North Pacific coast.

This series of complex stories from the extreme east and the extreme west of our continent leaves no doubt that each originated at one point.

The end of the story of the women who were married to stars differs somewhat in New England and on the Pacific coast. In the east the stars permit the women to return, while in the West they find the possibility of return by digging roots contrary to the commands of their husbands. In doing so they make a hole through the sky and see the earth. They then make a rope, which they fasten to their spades and let themselves down.

[1] Charles G. Leland, *The Algonquin Legends of New England* (Boston, 1885), pp. 142, 186.

[2] *Ibid.*, p. 145.

[3] *Ibid.*, p. 38.

We find the same incident in a story which Mr. A. S. Gatschet collected among the Kiowa. In the creation legend of this tribe, it is told that a woman was taken up to the sky. The analysis of the two legends reveals the following series of identical incidents: 1. A woman taken up to the sky. 2. Is forbidden to dig certain roots. 3. She disobeys her husband, and discovers a hole through which she can see the world. 4. She secretly makes a rope and lets herself down. In this case we may apply our first principle, and conclude that the tale in this form must have sprung from one center. This conclusion is strengthened by the fact that the rest of the Kiowa legend coincides with another tale from the Northwest coast, which is also a creation legend. The Kiowa tale continues telling how the son of the sun fed upon his mother's body. Then an old woman captured him by making arrows and a ball (which is used as a target) for him and inducing him to steal them. I have recorded this tale among the Tsimshian at the northern boundary of British Columbia.

The comparisons which we have made show that each group of legends has its peculiar province, and covers a certain portion of our continent. We found a number of tales common to the North Pacific and the Arctic coasts. Another series we found common to the territory between the North Atlantic and Middle Pacific coasts. The Kiowa tale and the Northwestern tale indicate a third group which seems to extend along the Rocky Mountains. I will not lay too much stress upon the last fact, as the province of these tales needs to be better defined. It appears however, clearly, that tales, and connected with it, we may add, other cultural elements, have spread from one center over the Arctic and North Pacific coasts, while there is hardly anything in common to the Eskimo and Algonquin. These facts strengthen our view that the Eskimo, before descending to the Arctic coast, inhabited the Mackenzie Basin, and were driven northward by the Athapascan. We must also assume that a certain cultural center corresponds to our second province of legends.

We will finally compare some American myths with such of the Old World, but we shall confine ourselves to those to which our first principle may be applied. I have found a series of complicated tales which are common to both. One of the most remarkable is the story of the cannibal witch who pursued children. Castrèn [1] has recorded the following Samoyede fairy tale: Two sisters escaped a cannibal witch who

---

[1] *Ethnologische Vorlesungen* (St. Petersburg, 1857), p. 165.

pursued them. One of the girls threw a whetstone over her shoulder. It was transformed into a cañon and stopped the pursuit of the witch. Eventually the latter crossed it, and when she almost reached the sisters, the elder threw a flint over her shoulder, which was transformed into a mountain and stopped her. Finally the girl threw a comb behind her, which was transformed into a thicket. On the North Pacific coast we find the identical story, the child throwing three objects over its shoulders,—a whetstone which became a mountain, a bottle of oil which became a lake, and a comb which became a thicket.

Among a series of Ainu tales published by Basil Hall Chamberlain I find four or five [1] which have very close analoga on the North Pacific coast.

Another very curious coincidence is found between a myth from the Pelew Islands and several from the North Pacific coast. J. Kubary [2] tells the following: A young man had lost his fish-hook, the line having been broken by a fish. He dived after it, and, on reaching the bottom of the sea, reached a pond, at which he sat down. A girl came out of a house to fetch some water for a sick woman. He was called in and cured her, while all her friends did not know what ailed her. In British Columbia we find the same story, an arrow being substituted for the hook, a land animal for the fish. There are a number of other remarkable coincidences in this tale with American tales from the Pacific coast. It is said, for instance, that a man owned a wonderful lamp, consisting of two mother-of-pearl shells, which he kept hidden, and which was finally taken away by a boy, exactly as the sun was stolen by the raven in Alaska.

It is true that comparisons ought to be restricted to two well-defined groups of people; coincidences among the tales of one people and a great variety of others have little value. Still, diffusion has taken place all along eastern and northern Asia. Setting aside the similarity of the Northwest American tales to those from Micronesia, I believe the facts justify the conclusion that transmission of tales between Asia and America has actually taken place, and, what is more remarkable, that the main points of coincidence are not found around Bering Strait, but farther south; so that it would appear that diffusion of tales, if it took place along the coast line, was previous to the arrival of the Eskimo in Alaska. I admit, however, that these conclusions are largely con-

---

[1] "Folk-Lore Journal," 1888, p. 1ff., nos. 6, 21, 27, 33, 36.
[2] A. Bastian, *Allerlei aus Volks- und Menschenkunde* (Berlin, 1888), vol. 1, p. 63.

jectural, and need corroboration from collections from eastern Asia and from Alaska, which, however, unfortunately do not exist.

I hope these brief notes will show that our method promises good results in the study of the history of folk-lore.

It is particularly important to emphasize the fact that our comparison proves many creation myths to be of complex growth, in so far as their elements occur variously combined in various regions. This makes it probable that many elements have been embodied ready-made in the myths, and that they have never had any meaning, at least not among the tribes in whose possession we find them. Therefore they cannot be explained as symbolizing or anthropomorphizing natural phenomena; neither can we assume that the etymologies of the names of the heroes or deities give a clue to their actual meaning, because there never was such a meaning. We understand that for an explanation of myths we need, first of all, a careful study of their component parts, and of their mode of dissemination, which must be followed by a study of the psychology of dissemination and amalgamation. Only after these have been done shall we be able to attack the problem of an explanation of myths with hope of success.

REVIEW OF G. W. LOCHER, "THE SERPENT IN KWAKIUTL RELIGION: A STUDY IN PRIMITIVE CULTURE"[1]

THE attempt has been made in a number of recent works to interpret from the viewpoint of systematic sociology the ethnological data relating to the Kwakiutl Indians which I have assembled over a long period of time. George Davy's work, "La foi jurée," V. Larock's, "Essai sur la valeur sacrée et la valeur sociale des noms de personnes dans les sociétés inférieurs" and the present volume belong in this category.

Dr. Locher's investigation is based on the assumption that every mythology must be systematic. He says, "Of much greater value than the statement that certain foreign elements have penetrated into a culture is the answer to the question, why and in what manner these elements have been accepted. And for this we need some insight into the cultural system as such. This is pre-eminently true of mythology, which is dominated by a strict system and which by no means consists of a fortuitous hodge-podge of figures and motifs."

There are no criticisms to be raised against the first part of this statement. The conditions under which cultural traits are accepted or rejected present one of the most important and, at the same time, most difficult subjects of ethnological investigation. On the other hand, I have grave doubts regarding the second part of the author's statement.

It has become customary to emphasize the unity of culture and to attempt to discover the "function" of each and every act or thought in the cultural system. The complaint has been made often and by every earnest student that the stereotyped ethnographical description provides us only with disconnected fragments of the living culture. If the old method is still being pursued, this is due rather to technical difficulties that often cannot be easily overcome than to a lack of recognition of the fact that a penetrating investigation would bring to light much that is important and new. However, it is not justifiable to con-

[1] *Deutsche Literaturzeitung* (1933), pp. 1182–1186.

clude from the defects of the available descriptions which do not reveal a unity of culture, that the whole culture must be a compact unit, that contradictions within a culture are impossible, and that all features must be parts of a system. We should rather ask in how far so-called primitive cultures possess a unity that covers all aspects of cultural life. Have we not reason to expect that here as well as in more complicated cultures, sex, generation, age, individuality, and social organization will give rise to the most manifold contradictions?

Dr. Locher seeks a systematic interpretation of mythology without asking himself whether there is such a thing as a mythological system. His method of proving this point, as that of other investigators who work toward a similar goal, appears to me as follows: Myths are not what they appear to be. They hide a deeper significance which we must discover. The investigation is based upon a comparison of the stories which are grouped around the different mythological figures, upon an examination of their names, attributes, actions and associations with other figures. It is hoped in this way to recognize their "true" significance which is unknown to the living native himself, in part, because the original meaning has been forgotten, in part, I presume, because it is taken for granted that the real "system" is just as little known to him as the grammatical system of his language.

It seems to me that such attempts to discover the "true" essence of myths are analogous to the primitive way of thinking as assumed by the same investigators. As myths to the student of mythology are not what they seem, so to the primitives sun, moon, stars, lightning, clouds are supposed to hide a deeper meaning. They are conceived as a system, as a form of human life endowed with greater powers. The logic in both cases appears to me the same.

If we assume that the mythological system was at one time clearer than it is today, we are obliged to examine this theory by means of an historical analysis. Thus we are thrown back upon the much-maligned analytical method which proves that the material of every mythology does not by any means represent an old system, but has been assembled from many sources, partly in times long gone by, partly quite recently. If in spite of this fact a system should exist, it would have arisen out of the reorganization of all the native and foreign material into a new unity.

It can be shown in many cases, and especially in the instance of the Kwakiutl and Bella Bella with whom Locher deals, that parts of the mythology have been introduced quite recently and have never been worked into a system.

I do not deny that in exceptional cases the whole mythology, or at least a great part of it, may have developed into a system. This is especially true when an orthodox mythology is being cultivated by a small priestly group, whose thoughts revolve essentially around matters of religion. Even in these cases the exoteric mythology seldom agrees with the esoteric system.

The second assumption which may be made by the interpreter of myths is that a system is present even though it never finds clear and conscious expression. This assumption is likewise contradicted by the constant changes of the contents of mythology which absorbs contradictory stories without any difficulty.

All this is particularly apparent in the material treated by Locher. In these tribes unity of culture is based essentially on the valuation of social position. Every individual must have something, possession of which raises his social standing above that of his fellow tribesmen, and this possession must be defended under all circumstances. We can clearly recognize the influence of this underlying principle upon the mythology. The tribes are divided into groups which are based essentially on blood relationship. Each group has its myths and each one embellishes its legends with ever-new additions in order to maintain its social standing.

My accounts of personal reminiscences of the Kwakiutl go back approximately to 1850, and a number of earlier dates are well authenticated, so that many details of their history can be traced back to the beginning of the nineteenth century. I conclude from these reports that the complete cycle of cannibal myths did not penetrate into Kwakiutl mythology before the first half of the nineteenth century, and that the related ritual has been introduced piecemeal as a result of intermarriage with northern tribes. Even at the present time the scene of the principal myth of this cycle is laid in Rivers Inlet, outside of Kwakiutl territory, and the myth is narrated as belonging to one of the subsidiary groups of that tribe. The countless stories in which the cannibal spirit has been substituted for wolves, bears, and other creatures, which bring supernatural gifts, are obviously new inventions to prove the rights of other groups to the highly esteemed ritual. The ceremonial "cannibal-post," the symbol of the house in which the ceremony takes place, was introduced about 1850; the woman associate of the cannibal, perhaps

1858. Not a single one of the myths[1] characteristic of the spirit presiding over her ceremonial has taken hold among the Kwakiutl.

One of the most interesting cases is the myth of the supernatural birth of the son of a dead woman, who later becomes the wanderer who is always hungry. I recorded the story for the first time in 1888 in Nahwittee, close to the northern tip of Vancouver Island; and again about 1900, this time also from a native of the same village. In 1931 no one in Nahwittee remembered this story. Inquiries with reference to the former narrators brought forth the information that the first one was the descendant of a man who had lived with the Tsimshian for a long time as a slave. Unfortunately I do not know how my second informant was connected with this family. The story belongs to the Tsimshian raven cycle, was for a time a favorite with a certain Kwakiutl family and inserted by them into the main cycle of this region.

Dr. Locher emphasizes particularly the tale of *Qā'tenats,* who discovers that the chief of the sea is the double-headed serpent. This is the only instance of this identification among the Kwakiutl. The name of the hero of this story, which comes from the southernmost part of the tribe, indicates that we are dealing here with a Comox story. Moreover, the same story is told by a Comox tribe.[2] The Comox narrator does not speak of the sea spirit, but rather of the double-headed serpent. Presumably the Kwakiutl narrator, who was not familiar with the double-headed serpent as an inhabitant of the sea, introduced in its place the sea spirit he knew. Consequently it may not be identified with the serpent.

The entire method by which the double-headed serpent is to be set down as the fundamental concept of Kwakiutl mythology seems to me to rest upon a complete misunderstanding of the relation of the Indian to his mythology and of the development of the mythology of these tribes. Objections such as those here touched upon, could be raised against practically every step of the author's consideration.

It seems to me that every non-historical explanation of myths which seeks to establish a systematic symbolism suffers from the same error in logic. It is probably possible, wherever sufficient material is available, to recognize that mythologies are not stable. According to the cultural character of the people, material of heterogeneous origin develops into

---

[1] "Bella Bella Tales," *Memoirs of the American Folk-Lore Society,* vol. 25 (1932), p. 74 *et seq.*

[2] *Zeitschrift für Ethnologie,* vol. 24 (1892), Verhandlungen, p. 63.

a loosely connected whole, influenced by the basic concepts and the art style of the tribe. Almost always it reveals gaps and breaks which go back to its origin. In a theoretical treatment, mythological narratives and mythological concepts should not be equalized; for social, psychological, and historical conditions affect both in different ways. A systematic explanation of mythological stories seems to me illusory. We may accept the fundamental concepts of the myths, the supernatural creatures of the sea, land, sky, and the underworld, for what they are; we may likewise assume their partial identification with natural phenomena; but the attempt to find in the stories a symbolic significance which is not immanent will rarely lead to acceptable conclusions.

MYTHOLOGY AND FOLK-TALES OF THE NORTH AMERICAN INDIANS[1]

I. MATERIAL

D URING the last twenty years a very considerable body of tales of the North American Indians has been collected. Before their publication, almost the only important collections available for scientific research were the Eskimo tales published by H. Rink,—material recorded in part by natives during the earlier part of the nineteenth century, and printed also in the native language in Greenland; the traditions collected by E. Petitot among the Athapascan tribes of northwestern Canada; the Ponca tales collected by J. O. Dorsey; a few Siouan tales recorded by Stephen R. Riggs; and the Klamath traditions collected by Albert S. Gatschet. The material published in Daniel G. Brinton's "Library of Aboriginal American Literature" also deserves notice. In all of these the attempt was made to give a faithful rendering of the native tales; and in this they differ fundamentally from the literary efforts of Schoolcraft, Kohl, and other writers. Owing to their scope, they are also much more valuable than the older records found in the accounts of missionaries and in books of travel and exploration.

Since those times, somewhat systematic collections have been made among a large number of tribes; and, although the continent is not by any means covered by the existing material, much has been gained to give us a better knowledge of the subject.

Two types of collection may be distinguished. The one includes tales taken down in English or in other European tongues directly from natives, or indirectly with the help of interpreters. Among American institutions, the Bureau of American Ethnology, the American Museum of Natural History, the Field Museum of Natural History (Field Columbian Museum) in Chicago, for a few years the Carnegie Institution of Washington, have worked in this field. Much material is also found in the "Journal of American Folk-Lore," and in the earlier volumes of the "American Anthropologist" and of the "American Antiquarian and

[1] *Journal of American Folk-Lore*, vol. 27 (1914), pp. 374–410.

451

Oriental Journal." The other type of collection contains tales taken down from dictation by natives, or recorded in the native language by natives, and later on revised and edited. So far, the latter form the smaller group.

With the increase of material, the demands for accuracy of record have become more and more stringent. While in the earlier period of collecting no great stress was laid upon the recording of variants and their provenience,—as, for instance, in Rink's collection, in which we have variants from different parts of the country combined into a single story,—we now desire that each tale be obtained from several informants and from several places, in order to enable us to gain an impression of its importance in the tribal lore, and to insure the full record of its contents and of its relations to other tales. Furthermore, the importance of the record in the original language has become more and more apparent. This is not only for the reason that the English translation gives a very inadequate impression of the tales, but also because often the interpreter's inadequate knowledge of English compels him to omit or modify important parts. Even the best translation cannot give us material for the study of literary form,—a subject that has received hardly any attention, and the importance of which, as I hope to show in the course of these remarks, cannot be overestimated.

It is doubtful whether all the records that have been collected in previous years are well adapted to this study, because the difficulty of taking down accurate rapid dictation from natives, and the difficulty which the natives encounter in telling in the traditional manner sufficiently slowly for the purpose of the recorder, almost always exert an appreciable influence upon the form of the tale. Owing to the multiplicity of American languages and to the exigencies of the situation in which students find themselves, the recorder has only rarely a practical command of the language; and for this reason the difficulty just mentioned cannot be readily overcome. Up to the present time, the most successful method has been to have the first record made by natives who have been taught to write their own language. After they have acquired sufficient ease in writing, the diction generally becomes satisfactory. A certain one-sidedness will remain, however, as long as all the material is written down by a single recorder. It has also been suggested that phonographic records be used, which may be written out from re-dictation; but so far, no extended series has been collected in this manner.

The experience of investigators in many regions suggests that the difficulty just mentioned is not as great as might be supposed. This is indicated by the fact that good informants often break down completely when requested to dictate descriptions of the events of everyday life. They will then state that they are well able to tell stories that have a fixed form, but that the slow dictation of descriptions to be made up new is too difficult for them. It would seem, therefore, that the form in which most of the tales are obtained must be fairly well fixed. Ordinarily a poor rendering of a story can easily be recognized by the fragmentary character of the contents, the briefness of sentences, by corrections and unnecessary repetitions. We also have many tales in which the same incident is repeated a number of times; and in those cases the form of the repetitions shows, on the whole, whether the narrator has a fairly good command of his subject. Furthermore, a great many native tales contain, besides the connected narrative, stereotyped formulas, which are always told in the same manner, and which are undoubtedly always given in correct form.

It has been the habit of most collectors to endeavor to find the "right" informant for tales, particularly when the stories refer to elaborate sacred rituals, or when they are the property of social groups possessing definite privileges. It may then be observed that certain tales are in the keeping of individuals, and are only superficially or partially known to the rest of the people. In these cases the recorder has often adopted the attitude of the Indian who possesses the most elaborate variant of the tale, and the fragmentary data given by the uninitiated are rejected as misleading. This view is based on the assumption of a permanence of form of tradition that is hardly justifiable, and does not take into consideration the fact that the esoteric variant which is developed by a small number of individuals is based on the exoteric variants afloat among the whole tribe. We shall revert to this subject later on.

This static view of Indian folk-lore is also expressed by the preference given throughout to the collection of purely Indian material unaffected by European or African elements, and by the reluctance of investigators to bestow as much care upon the gathering of the more recent forms of folk-lore as is given to those forms that were current before the advent of the Whites. For the study of the development of folk-tales the modern material is of particular value, because it may enable us to understand better the processes of assimilation and of adaptation, which undoubtedly have been of great importance in the history of folk tradition.

II. MYTH AND FOLK-TALE

In our American collections the two terms "myth" and "folk-tale" have been used somewhat indefinitely. This is a necessary result of the lack of a sharp line of demarcation between these two classes of tales. No matter which of the current definitions of mythology we may adopt, there will arise difficulties that cannot be settled without establishing arbitrary distinctions. If we define myths as tales that explain natural phenomena, and that may be considered in this sense as parts of an interpretation of nature, we are confronted with the difficulty that the same tale may be explanatory in one case, and a simple tale without explanatory features in another. The strict adherence to this principle of classification would therefore result in the separation of tales that are genetically connected, one being classed with myths, the other with folk-tales. It goes without saying that in this way unnecessary difficulties are created.

If we make the personification of animals, plants, and natural phenomena the standard of distinction, another difficulty arises, which is based on the lack of a clear distinction between myths, on the one hand, and tales relating to magical exploits that are considered as true and of recent occurrence, on the other, and also on the similarities between tales relating to the adventures of human beings and animals.

Of similar character are the obstacles that stand in the way of a definition of myths as tales relating to ritualistic performances.

In all these cases the same tales will have to be considered, in one case as myths, and in another as folk-tales, because they occur both in explanatory and non-explanatory forms, relating to personified animals or natural objects and to human beings, with ritualistic significance and without it. If we do accept any one of these definitions, it will therefore always be necessary to consider the two groups together, and to investigate their historical and psychological development without regard to the artificial limits implied in the definition. This difficulty cannot be met by assuming that the folk-tale originated from a myth and must be considered a degenerate myth, or by the hypothesis that conversely the myth originated from a folk-tale; for, if we do this, a theoretical point of view, that should be the end of the inquiry, is injected into our consideration.

For our purposes it seems desirable to adhere to the definition of myth given by the Indian himself. In the mind of the American native there exists almost always a clear distinction between two classes of tales. One group relates incidents which happened at a time when the world had not yet assumed its present form, and when mankind was not yet in possession of all the arts and customs that belong to our period. The other group contains tales of our modern period. In other words, tales of the first group are considered as myths; those of the other, as history. The tales of the former group are not by any means explanatory in character throughout. They treat mostly of the achievements of animals and of heroes. From our modern point of view, it might be doubtful sometimes whether such a tale should be considered as mythical, or historical, since, on account of the Indian's belief in the powers of animals, many of the historical tales consist of a series of incidents that might as well have happened in the mythological period; such as the appearance of animals that become supernatural helpers and perform marvellous exploits, or of those that initiate a person into a new ritual. It can be shown that historical tales may in the course of time become mythical tales by being transferred into the mythical period, and that historical tales may originate which parallel in the character and sequence of their incidents mythical tales. Nevertheless the psychological distinction between the two classes of tales is perfectly clear in the mind of the Indian. It is related, in a way, to the ancient concepts of the different ages as described by Hesiod.

For our analytical study we must bear in mind that the psychological distinction which the natives make between mythical and historical tales is, from an historical point of view, not more definitely and sharply drawn than the line of demarcation between myths and tales defined in other ways. The point of view, however, has the advantage that the myths correspond to concepts that are perfectly clear in the native mind. Although folk-tales and myths as defined in this manner must therefore still be studied as a unit, we have avoided the introduction of an arbitrary distinction through our modern cultural point of view, and retained instead the one that is present in the minds of the myth-telling people.

The mythical tales belong to a period that is long past, and cannot be repeated in our world, although the expectation may exist of a renewal of mythical conditions in the dim future. Only when we ourselves are transferred into the realm of mythical beings, that continue to exist somewhere in unknown parts of our world, may myths again become happenings. The mythological beings may thus become actors in historical folk-tales or in localized tradition, although they appear at the same time as actors in true myths. The Indian who disappears and is taken to the village of the Buffaloes is, in the mind of the Indian, the hero of an historical tale, although the Buffalo men are at the same time mythical personages. The novice initiated by the spirits of a secret society is taken away by them bodily; and when he re-appears among his tribesmen, he tells them his story, which deals with the gifts of mythical beings. The person who revives from a death-like trance has been in communion with the mythical world of the ghosts, although he has been allowed to return to our world and to follow his usual occupations.

It is therefore clear that in the mind of the Indian the appearance of mythical characters is not the criterion of what constitutes a myth. It is rather its distance in space or time that gives it its characteristic tone.

It appears from these remarks that in the study of the historical origin of myths and folk-tales of modern times, the widest latitude must be given to our researches. The types and distribution of the whole body of folk-tales and myths must form the subject of our inquiry. The reconstruction of their history will furnish the material which may help us to uncover the psychological processes involved.

I cannot agree with Bastian and Wundt,[1] who consider the discovery of the actual origin of tales as comparatively insignificant, because both, independently created and disseminated material are subject to the same psychological processes which may therefore be studied by an analytical treatment of the tales as they now exist. I do not see how this can be done without interpreting as an historical sequence a classification based entirely on psychological or other considerations,— a method that can never lead to satisfactory results, on account of the arbitrary, non-historical premises on which it is founded. If there is more than one classification of this type possible, the reconstructed psychological processes will differ accordingly; and we must still demand that the change from one type to another be demonstrated by actual historical evidence when available, by inferences based on distribution or similar data when no other method can be utilized. Here, as in all other ethnological problems, the principle must be recognized that phenomena apparently alike may develop in multitudinous ways. A geometrical design may be developed from a conventionalized realistic

---

[1] Wilhelm Wundt, *Völkerpsychologie*, vol. 2, part 3, Leipzig (1909), p. 62.

form, or it may develop directly through a play with elementary technical motives; a semi-realistic form may be a copy of nature, and may have been read into a pre-existing geometrical design; or both may have been borrowed and developed on new lines. A ritual may be a dramatic presentation of a myth, it may be an ancient rite to which a myth has become attached, or it may be a copy of foreign patterns. There is no *a priori* reason that tells us which has been the starting-point of a local development, for the modern forms may have grown up in any of these ways or by their joint action. At the same time, the psychological processes that come into play in one case or the other are distinct. For this reason we insist on the necessity of an inductive study of the sequence of events as the basis for all our work.

The results of these inquiries, however, do not touch upon another problem upon which much thought has been bestowed. The beings that appear as actors in mythological tales are creatures of the imagination, and differ in the most curious ways from the beings which are known in our every-day world. Animals that are at the same time men, human beings that consist of parts of a body or are covered with warts and blotches, beings that may at will increase or decrease in size, bodies that may be cut up and will readily re-unite and come to life, beings that are swallowed by animals or monsters and pass through them unharmed, are the ordinary inventory of folk-tales as well as of myths. Whatever is nowhere seen and whatever has never happened are here common every-day events.

The imagination of man knows no limits, and we must expect great varieties of form in mythical beings and happenings. While such diversity is found, there still exist certain features that occur with surprising frequency,—in fact, so often that their presence cannot be due to accident. The attention of many investigators has been directed to these similarities, which have led to the inference that those traits that are common to the myths and folk-tales of diverse peoples and races are the fundamental elements of mythology, and that our real problem is the discovery of the origin of those most widely spread.

It would seem that much of the conflict of current opinion is due to our failure to keep distinctly apart the two lines of inquiry here characterized,—the one, the investigation into the history of tales; the other, the investigation of the origin of traditions or ideas common to many or all mythologies.

III. DISSEMINATION OF FOLK-TALES

Our first problem deals with the development of modern folk-tales. During the last twenty years the tendency of American investigators has been to disregard the problem of the earliest history of American myths and tales, and to gain an insight into their recent growth. The first step in an inductive study of the development of folk-tales must be an investigation of the processes that may be observed at the present time, and these should form the basis of inquiries into earlier history. Therefore stress has been laid upon the accumulation of many variants of the same tale from different parts of the country, and these have been made the basis of a few theoretical studies.

Not more than twenty-five years ago Daniel G. Brinton asserted that the similarity of Iroquois and Algonquian mythologies was due to the sameness of the action of the human mind, not to transmission. Since that time such a vast amount of material has been accumulated, proving definite lines of transmission, that there is probably no investigator now who would be willing to defend Brinton's position. A detailed study of transmission among the tribes of the North Pacific coast, and a brief summary of the similarities between Navaho and Northwest American folk-tales, were followed by many annotated collections containing parallels from many parts of America. The importance of dissemination was brought out incidentally in Dr. Lowie's investigation on the test-theme in American mythology and by Dr. Waterman's study of the explanatory element in American folk-tales.

Two rules have been laid down as necessary for cautious progress.[1]

First, the tale or formula the distribution of which is investigated, and is to be explained as due to historical contact, must be so complex, that an independent origin of the sequence of non-related elements seems to be improbable. An example of such a tale is the Magic Flight, in which we find a combination of the following elements: flight from an ogre; objects thrown over the shoulder forming obstacles,—first a stone, which becomes a mountain; then a comb, which becomes a thicket; lastly a bottle of oil, which becomes a body of water. It is hardly conceivable that such a group of unrelated incidents should arise independently in regions far apart.

---

[1] See Boas, "Dissemination of Tales Among the Natives of North America," *Journal of American Folk-Lore*, vol. 4 (1891), pp. 13–20, pp. 437–445 of this volume; W. Wundt, *Völkerpsychologie*, vol. 2, part 3, p. 62; Van Gennep, *La formation des légendes* (1910), p. 49.

The second rule is, that for a satisfactory proof of dissemination, continuous distribution is required. The simpler the tale, the greater must be our insistence on this condition. It must of course be admitted that simple tales may be disseminated over wide areas. It must also be admitted that in all probability tales known at one time have been forgotten, so that intermediate links in an area of geographically continuous distribution may have been lost. This, however, does not touch upon our methodological point of view. We desire to find uncontestable evidence of transmission, not alone the possibility or plausibility of transmission ; and for this purpose our safeguards must be insisted on.

The study of the distribution of themes requires a ready means for their identification, and this necessitates a brief terminology : hence the attempts to establish a series of catch-words by means of which tales and incidents may readily be recognized. Frobenius, Ehrenreich, Lowie, and Kroeber [1] have contributed to this undertaking ; but an elaboration of a satisfactory system of catch-words requires more penetrating study of the tales than those that have hitherto been made. Certain results, however, have been obtained from the study of the distribution of themes. The material that has been collected suggests that, as inquiry progresses, we may be able to discern various areas of distribution of themes. Some of these are known over large portions of the continent. For instance, the story of the Bungling Host—of a person who is fed by the magic powers of his host, who tries to imitate him and fails ignominiously—occurs from New Mexico on, all over the eastern part of North America, and is lacking only, as it seems, in California and on the Arctic coast. Similar to this is the distribution of the story of the Rolling Rock, which pursues an offending person, and pins him down until he is finally freed by animals that break the rock. Perhaps this does not extend quite so far north and south as the former story. While the Bungling-Host tale is known on the coast of British Columbia, the Rolling-Rock story does not reach the Pacific coast, although related tales are found in parts of California. Still other tales are essentially confined to the Great Plains, but have followed the trade-routes that lead to the Pacific Ocean, and are found in isolated spots from British

[1] Leo Frobenius, *Im Zeitalter des Sonnengotts;* Paul Ehrenreich, *Die Mythen und Legenden der Südamerikanischen Urvölker,* pp. 34–59; Robert H. Lowie, "The Test-Theme in North American Mythology," *Journal of American Folk-Lore,* vol. 21 (1908), p. 101 ; A. L. Kroeber, "Catchwords in American Mythology," *ibid.,* vol. 21 (1908), p. 222; see also T. T. Waterman, "The Explanatory Element in the Folk-Tales of the North American Indians," *ibid.,* vol. 27 (1914), pp. 1–54.

Columbia southward to California. To this group belongs the story of the Dancing Birds, which are told by a trickster to dance with closed eyes, and then are killed by him, a few only escaping. Another story of this group is the characteristic Deluge story, which tells of the creation of a new earth by diving animals. During the Flood the animals save themselves on a raft. One after another dives, until finally the muskrat brings up some mud, of which the new earth is created. This story is known in a very wide area around the Great Lakes, and occurs in recognizable form on a few points along the Pacific coast. To this same group belongs the tale of the Star Husbands. Two girls sleep out of doors, see two stars, and each wishes one of these for her husband. When they awake the following morning, their wish is fulfilled. One of the stars is a beautiful man, the other is ugly. Eventually the girls return to earth. This tale is known from Nova Scotia, across the whole width of the continent, to the Western plateaus, Vancouver Island, and Alaska. Still other stories of the same area are those of the Blood-Clot Boy, who originates from some blood that has been thrown away, and who becomes a hero; the story of Thrown-Away, the name for a boy who is cast out, brought up in a magic way, and who becomes a hero; the Snaring of the Sun; and many others.

The second group has a decided Western distribution, and is found extensively on the Plateaus and on the Pacific coast; although some of the stories have also crossed the mountains, and are found on the Eastern Plains. To this group belongs the story of the Eye-Juggler; that is, of an animal that plays ball with his eyes, and finally loses them; of the ascent to the sky by means of a ladder of arrows; and the story of the contest between Beaver and Porcupine, Beaver inviting Porcupine to swim, while Porcupine invites Beaver to climb.[1]

A third area of distribution may be recognized in the peculiar migration legends of the Southwest and of the Mississippi basin, which have no analogues in the northern part of the continent.

The distribution of themes becomes the more interesting, the more carefully the tales are considered. Thus the widely spread story of the Bungling Host may be divided into a number of types, according to the tricks performed by the host. On the North Pacific coast occurs the trick of knocking the ankle, out of which salmon-eggs flow; on the Plateaus, the piercing of some part of the body with a sharp instrument and pulling out food; on the Plains, the transformation of bark into

[1] See T. T. Waterman, *op. cit.*, pp. 1–54.

food; and almost everywhere, the diving for fish from a perch.[1] There is little doubt that as collection proceeds, and the distribution of themes can be studied in greater detail, the areas of dissemination will stand out more clearly than now. The greatest difficulty at present lies in the absence of satisfactory material from the Southeast and from the Pueblo region.

Ehrenreich [2] has attempted to extend these comparisons to South America and to the Old World; but many of his cases do not conform to the methodological conditions previously outlined, and are therefore not quite convincing, although I readily admit the probability of dissemination between the southern and northern half of the continent. I am even more doubtful in regard to the examples given by Dähnhardt [3] and Frobenius.[4] If Dähnhardt finds, for instance, that we have in North America a group of tales relating how Raven liberated the sun, which was enclosed in a seamless round receptacle, that the Chukchee tell of Raven holding the sun under his tongue, that the Magyar tell a similar incident of one of the heroes of their fairy-tales, it does not follow that these are the same tales. The Chukchee and Magyar tales are alike, and I should be inclined to search for intermediate links. Among the Chukchee the story has been inserted in the Raven cycle, and it seems probable that the prominence of the raven in their folk-lore is due to Northwest-coast influences, or that it developed at the same time in northeastern Asia and northwestern America. However, I do not think that the two tales are sufficiently alike to allow us to claim that they have the same origin.

Still more is this true of the alleged relations between Melanesian and American tales. Frobenius, who makes much of these similarities, calls attention, for instance, to the motive of the arrow-ladder, which occurs in Melanesia and in Northwest America. It seems to me that the idea of a chain of arrows reaching from the earth to the sky is not so complicated as to allow us to assume necessarily a single origin. Furthermore, the distance between the two countries in which the element occurs is so great, and there is apparently such a complete absence of intermediate links, that I am not convinced of the sameness of the elements. Even

---

[1] Franz Boas, "Tsimshian Mythology," *31st Annual Report of the Bureau of American Ethnology* (1916), pp. 694 *et seq.*

[2] P. Ehrenreich, *Die Mythen und Legenden der südamerikanischen Urvölker und ihre Beziehungen zu denen Nordamerikas und der Alten Welt* (1905).

[3] O. Dähnhardt, *Natursagen*, vols. i–iv. References are given in the index to these volumes (Leipzig, 1907–1912).

[4] Leo Frobenius, *Die Weltanschauung der Naturvölker* (Weimar, 1898).

the apparently complicated story of the Invisible Fish-Hook, which was recorded by Codrington, and which is common to Melanesia and North-west America, does not convince me. The fisherman's hook is taken away by a shark; the fisherman loses his way, reaches the shark's village, where a person lies sick and cannot be cured by the shamans. The fisherman sees his hook in the sick person's mouth, takes it out, and thus cures him. In this formula we have the widely-spread idea that the weapons of spirits are invisible to mortals, and *vice versa;* and the story seems to develop without difficulty wherever this idea prevails. The markedly close psychological connection of the incidents of the tale sets it off clearly from the Magic Flight referred to before, in which the single elements are quite without inner connection. Therefore the sameness of the formula, connected with the lack of intermediate geographical links, makes the evidence for historical connection inconclusive.

I repeat, the question at issue is not whether these tales may be related, but whether their historical connection has been proved.

Transmission between the Old World and the New has been proved by the occurrence of a set of complex stories in both. The most notable among these are the Magic Flight (or obstacle myth), the story of the Island of Women (or of the toothed vagina), and that of the killing of the ogre whose head is infested with frogs instead of lice. The area of well-established Old-World influence upon the New World is confined to that part of North America limited in the southeast by a line running approximately from California to Labrador. Southeast of this line, only weak indications of this influence are noticeable. Owing to the restriction of the tales to a small part of America, and to their wide distribution in the Old World, we must infer that the direction of dissemination was from the west to the east, and not conversely. Every step forward from this well-established basis should be taken with the greatest caution.

A certain number of folk-tales are common to a more restricted area around the coasts of Bering Sea and the adjoining parts of Asia and America. Many of these may have had their origin in America. An extension of this inquiry is needed for clearing up the whole interrelation between the New World and the Old. The suggestion of analogies made by Ehrenreich, Dähnhardt, Frobenius, and others, is worthy of being followed up; but the proofs they have so far given are not convincing to me. The theft of the sun and the bringing-up of the earth, to both of which I referred before; the story of the Swan Maidens who put off their clothing on the shore of a lake, assume human form, and are compelled to marry the hero who takes away their clothing,—are common property of America, Asia, and Europe. The variations of these tales are considerable; and their complexity is not so great, nor their geographical distribution so continuous, as to claim that proof of their identity has been established.

We should also mention the possibility of contact between America and the Old World across the islands of the Pacific Ocean. Roland B. Dixon [1] has recently collected data that suggest possible contact along this line; and Von Hornbostel [2] has tried to show similarity on the basis of musical systems that in his opinion can be explained with difficulty only, unless there has been old historical contact. No convincing material, however, is found in the domain of folk-tales.

I have not considered in the preceding remarks the recent influx of foreign themes from Europe and Africa. A fairly large amount of European folk-lore material has been introduced into the United States and Canada. Among those Indian tribes, however, that still retain fresh in their memory the aboriginal mode of life, these tales are sharply set off from the older folk-tales. They are recognizable by distinctiveness of character, although their foreign origin is not always known to the natives. They belong largely to the fairy-tales of Europe, and most of them were probably carried to America by the French voyageurs. It is only in recent times that a more extensive amount of material of this kind has been accumulated.[3] Favorite stories of this group are "John the Bear," "Seven-Heads," and a few others of similar type.

In Nova Scotia and Quebec, where contact between the European settlers and the Indians has continued for a long period, the number of European elements in aboriginal folk-lore is much larger. They may have been derived in part from Scotch and Irish sources. Still the distinction between the types of aboriginal and foreign tales is fairly clear, even to the minds of the narrators.

In the Southern States, where a large Negro population has come into contact with the Indians, we find introduced into the aboriginal folk-lore, in addition to the fairy tales, animal tales foreign to America.

---

[1] Roland B. Dixon, "The Independence of the Culture of the American Indian," *Science,* 1912, pp. 46–55.

[2] O. von Hornbostel, "Über ein akustisches Kriterium für Kulturzusammenhänge," (*Zeitschrift für Ethnologie,* vol. 43, 1911, pp. 601–615).

[3] Most of this material has been published in the *Journal of American Folk-Lore,* vols. 25–27 (1912–14); see also Rand, *Legends of the Micmacs* (New York, 1894).

Since many of these are quite similar in type to aboriginal American folk-tales, the line of demarcation between the two groups has tended to become lost. Some of the foreign details have been incorporated in the folk-lore of the Southeastern Indians, and their distinct origin has been forgotten by them. A similar assimilation of the animal tale has been observed in isolated cases in other districts, as that of a La Fontaine fable among the Shuswap of British Columbia, and perhaps of a European folk-tale among the Zuñi. For this reason we may conclude that the complete amalgamation is due to their identity of type.

The conditions are quite different in Latin America, where, with the exception of the most isolated areas, native folk-tales have almost given way to European material. The bulk of the tales collected in Mexico and South America is of the same character as the folk-tales of the American Negroes, and belongs to the same cycle to which they belong. Since Negro influence cannot readily be shown over this whole district, and since much of the correlated material is clearly European, the origin of these tales is plausibly referred to Spanish and Portuguese sources. They were probably carried to America at the time of the Conquest, taken to Africa by the Portuguese, and later on imported into the United States by Negroes who had previously adopted them in Africa. The definite solution of this problem would require careful collections in Spain. The published Portuguese material is not unfavorable to this theory, which is also supported by the occurrence of the same tales in the Philippine Islands, that have been so long under Spanish influence. It is true that some tales of this group that are found in southern Asia may be due to East-Indian influences, but the form of those hitherto published is rather in favor of the theory of a late Spanish origin. It seems likely that along with these tales the Negroes brought some African stories of similar character into North America.

Among the elements that have been introduced into our continent in this way, I mention the Magic Flight, which has thus been carried in two currents into the New World,—an ancient one, coming from Siberia by way of Bering Strait; a recent one, arising in Spain, and passing into Latin America, and gradually extending northward until the two meet in northern California.

It is not easy to say when this superposition of the ancient American lore by new European material in Latin America was accomplished. There are, however, indications favoring the assumption that some of it has had time to influence American tribes that did not come directly into intimate contact with Spanish cultural elements. Thus the tale of the race between Turtle and Rabbit—in which Turtle places his brothers, who look just like him, all along various points of the race-track, and thus makes Rabbit believe that he has won—has entered northward into Oregon and British Columbia; and a number of incidents that occur in Vancouver Island and in the interior of British Columbia may have to be explained in the same way. The general question of the influence of European lore upon our aboriginal tradition deserves much more careful attention than it has hitherto received.

IV. CHARACTERISTICS OF MYTHOLOGICAL AREAS

We return to the discussion of the aboriginal lore as it is found in our times, disregarding those elements that can be proved to be of modern introduction. The material collected in different parts of the continent presents marked differences in type. These are due to several causes. In some cases the themes contained in the tales are distinct; in others the actors are different; the point of the stories shows certain local peculiarities; or the formal structure possesses local characteristics. Among these features, attention has been directed particularly to the first three, although no systematic attempts have been made to cover the whole field.

In the preceding chapter I have discussed the dissemination of tales, and at the same time pointed out that they are not evenly distributed over the whole continent. It does not seem possible to give a definite characterization of those themes that form the constituent elements of the folk-tales of these larger areas.

The actors that appear as the heroes of our tales differ greatly in various parts of the continent. While in Alaska and northern British Columbia the Raven is the hero of a large cycle of tales, we find that farther to the south, first the Mink, then the Bluejay, takes his place. On the Western Plateaus Coyote is the hero, and in many parts of the Plains the Rabbit is an important figure. In other regions, heroes of human form appear. These occur sporadically along the Pacific coast, but in much more pronounced form on the Great Plains and in the Mackenzie area, without, however, superseding entirely the animal heroes. Owing to this difference in the form of the actors, we find the same tales told of Rabbit, Coyote, Raven, Mink, and Bluejay, but also of such beings as culture-heroes or human tricksters among the Algonquin, Sioux, Ponca, and Blackfeet. There is almost no limit to these transfers from one actor to another. The story of the Bungling Host is, for instance, told of all these beings, and other themes are transferred from one to another with equal ease. Analogous transfers occur frequently in the case of other figures that are less prominent in the folk-tales. The sun is snared by Mouse, Rabbit, or beings in human form. Gull and a person appear as owners of the sun. Kingfisher, Water-Ouzel, or other birds, play the rôle of hosts. Chicken-Hawk, Gopher, Deer, or Eagle steal the fire. Fox, Opossum, or Rabbit dupe Coyote. In part, the animals that appear in tales are determined by the particular fauna of each habitat; but, even aside from this, numerous transfers occur. In how far these changes may be characteristic, aside from the changes of the main figure, has not yet been determined.

The third point in regard to which the materials of various areas show characteristic differences is their formal composition; for the impression that certain types of stories are characteristic of definite areas is not due mainly to the selection of themes that they contain, and of the actors, but to the fundamental ideas underlying the plots, and to their general composition—if I may use the term, to their literary style.

Here a remark should be made in regard to the manner in which the accumulated material has been utilized for the purpose of theoretical discussion. When it is merely a question of discussing themes and actors, it may be justifiable to remain satisfied with data collected without particular precautions. On the whole, I do not think that the study of the distribution of tales has been seriously vitiated by the use of unsatisfactory records, although even here a certain amount of caution must be demanded. When Dähnhardt makes use of a collection like Phillips's "Totem Tales," he vitiates his statements, because neither is the provenience of the tales given correctly—Alaskan tales, for instance, being told as collected in Puget Sound—nor are the contents sufficiently reliable to serve as a basis for conclusions. The tales are throughout changed and modified so as to satisfy the literary taste of the author. Too little attention has been paid by students to the necessity of a critical examination of their material. Such criticism becomes imperative when the formal composition is to be made the subject of serious study. It is necessary to know exactly what is native, and what may be due to the literary taste of the recorder; what may be due to the individual informant, and what may be tribal characteristic. It is here that the importance of unadulterated text-material becomes particularly apparent. The neglect of all critical precautions, which is so characteristic of the manner in which ethnological material is habitually used, has vitiated the results of students, not only in the field of mythology and folk-lore, but perhaps even more in the study of customs and beliefs; and the time has come when the indiscriminate use of unsifted material must end.

In a way we may speak of certain negative features that are common to the tales of the whole American continent. The moralizing fable, which is so widely spread in Europe, Asia, and Africa, seems to be entirely absent in America. Professor Van Gennep has claimed that all primitive folk-tales must be moral.[1] This is true in so far as the plots of all primitive folk-tales find a happy solution, and must therefore conform to those standards that are accepted by the narrators.[2] This, however, is not the same as the moralizing point of the story, that is the peculiar character of the fable of the Old World. Although the American tale may be and has been applied by Indians for inculcating moral truths, this tendency is nowhere part and parcel of the tale. Examples of the moral application of a tale have been given by Swanton [3] from Alaska, and by Miss Fletcher [4] from the Pawnee. In the none of these, however, has the tale itself the moral for its point. It is rather a more or less far-fetched application of the tale made by the narrator. The tale can therefore not be classed with the African, Asiatic, and European animal tales, the whole point of which is the moral that is expressed at the end. It seems to me very likely that the almost complete absence of proverbs among the American natives is connected with the absence of the moralizing literary form, which among the Indians seems to be confined to the art of the orator who sometimes conveys morals in the form of metaphoric expression.

The attempt has been made to characterize one or two areas according to peculiarities of literary form. It is perhaps easiest thus to describe the folk-tales of the Eskimo, which differ from other American tales in that the fanciful animal tale with its transformation elements does not predominate.[5]

In other cases, however, the formal elements can be given clear expres-

---

[1] *La formation des légendes* (1910, 1912), p. 16.

[2] Friedrich Panzer, *Märchen, Sage und Dichtung* (Munich, 1905), p. 14.

[3] John R. Swanton, "Tlingit Myths and Texts," *Bureau of American Ethnology, Bulletin 39* (1909).

[4] Alice C. Fletcher, "The Hako," *22d Annual Report of the Bureau of American Ethnology*, part 2 (1904).

[5] Dr. Paul Radin states that the tales from Smith Sound published by Knud Rasmussen show that in Eskimo folk-lore the animal tale is as marked as among the Indians. This view does not seem to me warranted by the facts. The type of trifling animal tales recorded in Smith Sound has long been known, and differs fundamentally from animal tales common to the rest of the continent (article "Eskimo," in Hastings' Cyclopedia of Religions).

sion only when the tales are grouped in a number of classes. Most important among these are the serious origin tales, the trickster tales, and tales the incidents of which develop entirely or essentially in human society. As soon as this division is made, it is found possible to distinguish a certain number of well-defined types.

We shall take up first of all the origin myths. It is a common trait of most American origin myths that they deal with the transition from a mythological period to the modern age, brought about by a number of disconnected incidents, sometimes centering pre-eminently around the acts of one particular figure, sometimes by incidents distributed over a mass of tales that have not even the actions of one being as their connecting link. On the whole, the mythical world, earth, water, fire, sun and moon, summer and winter, animals and plants, are assumed as existing, although they may not possess their present forms, or be kept and jealously guarded in some part of the world inaccessible to the human race. We are dealing, therefore, essentially with tales of expeditions in which, through cunning or force, the phenomena of nature are obtained for the use of all living beings; and with tales of transformation in which animals, land and water, obtain their present forms. We do not find in North America the genealogical sequence of worlds, one generated by another, that is so characteristic of Polynesia. The idea of creation, in the sense of a projection into objective existence of a world that pre-existed in the mind of a creator, is also almost entirely foreign to the American race. The thought that our world had a previous existence only as an idea in the mind of a superior being, and became objective reality by a will, is not the form in which the Indian conceives his mythology. There was no unorganized chaos preceding the origin of the world. Everything has always been in existence in objective form somewhere. This is even true of ceremonials and inventions, which were obtained by instruction given by beings of another world. There is, however, one notable exception to this general rule, for many California tribes possess origin tales which are expressions of the will of a powerful being who by his thoughts established the present order. When this type of tale became first known to us through the collections of Jeremiah Curtin, it appeared so strange, that the thought suggested itself that we might have here the expression of an individual mind rather than of tribal concepts, resulting either from the recorder's attitude or from that of an informant affected by foreign thought. Further collections, however, have corroborated the impression; and it now seems certain that in northern California there exists a group of true creation tales.

The statement here made needs some further restriction, inasmuch as we have quite a number of tales explaining the origin of animals and of mankind as the results of activities of superior beings. Thus we have stories which tell how men or food-animals were fashioned by the Creator out of wood, stone, clay, or grass; that they were given life, and thus became the beings that we see now. It is important to note that in these cases it is not a mere action of a creative will, but always the transformation of a material object, which forms the essential feature of the tale. Furthermore, I believe it can be shown that many of these tales do not refer to a general creation of the whole species, but that they rather supply a local or temporary want. For instance, the Creator carves salmon out of wood, but they are not fit to serve his purpose. This does not imply that no salmon were in existence before that time, for we hear later on in the same cycle that the real salmon were obtained by a party that captured the fish in the mythical salmon country. The Creator, therefore, had to make artificially an object resembling the real salmon that existed somewhere else, but his unsuccessful attempt resulted in the origin of a new species. In another way this point may be brought out in the story of the origin of death, which appears as part of the Raven cycle of the North Pacific coast. Here Raven tries to create man first from stone, then from leaves. Since his attempts to give life to stones were unsuccessful, and man originated from leaves, man dies like leaves. The men thus created were, however, not the only ones in existence. Raven tried to create them only in order to obtain helpers in a particular kind of work in which he was engaged. Nevertheless the generalized explanation of death is attached to this story.

There are also marked differences not only in the manner in which origins are accounted for, but also in the extent to which these elements enter into tales. While in a large collection of Eskimo stories only from thirty-five to fifty phenomena are explained, the number is infinitely greater on the Western Plateaus. In the essay quoted before, Waterman states that ninety-eight Eskimo tales contain thirty-four explanations, while in a hundred and eighty-seven Plateau tales, two hundred and twenty-five explanations are found. This quite agrees with the impression that we receive by the perusal of tales. In some cases almost every tale is an origin tale, in others these are few and far between. For the determination of this element as characteristic of various areas, we require, of course, extensive collections, such as are available from a few tribes only. It is particularly necessary that the tales should not be gathered from a one-sided standpoint,—as, for instance, for a study of celestial myths or of animal tales,—because this might give an entirely erroneous impression. That typical differences exist can be determined even now. It is particularly striking that in some regions, as on the Western Plateaus, the explanatory element appears often as the basis of the plot; while other tribes, like the Eskimo, have a number of very trifling origin stories almost resembling animal fables. If these are excluded from the whole mass of explanatory tales, the contrast between various groups in regard to the importance of the explanatory element becomes particularly striking.

Marked differences occur also in the selection of the phenomena that are explained. Among the southern Caddoan tribes the explanation of stars preponderates. Among the Plateau tribes the largest number of tales refer to characteristics of animals. Among the Blackfeet and Kwakiutl the mass of tales relate to ceremonials. Among the Southern tribes a great number are cosmogonic tales.

Related to this is also the more or less systematic grouping of the tales in larger cycles. It is but natural that in all those cases in which traits of animals form the subject of explanatory tales, the tales must be anecdotal in character and disconnected, even if one person should form the center of the cycle. It is only when the origin tales are brought together in such a way that the mythological concepts develop into a systematic whole, that the origin stories assume the form of a more complex cosmogony. This point may be illustrated by the long record of the origin legend of Alaska collected by Swanton,[1] in which obviously a thoughtful informant has tried to assemble the whole mass of explanatory tales in the form of a connected myth. Critical study shows not only the entire lack of cohesion of the parts, but also the arbitrary character of the arrangement, which is contradicted by all other versions from the same region. Unifying elements are completely missing, since there is no elaboration of a cosmogonic concept that forms the background of the tale.

The same is no less true of the Kwakiutl, among whom the disconnected character of the origin tales is perhaps even more pronounced, since they refer in different ways to various aspects of the world; the origin of animals being treated in one way, the rise of social differences

---

[1] John R. Swanton, Tlingit Myths and Texts, *op. cit., pp.* 80 *et seq.*

of the people in another way, and the supernatural basis of their religious ceremonials in still another manner. The contrast in form brought about by the systematization of mythical concepts may be seen clearly in the case of the Bella Coola, who have developed more definite notions of the organization of the world, and among whom, for this reason, the single stories, while still disconnected, are referred clearly to a background of systematized mythical concepts. The contrast between the disconnected origin tales and the elaborate cycles is most striking when we compare the disjointed tales of the Northwest with the long connected origin myths of the East as we find them among the Iroquois and Algonquin, and even more when we place them side by side with the complex myths from the Southwest.

On the whole, these features are characteristic of definite geographical areas. On the Western Plateaus it is almost entirely the grouping of the tales around one single hero that makes them into a loosely connected cycle. So far as we can discover, the single adventures are disconnected, and only exceptionally a definite sequence of incidents occurs. The same is largely true of the origin tales of the East and of the Upper Mississippi region, excepting their complicated introductory parts. In other districts—as on the Pacific coast between Vancouver Island and central California—a somewhat more definite order is introduced by the localization of the tales. A transformer travels over the country and performs a series of actions, which are told in a definite order as his journeyings take him from place to place. Thus we have a definite order, but no inner connection between the incidents. Quite distinct in type are the origin tales in which the people themselves are brought to their present home by long-continued migration. It is characteristic of the northern part of the continent that there is no migration legend to speak of, that the people consider themselves as autochthonous. In the Southwest and in Mexico, on the other hand, particular stress is laid upon the emergence of the tribe from a lower world and upon its migrations, with which are connected many of the origin stories. This type, which in its whole setting is quite distinct from that of the North, occurs wherever Southern influences can be traced, as among the Arikara, a Caddoan tribe that migrated from the south northward to the Missouri River.

We may also recognize local characteristics in the details of the methods by which the present order of things is established. In the Plateau area, among the Eskimo, and in part at least in eastern North America, something happens that accidentally determines the future. When Grizzly-Bear, in a tussle, scratches Chipmunk's back, this gives rise to his stripes. If an animal jumps out of a canoe and breaks off his tail on the gunwale, this is the reason why it has a short tail. Since an animal wears down the hair of its bushy tail, it has a hairless tail now. Because the frog leaped on the moon's face, it stays there. In this area incidents in which transformations are the result of an intentional activity are quite rare, although the idea is not quite absent. In the East the concept of intentional transformation appears particularly in the tales treating of the origin of the earth and of ceremonies; on the Plateau it appears from time to time either in the form of councils held by the animals in order to decide how the world is to be arranged, or in contests between two antagonistic animals which desire different conditions. Thus we find in the Plateaus the story of Chipmunk and Bear, to which I referred before, essentially a contest which is to determine whether it shall always be day or always night; and in the Coyote cycle a contest which is to decide whether man shall be immortal.

On this basis a number of types of origins may be distinguished,— first, origins due to accidental, unintentional occurrences; second, the formation of the present order according to the decisions of a council of animals; third, development due to the actions of two antagonistic beings, the one benevolent and wishing to make everything easy for man, the other one counteracting these intentions and creating the difficulties and hardships of life; as a fourth type we may distinguish the culture-hero tales, the narrative of the migration of men or deities who wander about and set things right. At the present time it is hardly possible to group the origin stories quite definitely from these points of view. In the extreme north the disorganized tale seems to prevail. On the plateaus of the northern United States and in part of the plains, the animal council plays an important rôle. California seems to be the principal home of the antagonistic formula, although this idea is also prominent among some Eastern tribes; and culture-hero tales appear locally on the North Pacific coast, but more prominently in the south.

We shall next turn to a consideration of the trickster tales. In a sense these have been referred to in the previous group, because many of the trickster tales are at the same time origin tales. If, for instance, Coyote tricks the birds by letting them dance near the fire, and their red eyes are accounted for in this way, we have here an origin story and a trickster tale. At present we are not concerned with this feature, but rather with the consideration of the question whether certain features can be found that are characteristic of the whole cycle as developed in various regions. First of all, it seems of interest to note the degree to which the whole group of tales is developed. It is absent among the Eskimo, moderately developed in California, probably not very prominent in the aboriginal myths of the Southwest, but most prolific on the Northwest coast, the Northern Plateaus, and in the East. Whether it is a marked feature of the Athapascan area cannot be decided at present. Some of the heroes of the trickster cycle have been noted before. Raven, Mink, Bluejay, on the Northwest coast; Coyote on the Plateaus; Old Man among the Blackfeet; Ishtiniki among the Ponca; Inktumni among the Assiniboin; Manabosho, Wishahka, and Glooscap among various Algonquin tribes,—are some of the prominent figures. Although a complete list of all the trickster incidents has not been made, it is fairly clear that a certain number are found practically wherever a trickster cycle occurs. I have already stated that one group of these tales is confined to the Western Plateaus, another one to the northern half of the continent. At present it is more important to note, that, besides these widely distributed elements, there seem to be in each area a number of local tales that have no such wide distribution. The characteristics of the tales appear most clearly when the whole mass of trickster tales in each region is studied. A comparison of the Raven, Mink, and Bluejay cycles is instructive. The background of the Raven stories is everywhere the greedy hunger of Raven. Most of the Raven tales treat of Raven's endeavors to get plenty of food without effort; and the adventures relate to his attempts to cheat people out of their provisions and to the punishment doled out to him by those who have suffered from his tricks. Quite different in type are the Mink stories. Here we find almost throughout an erotic background. Mink tries to get possession of girls and of the wives of his friends. Occasionally only a trick based on his fondness for sea-eggs is introduced. The Bluejay adventures may be characterized in still another way. Generally it is his ambition to outdo his betters in games, on the hunt or in war, that brings him into trouble or induces him to win by trickery. He has neither a pronounced erotic nor a notably greedy character. The tricks of the Plateau cycles are not so easy to characterize, because the deeds of Coyote partake of all the characteristics just mentioned. Coyote attempts to get food, and his erotic adventures are fairly numerous; but on the whole these two groups are considerably outnumbered by tricks in which he tries to outdo his rivals.

The identification of trickster and transformer is a feature which deserves special notice. I have called attention to the fact—borne out by most of the mythologies in which trickster and culture-hero appear as one person—that the benefactions bestowed by the culture-hero are not given in an altruistic spirit, but that they are means by which he supplies his own needs.[1] Even in his heroic achievements he remains a trickster bent upon the satisfaction of his own desires. This feature may be observed distinctly in the Raven cycle of the Northwest coast. He liberates the sun, not because he pities mankind, but because he desires it; and the first use he tries to make of it is to compel fishermen to give him part of their catch. He gets the fresh water because he is thirsty, and unwillingly spills it all over the world while he is making his escape. He liberates the fish because he is hungry, and gets the tides in order to be able to gather shellfish. Similar observations may be made in other mythological personages that embody the qualities of trickster and culture-hero. Wherever the desire to benefit mankind is a more marked trait of the cycle, there are generally two distinct persons,—one the trickster, the other the culture-hero. Thus the culture-hero of the Pacific coast gives man his arts, and is called "the one who sets things right." He is not a trickster, but all his actions have a distinct bearing upon the establishment of the modern order. Perhaps the most characteristic feature of these culture-hero tales is their lack of detail. Many are bare statements of the fact that something was different from the way it is now. The hero performs some very simple act, and ordains that these conditions shall be changed. It is only when the culture-hero concept rises to greater heights, as it does in the South, that these tales acquire greater complexity.

Here may also be mentioned the animal tales that belong neither to the trickster cycle nor to the origin tales. It is hardly possible to give a general characterization of these, and to distinguish local types, except in so far as the importance of the tale is concerned. In the Arctic and the adjoining parts of the continent, we find a considerable number of trifling animal stories that have hardly any plot. They are in part merely incidents descriptive of some characteristic of the animal. Some of these

[1] Introduction to James Teit, "Traditions of the Thompson River Indians of British Columbia," *Memoirs of the American Folk-lore Society,* vol. 7 (1898); see pp. 407 *et seq.* of this volume.

trifling stories are given the form of origin tales by making the incidents the cause from which arise certain bodily characteristics of the animals, but this is not often the case. In the more complex tales which occur all over the continent, the animals act according to their characteristic modes of life. Kingfisher dives, Fox is a swift runner, Beaver a good swimmer who lives in ponds, etc. Their character corresponds to their apparent behavior. Grizzly-Bear is overbearing and ill-tempered, Blue-jay and Coyote are tricky. A sharp individual characterization, however, is not common.

We shall now turn to the third group of tales, those dealing with human society. These can only in part be characterized in the manner adopted heretofore. Some of their local color is due to the peculiar distribution of incidents which has been discussed before. On the whole, however, it is rather the plot as a whole that is characteristic. This may be exemplified by the incident of the faithless wife, which occurs all over the continent. The special form of the plot of the woman who has an animal or supernatural being or some object for a lover, whose actions are discovered by her husband who disguises himself in her garments and who deceives and kills the paramour and later on his wife, is most characteristic of the Northern area, reaching from north-eastern Siberia and the Eskimo district southward to the Mississippi basin.

Individualization of form may also be illustrated by the widely distributed incident of the deserted child who rescues his people when they are in distress. The special form of the plot—in which the child makes his parents and uncles ashamed, is deserted and then helped by animals that send him larger and larger game until many houses are filled with provisions, and in which the people offer him their daughters as wives —is characteristic only of the North Pacific coast. On the Plains the deserted boy escapes by the help of his protector, and becomes a power-ful hunter. The analysis of the plots has not been carried through in such detail as to allow us to do more than point out the existence of characteristic types in definite areas.

Much more striking in this group of tales is their cultural setting, that reflects the principal occupation and interests of the people. I have attempted to give a reconstruction of the life of the Tsimshian, basing my data solely on the recorded mythology. As might perhaps be expected, all the essential features of their life—the village, its houses, the sea and land hunt, social relations—appear distinctly mirrored in this picture. It is, however, an incomplete picture. Certain aspects of life do not appeal to the imagination of the story-tellers, and are therefore not specifically expressed, not even implied in the setting of the story. It is very striking how little the animal tale—in the instance in question, the Raven cycle—contributes to this picture. It is also of interest to note that among the Tsimshian the secret societies—which, as we conclude from other evidence, have been introduced only lately —occupy a very unimportant part in the tales, while the potlatch and the use of crests are two of their most notable features. How accurately the cultural background of the life of the people is reflected by the form of its tales, appears in the diversity of form in which the life of various tribes of the North Pacific coast is mirrored in their traditional lore. Although the general form is much the same in all, the reconstructions based on the evidence of their tales exhibit sharp individualization, and emphasize the differences in social organization, in social customs, in the importance of the secret societies, and in the great diversity in the use of crests and other supernatural gifts. A perusal of the available collections makes it quite clear that in this sense the expression of the cultural life of the people contained in their tales gives to them a marked individuality, no matter what the incidents constituting the tales may be.

The reflection of the tribal life, which is characteristic of the tale, is also expressed in the mass of supernatural concepts that enter into it and form in part the scenic background on which the story develops, in part the machinery by means of which the action progresses.

Wundt [1] and Waterman have called attention to the importance of distinctions between mythical concepts and tales. The cosmological background does not enter with equal intensity into the folk-tales of various groups. The Eskimo, who have clearly defined notions regarding the universe, do not introduce them to any great extent into their tales; while the various classes of fabulous tribes and beings, shamanism and witchcraft, occupy a prominent place. On the North Pacific coast the notions regarding the universe are on the whole vague and contradictory; nevertheless visits to the sky play an important rôle in the tales. The ideas regarding a ladder leading to heaven, and journeys across the ocean to fabulous countries, also enter into the make-up of the Northwest-coast traditions. In the South, on the other hand, the notions in regard to the center of the world, the lower world, and the four points of the compass, are of importance.

[1] Wilhelm Wundt, *Völkerpsychologie*, vol. 2, part 3 (Leipzig, 1909), p. 19.

The groups of fabulous beings that appear in each area exhibit also sharp characteristics; as the ice giants of the Iroquois and eastern Algonquin, the stupid giants of the Shoshoni and Kutenai, or the water-monsters of the South, the horned serpents of eastern America, the double-headed serpent of the coast of British Columbia, the giant thunder-bird of Vancouver Island, and the various forms of thunderers that are found among the different tribes of the continent.

Skinner [1] has recently called attention to the magical machinery that appears in the tales of human adventure among the Central Algonquin tribes. These features also characterize the tales of different areas. This subject has not been analyzed in sufficient detail to allow a definite grouping, but enough is known to indicate that a natural arrangement will result which will largely conform to cultural divisions.

This feature is still further emphasized when we direct our attention to the main plot of the story. I have shown that among the Kwakiutl the plot of most stories is the authentication of the privileges of a social division or of a secret society. Wissler has brought out a similar point in his discussion of Blackfoot tales,[2] many of which seem to explain ritualistic origins, the rituals themselves being in part dramatic interpretations of the narratives. The Pawnee and Pueblo stories reflect in the same way the ritualistic interests of the people. In this sense we may perhaps say without exaggeration that the folk-tales of each tribe are markedly set off from those of all other tribes, because they give a faithful picture of the mode of life and of the chief interests that have prevailed among the people during the last few generations. These features appear most clearly in the study of their hero-tales. It is therefore particularly in this group that an analogy between the folk-tale and the modern novel is found. The tales dealing with the feats of men are more plastic than those relating to the exploits of animals, although the animal world, to the mind of the Indian, was not so very different from our own.

The events occurring among the animals are less individualized so far as the tribal mode of life is concerned. At best we may infer from them whether we deal with buffalo-hunters of the Plains, fishermen of the Western coast, people of the Arctic or of the Southern desert. The more complex activities of the tribe appear rarely pictured in them, and then only incidentally.

---

[1] A. Skinner, *Journal of American Folk-Lore*, vol. 27 (1914), pp. 97–100.

[2] Clark Wissler and D. C. Duvall, "Mythology of the Blackfoot Indians" (*Anthropological Papers, American Museum of Natural History*, vol. 2, p. 12).

In the human tale the narrator gives us a certain amount of characterization of individuals, of their emotions,—like pity and love,—of their courage and cowardice, on which rests the plot of the story. The development of individual character does not proceed beyond this point. We do not find more than schematic types, which are, however, forms that occur in the every-day life of the people. On the contrary, the origin and trickster cycles deal with types that are either so impersonal that they do not represent any individual, or are merely the personification of greed, amorousness, or silly ambition. Wherever there is individuality of character, it is rather the expression of the apparent nature of the personified animal, not the character that fits particularly well into human society.

Considering the characteristic of the human tale as a whole, we may say that in all probability future study will show that its principal characteristics may be well defined by the cultural areas of the continent. How close this correspondence may be remains to be seen. The problem is an interesting and important one, because it is obvious that the tales, while readily adaptable, do not follow all the aspects of tribal life with equal ease, and a certain lack of adjustment may become apparent. This will serve as a valuable clue in the further study of the development of tribal customs and of the history of the distribution of tales. I have pointed out the probability of such incomplete adjustment in the case of the Kwakiutl, and Wissler has made a similar point in regard to the Blackfeet.

While much remains to be done in the study of the local characteristics of folk-tales in regard to the points referred to, a still wider field of work is open in all that concerns their purely formal character, and I can do no more than point out the necessity of study of this subject. On the basis of the material hitherto collected, we are hardly in a position to speak of the literary form of the tales. I am inclined to count among their formal traits the typical repetition of the same incident that is found among many tribes; or the misfortunes that befall a number of brothers, until the last one is successful in his undertaking. These have the purpose of exciting the interest and leading the hearer to anticipate with increased eagerness the climax. Quite different from this is a device used by the Tsimshian, who lead up to a climax by letting an unfortunate person be helped in a very insignificant way. The help extended to him becomes more and more potent, until the climax is reached, in which the sufferer becomes the fortunate possessor of power and wealth.

Another artistic device that is used by many tribes to assist in the characterization of the actors is the use of artificial changes in speech. Thus among the Kwakiutl the Mink cannot pronounce the sound *ts*, among the Kutenai Coyote cannot pronounce *s*, among the Chinook the animals speak different dialects. Dr. Sapir [1] has called attention to the development of this feature among the Shoshoni and Nootka.

The literary style is most readily recognized in the poetic parts of tales; but, since these fall mostly outside of the purely narrative part of the stories, I do not enter into this subject. We may contrast the simplicity of style of the Northwest coast—where poems consist sometimes of the introduction of a single word into a musical line, the music being carried on by a burden, sometimes of a purely formal enumeration of the powers of supernatural beings—with the metaphoric expression and fine feeling for beauty that pervade the poetry of the Southwestern Indians. Equally distinct are the rhythmic structures that are used by the Indians of various areas.[2] We must be satisfied here with a mere hint at the significance of these data. The desire may be expressed, however, that greater care should be taken in the collection of the material to make possible a thorough study of this aspect of our subject.

V. RECENT HISTORY OF AMERICAN FOLK-TALES

Our considerations allow us to draw a number of inferences in regard to the history of American folk-tales. We have seen that there is no tribe in North America whose tales can be considered as purely local products uninfluenced by foreign elements. We have found that some tales are distributed over almost the whole continent, others over more or less extended parts of the country. We have seen, furthermore, that the tales of each particular area have developed a peculiar literary style, which is an expression of the mode of life and of the form of thought of the people; that the actors who appear in the various tales are quite distinct in different parts of the country; and that the associated ex-

---

[1] E. Sapir, "Song Recitative in Paiute Mythology" (*The Journal of American Folk-Lore*, vol. 23 (1910), pp. 456–457).

[2] See, for instance, Alice C. Fletcher, "The Hako" (*22d Annual Report of the Bureau of American Ethnology*, part 2, pp. 282–368).

planatory elements depend entirely upon the different styles of thought. In one case the tales are used to explain features of the heavenly bodies; in others, forms of the land, of animals or of rituals, according to the chief interests of the people. It is fully borne out by the facts brought forward, that actors, explanatory tendencies, cultural setting, and literary form, of all modern American tales, have undergone constant and fundamental changes. If we admit this, it follows that the explanations that are found in modern tales must be considered almost entirely as recent adaptations of the story, not as its integral parts; and neither they nor the names of the actors reveal to us what the story may have been in its original form—if we may speak of such a form. Everything appears rather in flux. For this reason the attempt to interpret the history of the modern tale as a reflection of the observation of nature is obviously not justifiable. The data of American folk-lore do not furnish us with a single example that would prove that this process has contributed to the modern development of folk-tales. It would almost seem safer to say that the creative power that has manifested itself in modern times is very weak, and that the bulk of our tales consist of combinations and recombinations of old themes. At the same time the marked differentiation in the style of composition shows that the mainspring in the formation of the modern tale must have been an artistic one. We observe in them not only the result of the play of imagination with favorite themes, but also the determination of the form of imaginative processes by antecedent types, which is the characteristic trait of artistic production of all times and of all races and peoples. I am therefore inclined to consider the folk-tale primarily and fundamentally as a work of primitive art. The explanatory element would then appear, not as an expression of native philosophy, but rather as an artistic finishing touch required for the tale wherever the art of story-telling demands it. Instead of being the mainspring of the story, it becomes in one case a stylistic embellishment, while in another it is required to give an impressive setting. In either case the occurrence of the explanation cannot be reduced to a rationalizing activity of primitive man.

In a sense these results of our studies of American folk-lore are unsatisfactory, because they lead us only to recognize a constant play with old themes, variations in explanatory elements attached to them, and the tendency to develop various types of artistic style. They do not bring us any nearer to an understanding of the origin of the themes, explanations, and styles. If we want to carry on our investigation into a remoter past, it may be well to ask, first of all, how long the present development of mosaics of different style may have continued; whether there is any proof that some tribes have been the originators from whom others derived much of their lore; and whether we have any evidence of spontaneous invention that may have influenced large territories.

Since historical data are not available, we are confined to the application of an inductive method of inquiry. We may ask how large a portion of the folk-tales of a tribe are its sole property, and how many they share with other tribes. If a comparison of this kind should show a large number of elements that are the sole property of one tribe, while others have only little that is their exclusive property, it would perhaps seem justifiable to consider the former as originators, the latter as recipients; and we may conclude either that their own older folk-tales have disappeared or that they possessed very few only. It is not easy to form a fair judgment of the originality of the folk-tales of each tribe in the manner here suggested, because the collections are unequally complete, and because collectors or narrators are liable to give preference to one particular kind of tale to the exclusion of others. It is always difficult to base inferences on the apparent absence of certain features that may be discovered, after all, to exist; and this seems particularly difficult in our case. Still it might be possible to compare at least certain definite cycles that have been collected fairly fully, and that occur with equal exuberance in various areas; as, for instance, the trickster cycles of the Plains. On the whole, I gain the impression that not a single tribe appears as possessing considerably more originality than another.

One interesting point appears with great clearness; namely, the power of tales of certain types to become a prolific source of tales of similar import, provided the original tales are of social importance in the life of the people. Thus the Kwakiutl have apparently a considerable originality among their neighbors on the North Pacific coast, because all the numerous social divisions and secret societies of the tribe possess origin tales of the same type; so that a complete list would probably include hundreds of stories more or less strictly built on the same pattern. The ritualistic tales of the Blackfeet form another group of this kind; and the same may be true of the tales of the Mackenzie area dealing with the marriages between human beings and animals. In these cases we deal with one particular style of story, that has gained great popularity, and therefore appears in an endless number of variants.

Another condition that may lead to a strong individuality in a certain group develops when the tales are placed in the keeping of a small class of priests or chiefs, as the case may be. The more important the tale becomes on account of its association with the privileges and rituals of certain sections of the tribe, and the greater the emotional and social values of the customs with which it is associated, the more have the keepers of the ritual brooded over it in all its aspects; and with this we find a systematic development of both tale and ritual. This accounts for the relation between the occurrence of complex rituals in charge of a priestly class or of chiefs, and of long myths which have an esoteric significance. The parallelism of distribution of religious or social groups led by single individuals and of complex mythologies is so striking, that there can be little doubt in regard to their psychological connection. The Mexicans, the Pueblo tribes, the Pawnee, the Bella Coola, the Maidu,[1] may be given as examples. The contrast between a disorganized mass of folk-tales and the more systematic mythologies seems to lie, therefore, in the introduction of an element of *individual* creativeness in the latter. The priest or chief as a poet or thinker takes hold of the folk-traditions and of isolated rituals and elaborates them in dramatic and poetic form. Their systematization is brought about by the centralization of thought in one mind. Under the social conditions in which the Indians live, the keeper transfers his sacred knowledge in an impressive manner to his successor. The forms in which the sacred teachings appear at the present time are therefore the cumulative effect of systematic elaboration by individuals, that has progressed through generations.

This origin of the complex of myth and ritual makes it also intelligible why among some tribes the myths of sub-groups should be contradictory. An instance of this are the Bella Coola, among whom the tradition is in the keeping of the chief of the village community, and among whom each community has its own concept in regard to its origins. These contradictory traditions are the result of individual thought in each community, and do not come into conflict, because the audience identifies itself with the reciting chief, and the truth of one poetic creation does not destroy the truth of another one.

For a correct interpretation of these art-productions we must also

---

[1] Roland B. Dixon, who has pointed out the systematic character of their mythology, finds some difficulty in accounting for it, considering the simple economic and artistic life of the people. His own descriptions, however, show the great importance of personal leadership in all religious affairs of the tribe (*Bull. Am. Mus. Nat. Hist.*, vol. 17).

bear in mind that the materials for the systematic composition are the disconnected folk-tales and lesser rites of the tribe, which have been welded into a whole. From a psychological point of view, it is therefore not justifiable to consider the exoteric tales, as is so often done, degenerate fragments of esoteric teaching. It is true that they themselves undergo changes due to the influence of the priestly doctrine, but there is a constant giving and taking; and nowhere in America has the individual artist freed himself of the fetters of the type of thought expressed in the disjointed folk-tales. The proof for this contention is found in the sameness of the elements that enter into the tales of tribes with systematic mythology and of those without it.

The only alternative explanation of the observed phenomenon would be the assumption that all this material had its origin in more highly developed and systematized mythologies. It might be claimed that the remains of the Ohio mounds, the highly-developed artistic industries of the ancient inhabitants of the Lower Mississippi, and of the cliff-dwellings, prove that a high type of culture must have existed in many parts of the country, where at a later period only less complex cultural forms were found. The elaborateness of religious ceremonial of these times is proved by the characteristics of archæological finds. It is quite true that in the border area of Mexico, including under this term the whole region just mentioned, many fluctuations in cultural development must have occurred; but this does not prove their existence over the whole continent. Furthermore, the individuality of each folk-loristic area is such, that we must count the imaginative productiveness of each tribe as an important element in the development of the present situation. From this point of view, inquiries into the independence of each area, rather than investigations of the effect of diffusion, will be of the greatest value. The theory of degeneration is not supported by any facts; and I fail entirely to see how the peculiar form of American systematic mythology can be explained, except as the result of an artistic elaboration of the disconnected folk-tales, and how its character, which parallels primitive concepts, can be interpreted, except as the result of priestly speculation based on the themes found in folk-tales.

VI. MYTHOLOGICAL CONCEPTS IN FOLK-TALES

Our consideration of American folk-tales has so far dealt with their later history. The result of this inquiry will help us in the treatment of the question, What may have been the origin of these tales? It is obvious that in an historical inquiry for which no literary record of ancient mythology is available, we must try first of all to establish the processes that are active at the present time. There is no reason for assuming that similar processes should not have been active in earlier times, at least as long as the types of human culture were approximately on the same level as they are now. The art-productions of the Magdalenian period show how far back the beginning of these conditions may be placed; and so far we have no evidence that indicates that the American race as such has ever passed through a time in which its mental characteristics were different from those of modern man. The antiquity of cultural achievement in Mexico, the finds made in ancient shell-heaps, prove that for thousands of years man in America has been in possession of a type of cultural development not inferior to that of the modern, more primitive tribes. It may therefore be inferred that the processes that are going on now have been going on for a very long period. Constant diffusion of the elements of stories, and elaboration of new local types of composition, must have been the essential characteristic of the history of folk-tales. On the whole, invention of new themes must have been rare; and where it occurred, it was determined by the prevailing type of composition.

Disregarding the actors who appear in the stories, their contents deal almost throughout with events that may occur in human society, sometimes with plausible events, more often with fantastic adventures that cannot have their origin in actual human experiences. From these facts two problems develop that have given rise to endless speculation and discussion,—the first, Why are these human tales told of animals, of the heavenly bodies, and of personified natural phenomena? the other, Why is it that certain fantastic elements have a world-wide distribution?

The transfer of human experience to animals and personified objects has given rise to the view that all tales of this type are nature myths or an expression of the naïve primitive conception of nature. It has been clearly recognized that the themes are taken from human life, and used to express the observation of nature. The first question to be answered is therefore, How does it happen that the tales are so often removed from the domain of human society? Wundt has discussed this question in his comprehensive work on mythology,[1] in so far as the personification of nature is concerned. This discussion refers to

---

[1] Völkerpsychologie, vol. 2, part 1 (1905), pp. 577 et seq.

mythological concepts, not to the tales as such. It is obvious, however, that once the human character of animals and objects is given, the tales become applicable to them.

Another element may have helped in the development of animal tales, once the personification was established. In folk-tales every human being is considered as a distinct individual, and the mere name of a person does not characterize the individual. Moreover, named individuals are not very common in American folk-tales. The animal, on the other hand, is immortal. From the bones of the killed game arises the same individual hale and sound, and thus continues its existence indefinitely. Therefore the species, particularly in the mythological period, is conceived as one individual, or at most as a family group. This may also have helped to create the normative character of the tales. If an animal rubbed the hair off its tail, then all animals that are its descendants have the same kind of a tail. If all the thunder-birds were killed except one, their loss of power becomes permanent. I presume the identification of species and of individuals which is inherent in the personification of nature was an important element contributing to the development of this concept. It goes without saying that the result was not obtained by conscious reasoning. The substitution of individual for species merely favored the explanatory features of animal tales. The tendency to substitute for these transformations others in which events were due to the decision of a council, or where they were ordained by a culture-hero, may be due to a feeling of dissatisfaction with the simple type of transformation and the condensation of the whole species into one individual.

In all these tales the explanatory element must be considered as an idea that arose in the mind of the narrator suddenly by an associative process. I differ from Wundt in the importance that I ascribe to the looseness of connection between explanatory elements and the tale, a phenomenon to which he also refers.[1] It is not simply the apperceptive process, in which the subjective emotions are transferred to the object, that gives rise to the explanatory element in the tales; but the elements of mythological concepts are thoughts suggested first of all by the appropriateness of the pre-existing tale, and therefore depend in the first instance upon its literary form. For this reason the great difference in the character of folk-tales of America and those of Africa does not appear to me as a difference in the stages of their development. The

[1] *Ibid.* Part 3, p. 183.

moralizing tendency of the African tale is an art-form that has been typical for the Negro, but foreign to the American; and I can see no genetic connection between the explanatory and the moralizing tale.

While these considerations make the animal tale intelligible, they are not by any means a satisfactory explanation of the great importance of animal and nature tales in the folk-lore of all the peoples of the world; and it would seem that at present we have to accept this as one of the fundamental facts of mythology, without being able to give an adequate reason for its development.

The last question that we have to discuss is the significance of those traits of folk-lore that are of world-wide occurrence. Particularly in reference to this fact the claim is made that the wide distribution of the same elements can be explained only when we assume that they are derived from a direct observation of nature, and that for this reason they appear to primitive man as obvious facts. This subject has been treated fully by Ehrenreich [1] and other representatives of that mythological school which derives the origin of myths from the impressions that man received from nature, particularly from the heavenly orbs.

So far as I can see, all that has been done by these investigations is to show that when we start with the hypothesis that myths are derived from the impressions conveyed by the heavenly bodies, we can fit the incidents of myths into this hypothesis by interpreting their features accordingly. Lessmann [2] even goes so far as to state definitely that whatever cannot be derived from characteristics of the moon is not mythology. This, of course, ends all possible discussion of the relation between folk-tales and myths. In the passage referred to, Ehrenreich says that the phases of the moon produce certain types of myths. The new moon is represented in the supernatural birth through the side of the mother, and in the incident of a new-born hero lying in a manger or shell. The full moon is the hero in the fulness of his power and after his victories over dark demons. The waning of the moon is the cutting-up or the slow swallowing of the hero's body. The new moon is represented in decapitations with a sword, in test by fire, or in the cutting of sinews. In this enumeration of interpretations I cannot see

---

[1] P. Ehrenreich, *Die allgemeine Mythologie und ihre ethnologischen Grundlagen* (Leipzig, 1910), pp. 100 *et seq.*

[2] H. Lessmann, "Aufgaben und Ziele der vergleichenden Mythenforschung" (Mythologische Bibliothek (Leipzig, 1908), I⁴, pp. 31 *et seq.*).

any proof of his thesis, since he does not show that the same ideas may not have developed in some other way.[1]

Ehrenreich and other adherents of the modern cosmogonic school make the fundamental assumption that myths must represent phenomena actually seen,—a theory that seems to me based on a misconception of the imaginative process. The productions of imagination are not by any means the images of sense-experiences, although they are dependent upon them; but in their creation the emotional life plays an important rôle. When we are filled with an ardent desire, imagination lets us see the desire fulfilled. As a phenomenon strikes us with wonder, its normal features will be weakened and the wonderful element will be emphasized. When we are threatened by danger, the cause of our fear will impress us as endowed with extraordinary powers. It is a common characteristic of all these situations that the actual sense-experience may either be exaggerated or turned into its opposite, and that the impossible fulfilment of a wish is realized. After the death of a dear relative, neither we nor primitive man speculate as to what may have become of his soul; but we feel a burning wish to undo what has happened, and in the free play of fancy we see the dead come back to life. The slain leader in battle whose dismembered body is found, is seen restored to full vigor. The warrior surrounded by enemies, when all means of retreat are cut off, will wish to pass unseen through the ranks of the foes, and in a strong imagination the wish will become a reality. Many of the ideas that are common to all mythologies may thus be readily understood, and there is no need to think of the waning and waxing moon when we hear of the cutting-up or flaying of a person, and of his revival. These are ideas that are readily suggested by the very fact that the ordinary processes of imagination must call them forth.

No less is this true of the forms of demons which can easily be understood as fanciful distortions of experiences. Laistner's theory of the importance of the nightmare [2] as giving rise to many of these forms is suggestive; perhaps not in the sense in which he formulates it,—because the form of the nightmare will in all probability depend upon the ideas that are current in the belief of the people,—but because dreams are simply one form in which the creations of imagination

[1] See also the criticism by A. van Gennep, in his *Réligions, mœurs et légendes,* pp. 111 *et seq.*

[2] Ludwig Laistner, *Das Rätsel der Sphinx,* Berlin, 1889.

appear, and because they indicate what unexpected forms the fear-inspiring apparition may take. Still other mythic forms may be explained by the æsthetic transformations produced by the power of imagination. It is not only that the beauty of form is exaggerated, but the comic or tragic elements lead equally to transformations of sense-experience. I think it is quite possible to explain in this way the beautiful shining persons with bright hair, and also the cripples with distorted bodies, covered with warts and other disfigurements.

In short, there is hardly a single trait of all the mythologies that does not reflect naturally, by exaggeration or by contrast, the ordinary sense-experiences of man. It is only when we deny that these processes are characteristic of the imagination that we are confronted with any diffi-culty, and that we have to look for the origin of these forms outside of human society. As compared to this very simple view of the origin of the elementary forms of myths, the attempt to seek their prototypes in the sky seems to my mind far-fetched. It may also be said in favor of this view, that the combination of features that are demanded as characteristic of the sun, the moon, or other personified beings, appear only seldom combined in one and the same mythical figure. This has been clearly demonstrated by Lowie.[1]

These considerations show also that psychological conditions may bring about similarity of ideas without an underlying historical con-nection, and that the emphasis laid on the historical side must be supported by careful inquiry into those features in the life of man that may be readily explained by similarities in the reactions of the mind. Methodologically the proof of such independent origin of similar phe-nomena offers much more serious difficulties than a satisfactory proof of historical connection. The safeguards that must be demanded here are analogous to those previously described.[2] As we demanded before, as criteria of historical connection, actual evidence of transmission, or at least clear proof of the existence of lines of transmission and of the identity of subject-matter, so we must now call for proof of the lack of historical connection or of the lack of identity of phenomena. Obvi-ously these proofs are much more difficult to give. If we were to confine ourselves to the evidence contained in folk-tales, it might be an impos-sible task to prove in a convincing manner the independent origin of

---

[1] Robert H. Lowie, "The Test-Theme," etc. (*Journal of American Folk-Lore,* vol. 21, 1908, p. 101).
[2] See p. 458 of this volume.

tales, because the possibility of the transmission of a single idea always exists. It is only on the basis of our knowledge of the limitations of areas over which inventions, art-forms, and other cultural achievements, have spread, that we can give a basis for safer conclusions. On account of the sharp contrast between America and the Old World in the material basis of civilization, and the restriction of imported material to the northwestern part of the continent, to which we have already referred, we are safe in assuming that similar cultural traits that occurred in pre-Columbian time in the southern parts of the two continental areas are of independent origin. In more restricted areas it is all but impossible to give satisfactory proof of the absence of contact.

More satisfactory are our means for determining the lack of identity of apparently analogous phenomena. Historical inquiry shows that similar ideas do not always arise from the same preceding conditions; that either their suggested identity does not exist or the similarity of form is due to an assimilation of phenomena that are distinct in origin, but develop under similar social stress. When a proof of this type can be given, and the psychological processes involved are clearly intelligible, there is good reason for assuming an independent origin of the ideas.

A case in point is presented by the so-called "sacred" numbers.[1] I am not inclined to look at these primarily as something of transcendental mystic value; it seems to me more plausible that the concept developed from the æsthetic values of rhythmic repetition. Its emotional effect is obviously inherent in the human mind; and the artistic use of repetition may be observed wherever the sacred number exists, and where it is not only used in reference to distinct objects, but also in rhythmic repetitions of tunes, words, elements of literary composition and of actions. Thus the difference in favorite rhythms may account for the occurrence of different sacred numbers; and since the preference for a definite number is a general psychological phenomenon, their occurrence is not necessarily due to historical transmission, but may be considered as based on general psychological factors. The differences between the sacred numbers would then appear as different manifestations of this mental reaction. In the same way the idea of revival of the dead, or of the power to escape unseen, is a simple reaction of the imagination, and is not due, wherever it occurs, to a common historical source. These ideas develop naturally into similar incidents in stories that occur in regions widely apart, and must be interpreted

[1] See also p. 478 of this volume.

as the effect of psychological processes that bring about a convergent development in certain aspects of the tales. An instructive example is presented by the tales of the origin of death. The idea of the origin of death is readily accounted for by the desire to see the dead alive again, which often must have been formulated as the wish that there should be no death. The behavior of man in all societies proves the truth of this statement. Thus the imaginative processes are set in motion which construct a deathless world, and from this initial point develop the stories of the introduction of death in accordance with the literary types of transformation stories. The mere occurrence of stories of the origin of death—in one place due to the miscarriage of a message conveyed by an animal, in others by a bet or a quarrel between two beings—is not a proof of common origin. This proof requires identity of the stories. We can even understand how, under these conditions, stories of similar literary type may become almost identical in form without having a common origin. Where the line is to be drawn between these two types of development cannot be definitely decided. In extreme cases it will be possible to determine this with a high degree of probability; but a wide range of material will always remain, in which no decision can be made.

The limitation of the application of the historical method described here defines also our attitude towards the Pan-Aryan, and Pan-Babylonian theories. The identification of the elements of different folk-tales made by the adherents of these theories are not acceptable from our methodological standpoint. The proofs of dissemination are not of the character demanded by us. The psychological basis for the assumption of an imaginative unproductiveness of all the races of man, with the exception of one or two, cannot be proved; and the origin of the myth in the manner demanded by the theories does not seem plausible.

The essential problem regarding the ultimate origin of mythologies remains—why human tales are preferably attached to animals, celestial bodies, and other personified phenomena of nature. It is clear enough that personification makes the transfer possible, and that the distinctness and individualization of species of animals and of personified phenomena set them off more clearly as characters of a tale than the undifferentiated members of mankind. It seems to me, however, that the reason for their preponderance in the tales of most tribes of the world has not been adequately given.

STYLISTIC ASPECTS OF PRIMITIVE LITERATURE [1]

IN THE following pages I propose to discuss in how far general mental traits account for the development of poetry and of the art of narrative, and in how far special historical conditions have exerted an important influence.

First of all it may be pointed out that the two fundamental forms, song and tale, are found among all the people of the world and must be considered the primary forms of literary activity. It does not require special mention that primitive poetry does not occur without music, and that it is frequently accompanied by expressive motions or by dance. It is, therefore, more correct to speak of song rather than of poetry.

In order to give greater precision to our problem we must point out an important difference between modern and primitive prose. The form of modern prose is largely determined by the fact that it is read, not spoken, while primitive prose is based on the art of oral delivery and is, therefore, more closely related to modern oratory than to the printed literary style. The stylistic difference between the two forms is considerable.

The investigation of primitive narrative as well as of poetry proves that repetition, particularly rhythmic repetition, is a fundamental trait. All prose narrative consists in part of free elements the form of which is dependent upon the taste and the ability of the narrator. Inserted among these passages we find others of fixed form which give the narrative to a great extent its formal attractiveness. Quite often these passages consist of conversation between the actors in which deviation from the fixed formula is not permitted. In other cases they are of rhythmic form and must be considered poetry or chants rather than prose.

It is very difficult to gain a correct understanding of the forms of primitive prose, because most of the available material has been recorded in European languages only, and it is impossible to determine

[1] *Journal of American Folk-Lore,* vol. 38 (1925), pp. 329–339.

the accuracy of the rendering. In most of the records there is an obvious attempt to adopt the European literary style. Even when the material is available in the original text we may assume that, at least in the majority of cases, it does not reach the standard of excellence of the native narrative. The difficulty of phonetic rendering of foreign languages requires such slowness of dictation that the artistic style necessarily suffers. The number of collectors who have complete mastery of the native language is altogether too small. The best approximation to the art of narrative of primitive people is probably found in those cases in which educated natives write down the texts, or in the records taken down by some missionaries who, in long years of personal, intimate contact with the people, have acquired complete control of their language, and who are willing to give us just what they hear.

In almost all reliable collections the fixed formal parts are of considerable importance. In a few cases, as among the Wailaki of California, the connective text disappears almost completely.

It is not easy to form a correct opinion regarding the rhythmic character of the formal prose; in part because the rhythmic sense of primitive people is much more highly developed than our own. The simplification of the rhythm of modern folk song, and of the poetry intended to appeal to popular taste, has dulled our feeling for rhythmic form. It requires careful study to understand the structure of primitive rhythm, more so in prose than in song, because in this case the help of the melodic pattern is lacking.

I believe the liking for the frequent repetition of single motives is in part due to the pleasure given by rhythmic repetition. For example, the tales of the Chinook Indians are always so constructed that five brothers, one after another, have the same adventure. The four eldest ones perish while the youngest one comes out successful. The tale is repeated verbatim for all the brothers, and its length, which to our ear and to our taste is intolerable, probably gives pleasure by the repeated form. Conditions are quite similar in European fairy tales relating to the fates of three brothers, two of whom perish or fail in their tasks, while the youngest one succeeds. Similar repetitions are found in the German tale of Red Ridinghood, in the widely spread European story of the rooster who goes to bury his mate, or in the story of the three bears. In Oriental tales the incidents of the tale are sometimes repeated verbatim, being retold by one of the heroes.

A few additional examples taken from the narratives of foreign peoples will illustrate the general occurrence of the tendency to repetition. In the Basuto tale called Kumonngoe a man leads his daughter into the wilderness where she is to be devoured by a cannibal. On the way he meets three animals and the son of a chief. In each case the same conversation ensues. "Where are you leading your daughter?"— "Ask herself, she is grown up." She replies:

> "I have given to Hlabakoane Kumonngoe,[1]
> To the herd of our cattle Kumonngoe
> I thought our cattle were going to stay in the
>   kraal, Kumonngoe,
> And so I gave him my father's Kumonngoe."

In an Omaha tale of a Snakeman it is related that a man flees from a serpent. Three helpers in succession give him moccasins which on the following morning return of their own accord to their owners, and every time the same conversation is repeated. When the serpent goes in pursuit it asks every animal for information in exactly the same words. In a tradition of the Kwakiutl of Vancouver Island the same formula is repeated forty times together with the description of the same ceremonial. In the tales of the Pueblo Indians the same incident is repeated four times as happening to four sisters; the yellow, red, blue, and white girl. In a Siberian tale of the Hare we hear that a hunter hides under the branches of a fallen willow tree. One hare after another appears in order to browse, espies the hunter and runs away. In a Papua tale from New Guinea the birds come one after another and try to peck open the stomach of a drowned person so as to let run out the water that he has swallowed. Still more strikingly appears this type of repetition in a tale from New Ireland. The birds try to throw the cassowary off from the branch of a tree on which he is perched. In order to accomplish this, one after another alights next to the cassowary on the same branch, but nearer the trunk. Thus he is compelled to move out farther and farther until finally he drops down.

Much more striking are the rhythmic repetitions in songs. Polynesian genealogies offer an excellent example. Thus we find in Hawaii the following song:

---

[1] The girl had a brother named Hlabakoane, to whom she had given a magical food, called Kumonngoe, that belonged to her father and that the girl had been forbidden to touch.

> Lii-ku-honua, the man,
> Ola-ku-honua, the woman,
> Kumo-honua, the man,
> Lalo-honua, the woman,

and so on through sixteen pairs. Or in a cradlesong of the Kwakiutl Indians:

> When I am a man, then I shall be a hunter, O father!
> Ya ha ha ha.
> When I am a man, then I shall be a harpooneer, O father!
> Ya ha ha ha.
> When I am a man, then I shall be a canoebuilder, O father!
> Ya ha ha ha.
> When I am a man, then I shall be a carpenter, O father!
> Ya ha ha ha.
> When I am a man, then I shall be an artisan, O father!
> Ya ha ha ha.
> That we may not be in want, O father!
> Ya ha ha ha.

In the Eskimo song of the raven and the geese, the raven sings:

> Oh, I am drowning, help me!
> Oh, now the waters reach my great ankles.
> Oh, I am drowning, help me!
> Oh, now the waters reach my great knees.

and so on through all the parts of the body up to the eyes.

Quite remarkable is the analogy between this song and the following Australian war song:

> Spear his forehead,
> Spear his chest,
> Spear his liver,
> Spear his heart, etc.

I believe this pleasure given by the rhythmic repetition of the same or similar elements, in prose as well as in poetry, shows that Bücher's theory, according to which all rhythm is derived from the movements accompanying work, cannot be maintained, certainly not in its totality. Wundt derives the rhythm of songs used in ceremonies from the dance, that of working songs from the movements required in the performance of work,—a theory practically identical with that proposed by Bücher, since the movements of the dance are quite homologous to those of work. There is no doubt that the feeling for rhythm is strengthened by dance and by the movements required in the execution of work, not only in the common work of groups of individuals who must try to keep time, but also in industrial work, such as basketry or pottery that require in their execution regularly repeated movements. The repetitions in prose narrative as well as the rhythms of decorative art, so far as they are not required by the technique, are proof of the inadequacy of the purely technical explanation. The pleasure given by regular repetition in embroidery, painting, and the stringing of beads cannot be explained as due to technically determined, regular movements, and there is no indication that would suggest that this kind of rhythm developed later than the one determined by motor habits.

As soon as we enter into the art forms of a single cultural group, we may observe that there are peculiar features which are not the common property of mankind. This is clearest in certain forms of cultural life that are spread over large areas without reaching universal distribution. It is striking that certain literary forms are found among all the races of the Old World while they are little known in America. Here belongs particularly the proverb. The important position held by the proverb in the literature of Africa, Asia, and also of Europe until quite recent times, is well known. In Africa particularly do we find the proverb in constant use. It is even the basis of court decisions. The importance of the proverb in Europe is illustrated by the way in which Sancho Panza applies it. Equally rich is Asiatic literature in proverbial sayings. On the contrary, hardly any proverbial sayings are known from American Indians.

The same conditions are found in regard to the riddle, one of the favorite pastimes of the Old World, which is almost entirely absent in America. Riddles are known from the Yukon River, a region in which Asiatic influences may be discovered in several cultural traits, and from the Eskimo of Labrador. In other parts of the continent careful questioning has failed to reveal their occurrence. It is striking that even in New Mexico and Arizona, where Indians and Spaniards have been living side by side for several centuries and where Indian literature is full of Spanish elements, the riddle, nevertheless, has not been adopted, although the Spaniards of this region are as fond of riddles as those of other parts of their country.

As a third example I mention the peculiar development of the animal tale. Common to mankind the world over is the animal fable by means of which form and habits of animals, or the forms of natural phenomena are explained. The moralizing fable, on the other hand, belongs to the Old World.

The distribution of epic poetry is also wide, but nevertheless limited to a fairly definitely circumscribed area, namely Europe and a considerable part of Central Asia. We know in America long, connected tribal traditions, but up to this time, no trace of a composition that might be called a romance or a true epic poem has ever been discovered. Neither can the Polynesian legends telling of the descent and deeds of their chiefs be designated as epic poetry. The distribution of this form can be understood only on the basis of the existence of ancient cultural relations.

On the ground of the distribution of these types two conclusions may be established: the one that these forms are not necessary steps in the development of literary form, but that they occur only under certain conditions; the other that the forms are not determined by race, but depend upon historical happenings.

If at the time when Europeans first came to the New World the literature of the Americans did not possess the three types of literature which we mentioned, it does not follow that they would have appeared at a later time. We have no reason whatever to assume that American literature was less developed than that of Africa. The art of narrative and poetry was highly developed in many parts of America. We must rather assume that the historical conditions have led to forms different from those of the Old World.

The distribution of these forms among Europeans, Mongols, Malay and Negro proves the independence of literary development from racial descent. It shows that it is one of the characteristics of the enormously extended cultural area, which embraces almost the whole of the Old World, and which in other features also appears in distinct contrast to the New World. I mention here only the development of a formal judicial procedure, founded on the taking of evidence, the oath and the ordeal, and the absence of this complex in America; and the weak development in America of the belief in obsession and of the evil eye so widely known in the Old World.

These conclusions are much strengthened by the study of the literature of more restricted areas. The investigation of European fairy tales has led to the conclusion that in contents and form they embrace many survivals of past times. Not only Grimm's theories but also Gomme's views are based on this opinion. It is quite evident that the modern European fairy tales do not reflect the conditions of the state of our times, nor the conditions of our daily life, but that they give us an imaginative picture of rural life in semifeudal times, and that, owing to the contradictions beween modern intellectualism and the ancient rural tradition, conflicts of viewpoints occur that may be interpreted as survivals. In the tales of primitive people it is otherwise. A detailed analysis of the traditional tales of a number of Indian tribes shows complete agreement of the conditions of life with those that may be abstracted from the tales. Beliefs and customs in life and in tales are in full accord. This is true not only of old native material but also of imported stories that have been borrowed some time ago. They are quickly adapted to the prevailing mode of life. The analysis of tales from the Northwest coast and from the Pueblos gives the same result. Only during the period of transition to new modes of life, such as are brought about by contact with Europeans, do contradictions develop. Thus it happens that in the tales of Laguna, one of the Pueblos of New Mexico, the visitor always enters through the roof of the house, although the modern houses have doors. The headman of the ceremonial organization plays an important rôle in many tales, although the organization itself has largely disappeared. The tales of the Plains Indians still tell of buffalo hunts, although the game has disappeared and the people have become tillers of the soil and laborers.

It would be erroneous to assume that the absence of survivals of an earlier time can be explained as due to the permanence of conditions, to a lack of historical change. Primitive culture is a product of historical development no less than modern civilization. Mode of life, customs and beliefs of primitive tribes are not stable; but the rate of change, unless disturbances from the outside occur, is slower than among ourselves. What is lacking is the pronounced social stratification of our times that brings it about that the various groups represent, as it were, different periods of development. So far as my knowledge goes we find the cultural, formal background of the art of narrative of primitive people almost entirely determined by the present cultural state. The only exceptions are found in periods of an unusually rapid change or of disintegration. However, in this case also a readjustment occurs. Thus the stories of the modern Negroes of Angola reflect the mixed culture of the west African coast. In the cultural background of the narrative, survivals do not play an important rôle, at least not under normal conditions. The plot may be old, but it undergoes radical changes.

These remarks relating to literature do not mean, of course, that in other aspects of life ancient customs and beliefs may not persist over long periods.

The differences of cultural life which are reflected in literature have a far-reaching effect not only upon the contents, but also upon the form of the narrative. The motives of action are determined by the mode of life and the chief interests of the people, and the plots give us a picture of these.

In many typical tales of the Chukchee of Siberia the subject of the tale is the tyranny and overmastering arrogance of an athletic hunter or warrior and the attempts of the villagers to free themselves. Among the Eskimo a group of brothers often take the place of the village bully. Among both groups of people who live in small settlements, without any hard and fast political organization, the fear of the strongest person plays an important rôle, no matter whether his power is founded on bodily strength or on supposed supernatural qualities. The story uses generally a weak, despised boy as savior of the community. Although tales of overbearing chiefs do occur among the Indians, they are not by any means a predominant type.

The principal theme of the Indians of British Columbia, whose thoughts are almost entirely taken up by the wish to obtain rank and high position in their community, is the tale of a poor man who attains high position or of the struggles between two chiefs who try to outdo each other in feats that will increase their social standing. Among the Blackfeet the principal theme is the acquisition of ceremonies, possession and practice of which is a most important element in their lives.

All these differences are not entirely those of content but they influence the form of the narrative, because the incidents are tied together in different ways. The same motive recurs over and over again in the tales of primitive people, so that a large mass of material collected from the same tribe is liable to be very monotonous, and after a certain point has been reached we obtain only new variants of old themes.

However, much more fundamental are the differences which are based on general difference of cultural outlook. The same story told by different tribes may bear an entirely different face. Not only is the setting distinct, the motivation and the main points of the tales are emphasized by different tribes in different ways, and take on a local coloring that can be understood only in relation to the whole culture. An example selected from among the tales of the North American

Indians will illustrate this point. I choose the story of the star husband, which is told on the prairies, in British Columbia, and on the North Atlantic coast. The prairie tribes tell that two maidens go out to dig roots and camp out. They see two stars and wish to be married to them. The next morning they find themselves in the sky married to the stars. They are forbidden to dig certain large roots, but the young women disobey the orders of their husbands and, through a hole in the ground they see the earth below. By means of a rope they climb down. From here on the story takes distinctive forms in different geographical areas. In one form the adventures of the women after their return are described, in the other the feats of the child borne by one of them. The central viewpoint of the same story as told by the Indians of British Columbia is completely changed. The girls of a village build a house in which they play and one day they talk about the stars, how happy they must be, because they are able to see the whole world. The next morning they awake in the sky, in front of the house of a great chief. The house is beautifully carved and painted. Suddenly a number of men appear who pretend to embrace the girls but kill them by sucking out their brains. Only the chief's daughter and her younger sister are saved. The elder sister becomes the wife of the chief of the stars. Finally the chief sends them back with the promise to help them whenever they are in need. They find the village deserted and the star chief sends down his house and the masks and whistles belonging to a ceremony which becomes the hereditary property of the woman's family. The tale ends with the acquisition of the house and the ceremony, matters that are almost the sole interest in the lives of the Indians. In this way the story becomes one of the long series of tales of similar import, although the contents belong to an entirely distinct group.

As a second example I mention the story of Amor and Psyche which has been cast into a new mould by the Pueblo Indians. Here the antelope appears in the form of a maiden. She marries a youth who is forbidden to see the girl. He transgresses this order and, by the light of a candle, looks upon her while she is asleep. Immediately the girl and house disappear and the young man finds himself in the wallow of an antelope.

Equally instructive are the transformations of biblical stories in the mouth of the native. Dr. Benedict and Dr. Parsons have recorded a -nativity story of the Zuni in which Jesus appears as a girl, the daughter of the sun. After the child is born the domestic animals lick it, only the mule refuses to do so and is punished with sterility. The whole story has been given a new aspect. It is made to account for the fertility of animals, and tells how fertility may be increased, a thought uppermost in the minds of the Pueblos.

In still other ways does the interest of the tribe enter into the character of their literature. A people that have an appreciation of beauty will express it in the form of their narrative. This explains the difference of style between some Polynesian tales with their highly colored descriptions and the barrenness of many Indian traditions; or the relative wealth of the tales of the Tsimshian when contrasted with those of the Plateau tribes. Let me give a few examples illustrating these points. In the Fornander collection of Hawaiian tales we read: "They admired the beauty of his appearance. His skin was like to a ripe banana. His eyeballs were like the young buds of a banana. His body was straight and without blemish and he was without an equal." In the story of Laieikawai it is said: "I am not the mistress of this shore. I come from inland, from the top of the mountain which is clothed in a white garment." It would be a vain task to search for similar passages in the literature of many a tribe.

Descriptions and poetic metaphor appear more frequently in songs. However, even these are not found everywhere. The songs of the Indians of the Southwest suggest that the phenomena of nature have impressed the poet deeply; but we must remember that most of the metaphors and descriptive terms are determined ceremonially. As an example I give the following song of the Navaho:[1]

On the trail marked with pollen, may I walk,
With grasshoppers about my feet, may I walk,
With dew about my feet, may I walk,
With beauty, may I walk,
With beauty before me, may I walk,
With beauty behind me, may I walk,
With beauty above me, may I walk,
With beauty under me, may I walk,
With beauty all around me, may I walk,
In old age wandering on a trail of beauty, lively, may I walk,
In old age wandering on a trail of beauty, living again, may I walk. It is
    finished in beauty.

Of similar character is the following song of the Apache:[2]

[1] Washington Matthews, "Navaho Myths, Prayers and Songs," *University of California Publications*, vol. 5, p. 48, lines 61–73.
[2] P. E. Goddard, "Myths and Tales from the White Mountain Apache," *Anthropological Papers of the American Museum of Natural History*, vol. 24 (1910), p. 131.

At the east where the black water lies, stands the large corn, with staying roots, its large stalk, its red silk, its long leaves, its tassel dark and spreading, on which there is the dew.

At the sunset where the yellow water lies, stands the large pumpkin with its tendrils, its long stem, its wide leaves, its yellow top on which there is pollen.

The following song of the Pima has also ceremonial significance:[1]

Wind now commences to sing;
Wind now commences to sing.
The land stretches before me,
Before me stretches away.

Wind's house now is thundering;
Wind's house now is thundering.
I go roaring over the land,
The land covered with thunder.

Over the windy mountains;
Over the windy mountains,
Came the myriad-legged wind.
The wind came running hither.

The Black Snake Wind came to me;
The Black Snake Wind came to me.
Came and wrapped itself about,
Came here running with its song.

The following Eskimo song which describes the beauty of nature is well known:[2]

The great Kunak mount yonder south, I do behold it;
The great Kunak mount yonder south, I regard it;
The shining brightness yonder south, I contemplate.
Outside of Kunak it is expanding,
The same that Kunak towards the seaside doth quite encompass.
Behold, how yonder south they shift and change.
Behold, how yonder south they tend to beautify each other,
While from the seaside it is enveloped in sheets still changing,
From the seaside enveloped to mutual embellishment.

Important differences are also found in the tendency of uniting single episodes to a more complex unit. Among some people the episodes are anecdotically short; among others the wish for a more complex structure is felt. Often this is accomplished by the meager device of con-

[1] Frank Russell, "The Pima Indians," *26th Annual Report of the Bureau of American Ethnology* (1908), p. 324.

[2] Henry Rink, *Tales and Traditions of the Eskimos* (London, 1875), p. 68.

centrating all the anecdotes around one personage. But in other cases there is an effort to bring about an inner connection between the tales. Thus the raven tales of Siberia and Alaska are on the whole connected only by the individuality of the raven and by his voracity. In southern British Columbia some of the elements of these tales have been brought into an inner connection: The thunderbird steals a woman. In order to recover her the raven makes a whale of wood and kills the gum because he needs it to calk the whale. In another tale the killing of the gum is the introduction to a visit to the sky. The sons of the murdered gum ascend to the sky to take revenge. Among the Pueblo Indians a large number of single incidents are combined into a connected origin tale.

It must not be assumed that the literary style of a people is uniform; the forms are often quite varied. Unity of style is not found in decorative art either, for many cases can be adduced in which different styles are used in different industries or among different groups of the population. Just so we find in a tribe complex tales that have definite structural cohesion, and brief anecdotes; some told with an evident enjoyment of diffuse detail, others almost reduced to a formula. An example of this are the long stories and the animal fables of the Eskimo. The former treat of events happening in human society, of adventurous travel, of encounters with monsters and supernatural beings, of deeds of shamans. They are novelistic tales. On the other hand many of the animal fables are mere formulas. Similar contrasts are found in the tales and fables of the Negroes.

The styles of songs vary also considerably according to the occasion for which they are composed. Among the Kwakiutl we find long songs in which the greatness of the ancestors is described in the form of recitatives. In religious festivals songs are used of rigid rhythmic structure, accompanying dances. In these the same words or syllables are repeated over and over, except that another appellation for the supernatural being in whose honor it is sung is introduced in each new stanza. Again of a different type are the love songs, which are not by any means rare.

We have found that the literatures of all the peoples about which we have information share one feature, namely rhythmic form; that, however, in detail there are great variations; particularly that some literary forms, like the proverb and the riddle that appear to us as the most natural products of literary activity are not by any means universal.

THE FOLK-LORE OF THE ESKIMO [1]

THE Eskimo inhabit the whole Arctic coast of America and many islands of the Arctic Archipelago. Their habitat extends on the Atlantic side from East Greenland to southern Labrador, and thence westward to Bering Strait. A few colonies are even located on the Asiatic shore of Bering Strait. Their culture throughout this vast area is remarkably uniform. A certain amount of differentiation may be observed in the region west of the Mackenzie River, where the neighboring Indian tribes, and probably also the tribes of the adjoining parts of Asia, have exerted some influence upon the Eskimo, whose physical type in this region somewhat approaches that of the neighboring Indian tribes. The foreign influences find expression particularly in a greater complexity of social life,—in a higher development of decorative art, in the occurrence of a few inventions unknown to the eastern Eskimo (such as pottery and the use of tobacco), and in religious observances, beliefs, and current tales not found in more eastern districts.

Unfortunately the folk-lore of the tribes west of the Mackenzie River is only imperfectly known, so that we cannot form a very clear idea of its character. Judging, however, from the fact that quite a number of Eskimo tales which are known east of Hudson Bay are known to the Chukchee of northeastern Siberia,[2] we are justified in assuming that these tales must also be known—or have been known—to the Alaskan Eskimo.

The present state of our knowledge of the Eskimo warrants us in assuming that the most typical forms of Eskimo culture are found east of the Mackenzie River, so that we may be allowed to base our description of Eskimo folk-lore on material collected in that area. A clear insight into the main characteristics of the folk-lore of the western Eskimo cannot be obtained at present, owing to the scantiness of the available material.

[1] *Journal of American Folk-Lore,* vol. 17 (1904), pp. 1–13.
[2] Waldemar Bogoras, "The Folk-Lore of Northeastern Asia as compared with that of Northwestern America," *American Anthropologist,* N.S. vol. 4 (1902), pp. 577–683.

The collections of eastern Eskimo folk-lore consist principally of H. Rink's Greenland Series,[1] G. Holm's tales from East Greenland,[2] A. L. Kroeber's account of Smith Sound traditions,[3] F. Boas's records from Baffin Land and Hudson Bay,[4] and Lucien M. Turner's collections from Ungava Bay.[5] From the region of the Mackenzie River and farther west we have to consider principally the tales collected on the Mackenzie River by E. Petitot,[6] and those recorded by E. W. Nelson,[7] Francis Barnum,[8] and John Murdoch[9] in Alaska.

The most striking feature of Eskimo folk-lore is its thoroughly human character. With the exception of a number of trifling tales and of a small number of longer tales, the events which form the subject of their traditions occur in human society as it exists now. There is no clear concept of a mythical age during which animals were men capable of assuming animal qualities by putting on their blankets, and consequently there is no well-defined series of creation or transformation legends. The world has always been as it is now; and in the few stories in which the origin of some animals and of natural phenomena is related, it is rarely clearly implied that these did not exist before.

I will first of all discuss the group of tales that may be interpreted as creation legends. Most important among these is the legend of the "Old Woman." It seems that all the Eskimo tribes believe that a female deity resides at the bottom of the sea; and that she furnishes, and at times withholds, the supply of sea-mammals, the chief source of subsistence of the Eskimo. The Central Eskimo say that at one time she

---

[1] H. Rink, *Eskimoiske Eventyr og Sagn* (Copenhagen, 1866) (second part), 1871; *Tales and Traditions of the Eskimo* (London, 1875), translation of part of the contents of the Danish edition; unless otherwise stated, this translation is quoted.

[2] G. Holm, "Sagn og Fortaellinger fra Angmagsalik," *Meddeleser om Grønland,* vol. 10.

[3] A. L. Kroeber, "Tales of the Smith Sound Eskimo," *Journal of American Folk-Lore,* vol. 12 (1899), pp. 166 *et seq.*

[4] F. Boas, "The Central Eskimo," *6th Annual Report of the Bureau of Ethnology* (1888), pp. 339–669; quoted Boas, 1; F. Boas, "The Eskimo of Baffin Land and Hudson Bay," *Bulletin American Museum of Natural History,* vol. 15 (1901), pp. 1–370; quoted Boas, 2.

[5] Lucien M. Turner, "Ethnology of the Ungava District, Hudson Bay Territory," *11th Annual Report of the Bureau of Ethnology* (1894), pp. 159 *et seq.*

[6] E. Petitot, *Traditions indiennes du Canada nord-ouest* (Paris, 1886).

[7] E. W. Nelson, "The Eskimo about Bering Strait," *18th Annual Report of the Bureau of Ethnology* (1899), pp. 1–518.

[8] Francis Barnum, *Grammatical Fundamentals of the Innuit Language* (Boston, 1901), pp. 384.

[9] John Murdoch, "A Few Legendary Fragments from the Point Barrow Eskimos," *American Naturalist* (1886), pp. 593–599.

had been a woman who escaped in her father's boat from her bird-husband, and who, on being pursued by her husband, was thrown overboard by her father. When she clung to the gunwale of the boat, her father chopped off her finger-joints one after another. These were transformed into seals, ground-seals, and whales (in the Alaska version, into salmon, seals, walrus, and the metacarpals into whales [1]). After this had happened, she was taken to the lower world, of which she became the ruler. In South Greenland, where this tale also occurs,[2] the "Old Woman" plays an important part in the beliefs and customs of the people, since she is believed to be the protectress of sea-mammals. Evidently the tale is known to all the tribes from Greenland westward to Alaska, since fragments have been recorded at many places.

In another tale the origin of the walrus and of the caribou are accounted for. It is said that they were created by an old woman who transformed parts of her clothing into these animals. The caribou was given tusks, while the walrus received antlers. With these they killed the hunters, and for this reason a change was made by which the walrus received tusks, and the caribou antlers.[3]

The different races of man, real and fabulous, are considered the descendants of a woman who married a dog, by whom she had many children who had the form of dogs. Later on they were sent in different directions by their mother; and some became the ancestors of the Eskimo, others those of the Whites, while still others became the ancestors of the Indians and of a number of fabulous tribes.[4]

In a legend which is common to all the Eskimo tribes,[5] it is told that Sun and Moon were brother and sister. Every night the sister was visited by a young man who made love to her. In order to ascertain the identity of her lover, she secretly blackened his back with soot while embracing him. Thus she discovered that her own brother was her lover. She ran away, carrying a lighted stick for trimming the lamps, and was pursued by her brother. Both were wafted up to the sky, where she became the sun, and he became the moon.[6]

---

[1] Boas, 2, p. 359. I give in the following footnotes references to this book, in which the versions from various regions have been collected.
[2] H. Rink, *The Eskimo Tribes* (Copenhagen, 1891), p. 17.
[3] Boas, 2, p. 361.
[4] *Ibid.*, p. 359.
[5] This story is also widely known among Indian tribes. See James Mooney in *19th Annual Report of the Bureau of Ethnology* (1900), pp. 256, 441.
[6] Boas, 2, p. 359.

It would seem that in the beginning man was immortal. According to Egede, a dispute arose between two men regarding the advantages of having man die. Since that time man is mortal.[1] This legend is not quite certain. If correct it must be related to the tradition of the origin of day and night told on the west coast of Hudson Bay,[2] and to the numerous analogous Indian tales.[3]

There are quite a number of insignificant stories of hunters, of people quarrelling, etc., who were wafted up to the sky and became constellations.[4] Thus an old man who was being teased by a boy tried to catch him, and both rose up to the sky, where they became stars. A number of bear-hunters, their sledge, and the bear which they were pursuing, rose to the sky and became the constellation Orion.[5]

Similar to these are a number of trifling stories telling of the origin of certain animals, and in which their peculiarities are explained. Examples of these are the story of the Owl and the Raven, in which it is told that the Raven makes a spotted dress for the Owl, while the latter, in a fit of anger, pours the contents of a lamp over the Raven, making him black; [6] and the story of the grandmother who kept on walking along the beach while her grandson was drifting out to sea until the soles of her boots turned up and she became a loon.[7] All these stories are brief, almost of the character of fables or anecdotes.

There are a few creation stories, in which the creation of a certain animal appears as an incident of a purely human story. Here belongs the tradition of the origin of the narwhal. A boy, wishing to take revenge on his mother, who had maltreated him while he was blind, pushed her into the sea, where she was transformed into a narwhal, her topknot becoming its tusk.[8] Similar in general character to this is the tradition of the girl who was maltreated by her parents, and who was gradually transformed into a black bear.[9]

[1] According to Egede. See Rink, p. 41; also David Cranz, *Historie von Groenland* (Barby, 1765), p. 262.

[2] Boas, 2, p. 306.

[3] G. B. Grinnell, *Blackfoot Lodge Tales*, pp. 138, 272; W. Matthews, *Navaho Legends*, p. 77; A. L. Kroeber, "Cheyenne Tales," *Journal of American Folk-Lore*, vol. 13 (1900), p. 161; C. G. Du Bois, "Mythology of the Diegueños," *Ibid.*, vol. 14 (1901), p. 183; James Mooney, "Myths of the Cherokee," *19th Annual Report of the Bureau of Ethnology* (1900), p. 436.

[4] Boas, 2, p. 174.

[5] *Ibid.*, p. 360.

[6] *Ibid.*, pp. 220, 320.

[7] *Ibid.*, p. 218.

[8] *Ibid.*, p. 168.

[9] *Ibid.*, p. 171.

Another tale explains how thunder and lightning are produced by two women who live by themselves; still another one tells that in olden times children were not born, but found in the snow, and that the new order of things originated when a child climbed into the womb of a woman along her shoe-strings, which had become unfastened.

It will be noticed that in none of these creation legends is there any inner connection between the whole trend of the story and the incident of creation. It is not clearly stated, and in many of these stories it is not even necessarily implied, that the animals created did not exist before the creation recorded in the story. The animals created are rather individuals than the first of their species. The general conditions of life supposed to prevail at the time of the story are the same as the conditions of life at the present time. This is exemplified in the story of the origin of the sea-mammals, in which it is in no way stated that the game animals were created to supply the needs of man. So far as the story shows, these animals might have existed before they were created from the finger joints of the "Old Woman." Neither does it appear from the tale of the origin of the sun and moon that there was no daylight before this event.

The complete absence of the idea that any of these transformations or creations were made for the benefit of man during a mythological period, and that these events changed the general aspect of the world, distinguishes Eskimo mythology from most Indian mythologies. Almost all of these have the conception of a mythological period, and of a series of events by means of which conditions as we know them now were established. It is true that in Indian legends also the story implies natural and social surroundings similar to those in which the Indians live, and that this sometimes leads to contradictions of which the Indians do not become conscious, the fact being forgotten that a number of things necessary for life had not yet been created. Nevertheless, the fundamental idea in Indian legends is, on the whole, the relation of the thing created to human life, which point of view does not appear at all in the myths of the Eskimo.

The absence of the idea that during the mythological period animals had human form, that the earth was inhabited by monsters, and that man did not possess all the arts which made him master of animals and plants, is closely connected with the striking scarcity of animal tales. While the bulk of Indian myths from almost all parts of our continent treat of the feats of animals, such stories are rare among the Eskimo.

The creation legends referred to before can hardly be classed in this group, because the animals do not appear as actors possessed of human qualities—excepting, perhaps, the story of the woman who married the dog. Here belongs, however, the legend of the man who married a goose.[1] This story, in its general character, is closely related to the swan-maiden legends of the Old World. A man surprises a number of girls bathing in a pond. He takes away their feather garments and marries one of their number, who later on resumes bird shape by placing feathers between her fingers, and flies back to the land of the birds, which is situated beyond the confines of our world, on the other side of the hole in the sky.

The incident in the story of the origin of the narwhal, of the goose which takes a blind boy to a lake and dives with him, thus restoring his eyesight, also belongs here. Furthermore, we must count here the widespread Eskimo story of the girls who married, the one a whale, the other an eagle, and who were rescued by their relatives; that of the woman who invited the animals to marry her daughter, but declined the offers of all until finally the foxes came and were admitted to the hut, where they were killed; and the tale of the man who married the fox, which, on taking off its skin, became a woman, with whom he lived until she was driven away by his remark that she smelled like a fox. Besides these, hardly any animal stories are found east of Alaska, excepting a very considerable number of trifling fables. These show a gradual transition to the more complex animal stories such as were mentioned before. An instance of this kind is the Greenland story of the man who was invited in first by the Raven, then by the Gull, and who was given such kinds of food as these birds eat. This story occurs in a much more trifling form in Baffin Land.[2]

It is remarkable that almost all the important animal stories are common to the Indian tribes and to the Eskimo. The dog-mother tradition is known over a large part of North America, along the North Pacific coast as far south as Oregon, on the Plains, in the Mackenzie basin, and on the Missouri and upper Mississippi. The second legend of the series, that of the man who married a goose, occurs among the Chukchee, and was found by John R. Swanton among the Haida of Queen Charlotte Islands. At present its occurrence in British Columbia seems

[1] Boas, 2, p. 360. References to the following stories will be found at the same place.
[2] Rink, p. 451; Boas, 2, p. 216.

isolated, but probably it will be found among the tribes of southern Alaska and among the Athapascan, since many stories appear to be common to this area. The whole first part of the story of the origin of the narwhal, which contains the incident of the boy whose eyesight is restored by a goose, is common to the Eskimo, to the Athapascan of the Mackenzie area, and to the tribes of the central coast of British Columbia.[1] I do not know the story of the girls who married the whale and the eagle from any tribe outside of the Eskimo and Chukchee; while the next one, the legend of the woman who called one animal after another to marry her daughter, reminds us forcibly of the Tsimshian story of Gauo's daughter.[2] The first part of the tale of the man who married the fox is identical with analogous tales of the Algonquian and Athapascan of the north.[3] It is the story of the faithless wife who was surprised by her husband when visiting her lover, a water-monster. The second part, in which it is told that the man married a fox who had taken off his skin, also finds its counterpart in a group of tales of similar character that belong to the Athapascans.[4]

Thus it will be seen that every single pure animal story of the Eskimo, with the exception of one, finds its counterpart in Indian folk-lore. Their total number is six. It is probable that the number of such tales in Alaska is much greater, since we know from Nelson's and Barnum's records that many of the animal tales of the Indians of the North Pacific coast and of the Athapascans have been introduced among them. A few additional animal tales have also been found on the west coast of Hudson Bay, but these are also of Indian origin throughout, being evidently borrowed comparatively recently by the Eskimo from their neighbors; otherwise they would have spread more widely among the Eskimo.

I think it is justifiable to infer from these facts that the animal myth proper was originally foreign to Eskimo folk-lore. The concept that animals, during a mythic age, were human beings who, on putting on their garments, became animals, and whose actions were primarily human, does not seem to have formed a fundamental part of their concepts.

[1] See Boas, 2, p. 366.
[2] See F. Boas, "Tsimshian Texts," *Bureau of American Ethnology,* Bulletin 27 (1902), p. 221; *Indianische Sagen von der Nordpacifischen Küste Amerikas,* p. 281.
[3] Rink, p. 143; Boas, 2, p. 222; Petitot, *loc. cit.,* p. 407.
[4] Boas, "Traditions of the Ts'ets'ā'ut," *Journal of American Folk-Lore,* vol. 9, pp. 263, 265; Petitot, *loc. cit.,* p. 120.

This does not exclude the clearly developed notion that, even at the present time, animals may become the protectors of men, to whom they will give instruction; and that man, by means of magic, may assume the form of animals. We also find that animals are conceived as human beings who retain animal characteristics in all their actions. A good example of this concept is the tale of the transmigrations of the soul of a woman,[1] in which the manner of life of various animals is described. The soul of the woman, upon entering an animal, converses with other individuals of the same species as though they were human beings, and their actions are like those of human beings. Another story of a similar kind describes a family wintering in a village of bears.[2] Stories of girls marrying monsters [3] may also be mentioned as examples of the anthropomorphic concept of animals.

The characteristic point in all these stories seems to be that the actions of the anthropomorphized animals are strictly confined to anthropomorphic interpretations of animal activities; as, for instance, in the tale of the transmigration of the soul of the woman, to explanations of how the walrus dives and how the wolves run, and in the tale of the bear, to remarks on the large size and voracity of the bear people. There do not seem to be any stories of undoubted Eskimo origin in which animals appear really as actors in complex adventures, as they do in the coyote, rabbit, or raven stories of the Indians, or in the fox stories of the Japanese, or in other animal stories of the Old World, in which the peculiarities of the animal determine only the general character of its human representative, while the scope of the adventures is entirely outside the range of animal activities, the stories being based on a variety of incidents that might happen in human society.

I consider this restriction of the field of animal tales one of the fundamental features of Eskimo folk-lore, and am inclined to believe the few tales of different character as foreign to their ancient culture.

The great mass of Eskimo folk-lore are hero-tales in which the supernatural plays a more or less important rôle. In this respect Eskimo folk-lore resembles that of Siberian tribes; although the adventures are, on the whole, of a quite distinct character, which is determined by the general culture of the Eskimo.

Many of these stories appear to us so trifling that we might be in-

---

[1] Boas, 2, pp. 232, 321.
[2] Rink, pp. 177 et seq.
[3] Ibid., pp. 186 et seq.

clined to consider them as quite recent, and as tales of incidents from the life of an individual not long since dead, distorted by the imagination of the story-teller. That this assumption is not tenable is shown by the wide distribution of some of these stories. A striking example of this kind is the story of Iavaranak, which is known in Greenland, Cumberland Sound, and in Labrador.[1] It tells of a girl of a tribe of inlanders who lived among the Eskimo, and who betrayed them to her own tribesmen. One day, while the Eskimo men were all absent, she led her friends to the Eskimo village, where all the women and children were killed. She returned inland with her friends, but eventually was killed by a party that had gone out to take revenge. Still more remarkable is the tale of Sikuliarsiujuitsok,[2] which occurs both in Labrador and Cumberland Sound. It is told that a very tall man, who was so heavy that he did not dare to hunt on new ice, was much hated because he took away the game from the villagers. One day he was induced to sleep in a small snow-house, in which he lay doubled up, and allowed his limbs to be tied in order to facilitate his keeping quiet in this awkward position. Then he was killed. A third story of this character is that of Aklaujak,[3] which is also known both in Labrador and in Cumberland Sound. It is the story of a man whose wife was abducted by his brothers. He frightened them away by showing his great strength. While sitting in his kayak, he seized two reindeer by the antlers and drowned them. Even the names of the heroes are the same in these tales. Since intercourse between the regions where these tales were collected is very slight,—in fact, ceased several centuries ago,—we must conclude that even these trifling stories are old. In fact, their great similarity arouses the suspicion that many of the apparently trifling tales of war and hunting, of feats of shamans and of starvation, may be quite old. The conservatism of the Eskimo in retaining such trifling stories is remarkable, but is quite in accord with the conservatism of their language, in which the names of animals that occur in southern latitudes are retained in the far north, where these animals are absent, and where the names, therefore, receive an altered meaning. Thus the names agdlaq ("black bear"), sigssik ("squirrel"), umingmak ("musk-ox"), are known on the west coast of Baffin Bay, although none of these animals occurs in that area. The amaroq ("wolf") and the avignaq ("lemming"), which

---

[1] Rink, pp. 174, 175; Boas, 2, p. 207.
[2] Rink, p. 449; Boas, 2, p. 292.
[3] Rink, p. 449; Boas, 2, p. 270.

are not found in West Greenland, are there considered as monsters. In the same way the adlet, the name for "Indians," occurs in Greenland and Baffin Land as a designation of a fabulous inland tribe.

The same conservatism manifests itself in the faithful retention of historical facts in the folk-lore of the people. In South Greenland the memory of the contests between the Eskimo and the Norsemen which took place between 1379 and 1450 survives.[1] In southern Baffin Land the visits of Frobisher in 1576–1578 are still remembered.[2]

The fabulous tribes described in Eskimo folk-lore are numerous. Those most frequently mentioned are the tornit, the adlet or erqigdlit, and the dwarfs.[3] The tornit are described as a race of great strength and stature, but rather awkward, who at an early period inhabited the country jointly with the Eskimo, but who were ultimately driven out. On the whole, they are good-natured, and the stories tell mostly of friendly visits, although hostile contests also occur.[4] The adlet or erqigdlit are described as having the lower part of the body like that of a dog, while the upper part is like that of man. They are ferocious and fleet of foot, and encounters between them and Eskimo visitors always terminate in a fierce battle, which generally ends with the death of the adlet. In some cases the visitors are saved by the kindness of a single individual.[5] The dwarfs are of enormous strength; they carry short spears, which never miss their aim.[6] They sometimes visit the villages. There are tales of intermarriages of all these fabulous people with the Eskimo.

Besides these fabulous tribes, giants and cannibals are often mentioned in the tales. There are giants [7] of such size that they scoop up hunters and their boats in the hollow of their hands. Their boots are so large that a man can hide in the eyelet through which the shoelacing is drawn. In tales of marriages between giants and man the incongruity of their sizes forms the subject of coarse jokes.

The tales of monsters relate of hunters who vanquish them after fierce combats [8] and of girls married to monsters.[9]

[1] Rink, pp. 308 et seq.
[2] Hall, Life with the Esquimaux (London, 1865), p. 247.
[3] Rink, pp. 46 et seq.
[4] Boas, 2, pp. 209 et seq., 315; Rink, pp. 47, 217, 438.
[5] Rink, p. 116; Boas, 2, pp. 302 et seq.
[6] Rink, p. 48; Boas, 2, pp. 200 et seq., 316.
[7] Boas, 2, p. 360; Rink, p. 430.
[8] Rink, p. 116.
[9] Ibid., p. 186.

The tales of quarrels and wars give us a clear insight into the passions that move Eskimo society. The overbearance of five brothers or cousins, the middle one being the most atrocious character, or simply of a number of men, their tyranny over a whole village, and their hostility against the suitor of their sister, form favorite themes.[1] We find also many tales of a powerful man who holds the whole village in terror,[2] and who is finally slain. Often those who attack the overbearing brothers or the master of the village are introduced as visitors from a distant place to which they have fled or which is their home. They are first hospitably treated, and afterwards the customary wrestling-match —which is a test between the residents and the new-comers—is arranged,[3] and in this match the quarrel is fought out.[4] Sometimes the theme of the tale is the maltreatment of a poor orphan boy by the whole village community, which is eventually punished for its malice.[5] In many cases the poor boy is described as living with his grandmother or with some other poor old woman, or with an old couple. While he is growing up, he secretly trains his body to acquire strength, and is admonished by those who take care of him not to forget his enemies.[6] Tales of poor maltreated children who later on become very powerful are a frequent and apparently a favorite subject of story-tellers.

A peculiar trait of Eskimo tales is the sudden springing up of hatred between men who had been the best of friends, which results in treacherous attempts on life.[7] The causes for this sudden change from love to hatred are often most trifling. In one of the stories quoted here the reason given is the failure of one of the friends to come back from the interior in season to take his share of the seals caught by his friend. In the second story the reason is that one man shoots the dog of another on being requested to do so. In the third no reason whatever is given.

No less curious is the boldness of visits of men to their enemies, whom they intend to kill, and among whom they settle down and live until finally the struggle begins.[8]

The reasons for quarrels are generally disputes over property rights, jealousies, tale-bearing of old women, and often resentment against

---

[1] Rink, pp. 346, 351, 362; Boas 2, p. 288.
[2] Rink, p. 135; Boas, 2, pp. 283, 290.
[3] Boas, 2, p. 116.
[4] Rink, pp. 206, 211.
[5] *Ibid.,* p. 83.
[6] *Ibid.,* pp. 202, 339, 347, 364.
[7] *Ibid.,* pp. 119, 215, 333.
[8] *Ibid.,* p. 205.

tyranny. Many stories begin with an incident of this kind, and end with the tale of revenge. In a few cases the reason for a person becoming a murderer is his despair over the loss of a relative.[1]

Tales of shamans are quite numerous. Some tell of their visits to other worlds, while others illustrate their supernatural powers. These stories presuppose a knowledge of the fundamental mythical concepts of the Eskimo, who believe in a number of worlds above and below to which the spirits of the dead go. The mistress of the lower world is the "Old Woman," the mother of sea-mammals, which she withholds whenever she is offended by man. Therefore many tales tell of the shaman's visit to her abode, whither he goes to propitiate her. His body is tied with thongs; he invokes his guardian spirits, and his soul departs. The difficulties of approach to her are described in great detail in the Greenland traditions.[2] It is worthy of notice that some of the dangers the shaman has to pass on his way to her are described also by the Central Eskimo as found on the trail to the country of the birds beyond the hole in the sky.[3] The Greenland tradition mentions that on the way to the dwellings of the happy dead, an abyss and a boiling kettle have to be passed, and that terrible monsters guard her house, while in the entrance of her house is an abyss that must be crossed on the edge of a knife. The dangers on the trail to the land beyond the sky are the boiling kettle, a large burning lamp, the guardian monsters, two rocks which strike together and open again, and a pelvis bone. The principal office of the shaman, after reaching the "Old Woman," is to free her of the unconfessed abortions—the greatest sin in the eyes of the Eskimo—which infest her and cause her anger.[4]

Other shamans' tales relate of a visit to the Moon,[5] who is described as a man who lives in a house, in the annex of which the Sun resides. The visitor has to witness without laughing the antics of an old woman, otherwise she will cut out his entrails and give them to her dogs to eat.

The shamans perform their supernatural feats by the help of their guardian spirits, which are mostly animals, but also the spirits of the dead or those residing in certain localities or in inanimate objects. The

[1] Rink, p. 213; Boas, 2, p. 299. This attitude is also found among Indians who wish to recover their equanimity by making others suffer in the same way as they have suffered.

[2] Rink, p. 40.

[3] Boas, 2, p. 337.

[4] Rink, p. 40; Boas, 2, pp. 120 et seq.

[5] Boas, 2, p. 359.

obeying spirit appears on the summons of the shaman, and takes him away to distant countries [1] or assists him against his enemies.[2] Amulets consisting of pieces of skin of animals enable the wearers to assume the form of the animal.[3] Shamans are able to change their sex,[4] and to frighten to death their enemies by tearing the skin off their faces or by other means.[5] Many tales also deal with witchcraft and with shamans overcoming the wiles of witches.[6] Witchcraft is practiced by means of spells or by means of bringing the food of an enemy into contact with a corpse, which results in making the person who eats it a raving maniac.[7] Spiders and insects are also used for purposes of witchcraft.

The sexual element, which plays a prominent part in the tales of the Indians of the Pacific coast, is present only to a slight degree in Eskimo tales. Among the whole mass of Eskimo traditions collected and retold without omission of passages that in our state of society would be deemed improper, very few obscene incidents are found.

All the ideas, the most important of which I have briefly described here, are welded into the hero-tales of the Eskimo. The tales themselves may be roughly grouped into those describing visits to fabulous tribes and encounters with monsters, tales of quarrels and wars, and those of shamanism and witchcraft. Of course, all these elements appear often intimately interwoven; but still the stories may readily be grouped with one or another of these types.

The first group, the tales of visits to fabulous tribes, embraces many legends of the adventures of hunters who travelled all over the world. The best known of these is perhaps the story of Kiviuk,[8] who went out in his kayak, and, after passing many dangerous obstructions, reached a coast, where he fell in with an old witch, who killed her visitors with her sharp tail, by sitting on them. After escaping from her by covering his chest with a flat stone, he came to two women who lived by themselves, and whom he assisted in obtaining fish. Finally he travelled home and found his son grown up. Characteristic of Greenland are the numerous traditions of visits to a country beyond the sea, and of adventures there.

[1] Rink, p. 45.
[2] Boas, 2, p. 184.
[3] Rink, pp. 7, 16, 23.
[4] Boas, 2, pp. 248, 249.
[5] Rink, p. 52; Boas, 2, pp. 249, 255.
[6] Rink, p. 69.
[7] *Ibid.,* p. 6.
[8] *Ibid.,* p. 157; Boas, 2, p. 182; Kroeber, *loc. cit.,* p. 177. See also Rink, p. 222; Holm, p. 48.

These do not seem to be so common among the central tribes, although among them similar tales are not missing.[1] An example of these is the tale of two sisters who were carried away by the ice to the land beyond the sea, where they subsisted for some time on salmon and seals which they caught. They were discovered by two men whom they married. They gave birth to two daughters, whereupon the husband of the one threatened to kill his wife if she should give birth to another daughter. Therefore they made their escape back to their own country across the ice. Their brother, induced by their tales of the abundance of game in the country across the sea, set out on a visit, giving his boat three coverings, which he cut off in succession when they became wet. He caught much game, and killed the men who had threatened his sisters by causing them to drink water mixed with caribou-hair taken from the stocking of a dead person. By this means the enemies were transformed into caribou, which he shot.[2]

The most famous among the tales of cannibals is that of the man who fattened his wives and ate them, until the last one made good her escape and reached her brothers, who killed the cannibal.[3]

Among all these hero-tales very few, if any, stories, or even elements of stories, are found which are common to the Eskimo and to their Indian neighbors, while some of these tales are quite similar to those of the Chukchee and even of the Koryak, whose culture has been directly influenced by that of the Eskimo. We may, therefore, consider them the most characteristic part of the Eskimo folk-tales. They reflect with remarkable faithfulness the social conditions and customs of the people. They give, on the whole, the impression of a lack of imaginative power. I indicated before that the few animal tales of the Eskimo are largely the common property of the Indian tribes of the Mackenzie basin and of the Eskimo. Although a few of them—such as the story of the man who recovered his eyesight—have been found as far east as Greenland, the greater number of such stories are found on the coasts of Hudson Bay, where the Eskimo are neighbors of the Athapascans, and we have seen that they are probably originally foreign to the Eskimo. Nevertheless they have come to be among the most important and most popular tales of the Eskimo tribes.

[1] Rink, pp. 169, 248, 270; Boas, 2, p. 191.
[2] Rink, p. 169.
[3] Boas, 2, p. 360.

ROMANCE FOLK-LORE AMONG
AMERICAN INDIANS[1]

RECENT collections of American Indian folk-lore prove more and more clearly that a great deal of European material has been assimilated by the natives of our continent. Many stories that are at present found among American Indians are versions of well-known European tales, while others that are more thoroughly assimilated can also be shown to be derived from Europe.

The imported material goes back almost entirely to three distinctive sources, French, Spanish and Portuguese, and Negro. The early French settlers brought their tales and beliefs to our continent. How great the wealth of this material was may be seen from the collections of French Canadian folk-lore published in the *Journal of American Folk-Lore*.[2] As employees of the Hudson's Bay Company and as independent fur traders they carried their lore over extended areas of the continent.

Quite a variety of French material has become part of Indian lore. Fairy tales like the story of Seven-Heads and John the Bear are found wherever the French fur trader went. Generally these tales retain so much of their European setting that they may be readily recognized as foreign elements, although there are cases in which assimilation has progressed so far that we might be doubtful in regard to their origin, if the plot did not show so clearly their European connections. One of the most widely spread types of French tales includes those relating to the young hero, P'tit Jean, partly fairy tales in which he is made the hero, partly trickster and noodle tales. Even the name has been taken over by the Indians and appears in more or less distorted form, for instance, as Buchetsá among the Shuswap Indians of British Columbia.[3]

We have records of French stories all over the northern part of the continent from Quebec and Nova Scotia to British Columbia, as well

[1] *The Romanic Review,* vol. 16 (1925), pp. 199–207.
[2] *Journal of American Folk-Lore,* vol. 29, No. 111 (1916); vol. 30, No. 115 (1917); vol. 32, No. 123 (1919); vol. 33, No. 129 (1920), vol. 36, No. 141 (1923).
[3] James A. Teit, "The Shuswap Indians," *Publications of the Jesup North Pacific Expedition,* vol. 2, part 7 (1909), p. 733.

as on the southern plains where French influence was important at an early time. A useful survey of this material has been made by Prof. Stith Thompson.[1]

The region in which Spanish tales are found centers naturally in Spanish America, extending from California, Arizona, New Mexico and Texas southward through the American continent wherever the Spaniards came into close contact with the natives. In Brazil Portuguese material, which, however, is practically identical in content with the Spanish material, takes its place. The investigations of Prof. Aurelio M. Espinosa, Dr. Elsie Clews Parsons and my own [2] have shown clearly that a great amount of American Indian material can be traced directly to Spanish sources. We find numerous fairy tales such as Cinderella, Amor and Psyche, Doctor Allwissend, the Swan Maidens, which are general European property and are known to occur in Spain. Many of these are identical with French tales, and we may often be doubtful whether we are dealing with material of French or Spanish origin. This is true particularly of the most widely distributed stories, such as John the Bear or Seven-Heads which are found over the greater ·part of the continent. Still more extended is the distribution of the Magic Flight story, which in the Old World occurs from Morocco to East Siberia, crosses to the American continent and occurs throughout the whole of the Northwest Coast area in a form that makes it quite certain that it came here before White influence made itself felt. We conclude this from the very intimate connection between this story and the religious concepts of the people, as well as from the close analogy with East Siberian forms of the tale. On the other hand, the same story has been imported into America by French and Spanish colonists, so that it has circled the whole world, and the two currents of dissemination meet on the North Pacific Coast.

The numerous noodle stories of the Southwest are also derived from Spanish sources. This group is not absent in the area in which French material prevails, but so far as our present knowledge goes, tales of this type are not so plentiful there. A few have been recorded by Mr. Teit from the Thompson Indians [3] in British Columbia, and others are men-

---

[1] "European Tales among the North American Indians," *Colorado College Publications, Language Series,* vol. 2, No. 34 (1919), pp. 319–471.

[2] See *Journal of American Folk-Lore,* vol. 23 (1910), p. 3; vol. 24 (1911), p. 398; vol. 27 (1914), p. 211 (Espinosa, for New Mexican Spanish tales); vol. 25 (1912), p. 247 (Boas); vol. 31 (1918), p. 216 (Parsons).

[3] James A. Teit, "European Tales from the Upper Thompson Indians," *Journal of American Folk-Lore,* vol. 29 (1916), pp. 313 *et seq.*

tioned by Prof. Thompson in his general survey of the subject. In the Southwest where Spanish influence predominates they are quite numerous and include stories of the foolish bridegroom, others from the Pedro Urdimales group and many others.

Animal tales of European origin are also quite frequent. Of special interest is the Shuswap tale of the grasshopper contained in Teit's collection,[1] who amuses himself rather than help the people catch salmon. Later on he starves and is punished by being transformed into a grasshopper which must always jump about and dance and live on grass. This is evidently the well-known La Fontaine fable changed from a moralizing fable into a typical Indian explanatory tale.

In Spanish territory the animal fable of foreign origin is more fully developed. It is particularly fully represented in the Coyote cycle of the Southwest and in the corresponding Tiger cycle of South America.

In order to understand the distribution of these tales we have to consider the dissemination of material apparently of Negro origin. Many of the Indian animal tales of foreign origin are decidedly more similar to American Negro tales than to European ones, and the two groups must have had the same origin. In many cases it is difficult to decide whether their home must be looked for in Spain or in Africa. Collections like those from Angola by Elie Chatelain [2] and those from Portuguese Southeast Africa [3] contain numerous examples showing that Portuguese folk-lore has penetrated Africa, being carried there at the time of colonization.

The problems presented by animal stories are more difficult. Parallel forms that occur in America and in Africa are common. Striking examples of this type are the Tar Baby stories and the race between a slow and a fleet animal. Many of this group of tales, but not all, are the common property of Europe and Africa, and the question arises as to the relation between these two areas. Gerber [4] assumed that the American tales are due to Negro influence. This is undoubtedly true in the Southeast and in many parts of Brazil and in other countries where Negro influence is strong. Espinosa and myself have held to the theory that most of these tales are of Spanish provenience and came to America

[1] *Publications of Jesup North Pacific Expedition,* vol. 2, part 7, p. 655.

[2] "Folk-Tales of Angola," *Memoirs of the American Folk-Lore Society,* vol. 1 (1894).

[3] F. Boas and C. Kamba Simango, "Tales and Proverbs of the Vandau of Portuguese South Africa," *Journal of American Folk-Lore,* vol. 35 (1922), pp. 151–204.

[4] A. Gerber, "Uncle Remus Traced to the Old World," *Journal of American Folk-Lore,* vol. 6 (1893), pp. 245 *et seq.*

in part directly and in part indirectly from Spain, the latter group being brought here by Negroes who learned the tales in Africa from Spaniards and Portuguese.

We are confronted here with the difficulty that we are lacking evidence of the occurrence of several of these tales in Europe. The Tar Baby story to which I referred before is a characteristic example. Its general distribution among American Indians is such that we must conclude that the story has the same provenience as a large group of stories which can be shown to have come from Spain, but no exact parallel has been recorded in Spain. Prof. Espinosa on his recent collecting trip found a Spanish story which undoubtedly belongs to the general cycle of Tar Baby stories, but which differs considerably from the cycle as found among the Negroes and the American Indians. The peculiar distribution of this tale in America and in other Spanish colonies, such as the Philippines,[1] suggests to my mind that it must have been carried into these areas by the Spaniards shortly after the time of discovery. In North America its distribution coincides essentially with the area of Negro influence, but in Central America and South America it occurs in districts in which assimilation from Negro sources is very unlikely, and where we should be more inclined to look for Spanish sources. The intensity of Spanish influence in the Philippines is best illustrated by the rich Romance literature which is directly derived from Spanish literary and oral sources.[2] Although the essential form of the Tar Baby story occurs in the East Indies, the similarity of its setting in America, Africa and the Philippines shows that the forms in these three areas must go back to a common source. The question now arises whether we have the right to assume that the tale is of Spanish origin and was carried by the Spaniards to Africa and later on by African slaves to America. It seems to my mind that we may well consider here the question whether the numerous slaves of African descent who were imported into Portugal and there employed as agricultural laborers may not have had an influence on Portuguese folk-lore and indirectly on Spanish folk-lore. It is not improbable that folk tales from equatorial Africa may have been imported into Europe in this manner during the fifteenth

---

[1] D. S. Fansler, "Filipino Popular Tales," *Memoirs of the American Folk-Lore Society,* vol. 12 (1921), p. 327, N. Y.; Espinosa, *Cuentos populares españoles* (Stanford Univ., 1923), p. 80.

[2] Dean S. Fansler, "Metrical Romances in the Philippines," *Journal of American Folk-Lore,* vol. 29 (1916), pp. 203 *et seq.*

century and may have been afloat there for some time without taking as firm root as the older folk tales, and that in this way the Portuguese and Spaniards were instrumental in disseminating tales of Negro origin. With the material in our hands at present it is impossible to decide just what happened. A thorough search in southern Spain and Portugal for tales belonging to this group may perhaps help us to clear up this important question.

A similar difficulty arises in regard to the tale of the attempted execution of Br'er Rabbit, who boasts that various methods proposed for killing him will be ineffectual, but says that he fears to be thrown into briar bushes. We find this tale widely distributed in the area of Negro influence in America, but in another part of the continent Turtle takes the place of Br'er Rabbit. The tale in which this occurs, "Turtle's War Party," is evidently an Indian tale, but it is difficult to believe that the incident here referred to could have arisen independently.

The problem that confronts us in regard to the Tar Baby story appears still more clearly in the story of the race between a slow and a fleet animal. In Asia and in Central Africa the story refers to a race between Turtle and some fleet runner. In Europe Turtle never appears in this rôle. Proof of direct European origin can best be given for the Laguna version of the tale. In the earliest recorded European version of the thirteenth century [1] the two runners contend in regard to the ownership of a field, and the same incident occurs in the Laguna form.[2] It is absent in the African versions and we must, therefore, conclude that the Laguna tale is of European origin. In the area of Spanish influence we find the Frog as the slow animal, as in the French and Italian versions.[3] The Frog as one of the two competitors appears in Laguna, among the Apache, in northern Mexico, Oaxaca and Chile. Among the Zuni the Gopher (or Mole) takes its place. Among the Cora of Mexico,[4] the Locust. In the territory subject to French influence we find the Frog among the Kutenai.[5] Among the Chiriguano the tick is the slow ani-

---

[1] Bolte and Polívka, *Anmerkungen zu den Kinder- und Hausmärchen der Brüder Grimm* (1913–18), vol. 3, p. 343; Oskar Dähnhardt, *Natursagen* (Leipzig, 1907–12), vol. 4, p. 470.

[2] F. Boas, "Keresan Texts," *Publications of the American Ethnological Society*, vol. 8, part 2, p. 261, and corresponding translation in Part 1 (1925).

[3] Bolte and Polívka, vol. 3, p. 347.

[4] K. T. Preuss, *Die Nayarit-Expedition* (Leipzig, 1912), p. 209.

[5] F. Boas, "Kutenai Tales," *Bureau of American Ethnology, Bulletin 59* (1918), pp. 43, 307.

mal; [1] in the Philippines the snail; [2] in Borneo [3] the crab. In other parts of America the slow competitor is the Turtle as in all parts of Africa and in the Aesopian fable. In the southeastern United States where Negro influence is all important it is easily understood why the African form should prevail, but it is not clear why we should find in the northern area, among the Arikara, the Salish of Washington, the Ojibwa, the Wyandotte and others, the Turtle. It seems very unlikely that these tales should have been derived from Negro sources. We may therefore ask ourselves whether unrecorded French or Spanish versions do not exist in which Turtle appears as an actor.

Still another analogous case is presented by the story of the escape up the tree, which has been fully discussed by Dr. Elsie Clews Parsons.[4] She gives a number of African versions, some from American Negroes and others from American Indians located on the western plains and plateaus. Recently a new version has been recorded from Puget Sound. In this case European parallels are also missing. Furthermore the tale is very thoroughly assimilated and forms part of stories of purely Indian form. Nevertheless the incident must be considered as imported from Africa or Europe. I am under the impression that a slow infiltration of elements of this type has occurred on the western plateaus, perhaps also in California, proceeding from Mexico northward; and that this current of dissemination is so old that most of the foreign material has been thoroughly embodied in native folk tales. This process is probably also the cause of the occurrence of the Swan Maiden element in some of the most important tales of the southwestern plateaus.[5]

Assimilation occurs perhaps more rapidly than is ordinarily assumed. Proof of this is the change of the moralizing fable into an explanatory Indian tale like the one referred to before, or the Sans Poil story of the race between Turtle and Frog,[6] in which both animals stake their tails. Frog loses and for this reason the pollywog loses its tail.

While the material previously discussed is derived from the intimate

---

[1] Erland Nordenskiold, *Indianersagen*, p. 292.

[2] Dean S. Fansler, "Filipino Popular Tales," *op. cit.,* p. 429; W. H. Millington and Berton L. Maxfield, *Journal of American Folk-Lore*, vol. 20 (1907), p. 315.

[3] I. H. N. Evans, "Folk Stories of the Tempanouk and Tuarun Districts," *Journal of the Royal Anthropological Institute*, vol. 43 (1913), p. 475.

[4] *Zeitschrift für Ethnologie*, vol. 45 (1922), pp. 1–29.

[5] F. Alden Mason, "Myths of the Uintah Utes," *Journal of American Folk-Lore*, vol. 23 (1910), p. 322; R. H. Lowie, "Shoshonean Tales," *ibid.*, vol. 37 (1924), p. 86.

[6] "Folk-Tales of Salishan and Sahaptin Tribes," *Memoirs of the American Folk-Lore Society*, vol. 11 (1917), p. 111.

intercourse between colonists or hunters and Indians, there is another group of tales that has been disseminated through the influence of missionaries. These are partly Biblical tales, partly moralizing fables used for the purposes of instruction. The latter group has been found particularly in Spanish territory where the Catholic clergy used them. Here belong a number of the Aesopian fables like that of the snake which in return for being freed by a man threatens to kill him. Stories of saints are also found in this territory. So far they have not been collected in other districts where Catholic missionaries have been working, but they may occur there. On the whole, this group of tales is very slightly modified.

The fate of Biblical stories has been quite different and often they are found assimilated to the native style of mythology and of story-telling. Examples are the Biblical tales of the Thompson Indians.[1] They believe that in the beginning all trees bore fruit, and that the pine particularly had large sweet fruit. God told man that he would come soon and tell them what they might eat. Meanwhile the Devil asked Eem (Eve) to eat of the fruit of the white pine, which was particularly good. She mistook the Devil for God, and as a punishment she was sent to live with the Devil and the fruits of all trees shrivelled up to the size of seeds and berries. Then God created a new wife for Atam (Adam) by taking out one of his ribs.

Christ is said to be the son of Patliam (Bethlehem). He is deserted by his mother in a swamp where a sheep and a rooster take care of him. The latter announces that the child is a god. A cow is sent by God to feed him, and his mother takes him back from the swamp and travels with the child until she reaches a stream. Until that time human beings had no fingers and no toes, and when they stepped into the water in order to cross the stream (baptism) all of a sudden her feet and her hands assumed their present form.

Thorough assimilation is also found in the nativity tale of Zuni. Two versions have been recorded, one by Dr. Elsie Clews Parsons,[2] one by Dr. Ruth Benedict.[3] The most characteristic feature of this tale is that the child was born in a manger and that the animals came to bless it. The pig blesses it first and is recompensed by the mother by being given a large number of offspring. The sheep comes next and is given two off-

[1] James A. Teit, "Mythology of the Thompson Indians," *Publications of the Jesup North Pacific Expedition,* vol. 8 (1913), pp. 399 *et seq.*

[2] *Journal of American Folk-Lore,* vol. 31 (1918), pp. 258, 259.

[3] Zuni Mythology, vol. I, pp. 279, 280.

spring at a time. The mule refuses to bless the child and is punished with barrenness.

Many of the deluge tales of North American Indians are obviously derived from Biblical sources. There are also a large number of native deluge tales. The assimilation between the two groups is very thorough and in a great many cases it is difficult to decide whether we are dealing with a Biblical or a native story.

Not all the problems relating to the origin and development of contents and style of American mythology can be solved at the present time, but there is no doubt that Romance sources have added a great deal to the lore of America and that in some cases even stylistic characteristics of Romance story-telling may be traced in native tales.

SOME PROBLEMS IN NORTH AMERICAN
ARCHAEOLOGY [1]

IN the study of American archaeology we are compelled to apply methods somewhat different from those used in the archaeology of the Old World. While the archaeology of the Mediterranean country and of a large portion of Asia deals with the early remains of peoples that possessed a literature, and whose history is partly known from literary sources, we find in America, almost exclusively, remains of people unfamiliar with the art of writing, and whose history is entirely unknown. The problem, therefore, with which we are dealing is allied to the problem of the prehistoric archaeology of the Old World. The method that is pursued in dealing with the ancient remains of the lake-dwellers, of the kitchen-middens, and of other prehistoric sites, of which we have no literary knowledge, must be pursued in investigations in American archaeology. But even in this case the conditions are not quite comparable. The ancient culture of the people who left their remains in Europe has completely disappeared, and has given way to civilization of modern type. It seems probable that the remains found in most of the archaeological sites of America were left by a people similar in culture to the present Indians. For this reason, the ethnological study of the Indians must be considered as a powerful means of elucidating the significance of archaeological remains. It is hardly possible to understand the significance of American archaeological remains without having recourse to ethnological observations, which frequently explain the significance of prehistoric finds.

It is only in Central America, and, to a certain extent, in western South America, that the archaeological remains have a character similar to those of the Mediterranean area. Only in these regions do we find ruined buildings and monuments that bear inscriptions that may, perhaps, serve to explain their significance.

The problems of American archaeology deal principally with the

[1] *American Journal of Archaeology, Second Series,* vol. 6 (1902), pp. 1–6.

earliest history of the inhabitants of this country. In some cases the results of archaeological investigation indicate to us fundamental changes in the state of culture prevailing in certain areas, and even demonstrate the migrations of certain tribes. I wish to call attention to some problems of this character that are met with on the Pacific Coast of our continent.

At the present time the Pacific Coast of North America is inhabited by an enormous number of tribes, diverse in culture. The present distribution of languages suggests that, in early times, extensive migrations must have taken place. The most remarkable fact that we observe in the distribution of languages is the occurrence of a number of isolated regions in which Athapascan dialects are spoken. Athapascan is the prevailing language of the whole interior of Alaska and of the Mackenzie basin. It occupies the whole northwestern part of our continent, as far south as a line drawn west from Hudson Bay to the Rocky Mountains. South of this line a large number of small tribes are met with, speaking Athapascan dialects. All of these are located near the Pacific Coast, in British Columbia, Washington, Oregon, and California. In the far south we meet, again, with a large body of Athapascan tribes, consisting principally of the Navaho and Apache. This peculiar distribution of the Athapascan language, in connection with the irregular distribution of other languages, makes it quite certain that great disturbances must have taken place in that area. In regard to culture we may distinguish four fundamental types on the Pacific Coast,—the Eskimo of the Arctic, the Indian of Alaska and British Columbia, the type of culture of Columbia River, and that of California. I will not enter into a detailed description of these. The line between the Eskimo type in the north and the Alaskan Indian type is quite sharp, while the other groups gradually merge into one another.

The distribution of physical types also proves the great diversity in the origin of the tribes of the North Pacific Coast. It is not possible at present to affiliate each type definitely with other known types, but the diversity of form found in the Coast types between Alaska and Southern California is so great that we must suppose that the diversity is a very ancient one.

It is possible to follow, to a certain extent, the history of this area by ethnological methods. When we find certain customs distributed over a definite continuous area, and absent in others, we may suppose that they originated among the people inhabiting this district. In this manner, the study of the ethnological distribution of customs and beliefs may, to a certain extent, clear up the history of tribes.

The study of the beliefs and traditions of the Eskimo of Alaska shows that the fundamental features of their beliefs are common to them and to the Eastern Eskimo, and makes it quite certain that these beliefs must have been the ancient property of the Eskimo. The culture of the Alaskan Eskimo shows, however, certain remarkable differences from the culture of the eastern Eskimo tribes. All of these features can be explained as due to the influence of the Indians of Alaska, so that we are justified in drawing the inference, in this case, that the whole Eskimo culture has been modified by a later influence. When we follow the Pacific Coast southwest, we find that a sudden change in customs, beliefs, and folk-lore takes place near the central part of the coast of British Columbia, and that particularly the Tsimshian, of the tribes of this area, show a great many features that differentiate them from other neighboring tribes, so that we may conclude that they are, comparatively speaking, new arrivals in this district. It can also be shown that the Columbia River must have been one of the great routes along which Eastern influences were imported on the Pacific Coast. The mythology of the tribes living at the mouth of the Columbia River shows a great number of elements which can have had their origin only east of the Rocky Mountains. Evidently an old connection between the Pacific Coast and the East has existed here for a very long time. Naturally it is impossible to utilize historical traditions of the tribes for the construction of their history, because all of them are more or less of a mythical character. It is possible to reconstruct the history only by a comparative study of all the elements of their culture.

The study of the ethnology of this region shows, therefore, clearly, that there have been great changes in the distribution of the tribes, but it seems impossible to unravel the early history of these changes. The question, accordingly, arises, In how far can archaeological methods supplement ethnological information? There are two places particularly at which these investigations seem to give promising results. The distribution of languages and customs in Southern British Columbia makes it clear that here important dislocations must have taken place. I pointed out before that the Columbia River must have been the course along which Eastern culture was imported to the Pacific Coast. We may also seek by archaeological methods a solution of the question regarding the early influence of the Indian upon the Eskimo.

The archaeology of Southern British Columbia, the first of the areas which I mentioned here, has been investigated in some detail. This work has been done by the Jesup North Pacific Expedition of the American Museum of Natural History, under the direction of Harlan I. Smith. His investigations prove clearly that not only have the customs of the people undergone material changes, but also that in early times an entirely different type of man inhabited the area in question. At present the Indians bury their dead in boxes, which are either placed in trees or deposited in caves. In olden times the method of burial was to construct large stone cairns with a central chamber for the bodies. The peculiar style of carving found in prehistoric remains is in some respects similar to the style of carving found on the plateaus of British Columbia. Pipes are found here which in their type are identical with those of the inland and of the plateaus farther to the south. It is difficult to identify the prehistoric type of this district with any other known type of the Pacific Coast, but its affiliations are decidedly more with the people of the interior and of the Columbia River than with the present inhabitants of the coast of British Columbia.

It would seem from all this, that in early times the affiliation between the coast and the interior was much closer than it is now, and this fact is in accord with the distribution of languages in this area. Tribes belonging to the same linguistic stock inhabit the interior of British Columbia and Washington, and the coasts of Washington and of Southern British Columbia. Although the stock is divided into a great many different languages, their affinities are quite clear. The archaeological finds make it probable that this stock was in later times assimilated by the northern coast tribes in bodily form as well as in culture.

The archaeology of Alaska offers a problem that is no less interesting. If it is true that the ancient culture of the Eskimo of this district has been affected by the Indians, the questions arises, whether the Eskimo were the original inhabitants. There are weighty reasons which seem to favor the theory that in former times this country was inhabited by different tribes. A study of the ethnology of the tribes of Northeastern Siberia seems to reveal the fact that they are more closely associated in culture and in physical form with the Indians of the North Pacific Coast than with the Eskimo of Alaska. If this is true, the inference seems justifiable that the Eskimo are recent intruders in this district. It is not probable that the Eskimo tribes of Alaska can be considered as Eskimo of pure descent, because in them the most characteristic physical features of that type are much weakened. The height of skull, length of skull, and width of face—which must be considered the fundamental characteristics of the Eskimo tribe—are not as marked here as they are farther to the east.

Attention may also be called to the curious distribution of the art of pottery in this area. At the present time, pottery is made only by the Athapascan and Eskimo tribes of the Yukon River. On no other part of the North Pacific Coast is pottery known. It is also unknown to the present inhabitants of Northeastern Siberia. Archaeological investigations made on the northern coast of the Sea of Okhotsk show, however, the existence of pottery among the prehistoric people of that district. Since this is the only place on the whole Pacific Coast, from the Amur River in Siberia northward to Bering Strait, and along the American coast south to California, where pottery is found, it seems to me to speak for an early connection between the inhabitants of these districts.

The problem of the earliest inhabitants of Alaska can certainly be solved by the archaeological investigations. The implements of the Eskimo and their physical type are so characteristic that they cannot be mistaken for anything else. If the most ancient shell-mounds of the east coast of Bering Sea, of which there are a great number, should reveal a type different from the Eskimo and a culture different from that of the Eskimo, we should have a distinct proof of a population preceding the present inhabitants of Alaska. All the evidences we find seem to make it probable that such a change of culture and of type may be found here, and I consider the investigation of this area as one of the important problems of American archaeology.

We may expect that if archaeology in America is applied hand in hand with ethnological and linguistic methods, it will be a most powerful help in unravelling the history of our continent.

ARCHAEOLOGICAL INVESTIGATIONS IN THE VALLEY OF MEXICO BY THE INTERNATIONAL SCHOOL, 1911–12 [1]

D URING the season of 1911–12, when I had charge of the International School of American Ethnology and Archaeology in Mexico City, we gave much attention to the question of the sequence of ancient cultures in the valley. Some years ago Mr. William Niven had called attention to the wealth of material to be found in the brickyards of Atzcapotzalco, and Professor Seler proved by investigation that comparatively few objects belonging to the Aztec culture were found there, while the majority were of the type of Teotihuacan. He had also noticed a number of very curious types which were found in gravels at Atzcapotzalco and had evidently been rolled in river beds.

To ascertain the relative age of these archaeological deposits, I entrusted an excavation in one of the brickyards to Sr. M. Gamio, a Fellow of the School. I also made a somewhat extended reconnaissance in the Sierra de Guadalupe to see whether the Teotihuacan type would be found there, either in surface layers or at a greater depth. I wish to express here my thanks to M. Jorge Engerrand for giving us most valuable aid in the geological interpretation of the strata investigated.

The part of the valley of Mexico in which our researches were made lies between the Sierra de Sta. Cruz and that of Guadalupe. The bottom of the valley rises gradually northward from the Lake of Texcoco. At San Miguel Amantla, where our excavations were made, the valley is probably not more than 3 or 4 meters above the present level of the lake. The surface is irregular, partly from the effects of erosion, partly owing to the removal of considerable masses of soil which have been used for centuries for the manufacture of adobes. The surface consists of vegetable mould and decomposed volcanic tufa deposited in the form of dust. In many places, one or more layers of tepetate are found at a depth of about 1 meter. This is a calcareous deposit due to the oozing

[1] *Proceedings of the 18th International Congress of Americanists* (1912), pp. 176–179.

out and redepositing of calcareous matter. The tepetate had been used for buildings in some places, and appears in such combination with layers of pebbles as to make an artificial origin at least plausible. Mounds of varying size are found above the tepetate all over the valley, and often rise over a paved floor, which is almost always accompanied by layers of tepetate.

At San Miguel Amantla, the deeper layers were examined. In the first excavation Sr. Gamio found loose decomposed tufa under the tepetate, and at a depth of about two meters and a half he came to the foundation of a house. The remains of an excavation and of a large hearth indicated that at this level the site had been inhabited. Deeper down followed more decomposed tufa but much more solidly packed, and fine and coarse sands were found in between. The whole structure of the deposit indicates that it must be considered as a subaërial deposit from which the finest particles were washed out by water during wet seasons, leaving the volcanic sand, which shows, in some places, stratification due to small watercourses. At a depth of 7 meters the volcanic tufa ceases almost suddenly and is followed by very coarse gravel alternating with sand, clearly the remains of a stream which crossed the valley. The gravel is about 2 meters thick. It also ends suddenly, resting on a very hard black clay which contains impressions of plants and is evidently an old swamp. This clay is filled with much decomposed tufa. Under it is found a whitish sand, a lake deposit. The present water table, at the end of the dry season, is in the hard swamp clay. A number of control diggings showed that the swamp had a considerable extension, and that the gravel bed represents a river 100 meters in width. At the sides of the river a sandy soil is found in place of the gravel, probably indicating that more of the fine material was washed away there than in the higher levels. This old river-bed seems to lie under a former level of the Lake of Texcoco, which would indicate considerable climatic changes in the valley of Mexico since the deposition of the swamp clay.

In the region of San Miguel Amantla and Tacuba, Aztec remains are confined to the mounds and to surface layers. As soon as the undisturbed decomposed tufa is reached, specimens typical of the culture of Teotihuacan are found. The remains of houses belong to this type, which persists to the depth where the river gravel is reached. The remains are plentiful everywhere, but mostly so on and under the level of the house-foundations.

Still deeper in the gravel, rolled pieces of pottery were found. So far as their character can be determined, these do not belong to the Teotihuacan culture, but are of an entirely distinct technique. Remains of this kind have been found wherever the gravel of this river course has been examined. In the swamp and underlying sand no artifacts have been found. It is, therefore, clear that the decomposed tufa represents a long period of occupancy by people who had the cultural type of Teotihuacan, while the Aztec period was very much shorter. If it should turn out that the geographical and climatic conditions have not changed considerably since the disappearance of the river course we must assume a very long time for the Teotihuacan period.

The most difficult question involved in this investigation is the identification of the cultural type of the river gravel period. The pebbles in the gravels come from the Santa Cruz mountains, and although the bits of rolled pottery might have had the same origin, it seemed to me that many were not sufficiently rounded to have undergone transportation over long distances in a rapid river filled with pebbles, and for this reason a search in the valley seemed necessary. In this we were favored by luck, and Sr. Gamio found objects of this type in his fifth excavation quite plentifully and in undisturbed position. His finds consist of small figures and fragments of pottery with painted surfaces. Here he made the important observation that in the lower sands these older types occurred with the types of Teotihuacan and that the latter seemed to disappear in the lowest layers of the sand. It would seem, therefore, that there has been a gradual transition from the oldest culture to that of Teotihuacan. We had reached this conclusion before, from the types of small pottery heads, some of which showed distinct technical affiliations with the oldest culture. In the Museum at Teotihuacan a number of figurines of the same type are shown and recently objects of the same class were found at the lowest levels of the subterranean structures. These finds were made by Sr. Rodriguez, Inspector-General of Monuments, and are important because they show that in Teotihuacan also the same primitive culture occurs.

My own inquiries in the Sierra de Guadalupe enabled us to give a better identification of this culture. In the autumn of 1911, when searching with Dr. von Hoerschelmann for some point in the Sierra de Guadalupe where the Teotihuacan type might occur, our attention was called to a pile of potsherds on the slope of the hill of Zacatenco, and the similarity of the types to those of the Cerro de la Estrella, as well as the difference between these types and the valley types was at once apparent.

In the course of the following months I succeeded in locating two other places with the same type in the Sierra de Guadalupe, and further objects of the same character, although not in such quantity, were secured from the Peñon de los Baños and Los Reyes. I was able to bring together a considerable collection of specimens and these are identical in type with the oldest culture of San Miguel Amantla. The whole impression of these remains is that they are closely akin to those of the State of Colima and of parts of Michoacan, so that we may conclude that a technical culture fairly uniform in its fundamental forms extended in early times from the Pacific Ocean to the Valley of Mexico, and northward to the state of Zacatecas.

The principal characteristics of the type of pottery found in the sites mentioned are: great thickness, frequent occurrence of moulded rims; designs punched in with a dull point; others painted in red, often with scratched outlines which the color does not follow evenly; a white slip with scratched designs; the occurrence of grecques somewhat similar to those of the Pueblos of New Mexico; feet of very large size, and handles in form of hands. Small heads are very numerous; they were never made in moulds, but the various ornaments were built up of bits of clay, and the eye generally consists of a clay pellet with two impressions made with the point of a stick. The legs of female figures show enormous dimensions of the thighs, while those of male figures are thin. Almost all the figures are naked, but provided with neck, ear, and hair ornaments. They were painted red and perhaps white. It may be remarked here that on the eastern slope of the Guadalupe mountains a site was found, which was covered with the remains of the Teotihuacan type.

Across the Valley, on the Cerro de la Estrella, remains of the oldest type were found, while at the foot of this mountain, at Culhuacan, enormous quantities of Aztec pottery occur. Nevertheless, in the ditches that cross this district, numerous specimens with engraved line designs are found. Since the bulk of the pottery found here has a character quite distinct from other Aztec pottery, it seemed desirable to investigate the succession of types. The characteristic yellow ware of the Valley of Mexico may be divided into three groups; one, of very fine pottery of light color with regular delicate line-and-dot designs; a second, a little coarser, and perhaps a little darker, with broader line-and-curve designs; and a third type much coarser, and darker in color, with complex designs which bear evidence of having been executed very rapidly and carelessly. A number of small excavations which were made by Miss

Ramirez Castañeda show that at Culhuacan the first-named type is the most recent. Where the soil has not been disturbed it occurs only in superficial layers. Deeper down, the third type only is found until the water table is reached, and it occurs in very great profusion. It seems likely that the older type of Culhuacan pottery had its prototype in earlier forms, since the rapidity of execution of the designs cannot be understood unless we assume that the potters were familiar with certain definite patterns and executed them with the same rapidity and individuality as we do handwriting.

Pottery with incised designs was found only in the deeper layers, although not very plentifully. A few specimens of identical type occur in the oldest Guadalupe sites, but there is not enough material available to associate these remains definitely with any cultural period. At the level of the water table the yellow pottery of the Valley of Mexico disappears and, farther down, the amount of pottery found is rather small; all the objects of this level that can be identified have the type of Teotihuacan. I consider a more thorough search in these deeper layers very promising, because the muck has preserved objects of wood which may throw much light upon the ancient civilization. The fact that objects of pottery are found here as much as 3 meters under the water table does not necessarily indicate great antiquity, for it may well be that the so-called "floating gardens" existed in this area for a long time. A constant sinking of the soil and oozing out at the bottom occurs in these gardens and would gradually carry the old surface layers to considerable depths.

The principal results of the archaeological work may thus be summarized by saying that we have obtained the proof of a very old culture widely spread in Mexico and antedating the culture of Teotihuacan. Whether the remains found in the hills indicate a late persistence of this culture cannot be stated definitely. Later on there followed a long period in which the culture of Teotihuacan prevailed. Apparently there was a gradual transition from the first to the second period. No such transition was noted between the culture of Teotihuacan and the Aztec culture; the latter seems to have lasted, comparatively speaking, a very short time. What preceded the oldest culture is not known, for in the place investigated, no earlier remains have been found. It is quite possible that in regions located on higher ground outside the limits of the ancient lake and swamp, the conditions for further research may be more favorable.

REPRESENTATIVE ART OF PRIMITIVE PEOPLE[1]

W̲HEN studying the graphic and plastic arts of primitive people, two aspects have to be distinguished—the type of art which develops from the mastery of technique, and the other which develops from the attempts at a graphic representation of objects which interest the people.

When we speak of art, we have to bear in mind that all art implies technical skill. It is therefore an improper use of the term to speak of primitive art when we refer to objects in which the producer does not possess that mastery of technique that makes the product of his labors a work of art. A basket, a pot, or a wooden object, crudely made and irregular in outline, cannot claim the term of a product of artistic activity. On the other hand, the increase in skill brings it about that the products of the handicraft of man attain an artistic value. An inexperienced basket-maker who does not control the movements of her hands will produce an uneven fabric, the stitches of which will be different in size and different in texture, and which will for this reason possess an irregular surface. On the other hand, the expert basket-weaver will have such control over her movements that all the various operations will be performed in an automatic manner; so that the intensity of pull and the manner of twisting that are necessary in these operations will be performed with even intensity. For this reason the stitches will be absolutely regular, and the regularity itself will produce an esthetic effect. The same is true in the case of woodwork, where the use of the ax or of the adz in the hands of the expert workman will be so automatic that perfectly regular lines and surfaces will be produced. This virtuosity in the handling of tools and of materials is the very essence of artistic skill; and we may safely say that in many cases the esthetic effect of the manufactured objects is not due to a primary intention on the part of the manufacturer, but is a secondary product of the possession of masterly skill.

[1] *Holmes Anniversary Volume* (Washington, 1916), pp. 18–23.

While this skill may produce regularity of outline, it does not necessarily result in designs. As soon, however, as the workman begins to play with his technique—an occupation that is enjoyed by every virtuoso—then the opportunity is given for the origin of design. The potter who in turning her pot gives it regular impressions with the nail of her thumb, the basket-maker who in playing with her technique develops the art of twilling, or the woodworker who varies the form of the surfaces over which he works with his adz, are led at once, by this very play with the technique, to the creation of decorative designs.

In all these matters we do not presuppose any impulse that has for its primary object the creation of esthetic forms: the esthetic forms appear rather as secondary products of virtuosity. Neither do we need to presuppose in this line of activities any desire to represent forms, and to convey ideas by means of decorative forms.

It is obvious, however, that these technical activities do not exhaust the range of forms that are found as products of the artistic skill of primitive man. We find everywhere attempts to convey definite meanings by means of graphic outlines or sculptural forms. These may be simply what has been called "Augenblickskunst" by Wilhelm Wundt; that is, forms which are intended only for the use of the moment, and that are designed to represent to the mind of the maker or to that of others certain impressions received from the experience of the moment. In these productions the artistic element is practically absent, because the outlines are always crude, and there is no technical skill exhibited in their execution.

It is characteristic of the development of representative art, however, that the technical skill which is acquired in the development of technical art is applied also in the execution of representative forms; and it is in this case that we actually find the beginnings of representative art.

It is not my purpose to discuss in the following lines the intimate relations between decorative and representative art that do develop in many cases, and that are found particularly close in primitive life. This subject has been discussed fully and extensively in many publications among which must be mentioned the excellent contributions by Professor William H. Holmes, published in the Annual Reports of the Bureau of American Ethnology. It may be sufficient to point out that, according to our present point of view, it seems futile to discuss the question whether representative decorative art is older than geometrical decorative art, but that it rather appears that we are dealing here with two different sources of artistic activity, which tend to merge into the development of graphic and plastic arts. We may recognize both a tendency to geometrical conventionalization of representative design whenever it is used for decorative purposes, and we may also recognize the tendency to read meaning into geometrical decorative design when it is given representative value.

Considerable interest attaches to the question of characteristics of both the crude and more highly developed representative designs that occur in various cultural stages.

We will direct our attention here particularly to the attempts at representation on a surface; that is to say, to the graphic arts of drawing, engraving, and painting.

It is clear that whenever man tries to represent objects of nature in this manner, he is confronted with the problem of showing a three-dimensional object on a surface. The complete presentation of the object in all its aspects cannot be given; and the question therefore arises of solving the problem how to represent in an adequate way a three-dimensional space.

When we examine the products of the art of primitive people, we find that on the whole a method is used which is apparently quite foreign to our modern feeling. While in our modern perspective drawing the painter tries to give the visual impression of the object, showing only what we believe we see at any given moment, we find that in more primitive forms of art this solution of the problem appears unsatisfactory, for the reason that the momentary position of the object will not exhibit certain features that are essential for its recognition. For instance, if a person it seen from the back, the eyes, the nose, and the mouth are not visible; but at the same time we know that eyes, nose, and mouth are essential characteristic elements of the human form. This idea is so fundamental in the view of most primitive people that we find practically in every case the endeavor to represent those elements that are considered as essential characteristics of the object. It is obvious that when this is to be done, the idea of rendering the momentary impression must be given up, because it may not be possible to see all these different features at the same time; and thus we find that one of the characteristic traits of primitive art is the disregard of the relative position of the essential elements of the object of representation.

It is interesting to note that the same problem presents itself to the child when it first tries to draw, and that the solution of the problem generally follows the same line that is adopted by primitive man; namely, the endeavor to represent all those elements that are considered as essential and characteristic rather than the actual spatial relations as they appear at any given moment. We must explain from this point of view the profiles with two eyes, or the outlines of the body under the garments, which occur in the drawings of both children and primitive tribes.

However, it must not be assumed that this tendency is independent of certain traditional characteristics that determine style. This may be observed even in cases where we are dealing with realistic representations executed in very crude outlines. Thus the human form as represented in certain South American drawings consists very often of a triangle with point downward, the two descending sides of the triangle being continued as legs, while the horizontal line on top represents the shoulder line, and is continued outward so as to represent the arms. In other regions we find that the human body is often represented by a curved line which is open below and terminates in the legs and feet. The Eskimo, on the other hand, never utilize a form of this kind, but always execute their drawings in the form of silhouettes. On account of their tendency to show silhouettes, attention is directed only to the outlines, which are executed in many cases with a remarkable degree of fidelity to nature. On the other hand, the artist of the Magdalenian period was not satisfied with the mere outline, but tried to fill in details that the Eskimo habitually disregards. The treatment of the body by the Bushman shows again other characteristics. Cases of this kind indicate that we have to speak of traditional style even in those cases in which the forms seem at first glance to be a result of the naïve attempt at representing essential elements of the object to be represented. This stylistic character is expressed both in the outline and in the traits which are selected for representation.

The fundamental idea that in the representation of an object its essential traits must be shown has led to the development of artistic styles which demonstrate a high technical skill, but which are quite foreign to our feeling. Perhaps the most characteristic case is that of the art of the Indians of the North Pacific coast of America, in which the principle of representation of an object by means of symbols is carried to extremes. The conventional form in which an animal body is shown does not differ much for various types of animals; but the fundamental rule underlying the art is that the characteristic parts of the animals *must* be shown. Thus a beaver, which is characterized by the large incisors and by the tail, *must* contain these elements, no matter how the rest of the body may be treated. The killerwhale *must* show the large dorsal fin, no matter how the rest of the body may be presented.

Since the art of the Northwest coast is at the same time, on the whole, a decorative art, in which definite principles have developed in regard to the treatment of the decorative field, we find that the method of representation consists always in the attempt to squeeze the symbols of the animal that is to be represented into the decorative field and follow the rules of the treatment of surfaces that are presented by the style of the Northwest coast art.

When we compare the art of the North Pacific coast, which has developed this tendency to an extreme degree with our modern art, it might appear that the principles are fundamentally opposed to each other. Nevertheless it is easy to show that modern art is only slowly and by degrees emancipating itself from the idea that the representation of a three-dimensional object should contain the essential permanent characteristics of the object. If we remember that the imagination of the primitive artist is given its direction by the desire to represent all the essential parts of his subject, no matter whether they may be visible at a given moment or not, we can see that those paintings, in which different scenes of the same incident are represented as parts of one composition, follow out to a certain extent the same idea. Thus if we see in one painting Adam and Eve in Paradise on the left, the serpent in the middle, and the expulsion from Paradise on the right, it is clear that the artist followed in a way the same principle of showing the essential scenes in the same painting, although they do not belong to the same visual impression. But we can go a step farther. Large groups, like those of the Dutch painters, in which, on a large canvas, many individuals are shown with equal distinctness, do not represent the momentary visual impression. We see with distinctness only a small part of the visual field, while the rest appears blurred, and the painting therefore represents, not a momentary visual impression, but a picture reconstructed from a succession of impressions that are obtained when the eye moves over the whole field of vision. The discrepancy between the momentary impression and the painting is particularly striking in those cases in which the picture itself is small and can be taken in at a single glance. Then the sharpness of outline with which all the figures stand out is contradicted by our everyday experience. It is only quite recently that pictorial art has used this phenomenon to any extent in order to compel the viewer to direct his attention to that point that is prominent in the mind of the painter.

Similar observations may be made in regard to color. We find that almost throughout, the colors which are utilized are those in which an object appears to us permanently. It is only with difficulty that most of us get accustomed to green faces, such as appear in the shadow of a tree, or red faces that may be produced by red curtains or the reflection of a brick wall. In these cases the abstraction from the momentary impression is so strong that most of us are not even aware that we actually do see these passing color effects.

It appears from this point of view that the principle of painting what may be called the permanent characteristics of an object have not by any means disappeared from modern art, and that, although the conflict between the momentary visual impression and what we consider the permanent form is not as fundamental as it is in many forms of primitive art, its effect may be traced even in modern times.

It is easy to show that the absence of realistic forms in the representative art of primitive tribes is not due to lack of skill. For instance, in those rare cases in which it is the object of the artist to deceive by the truthfulness of his representation, we find that the narrow lines imposed by conventional style may be broken through. Thus the wood-carvers of the North Pacific coast, who are hemmed in so rigidly by the conventional style of that region, succeed in carving heads remarkably true to nature, which are used in their winter ceremonies, and which are intended to give the impression that a certain person has been decapitated. A remarkable specimen of this kind has been illustrated in the Annual Report of the United States National Museum for 1895 (page 504). Equally convincing are some attempts of these Indians to reproduce in wood carving classical statues that have been shown to them. We must rather seek for the condition of their art in the depth of the feeling which demands the representation of the permanent characteristics of the object in the representative design.

REVIEW OF MacCURDY, "STUDY OF
CHIRIQUIAN ANTIQUITIES"[1]

DOCTOR MacCURDY in his study of Chiriquian Antiquities (*Memoirs of the Connecticut Academy of Arts and Sciences*, vol. 3 [1911]) tries to prove that the geometrical ornamentation is derived from representative designs.

The difficulty in proving or disproving this theory lies in the fact that the material studied is not dated, that we do not know whether some forms are older than others, or whether all belong to the same time. That changes of artistic style have occurred in these areas is more than likely, notwithstanding the meagerness of proofs of cultural sequences on our continent. Dr. Spinden's demonstration of changes in the technique of an art style in Central America, the analogous phenomena observed among the cruder cultures of the Northwest coast, are important from this point of view which should receive the closest attention of archaeologists.

It seems to the writer that the chief objections to the attempted interpretation of the development of an artistic style from a study of the undated object alone lie in the formal character of the treatment of the problem. Dr. MacCurdy, like his predecessors, has given us a careful classification of form and ornament, arranged according to considerations of technique, and of greater or lesser complexity of form. Among these he selects the forms which seem most plausible as the starting point of the series and the rest are then arranged in order, a time sequence being substituted for a series based on similarities of form. It may be that the investigator happens to strike the correct arrangement, but, considering the complexity of the problem and the possibilities of development in various directions, the probability of having reached a true historical explanation is not very great.

Dr. MacCurdy sums up the series of processes that lead to conven-

[1] *Science,* N.S., vol. 34 (1911), pp. 442–446.

tionalization as due to reduplication, exaggeration, elimination or fusion of parts of units; transposition, shifting and substitution; isolation of parts and their use independently of the whole; wholesale reduction and simplification; adaptation to fit a given space (pp. 127, 229). All these may occur, but they do not prove an historical development, because they are merely an enunciation of the principles of classification or seriation chosen by the student.

Wilhelm Wundt, in his *Völkerpsychologie,* has pointed out that in our studies of the development of art the psychological processes of the artist are the essentials for a clear understanding of the history of art, and I think this point of view must be kept in mind constantly.

For this reason it seems to me that the purely classificatory method, as followed by Dr. MacCurdy as well as by previous students, is not likely to give us the desired clue. Neither can it be found in ethnological inquiry and the most copious explanatory notes, which must always be open to the suspicion of having been read into the designs by the natives.

We have to bring before our minds more clearly the procedure of the native artist, the conditions under which he works and the extent of his originality. The term conventionalization, which we so readily employ, should be taken in a stricter sense, and we must understand what happens in the mind of the artist—including under this term subconscious processes—who either conventionalizes a realistic representation or develops a realistic form out of a geometrical form. Thus the problem presents itself of discovering the fundamental art forms that exert a domineering influence over the artist.

From this point of view, it seems to my mind that the first element to be determined is what is stable in each art form. Dr. MacCurdy does this in his careful classification of the material; and the association between lack of painting and presence of attached decorative elements modeled in the round,—a conclusion which I think has quite a general validity;—the presence of painting and lack of relief decoration; and other more detailed characteristics of certain forms, like the presence of the rim in vessels with neck decoration are brought out clearly.

The next step in the discussion of the ware with attached ornaments, however, does not seem to me well taken. Dr. MacCurdy points out the great frequency of armadillo-like forms, and the peculiar character of carapace, foot, eye and tail ornaments. From these he concludes, if I understand him rightly, that the life motive is older than the elements just described, which are derived from it. The relationship of the ware with relief decoration to analogous types of neighboring districts does not seem to me to favor this view. It is the essential characteristic of all this ware, that the decorative elements consist of small nodes or fillets which are applied to the surface of the vessel or to some of its parts, like feet, neck, shoulder or handle; and which are decorated by a series of short parallel impressions. An oval node with single medial lines is often used to indicate an eye; a similar nodule with a number of parallel lines indicates the foot, a series of parallel, short fillets with parallel short crosslines, are applied to the bodies of animal forms, but also to the bodies of vases. Hartman [1] describes analogous technical motives from Chircot and Orosi in Costa Rica (for instance Pl. 22, Fig. 2; Pl. 27, Fig. 2; Pl. 37, Figs. 5, 6; Pl. 39, Fig. 1; Pl. 51, Fig. 8; Pl. 64, Fig. 7) which in technical character are so much like the Chiriqui specimens that we can hardly doubt that they are derived from the same device. It might seem that this method of decoration is so easily discovered that little weight can be attached to it. Its extended use in South and Central America and in the West Indies [2] is, however, quite characteristic of that area. In North America it is not common, except in the Gulf region.[3] In contrast with its frequency in the highly developed pottery of Central America its almost complete absence may be noted in Africa, where highly decorated pottery forms are by no means absent, and where lids with animal figures might seem to suggest readily the application of the device.[4] This is true also of the prehistoric pottery of Europe. Only in the slip (barbotine) decorations of the terra sigillata do we find anything resembling the American appliqué ornamentation, but since the material is applied in a semifluid state, it does not attain the same freedom of treatment. Nodes that do occur in European prehistoric pottery seem to have been made rather in imitation of punched bronze decorations and belong to a late period. Attached animal figures, made in clay, like those found at Oedenburg, also seem to be imitations

[1] C. V. Hartman, *Archeological Researches in Costa Rica* (Stockholm, 1901).

[2] See, for instance, W. J. Fewkes, "The Aborigines of Puerto Rico," *25th Annual Report Bureau of American Ethnology* (1907), Fig. 36, p. 185; Pl. 76, Fig. c; Pl. 78; Pl. 79.

[3] G. P. Thurston, *The Antiquities of Tennessee* (Cincinnati, 1890), p. 146; Pl. 7; W. H. Holmes, "Aboriginal Pottery of the Eastern United States," *20th Annual Report Bureau of American Ethnology* (1903); for references see index under "fillets" and "nodes."

[4] "Notes analytiques sur les collections ethnographiques du Musée du Congo," vol. 2, "Les industries indigènes"; part 1, "La céramique." (Fig. 293a is the only one that may exhibit this technique.)

of metal work and have never reached that development which is so characteristic of Central American ceramic art.[1]

The characteristics slit rattle feet of Chiriqui pottery prove even more conclusively than the application of fillets and nodes, that the art forms of this province must be considered as a special development of forms characteristic of a much wider area. This type of foot is so well known that no special reference to its occurrences outside of the Chiriqui territory need be given.

We are thus led to the conclusion that the armadillo motive of the author is historically related to the method of decorating and building up vessels from separate pieces, nodes and fillets, the nodes and fillets being in many regions decorated by parallel incised lines, or by dots. If this is true, the armadillo motive can only be a specialized application of the building up of animal motives from the elements in question, and neither can the elements themselves be considered primarily as symbols of the armadillo (p. 61), nor can all the animals built up of these elements be interpreted as armadillos.

For the same reason I am inclined to doubt the correctness of the interpretation of the alligator group, which was first given by Professor Holmes in the work before referred to. The upturned snout, of which much is made as a means of identification, is a character of much wider distribution than the alligator motive. The monkeys on Plates 27 and 32a of Dr. MacCurdy's book have it, and we find it as well in the interior of Costa Rica [2] as in parts of South America. This is no less true of the curious "nuchal appendage" which occurs in Costa Rica [3] as well as in South America,[4] and of the dotted triangle.

It seems to me that the essential point of this consideration lies in the technical and formal motives that are common to a large area, although differing in details in its provinces. These are the materials with which the artist operates and they determine the particular form which a geometrical motive or a life motive takes. If the notched fillet and node

---

[1] Relief ornaments consisting of fillets have been described from northern Germany, Bohemia, Bosnia and Italy. See, for instance, Radinsky, Butmir, Vienna, 1895; K. Koenen, *Gefässkunde der vorrömischen, römischen und fränkischen Zeit in den Rheinlanden* (Bonn, 1895), Pl. 3, Fig. 12.

[2] Hartman, *loc. cit.*, Fig. 2; Pl. 35; Pl. 81; Fig. 286, p. 128. The region in question has more frequently a proboscis-like appendage, rolled downward.

[3] Hartman, *loc. cit.*, Fig. 2; Pl. 35.

[4] M. H. Saville, "The Antiquities of Manabi, Ecuador," *Contributions to South American Archaeology. The George G. Heye Expedition* (1907), Pl. 8. See also E. Seler, "Archäologische Untersuchungen in Costarica," *Globus*, vol. 85 (1904), p. 237.

are the material with which the hand and the mind of the artist operate, they will occur in all his representations. If the conventional outline of the animal body has a definite form, all animals will tend to be represented in that manner. I have tried to emphasize at a previous time [1] the importance of such fixed traditional forms in determining the conventional style of decorations.

In his further descriptions of the art work of Chiriqui Dr. MacCurdy notes the similarity of motives used in metal castings, notably in the gold castings, and the armadillo pottery, a similarity which consists essentially in the use of detached figures, nodes and fillets, as described before. He also calls attention to the frequent occurrence of the head with upturned snout—the alligator-head design of painted pottery— in this technique, a feature that had escaped the attention of previous students. At least one of them has, however, the type of proboscis rolled down (Pl. 58, Fig. g) which is so common on the plateaus of Costa Rica. In this case also the rigidity of the fundamental form seems particularly suggestive to the writer, because a variety of animals have all been presented in analogous outlines.

[1] Notes to G. T. Emmons, "The Chilcat Blanket," *Memoirs of the American Mueum of Natural History,* vol. 3, part 4, pp. 355 *et seq.*

THE DECORATIVE ART OF THE
NORTH AMERICAN INDIANS [1]

THE extended investigations on primitive decorative art which have been made during the last twenty years have clearly shown that almost everywhere the decorative designs used by primitive man do not serve purely esthetic ends, but that they suggest to his mind certain definite concepts. They are not only decorations, but symbols of definite ideas.

Much has been written on this subject; and for a time the opinion prevailed that wherever an ornament is explained as a representation of a certain object, its origin has been in a realistic representation of that object, and that it has gradually assumed a more and more conventionalized form, which has often developed into a purely geometrical motive.[2] On the other hand, Cushing and Holmes have pointed out the important influence of material and technique in the evolution of design, and, following Semper, have called attention to the frequent transfer of designs developed in one technique to another. Thus, according to Semper, forms developed in wood architecture were imitated in stone, and Cushing and Holmes showed that textile designs are imitated on pottery.

The origin of certain designs from technical forms is now recognized as an important factor, and it must therefore be assumed that in many cases the interpretation has been read into the design. The existence of this tendency has recently been pointed out by H. Schurtz [3] and by Professor A. D. F. Hamlin,[4] who has treated in a series of essays the evolution of decorative motives.

In speaking of the process of conventionalization or degeneration of realistic motives, Professor Hamlin says: "Indeed, this degeneration may reasonably be accepted as suggesting that the geometric forms

[1] *The Popular Science Monthly* (Oct., 1903).
[2] A. C. Haddon, *Evolution in Art* (London, 1902).
[3] H. Schurtz, *Urgeschichte der Kultur* (Leipzig and Vienna, 1900), p. 540.
[4] *The American Architect and Building News*, 1898.

which it approaches were already in habitual use when it began, and that the direction of the degeneration was determined by a pre-existing habit or 'expectancy' (as Dr. Colley March calls it) of geometric form acquired in skeuomorphic decoration" [1] (*i.e.*, in a form developed from technical motives). At another place [2] he says: "After having undergone in its own home such series of modifications, the motive becomes known to the artists of some race or civilization through the agency either of commerce or of conquest. It is carried across seas and lands, and in new hands receives still another dress in combinations still more incongruous with its original significance. It is no longer a symbol, but an arbitrary ornament, wholly conventional, modified to suit the taste and the arts of the foreigners who have adopted it. In many cases it undergoes modification in two or more directions, resulting in divergent developments, which in time produce as many distinct motives— cousins, as it were, of each other—each of which runs its own course independently of the others. This phenomenon we may call 'divergence.' A common cause of divergence is the tendency to assimilate a borrowed motive to some indigenous and familiar form, usually a natural object, thus setting up a new method of treatment quite foreign to the origin of the motive."

I intend to show in the following pages that the same processes, which Professor Hamlin traces by historical evidence in the art of the civilized peoples of the Old World, have occurred among the primitive tribes of North America. [3]

Before taking up this subject, attention may be called to a peculiar difference between the decorative style applied in ceremonial objects and that employed in articles of every-day use. We find a considerable number of cases which demonstrate the fact that, on the whole, the decoration of ceremonial objects is much more realistic than that of ordinary objects. Thus we find the garments for ceremonial dances of the Arapaho covered with pictographic representations of animals, their sacred pipe covered with human and other forms, while their painted blankets for ordinary wear are generally adorned with geometrical designs. Among the Thompson Indians ceremonial blankets are also

---

[1] *Ibid.*, p. 93.   [2] *Ibid.*, p. 35.

[3] The examples and illustrations here represented are taken, unless otherwise stated, from specimens in the American Museum of Natural History. The information and material used were collected by Dr. Roland B. Dixon, Professor Livingston Farrand, Dr. A. L. Kroeber, Dr. Berthold Laufer, Dr. Carl Lumholtz, Mr. H. H. St. Clair, Mr. James Teit and Dr. Clark Wissler, all of whom have contributed to the systematic study of decorative art undertaken by the museum.

covered with pictographic designs, while ordinary wearing-apparel and basketry are decorated with very simple geometrical motives. On the stem of a shaman's pipe we find a series of pictographs, while an ordinary pipe shows geometric forms. Even among the eastern Eskimo, whose decorative art, on the whole, is very rudimentary, a shamanistic coat has been found which has a number of realistic motives, while the ordinary dress of the same tribe shows no trace of such decoration (Figs.

Fig. 1. Shaman's coat. Eskimo, Iglulik.

1, 2). The same phenomenon may also be observed outside of America, as is demonstrated by the difference in style between the shaman's coat and the ordinary coat of the Gold of the Amur River (Figs. 3, 4). The most striking examples of this kind are the woven designs of the Huichol Indians of Mexico. All their ceremonial weavings are covered with more or less realistic designs, while all their ordinary wearing-apparel presents rigid geometrical motives. In fact, the style of the two is so different that it hardly seems to belong to the same tribe

FIG. 2. Man's costume. Eskimo, Aivilik.

FIG. 3. Shaman's coat. Gold.

Fig. 4. Decorated fish skin coat. Gold.

(Fig. 5). We may perhaps recognize the same tendency in the style of decoration of modern dwelling-rooms and in that of public buildings. The designs on the stained glass of house-windows are usually arranged in geometrical forms; those of churches represent pictures. The wall decorations of houses are wall papers of more or less geometrical character; those of halls devoted to public uses are generally adorned with symbolic pictures.

This difference in the treatment of ceremonial and common objects shows clearly that the reason for the conventionalization of motives can not be solely a technical one, for if so, it would act in one case as well

FIG. 5. Ceremonial shield and belt for ordinary wear. Huichol.
After Lumholtz.

as in the other. In ceremonial objects the ideas represented are more important than the decorative effect, and it is intelligible that the resistance to conventionalism may be strong; although in some cases the very sacredness of the idea represented might induce the artist to obscure his meaning intentionally, in order to keep the significance of the design from profane eyes. It may, therefore, be assumed that, if a tendency to conventionalization exists, it will manifest itself differently, even among the same tribe, according to the preponderance of the decorative or descriptive value of the design.

On the other hand, the general prevalence of symbolic significance in ordinary decoration shows that this is an important aspect of decorative art, and a tendency to retain the realistic form might be expected, provided its origin were from realistic forms. If, therefore, the whole decorative art of some tribes shows no trace of realism, it may well be

Fig. 6. Parfleches. Left, Arapaho; right, Shoshone.

doubted whether their ordinary decorative designs were originally realistic.

The history of decorative design can best be investigated by analyzing the styles of form and interpretation prevailing over a limited area. If the style of art were entirely indigenous in a given tribe, and developed either from conventionalization of realistic designs or from the elaboration of technical motives, we should expect to find a different style and different motives in each tribe. The general customs and beliefs might be expected to determine the subjects chosen for decoration, or the ideas that are read into the technical designs.

As a matter of fact, the native art of North America shows a very different state of affairs. All over the Great Plains and in a large portion of the western plateaus an art is found which, notwithstanding local peculiarities, is of a uniform type. It is characterized by the appli-

cation of colored triangles and quadrangles in both painting and embroidery in a manner which is found in no other part of the world.

The slight differences of styles which occur are well exemplified in the style of painted rawhide bags or envelopes, the so-called 'parfleches.' Mr. St. Clair has observed that the Arapaho are in the habit of laying on the colors rather delicately, in areas of moderate size, and of following out a general arrangement of their motives in stripes; that the Shoshone, on the other hand, like large areas of solid colors, bordered by heavy blue bands, and an arrangement in which a central field is set off rather prominently from the rest of the design (Fig. 6). This difference is so marked that it is easy to tell a Shoshone parfleche that has found its way to the Arapaho from parfleches of Arapaho manu-

FIG. 7. Moccasin.

facture. In other cases the most characteristic difference consists in the place on the parfleche to which the design is applied. The Arapaho and the Shoshone never decorate the sides of a bag, only its flaps, while the tribes of Idaho and Montana always decorate the sides. Another peculiarity of Arapaho parfleche-painting, as compared to that of the Shoshone, is the predilection for two right-angled triangles standing on the same line, their right angles facing each other—a motive of common occurrence all over the southern part of the Plains and in the southwestern territories; while the Shoshone generally place these triangles with facing acute angles. A detailed study of the art brings out many minor differences of this sort, although the general type is very uniform.

Certain types of designs are so much alike that they might belong to one tribe as well as to another. A type of moccasin used by the Shoshone, Sioux and Arapaho (Fig. 7) will serve as a good example. Its characteristic form is a cross on the uppers, connected with a bar on the instep, from which arise at each end two short lines. This design is so complex that evidently it must have had a single origin. It is of great importance to note that nevertheless the explanations given by the various tribes are quite different. The design is interpreted by the Arapaho as the morning star; the bar on the instep, as the horizon; the short lines, as the twinkling of the star. To the mind of the Sioux the design conveys the idea of feathers, when applied to a woman's moccasin; when found on a man's moccasin, it symbolizes the sacred shield suspended from tent-poles. The identical design was explained by the Shoshone as signifying the sun (the center) and its rays; but also the thunderbird, the cross-arms of the cross evidently being the wings; the part nearest the toe, the tail, and the upper part, the neck with two strongly conventionalized heads attached. If these are the ideas conveyed by this design to the makers, it is clear that they must have developed after the invention or introduction of the design; that the design is primary, the idea secondary, and that the idea has nothing to do with the historical development of the design itself.

Fig. 8. Embroidered design. Arapaho.

It may be well to give a few additional examples of such similarity of design and difference of symbolism. One of the typical designs of this area is a cross to the ends of which deeply notched squares are attached (Fig. 8). Dr. Kroeber [1] received the following explanation of this design from an Arapaho: the diamond in the center represents a person; the four forked ornaments surrounding it are buffalo hoofs or tracks. Dr. Wissler found the design on a pair of woman's leggings of the Sioux. In this case the diamond-shaped center of the design represents the breast of a turtle; green lines forming the cross indicate the four points of the compass; the forked ornaments symbolize forks of trees struck by hailstones, which are indicated by small white

[1] A. L. Kroeber, "The Arapaho," *Bulletin American Museum of Natural History,* vol. 18 (1902–1904).

rectangles. Mr. St. Clair came across the same design among the Shoshone, where it was found on a cowhide bag. The central diamond was interpreted as the sun and clouds; the notched designs were explained as mountain-sheep hoofs. There is a certain similarity in this case between the explanations given by the Arapaho and those of the Shoshone, while the Sioux connect ideas of a different type with the design.

Such differences of interpretation are also found on painted designs. The Shoshone sometimes imagine they see a battle scene in the squares and triangles of their parfleche designs. The square in the center of

Fig. 9 was explained to Mr. St. Clair as an enclosure in which the enemy was kept by a besieging party, represented by the marginal squares. The narrow central line is the trail by which the enemy made good his escape. Many others represent geographical features, such as mountains and valleys. Such geographical ideas are represented on some Arapaho parfleches, while others exhibit a more complex symbolic significance. Battle scenes, however, are not found in interpretations given by the Arapaho.

FIG. 9. Parfleche. Shoshone.

The similarity of complex designs, combined with dissimilarity of interpretation, justifies a comparison of simpler forms. These might be believed to have originated independently; but the sameness of the complex forms proves that their component elements must have had a common origin, or at least have been assimilated by the same forms. One of the striking examples of this kind is the cross. Among the Arapaho it signifies almost invariably the morning star. To the mind of the Shoshone it conveys the idea of barter. The Sioux recognizes in it a man slain in battle and lying flat on the ground with arms outstretched. The Thompson Indians of British Columbia recognize in it the crossing trails at which sacrifices are made.

The simple straight red lines with which skin bags are decorated are another good example. A specimen was collected by Dr. Kroeber among the Arapaho (Fig. 10, front and side). He explains the stripes on the beaded design on the narrow sides and on the flaps of the bag as camp trails; the shorter transverse stripes intersecting these longitudinal lines, as ravines, that is, camping-places. On the front of the bag the horizontal lines of quill-work, which resemble the lines on buffalo-robes, are paths. Bunches of feathers on these lines represent buffalo-meat hung up to dry. Adjoining the bead-work are small tin cylinders with tufts of red hair; these represent pendants or rattles on tents. Mr. St. Clair obtained the following explanation of a Shoshone bag of almost identical design: The porcupine-quill work on the front of the bag repre-

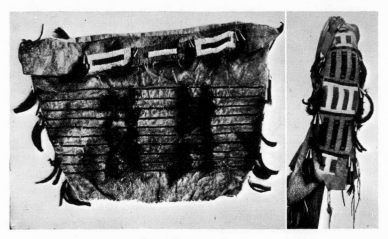

Fig. 10. Embroidered skin bag. Arapaho.

sents horse-trails. The red horse-hair tassels at each side are horses stolen by people of one village from those of another, the villages being represented by the bead-work at the sides of the bag. The bead-work on the flap represents the owners of the horses indicated by the horse-hair tassels on the flap. Among the Sioux the same design is used in the puberty ceremonial, and symbolizes the path of life.

It must not be believed that the interpretation of a certain motive, or even of a complex figure when used by the members of one tribe, is always the same. As a matter of fact, the number of ideas expressed by it is often quite varied. We find, for instance, an obtuse triangle with enclosed rectangle (see Fig. 11) explained by the Arapaho as the mythic cave from which the buffalo issued, as cattle-tracks, as a mountain, cloud, brush hut and tent; an acute triangle, with small triangles attached to its base, as a bird-tail, frog, tent and bear-foot.

Nevertheless the explanations given by various tribes show peculiar characteristics in which they differ from those of other tribes. The explanations possess no less a style of their own than the art itself. Triangles are explained as tents by all the tribes, and mountains or hills form a prominent feature of their descriptions; but among the three tribes mentioned only the Sioux see wounds, battle scenes with moving masses of men, horses, the pursuit of enemies, the flight of arrows, in their conventional designs; only the Shoshone see in them pictures of forts and stones piled up in memory of battles; only the Arapaho recognize in them prayers for life directed to the morning star.

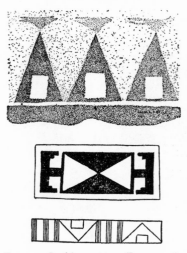

FIG. 11. Pueblo patterns. From specimens in the U. S. National Museum.

We find, therefore, that in this area the same style of art is widely distributed, while the style of explanation differs materially among its various tribes.

It may be worth while to review briefly the distribution of the style of art here discussed. On the whole, it is confined to the Plains Indians, west of the eastern wooded area. It would seem that it has been carried into the plateau region rather recently, where, however, it has affected almost all of the tribes east of the Cascade Range and of the Sierra Nevada. We find the acute triangle with small supporting triangles, and the obtuse triangle with enclosed rectangle, in the characteristic arrangement of the parfleches, on bags of the Nez Percés. At first glance, the art of the Pueblos seems quite different from the one that we are discussing here; but I believe that an intimate association of the two may be traced. The ancient pottery described by Dr. Fewkes, for instance, shows a number of the peculiar triangle and square motives which are so characteristic of the art of the Indians of the Plains (Fig. 11). The same triangle with supporting lines, the same triangle with the enclosed square, is found here. It seems very plain to my mind that the transfer of this art from pottery to embroidery and painting on flat surfaces has brought about the introduction of the triangular and rectangular forms which are the prime characteristic of this type of art.

In the prehistoric art of the northern plateaus, in California, on the North Pacific coast, in the Mackenzie basin, in the wooded area of the Atlantic coast, we find styles of art which differ from the art of the Plains, and which have much less in common with Pueblo art. Therefore I am inclined to consider the art of the Plains Indians in many of its traits as developed from the art of the Pueblos. I think the general

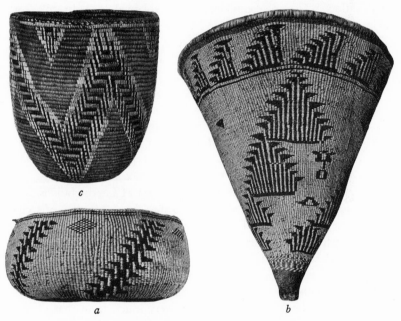

FIG. 12. Quail-tip designs on California and Oregon baskets.

facts of the culture of these tribes are fairly in accord with this notion, since it would seem that the complex social and religious rites of the southwest gradually become simpler and less definite as we proceed northward. If this opinion regarding the origin of the art of the Plains is correct, we are led to the conclusion that the tent with its pegs is the same form in origin as the rain-clouds of the Pueblos, so that the scope of interpretations of the same form is still more enlarged. Under these conditions, we must conclude that the interpretation is probably secondary throughout, and has become associated with the form which was obtained by borrowing. With this we are brought face to face with the skeuomorphic origin of the triangular design from basketry motives, which has been so much discussed of recent years.

The so-called "quail-tip" design of California is another example of the continuous distribution of a motive over a wide area, the occurrence of which in the outlying districts must be due to borrowing. The characteristic feature of this design, which occurs in the basketry of California and Oregon, is a vertical line, suddenly turning outward at its end. This motive occurs on both twined and coiled basketry, and with many explanations.[1] In some combinations it is explained as the lizard's foot (Fig. 12, a), in others as the pine cone or the mountain (Fig. 12, b). The gradual distribution of this motive over a wide area can best be proved in this case by a comparison with the distribution of the technique in which it is applied. The design occurs all over central and northern California. On Columbia River it is found on the Klickitat baskets. These are of the peculiar imbricated basketry which is made from this point on, northward. While the designs on imbricated basketry found in British Columbia are of a peculiar character, the Klickitat baskets of the same make (Fig. 12, c) have the typical California designs which also occur on the twined bags of this district.

Thus we find, not only that the distribution of interpretations and that of motives do not coincide, but also that the distribution of technique does not agree with that of motives. I think we can also demonstrate that the limits of styles of interpretation in some cases overlap the limits of styles of art. We have seen that on the Plains the style of art covers a wider area than the style of interpretation. It would seem that in other regions the reverse is the case. For instance, the style of art of the Nootka tribes differs very much from that of the Kwakiutl. Although both apply animal motives, the Nootka use very little surface decoration consisting of combinations of characteristic curved lines, which play an important part in Kwakiutl art, and which serve to symbolize various parts of the body. Nootka art is more realistic and at the same time cruder than Kwakiutl art. The ideas expressed in the art of both tribes, however, are practically the same. In the southwest we find that the culture of the Pueblos has deeply influenced the neighboring Athapascan and Sonoran tribes, while at the same time the decoration of their basketry bears a close relation to that of Californian

---

[1] Roland B. Dixon, "Basketry Designs of the Indians of Northern California," *Bulletin American Museum of Natural History,* vol. 17 (1902), pp. 2 et seq.

basketry. Although I do not know the interpretations of designs given by the Apache, Pima and Navaho, it seems probable that they have been influenced by the ideas current among the Pueblos. Among the Pueblos themselves—and in these I include the tribes of northern Mexico, such as the Huichol—there are well-marked local styles of technique and of decoration, and a general similarity of interpretation. I think the marked prevalence of geographical interpretations found among the Salish tribes of British Columbia, the Shoshone and the Arapaho is

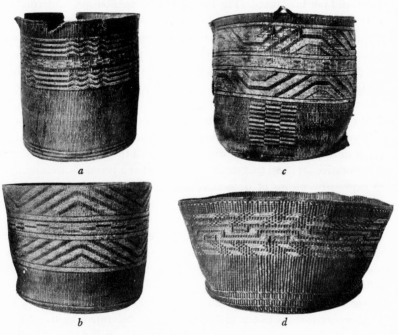

a   c

b   d

FIG. 13. Tlingit baskets. After Emmons.

another instance of distribution of a style of interpretation over an area including divers styles of art.

In a few cases it seems almost self-evident, from a consideration of the interpretations themselves, that they cannot have developed from realistic forms. The multiplicity of Arapaho explanations for the triangles which I mentioned before suggest this. According to G. T. Emmons,[1] the zigzag and the closely allied meander in Tlingit basketry

---

[1] "The Basketry of the Tlingit," *Memoirs American Museum of Natural History,* vol. 3 (1903), pp. 263 *et seq.*

have a variety of meanings. The zigzag may represent the tail of the land-otter (Fig. 13, a), the hood of the raven (Fig. 13, b), the butterfly (Fig. 13, c), or, when given a rectangular form (Fig. 13, d), waves and floating objects. It is evident, in view of the data here discussed, that these must be different interpretations of motives of similar origin.

We conclude from all this that the explanation of designs is secondary almost throughout and due to a late association of ideas and forms, and that as a rule a gradual transition from realistic motives to geometric forms did not take place. The two groups of phenomena—interpretation and style—appear to be independent. We may say that in many, perhaps in most cases, designs are considered significant. Different tribes may interpret the same style by distinct groups of ideas. On the other hand, certain groups of ideas may be spread over tribes whose decorative art follows different styles, so that the same ideas are expressed by different styles of art.

We may express this fact also by saying that the history of the artistic development of a people, and the style that they have developed at any given time, predetermine the method by which they express their ideas in decorative art; and that the type of ideas that a people is accustomed to express by means of decorative art predetermines the explanation that will be given to a new design. It would therefore seem that there are certain typical associations between ideas and forms which become established, and which are used for artistic expression. The idea which a design expresses at the present time is not necessarily a clue to its history. It seems probable that idea and style exist independently, and influence each other constantly.

For the present it remains an open question, why the tendency to form associations between certain ideas and decorative motives is so strong among primitive people. The tendency is evidently similar to that observed among children who enjoy interpreting simple forms as objects to which the form has a slight resemblance; and this, in turn, may bear some relation to the peculiar character of realism in primitive art, to which I believe Von den Steinen [1] was the first to draw attention. The primitive artist does not attempt to draw what he sees, but merely combines what are to his mind the characteristic features of an object, without regard to their actual space relation in the visual image. For this reason he may also be more ready than we are to consider some

[1] *Unter den Naturvölkern Zentral-Brasiliens* (Berlin, 1894), pp. 250 *et seq.*

characteristic feature as symbolic of an object, and thus associate forms and objects in ways that seem to us unexpected.

It may be worth while to mention one general point of view that is suggested by our remarks. The explanations of decorative design given by the native suggest that to his mind the form of the design is a result of attempts to represent by means of decorative art a certain idea. We have seen that this cannot be the true history of the design, but that it probably originated in an entirely different manner. What is true in the case of decorative art is true of other ethnic phenomena. The historical explanation of customs given by the native is generally a result of speculation, not by any means a true historical explanation. The mythical explanation of rites and customs is seldom of historical value, but is generally due to associations formed in the course of events, while the early history of myths and rites must be looked for in entirely different causes, and interpreted by different methods. Native explanations of laws, of the origin of the form of society, must have developed in the same manner, and therefore cannot give any clue in regard to historical events, while the association of ideas of which they are the expression furnishes most valuable psychological material.

DECORATIVE DESIGNS OF ALASKAN NEEDLE-
CASES: A STUDY IN THE HISTORY OF
CONVENTIONAL DESIGNS, BASED
ON MATERIALS IN THE U. S.
NATIONAL MUSEUM[1]

IN 1878 and the following years, Professor F. W. Putnam[2] described in detail the decorative designs found in the pottery of the Chiriqui Indians, and was the first, I believe, to propound clearly the theory that conventional designs develop from attempts at realistic representations, which gradually degenerate so that ultimately a purely conventional design remains in which the realistic origin can hardly be recognized. Since that time this theory has been independently stated by a number of investigators, particularly by H. Stolpe[3] and H. Balfour.[4] It has been applied extensively to explanations of primitive ornamental art. The most noteworthy contributions on this subject are those by Karl von den Steinen,[5] on the art of the Brazilian Indians, and by A. C. Haddon,[6] on the art of the natives of New Guinea.

Opposed to this view has been the theory propounded by Semper, who emphasizes the influence of material upon the development of the design, and that proposed by Cushing and Holmes,[7] who emphasize the importance of technique upon the development of geometrical design. More recently Karl von den Steinen[8] has also emphasized the importance of technical conditions upon the development of design, and his arguments have been followed and elaborated by Max Schmidt

---

[1] *Proceedings of the U. S. National Museum*, vol. 34 (1908), pp. 321–344.

[2] "Conventionalism in American Art," *Bulletin of the Essex Institute*, vol. 18 (1887).

[3] "Entwicklungserscheinungen in der Ornamentik der Naturvölker," *Mitteilungen der Anthropologischen Gesellschaft in Wien*, vol. 22 (1892), pp. 19 *et seq.*

[4] *The Evolution of Decorative Art* (London, 1893).

[5] *Unter den Naturvölkern Zentral-Brasiliens* (Berlin, 1894), pp. 258 *et seq.*

[6] *Evolution in Art* (1895).

[7] W. H. Holmes, "Textile Art in Relation to Form and Ornament," *6th Annual Report of the Bureau of Ethnology* (1884–85), p. 223.

[8] *Korrespondenzblatt der deutschen Gesellschaft für Anthropologie, Ethnologie und Urgeschichte*, vol. 35 (1905), p. 126.

in discussions of South American designs.[1] Th. Koch-Grünberg [2] follows in the same line of argument, showing that at least in Brazil a considerable number of cases may be found in which designs that have developed from technical motives receive a realistic significance.

From a wider point of view, the secondary development of motives and their re-interpretation as realistic designs have been claimed by Heinrich Schurtz [3] and by Professor Hamlin [4] in a discussion of the development of architectural decorative forms. The secondary character of symbolic interpretation has also been set forth by A. L. Kroeber,[5] Clark Wissler,[6] and by myself.[7]

We have therefore at the present time three distinct theories regarding the development of decorative design : First, the theory of the realistic origin of conventional motives; second, that of the technical origin of conventional motives; and, third, the theory that the explanations of conventional motives are essentially secondary in character, and due to a later association of the existing decorative forms with realistic forms.

I shall discuss in the following pages the decorative designs of Alaskan needlecases, largely from the region between the mouth of the Yukon River and the western part of Norton Sound, which seem to throw considerable light upon the history of decorative design, and illustrate the applicability of these various theories.

Among the carvings of Alaskan Eskimo we find a very large number of needlecases of peculiar form. They are of the characteristic tubular type of the Eskimo needlecase, in which the needle is inserted in a strip of skin pulled into a tube, which protects the needle against breakage. The peculiar type to which I here refer has, on the whole, a tube slightly bulging in the middle, and expanding into two wings or flanges at the upper end. It is characteristic of almost all these specimens that at a short distance below the flanges there are two small knobs on opposite sides of the tube. In some cases these are well marked, while in others they are so diminutive that they cannot

---

[1] *Indianerstudien in Zentralbrasilien* (Berlin, 1905), pp. 330 *et seq.*

[2] *Anfänge der Kunst im Urwald* (Berlin, 1905).

[3] *Urgeschichte der Kultur* (Leipzig, 1900), p. 540.

[4] *The American Architect and Building News* (1898).

[5] "Decorative Symbolism of the Arapaho," *American Anthropologist,* N.S., vol. 3 (1901), p. 329.

[6] "Decorative Art of the Sioux Indians," *Bulletin American Museum of Natural History,* vol. 18 (1904), pp. 231 *et seq.*

[7] "The Decorative Art of the North American Indians," *Popular Science Monthly* (1903), pp. 481 *et seq.,* see pp. 546 *et seq.* of this volume.

be seen at all, although they can be felt when moving the finger gently over the surface of the tube. They are a characteristic feature of this type, which is so well defined, and whose distribution is so restricted that there cannot be the slightest doubt as to the unity of its origin.

These needlecases have also a characteristic decoration. On the whole there is a tendency to set off a slightly concave surface, which extends along the faces of the tube, between the flanges and farther down. This concave face may be observed on the needlecases shown on figures 1 and 2. The flanges and the upper border of the tube are

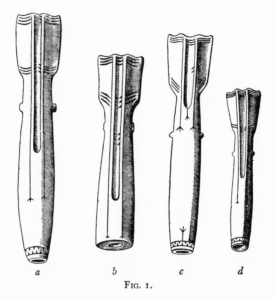

a   b   c   d

FIG. 1.

generally decorated by a design consisting of a number of parallel lines, which is repeated near the lower end of the flanges, where the parallel lines almost always slope slightly downward towards the tube. Similar line designs are also found on the concave face of the tube. In many cases these lines meet the lower lines on the flanges at an angle, being incised so that they slope downward from the middle line of the tube outward. In other cases they continue in the same direction as the lines on the flanges (figs. 1 *b*; 2 *a, b*). Many of the needlecases are so much polished and rubbed off by use that the design lines cannot be recognized distinctly. In other cases broken ends have been cut off (fig. 1 *b*), with the result that some of the characteristic decorative traits have become obscure. It would seem, however, that in all the better specimens of this simple type the central concave face of the needlecase is set off by two parallel incised lines, which extend downward to about the middle of the tubing, and which end at this place in two or three small spurs. The border designs on the flanges do not extend beyond these lines inward, so that they form the limits of the flanges. The parallel lines near the lower border of the flanges also generally end at the vertical lines.

Another characteristic decorative design of these needlecases is a narrow band extending around the lower end. This consists always,

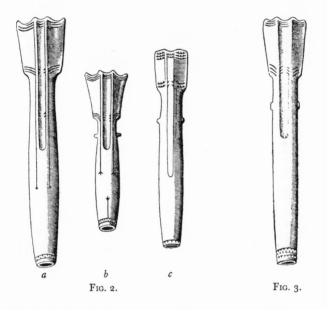

a   b   c

Fig. 2.   Fig. 3.

wherever it can be distinctly recognized, of two parallel lines with short alternating spurs directed toward the space between the two lines. Whenever these spurs are given a greater width this design assumes more or less the form of a zigzag band. A study of a considerable number shows clearly that the primary idea is not the zigzag band, but rather the two lines with alternating spurs. This is best shown by the fact that in those cases in which the lines are thin the alternation is often quite irregular. This may be observed, for instance, in the specimen shown in figure 3. On the whole, however, an alternation is observed. Bands of this kind may be recognized clearly in figures 1 *a, c, d*. Sometimes the band at the lower end appears doubled, or elaborated by the addition of short vertical lines with short spurs at their ends (figs. 1 c, 2b, 4). These lines are usually four in number. In the specimen shown in figure 5 a, two of these lines are absent, because their space is occupied by a long alternate-spur band which runs down the whole side of the needlecase. In another specimen one is absent, probably because the ivory at the place where it would be shows the soft inner part of the tusk, and has besides other defects. In figure 5 b, there is one of these lines on each side of the needlecase. In one specimen in the Ethnographical Museum of Berlin (IV A 5892) the number of these lines is more than four.

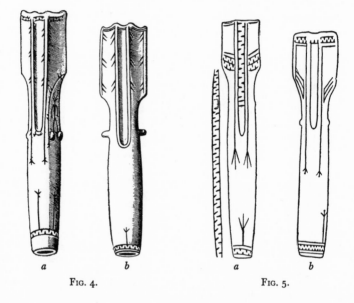

a   b   a   b

FIG. 4.   FIG. 5.

A partial doubling of the spur band may be observed on figs. 3 and 5 a.

The features here enumerated comprise those of the most generalized type of these needlecases. They may be briefly summed up as (1) a tube slightly bulging in the middle, (2) flanges at the upper end, (3) small knobs under the flanges, (4) long concave faces on opposite sides at the upper end of the tube, (5) long parallel lines with small forks at their lower ends setting off the concave faces, (6) border designs consisting of lines at the upper and lower ends of the flanges and on the concave face, and (7) an alternate-spur band at the lower end of the tube.

In order to understand the significance of this peculiar type of needle-case, we must bear in mind that the two design elements which are most characteristic of these specimens—namely, the line design with short branches and the alternate-spur design—are characteristic Eskimo motives over the greater part of the Arctic coast. The alternate spur band design is found on a number of very old specimens from Southampton Island and Lyons Inlet, collected by Capt. G. Comer, which are reproduced here in fig. 6 *a* and *c*. In the same region the forked-line design is found on bone engravings (fig. 6 *b*). It may be observed in a few of the specimens found by Parry in Fury and Hecla Straits in 1820 and on

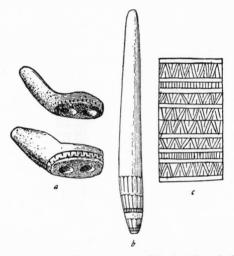

Fig. 6. *a*, Ivory attachment to line, west coast of Hudson Bay. *b*, Creaser, Iglulik. *c*, Design of needlecase, King William Land.

an ancient pair of ivory snow-goggles from Cumberland Sound (Ethn. Museum Berlin IV A 6833). It is also commonly found in tattooings. It occurs in the tattooings from the west coast of Hudson Bay, as well as in those from Baffin Land (fig. 7). Unfortunately I have not had opportunity to examine extensive collections from Greenland, in order to ascertain the occurrence of these designs. In view of their wide distribution over the whole Eskimo area, it seems justifiable to consider them as a very old possession of the Eskimo, and to assume that originally they bore no relation to the needlecases on which they are found with such great regularity. Incidentally it may be remarked that the explanations of these forms as bushes and whales' tails, which are given by the

Alaskan Eskimo, appear so one-sided that they cannot be accepted as a general interpretation.

The designs here mentioned do not seem to occur in parts of America or Asia which are outside of Eskimo influence. I have not been able to discover them on any objects of Indian manufacture except on a few specimens from the Yukon River made by Athapascan tribes directly under Eskimo influence. In Asia similar designs occur among the Koryak and Chukchee (fig. 8), while farther to the west and south I have not been able to find them. I am not certain whether the alternate-spur-line design does occur in the art of the Samoyed, but I have not discovered a single example in a large collection of Yakut specimens

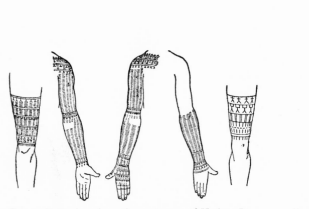

Fig. 7. Tattooings from the west coast of Hudson Bay and Hudson Strait.

Fig. 8. Ear-spoon, Kamchatka.

brought together by Mr. Jochelson; and it does not seem to occur among the Gilyak, Ainu, and southeastern Tungus tribes. It seems that the design occurs occasionally in Polynesian and Micronesian art, but I should not venture to conclude from this an historical relation, notwithstanding the rather large number of peculiar analogies between the northeast coast of the Pacific Ocean and the islands northeast of Australia.

Considering the continuous area in which the two designs occur, we may say that their essential home seems to be the Eskimo region, beginning with Alaska, and extending eastward and northeastward to Hudson Bay and Smith Sound, and that a few of the neighboring Indian tribes may have adopted them, and that they also occur among the neighboring Chukchee and Koryak.

One needlecase that has been found in the region of Southampton Island seems to me of particular importance in this connection (fig. 11 *a*). It will be seen that it also consists of a tube, like most Eskimo needlecases; that it expands widely near its upper end, the whole tube being flattened; and that near the middle there are two large wings, which correspond in their position to the small knobs of the Alaskan needlecases. This specimen has also the characteristic alternate-spur band of the Alaskan needlecases at its upper end, and the decoration is

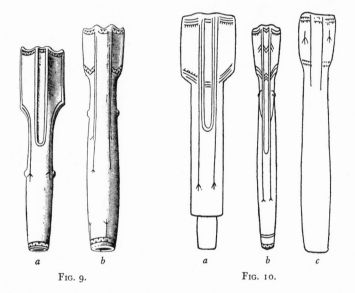

a	*b*	*a*	*b*	*c*
Fig. 9.		Fig. 10.		

repeated here in two parallel lines. Attention may be called to the occurrence of the same pattern at the same place in a number of the more complex specimens from Alaska, shown in figures 4 *b*, 5 *b*, 9. These and other similar occurrences show that the Eskimo often substituted this design for the single parallel lines.

The alternate-spur-band design is releated to the single spurred line, a pattern which is very common in many parts of the world. In the decorative art of the Eskimo it appears often in place of the alternate-spur band; for instance, on some needlecases of the type here discussed (see figs. 2 *c*, 10). In other cases the alternate-spur band is replaced by a ladder design (fig. 15 a) which on account of its rarity, may be considered as a degenerate form of the alternate-spur band.

A group of needlecases similar to the one just described from Southampton Island has been found in the district between Southampton Island and Smith Sound (figs. 11, 12). The only type of needlecase known from Smith Sound has this peculiar character. Unfortunately the specimens which I have seen are all exceedingly rough; but they all consist of a flattened tube, very wide at the upper end, and small

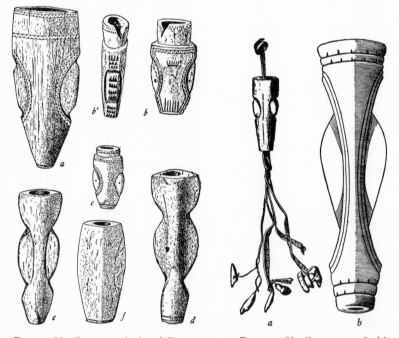

FIG. 11. Needlecases. *a, b, d, e, f*, Frozen Strait. *c*, Pond's Bay.

FIG. 12. Needlecases. *a*, Smith Sound. *b*, Rawlings Bay, west coast of Smith Sound.

and round at the lower end, provided at the sides with two characteristic wings (fig. 12 a). The same type with some dot decorations has been collected at Ponds Bay in the northern part of Baffin Land (fig. 11 c), while the older specimens from the northern part of Hudson Bay are much more elongated, and have the wings and flanges set off more clearly from the body of the needlecase (fig. 11 d, e).

A specimen in the British Museum from Rawlings Bay on the West coast of Smith Sound is of similar type (fig. 12 b).[1] It proves that this type extended from Hudson Bay northward over Grinnell Land to north Greenland.

It seems plausible that the Alaskan type and the Eastern type represent specialized developments of the same older type of needlecase, and that the flanges and diminutive knobs of the Alaskan specimens are homologous to the flanges and large wings of the Eastern specimens. When the first specimens of this kind were collected, Prof. O. T. Mason, according to information which he has kindly given to me, was inclined to believe that they were of foreign origin. In a note on the specimen shown in fig. 9 b, he wrote at that time:

"This specimen is a needlecase from St. Michael, Alaska. It is made of walrus ivory and carved in a form which suggests the butt end of an arrow, with two feathers projecting from opposite sides on the shaft. The likeness is made more striking by the fluting on the butt end, which resembles the nock of the arrow. A little in front of the two feathers are projecting bosses. The tube of the needlecase is slightly expanded in the middle and contracted at the smaller end. The ornamentation consists of narrow bands across the shaft, and the feathers at their extremities cut out in zigzag line very much in the style of Polynesian ornamentation. At the smaller end there is also a similarly ornamented band from which rise four symbols of shrubs. An exactly similar piece is figured in N. A. E. Nordenskiöld [2] and labeled "knife handle from Port Clarence." There are four of these objects in the United States National Museum and, compared with hundreds of others, they place themselves unmistakably in the class of needlecases. There is no doubt that these six specimens—five in the United States National Museum and one shown by Nordenskiöld—are not aboriginal in form or ornament; that they belong to a style of art introduced into Alaska after the advent of the Russians.

In Seebohm [3] will be seen the figure of a Samoyed needlecase with a tube of metal, inclosed at its top in a belt, and riveted along the side. The suggestion is here thrown out that the Eskimo artist has endeavored to reproduce in ivory a facsimile of this metal tube and a portion of the leather belt, even to the projecting rivets. The Nordenskiöld specimen has, in addition, walrus heads and seals carved on the side of the tube.

This Polynesian style of ornamentation is common on hundreds of Eskimo objects in and about St. Michael; for, after the advent of the Russians and intercourse with sailors of the Pacific Ocean, the arts of the two areas became very much entangled."

[1] *American Anthropologist*, N.S., vol. 11 (1909), p. 135.
[2] *Voyage of the Vega* (London, 1881), vol. 2, p. 241.
[3] *Siberia in Asia* (London, 1882), p. 56.

Considering the antiquity of the eastern specimens, it does not seem plausible that the Alaskan specimens are a newly developed type. Their great frequency and the fixity of the type are also not in favor of this view.

It might perhaps also be argued that the knobs serve for firmly attaching the needlecase to a skin strap, but there is no evidence whatever that the needlecases were thus suspended. They seem to have been carried like all other Eskimo needlecases, by an attachment to the strip of skin into which the needles are inserted.

It seems certain, therefore, that the diminutive knob of the Alaskan needlecase serves no practical end whatever, and that it is a purely conventional feature in the form of the utensil. It is true that the large wings and flanges of the Eastern needlecases also serve no practical end; but it seems well to bear in mind the close resemblance of the two types.

It is interesting to compare the simple types heretofore described with a number of more complex needlecases which clearly belong to the same type.

It would seem that, first of all, the strong inclination of the Alaskan Eskimo to decorate carved objects by means of incised designs has led to further developments of the patterns heretofore described. Examples of this kind may be observed in many specimens. In fig. 4 b, the same typical arrangement of flanges, knobs, and faces may be observed; but the concave face and vertical line are further decorated by oblique spurs placed in pairs, and the lower border design of the flange is elaborated as a single line with double oblique spurs also. On both sides of the needlecase, and surrounded by the line running downward along the lower border of the flange and on the body of the tube, is a design of what seems to be a human being with a caribou head, which stands on a line extending across the side of the needlecase, just over two knobs, the single knob on each side being doubled in this case. On the lowest point of the line surrounding the concave face stands a quadruped with long body and bent legs. Another type of elaboration and modification of the design is shown in figure 4 a, where the lines with pairs of oblique spurs have also been made use of. Many needlecases are so much worn down that the designs have become quite indistinct; but often the middle concave face was never well marked. These specimens resemble in general shape the characteristic designs, the forms are rounded off, and have lost many of their decorative traits. On the reverse side of one of these specimens (fig. 13), a double line with oblique spurs running outward from the lines is shown, but not in the middle of the needlecase. Its position is so irregular that it cannot be compared with the decorations of the specimens heretofore described. The specimen has quite an irregular line decoration on the flanges. A modern, roughly finished specimen (U.S.N.M. 33697) of the usual type has the concave face hollowed out deeply, and the flanges are set off more markedly than in the majority of specimens. The knobs have been moved very far downward. Fig. 9 *a* also seems to be a modern specimen, in which the vertical border lines of the concave face have been moved toward the border of the flanges, and where the upper border is replaced by an alternate-spur band. In this specimen the knobs are also moved very far downward. The specimen shown in figure 14, resembles in many respects

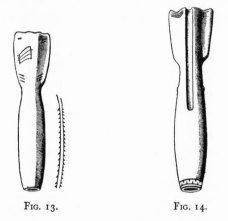

FIG. 13.   FIG. 14.

the one show in fig. 9 *a,* particularly in the depth of the concave faces and in the sharp angle formed by the flanges where they are set off from the body of the tube.

In figure 9 *b,* the border lines of the concave face consist of two forked lines on each side, and the border lines of the flanges have been transformed into alternate-spur bands. In fig. 10 *c* the same lines are etched as spur bands, and the forked-line design is placed on the flanges. There is no indication of knobs. In the specimen shown in fig. 5 *a* we find on the concave face of the tube an alternate-spur band added, which ends below, on the reverse and the obverse, with two parallel cross-lines. On the lower part of the flanges is shown, on one side a double alternate-spur band. The opposite side is laid out on the same plan, with the only exception that the cross-lines between the lowest pair of border lines are drawn right across (as in the bands in fig. 15 a). The whole side of this needlecase is flattened, beginning under the flange, down to the lower border. This flat field is occupied in its whole length by an alternate-spur band.

The bands in fig. 15 a are occupied by ladder designs instead of alternate-spur designs. Presumably this is the result of careless execution of the older spur design. Fig. 15 b shows a very careful technique, and it is characterized by a strict adherence to the general type, extreme smallness of the knobs, and elaboration of the decorative motives. Thus the

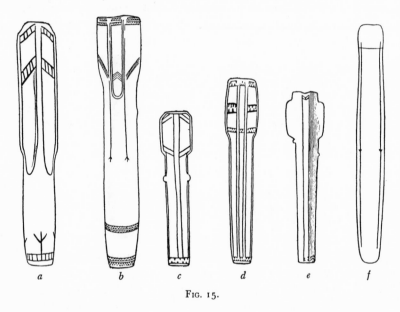

FIG. 15.

upper border consists here of two alternate-spur bands; the lower border of the flanges of a number of parallel lines which are very close together. The same kind of lines occur on the middle field. The decorative band at the lower end is also doubled, and repeated at a short distance above the lower end.

Other modifications are found in the following specimens. In fig. 15 c there is no middle concave face, but in its place we find two parallel lines which are carried down to the lower border. There are also two parallel lines on each side running down from the flanges to the lower border, and to the upper and lower border lines of the flanges are added vertical border lines, so that the whole flanges appear framed. The cross-section of this specimen is angular. In fig. 15 *d* two parallel lines are substituted for the concave face, as in the specimen just described. The sides of this needlecase are also flat while the back shows no vertical design and a rounded surface. Its only decoration consists of a continuous alternate-spur band design on top and at the lower end of the small flanges, continuing the corresponding bands on the front of the specimen and on the narrow sides of the flanges. This specimen has no indication of knobs.

Fig. 15 *e* is in many respects peculiar, particularly in so far as the two small knobs are not on the same level. The middle concave field is carried down to the lower end of the needlecase, as in the two preceding cases, and the whole needlecase is angular in cross-section. It has eight faces, which taper down toward the lower end. On the three faces on the right-hand side is the small double-angle decoration which has been indicated in our illustration. A double angle turned with its apex downward is also found on the lateral face on the right-hand side. As shown in the illustration, the flanges do not extend up to the top of the needlecase, as is the case in most specimens.

The needlecase represented in fig. 15 *f* illustrates a very peculiar reduction in the general form. The flanges have almost disappeared, and with them the upper and lower decorative border, as well as the border at the lower end of the tube; and all that remains to remind us of the form here discussed are four parallel forked lines, which, however, are continued beyond the forks. Nevertheless the impression given by the specimen in connection with the whole series is such that I do not doubt for a moment that it belonged originally to the series under discussion.

The series represented in the following figures seem to me of special interest from a theoretical point of view. The identity of the types of needlecases here shown with the preceding ones is perfectly obvious. The specimens collected in figures 16 and 17 show with perfect distinctness the bulging tube, the flange with its decoration, the knobs, and the concave face of the tube. Here part of the specimen seems to be conceived of as an animal. The bulging tube is the body of the animal, whose head has been added at the lower end. Although the transformation of the lower end of the needlecase into an animal has been perfected; it does not seem likely that the whole object was conceived as an animal form. If this were the case, the flanges, when transformed into the tail of a sea

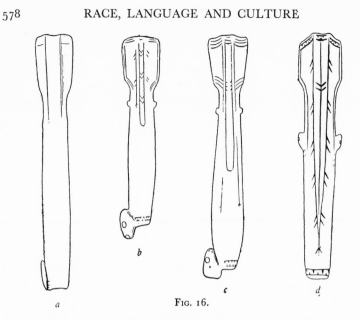

FIG. 16.

mammal, would probably have been modified, and the position of the head would be so changed as to be in proper relation to the tail.

It seems entirely artificial to assume that in this case the animal form as such could possibly have preceded the typical needlecase as before described, but that we are dealing here evidently with a secondary inter-

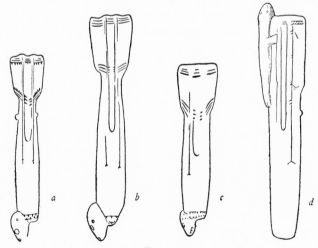

FIG. 17.

pretation of the design, which finds expression in the addition of the animal head and in other later additions to the whole form. In figs. 16 *b, c* and 17 *a-c,* the entire old design may be recognized in all its details; even the alternate-spur band remains, although it interferes with the form of the seal's head which has been added. In fig. 16 *c* the head of the animal has been turned, so that the lower part of the needle-case looks like a sea animal swimming on its back. A similar specimen from the Ethnographical Museum in Berlin is shown in fig. 18. It has a unilateral small knob. In fig. 16 *a* we find what may be a still further development of the original design here described. The seal's head has

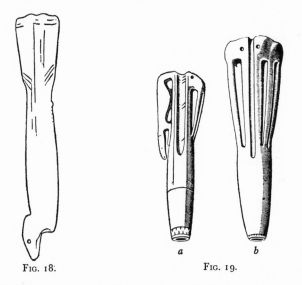

FIG. 18.   FIG. 19.

disappeared again, and in its place we find a simple knob. There are three parallel lines near the lower ends of this knob, which makes the whole area, seen from the top, look a little like a small crustacean. The knobs in this specimen are very small. I consider it quite possible that here we may have a case where, under the stress of older forms of the needlecases, a partial reversion to the original type has taken place.

The strong tendency of the Eskimo to utilize animal motives has found expression in another manner in the specimen represented in fig. 16.*d.* Here the small lateral knobs have been considerably enlarged and have been given the form of seals' heads. I believe that here also there can be no doubt in regard to the question whether the seal's head or the knobs are older. If the knob had to be considered as a degenerate form of the seal's head, it would hardly be intelligible why only one or two specimens out of a great number should retain the heads in this place, while in practically all other cases the reduction to a simple knob, sometimes so small that it can hardly be felt, should have occurred. It

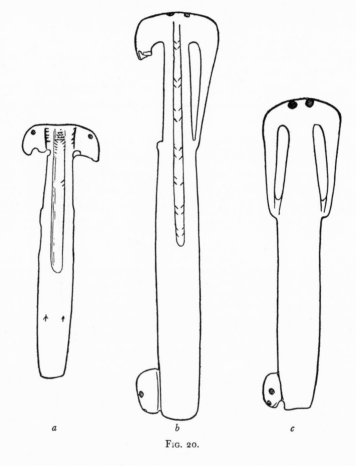

a   b   c

FIG. 20.

seems quite evident that in this case the imagination of the artist was stimulated by the traditional knob, and that it has been developed, owing to a desire to further decorate the utensil, into a seal's head. The modification of the central concave face of this specimen is quite in accord with other modifications of the same surface, which have been described before. On the reverse of this needlecase the pairs of oblique spurs attached to the converging lines are directed toward the upper part of the needlecase.

In the following figures a number of specimens have been collected, in which another part of the needlecase has been modified through the general tendency of the Eskimo artists to introduce animal designs. Instead of the lower end, the flange has been thus developed. The procedure appears perhaps clearest in the specimen shown in fig. 19 *a,* where on one side the flange shows a number of perforations and modifications, by means of which it has been developed into a quadruped, while on the other side a walrus head has been developed by making a long slit along the body of the tube and by inserting an eye, and lines indicating nostrils and mouth, near the upper border. Thus the outer sides of the flanges form the tusks of the walrus head, while the top forms the head itself. The specimen here referred to shows clearly its close relation to the original type of needlecase. The decoration of the lower part and the concave face may still be observed. The characteristic decorations of the concave face are also indicated. In fig. 20 we find the same type of needlecase with a double walrus head at the top. In most of the specimens the tusks have been broken off. In fig. 20 *a* traces of the vertical forked lines bordering the middle field also remain. In the specimens shown in fig. 20 *a* and *b* the middle concave face is quite distinct. In figs. 20 *b* and *c* two specimens are represented which combine a modification of the lower end of the needlecase with that of the upper end. At the lower end a seal head is shown on one side, as in the specimens previously discussed, while at the upper end the double walrus head is found. In one of these specimens the middle concave face is well marked, although it is not bordered by an incised line.

Fig. 21.

The next group of modifications of the old type of needlecase follows the same direction as those just desribed, the flanges being modified so as to represent an animal on each side. A specimen of this type is shown in fig. 21, where a walrus with head stretched forward is shown. The tusks touch the upper end of the tube, while the two flippers are shown at the lower end. Two seals are shown in the same position on fig. 22 *g,* while two quadrupeds occupy the position of the flanges in figs. 22 *a, f.* In fig. 22 *d* the quadrupeds appear doubled; and in fig. 22 *h* the seals have so much increased in size that they occupy the whole side of the needlecase. However, in this case also, the close relation between all these types can easily be demonstrated by an examination of figs. 22 *d* and *g* which retain all the characteristic traits of the simple type. The two animals in fig. 22 *f* seem to represent lemmings. They are placed somewhat differently from the ordinary form of the flanges, but are

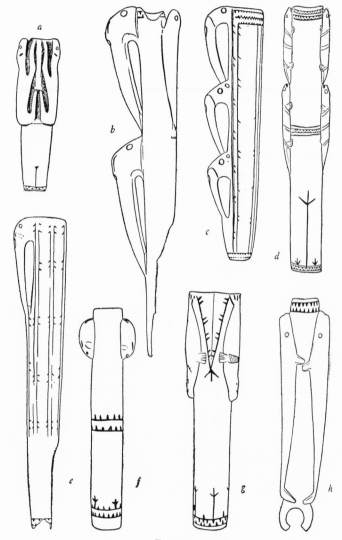

Fɪɢ. 22.

evidently developed from forms like those shown in figs. 22 *a* and *g*. A specimen in which the one side of the needlecase retains the ordinary shape, while the opposite side of the flange has been transformed into an animal, is represented in fig. 17 *d*.

In this case also it would seem exceedingly difficult to interpret the simple geometrical form of the needlecase as a later development from the animal representations here discussed. In this case, similarities of the decorative designs on the tubings would be entirely unintelligible, while the assumption that the animal forms have developed from the geometrical forms seems to give a very plausible explanation of the forms.

The specimens in which the upper end has been so modified as to become a double walrus head lead us to another group in which the walrus head is repeated a number of times along the sides of the tube. Specimens of this kind are represented in figs. 22 *b* and *c*. In both of these traces of the old upper and lower border decoration remain, and fig. 22 *c* also shows the typical oblique spurs in pairs in the same position which has been described several times. It therefore seems perfectly natural to interpret these forms as the result of repetitions of the animal design, which was first developed from the flanges of the needlecase. Figs. 22 *c* and *e* differ from other specimens of their kind in that they have the walrus head developed only on one side, while on the opposite side the flange is suppressed.

As has been indicated, the geometrical decorations of the typical flanged needlecases reappear in many of these highly modified specimens. Attention may also be called to the forked-line designs which rise from the lower border in the usual number in the specimens shown in figs. 22 *d*, *f* and *g*. In the last named specimen the number of these lines is five. The deviation in number may be due to inaccuracy in laying out the ornament. In fig. 22 *d* there are two forked designs on opposite sides, while on each side from the tails of the animals down to the lower border runs an alternate-spur band. Between the alternate-spur bands and the long forked lines there are short forked lines, as indicated in the illustration. Only in fig. 22 *h* do we find an important modification of the lower end of the needlecase, which forms a ring. That in our specimen has been broken. The backs of the two needlecases shown in figs. 22 *c* and *e* are somewhat flat. It is of interest to compare the line decoration of the latter needlecase with the one shown in fig. 4 *b,* which is a simple modification of the fundamental type.

The illustrations, figs. 23 *a* and *b,* of two needlecases in human form, are not quite as convincing as the specimens themselves; but a comparison of these forms with the other needlecases of this series seems to me to suggest with great force that the human figures here shown are related to the same type of needlecase that we are discussing. The whole human

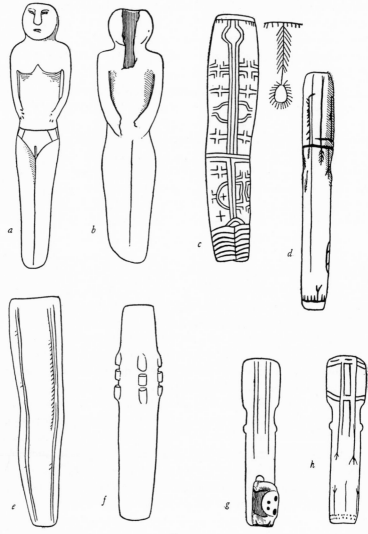

FIG. 23.

figure is treated as a tube, and it is my opinion that the bulging hips correspond to the bulging middle part of the needlecase, while the arms correspond to the flanges, and perhaps more particularly to developments of the flanges similar to the walrus-head developments, while the head is a later development of the upper border, suggested by the perception of the similarity of the whole form to a human figure. I do not wish to imply that the human figure in this case has necessarily developed from the type of needlecase first discussed; but it seems plausible to me that an assimilation between the human figure and this type has taken place in the two specimens here illustrated. It seems likely that the animal figure shown in fig. 24 must be considered in a similar manner. There is no doubt that the vivid representation of the animal lying down has very little to do with our type of needlecase; nevertheless I cannot free myself from the impression that the artist, in his treatment of the subject, has been influenced by the treatment of the flanges of needlecases and by the general form of this utensil. There is a certain similarity between the position of the feet and the positions of the walrus tusks shown in figs. 19 and 20, which is not explained by a realistic treatment of the animal alone; and the same is true of the position of the neck and head and of the curves in the hind part of the body.

Fɪɢ. 24.

The similarities which I am discussing here are even less clear in some of the other specimens represented here. Fig. 23 c evidently represents a human leg, the design on one side being a representation of tattooing. In this case faint traces of the upper border design and of the lower border design remain, and the outline of the whole specimen still recalls to a certain extent the bulging tube below and the wider part with its flanges above. If we agree to accept this specimen as belonging to the present series, the specimen shown in fig. 23 e, must be considered as belonging here also. There is no doubt that fig. 23 d belongs to our series. The tube and the knobs are the same as those occurring in the most typical specimens. Instead of the concave faces, we have merely flat surfaces, and the flanges have been much reduced in size, but are perfectly distinct and sharply set off. The ornamentation, however, differs on the flanges and concave faces from the ordinary decoration. Besides the designs shown in the illustration, we have on the back of the flange to the right, a line with two pairs of one-sided oblique spurs running downward and a forked line running down from the black ring, like the one shown on the right-hand side of the illustration. On the right-hand side of the lower part of the needlecase an etched design, representing a quadruped with long tail, will be observed. Fig. 23 *f* shows a simple tube with four groups of knobs, which may have been suggested by the knobs of the specimens here described. Figs. 23 *g* and *h* represent a needlecase, which on one side shows the typical form of the flanged specimens, while on the opposite side the head, neck, and fore-paws of an animal are set off.

Another geometrical development of the ordinary type is represented in fig. 25 *a*. In this specimen the general outline of the flanged tube is

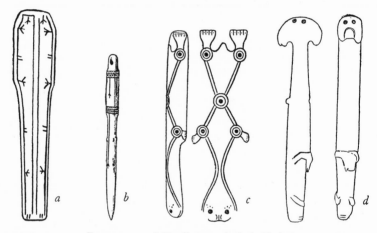

FIG. 25. *a, c, d*, Needlecases. *b*, Awl, Alaska.

readily recognized, but all the other characteristic features have disappeared.

In fig. 26 specimens are illustrated the relations of which to the flanged type are very doubtful. The knobs in fig. 26 *a*, which are doubled in the axial direction and appear on four sides of the tube, are analogous to those shown in fig. 23 *f*; and these two types are undoubtedly closely related. Attention may be called to the awl-like implement illustrated in fig. 25 *b*, which shows the same four knobs here described, and which therefore in its origin may well be related to the decorative designs on the needlecases. The animal types figs. 26 *b-e* and fig. 25 *c*, diverge so much from the flanged type that their relationship seems very doubtful. Still I cannot free myself of the impression of a certain

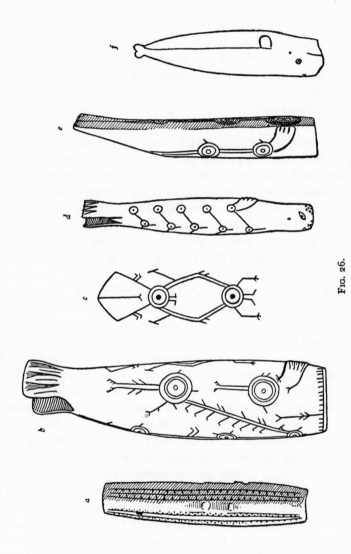

Fig. 26.

influence of the flanged types upon these forms also. This becomes apparent by a comparison of the needlecase shown in fig. 25 *d* with the animal types here discussed. It is quite evident that this specimen has its affiliations both with the animal types and the walrus-head types shown in figs. 19 and 20. It is, however, also possible that its form has originated by assimilation of two distinct types.

The conclusion which I draw from a comparison of the types of needlecases here represented is that the flanged needlecase represents an old conventional style, which is ever present in the mind of the Eskimo artist who sets about to carve a needlecase. The various parts of the flanged needlecase excite his imagination; and a geometrical element here or there is developed by him, in accordance with the general tendencies of Eskimo art, into the representation of whole animals or of parts of animals. In this manner, the small knobs or the flanges are developed into heads of animals. After this modification has once set in, the animal figures may be repeated on other parts of the implement. Besides this, associations between animal forms and the form of the whole needlecase seem to have taken place, which have to a certain extent modified the manner of representing animal forms which were adapted to use as needlecases; so that the old form and style of the needlecase determined the treatment of the animal form.

If we were to apply to the present series the theory of the origin of conventional form from realistic motives, it would be exceedingly difficult to account for the general uniformity of the fundamental type. It seems to me that, on the basis of this theory, we could not account for the diversity of realistic forms and the uniformity of general type. Neither does it seem possible to account for the series of types by assumption of any influence of technique; and my impression is that the only satisfactory explanation lies in the theory that the multifarious forms are due to the play of the imagination with a fixed conventional form, the origin of which remains entirely obscure. This I freely acknowledge. If, however, we are to form an acceptable theory of the origin of decorative designs, it seems a safer method to form our judgment based on examples the history of which can be traced with a fair degree of certainty, rather than on speculations in regard to the origin of remote forms for the development of which no data are available.

I believe a considerable amount of other evidence can be brought forward sustaining the point of view that I have tried to develop, namely, that decorative forms may be largely explained as results of the play of the imagination under the restricting influence of a fixed conventional style. Looking at this matter from a purely theoretical point of view, it is quite obvious that in any series in which we have at one end a realistic figure and at the other end a conventional figure, the arrangement is due entirely to our judgment regarding similarities. If, without further proof, we interpret such a series as a genetic series, we simply substitute for the classificatory principle which has guided us in the arrangement of the series a new principle which has nothing to do with the principle of our classification. No proof whatever can be given that the series selected according to similarities really represents an historical sequence. It is just as conceivable that the same series may begin at the conventional end and that realistic forms have been read into it, and we might interpret the series, therefore, as an historical series beginning at the opposite end. Since both of these tendencies are active in the human mind at the present time, it seems much more likely that both processes have been at work constantly, and that neither the one nor the other theory really represents the historical development of decorative design.

The assumption of a development from realistic design to conventional design also omits the consideration of one exceedingly important element, namely, the style of convention that prevails in the types of art of different areas. If geometrical designs developed from realistic motives the world over, it still would remain to be proved why a certain style of conventionalism belongs to one art and another style to another art; and in order to explain in a satisfactory way the different styles of art, we should have to accept these as given at a very early stage during the process of conventionalization of realistic designs.

The attempt to explain the processes of conventionalization by the theory of the influence of technical motives does not seem to offer an entirely adequate solution of this problem. It is true that certain very simple designs seem to be due almost entirely to the influence of technique upon simple decorative tendencies. This influence, however, does not reach so far as to determine in detail the character of design in the same kind of material or in the same technique. As examples of such differences may be mentioned, for instance, the designs in woven checkered mattings from West Africa, where peculiar realistic figures alternate with geometrical band designs; the designs of cedar-bark mattings of the Ojibwa and of those of the North Pacific coast, and of designs made in the same technique by the South American Indians. In all these cases the technical conditions are practically the same, but the styles differ vastly. It seems necessary, therefore, to assume in the development of design the existence of tendencies which are due to causes different from the technique, and unrelated to the realistic motives which may be current or may have been current.

I have no theory to offer in regard to the origin of these types of convention, which presumably was connected with a whole series of activities determining the perception and reproduction of forms; but it seems desirable to illustrate by a number of instances the fixity of these conventional forms and the deep influence that they have had even in apparently realistic forms. I have pointed out in the discussion of the designs of the blankets of the Chilkat Indians that a great many of the older forms can be reduced to two fundamental types, and that, no matter what animal may be represented in the art of the weaver, it is almost always reduced to one of these two forms.[1] In the same place I have shown that the treatment of the animal figure on carved boxes of the Tlingit has other fixed conventional forms, which, although closely related to the blanket design, are quite permanent and applied only in the manufacture of boxes.[2]

In a quite different region, among the Tungus tribes of the Amur River, Dr. Berthold Laufer has shown that one of the essential types determining the whole arrangement of decorative designs, which consist of realistic figures as well as of curved lines, is based on the type of "cocks combatant." [3]

It is also important to note that figures conforming to such fundamental types may be interpreted in a great variety of ways by the people who use them. I have pointed out such a similarity of type and fundamental difference of interpretation in explanations given by the Huichol Indians.[4] Here we find practically the same figures once interpreted as the freshwater crab, and then as oak leaves and stems. Other more extended series of such ambiguous interpretations may be found in the art of the Plains Indians as well as in those of other parts of the world.[5]

I have suggested before that in many cases these forms seem to compel

[1] G. T. Emmons, "The Chilkat Blanket," *Memoirs of the American Museum of Natural History*, vol. 3 (1907), p. 355.

[2] *Ibid.*, pp. 357 *et seq.*

[3] *Publications of the Jesup North Pacific Expedition*, vol. 4 (1902), pp. 22 *et seq.*

[4] Carl Lumholtz, "Decorative Art of the Huichol Indians," *Memoirs of the American Museum of Natural History*, vol. 3 (1900), p. 287 and Figs. 451 and 465.

[5] A. L. Kroeber, "The Arapaho," *Bulletin of the American Museum of Natural History*, vol. 18 (1902); Clark Wissler, "Decorative Art of the Sioux Indians," *ibid.*, vol. 18, part 3 (1904).

us to assume that the interpretations of many simple forms are entirely secondary; that often the forms have been borrowed; and that later on, according to their use in the life of the people, they have been given a fitting interpretation.[1]

I think evidence can be brought forward also to show that the tendency to play, and the play of the imagination with existing forms, have deeply influenced the decorative art of primitive tribes as we find it at the present time.

The first of these traits appears with particular clearness in the tendency to use rhythmic repetitions of varying forms. Bead necklaces are one of the most striking examples of the pleasure that man receives through the use of rhythmic repetition of colors and forms. Among primitive tribes the rhythmic and symmetrical order of such arrangements are often exceedingly complex,—so complex, in fact, that they can be recognized by us only by a close study of the arrangement. A case of this kind occurs in the fringe on a pair of leggings collected among the Thompson Indians, which I have described.[2] In this specimen we have a fringe which hangs down in a very disorderly fashion, so that the constituent elements cannot be seen distinctly. Nevertheless a most painstaking arrangement of the component elements is adhered to, the rhythmic unit consisting of five elements,—one string having one glass bead and two bone beads in alternating order, one undecorated string, one having alternating glass and bone beads, one undecorated, and one having one glass bead and two bone beads in alternating order. I have found still more complex rhythmic repetitions and symmetrical arrangements on the embroidered borders of coats of the Koryak. These contained sometimes ten and more elements in one group.[3] Still another case of similar kind, from Peru, has been described by Mr. Mead.[4] Here a rhythmic repetition of six units seems to be very common.

I consider it particularly important to observe that in the first of these specimens the rhythmic repetition cannot be seen when the leggings are in use, because this suggests strongly that the reason for the application of the rhythmic repetition is not the aesthetic pleasure in the effect which it produces, but the pleasure felt by the maker. If this is true, then we

---

[1] See p. 562 of this volume.
[2] *Publications of the Jesup North Pacific Expedition*, vol. 1 (1906), p. 384, fig. 313.
[3] *Publications of the Jesup North Pacific Expedition*, vol. 6, part 2 (1908), pp. 689 *et seq.*
[4] *Boas Anniversary Volume* (1906), pp. 193 *et seq.*

do not need to assume that in the other cases a much more highly developed appreciation of complex rhythm is found among primitive people than the one we possess. Corroborative evidence in regard to this point is offered by the basketry of the Thompson and Lillooet Indians. I have noticed that here, where in a fine imbricated technique color bands are produced, the basket weavers tend to use with great regularity certain groupings of the number of stitches belonging to each color, although, owing to the irregularity of the size of the stitches, these modifications can hardly be observed.[1] If these facts have a wider application, it would seem that on the whole the pleasure given by much of the decorative work of primitive people must not be looked for in the beauty of the finished product, but rather in the enjoyment which the maker feels at his own cleverness in playing with the technical elements that he is using. In other words, one of the most important sources in the development of primitive decorative art is analogous to the pleasure that is given by the achievements of the virtuoso.

Examples may also be given illustrating the effect of the play of imagination upon the development of design. One of the best examples of this kind is offered by the decorated bag of the Thompson Indians illustrated by Professor Farrand.[2] The analogy of this soft rectangular bag, which is decorated with rows of large diamonds, to other similar bags shows quite clearly that the rows of diamonds have the same origin as the rows of diamonds which are painted on parfleches of the Plains Indians. In this case the diamonds suggested the idea of ponds; and, in order to emphasize this idea, which came to the mind of the woman who used the bag, she added a number of birds flying toward these ponds. Other examples of this kind have been mentioned by Doctor Koch-Grünberg in his observations on the drawings of South American Indians. The development of the triangles in the designs of the Plains Indians to tent designs or cloud designs brings out similar points.

Thus it would seem that the development of decorative designs cannot be simply interpreted by the assumption of a general tendency toward conventionalism or by the theory of an evolution of technical motives into realistic motives by a process of reading in, but that a considerable number of other psychic processes must be taken into consideration if we desire to obtain a clear insight into the history of art.

[1] *Publications of the Jesup North Pacific Expedition*, vol. 2 (1906), p. 206.
[2] *Ibid.*, vol. 1, Plate xxxiii, fig. 1.

THE RELATIONSHIPS OF THE ESKIMOS OF
EAST GREENLAND [1]

D R. W. THALBITZER describes in the "Meddelelser om Grønland," vol. XXVIII, the Amdrup collection from east Greenland,
which comprises objects found between the sixty-eighth and seventy-
fifth degrees of north latitude. The publication is of great interest, because it brings out conclusively the close relationship between the culture
of the northeast coast of Greenland and that of Ellesmere Land, northern Baffin Land and the northwestern part of Hudson Bay. The similarities are so far-reaching that I do not hesitate to express the opinion
that the line of migration and cultural connection between northeast
Greenland and the more southwesterly regions must have followed the
shores of Ellesmere Land, the northern coast of Greenland, and then
southward along the east coast. One of the most suggestive types found
in Dr. Thalbitzer's publication is a needlecase, page 421 (fig. 1). I
have called attention to the distribution of this type of needlecase in my
paper on the "Eskimo of Baffin Land and Hudson Bay," [2] and in the
discussion of the decorative designs of Alaskan needlecases. [3] The specimens described in these two publications are from Frozen Strait in Hudson Bay, Ponds Bay and Smith Sound. Later on I discussed another
needle-case of the same type from Rawlings Bay in Ellesmere Land, [4]
(fig. 12 b, p. 572 of this volume). Among these only those from Ponds Bay
and Smith Sound were found in actual use, while the others were collected from ancient house-sites. Two similar specimens are figured by
Dr. Thalbitzer. These were found in the region of northwestern Greenland, that is, near the island of Disco. The ornamentation on the specimens here is identical with the alternating spur decoration which was
discussed by Stolpe in his studies of American ornament, and by myself
in the discussion of Alaskan needle-cases before referred to. The same

[1] From *Science*, N.S., vol. 30, No. 772 (Oct. 15, 1909), pp. 535–536.
[2] *Bulletin American Museum of Natural History*, vol. 15, part 2 (1907), p. 433.
[3] *Proceedings of the U. S. National Museum*, vol. 34 (1908), p. 326. (See pp. 571
of this volume.)
[4] *American Anthropologist*, N.S., vol. 2 (1909), p. 135; see p. 572 of this volume.

ornament occurs in the ornamentation of a comb shown on page 472 of Dr. Thalbitzer's publication.

Among the other specimens, sealing-stools (pp. 430, 431) seem to be particularly important. They are very similar in form to a specimen found by Peary in Grinnell Land.[1] The ice-scraper of bone figured on page 438 must be compared with the set of implements shown on page 409, "Eskimo of Baffin Land and Hudson Bay." Even the perforation for suspending the scraper agrees with those of specimens from Southampton Island. There seems to me little doubt that the hammer-like implement illustrated on page 442 of Dr. Thalbitzer's publication is a

FIG. 1. Needlecases, east Greenland.

blubber-pounder similar to those made of musk-ox horn illustrated on page 402 of my paper on the "Eskimo of Baffin Land." The bone heads of adzes [2] agree fairly well with those shown on page 381.[3] The decoration on the handles of the bodkins [4] may perhaps be compared to the handles of the wick-trimmers from Melville Peninsula.[5]

All these types which show close correspondence in form are so much specialized that they must be considered as evidence of old contact or of sameness of origin. So far as I am aware, none of these types have been

[1] "Eskimo of Baffin Land and Hudson Bay," *op. cit.*, p. 463.
[2] Thalbitzer, p. 449.
[3] Boas, "Eskimo of Baffin Land, etc.," compare also *ibid.*, p. 416.
[4] Thalbitzer, p. 399.
[5] Boas, *op. cit.*, p. 403.

found in the region between Disco and Cape Farewell, nor do they occur in Angmagsalik. If this is true, the conclusion seems unavoidable that the Eskimos reached the northeast coast of Greenland by way of the north coast.

C. Ryder has called attention to the similarity of some of the east Greenland types to those from Alaska, and Thalbitzer again calls attention to the similarity of the harpoon-shafts to those of Point Barrow (p. 444). I have called attention to several other similarities of this kind, particularly the alternating spur decoration,[1] to which Thalbitzer also refers (p. 472), and the forms of several specimens.[2] Similarities between the Ponds Bay region and the western regions have also been pointed out by Dr. Wissler in his description of a collection made by Captain James Mutch in that region.[3] The distribution of types suggests very strongly that a line of migration or of cultural contact may have extended from the Mackenzie region northeastward over the Arctic Archipelago to north Greenland, passing over the most northerly part of Baffin Land, and that the culture of southwestern Greenland, and that of southeastern Baffin Land and of Labrador, must be considered as specialized types.

[1] See p. 567 of this volume.
[2] Boas, *op. cit.*, pp. 461–464.
[3] *Anthropological Papers of the American Museum of Natural History,* vol. 2, part 3 (1909), pp. 316–318.

THE IDEA OF THE FUTURE LIFE AMONG
PRIMITIVE TRIBES [1]

A MONG the many attempts that have been made to describe and
explain the origin and development of the concepts of soul and
immortality the one made by Edward B. Tylor in his "Primitive Culture" is most exhaustive and carefully thought out. Although since the
publication of his work, much new evidence has been accumulated, the
new data may well be fitted into his general treatment of the subject.

We are, however, no longer quite ready to accept his interpretation
of the material which he has so assiduously collected and marshalled in
logical order. To him the ideas by which primitive man expresses his
sense experience are a result of speculative thought, of reasoning that
leads to a consistent view of the world. These thoughts, being determined by the general state of cultural life, lead to concepts which naturally develop one from the other and represent a typical series which
arises regardless of race and of historical affiliations. It is true that,
sometimes, he sets aside the latter point of view and recognizes specific
forms of thought which belong to various cultural groups, such as the
Indo-Europeans on the one hand, the Semites on the other, but these
approaches to an historical treatment are entirely subordinated to the
general evolutional viewpoint in which certain cultural types appear as
belonging to the evolutionary stages of primitive, barbaric or civilized
society.

We are, at present, more inclined to consider the growth of ideas, not
as a result of rational processes, but rather as an involuntary growth,
and their interpretation as the outcome of rationalization when, together
with correlated action, they rise into consciousness. We recognize that
the rationalizing interpretation of an idea does not by any means necessarily represent its historical growth, and that a classification of ideas
from a definite viewpoint, beginning with those that seem to be simple
and proceeding to those that seem complex, cannot without further

[1] *Religion and the Future Life,* edited by E. Hershey Sneath (New York, 1922),
pp. 9–26. With permission of Fleming H. Revell Company.

proof be interpreted as historical sequence, but may give an entirely distorted picture of historical happenings.

We may trace the development of the concepts "soul" and "immortality" in the history of Europe and of other countries in which historical data are available, but the attempt to give an historical interpretation for people without recorded history is liable to lead to quite fallacious results if based on nothing else than a classification of data according to their complexity.

Nevertheless, the problem that Tylor set himself remains. There are decided similarities in the views held regarding "soul" and "immortality" among peoples that in measurable time cannot have had any historical connection. There is, however, danger of overlooking, on account of a general resemblance, significant dissimilarities which may have value from an historical point of view. It is unavoidable that we should base our considerations, as Tylor did, on the data of individual psychology and that we should try to understand how, in a given cultural setting, man may be led to form certain concepts. In following out this method, we should, however, take into consideration the effects of secondary rationalization and the historical facts that may have influenced the ways by which simple ideas grew into complex dogma.

From this point of view Tylor's treatment appears to us as too schematic. He does not take into consideration the multifarious mental conditions that may lead to the concepts "soul" and "immortality," but he selects a few and bases his conclusions upon their general applicability. Now and then he does mention the possibility of alternative mental states that might lead to similar results, only to revert to his main explanation.

The difference in point of view appears most clearly in Tylor's summing up of his explanation of the occurrence of the belief in multiple souls: [1] "Terms corresponding with those of life, mind, soul, spirit, ghost, and so forth, are not thought of as describing really separate entities, so much as the several forms and functions of one individual being. Thus the confusion which prevails in our own thought and language, in a manner typical of the thought and language of mankind in general, is in fact due not merely to vagueness of terms, but to an ancient theory of substantial unity which underlies them."

We are inclined to take for our starting point precisely the opposite point of view.

[1] Edward B. Tylor, *Primitive Culture* (London, 1891), vol. 1, p. 435.

The unconscious growth of concepts is expressed nowhere more clearly than in language. In many languages we find the tendency to conceptualize a quality, a condition, or even an habitual action, which then appears in the form of a noun. It is not by any means necessary that the occurrence of such concepts must lead to an imaginative process by means of which they are given concrete form, but it gives ready opportunity for such development. We still feel the force in the use of metaphorical expressions which are based on the concrete form given to a term that from a logical point of view, is of attributive character. These metaphors may be modern or based on ancient patterns.

It is noticeable that particularly the states and functions of physical and mental life do not appear to primitive man as qualities, conditions or actions, but as definite concepts which tend to take on concrete form. Even in modern science we are still struggling with the confusion between substance and attribute in the analysis of such concepts as matter and energy.

We do not mean to imply by this that mythology, as Max Müller states, "is a disease of language," that all mythological concepts originate from misinterpreted or reinterpreted linguistic forms; we rather mean that the formation of concepts is not the same in all languages and that in particular the grouping of what is substance and what attribute, is not always made in the same way, and that many attributes are conceived as substance. It does not seem plausible that linguistic form should be subsequent to the conscious conceptualization of an attribute as a substance. The two must rather be considered as concomitant and interdependent phenomena. It is quite conceivable that where the tendency to objectivation of attributes prevails, later on the transformation of other attributes into objects may follow by analogy, but the primary basis cannot be considered in any way as due to a conscious classification,—just as little as the classification of the spectrum into a limited number of fundamental color terms can be due to conscious conceptualization of a number of selected colors.

On the basis of these considerations we interpret the fact that many manifestations of life take concrete forms as an effect of the tendency to conceive certain classes of attributes as substances. In modern languages terms like hunger, courage, love, sin, consciousness, death, are either owing to traditional usage or to poetic imagination, endowed with qualities, even with concrete forms.

The more distinctly a quality is conceived as a concrete substance, the less will its existence be bound up with the object possessing the quality in question. If success in hunting is conceived as a substance that may associate itself with a person, it will exist independently of the person who may acquire it or lose it and after his death it will continue to exist as it existed before its acquisition. When a sin is conceived as a substance, as is done by the Eskimo, it has an independent existence. It attaches itself to a person ; it may be separated from the sinner, and continue to exist independently until attached to some other person. They are no longer qualities that die with the individual to whom they belong. Sickness is often conceived not as a condition of the body, but as an extraneous object that may enter the body of a person and may be extracted again, or that may be thrown into it. This foreign substance that acts upon the living being may be as permanent in its existence as the earth, the heavens and the waters.

In all these cases there is no integral association between the object and its objectivated quality. Each leads an independent existence. The quality of the expert hunter, or the faculty of the shaman may be conceived as objects or as personalities that assist the man with whom they are associated. They are different from his own personality and we designate them as magical objects or as helping spirits.

There is, however, another group of qualities considered as substances which are most intimately connected with human life and without which a person is not a complete living being. Life, power of action, personality belong to this group. Wherever they occur in one form or another we designate them as "soul." The soul represents the objectivated qualities which constitute either the ideal human being or the individual personality. A study of the terms which are ordinarily translated as "soul" shows clearly that the equivalents in primitive tongues represent a variety of qualities of living man, and that their meaning varies accordingly.

Often the term "life" corresponds to what we call "soul." Thus the Chinook Indian of Northwest America says that when "life" leaves the body man must die, and that if it is returned to the body, he will recover. "Life" is an objectivation of all that differentiates the living person from the dead body. It leads a separate existence and, therefore, continues to exist after death.

"Life" itself is not always conceived as a unit. When a paralyzed arm or leg has lost its power of motion, its separate "life" has gone, but the person continues to live as long as the "great life" that belongs to the whole body stays with him. It is not by any means necessary that the "life" should be conceived in anthropomorphic form; it is sometimes considered as an object or as an animal such as a butterfly. As long as it stays in the body, its owner is alive; when it leaves, he dies; when it is hurt, he sickens.

In a wider sense the power to act, the will power, is classified not as a function of the living body, but as something substantial, of independent existence. We might call it the personality separated from the person. In a way it is another form under which life is conceptualized. On account of its closer association with the form of living man, it is very liable to appear in anthropomorphic form.

There is no sharp line that separates this concept from the products of imagery, in so far as these are not understood as functions of mental life, but as independent objects. Tylor and others have discussed fully and adequately the effects of the products of imagination in dreams and trance experiences in which man finds his body in one place while his mind visits distant persons and sees distant scenes, or when he finds conversely distant scenes and persons appearing before his mental eye. These are based on memory images which attain at times unusual intensity. Not by a logical process, but by the natural and involuntary process of classification of experience, man is led to the concept of the objective existence of the memory-image. Its formation is due to the experiences of visual and auditory imagery.

We may recognize the objectivation of life and of the memory-image as the principal sources from which the manifold forms of soul concepts spring. As the life-soul may vary in form, so the memory-image soul may take varying forms according to the particular aspect of the personality that predominates. These two concepts of the soul do not remain isolated, but the one always influences the other. A detailed study of their interrelation and of the variety of meanings that corresponds to our term "soul" would require a close study of the forms of thought that have grown up on this general psychological background, partly through an inner development, partly owing to diffusion of ideas.

The most important results of these considerations for our problem is the recognition of the fact that those qualities, conditions, and functions which we combine under the term "soul" are looked upon as substances and that, for this reason, body and soul have separate existence and their lives are not encompassed in the same space of time.

In fact, there is probably not a single primitive people that holds rigidly to the belief that the existence of the soul coincides with the actual span of life of the individual. The soul may be considered as existing before the birth of its owner and it may continue to exist after his death. However, the idea of immortality, of a continued existence without beginning in the past and without end in the future is not necessarily implied in these beliefs.

Pre-existence is necessarily connected with the idea of rebirth. It is another expression of the primitive mythological thought which assumes that nothing has a beginning, that there is no creation of anything new, but that everything came into being by transformations. The animals, plants, striking features of the landscape are commonly accounted for as due to the transformation of human beings into new forms. Thus also the birth of a child is accounted for as a result of the transformation of a pre-existing being. If the Eskimo believe that children, like eggs, live in the snow and crawl into the mother's womb, if some Australian tribes believe that a totem or ancestral spirit enters the mother's body, if some Indian tribes of America believe that salmon may be reborn as children, or that a deceased person may come back to be born again by a woman of his own family, this is not necessarily due to a complete lack of knowledge of the physiological process of conception, but should rather be interpreted as a particular aspect of the concept of "life" or "soul," as independent of bodily existence. This appears very clearly in the case of the Eskimo who misinterpret sexual intercourse as intended to feed the child that has entered the mother's womb. These ideas are presumably analogous to the ideas surviving in our folk-lore in which children are presented as pre-existing. The belief in transmigration shows most clearly that we are dealing here with the soul which exists before the birth of the child.

The term "immortality" is, however, applied more specifically to life after death. We have pointed out before that the visualization of the form of a person, due to imagery, is one of the principal sources of the concept of "soul." This form survives after the death of the individual as his memory-image. For this very reason the image-soul cannot possibly die with the death of the person, but will survive at least as long as his friends survive. The importance of the recollection of a person for the future life of the soul is brought out in the beliefs of many Bantu tribes of Africa. Thus among the Vandau, the soul of a person who s remembered will be kindly disposed toward his friends. When the deceased is forgotten, his soul becomes a malignant being that is feared and must be driven away.

The memory-image is intangible, it arises suddenly and vanishes again when the calls of every-day life repress imaginative thought. It partakes of all the features of the departed and even his voice may dimly sound in the imagination of the surviving friend. In memory the departed will appear as he was known in life, in his usual dress and engaged in his usual occupations so that with his image appear also his property that he used in his lifetime. The inanimate property partakes in a peculiar way in the continued existence of the memory-image even after the objects have been destroyed. It is hardly necessary to assume with Tylor that the belief in this continued existence of proprietary objects is due to an animistic belief. In many cases it may be based merely on the continued existence of the memory-image.

The importance of the memory-image in the formation of the soul concept is nowhere clearer than in those cases in which the dead one is believed to continue to exist in the land of souls in the same condition in which he was at the time of death. When the aging Chukchee demands to be killed before he is infirm and unable to withstand the hardships of life, he acts under the assumption that his soul will continue in the same condition in which he finds himself at the time of death. Whether or not this is the historical source of the custom is irrelevant for its modern interpretation by the Chukchee. In the same way the belief of the Eskimo that a person who dies of old age or of a lingering illness will be unhappy in future life, while he who is suddenly taken away in full vigor, as a man who dies a violent death or a woman who dies in childbirth, will be strong and happy in future life is expressive of the memory-image that the deceased leaves in the minds of his survivors.

If the belief in continued existence is based on the persistence of the objectivated memory-image, it might be inferred that there should be a widespread belief of the death of the soul at the time when all those who knew the deceased are dead and gone. As a matter of fact, we find indications of a belief in a second death that conform with this idea, but in the majority of cases the soul is believed to be immortal. There are a considerable number of cases in which the second death of a soul is described, but most of these are not of a character that may easily be reduced to the fact that the deceased is forgotten. They seem rather to be due to the imaginative elaboration of the continued life of the soul which is necessarily thought to be analogous to our own life and in which, therefore, death is a natural incident.

It does not seem difficult to understand why the objectivation of the memory-image should lead to the belief in immortality rather than in a limited existence after death. To the surviving friend the memory-image is a substance and he will talk of it as having permanent existence. It will, therefore, be assumed by his friends who may not have known the deceased, in the same way, and will continue to exist in their minds in the same way as all other qualities that are, according to the views held by their society, conceived as substances.

Knowledge of the presence and actual decomposition of the body and the long preservation of the skeleton is the source of a number of other concepts that are related to the idea of immortality. When we speak of ghosts, we are apt to think more of the disembodied souls which wait to be redeemed, than of the skeletal remains that are thought to be endowed with life. Nevertheless we find, every now and then, that the ghost is not described as the transparent or vaporous apparition of the memory-image, but as bearing the features of a skeleton, often with grotesque additions of luminous orbits and nasal aperture. In this form the ghost is, of course, not the memory-image of the living, but a concept representing the remains of the dead body endowed with life. For this reason it happens often that these "immortals" are not individualized, but are conceived as very impersonal beings who may wage war among themselves, or against man, who may waylay the unwary and form a hostile tribe of foreigners, as though they were ordinary living beings, but endowed with unusual powers. The lack of individuality of this type of ghost appears very clearly among many American tribes, while the idea does not seem to prevail in Africa. We can hardly consider these ghosts as immortal souls, because they lack completely individuality.

Nevertheless there arises at times confusion between the two concepts. The ghosts have their village or villages and often, when the soul,—in the sense of life and memory-images,—of the departed leaves the body, it is said to go to the village of the ghosts where it meets previously departed friends and many persons whom it does not know,—those who died long ago. This contradiction is not surprising, because there are many associative bonds between the two groups of ideas, so that the one calls forth the other and a sharp line between the two concepts is, therefore, not established.

It is most important, for a clear understanding of the questions with which we are dealing and of similar problems, that we must not expect a consistent system of beliefs in primitive thought. We must remember that concepts originating from different principles of unconscious classification must overlap, and that for this reason, if for no other, the same concept may belong to conflicting categories. Only when conscious rationalization sets in and a standardization of beliefs develops may some of these conflicting or even contradictory views be harmonized.

It would seem, therefore, best not to include in the idea of immortality of the soul, the idea of separate existence which is attached to the acquaintance with the decomposing body and the relative permanence of the skeleton, just as little as we can consider the permanence and separate existence of objectivated spiritual powers, such as skill and success as immortal souls. They appear to us rather as helpful spiritual beings or objects.

The fundamental differences between the various forms of the soul concept and between the feelings and thoughts that lead to the assumption of a separate existence of the soul are the source also of many conflicting views regarding the abode of the soul before birth, during life and after death. Except in the cases of a well-developed belief in transmigration, there is no clearly formulated concept of the places and conditions in which souls exist before birth. Even when they are believed to be returned ancestors, there does not seem to be a well-defined belief regarding the mode of life of a pre-existing soul. This may be due to the lack of congruity between the behavior of the new-born infant and the memory-image which is ordinarily associated with the full-grown person. This makes it difficult to bridge the gap between the existence of the soul and the birth of the child.

During life, more particularly during healthy life, the seat of the soul is conceived to be in the body, or at least, closely associated with the body. Quite often the concepts of the relations between body and soul lack in definiteness. The distinction between a spiritual helper or a protecting object and the "soul" shows, however, very clearly that the former is thought of as existing apart from the body, while the latter is closely associated with it. We pointed out before that we find in both groups conceptualized attributes, but that the former are less firmly connected with the fundamental phenomena of life. In many cases, the "life-soul" is believed to permeate the whole body, or the special part of the body to which it belongs. When the soul is considered as an object, it may be thought to be located in some vital part, as in the nape of the neck; or, still more commonly, it is identified with those functions of the body that cease with death, such as the breath, the flowing blood, or the moving eye. So far as these are visible and tangible objects of temporary existence, they are considered the seat of the "life-soul" itself. However, the latter always remains the objectivation of the functions of life.

The concept of the memory-image soul leads to different beliefs in regard to its localization. Its essential feature is that it is a fleeting image of the personality and that, for this reason, it is identical in form with the person. Shadows and reflections on water partake of these unsubstantial, fleeting characteristics of the image of the person. Probably for this reason they are often identified with the memory-image soul. There are, however, also mixed concepts, as that of a "life-soul" which, after leaving the body, appear in the form of its owner, but of diminutive size.

Much clearer than the idea of localization of the pre-existing soul and of the soul of the living are those relating to the conditions of the souls after death. In imaginative stories, the details of life after death are often elaborated. They are confirmed and further embellished by the reports of people who, in a trance, believe they have visited the country of the souls.

The presence of the bodily remains, the departure of life, and the persistence of the memory-image lead to many conflicting views which have certainly helped in the development of the belief in multiple souls. While the idea of a life-soul combined with the belief in a continued existence of the personality, creates readily the formation of the concepts of a distant country of the dead, the memory-image based on the remembrance of the daily intercourse of the deceased with his survivors and the presence of his tangible grave lead rather to the belief in the continued presence of the soul. In the conflicting tendencies which are thus established, and in the elaboration of detail which is necessarily involved in tales regarding future life, historical diffusion plays a much more important part than in the formation of the mere concepts of soul and immortality, and it would be quite impossible to understand the multifarious forms of description of the land of the dead without taking into consideration the actual interrelations between tribes. An attempt at a purely psychological analysis would be quite misleading. We find, for instance, in Africa a widespread idea of sacred groves in which

ancestral souls reside; this must be taken as a result of historical adaptation, not as the necessary development of psychological causes that lead
to the same result anywhere,—in the same way, as the characteristic
belief in the different behavior of remembered and forgotten ancestral
souls which is common to many South African tribes, must be due to
historical assimilation. This is proved by the definite localization of
these beliefs in well-circumscribed areas.

Nevertheless a number of features may be recognized which are of
remarkably wide distribution and for which, therefore, a common
psychological cause may be sought.

The belief in a temporary presence of the soul in or near the place
of death is quite common and may be based on the condition of mind
which prevails until the survivors have adapted themselves to the absence of the deceased. It may be interpreted as the objectivation of the
haunting consciousness of his previous presence in all the little acts of
everyday life, and in the feeling that he ought still to be present. As
this feeling wears down, he departs to the land of the souls. In the
same way the difficulty of separating the dead body from the remembrance of the body in action may be the cause of the belief that the soul
hovers for some time around the grave, to leave only when the body
begins to decompose.

The ideas relating to the permanent abode of the souls are not easily
interpreted, largely on account of their complex mythological character
which requires a detailed historical investigation. Nevertheless there
are a few general features that are so widely distributed that they may
be briefly touched upon. Generally the village of the dead is thought
to be very far away, at the western confines of our world where the sun
and moon disappear, below the ground or in the sky, and difficult to
reach. Among the obstacles in the way, we find particularly a river that
must be crossed by the soul, or dangerous passages over chasms. It is
but natural that the souls should be conceived as living in the same way
as human beings do. The experiences of primitive man give no other
basis for his imagination to work on. Their occupations are the same,
they hunt, eat and drink, play and dance. A living person who takes
part in their daily life, particularly if he taste of their food, cannot return to the land of the living. The objects which the immortal souls
use are also immortal, but they appear to the living as old and useless,
often in the form in which they are disposed of at the funeral ceremonies. Notwithstanding the identity of the social life of the dead and

of the living, there is a consciousness that things cannot be the same there as here, and this thought is given expression in the belief that everything there is the opposite of what it is here. When we have winter, it is summer there, when we sleep, the souls of the dead are awake.

We cannot enter into the great variety of beliefs regarding the land of the souls without overstepping the bounds of a socio-psychological discussion.

The belief in a number of different countries of the dead, however, requires brief mention. We are accustomed to think of these distinctions from an ethical point of view, of heaven for the souls of the good, of hell for the souls of the bad. It is doubtful whether in primitive life this concept ever exists. The difference in the locations of the countries of the dead and of their conditions is rather determined by the memory-image of the person at the time of his death. The strong and vigorous who live a happy life, are assembled in one place—the weak and sickly at another place. When other principles of separation prevail, they may be reduced to other classificatory concepts. In simple economic conditions the whole community is equally affected by favorable and unfavorable conditions. Among the Eskimo, when the weather is propitious, the whole village has enough food, and every healthy person is happy. When, on the other hand, no game can be obtained on account of continued tempests, the whole village is in distress. Therefore a conception of future life in which in the same village a considerable part of the people are unhappy, another considerable part happy, does not coincide with the experience of Eskimo life and we may, perhaps, recognize in social conditions of this type a cause that leads to a differentiation of abodes of the dead.

In the preceding discussion, we have considered only the general socio-psychological basis on which the concepts of "soul" and "immortality" have arisen. It is necessary to repeat, that for a clear understanding of the great variety of forms which these beliefs take, the historical relations between groups of tribes must be considered, not only of those that are at present in close contact, but also of those which belong to larger cultural areas in which intertribal cultural influences may belong to early periods.

THE CONCEPT OF SOUL AMONG THE VANDAU[1]

THE following is a description of the concepts relating to the soul among the Vandau of Portuguese Southeast Africa, as developed in conversations with K'amba Simango, a young Mundau who was studying in New York in 1919. He seemed to be well informed in regard to the customs and beliefs of his people. He speaks both Chindau and Zulu.

"Life" is called *vγomi*[2] (Zulu *ubut'oηgo*). The Zulu word is also used in Chindau in the form *vut'oηgo*. The prefix shows that it is an abstract term. Living man has a body (*muvili* pl. *mivili*) and a *bvuli* (pl. *mabvuli;* Zulu *isit'u·ndzi*). The *bvuli* is alive and indestructible. It is not indissolubly connected with the body. The shadow or reflection of an object is also called *bvuli*. The *bvuli* is an essential part of existence only in man. In dreams the *bvuli* appears or leaves the body, and both *bvuli* and body have "life" (*vγomi*). The *bvuli* is never sick. When a person dies the body is without "life" which stays with the *bvuli*, that is, the *bvuli* remains alive while the body is dead.

After the death of a person the *bvuli* becomes a *mulu·ηgu* (pl. *valu·-ηgu*), synonym *mudjimu* (pl. *vadjimu*). The latter term may be derived from the stem *djima* (*k'udjima* to extinguish). The corresponding Zulu terms are *it'o·ηgo* (pl. *amat'o·ηgo*), used also in Chindau in the form *t'o·ηgo* (pl. *mat'o·ηgo*); synonym *isit'ut'a* (pl. *izit'ut'a*), used in Chindau in the form *tšit'ut'a* (pl. *zit'ut'a*). This term may be derived from Zulu *uk'ut'ut'a* to wander about. The *mulu·ηgu* has the form and

---

[1] *Zeitschrift für Ethnologie,* vol. 52, part 1 (1920–21), pp. 1–5.

[2]
v, f	bilabial
p', t', k'	glottalized surds
p', t', k'	strongly aspirated surds
η	middle palatal nasal
γ	middle palatal fricative
ż	labialized sonant *z*, like a whispered *zü*
š	English *sh*
tš	English *ch*
dj	English *j*
l	with strong vibration of sides of tongue
·	long vowels
.	separates vowels that do not form diphthongs
e, o	always open

character of the deceased. The term *bvuli* is also used for the *mulu·ŋgu,* meaning that he is the shadowy, unsubstantial image of the dead one. With this meaning the *mulu·ŋgu* is also called *moya,* wind, air, and *mpʿepʾo* wind, because, like the air, it cannot be touched and held. The *mulu·ŋgu* does not stay with the body but follows the family. The *mulu·ŋgu* retains the name of the deceased. He is immortal and cannot be reborn. Every family venerates its own *valu·ŋgu.*

When all the relatives of *malu·ŋgu* are dead and his memory is forgotten, or when he goes to a strange tribe in which he has neither relatives nor friends, he wanders about and becomes a *tšilo·mbo* (pl. *zilo·mbo*) or a *dzokʾa* (*kʾudzokʾa* to rattle in the throat), because a person possessed for the first time by a *dzokʾa* produces a rattling noise in the throat. A synonym for *dzokʾa* is *zintʿikʾi* (pl. *mantʿikʾi,* usually meaning "ceremonial song"; compare *kʾuntʿikʾinya* to throttle). The Zulu call the *tšilo·mbo idlozi* (pl. *amadlozi*) used in Chindau in the form *dlozi.* The Zulu call the *dzokʾa muŋgo·ma.* Since all of these belong to persons who have been forgotten they have no known personal names, but they reveal their names when they come into personal contact with the living. The *tšilo·mbo* is similar to the *dzokʾa,* but weaker. A *tšilo·mbo* who brings misfortune is also called *kʿombo,* i.e. bent, because he bends the straight road of life. The *tšilo·mbo* accompanies and directs the *beze* (pl. *madjibeze*), the experienced *naŋga* and the expert *dotʾa.* These three are medical practitioners who by the use of herbs and by means of prophetic bones (*ze·mbe*) advise and cure the sick.

The *dzokʾa* are unknown deceased persons who possess the *nyamsolo* (fuller form *nyamusolo; nya* head) and with whose assistance they take the scent (*kʾufemba*) of the *mulu·ŋgu* who causes sickness. The word *nyamsolo* (pl. *madjinyamsolo*), or in form of respect *vanyamsolo* may be derived from *solo* head (?). After the *dzokʾa* has taken the scent of the *mulu·ŋgu,* he overpowers him, takes hold of him if he tries to escape and forces him into the body of the *nyamsolo.* Then the *mulu·ŋgu* speaks through the mouth of the *nyamsolo.* The *dzokʾa* takes no part in these proceedings. By means of a slight indisposition of a person, his departed grandfather may wish to indicate his desire for attention. Then the *dzokʾa* of the *nyamsolo* takes the scent of the *mulu·ŋgu* who is forced into the body of the *nyamsolo.* The *mulu·ŋgu* states his name and wishes. As soon as this is done the *nyamsolo* sneezes *"wensya"* and thus removes the *mulu·ŋgu* from his body. The *mulu·ŋgu* of a relative does not cause serious sickness. When the *mulu·ŋgu* of a person not a member of his own family attacks a person he is taken seriously ill. Then the *mulu·ŋgu* is bribed by presents to desist. After the *mulu·ŋgu*, through the mouth of the *nyamsolo,* has expressed his willingness to accept the presents, the *nyamsolo* sends out his attendants (*muliša,* pl. *valisă*) who deposit the presents outside in the grass. Then the *nyamsolo* sneezes "*wensya*" and thus dismisses the *mulu·ŋgu.* The *mulu·ŋgu* who is sent out against a person attacks only the body, not the *bvuli.* He tries to throttle the patient, to break his neck or to kill him in some other way. The nature of his attacks is shown by the symptoms of the sickness. Often he tries to kill a person by the same sickness that killed him. A *dzok'a* belonging to a foreign tribe is designated by the word that belongs to the language of that tribe. Thus a Zulu *dzok'a* is called *muŋgo·ma.* Others are simply indicated by tribal names, as, for instance, *lo·zi,* a *dzok'a* of the Vandau of Rhodesia.

Generally a *dzok'a* is acquired unintentionally. A person who is walking about may accidentally pass a *dzok'a* who will accompany him. Then the person feels ill. A *ŋaŋga* or *nyamsolo* is called who tries to drive away the *dzok'a.* If the person wishes to keep the *dzok'a* he will stay with him and after an initiation the person will be a *nyamsolo.*

Some *nyamsolo* have from ten to fifteen *dzok'a.* At the initiation, when the *dzok'a* enters the person's body for the first time, he fills the upper part of the body of the novice who breathes with rattling in the throat. At later times, when the *dzok'a* is asked to find the *mulu·ŋgu* causing sickness he does not cause any discomfort.

The *bvuli* of children, old people, and mentally affected are called *nšimu* (sing. and pl.), synonym *salavusa* (pl. *masalavusa*) said to be derived from *k'usala* to stay, remain, and *vušwa* grass). They lie in the grass and attach themselves to anyone who happens to pass by. Their presence is indicated by a slight feeling of discomfort or by itching of the body. Therefore, when a person has these feelings it is said, *ndatšik'a salavusa,* "I stepped on a *salavusa.*" When a few crumbs of food are thrown to them they leave and repeat the same game with the next passer-by.

Several kinds of *mulu·ŋgu* have special names. A *mupfukwa* is the *mulu·ŋgu* of a person who has been murdered and who comes to take revenge. (*K'upfuk'a* means "to emerge", "to take revenge".) Other *mulu·ŋgu* are instigated by witches, male or female (*valo·yi*), to attack

their enemies. The *mupfukwa* pursues his murderer at his own initia-
tive.

Ba·ndu is a special term for a particularly merciless *mulu·ŋgu*.

The *mpʻo·ŋgo* is the *mulu·ŋgu* of a member of the chief's family,
particularly of a past generation, presumably of an individual who has
been forgotten. Some member of the chief's family, one who is observing the prescribed customs meticulously, is liable to be attacked by him.
In this case he is also called *mpʻo·ŋgo* because the *mpʻo·ŋgo* speaks
through him. The *mpʻo·ŋgo* does not cause sickness of individuals but
affects the welfare of the whole tribe.

My informant declares that the Vandau do not believe that dead
ancestors turn into snakes. The *valu·ŋgu* keep snakes in the way we keep
dogs, and snakes are treated with respect because they are the property of
the *valu·ŋgu*. Groves are not venerated, but since graves are placed in
groves they are feared and respected as property of the *valu·ŋgu*.

Since "life" (*vγomi*) is considered as an abstract power, man, according to our informant, has only one soul which, according to its state and
actions, is designated by various names:

During life of the owner	*bvuli* (shadow, reflection)
After death, but while the owner is remem- bered	*mulu·ŋgu* or *mudjimu*
On account of its unsubstantiality	*moya* or *mpʻepʻo* (wind)
Souls of children, old or mentally unsound persons	*nšimu* or *salavusa*
After death, when forgotten	*tšilo·mbo* (if weak) *dzokʼa* (if strong)
The *mulu·ŋgu* of a member of the chief's family	*mpʻo·ŋgo*

RELIGIOUS TERMINOLOGY OF THE
KWAKIUTL[1]

THE general term for the supernatural, the wonderful, is *na'walak*[u].[2] The term is used as a noun to indicate beings endowed with supernatural power. The salmon (R 609.4[3]), the lark (R 1329.35), the cedar (R 617.13), the trees (R 1327.6) are addressed in prayers as *na'walak*[u]. Supernatural beings that appear in visions are always designated by this term (R 631.16; 1185.35; 1218.25). Twins who are believed to have supernatural powers (R 633.39) are called *na'walak*[u] and so are the initiated participants in religious ceremonies (J III 59.40).

Frequently the term is used as an attribute. We find "supernatural (wonderful) woman" (*na'walak*[u] *ts!Edā'q* J III 66.31) ; "supernatural wife" (*na'walak*[u] *gEnE'm* J III 69.9) ; "country" (*na'walak*[u] *awī'-*[ε]*nak!wEs* R 1183.92 ; *na'walak!wEdzas* R 914.10) ; "lake" (*na'walak*[u] *dzE*[ε]*lā'l* R 1183.94) ; "mat" (*na'walagwEdzo lē'*[ε]*we*[ε] R 1199.14). The tips of hemlock trees which are believed to have wonderful powers are called "supernatural tips" (*na'walagwEtâ*[ε]*ye* R 725.64). Pathologically shortened twigs bearing closely condensed leaves are called "supernatural twigs" (*nEna'walagwExLawe*[ε]). As quality it appears also in the term "to make supernatural" (*na'walakwamas* R 707.42).

The term is also used to express the quality of being supernatural (*na'walak!wene*[ε] R 741.75), in the same way as *bEgwā'nEmene*[ε] designates the abstract term "manhood".

On other occasions the term is used to express the wonderful, supernatural power of beings. We find "the supernatural power of the trees (*na'walakwasa Lax*[u]*Lā'se* R 1328.20), and "there is no supernatural power greater than that of the house of Cannibal-at-North-End-of-World" (*k·!eyâ'se na'walakwagawese ō'gwE*[ε]*la lax g·ō'kwas ba'x*[u]*ba-kwa'lanux*[u]*sī'wa*[ε]*ya* R 1184.96) ; or "the supernatural power of being cut up" (and reviving) (*na'walakwases t!ōt!Ets!ālasE*[ε]*we* R 1135.16).

---

[1] Festschrift Meinhof, Hamburg, 1927, pp. 386–392.
[2] For explanation of alphabet see p. 232 of this volume.
[3] For abbreviations of references see p. 232 of this volume.

According to this use of the term they say "to try to get supernatural power" (*năʼᵋnawalak!wa* R 1208.95) ; "to use supernatural power" (*neᵋna'walax"sila* R 635.50). When beings who possess supernatural powers do not show them and then, suddenly prove their wonderful qualities, it is said "he becomes supernatural" (*na'walagwEłEla* R 1201.42). At another place a novice is called into a house "to be made supernatural by the supernatural power of the house" (*qaᵋ wä'g·ilaxseᵋ na'walakwEliłasoᵋsa nax·na'walagwiłaxsa lō'bEkwex* R 734.18). The source of supernatural power is also called *na'walagwEm*. When the cedar, a *na'walak"*, is compelled by the magical use of ax chippings to fall in a certain direction, the woodchopper says, "supernatural one, now you will follow the source of your supernatural power" (*wa, na'- walakwai', laᵋE'ms lāl lā'sgEmiłxes na'walagwEmos,* R 617.13). A being is called "owner of the source of supernatural power" (*naᵋna'- walagwEmnuk"* M 703.8).

The *na'walak"* is all-powerful, "for nothing is unattainable for the great, true supernatural one" (*qaᵋxs k·!eyâ'säex wEyō'ĻanEma naᵋna'- walax"dzek·as* R 1327.12).

On account of their sacred character the whistles which are used in sacred ceremonies are also called *na'walak"*. A certain ceremony is called "the grizzly bear with whistles of the door of the house of Canni- bal-at-North-End-of-World" (*na'walagwade nEnᵋstâ'liłas t!Ex·Eläs g·ō'kwas ba'x"bakwā'lanux"siwaᵋ ye* R 856.52) ; and it is told "therefore, it is said, sounded at once the roof of the house, namely the whistles of the *nō'nłEm*" (*hē'x·ᵋidaᵋEmᵋla'wise hē'k·!Eg·ale ō'gwäsasa g·ō'kwe, yEx na'walakwasa nō'nłEme* R 1037.52).

The soil from a land otter slide which is used as a magic means for influencing weather is called *na'walak"*. It is said, "do not handle too roughly this supernatural one (namely the soil), otherwise our weather will be too rough" (*gwa'la âłElisaxwa na'walakwex ā'Lox â'łElisEnts ᵋnā'lax* R 628.7).

These examples show that the word *na'walak"* has a very wide mean- ing. It may be used to designate a person, but it also expresses the attri- bute or the abstract idea of supernatural power—just like the term "manitou", or "saintly, the saint, sanctity, sanctuary", or German "heilig, der Heilige, Heiligkeit, Heiligtum". The quotations given here prove that the term has neither an exclusively anthropomorphic nor a general mana meaning. The one or the other prevails according to circumstances.

Opposite the wonderful, supernatural, is the ordinary, the profane (*ba'xwɛs*). It is said that twins and seal hunters are supernatural, other people ordinary (R 716.72). In the religious ceremonials the uninitiated are designated as profane (R 1158.27). A novice who is excited by the supernatural beings becomes quiet and "becomes ordinary" (*bā'xwɛsᵉid* R 920.21). The ancestors who came down from the sky in the shape of birds took off their masks and became ordinary (M 675.10). An uninitiated person who is present at a sacred ceremony profanes it. It is said, "Go and ask our great friend here, why he has come to this our supernatural place; whether it is good or bad; whether he has come to make us profane" (*wä'g·il wɛLä'Lɛxg·ɛnts ᵉnɛmō'x^udzek· lax g·ā'xełasox lä'xɛnts na'walak! wäsex ḷoᵉ ē'k·e ḷoᵉ ᵉya'x·sɛme ḷoᵉ g·äx bɛba'xwɛyɛla g·ā'xɛnts* R 1185.34). To betray the secrets of supernatural beings or powers is "to make them profane" (*bā'xwɛs-ᵉidā'mas* R 716.83). Smoke of excrements and broken taboos have the same effect (R 747.27).

The term *bā'xwɛs*, just like *na'walak^u* is used as a substantive and as an attribute. A feather, in contrast to another one, is called *ba'xwɛs ts!ɛ'lts!ɛlk·* (J III 17.13) "a common feather", and "common, i.e. profane, men" (*ba'xwɛs bɛgwā'nɛm* J III 44.32) are mentioned.

The term *ba'xwɛs* also designates the season in which the sacred ceremonials (*ts!a'eqa*) are not performed. Everything that refers to the profane summer season is called *ba'xwɛs*. There are *ba'xwɛs* names (*ba'xwɛdzɛxLäᵉyu* R 925.32); "a potlatch given in the *ba'xwɛs* season" *ba'xwɛstala* (R 903.64). At the beginning of the winter ceremonials the profane quality is wiped out of the eyes (*ḷā'xᵉwid qaᵉs la'os ᵉwīᵉla ts!ō'xᵉstoda qaᵉ lä'wäyeᵉsos bā'baxwɛstâᵉyaq!os* (R 914.2; 'arise and go wash your eyes, so that the profane may go out of your eyes').

Another term which expresses the ordinary, the lack of supernatural power, is *ăō'ms*. It is used almost always with the negation. *k·!ēᵉs ăō'ms* means the possession of supernatural power: people (J III 33.35); a bird (J III 61.40); a lake (J III 143.4) are so designated. At one place it occurs together with *na'walak^u* (*k·!ēᵉs ăō'ms na'walak^u* R 1326.61).

Supernatural beings who protect or harm man are often called *ha'ya-łilagas* "woman setting right." The mother of twins protects her newborn children against these beings by washing them with urine, of which the spirits are afraid (R 668.47). These spirits are fond of sea eggs. If they should touch the remains of a meal of sea eggs all those who have shared in the meal will be sick (R 614.22). They look at canoes that are being built and by doing so spoil them unless the canoes are magically protected (R 616.55). In this case they are identified with the souls of dead canoe builders (R 616.52). They take away the souls of people who are dying (R 705.2). They are also called "the women setting right of the farthest inland" (*ha'yalilagasasɛnts ā'Lagawe*ᵉ R 706.33). Some Indians designate the benevolent spirit of the fire of the house (*k!wax·Lā'la* 'the one sitting on the flames') by the term *ha'yalilagas* (R 1332.29). Others say it is a soul (*bɛxᵉwɛnē'ᵉ* R 1332.31). The spirits that appear to the novice and bestow their gifts upon him are often designated by the term *ha'yalilagas* (R 1202.75). In general the dead as malevolent spirits are so designated. In C II 322.5 it is specifically stated that this term is so used by the Koskimo and Nahwittee while the Kwakiutl use the term *lâ'ᵉlenoxᵘ* (*ha'yalilagasax, yɛk·asxoᵉ gwɛᵉyō'-kwasaxse Kwā'g·ule lâ'ᵉlenoxwa*). In a Nahwittee ceremony (R 919.93) the spirit of the deceased is called *ha'yalilagas;* also in the Kwakiutl tale R 1119.49. In C III 20.22 it is also said that the *lâ'ᵉlenoxᵘ* are called *ha'yalilagas* (*ha'ăyalilagas yɛxɛnts gwɛᵉyō' leslâ'ᵉlenoxᵘ*). In J III 423.2 it is said that the *ha'yalilagas* causes sickness. In songs the thunderbird (M 711.1) and "the Snake-in-Stomach" (M 717.7) are called *ha'yalilagas*.

Judging from its form the word belongs to the Bella Bella dialect; *ha'yalila* means "to set right", -*gas* woman. However, these spirits as well as many others are not always conceived as female.

The term *lâ'ᵉlenox* is used both for a complete corpse and for the spirit of the dead (J III 106.1 ; R 713.60) : "The spirit of the dead is not the soul, for he is only seen when he warns whom he wishes to see him, and he has a body like a living person and his bones are those of men long dead" (*lä k·!ē*ᵉ*s bɛxᵉwɛnaᵉya lâ'ᵉlenoxwe, yɛxs lē'x·aᵉmăe dō'xᵉwaḷɛlasqes â'ᵉmăe q!ē'q!ayak·ilaxes gwɛᵉyō' qaᵉ dō'xᵉwaLɛlaq, yɛqē'xs sɛnā'laᵉmăe bɛgwā'nɛm Ḷɛᵉwis xā'qexa la gä'la ḷɛᵉla' bɛgwā'-nɛma* R 727.10). The word is derived from the stem *lɛwal-*, 'the dead one touches a person and causes sickness' (*lɛwa'lkᵘ* 'touched by a ghost' R 918.77 ; *lâ'la* 'a ghost touches').

The soul "has no bone and no blood, for it is like smoke or like a shadow." It has no abode outside of the body to which it belongs (*la k·!eyâ's g·ōx̣ᵘs ō'gwɛᵉlä lā'xɛnts ō'k!winaᵉyex lax ō'kwinaᵉyas bɛxᵉwɛna'yide,* R 728.15). The soul is called *bɛxᵉwɛnē'ᵉ* 'human long body'. The Koskimo call it *bɛkwa'ᵉe* 'something human'; the ᵉnā'-

k!wax·da^εx^u call it often *bεgwā'nεmgεmł* 'human mask'. In Knight Inlet the term *q!wε^εlā'yu* 'means of life' is said to be used ; in Nahwittee *ts!ē'k!wa* 'bird'. Trees, bushes, birds, small and large animals have souls "for all are human" (R 1220.68). The halibut (R 1322.69) and the salmon (R 612.63) have souls. The soul sits on the crown of the head (*yu'^εmǎas k!wā'łεnts ō'xLǟ^εyex* R 715.48). In sleep it is able to leave the body. While it is absent its owner is weak. If it stays away too long, or if it is abducted, its owner falls sick. Then the shaman searches for it (*bā'bakwayoL!a* 'he tries to obtain the soul' R 721.79). I have not found any indication of the belief that soul and life are considered as identical. The powers are called life givers (*q!wεlā'la^εyu* 'means of being alive' R 1297.3, line 1 ; *q!wē'q!wεlag·i^εla^εyu* 'means of making alive' R 1294.4 ; *g·ε'lg·εldokwila* 'prolonging life' R 618.19), but it is nowhere said that the soul is life, except in the abnormal and rare Knight Inlet term given before.

The soul is identified with the owl and every person has his own owl. If it is killed his soul is killed.

The gifts which human beings receive from spirits are called treasures (*Ļō'gwe^ε*). This term does not refer to supernatural gifts exclusively. Children are so designated. However, its most common use is for supernatural gifts. Stones found in the stomachs of halibut bring luck and "are found as treasures by fishermen" (*Ļā'Ļogwalaso^εsa ba'kwa^εle'noxwe* R 1324.8). Ceremonies received in visions (J III 56.34) ; magic objects by means of which wealth is secured (J III 108.1) ; the instrument that kills enemies (C II 182.2) ; the self-paddling canoe (J III 130.28) ; the meeting with supernatural beings are *Ļō'gwe^ε*. The person who has such a treasure is *Ļō'gwala* (J III 78.2 ; R 1139.93). The owner of a treasure is called *Ļō'gwe^εnuk^u* (C II 378.21) and the attempt to secure a treasure *Ļā'Ļogẇasd*, etymologically an unusual form. To use one's treasure is called *Ļā'Ļox^usila* (C 26.7).

One type of the gifts received from supernatural beings is the sacred song (*yä'lagwεm* C II 90.7) which is sung (*yä'laqwεla* R 708.61) by the shaman and others who have received supernatural gifts, when they return from their encounter with the spirits and whenever they show their gifts.

The applicant who wishes to obtain the friendship of the spirits must be pure. Bathing in cold water, rubbing the body with twigs of the hemlock tree until blood shows (C II 372.17 ; R 1122.26), washing with urine (C II 326.19) ; rubbing the body with wrappings of a corpse (CXXVI 106.61) ; rubbing with hellebore (CXXVI 125.64) are means of purification which is called *g·ī'g·Eltala* or *q!ē'qEla* (J III 105.28). An object used for magical purposes, perhaps as an amulet, is called *q!ē'qaleᵉ*, presumably because it serves as a means of purification.

To observe taboos and to be careful in ordinary pursuits are called "to treat well" (*ǎē'k·ila*). Thus it is used in one passage to express "to handle (berries) carefully" (R 280.1) ; at another place that the woman must be careful and stay at home when her husband is out hunting (R 638.28). It also has the general meaning of "observing taboos" (R 649.3).

To break a taboo is called *ǎǎ'ms* 'to spoil, to cause misfortune' (R 575.35 ; 607.1), from this stem *ǎᵉmē'lEla* to be unfortunate (R 922.26), and *ǎǎ'msila* 'widow' (the one who causes misfortune R 604.27).

Widows and sick people are isolated in a taboo shelter, outside the house (*hoᵉs* R 719.37 ; 1118.23). When the tabooed one is in the taboo shelter it is called *hōᵉdzats!e* 'taboo receptacle'.

To practice shamanism is *pExa'* (e.g. *pExa'sEᵉweda ᵉwap* 'the water was treated by the shaman' C II 100.16) ; abstract *pExᵉē'neᵉ* quality of a shaman (*hē'ᵉEm Ḻē'gEms lā'xes pExᵉē'naᵉye* 'that was his name in his quality as a shaman' R 718.3). The shaman is called *pExǎla* (R 700.13 ; 731.67). In the winter ceremonial the initiated are also called *pExǎla*, their head *pExEmē'ᵉ* (R 728.1).

The supernatural powers and, with their help the shaman, cure sick people (*hē'lik·a* R 707.36 ; 729.32 ; *hē'lixᵉid* 'to begin to heal' R 731.61), or they sanctify objects (*lā'ᵉlǎe hē'lik·asEᵉweda ᵉwap* 'then, it is said, the water was made sacred' C II 100.16). Therefore the assistant of the cannibal, the highest order of the members of the winter ceremonial, is called "mouth healer" (*hē'lig·Exsteᵉ* C II 300.28), and it is said of a spirit that he is "the owner of the means of healing" (*hē'lig·ayunukᵘ* R 737.92).

Both the spirits and the shamans are paid for their services (*a'ya* C II 50.20 ; 350.5 ; R 635.52). This term is not used for other kinds of payments.

To pray is called *ts!E'lwaqa*. It means also "to thank, to praise, to ask favors." The salmon is thanked (R 610.27), also fish, game and trees (R 619.25) who are at the same time asked help. In human intercourse it means "to praise, to console."

Anyone may practice witchcraft ($\check{e}'qa$) provided he knows the method. It is not based on supernatural gifts but based on knowledge of the ways of doing harm by magical means. It is practiced by the $eq!\check{e}'$-nox^u. It can be warded off either by repeating the witchcraft procedure or by destroying the magical objects.

MISCELLANEOUS

ADVANCES IN METHODS OF TEACHING [1]

A NTHROPOLOGY is one of the subjects that have been added to the university curriculum quite recently. For this reason I will devote my remarks to a consideration of the field that anthropological instruction is intended to cover and of its relations to allied sciences rather than to a discussion of methods of instruction.

According to purely theoretical definitions, anthropology is the science of man and might be understood to cover a vast range of subjects. The physical as well as the mental characters of man may be considered in a certain way as the proper field of anthropology. But sciences do not grow up according to definitions. They are the result of historical development. The subject-matter of anthropology has been accumulated principally by travellers who have made us acquainted with the people inhabiting distant countries. Another part of the subject-matter of anthropology is due to the investigation of prehistoric remains found in civilized countries. Only after certain methods had developed which were based largely on the information thus collected was the White race made the subject of investigation.

For this reason the aim of anthropology has been largely to explain the phenomena observed among tribes of foreign culture. These phenomena are naturally divided into three groups: (1) the physical appearance of man; (2) the languages of man, and (3) the customs and beliefs of man. In this manner three branches of anthropology have developed: (1) somatology, or physical anthropology; (2) linguistics, and (3) ethnology. Up to this time anthropological investigation has dealt almost exclusively with subjects that may be classed under these three headings. These subjects are not taken up by any other branch of science, and in developing them anthropology fills a vacant place in the system of sciences.

The treatment of these three subjects requires close co-operation between anthropology and a number of sciences. The investigation of the

[1] Discussion before the New York meeting of the American Naturalists and Affiliated Societies (Dec., 1898). *Science,* N.S., vol. 9 (1899), pp. 93–96.

physical characteristics of man has also been taken up by anatomists, but the point of view of the anatomist and that of the anthropologist are quite different. While the former is primarily interested in the occurrence of certain modifications of the human form and in their genetic interpretation, the anthropologist is interested in the geographical distribution of varieties of form, in the variability of the human species in different areas and in their interpretation. The thorough study of physical anthropology, or somatology, requires the combined training of the anatomist and of the anthropologist.

In the study of linguistics the anthropologist deals with a subject that has been partially taken up by the student of special linguistic stocks. The study of the structure of the Aryan languages, of the Semitic languages and of the Mongol languages has been carried on with great success by philologists; but the anthropological problem is a wider one —it deals with the general question of human language.

In the study of ethnology the field of investigation of the anthropologist adjoins that of the field of research of the psychologist and of the sociologist. The development of a truly empirical psychology makes it necessary to draw largely upon material furnished by anthropological studies. On the other hand, sociologists have found that the analysis of the culture of civilized society cannot be carried out successfully without a comparative study of primitive society, which is the subject-matter of anthropological research.

The method of anthropology is an inductive method, and the science must be placed side by side with the other inductive sciences. Our conclusions are based on comparisons between the forms of development of the human body, of human language, of human activities, and must be as truly inductive as those of any other science. By including psychology and anthropology in the present discussion on the methods of teaching science, we have given expression to the conviction that the method of investigation of mental phenomena must be no less an inductive method than that of physical phenomena.

The teaching of anthropology may be made to supplement in many ways the teaching of allied subjects, and I will briefly outline its functions in the university curriculum.

Physical anthropology has come to be primarily a study of the varieties of man. The differences between different types of man, defined either geographically or socially, are slight—so slight, indeed, that the biologist, until quite recent times, would have disregarded them entirely.

Slight differences in type have been of importance to the student of anthropology at an earlier time than to the student of zoology, because we are more deeply interested in the slight differences that occur in our own species than in those found among animals. For this reason in anthropology sooner than in zoology the insufficiency of description was felt. Anthropology was the first of the biological sciences to substitute measurement for description and the exact number for the vague word. The method of measuring variable phenomena—in the case of anthropology, of the variations composing a type—had to be developed. It is only natural that in the course of this development mistakes were committed which had to be rectified, and that the sound method of metric description developed slowly. It would seem that at present we have reached the stage where the methods of metric description may be clearly recognized, and we may, therefore, expect confidently a rapid and wholesome development of physical anthropology. A glance at recent biological literature shows very clearly that descriptive zoology and descriptive botany are passing at present to the substitution of metric description for verbal description that took place in anthropology some time ago. The study of anthropological methods may prevent biologists from repeating the same errors that were committed in the early days of anthropology. Anthropological subjects will, for a long time to come, remain the most available material for metrical studies of variations in the higher forms of life, because the material can be obtained in greater numbers and with greater ease than in studies of most of the higher animal forms. The metric method, which is at present principally an anthropological method, will, in a very short time, become of great importance to the student of biology, who ought, for this reason, to profit by the experiences of the anthropologist.

The fuller development of physical anthropology will lead to a study of the physiology and experimental psychology of the races of man. But in these lines of work we have hardly made a beginning. The relation of these inquiries to physiology and to psychology will be the same as that of physical anthropology to anatomy.

I may be allowed to pass by briefly the relations of the linguistic method of anthropology to other sciences. You will recognize at once that this subject, as well as its methods, must have a stimulating effect upon the teaching of philology, because its conclusions are based upon the broad grounds of human language; not on the studies of a single family of languages. The science of linguistics is growing slowly on account of its intrinsic difficulties. These difficulties are based on the lack of satisfactory material as well as on the amount of labor involved in the acquisition of knowledge in its particular line of research. Work in this field is most urgently needed, because the languages of primitive man are disappearing rapidly, thus depriving us of valuable material for comparative study.

Ethnology, the last division of anthropology, covers a vast field. Its main object may be briefly described as the discovery of the laws governing the activities of the human mind, and also the reconstruction of the history of human culture and civilization. The methods applied by ethnologists are twofold. The investigation of the history of the culture of definite areas is carried on by means of geographical and of archæological methods. The methods are geographical in so far as the types inhabiting a country, their languages and their customs, are compared with those of neighboring tribes. They are archæological in so far as they deal with the prehistoric remains found in the country in question. In this case we apply inductive methods for the solution of historical questions. The investigation of the laws governing the growth of human culture is carried out by means of comparative methods, and is based on the results of the historical analysis referred to before. These laws are largely of a psychological nature. Their great value for the study of the human mind lies in the fact that the forms of thought which are the subject of investigation have grown up entirely outside of the conditions which govern our own thoughts. They furnish, therefore, material for a truly comparative psychology. The results of the study of comparative linguistics form an important portion of this material, because the forms of thought find their clearest expressions in the forms of language.

It appears, from these brief statements of the scope and methods of anthropological research, that an acquaintance with the whole field is indispensable for the sociologist; that a knowledge of results and methods will be of advantage to the psychologist, and that the statistical method developed in physical anthropology will be very helpful to the student of biology. In a general way, a knowledge of the outlines of anthropology seems to be of educational value, particularly in so far as it broadens the historical views of the student, because it extends his view over cultures and civilizations that have grown up uninfluenced by our own. The advances made by our own race will appear to him in a truer light when he is able to compare them with the work done by other peoples and races, and if he understands how much our own civilization owes to the achievements of people who appear to be at present on a low level of culture. The methodological value of the teaching of anthropology lies in the fact that it shows the possibility of applying inductive methods to the study of social phenomena

THE AIMS OF ETHNOLOGY [1]

M ANY books of travel give us descriptions drawn in the most abhor-
rent lines of the people inhabiting foreign countries, describing
their mode of life as similar to that of wild beasts, denying that there is
any indication of emotional or rational life deserving of our sympathy.
In early descriptions of Australians, Bushmen, Fuegians they are often
described as the lowest forms of mankind, void of all feeling for social
obligations, without law and order, without imagination, even without
shelter and tools.

If travellers who have seen those people give us descriptions of this
type, it is not surprising that others who have never been in contact
with primitive people accept their views and we begin to understand
the reason for the oft-repeated question: What is the use of studying the
life of primitive people?

Even the rudest tribes do not conform to the picture that is drawn
by many a superficial traveller. Many examples may be culled from
the extensive literature of travel showing the superficiality of the reports
given. The well-known traveller Burchell met near the Garib a group
of Bushmen and gives us the most wonderful report of their complete
lack of reasoning power. He asked the question: What is the difference
between a good and an evil action? and since they could not answer
to his satisfaction he declared them to have no power of reasoning and
judging. In a similar way the Fuegians were asked about their religious
ideas in terms that were necessarily unintelligible to them, and since
they could not answer it was said that they cannot grasp any idea that
transcends the barest needs of everyday life. Nowadays we know better,
and no scientifically prepared traveller would dare to make statements
of this kind. We know now that the Bushmen, whom Burchell described as little different from wild beasts, have a well-developed music,
a wide range of tales and traditions; they enjoy poetry and are excel-

---

[1] Lecture given before the Deutscher Gesellig-Wissenschaftlicher Verein von New
York, March 8, 1888; New York, Hermann Bartsch, 1889. I have included this paper
in the present series because it illustrates my early views regarding ethnological
problems.

lent narrators. Their rock paintings show a high degree of skill and a remarkable understanding of perspective. We also know that the Fuegians have a well-developed social organization and that their customs are proof of a deep-seated religious attitude.

The Andamanese are another people that owe their ill repute to the reports of early travellers. Marco Polo, who visited them in 1285, said: "These people are like wild beasts, and I assure you that all the men of this island Angamanain have heads like those of dogs, and teeth and eyes of the same kind; in fact, their faces look like those of bulldogs." An Arabic writer of the ninth century says: "The color of their skin is terrifying; their feet are large, almost a cubit long, and they are absolutely without clothing." Compare this with the description of E. H. Man, to whom we are indebted for a better knowledge of this interesting people. He says: "It has been asserted that the communal marriage system prevails among them, and that marriage is nothing more than taking a female slave, but so far from the contract being regarded as a merely temporary arrangement, to be set aside at the will of either party, no incompatibility of temper or other cause is allowed to dissolve the union, and while bigamy, polygamy, polyandry, and divorce are unknown, conjugal fidelity till death is not the exception, but the rule. . . . One of the most striking features of their social relations is the marked equality and affection which subsists between husband and wife." Even if this description should be considered as somewhat colored, it shows nevertheless that these people are not "like wild beasts."

Thus a closer study shows that some of the peoples of worst repute are not as crude as superficial reports would make us believe, and we are led to suspect that the cultural conditions among all primitive peoples may be higher than is commonly assumed.

Our knowledge of primitive tribes the world over justifies the statement that there is no people that lacks definite religious ideas and traditions; that has not made inventions, that does not live under the rule of customary laws regulating the relations between the members of the tribe. And there is no people without language.

The task of ethnology is the study of the total range of phenomena of social life. Language, customs, migrations, bodily characteristics are subjects of our studies. Thus its very first and most immediate object is the study of the history of mankind; not that of civilized nations alone, but that of the whole of mankind, from its earliest traces found in the deposits of the ice age, up to modern times. We must follow the gradual development of the manifestations of culture. The aim we have in view may be illustrated by an example.

The wealth of tales and traditions of Europe, and their innumerable customs that persist even at the present time are well known. The collections of fairy tales by Grimm and the folk songs gathered in Brentano's *Wunderhorn* are perhaps the earliest systematic attempts to gather the available material. Grimm considered the tales and customs as survivals of ancient Germanic paganism being modified by the changes of cultural life. The deities of early times were interpreted as personified forces of nature. When the collected material increased, this theory proved to be inadequate. It was found that certain tales and songs or superstitions that were first considered as of ancient pagan origin were introduced in recent times, and in many cases it was shown that they originated in far-distant lands. As late as the middle ages Europe received a considerable amount of its customs, beliefs and traditions from the East, and these were modified according to European cultural patterns. The new ideas exerted their influence upon the social conditions of Europe. For example, M. Gaster has tried to prove that the belief in witches of the middle ages that persists to the present time was introduced into western Europe during the fourteenth century in connection with the dualistic teachings of the schismatics who defended the dogma of the power of Satan and the protection of the Saints. These teachings originated among the Bulgarian Christians of southeastern Europe. Although the views of Gaster are not entirely acceptable they prove the strong influence of the teachings of the heretics upon popular belief and popular literature. Besides these foreign elements, customs and traditions are directly derived from pagan times, so that the study of modern life leads us back to the cultural forms of primitive times.

In primitive society cultural contact exerts an even more marked influence than in our complex civilization.

The famous story of the race of turtle and hare, or swinegel and rabbit may serve as an example. It is found in Morocco where hedgehog and jackal are the contestants. In Cameroon elephant and turtle, among the Hottentot ostrich and turtle are the heroes. The Tupi Indians of Brazil tell the same story about deer and turtle, and it seems plausible that they learned it from African slaves. The tales of American Negroes offer one of the most remarkable examples of transmission, since they represent a mixture of African and European ideas which, in turn, have influenced the folk-tales of the American Indians.

Such transfers are found not only in customs and popular tales, but also in mythology, which show many traces of foreign origin. The Semitic elements of Greek mythology are well known. We need only mention Aphrodite and Heracles. I may add an example taken from my own observations among the Indians of British Columbia. In the south are found many tales referring to the sun, his origin and wars between the animals and the heavenly bodies. In southern Alaska the Raven is the creator who made man, the country, fire and water. He gave to man food and shelter, inventions and customary law. Both groups of ideas, although quite distinct, have spread along the coast so that the mythology is an inextricable mixture of these fundamental ideas.

These observations indicate that the first aim of ethnological inquiry must be critical analysis of the characteristics of each people. This is the only way of attaining a satisfactory understanding of the cultures found in wider areas. The means at our disposal for making such an analysis are varied: bodily form, language and culture are results of historical processes and may, therefore, be utilized for the study of history. For prehistoric times we have to be satisfied with the study of remains.

Bodily form is inherited from one generation to the next. Therefore it is the first task of the investigator to find the permanent forms characteristic of each area. Since some time it has become customary to look for the principal characteristics in the skull forms, partly because they are quite stable, partly for practical reasons since it is easier to collect skulls than other parts of the skeleton, excepting the long bones. In the complicated forms of the skull the individuality of the group is most clearly expressed and its form is not subject to habits of life to the same degree as some other bones. Skulls are often preserved when other bones are decomposed, broken or scattered, so that they are the most available material for the study of populations of earlier periods. Data based on skull measurements are merely a means of expressing in brief terms characteristics of bodily build. Among people that form a unit as far as language and culture are concerned, a mixed origin may be shown. Thus Asia Minor is inhabited by people speaking Turkish, excepting, however, Greeks and Armenians. Dr. von Luschan, who has recently studied the bodily form of these people, shows that in bodily form they do not conform to other Turkish-speaking peoples, but that the majority are in type like the Armenians. In the west Greek, and in the south Arabic types prevail. Many of the Greek-speaking people of Asia Minor are also of Armenian type, while those of the south coast are Hellenized Arabs. We conclude from these data that the earlier inhabitants of Asia Minor have been assimilated linguistically and culturally by the invading Turks.

As another example showing the importance of these inquiries we may mention the distribution of the Pygmies to which the French anthropologist De Quatrefages has paid particular attention. I mentioned before the Bushmen, a pygmy people. Tribes of small stature have been found in many parts of Central Africa as far as the Lake region at the sources of the Nile. Recently their occurrence in West Africa has also been reported so that the ancient reports of Herodotus are confirmed by modern observation. Equally short are the Andamanese and some of the tribes of the mountains of India, the Malay Peninsula, the Philippines and Formosa, and similar traits may be observed among tribes of New Guinea and neighboring islands where they seem to have intermarried with their neighbors. The males among most of these people measure not more than about 140 cm. The Akka of Central Africa are even shorter, measuring not more than 120 or 130 cm. Although these types are not by any means of identical anatomical form they have some traits in common, particularly the small size and the stiff, frizzly hair. Their presence in all parts of the southern border of the Old World—in which we include Africa—makes it likely that they are the remnants of an ancient race which was overcome by the immigration of the tall Negroes in Africa, by the invasion of southern Asia by people who came from the West and the North.

Thus the investigation of the types of man leads us back into the earliest periods of human life. The method is founded on the permanence of anatomical forms.

Another important means for investigating early history is language. Many languages have succumbed under the influx of conquerors, while in other cases they have survived slightly altered and the languages of the conquerors have been lost. In still other cases ancient languages survive in protected areas, in remote villages, in infertile, swampy districts or on islands. Such are a number of Romance dialects, the Basque, the numerous languages of the Caucasus, of California and of West Africa. The history of the Athapascans is illuminated by the fact that isolated tribes of the Pacific coast, the Navaho and Apache of our southwestern States and the people of the Mackenzie area speak dialects belonging to this linguistic family. The discovery of Carib languages in Brazil throws new light on the history of these peoples.

Another trait of language is of importance. While anatomical characteristics are important on account of their permanence, languages change more readily and the changes are such that they throw much light on their history. New languages originate, grow and disappear. From earlier languages new ones arise through mixture (like English) ; and they disintegrate according to their phonetic character and grammatical processes and according to the fates of the people speaking them, and form new dialects. These changes, due to mixture or inner development, are a fruitful source of historical inferences. The methods of study have been developed through the study of Indo-European languages, but beginnings are being made to apply these results to other linguistic families. The analysis of dialects enables us to follow the history of words and of concepts through long periods of time and over distant areas. The introduction of new inventions and migration into distant countries are often indicated by the appearance of new words the origins of which may be ascertained. Thus the history of language reflects the history of culture. Schrader and Penka have applied this method to investigations on the early home of Aryan-speaking peoples. Our knowledge of the languages of primitive people is, on the whole, not far enough advanced to permit a similar analysis. To make this possible we need a literature of these languages. At present we have hardly adequate vocabularies.

The third means for the investigation of early history of peoples that have no written records is the study of their culture. It is not too much to say that there is no people whose customs have developed uninfluenced by foreign culture, that has not borrowed arts and ideas which it has developed in its own way.

A noteworthy example of this kind is found among the Fan, a tribe living north of the lower Congo. When the Portuguese discovered the Congo about 450 years ago, they found bows and arrows used by the Negroes. The Portuguese influenced the culture of the Negroes in many ways and they learned from them the use of the crossbow. Later on, when Portuguese influence declined, the Fan retained the use of the crossbow. Being unable to imitate the complicated mechanism of the Portuguese crossbow, they invented a new release. The new form was not strong enough to fly the bolt over long distances, therefore they used poisoned bolts to make them effective. When the Fan were rediscovered in the nineteenth century they were found in possession of this curious weapon, the origin of which seemed at first quite unexplainable. Similar imitations of European objects are found on the islands of the Pacific Ocean. Thus the Fiji Islanders gave to their clubs the forms of European guns, and the chiefs of New Britain adopted as headdress the hat form of British Admirals. There are some cases of double imitation. The steel harpoon used by American and Scotch whalers is a slightly modified imitation of the Eskimo harpoon. These were again imitated by the Eskimo.

In some cases imitations are not confined to single inventions. Cases are known in which the bulk of the culture of a people is adopted by their neighbors. Thus an African tribe which was subject to attack of the warlike Zulu sought protection by assuming Zulu customs and manners.

On the other hand, there exists a decided conservatism, minute peculiarities being retained while the general life of the people may undergo important changes. Thus Edward Morse proved that the peoples of large continental areas have in common methods of arrow-release, which differ from those used in other extended areas.

The style of ornament, the forms of implements and weapons are generally preserved tenaciously. When a new material is introduced the earlier forms are often maintained. Thus tribes that learned the art of pottery and that had used in earlier times basketry in its place, often imitate basketry forms in clay. Weapons set with spines or teeth are imitated in woodcarving or stone. New forms may also be imitated in familiar material. Thus the bronze axes of early Europe were imitated in stone.

Traditions, and particularly verses and tunes contained in them, are often retained with great tenacity. The songs, being transmitted from one generation to the other, may differ so much from current speech that they come to be mysterious and unintelligible.

We recognize that the life of a people in all its aspects is a result of its history, in which are reflected the tribal tradition as well as the features learned by contact with neighbors. To the ethnologist the most trifling features of social life are important because they are expressions of historical happenings. They are part of the data from which the past has to be reconstructed.

It may be said that what we describe here is history of culture, not ethnology. This is true. Ethnography is part of the history of culture, and cannot be separated from it. Owing to our increasing ethnological knowledge we appreciate that the history of civilization cannot be understood without a knowledge of that of primitive man. At the same time the development of ethnology is largely due to the general recognition of the principle of biological evolution. It is a common feature of all forms of evolutionary theory that every living being is considered as the result of an historical development. The fate of an individual does not influence himself alone, but also all the succeeding generations. Therefore, in order to understand an organism it is not sufficient to study it as a stable form, but it must be compared with all its ascendants and descendants. This point of view introduced an historical perspective into the natural sciences and revolutionized their methods. The development of ethnology is largely due to the adoption of the evolutionary standpoint, because it impressed the conviction upon us that no event in the life of a people passes without leaving its effect upon later generations. The myths told by our ancestors and in which they believed have left their impress upon the ways of thinking of their descendants who were subjected to the influence of a foreign civilization. Even the most brilliant genius is influenced by the spirit of the time in which he lives, by his environment, which is a product of events of the past. Thus the history of culture teaches the continuity of ideas and inventions beginning with the stages on which we find the primitive tribes of our times. The history of science, invention and religion must be based on the study of the lives of primitive tribes.

I have used here throughout the term "primitives" without further explanation. I hope this has not conveyed the impression that I consider these tribes as living in an original state of nature, such as Rousseau imagined. On the contrary, we must remember that every primitive people has had a long history. It may have descended by decay from a stage of higher development or it may have risen to its present stage battling against vicissitudes. There is no primitive tribe that is not hemmed in by conventional laws and customs. The more primitive it is the greater is the number of restrictions that determine every action.

If we found that ethnology as an historical science is intimately related to the history of culture, this connection appears still closer when we turn to the second important task of our science. A comparison of the social life of different peoples proves that the foundations of their cultural development are remarkably uniform. It follows from this that there are laws to which this development is subject. Their discovery is the second, perhaps the more important aim of our science.

There is no fundamental contrast between these aims, for the general law is expressed in the individual phenomenon just as much as the individual phenomenon is interpreted as an exemplification of the general law. However, the method used in discovering these laws is distinctive and throws light upon the individual case, for it shows which of its features are accidental and which are of general applicability. Therefore the purely historical method without a comparative study will be incomplete. The detailed study of the individual case compels us to fall back on the comparative method, for the means at our disposal for clearing up the actual history of cultures are limited. Written records do not reach back into hoary antiquity and are available only for a few cultures. The other methods which we have discussed are also too often of little avail. In all these cases nothing is left but to compare the social phenomena of distinct areas and to base our deductions on their similarities and dissimilarities. In the pursuit of these studies we find that the same custom, the same idea, occurs among people for whom we cannot establish any historical connection, so that a common historical origin may not be assumed and it becomes necessary to decide whether there are laws that result in the same, or at least similar phenomena independently of historical causes; in other words whether the development of the human mind follows definite laws. Thus develops the second important task of ethnology, the investigation of the laws governing social life, or as it is generally called, the study of folk psychology.

The very first question to be answered is whether there are laws according to which culture progresses or whether its development is due to accident. We mentioned before examples of the occurrence of similar phenomena in regions far apart. In these cases the ethnologist is always confronted with two equally possible explanations. The two phenomena may have originated from a common historical source or they may have developed independently of each other. Only in a few very general cases there can be no doubt. For instance the fact that there are no peoples without religion or without art; that everywhere some form of social organization is found, that everywhere with progressing culture the individual becomes freer, because the innumerable arbitrary rules governing his conduct tend to disappear—all these may be justly explained as due to the mental characteristics of mankind.

The method of inquiry of the student of folk psychology may also be illustrated by an example. The results obtained by recent inquiries into the history of the family present an excellent example.

The results of philological and historical investigations referring to peoples speaking Indo-European languages demonstrated that the fam-- ily was the foundation of society and that on this basis the tribe and state developed. From this point of view it seemed strange that among some peoples the father was not the head of the family but that often the mother had rights which in later time belonged to the father. Thus Herodotus tells that among the Lycians the daughters inherited from their parents, not the sons. It is told that in Athens at the time of Cecrops the children took their names from their mothers, and according to Tacitus the mother's brother enjoyed particular respect. The numerous tales of Amazons may also be mentioned. From the standpoint of our culture these customs were unexplainable, but when the customs of primitive people came to be known the history of the development of the family was more readily understood.[1] (Among many primitive tribes descent is unilateral, the child being counted as a member of either the father's or the mother's line; not a member of both. When the child belongs to the mother's line and position or other rights are held by males conflicts develop; because the child does not inherit these from his father, but from the men of his mother's line, that is to say from his maternal uncle. When the family consisting of parents and children form an economic and social unit this type of organization leads easily to conflicts between father and sons, and between a man and his wife's brothers. Therefore there is an element of instability in these institutions and they are liable to break down and change to a form in which either the child belongs to the father's line, so that conflicts are avoided, or that it belongs to both lines.)

A conclusion based on investigations of this type should be emphasized. It shows that emotional reactions which we feel as natural are in reality culturally determined. It is not easy for us to understand that the emotional relation between father and son should be different from the one to which we are accustomed, but a knowledge of the life of

---

[1] The following passage has been changed, because the current view of a necessary precedence of matrilineal forms of family organization was accepted. This view is not tenable since it is impossible to derive all forms of family organization from a single source.

people with a social organization different from ours brings about situations in which conflicts or mutual obligations arise of a character quite opposed to those we are accustomed to and that run counter to what we consider "natural" emotional reactions to those to whom we are related by blood.

The data of ethnology prove that not only our knowledge, but also our emotions are the result of the form of our social life and of the history of the people to whom we belong. If we desire to understand the development of human culture we must try to free ourselves of these shackles. This is possible only to those who are willing to adapt themselves to the strange ways of thinking and feeling of primitive people. If we attempt to interpret the actions of our remote ancestors by our rational and emotional attitudes we cannot reach truthful results, for their feeling and thinking was different from ours. We must lay aside many points of view that seem to us self-evident, because in early times they were not self-evident. It is impossible to determine *a priori* those parts of our mental life that are common to mankind as a whole and those due to the culture in which we live. A knowledge of the data of ethnology enables us to attain this insight. Therefore it enables us also to view our own civilization objectively.

When it is recognized that similar customs may spring up independently, we are no longer prone to infer from superficial similarities community of origin of peoples. How often have the lost tribes of Israel been rediscovered—in America, Polynesia and Africa! How often have lost tribes of antiquity been supposed to have migrated by way of the fabulous Atlantis to America! The argument for such extravagant theories is generally the occurrence of some taboo or of an ornament found in widely separated regions.

It is indeed most remarkable that the same cultural phenomena recur in the most remote parts of the world and that the varied complex forms of thought and action which the human mind develops are repeated and so distributed that historical connection is almost unthinkable. The Phaëthon tale is a good example. It is the story of the son of the Sun who drives the heavenly chariot and is cast down by the thunderbolt of Zeus when he scorches the earth. Among the Indians of British Columbia the mink visits his father, the sun, carries the sun in his stead and is cast down by his own father when he scorches the earth. The custom of wearing large ornaments in the lips is found in parts of America, but also in equatorial Africa. Recently Bastian has treated modern spiritism from the same point of view, showing its similarity with the practices of spiritism among primitive people.

The frequent occurrence of similar phenomena in cultural areas that have no historical contact suggests that important results may be derived from their study, for it shows that the human mind develops everywhere according to the same laws.

The discovery of these is the greatest aim of our science. To attain it many methods of inquiry and the assistance of many other sciences will be needed. Up to this time the number of investigations is small, but the foundations have been laid by the labors of men like Tylor, Bastian, Morgan and Bachofen. As in other new branches of science there is no lack of hasty theorizing that does not contribute to healthy growth. Far-reaching theories have been built on weak foundations. Here belongs the attempt to explain history as determined by the nature of the country in which the people live. A relation between soil and history cannot be denied, but we are not in a position to explain social and mental behavior on this basis and anthropo-geographical "laws" are valid only as vague, empty generalities. Climate and soil exert an influence upon the body and its functions, but it is not possible to prove that the character of the country finds immediate expression in that of its inhabitants. It is said that the Negro, living in tropical Africa and not troubled by lack of food, is lazy and does not take the trouble to clothe his body. The Eskimo also is said to be made lazy by the long Polar night which dwarfs his imagination. Unfortunately such generalizations are entirely misleading. There are Negro tribes which punish anyone who appears in public improperly clothed; while the tribes of Tierra del Fuego which live in an inhospitable climate are scantily clothed. The Eskimo, during the long winter night, find entertainment in dance, song and story telling.

Furthermore, the principles of biological evolution were easily applied to the phenomena of cultural history and so one system after another developed telling us how mankind from the lowest levels of barbarism was led to the highest levels of civilization. The cautious scientist cannot follow those vagaries. We have attempts to construe the development of modern ethics from ethnological data starting with the simple assumption that consideration of the welfare of fellow-men was useful to the individual. Fear of revenge and desire for security are said to be the basis of all ethical concepts. Customary law may have developed in a manner similar to these ideas, but it is not justifiable to conclude that this is the basis, the only basis of the concepts of good and evil. It would take us too far afield to enter into this subject in greater detail, but it seemed necessary to define the limitations of ethnological science. It will not give us information regarding the fundamental traits of the human mind. Ethnology will give us no information on the origin of the concepts of space and time, or of causality.

On the other hand ethnology may contribute new ideas to other sciences, such as psychology, philosophy and history. We have seen that ethnology deals with the history of primitive peoples. Their fates repeat under simpler conditions, on a lesser scale, the same kinds of events that occur in the history of our complex civilization. New ideas are assimilated according to the culture of the recipient people. They are developed or disappear again. It is instructive to see how difficult it is to adopt new ideas. The invention is not difficult. Difficult is the retention and further development. Therefore the development is the slower the lower the cultural status. On the other hand it is important to observe the fight of individuals against tribal customs. The same kind of struggle that the genius has to undergo among ourselves in his battle against dominant ideas or dominant prejudice occurs among primitives and it is of particular interest to see in how far the strong individual is able to free himself from the fetters of convention.

Ethnology may also contribute much to the study of psychology. Nothing is more instructive for the student of the human mind than an understanding of human error and for this subject ethnology furnishes a plethora of materials. The eternal war between rational thought and emotion and the historical development of the progress of reason over tradition must find its principal source in the data of ethnology.

I have hastily sketched the scope of our science. I have not been able to do more than to mark the broadest outlines of the aims we have in mind. With a few words I have tried to indicate the methodological means at our disposal. The history of mankind·is to be reconstructed by investigations of bodily form, languages, and customs. We wish to discover the laws governing the development of the mind by a careful comparison of its varied manifestations; and I have tried to indicate the limits beyond which ethnology cannot proceed.

I hope I may have succeeded in my task: to show that it is not idle curiosity or fondness of adventure that induces the scientist to visit distant people of apparently low grades of culture; that we are conscious of a task well worthy of the most strenuous efforts when we collect the languages, customs and tales of tribes whose life differs in fundamental aspects from our own.

THE STUDY OF GEOGRAPHY[1]

IT IS a remarkable fact, that, in the recent literature of geography, researches on the method and limits of that science occupy a prominent place. Almost every distinguished geographer has felt the necessity of expressing his views on its aim and scope, and of defending it from being disintegrated and swallowed up by geology, botany, history, and other sciences treating on subjects similar to or identical with those of geography. If the representatives of a science as young as geography spend a great part of their time in discussions of this kind, though the material for investigation is still unlimited; if they feel compelled to defend their field of research against assaults of their fellow-workers and outsiders,—the reason for this fact must be looked for in a deep discrepancy between their fundamental views of science and those of their adversaries.

Formerly, when the greater part of the earth's surface was undiscovered, and European vessels sailed only over their well-known routes from continent to continent, careful not to stray from the old path and fearing the dangers of unknown regions, the mere thought of these vast territories which had never been sighted by a European could fill the mind of geographers with ardent longing for extended knowledge; with the desire of unveiling the secrets of regions enlivened by imagination with figures of unknown animals and peoples. But the more completely the outlines of continents and islands became known the stronger grew the desire to *understand* the phenomena of the newly discovered regions by comparing them with those of one's own country. Instead of merely extending their study over new areas, scientists began to be absorbed in examining the phenomena more intently, and comparing them with the results of observations already made. Thus Humboldt's admirable works and Karl Ritter's comparative geography arose out of the rapidly extending knowledge of the earth.

The fact that the rapid disclosure of the most remote parts of the globe coincided with the no less rapid development of physical sciences has had a deep influence upon the development of geography; for while the circle of phenomena became wider every day, the idea became prev-

[1] *Science,* vol. 9 (1887), pp. 137–141.

alent that a single phenomenon is not of great avail, but that it is the aim of science to deduce laws from phenomena; and the wider their scope, the more valuable they are considered. The descriptive sciences were deemed inferior in value to researches which had hitherto been outside their range. Instead of systematic botany and zoology, biology became the favorite study; theoretical philosophy was supplanted by experimental psychology; and, by the same process, geography disintegrated into geology, meteorology, etc.

Ever since, these sciences have rapidly developed, but geography itself has for a long time been almost overshadowed by its growing children. However, we do not think they can fill its place, and wish to prove that its neglect cannot be remedied by the attentive cultivation of those sciences separately.

Those accustomed to value a study according to the scope of the laws found by means of it are not content with researches on phenomena such as are the object of geography. They consider them from a physical standpoint, and find them to be physical, meteorological, or ethnological; and, after having explained them by means of physical, physiological, or psychological laws, have finished their work. It is instructive to consider thoroughly their definition of geography. They declare that the domain of this science comprises neither magnetical and meteorological nor geological phenomena and processes. They generously grant it the study of the distribution of animals and plants, as far as physiologists and evolutionists will permit; but all agree that anthropo-geography —the life of man as far as it depends on the country he lives in—is the true domain of geography.

It is not difficult to discover the principle on which this segregation is founded. Physical phenomena are subject to physical laws which are known, or which will assuredly be found by the methods used in discovering those that are known. Physiological, and, to a still higher degree, psychological laws are not sufficiently well known to allow their being treated in the same way as physical laws. The conditions of the phenomena are generally so complicated that, even if the most general laws were known, a strict conclusion cannot easily be drawn. But were those auxiliary sciences just as far developed as physics, no doubt the same scientists who at the present time concede them willingly to geography would not hesitate to claim them for physiology and psychology. It is evident that there is no middle way: geography must either be maintained in its full extent or it must be given up altogether.

As soon as we agree that the purpose of every science is accomplished when the laws which govern its phenomena are discovered, we must admit that the subject of geography is distributed among a great number of sciences; if, however, we would maintain its independence, we must prove that there exists another object for science besides the deduction of laws from phenomena. And it is our opinion that there is another object,—the thorough understanding of phenomena. Thus we find that the contest between geographers and their adversaries is identical with the old controversy between historical and physical methods. One party claims that the ideal aim of science ought to be the discovery of general laws; the other maintains that it is the investigation of phenomena themselves.

It is easily understood, therefore, why in geography the contest between these views is particularly lively. Here naturalists and historians meet in a common field of work. A great number of modern geographers have been educated as historians, and they must try to come to an agreement with the naturalists, who, in turn, must learn to accommodate their views to those of the historians. It is evident that an answer to this fundamental question on the value of historical and physical science can only be found by a methodological investigation of their relation to each other.

All agree that the establishment of facts is the foundation and starting-point of science. The physicist compares a series of similar facts, from which he isolates the general phenomenon which is common to all of them. Henceforth the single facts become less important to him, as he lays stress on the general law alone. On the other hand, the facts are the object which is of importance and interest to the historian. An example will explain our meaning more satisfactorily than a theoretical discussion.

When Newton studied the motion of the planets, the distribution of those celestial bodies in space and time was the means, not the object, of his researches. His problem was the action of two bodies upon each other, and thus he found the law of gravitation. On the other hand, Kant and Laplace, in studying the solar system, asked the question, Why is every one of the bodies constituting the solar system in the place it occupies? They took the law as granted, and applied it to the phenomena from which it had been deduced, in order to study the history of the solar system. Newton's work was at an end as soon as he had found the law of gravitation while this law was the preliminary condition of Kant's work.

Here is another example: according to Buckle's conception, historical facts must be considered as being caused by physiological and psychological laws. Accordingly, he does not describe men and their actions as arising from their own character and the events influencing their lives, but calls our attention to the laws governing the history of mankind. The object of the historian is a different one. He is absorbed in the study of the facts, and dwells admiringly on the character of his heroes. He takes the most lively interest in the persons and nations he treats of, but is unwilling to consider them as subject to stringent laws.

We believe that the physical conception is nowhere else expressed as clearly as in Comte's system of sciences. Setting aside astronomy, which has been placed rather arbitrarily between mathematics and physics, all his sciences have the one aim, to deduce laws from phenomena. The single phenomenon itself is insignificant: it is only valuable because it is an exemplification of a law, and serves to find new laws or to corroborate old ones. To this system of sciences Humboldt's "Cosmos" is opposed in principle. Cosmography, as we may call this science, considers every phenomenon as worthy of being studied for its own sake. Its mere existence entitles it to a full share of our attention; and the knowledge of its existence and evolution in space and time fully satisfies the student, without regard to the laws which it corroborates or which may be deduced from it.

Physicists will acknowledge that the study of the history of many phenomena is a work of scientific value. Nobody doubts the importance of Kant's researches on the solar system; nobody derogates from that of investigations upon the evolution of organisms. However, there is another class of phenomena the study of which is not considered of equal value, and among them are the geographical ones. In considering the geography of a country, it seems that the geological, meteorological, and anthropo-geographical phenomena form an incidental conglomerate, having no natural tie or relation to one another, while, for instance, the evolutionist's subject of study forms a natural unity. We may be allowed to say that the naturalist demands an objective connection between the phenomena he studies, which the geographical phenomena seem to lack. Their connection seems to be subjective, originating in the mind of the observer.

Accordingly there are two principal questions which must be answered: first, the one referring to the opposition between physicists and cosmographers, i.e., Is the study of phenomena for their own sake equal in value to the deduction of laws? second, Is the study of a series of phenomena having a merely subjective connection equal in value to researches on the history of those forming an objective unity?

We shall first discuss the difference of opinion between physicists and cosmographers. The two parties are strongly opposed to each other; and it is a hard task to evaluate fairly the arguments of opponents whose method of thinking and way of feeling are entirely opposed to one's own. An unbiased judgment cannot be formed without severe mental struggles which destroy convictions that were considered immovable, and had become dear to us. But those struggles lead to the grander conviction that both parties, though in a permanent state of conflict, aspire to the same end,—to find the eternal truth.

The origin of every science we find in two different desires of the human mind,—its aesthetic wants, and its interest in the individual phenomenon. It must have been an early desire of developing mankind to arrange systematically the phenomena seen by the observer in overwhelming number, and thus to put the confused impressions in order. This desire must be considered an emanation of the aesthetic disposition, which is offended by confusion and want of clearness. When occupied in satisfying this desire, the regularity of the processes and phenomena would attain a far greater importance than the single phenomenon, which is only considered important as being a specimen of the class to which it belongs. The more clearly all phenomena are arranged, the better will the aesthetic desire be satisfied, and, for that reason, the most general laws and ideas are considered the most valuable results of science.

From this point of view, the philosophical ideas of Epicurus are very interesting, as they may be considered the extreme position to which this aesthetic desire can lead if the pleasure one enjoys in arranging phenomena in a clear system is the only incentive. He considered any explanation of a phenomenon sufficient, provided it be natural. It does not matter, he taught, if an hypothesis is true, but all probable explanations are of the same value, and the choice between them is quite insignificant. We believe this opinion is called to new life by a number of modern scientists, i.e., by those who try to construct the evolution of organisms in details which, at the present time at least, can neither be proved nor refuted. If, for instance, Müller describes the history of flowers, he gives only a probable way of development, without any better proof than that it seems to be the simplest and therefore the most plausible. But this construction of a probable hypothesis as to the origin of phenomena gives a satisfaction to our aesthetic desire to bring the confusion of forms and species into a system. But it should be borne in mind that a theory must be true, and that its truth is the standard by which its value is measured. Therefore naturalists are always engaged in examining the truth of their theories by applying them to new phenomena, and in these researches those phenomena are the most important which seem to be opposed to the theories. As soon as the question whether the theory is applicable to the class of phenomena is solved, the whole class is of little further interest to the investigator.

While physical science arises from the logical and aesthetic demands of the human mind, cosmography has its source in the personal feeling of man towards the world, towards the phenomena surrounding him. We may call this an "affective" impulse, in contrast to the aesthetic impulse. Goethe has expressed this idea with admirable clearness: "It seems to me that every phenomenon, every fact, itself is the really interesting object. Whoever explains it, or connects it with other events, usually only amuses himself or makes sport of us, as, for instance, the naturalist or historian. But a single action or event is interesting, not because it is explainable, but because it is true." (*Unterhaltungen deutscher Ausgewanderter.*)

The mere occurrence of an event claims the full attention of our mind, because we are affected by it, and it is studied without any regard to its place in a system. This continuous impulse is the important counterbalance against the one-sidedness of a science arisen from merely aesthetic impulses. As the truth of every phenomenon causes us to study it, a true history of its evolution alone can satisfy the investigator's mind, and it is for this reason that Epicurus's probable or possible explanation is not at all satisfactory for science, but that every approach to truth is considered a progress by far superior to the most elaborate system which may give proof of a subtle mind and scrupulous thought, but claims to be only one among many possible systems.

Naturalists will not deny the importance of every phenomenon, but do not consider it worthy of study for its own sake. It is only a proof or a refutation of their laws, systems, and hypotheses (as they are deduced from true phenomena), which they feel obliged to bring as near the truth as possible. The deductions, however, are their main interest; and the reward of the indefatigable student is to review, from the summit of his most general deductions, the vast field of phenomena. Joyfully he sees that every process and every phenomenon which seem to the stranger an irregular and incomprehensible conglomerate is a link in a long chain. Losing sight of the single facts, he sees only the beautiful order of the world.

The cosmographer, on the other hand, holds to the phenomenon which is the object of his study, may it occupy a high or a low rank in the system of physical sciences, and lovingly tries to penetrate into its secrets until every feature is plain and clear. This occupation with the object of his affection affords him a delight not inferior to that which the physicist enjoys in his systematical arrangement of the world.

Our inquiry leads us to the conclusion that it is in vain to search for an answer to the question, Which of the two methods is of a higher value? as each originates in a different desire of the human mind. An answer can only be subjective, being a confession of the answerer as to which is dearer to him,—his personal feeling towards the phenomena surrounding him, or his inclination for abstractions; whether he prefers to recognize the individuality in the totality, or the totality in the individuality.

Let us now turn to the discussion of the second point. We have seen that physicists are inclined to acknowledge the value of a certain class of cosmographical studies. It is the characteristic quality of those phenomena that they are the result of the action of incidental causes upon one group of forces, or upon the elements of phenomena. The physicist does not study the whole phenomenon as it represents itself to the human mind, but resolves it into its elements, which he investigates separately. The investigation of the history of these elements of phenomena leads to a systematical arrangement, which gives to the aesthetic desire as much satisfaction as the formulation of laws. The end which evolutional and astronomical researches tend to is the best proof of this fact. A study of groups of phenomena which seem to be connected only in the mind of the observer, and admit of being resolved into their elements, cannot lead to a similar result, and is therefore considered of inferior value. However, we have tried to prove that the source of cosmographical researches is an affective one. If this be right, we cannot distinguish between complex and simple phenomena, as the physicist tries to do, and neglect their subjective unity,—the connection in which they appear to the mind of the observer. The whole phenomenon, and not its elements, is the object of the cosmographer's study. Thus the physiognomy of a country is of no interest to the physicist, while it is important to the cosmographer.

From the stand-point we occupy, a discussion of the value of these researches is of just as little avail as that of the value of the two branches of science, for the judgment will be founded on the mental disposition of the judge, and be only a confession as to which impulse predominates, the aesthetic or the affective. However, one fact appears from our inquiry : cosmography is closely related to the arts, as the way in which the mind is affected by phenomena forms an important branch of the study. It therefore requires a different treatment from that of the physical sciences.

We will apply these results to the study of geography. Its objects are, the phenomena caused by the distribution of land and water, by the vertical forms of the earth's surface and by the mutual influence of the earth and its inhabitants upon each other.

What does the physicist do with this object of study ? He selects a single element out of phenomena which are observed at a certain point of the earth's surface, and compares it with another one found at another place. He continues in this way searching for similar phenomena, and loses sight altogether of the spot from which he started. Thus he becomes the founder of the sciences into which geography has gradually been resolved, as his studies are either directed to geological phenomena alone, or to meteorological, botanical, or whatever it may be. The most general deductions which can be reached in the pursuit of these studies still have a close connection with the single object, as they cannot be carried further than to the most general geographical ideas, as mountain ranges, running water, oceans, etc. The most general results of his investigations will therefore be a general history of the earth's surface. When he brings these results into a system, he acts, as it seems to us, against the cosmographical character of the science. For instance, a system of all possible actions of water as forming the earth's surface seems to us of little value, except from a practical stand-point as being useful in studying the geological history of a district or of the earth's surface. Therefore these systems must be considered as important auxiliary sciences, but they are not geography itself. Their value is founded only on their applicability to the study of geography. The invention of geographical systems, so far as they do not serve this purpose, must be considered as useless, and classifications must be made only as far as geographical phenomena of a similar kind must be explained by different causes.

But there is another branch of geography besides this, equal to it in value—the physiognomy of the earth. It cannot afford a satisfactory object of study to the physicist, as its unity is a merely subjective one; and the geographer, in treating these subjects, approaches the domain of art, as the results of his study principally affect the feeling, and therefore must be described in an artistic way in order to satisfy the feeling in which it originated.

Our consideration leads us to the conclusion that geography is part of cosmography, and has its source in the affective impulse, in the desire to understand the phenomena and history of a country or of the whole earth, the home of mankind. It depends upon the inclination of the scientist towards physical or cosmographical method, whether he studies the history of the whole earth, or whether he prefers to learn that of a single country. From our point of view, the discussion whether geology or meteorology belongs to geography is of little importance, and we are willing to call all scientists geographers who study the phenomena of the earth's surface. We give geology no preference over the other branches of science, as many modern scientists are inclined to do. The study of the earth's surface implies geological researches as well as meteorological, ethnological, and others, as none of them cover the scope of geography, its aim being to delineate the picture of the earth's surface.

Many are the sciences that must help to reach this end; many are the studies and researches that must be pursued to add new features to the incomplete picture; but every step that brings us nearer the end gives ampler satisfaction to the impulse which induces us to devote our time and work to this study, gratifying the love for the country we inhabit, and the nature that surrounds us.

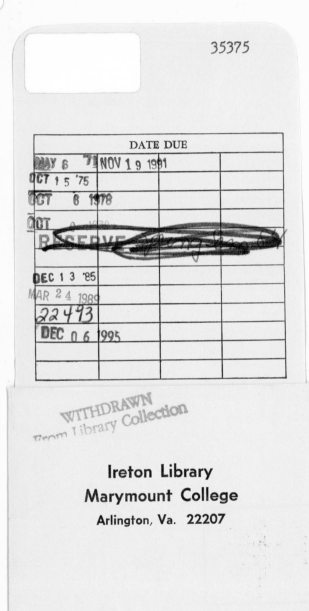